INTERNATIONAL ACCOUNTING

FOURTH EDITION

INTERNATIONAL ACCOUNTING

Frederick D. S. Choi

New York University

Carol Ann Frost

Research Associate
Dartmouth College

Gary K. Meek

Oklahoma State University

Prentice
Hall

UPPER SADDLE RIVER, NJ 07458

Library of Congress Cataloging-in-Publication Data

Choi, Frederick D. S., 1942–
   International accounting / Frederick D. S. Choi, Carol Ann Frost, Gary K. Meek —
4th ed.
     p. cm.
   Includes bibliographical references and index.
   ISBN 0-13-033272-0
   1. International business enterprises—Accounting.   I. Frost, Carol Ann.
II. Meek, Gary K., 1949–   III. Title.

   HF5686.I56 C53 2001
   657′.95—dc21   2001036063

Acquisitions Editor: Thomas Sigel
Editor-in-Chief: P. J. Boardman
Associate Editor: Kasey Sheehan
Editorial Assistant: Fran Toepfer
Media Project Manager: Nancy Welcher
Executive Marketing Manager: Beth Toland
Marketing Assistant: Brian Rappelfeld
Managing Editor (Production): John Roberts
Production Editor: Kelly Warsak
Permissions Coordinator: Suzanne Grappi
Associate Director, Manufacturing: Vincent Scelta
Manufacturing Buyer: Diane Peirano
Cover Design: Bruce Kenselaar
Composition: BookMasters, Inc.
Full-Service Project Management: BookMasters, Inc.
Printer/Binder: The Maple Press Company
Cover Printer: Phoenix Color Corp.

Credits and acknowledgments borrowed from other sources and reproduced, with permission, in this textbook appear on appropriate page within text.

10 9 8 7 6 5 4 3 2 1
ISBN 0-13-033272-0

To our families.

CONTENTS

PREFACE

This book is written with the express purpose of sensitizing students to the international dimensions of accounting and financial reporting. The world in which they will pursue their professional careers is a world dominated by global business and investment decisions. As most of these decisions are premised on financial data, a knowledge of international accounting is crucial for achieving proper understanding in international business and financial communications. Although ideal for upper division undergraduate students and masters students, we are pleased that contents of this award-winning effort have also benefited practicing accountants, financial executives, investment managers, accounting educators, and professional administrators around the world.

Our revision of a work that has spanned three decades features a number of enhancements. These include:

- Capital market, managerial, taxation, and institutional updates reflective of current trends and issues
- Discussion of the newly restructured International Accounting Standards Board
- Revised discussion of reporting and disclosure practices with many new examples from both developed and emerging market countries
- Expanded listings of relevant international Web site addresses and data sources
- Many new discussion questions, exercises, and cases

A growing number of academics are writing on the international dimensions of accounting and their contributions have benefited our work. We have also benefited from the professional literature and from many of our students and faculty colleagues who have triggered new ideas for us to consider.

In addition, we wish to acknowledge the following individuals for reviewing, providing data, or offering constructive suggestions for improving our work:

Ben-Hsien Bao–Hong Kong Polytechnic University
Ted Berg–Lehman Brothers
William F. Blosel–California University of Pennsylvania
Sarah Buckingham–Dartmouth College, Tuck School of Business
Iva Černa–Česká Rafinérská
Nils Crasselt–Ruhr-Universität Bochum
Paquita Davis-Friday–University of Notre Dame
Scott Foster–Lehman Brothers
Bambi A. Hora–Central Oklahoma University
Tatsuo Inoue–Kwansei Gakuin University
Cynthia G. Jeffrey–Iowa State University

Kurt Ramin–International Accounting Standards Board
Juan Rivera–University of Notre Dame
Hervé Stolowy–HEC School of Management
Judyth A. Swingen–Florida Gulf Coast University
Jiliang Yang–Hong Kong University of Science and Technology

Many individuals furnished able assistance in producing the manuscript. We especially wish to thank Clarke Cogsdill, who graciously edited all of our chapters with patience and humor; Alice Charney and Maureen Mamarella at New York University and Cynthia A. Conway at Oklahoma State University for their able typing assistance; and Thomas Sigel, Fran Toepfer, and Kelly Warsak at Prentice Hall and Sharon Anderson of BookMasters for their patience, encouragement, and editorial support.

However hard one tries to avoid them, errors are bound to occur in a work of this type. As authors, we accept full responsibility for all errors and omissions in the manuscript. We welcome constructive comments from all who use this book.

F. D. S. Choi

C. A. Frost

G. K. Meek

INTERNATIONAL ACCOUNTING

CHAPTER 1

INTRODUCTION

Accounting is a branch of applied economics that provides information about business and financial transactions for users of that information. International accounting is distinct because the information concerns a multinational enterprise (MNE) with foreign operations and transactions, or the users of the information are in a different domicile than the reporting entity.

Those who want to manage business, or obtain or supply financing across national borders, need to understand the international dimensions of accounting. Accounting amounts may vary significantly according to the principles that govern them. Differences in culture, business practices, political and regulatory structures, legal systems, currency values, foreign exchange rates, local inflation rates, business risks, and tax codes all affect how the MNE conducts its operations and financial reporting around the world. Financial statements and other disclosures are impossible to understand without an awareness of the underlying accounting principles and business culture.

We view accounting as consisting of three broad areas: measurement, disclosure, and auditing. *Measurement* is the process of identifying, categorizing, and quantifying economic activities or transactions. The intent of accounting measurements is to provide users with information that will facilitate economic decisions. *Disclosure* is the process by which accounting measurements are transmitted to their users. This area focuses on issues such as what is to be disclosed, when, by what means, and to whom. Disclosure includes accounting disclosures to external parties and the internal use of accounting information. Finally, *auditing* is the process by which specialized accounting professionals (auditors) examine and verify the adequacy of a company's financial and control systems and the accuracy of its financial records. Internal auditors are company employees who answer to management; external auditors are non-employees who are responsible for attesting that the company's financial statements are prepared in accordance with some generally accepted standards.

The importance of understanding international accounting increases as business and financial markets become more global. Exhibit 1-1 shows that the dollar volume of cross-border equity offerings almost tripled between 1995 and 1999, with over US$500 billion raised during the 5-year period. International offerings in bonds, syndicated loans, and other debt instruments also grew dramatically during the 1990s.

National controls on capital flows, foreign exchange, foreign direct investment, and related transactions have been dramatically liberalized in recent years, reducing the

EXHIBIT 1-1	Geographical Analysis of International Equity Offerings Made by Companies from Five Geographic Regions 1995–1998. ($US millions) (Including Only the Sales of Securities Outside the Domestic Market)					
	1995	*1996*	*1997*	*1998*	*1999*	*Total*
North America	11,307	13,759	15,167	22,139	23,963	86,335
Europe	31,526	49,873	68,180	56,158	82,809	288,546
Africa/Middle East	1,779	1,612	3,346	2,232	3,174	13,142
Asia-Pacific	12,235	21,687	29,247	19,789	41,219	124,177
Latin America	878	5,204	6,353	252	721	13,408
Total Market	**57,725**	**93,134**	**122,293**	**100,570**	**151,887**	**525,609**

Source: PricewaterhouseCoopers, *Entering the European Capital Markets: A Guide for Companies and Advisers* (London: 2001).

barriers to international business. Exhibit 1-2 presents selected information on changes in financial sector policy in 34 nations during 1973–1996, and illustrates efforts by national governments to open their economies to private enterprise and international investors and business. This exhibit shows that, with a few exceptions, there was a strong trend worldwide during this period to privatize government-owned financial enterprises (especially banks) and to reduce or eliminate foreign exchange controls and limits on cross-border investment.

A BRIEF HISTORY OF INTERNATIONAL ACCOUNTING[1]

Accounting has evolved throughout recorded history to meet the needs of those who conduct economic transactions. As business has developed international dimensions, accounting has kept pace. For example, the growth of international commerce in northern Italy during the late Middle Ages (and the desire of government to find ways to tax commercial transactions) led to the invention of double entry record keeping that became fully developed in the fourteenth century.

Since then, and at an accelerating rate, business has become more international and the associated accounting issues have become more complex. The development of the British Empire created unprecedented needs for British commercial interests to manage and control enterprises in the colonies, and for the records of their colonial enterprises to be reviewed and verified. These needs led to the emergence of accounting societies in the 1850s and an organized public accounting profession in Scotland and England during the 1870s. Since then there has been "a mutual interaction between auditors and accountants to find a generally accepted framework of accounting procedures and techniques that would allow accurate and understandable financial statements to be reviewed and reported."[2]

Accounting has been remarkably successful in its ability to be transplanted from one national setting to another while allowing for continued development in theory and

---

[1]A classic overview of this subject is Vernon K. Zimmerman, "Introducing the International Dimension of Accounting," in *International Accounting*, Peter Holzer, ed., 1984, 3–16.
[2]Ibid., 7.

EXHIBIT 1-2 Changes in Financial Sector Policy in 34 Nations 1973–1996

Country	Privatization	International Capital Flows
Industrialized Countries		
United States	None	Limited controls imposed in the 1960s, abolished in 1974
Canada	None	None
Japan	Government controls roughly 15% of financial assets through the postal savings system.	Controls on capital inflows eased after 1979. Controls on capital outflows eased in the mid-1980s. Foreign exchange restrictions eased in 1980. Remaining restrictions on cross-border transactions removed in 1995.
United Kingdom	None	All remaining controls on foreign-exchange purchase eliminated in 1979.
France	Some banks nationalized since 1945. All larger banks nationalized in 1982. Several French banks privatized in 1987 and 1993, including Banque Nationale de Paris.	Capital flows in and out of the country largely liberalized during 1986–1988. Liberalization was completed in 1990.
Germany	None	Most capital controls dismantled in 1973.
Italy	Credito Italiano and some other public banks privatized in 1993–1994.	Foreign exchange and capital controls eliminated by May 1990.
Australia	Some state-owned banks privatized in the 1990s. Commonwealth Bank of Australia privatized in 1997.	Capital and exchange controls tightened in late 1970s after the move to indirect monetary policy increased capital inflows. Capital account liberalized in 1984.
New Zealand	Bank of New Zealand (one of the four largest banks) privatized in the early 1990s. Development Finance Corporation closed. Government sold all remaining shares in state-owned banks by 1992.	All controls on inward and outward foreign exchange transactions removed in 1984. Controls on outward investment lifted in 1985. Restrictions on foreign-owned companies' access to domestic financial markets removed in late 1984. Controls on foreign direct and portfolio investment and repatriation of profits eased in 1985.
East Asia		
Hong Kong	None	None
Indonesia	Stock exchange privatized in 1990.	Most transactions on the capital account liberalized in 1971. Some restrictions on inflows remain. The regulation requiring exporters to sell their foreign-exchange holdings to banks abolished in 1982. Foreign direct investment regulations eased further in 1992.
Korea	Government divested its shares in commercial banks in the early 1980s. State-owned banks' share of total assets 13% in 1994.	Controls on foreign borrowing under US$200,000 with maturities of less than three years eased in 1979. Restriction on foreign borrowing under US$1 million eased in 1982. Controls on outward and inward foreign investment gradually eased since 1985. Significant restrictions on inward investment in place until 1998.
Malaysia	Share of state-owned banks in total assets of the financial sector 8% in 1994 (BIS estimate). Government is the majority shareholder in the country's largest bank and wholly owns the second largest bank.	Capital account mostly liberalized in the 1970s. Inward foreign direct and portfolio investment deregulated further in the mid-1980s. Controls on short-term and portfolio inflows temporarily reimposed in 1994.

EXHIBIT 1-2 *(cont.)*

Country	*Privatization*	*International Capital Flows*
Philippines	Government took over some failed financial institutions during the early 1980s. Government's share of total bank assets was lowered to 22% by 1996. Government reduced its stake in PNB to 47% in December 1995.	Foreign exchange and investment channeled through government in the 1970s. Interbank foreign exchange trading limited to 30 minutes per day after 1983. Off-floor trading introduced in 1992. Restrictions on all current and most capital transactions eliminated over 1992–1995.
Singapore	None	Government freed exchange and capital controls by 1978. (Exception: Offshore banks may not transact in Singapore dollars.)
Taiwan	Privatization effort blocked by controlling interests in 1989.	Foreign-exchange controls removed in 1987. Inward and outward capital flows limited to US$5 million per person per year.
Thailand	Share of state-owned banks in total assets 8% in 1994 (BIS estimate).	Restrictions on inward long-term investment eased in the mid-1980s. Controls on short-term flows and outward investment eased in the 1990s. The reserve requirement on short-term foreign borrowing is 7%. Currency controls introduced in May and June 1997 to deter currency speculators. Limits on foreign ownership of domestic financial institutions relaxed in October 1997.
Latin America		
Argentina	Fifteen percent of the loan market privatized since 1992. Government still owns the largest commercial bank, Banco de la Nación Argentina.	Multiple exchange rate system unified between 1976 and 1978. Foreign loans at market exchange rates permitted in 1978. Controls on inward and outward capital flows loosened in 1977. Liberalization measures reversed in 1982. Capital and exchange controls eliminated in 1991.
Brazil	None	System of comprehensive foreign exchange controls abolished in 1984. Most capital outflows restricted in the 1980s. Controls on capital inflows strengthened and controls on outflows loosened in the 1990s.
Chile	Nineteen domestic commercial banks privatized in 1974. Banks nationalized during the 1982 crisis were reprivatized in the mid-1980s.	Capital controls gradually eased since 1979. Controls reimposed in 1982 and eased again in mid-1980s. Foreign direct and portfolio investment subject to a one-year minimum holding period. Foreign loans subject to a 30% reserve requirement.
Colombia	Two large banks and a large finance company nationalized in 1982. Government intervened in over 20 financial institutions between 1982 and 1986. 30% of loan market privatized by 1995.	Controls on capital inflows relaxed in 1991. Exchange controls also reduced. Large capital inflows in the early 1990s led to the reimposition of reserve requirements on foreign loans in 1993.
Mexico	Authorities nationalized 18 commercial banks in 1982. Nationalized banks privatized in 1991.	Government given discretion over foreign direct investment in 1972. Ambiguous restrictions on foreign direct investment rationalized in 1989. Portfolio flows decontrolled further in 1989.
Peru	All five public development banks closed in early 1990s. All seven public commercial banks liquidated or divested over 1991–1995.	Capital controls removed in December 1990.

EXHIBIT 1-2 *(cont.)*

Country	Privatization	International Capital Flows
Venezuela	Four small public commercial banks liquidated or privatized in 1989. Public sector banks' share of total deposits 9% in 1993. Share increased to 29% after the nationalization of several banks during 1994–1996.	Foreign direct investment regime largely liberalized over 1989–1990. Exchange controls on all current and capital transactions imposed in 1994. System of comprehensive foreign exchange controls abandoned in April 1996.
Middle East and Africa		
Egypt	Some privatization of smaller state banks. The four largest public banks not slated for privatization as of 1996.	Foreign exchange system decontrolled and unified in 1991. Some controls on inward portfolio and direct investment lifted in 1990s.
Israel	Government nationalized leading banks in 1983. Union Bank (part of Bank Leumi) privatized in 1990s. 43% of Bank Hapoalim sold to Israeli-American consortium in 1997.	Capital controls eliminated in 1977 and reimposed in 1979. After 1987, restrictions on capital inflows gradually eliminated and restrictions on capital outflows gradually eased.
Morocco	The Casablanca stock market is state-owned. One state-owned bank was privatized in 1995.	Current account convertibility achieved in the 1990s. Surrender requirements or export revenue and outward investment restrictions relaxed in the early 1990s. Restrictions on inward foreign direct and portfolio investment and external borrowing by residents eased after 1993.
South Africa	None	Capital controls tightened in 1985. Exchange controls on nonresidents eliminated in 1995. Controls on residents relaxed in 1995.
Turkey	State-owned banks' share in total assets of the bank system remained constant over 1980–1990, at approximately 52%.	Capital flows liberalized in 1989.
South Asia		
Bangladesh	Commercial banks nationalized in the 1970s. Two state-owned banks sold back to original owners in early 1980s. (These banks remain uncompetitive.)	Foreign exchange markets unified in 1991–1992. Restrictions on current transactions eliminated in 1994. Controls on capital inflows eased after 1991.
India	All large banks nationalized in 1969. Government divested part of its equity position in some public banks in the 1990s.	Regulations on portfolio and direct investment eased since 1991. The exchange rate was unified in 1993–1994. Current-account convertibility achieved in 1994.
Nepal	Two large public sector banks hold over half of total bank deposits. Government share of Nepal Bank Limited reduced to 41%.	Dual exchange rate system introduced in 1992. Current account became fully convertible in 1994. Some capital transactions liberalized in the 1990s, but restrictions remain.
Pakistan	Muslim Commercial Bank privatized in 1991. Allied Bank privatized in stages between 1991 and 1993. First Women Bank privatized in 1997.	Rupee convertible for current transactions since July 1994. Capital controls eased in the 1990s.
Sri Lanka	Two development finance banks privatized in 1990s.	Exchange rate unified in 1978. Rupee made convertible for current transactions in 1994. Capital controls on inflows eased in 1978. Foreign portfolio investment restrictions eased further in 1991. Restrictions on capital outflows remain.

Source: John Williamson and Molly Mahar, *A Survey of Financial Liberalization* (Princeton, New Jersey: Princeton University International Finance Section, Essays in International Finance #211).

practice worldwide. Developments in telecommunications and computer technology allow information to be recorded, transmitted, and reviewed with a speed and accuracy that was all but unimaginable a few years ago. The World Wide Web, a curiosity in the early 1990s, is now indispensable for obtaining international financial information.

Along with an increasing international dimension has come the realization that accounting does not serve only the interests of business managers and owners. Governments, labor and consumer groups, environmentalists and other social activists, creditors, and investors all have interests (economic and otherwise) in the activities of businesses. They, as well as managers and owners, need access to complete and accurate financial information.

Many of the most interesting issues in accounting today result from its international dimensions. The explosive growth in cross-border transactions and the increase in companies seeking capital in international markets have made international accounting problems a daily fact of life for people in business around the world.

ROLE OF ACCOUNTING IN BUSINESS AND GLOBAL CAPITAL MARKETS

THE GLOBAL ENVIRONMENT OF BUSINESS

The international dimensions of internal (managerial) accounting are critically important. Managerial accounting from an international perspective includes possibly the most complex and detailed material in this book. We focus on three broad areas: managerial planning and control, multinational risk management, and the closely linked topics of taxation and transfer pricing.

A multinational business must understand the effects of environmental complexities on its accounting measurements. For example, understanding the effects of changes in foreign exchange and inflation rates is critical in areas such as the preparation of short- and long-term budgets for parent companies and their subsidiaries (or branches), measuring and evaluating the performance of local business units and managers, and making corporate-wide decisions on the allocation of investment capital and retained earnings, among others. To make matters more complex, foreign exchange and inflation rates do not work in tandem. The effect on accounting measurements of changes in foreign exchange rates and foreign inflation is so pervasive that managing the risks involved in these changes is a subject of its own. The multinational corporate treasury needs to identify the enterprise's exposure to exchange rate and inflation risk, to decide which risks to hedge against, and to evaluate the results of its risk management strategy.

Businesses that operate in more than one country need to carefully examine and manage their tax exposure. Knowledge of tax codes and currency values is only the beginning. It is very possible that steps taken to lower taxes in one place will raise taxes elsewhere, possibly by an amount greater than the reduction. The effects of tax strategies on corporate budgeting and control procedures must be considered carefully. For example, a good strategy to reduce taxes might have unwanted effects on the performance evaluation system.

Transfer prices—the prices charged to business units for internal transactions that cross national borders—frequently are set with tax minimization in mind. The basic idea is to concentrate expenses (as far as possible) in high-tax countries, and to concentrate revenues in low-tax countries, thus maximizing overall profit. Governments are well aware of this strategy and have adopted complex rules to prevent abusive use of this strategy. While the notion of the "arm's-length" price is widespread, its definition and the methods for calculating it have many variations. On top of all this, unexpected changes in exchange rates or inflation rates can wreak havoc on tax planning strategy. Generally it is necessary to use complex computer modeling to calculate the overall expected impact of a company's tax strategy.

CAPITAL MARKETS

Accounting plays a critical role in the efficient functioning of capital markets. Lenders, investors, financial analysts, regulators, and stock exchanges require information about the financial performance, position, and the future prospects of companies seeking financing. The needs of capital market participants have strongly shaped the development of accounting practice, as discussed in Chapter 2. Furthermore, the *relative* influence on accounting development of global capital market participants grows as these markets become an increasingly important source of finance. Demands of market participants strongly influence companies' accounting and disclosure choices, and national and international efforts to harmonize accounting measurement, disclosure, and auditing practices around the world.

AN INTRODUCTION TO GLOBAL EQUITY MARKETS

Most major equity markets around the world grew dramatically during the 1990s. For example, Exhibit 1-3 shows that during 1995 through 2000, growth in stock market capitalization[3] almost doubled in Sweden, Switzerland, and the United Kingdom, and more than doubled in China, Hong Kong, France, Germany, Italy, the Netherlands, Spain (Madrid), Canada (Toronto), and the United States.[4]

Exhibit 1-4 shows that equity market capitalization as a percentage of gross domestic product (GDP) increased during the period 1995 to 1999 in almost all countries shown. The percentage more than doubled in Australia, Belgium, and Switzerland, and more than tripled in China, France, Italy, the Netherlands, and Spain. This indicates generally significant and, in many markets, striking growth in the relative importance of equity markets in national economies during the period examined.

Exhibit 1-5 shows that the number of domestic companies with shares listed increased in some markets and decreased in others during 1995 through 2000. However, the average sizes and annual trading volumes of listed companies have grown

---

[3]Stock market capitalization is the total number of issued shares of companies (including all classes) multiplied by their prices at a given time. The measure excludes investment funds, rights, warrants, options, and futures [see the *FIBV (International Federation of Stock Exchanges) Annual Report 1999*, 2000, 154].
[4]Stock exchange data must be interpreted with great caution. Some national statistics cover only the main market, while others include parallel (secondary) markets and/or all regional exchanges. Market capitalization data are distorted by cross-shareholdings of listed companies. Even the term *listed company* can be ambiguous. Stock exchanges in Germany and several other countries have been accused of using measurement approaches that inflate their trade volume and numbers of foreign companies with shares listed.

EXHIBIT 1-3 Market Capitalization of Shares of Domestic Companies Listed on 26 Stock Exchanges ($US millions)

Country	Dec. 31, 2000	Dec. 31, 1995	% change 2000/1995
Asia-Pacific			
Australia	372,794.4	244,338.3	52.6
China (PRC)[1]	330,703.0	42,055.0	686.4
Hong Kong	623,397.8	303,705.3	105.3
Japan (Tokyo)	3,157,221.8	3,545,306.5	−10.9
Korea	148,361.2	181,954.8	−18.5
New Zealand	18,613.0	31,949.8	−41.7
Singapore	152,826.7	150,958.6	1.2
Taiwan	247,601.9	187,211.4	32.3
Europe-Africa			
Belgium	182,481.0	101,752.3	79.3
Czech Republic[2]	11,796.0	15,664.0	−24.7
France	1,446,634.1	499,989.6	189.3
Germany	1,270,243.2	577,364.8	120.0
Italy	768,363.5	209,522.5	266.7
Luxembourg	34,016.4	30,443.3	11.7
Netherlands	640,456.3	286,651.5	123.4
South Africa	204,300.8	258,607.0	−21.0
Spain (Madrid)	504,219.3	150,914.2	234.1
Sweden	328,339.1	172,550.3	90.3
Switzerland	792,316.0	398,088.1	99.0
UK	2,576,991.9	1,346,640.7	91.4
North America			
Canada (Toronto)	770,116.2	366,344.6	110.2
Mexico	125,203.9	123,551.0	1.3
USA−Amex	86,775.3	103,147.0	−15.9
USA−Nasdaq	3,578,592.9	1,159,939.8	208.5
USA−NYSE	11,442,383.3	5,654,815.4	102.3
South America			
Brazil[3]	205,832.0	147,635.8	39.4

[1]China (PRC) market capitalization shown in the Dec. 31, 2000 column is for the combined Shenzhen and Shanghai Stock Exchanges as of Dec. 31, 1999.

[2]Czech Republic market capitalization shown in the Dec. 31, 2000 column is as of Dec. 31, 1999.

[3]Brazil market capitalization shown in the Dec. 31, 2000 column is as of Dec. 31, 1999.

Sources: International Federation of Stock Exchanges (FIBV); Meridian Securities Markets, *World Stock Exchange Fact Book 2000* (Round Rock, TX: Meridian Securities Markets LLC, 1995); *Standard & Poor's Emerging Stock Markets Factbook 2000* (New York: McGraw-Hill Company, 2000).

EXHIBIT 1-4	Relative Importance of Equity Markets in 17 National Economies—Market Capitalization as a Percentage of Gross Domestic Product (GDP) (End-of-Period Levels)					

Country	GDP ($US bill)	1999 Market Cap. ($US bill)	%	GDP ($US bill)	1995 Market Cap. ($US bill)	%
Asia-Pacific						
Australia	302.3	424.8	141%	348.8	244.3	70%
China (PRC)[1]	959.0	330.7	34%	700.2	42.0	6%
Hong Kong	159.2	608.3	382%	111.9	335.7	300%
Japan	4,849.1	4,470.9	92%	4,393.8	3,667.3	83%
Taiwan	296.7	376.1	127%	260.2	187.2	72%
Europe						
Belgium	230.8	184.4	80%	263.5	101.8	39%
Czech Republic	53.0 (est.)	13.4	25% (est.)	52.0	15.7	30%
France	1,178.5	1,296.3	110%	1,566.8	500.0	32%
Germany	3,843.8	1,422.2	37%	2,259.3	577.4	26%
Italy	1,096.9	710.8	65%	1,118.7	209.5	19%
Netherlands	349.2	806.6	231%	395.6	286.7	72%
Spain[2]	525.8	844.3	161%	574.3	150.9	26%
Switzerland	209.8	681.8	325%	287.2	398.2	139%
U.K.	1,162.4	2,394.6	206%	1,106.7	1,346.6	122%
North America						
Canada[3]	843.5	543.4	64%	568.6	366.3	64%
Mexico	530.9	153.5	29%	363.3	90.7	25%
United States	9,507.5	17,642.8	186%	7,245.8	6,917.7	95%

[1]For China (PRC), the GDP for 1999 is as of 1998.

[2]For Spain: Market capitalization and % of GDP for 1999 are for the combined Barcelona and Madrid Stock Exchanges; for 1995 these figures are for Madrid only.

[3]Canada market capitalization for 1999 is for the combined Montreal and Toronto Stock Exchanges; for 1995 it is for Toronto only.

Sources: International Federation of Stock Exchanges (FIBV); David Rathborne and Deborah Ritchie, eds., *The Salomon Smith Barney Guide to World Equity Markets 2000* (London: Euromoney Books and Salomon Smith Barney, 2000); Meridian Securities Markets, *World Stock Exchange Fact Book 2000* (Round Rock, TX: 2000); and Standards & Poor's, *Emerging Markets Factbook 2000* (New York: May, 2000).

EXHIBIT 1-5 Numbers of Companies with Shares Listed on 26 Stock Exchanges

Countries	Number of Companies as of December 31, 2000			Number of Companies as of December 31, 1995		
	Total	*Domestic*	*Foreign*	*Total*	*Domestic*	*Foreign*
Asia-Pacific						
Australia	**1,409**	1,333	76	**1,176**	1,127	49
China (PRC)[1]	**950**	950	0	**323**	323	0
Hong Kong	**790**	779	11	**542**	518	24
Korea	**702**	702	0	**721**	721	0
Japan (Tokyo)	**2,096**	2,055	41	**1,791**	1,714	77
New Zealand	**185**	131	54	**205**	145	60
Singapore	**377**	328	49	**445**	423	22
Taiwan	**531**	531	0	**347**	347	0
Europe-Africa						
Belgium	**265**	161	104	**281**	143	138
Czech Republic[2]	**164**	164	0	**1,635**	1,635	0
France	**1,185**	1,021	164	**904**	710	194
Germany	**989**	744	245	**1,622**	678	944
Italy	**297**	291	6	**221**	221	0
Luxembourg	**270**	54	216	**283**	55	228
Netherlands	**392**	234	158	**532**	347	185
South Africa	**616**	604	12	**639**	613	26
Spain (Madrid)[3]	**727**	718	9	**373**	369	4
Sweden	**311**	292	19	**236**	223	13
Switzerland	**416**	252	164	**438**	215	223
UK	**2,929**	2,428	501	**2,603**	2,078	525
North America						
Canada (Toronto)	**1,421**	1,379	42	**1,258**	1,196	62
Mexico[4]	**179**	175	4	**185**	185	0
USA—Amex	**693**	643	50	**791**	727	64
USA—Nasdaq	**4,726**	4,239	487	**5,122**	4,873	249
USA—NYSE	**2,468**	2,035	433	**2,675**	2,428	247
South America						
Brazil[5]	**460**	457	3	**543**	543	0

[1]China (PRC) numbers of companies shown in the Dec. 31, 2000 column are for the combined Shenzhen and Shanghai Stock Exchanges as of Dec. 31, 1999.

[2]Numbers of companies shown in the Dec. 31, 2000 columns are as of Dec. 31, 1999.

[3]Numbers of companies shown in the Dec. 31, 2000 columns are as of Dec. 31, 1999.

[4]The four foreign companies listed as of Dec. 31, 2000 are quoted on the International Quotation System, not listed on the Main Market.

[5]Numbers of companies shown in the Dec. 31, 2000 columns are as of Dec. 31, 1999.

Sources: International Federation of Stock Exchanges (FIBV); Meridian Securities Markets, *World Stock Exchange Fact Book 2000* (Round Rock, TX: 2000); and Standard & Poor's, *Emerging Markets Factbook 2000* (New York: May, 2000).

substantially, in part due to mergers and acquisitions, which also result in delistings of some of entities involved.

Hundreds of foreign issuers[5] have had their equity listed on European, North American, and Japanese stock exchanges for years. However, Exhibit 1-5 shows that the numbers of foreign companies listed in most markets other than the NYSE and Nasdaq have been declining. This suggests that many issuers question the benefits of such listings, and that the benefits of a foreign listing generally are greater in the United States than elsewhere.

However, *increasing* numbers of foreign issuers are listing on Europe's "new markets" (especially Germany's Neuer Markt), and represent a new trend in listing and capital raising by foreign issuers in Continental Europe.[6] The new markets are designed to meet the needs of young high-growth companies seeking new capital. Their listing standards are more flexible, and their financial reporting and corporate governance[7] standards are often more stringent than on the main markets.[8]

Exhibit 1-6 shows that the value of domestic share trading increased (in many cases, dramatically) between 1995 and 2000 in each of the equity markets shown. Foreign share trading dollar volume also increased in each of the markets except in the markets where no foreign shares were listed (China, Korea, Taiwan, and the Czech Republic), Japan, Singapore, and South Africa. The 1995 through 2000 increase in foreign share trading volume exceeded 300 percent in Australia, New Zealand, Germany, Italy, the Netherlands, Spain, Sweden, the United Kingdom, Mexico, Nasdaq (USA), and in Brazil.

THE THREE MAJOR EQUITY MARKET REGIONS

The three largest equity market regions[9] are North America, Europe, and Asia-Pacific.

NORTH AMERICA

The U.S. economy and its stock markets had unprecedented growth during the 1990s. By 2000 both the New York Stock Exchange, Inc. (NYSE) and The Nasdaq Stock Market, Inc. (Nasdaq) dominated other stock exchanges worldwide in terms of market capitalization, value of trading in domestic shares, value of trading in foreign shares (except for the London Stock Exchange [LSE]), capital raised by newly admitted companies, numbers of domestic listed companies, and numbers of foreign listed companies.

---

[5]An *issuer* is an entity that raises capital or has shares listed (with no capital raised) on a stock exchange. A *foreign issuer* is an issuer whose home country is different than the country of the capital market.
[6]Refer to the case at the end of this chapter, which discusses the initial public offering by the American company e-centives in October 2000. New markets have also recently been launched in Japan, Brazil, and many other non-European equity markets.
[7]Corporate governance refers to the structure of relationships and responsibilities among shareholders, board members, and managers designed to meet corporate objectives.
[8]Very few foreign issuers have raised capital on Continental Europe's more established main markets.
[9]Each equity market region is comprised of equity markets in multiple countries, and some of these national equity markets are comprised of several stock exchanges (as well as off-exchange trading systems). (For example, four stock exchanges operate in Spain, and eight stock exchanges operate in the United States.) A *stock exchange* is an entity that plays a central role in the regulation of trading markets, and that develops, operates, and manages those markets.

EXHIBIT 1-6 Value of Domestic and Foreign Share Trading on 26 Stock Exchanges ($US millions)

Countries	2000 Total	2000 Domestic	2000 Foreign	1995 Total	1995 Domestic	1995 Foreign
Asia-Pacific						
Australia	226,484.9	222,845.7	3,639.2	98,310.3	97,543.9	766.4
China (PRC)[1]	377,099.0	377,099.0	0.0	49,774.0	49,774.0	0.00
Hong Kong	376,664.1	373,401.2	699.4	95,832.0	95,588.9	243.2
Japan (Tokyo)	2,315,501.8	2,314,660.0	627.1	884,000.4	882,961.0	1,039.4
Korea	556,246.3	555,807.0	0.0	185,427.5	185,427.5	0.0
New Zealand	12,315.3	10,282.0	1,820.6	8,718.7	8,452.9	194.3
Singapore	95,153.1	95,153.1	0.0	63,983.2	63,983.2	0.0
Taiwan	983,782.1	983,782.1	0.0	389,272.7	383,505.6	0.0
Europe-Africa						
Belgium	43,786.8	37,780.5	5,733.1	18,342.9	15,196.2	3,077.1
Czech Rep[2]	4,120.0	4,120.0	0.0	3,630.0	3,630.0	0.0
France	1,064,866.0	1,054,475.7	10,390.3	213,161.0	209,545.0	3,616.0
Germany	2,120,128.5	1,798,461.6	321,323.1	593,936.2	580,134.7	13,801.5
Italy	1,019,625.3	989,553.6	30,071.7	87,117.6	87,085.1	32.5
Luxembourg	1,689.3	1,213.0	22.3	486.5	207.1	10.9
Netherlands	678,763.7	633,856.8	2,402.1	125,684.1	115,795.8	192.6
South Africa	77,446.1	76,967.1	0.0	17,425.4	15,947.9	1,234.0
Spain (Madrid)[3]	1,035,595.4	1,033,387.7	2,207.7	54,029.0	54,104.7	14.3
Sweden	485,288.3	389,744.0	95,544.3	94,209.9	93,223.3	986.6
Switzerland	638,374.6	607,719.6	28,851.3	340,114.4	319,117.0	17,600.8
UK	4,558,663.0	1,862,588.6	2,669,122.1	1,153,221.3	512,323.4	626,862.9
North America						
Canada (Toronto)	636,535.3	635,543.7	991.6	151,559.1	151,131.0	428.1
Mexico	45,768.4	45,272.7	495.7	35,037.2	34,191.8	0.0
USA—Amex	945,390.7	not avail.	not avail.	72,716.8	not avail.	not avail.
USA—Nasdaq	19,798,799.3	18,950,660.3	844,399.8	2,398,213.0	2,316,860.0	81,353.0
USA—NYSE	11,060,046.0	9,885,993.0	1,141,896.0	3,082,916.1	2,789,054.0	260,643.4
South America						
Brazil	101,537.4	100,670.2	860.2	69,031.3	69,031.3	0.0

[1]China (PRC) trade volume shown in the Dec. 31, 2000 columns are for the combined Shenzhen and Shanghai Stock Exchanges as of Dec. 31, 1999.

[2]Czech Republic trade volumes shown in the Dec. 31, 2000 columns are as of Dec. 31, 1999.

[3]Spain (Madrid) trade volumes shown in the Dec. 31, 2000 columns are as of Dec. 31, 1999.

Sources: International Federation of Stock Exchanges (FIBV); Meridian Securities Markets, *World Stock Exchange Fact Book 2000* (Round Rock, TX: 2000); and Standard & Poor's, *Emerging Markets Factbook 2000* (New York: May, 2000).

Also, the *relative* importance of North America in the global equity market has increased: Market capitalization in North America as a percentage of the global total increased from 31.6 percent at year-end 1990 to 57.2 percent by year-end 1999.[10]

ASIA

Until recently, many experts predicted that Asia would become the second most important equity market region. While European capital markets appeared moribund in the 1980s, Japan was recognized as one of the three leading world capital markets (along with the United States and United Kingdom). The People's Republic of China (China) emerged as a major global economy, and the "Asian Tiger" nations experienced phenomenal growth and development. However, several Asian financial crises in the 1990s highlighted the fragility and immaturity of these economies, and slowed the growth of capital markets in the region.

The "East Asian Crisis" began in July 1997. On July 2, Thailand floated the baht, which had been linked to the U.S. dollar for over a decade, and the baht lost 17 percent against the U.S. dollar. Other currencies in the region then lost value, leading to large investor losses, a reduction in global trade, and sharp drops in major stock markets.

The 1990s were a time of economic drift for Japan. During 1990, the Tokyo stock market collapsed, property values crashed, and banks faced huge loan losses. The 1997 East Asian Crisis increased worries about the strength of Japan's economy. The Japanese government began to intervene more actively in the economy during the late 1990s, but with disappointing results. The market capitalization of domestic shares on the Tokyo Stock Exchange increased 83 percent during 1999 (from US$2,440 to US$4,455 billion), but fell to US$3,667 billion by December 31, 2000.[11]

Finally, during the mid- to late 1990s, China had slower economic growth, tougher business conditions, major investor losses, and a decrease in foreign investment.[12]

Critics argue that Asian accounting measurement, disclosure, and auditing standards and the monitoring and enforcement of those standards are weak.[13] A number of Asian listed companies and market participants are involved in organized crime, insider dealings, and other activities that deter potential investors.[14] Also, some Asian governments periodically announce that they will intervene in equity markets to boost share prices, and market manipulation is not uncommon.[15]

---

[10]*International Federation of Stock Exchanges (FIBV) 1996 Annual Report*, Paris: FIBV, 1997; *International Federation of Stock Exchanges (FIBV) 1999 Annual Report*, Paris: FIBV, 2000.

[11]Statistics are from the *International Federation of Stock Exchanges (FIBV) 1999 Annual Report*, Paris: FIBV, 2000, and the FIBV Web site (*www.FIBV.com*).

[12]See Stephen Valdez, *An Introduction to Global Financial Markets*, 3d ed., London: Macmillan Press Ltd., chap. 15, 2000, for discussion of global financial crises.

[13]These attributes are neither good nor bad. Each market develops in response to economic conditions, the nature of its investors, sources of financing, and other factors. In Japan, for example, banks have long been the primary sources of finance. These banks have had full access to inside information about Japanese companies, and so there has been less demand in Japan for credible external financial reporting.

[14]For example, in an "unusually aggressive" move, the Osaka Securities Exchange launched a campaign to bar companies linked with organized crime from Nasdaq Japan in November 2000 Harney, Alexandra, "Osaka Market Targets Crime, *Financial Times* (November 16, 2000): 18.

[15]For example, Taiwan announced in November 2000 that it would institute emergency action to support share prices after a recent, dramatic fall. Mure Dickie, "Taiwan Offers Support as Share Prices Fall

However, the prospects for future growth in Asian equity markets are strong. Market capitalization as a percentage of GDP in Asia is low compared with that in the United States and several major European markets (see Exhibit 1-4), suggesting that equity markets can play a much larger role in many Asian economies. Also, Asian governments and stock exchanges are under pressure to improve market quality and credibility to attract investors.[16] A few Asian markets (e.g., Korea, Taiwan, and Hong Kong) have grown rapidly, and have experienced heavy trading volume relative to market capitalization.

WESTERN EUROPE

Europe is the second largest equity market region in the world in terms of market capitalization and trading volume.[17] Exhibit 1-3 shows the dramatic growth of many Continental European markets from 1995 through 2000. Market capitalization more than doubled in France, Germany, Italy, the Netherlands, and Spain (Madrid). Exhibit 1-4 shows that Europe outranks North America in terms of the number of foreign listed companies. Thus, even relative to the more mature United States equity market, the European equity market is large, active, and international.

Economic expansion significantly contributed to the rapid growth in European equity markets during the second half of the 1990s. A related factor in Continental Europe has been a gradual shift to an *equity orientation* that long has characterized the London and North American equity markets.[18] Privatizations of large government entities have made European equity markets more prominent and have attracted non-institutional investors, who until recently were not active in Continental Europe. Finally, confidence in European markets has grown with the success of the European Monetary Union (EMU).

The recent success of the "new markets" for fast growing technology companies (most notably Germany's Neuer Markt) reflects (and has helped cause) the growing importance of equity markets in Western Europe. Growing risk tolerance of investors and low-cost access to information on the World Wide Web have contributed to the growth of these new markets.

The "new markets" concept is not new. For many years, European stock exchanges created new markets to provide credible market segments for new types of issuers during times of market expansion. Later, the new markets lost their attractiveness and

---

Sharply," *Financial Times* (November 21, 2000): 16]. Also see Chris Cockerill, "The Two Faces of Chinese Capital," *Euromoney* (December 2000): 46.

[16]The Singapore Exchange, for example, has moved aggressively to position itself as the premier financial exchange in Asia outside of Japan. The exchange recently implemented new listing rules and more stringent disclosure requirements to attract new domestic and foreign listings [See PricewaterhouseCoopers' *International Briefings*, (May, June, and September 2000). As a second example, see "An End to Make-Believe Accounting (in Japan)," *Financial Times* (April 5, 2000)].

[17]International Federation of Stock Exchanges (FIBV) 1999 Annual Report, Paris: FIBV, 2000.

[18]Developed countries around the world can be divided roughly into those having a common law (English) orientation and those having a code law (Continental Europe) orientation (see Chapter 2). Common law countries include the United Kingdom, Canada, the United States, and Australia. In these countries, equity investors are widely dispersed and are the most important suppliers of capital. As a result, capital markets in many common law countries have evolved credible and open disclosure and accounting systems, and relatively stringent market regulation. In code law countries such as France, Germany, and Japan, banks provide most of the financing, and ownership tends to be concentrated among small groups of insiders. Demand for detailed public disclosure is generally lower in these countries than in common law countries, but is increasing.

were replaced by even newer markets. For example, during the 1980s the LSE created the Unlisted Securities Market (USM) for small companies ineligible for Official Listings. By the mid-1990s the USM's reputation had eroded. In response, the LSE created the Alternative Investment Market (AIM), and required all USM companies to transfer to AIM.

European equity markets will continue to grow. Stock market capitalization in the 11 members of the EMU was only 63 percent of GDP at year-end 1998, in contrast to 145 percent in the U.S. market and 156 percent in the U.K. market,[19] indicating significant growth potential. In addition, pension reform will create new demand for investment opportunities.[20] Also, more and more foreign investors are entering European equity markets. Cross-border equity flows are increasing as a percentage of cross-border bond flows, in part because equity has been a profitable investment since the market crash of October 1987.[21] The advent of the euro in early 1999 prompted a rush of cross-border mergers, which are expected to continue.

The rapid growth in global capital markets and cross-border investment activity means that the international dimensions of accounting are more important than ever for professionals who have to deal in any way with these areas.

EUROPEAN EQUITY MARKETS—A CLOSER LOOK

There are several good reasons to take a closer look at European equity markets. European capital markets are undergoing major, rapid changes, in part due to the globalization of the world economy and the increasing economic integration of the European Union. These changes reflect and exemplify changes taking place in capital markets around the world. Thus, a closer look at European equity markets will help lay the foundation for a better understanding of equity markets in general.

CONTINENTAL EUROPE'S NEW EQUITY CULTURE

A further basis for predicting continued growth in European equity markets is the growing equity culture in Europe. The successful hostile takeover in 1999 of Mannesmann, the third largest German company in market capitalization, by Vodafone, a British company, at a value estimated at US$175 billion, was a watershed example of the growth in shareholder power. At first most observers expected Mannesmann to mount a successful traditional defense, but pressure from large shareholders forced management to accept the deal. "The shareholder is king," said Mannesmann's chairman, Klaus Esser, when he finally conceded.[22]

Intense rivalry among European stock exchanges has contributed to the development of an equity culture. During the 1990s Continental European markets became

---

[19]Stephen Valdez, *An Introduction to Global Financial Markets*, 3d ed. London: Macmillan Press Ltd., 2000.
[20]With aging populations causing the numbers of pensioners to increase, a major initiative across much of Europe has been to move toward the private funding of pensions. The goal is to relieve the strain on "pay-as-you-go" state pension schemes. The growing numbers of private pension funds are allocating more of their assets to equities to increase returns. Also, some countries are liberalizing restrictions on pension fund investment.
[21]See "Shares Flow More Freely," *The Economist* (August 19, 2000): 66.
[22]See "Bidding for the Future," *The Economist* (February 12, 2000): 71.

more investor oriented to increase their credibility and attract new listings. External investors, in particular foreign investors and institutional investors, are demanding expanded disclosure and improved corporate governance. In addition, equity market development has become increasingly important to national governments and regulators, who also compete for recognition and prestige. Many European securities regulators and stock exchanges have implemented more stringent market rules, and are strengthening their enforcement efforts.

However, intense rivalry has also led stock exchanges and national regulators to ease listing rules and grant special exemptions to issuers. For example, the Paris Bourse exempted a French company (LibertySurf) from key requirements for admission to its main market after LibertySurf threatened to seek a listing on the Deutsche Börse if its demands were not met.[23] The Neuer Markt has also made concessions to attract new listings.

Continental European companies started to increase their disclosure levels, improve their financial reporting, and strengthen their corporate governance during the 1990s to attract new capital and investor interest. However, many of these companies, including some of the world's largest, still fall short of British and North American disclosure and listing standards.[24]

CONVERGENCE AND INTEGRATION OF EQUITY MARKETS

The growth of an equity culture in Europe has led to market convergence, as national equity markets become more similar. Market convergence is one step toward market integration. Perfect integration means that location (of the investor, the seeker of finance, the technology, and the regulation) no longer matters. In a perfectly integrated European capital market, a person or entity from any European nation would be able to trade any instrument regulated in any European market from any European location at the same cost.

One of the most important barriers to European capital market integration is fragmentation of clearing and settlement.[25] Settlement in Europe costs up to 10 times as much as in the United States.[26] A further problem is the large number of stock exchanges and the complex array of stock exchange alliances and mergers. Market participants also complain that they need to work with too many trading rule books and too many trading systems. The fragmentation of the securities trading infrastructure in Europe makes cross-border trading unacceptably expensive.[27]

---

[23]See S. Iskandar and B. Benoit, "Growing Competition Threatens Confidence," *Financial Times* (May 1, 2000).

[24]For example, *The Economist* (October 7, 2000): 73–74 discusses the ambivalence of French companies toward outside scrutiny and investor-oriented corporate governance.

[25]Clearing is the process of determining what each party is due to receive. Settlement involves the actual transfer of securities from the seller to the buyer, with an offsetting payment in cash.

[26]"European Stock Exchanges — Two into Three," *The Economist* (July 22, 2000): 98.

[27]These points were made in Richard Meier, *The European Stock Exchanges in Turmoil — A Swiss Perspective*, Zurich: SWX Swiss Exchanges, 2000.

Technological advances and competition will help reduce transaction costs and market fragmentation in cross-border trading. However, national differences in language, culture, legal and tax systems, and market regulation will continue into the foreseeable future. National regulators and stock exchanges strongly endorse the concept of a single European equity market, but at the same time create barriers to prevent it from happening.

European Union (EU) activities and the EMU have facilitated European equity market integration.[28] At the same time, EU developments illustrate the extent to which strong national interests interfere with financial market integration. For example, national competitive interests have been blamed for some of the most serious failures of the EU's Investment Services Directive (ISD), the umbrella framework for the integration of Europe's capital markets (see Chapter 8). A key weakness of the ISD is that some of its provisions have proved ambiguous in practice and have led to a range of different applications. National authorities have been accused of using the ISD as a protectionist weapon. Even when EU Directives lay down specific rules, their implementation differs from one Member State to another.[29]

Many have argued that a single European securities regulator is necessary for an integrated European capital market. However, most market experts agree that a "European SEC" is not the best way to regulate capital markets in Europe. In an informal discussion in October 2000, one European stock exchange executive said:

> "National regulators do not want to be replaced by a European regulator. Market participants are fearful of a new regulator who will introduce new rules and establish far-reaching regulations. Germans fear English regulation, and the French fear German regulation. Some fear that the U.K. FSA [Financial Services Authority] will take over Europe. Even more threatening is a complex mixture of London-, Frankfurt-, and Paris-based regulation. Although everyone agrees that a single European Capital Market is desirable, everyone also takes steps to prevent it from happening."[30]

STOCK EXCHANGE ALLIANCES AND MERGERS

Stock exchange alliances and mergers have made the European capital market landscape exceptionally complex. These alliances involve the sharing of various stock exchange functions, which may include marketing, listing, order routing, information

---

[28] Many other international organizations are seeking to reduce barriers to cross-border equity flows. As one example, IOSCO (International Organisation of Securities Commissions), which is comprised of securities regulators from more than eighty countries, has played a key role in the development of the International Accounting Standards and harmonization of disclosure standards for use in cross-border securities offerings (see *www.iosco.org*).

[29] See European Union Internal Market D.G. "European Securities Regulation—Set up of an Independent Committee." *Single Market News* (November 23, October 2000): 5.

[30] For formal arguments against the appropriateness of a "European SEC" and critical analysis of the ISD, refer to the European Commission Internal Market Web site (*http://europa.eu.int/comm/internal_market*); Benn Steil, *The European Equity Markets—The State of the Union and an Agenda for the Millennium.* London: Royal Institute of International Affairs, 1996; and the *FESE (Federation of European Stock Exchanges) Newsletter* (October, 2000).

dissemination, order execution, matching, clearing, settlement, and administration. Normally, a primary goal for any stock exchange entering an alliance is to reduce costs and thus gain a competitive advantage over its rivals. Relevant costs are those borne by the exchange and those borne by all stock exchange participants.[31]

Stock exchange alliances illustrate the internal contradictions in European capital market development. Stock exchange linkages involve cooperative agreements designed to benefit each member. However, the alliance members themselves are rivals, and often encounter significant problems because they cannot cooperate. A key problem is that it is difficult to create credible contractual commitments between the alliance partners.

Appendix 1-1 briefly describes Europe's most significant stock exchange alliances when this book went to press. The appendix includes discussions of globalization initiatives underway at the NYSE, Nasdaq, and The American Stock Exchange (Amex). These three U.S. stock markets have all been pursuing alliances in Europe.

CROSS-BORDER EQUITY LISTING AND ISSUANCE

The current wave of interest in cross-border listings on the European new markets follows a period during the 1980s when hundreds of foreign companies listed on European stock exchanges. Listing costs were relatively low, and "everyone was doing it."

Evidence suggests that issuers seek cross-border listings in Europe to broaden their shareholder base, promote awareness in their products, and/or build public awareness of the company, particularly in countries where the company has significant operations and/or major customers. (European stock exchanges long have promoted these potential benefits.) However, there is little evidence that such benefits are realized in European markets. Most foreign equities in Continental Europe are thinly traded or are not traded at all, and have few local shareholders. As noted earlier, during the 1990s many foreign companies delisted from European stock exchanges after realizing minimal benefits from those listings.

However, foreign issuers increasingly are raising capital in the European new markets. The rapid growth in Europe's new markets reflects a fundamental shift in Europe as retail (individual, non-institutional) investors become more active and an equity culture develops. The success of the new markets in turn creates further interest by retail investors. Continental European markets are becoming more credible and, therefore, potentially more attractive to foreign issuers.

National regulators and stock exchanges compete fiercely for foreign listings and trade volume, considered necessary for any stock exchange that seeks to become or remain a global leader. In response, European exchanges and market regulators have worked to make access faster and less costly for foreign issuers and at the same time increase their markets' credibility. As European markets become more specialized, each can offer unique benefits to foreign issuers.

Many European companies have difficulty deciding where to raise capital or list their shares. Knowledge of many equity markets with different laws, regulations, and in-

---

[31]Ruben Lee, *What is an Exchange? The Automation, Management, and Regulation of Financial Markets*, Oxford, England: Oxford University Press, Chaps. 4 and 5, 1998, presents a detailed discussion of stock exchange competition and cooperation.

stitutional features now is required. Also required is an understanding of how issuer and stock exchange characteristics interact. The issuer's home country, industry, and offering size are just some of the factors that need to be considered.[32] In addition, the costs and benefits of different market combinations need to be understood. One entrepreneur planning to raise capital said: "I spoke to three investment banks about it, and I had three different answers about which would be the right market for me." A London broker who advises companies on where to raise capital states that "The landscape is moving so fast that no one knows what it's going to be like in 6 months' time."[33] Exhibit 1-7 presents a more detailed list of factors companies consider in choosing a foreign capital market.[34]

The rapid pace of change in European capital markets, including the growing importance of stock exchange alliances, the emergence of Europe's new markets, and alternative trading systems, presents a highly complex setting. However, although financial reporting regulation will remain complex, the differences in rules will continue to lessen from one country to the next.

AN EXAMPLE—NIKKEN CHEMICALS CO., LIMITED

Appendix 1-2 contains the financial statements (including notes) and auditor's report (Report of Independent Certified Public Accountants) from Nikken Chemicals Co., Ltd.'s 2000 Annual Report. Nikken Chemicals, founded in 1947, develops, manufactures, and markets pharmaceuticals. Nikken Chemicals' common stock is listed on the Tokyo Stock Exchange but not on any overseas markets. The company reported 2000 net sales of more than US$550 million.

A potential investor or business partner from outside Japan would need to consider many international accounting issues to effectively use the information in Nikken's Annual Report. What accounting principles are used? Should the financial statements be restated to a different set of accounting principles to be more useful? What types of information does Nikken *not* disclose that one would expect to find in financial statements of companies from the United States, the United Kingdom, or Canada? How does one compensate for Nikken's limited disclosure? What does the auditor's report reveal about the level of audit quality? What auditing standards were used? Are they acceptable? Does the auditor's opinion mean the same thing in Japan as it does in the reader's home country? How does Nikken account for marketable securities (refer to

---

[32]*Home country* is relevant because companies can raise capital more easily in foreign countries that have legal and regulatory environments similar to their own. For example, an Australian company can probably access the U.K. equity market more easily than the French equity market. *Industry* is important because, other things equal, issuers seek to raise capital in markets where other companies in the same industry are listed, in order to improve the chances for adequate attention by financial analysts. For example, the SWX Swiss Exchange's New Market is attractive to biotechnology companies in part because Novartis and Roche (two of the world's largest pharmaceutical companies) are listed on the SWX Swiss Exchange and have attracted many pharmaceutical/biotech analysts to Zurich. Offering size is important because only relatively large offerings attract sufficient attention in the United States. Much smaller IPOs are common in Europe's new markets.

[33]Charles Fleming, "Europe's IPOs: Tough Choices on Just Where to Go Public," *The Wall Street Journal* (July 11, 2000), page C1.

[34]Appendix 1-3 presents Web site addresses for stock exchanges in more than 50 countries. Many stock exchange Web sites include information on unique stock exchange features that may attract foreign companies considering listing or raising capital in those markets.

EXHIBIT 1-7 Factors Relevant in Choosing an Overseas Market[35]

1. What is the extent of interest in a company shown by financial analysts and investors who normally participate in a market?
2. What is the level of trading activity on the exchange? Higher trading volume means more potential buyers of a company's securities.
3. How easy is it to raise capital? Some jurisdictions have complex listing or ongoing reporting requirements that may be difficult or impossible for a smaller company to meet.
4. What is the availability of capital in a market?
5. What is the reputation of the exchange? A growing international company may want the increased credibility and recognition that come with listing on a preeminent market such as the New York Stock Exchange.
6. To what extent does the company desire to raise its profile and establish its brand identity in a particular market? A stock exchange listing can benefit companies that operate or plan to operate in an overseas country.
7. To what extent are the market's regulatory environment and language similar to those in the company's home market? For example, a company from an English-speaking country with a common law (British-American) legal and regulatory system, such as Australia, might find it easier to list in the United Kingdom than in Continental Europe.
8. To what extent do institutional investors face statutory or self-imposed restrictions on the proportion of their investment portfolio that they can hold in securities of foreign companies? Sometimes these restrictions force a large international company to list on many stock exchanges to have access to sufficient institutional capital. These restrictions are difficult to overcome in some jurisdictions.
9. What are the nature and activities of investors in the market? For example, large pension funds in the Netherlands, Switzerland, and the United Kingdom invest heavily in equities of both domestic and foreign companies.
10. What is the likelihood that the company will be required to have locally listed shares to carry out a merger or acquisition in a particular country?
11. Will there be a need for locally listed shares to be used in employee stock option plans?

notes 2 and 5 in its financial statements)? Is this approach different from or similar to the accounting approach used in financial statements from the reader's home country?

Nikken's financial statements also raise many managerial and tax issues with international dimensions. How are transactions in foreign currencies and financial instruments accounted for? What are the related financial statement disclosures? Does the financial reporting of these items provide useful information to managers for managing transactions in these areas? Does Nikken's tax expense reflect domestic taxes only? What are the tax consequences to Nikken of doing business abroad?

Nikken's financial statements pose questions that any reader of nondomestic financial statements needs to address. Such questions and their answers provide the motivation for the following chapters.

---

[35]See PricewaterhouseCoopers LLC, *Accessing International Capital Markets*, New York: Pricewaterhouse-Coopers Global Capital Market Group, 2001.

Stock Exchange Alliances and Mergers

AMERICAN STOCK EXCHANGE ALLIANCES

Amex has been forming alliances with stock exchanges around the world to cross-list and trade exchange-traded funds (ETFs), which consist of baskets of stocks (such as Standard and Poor's Depository Receipts) that trade throughout the day in the same way as individual stocks. To date, Amex has announced joint agreements with Euronext NV (see the following) and the Singapore Exchange.

EURONEXT NV

Euronext NV is the first totally integrated cross-border, single-currency European stock and derivatives market, created by the merger of the Amsterdam, Brussels, and Paris Exchanges in September 2000. Euronext is divided into three main segments: (1) top stocks; (2) next economy stocks; and (3) mid and small caps. The Lisbon Stock Exchange will join Euronext in 2001, and the Luxembourg Stock Exchange has signed a cross-membership and cross-access agreement with Euronext. Euronext has a decentralized regulatory structure with entry points in the three financial centers (Amsterdam, Brussels, and Paris). Euronext will provide the benefits of a consolidated exchange organization, but will remain based in the local markets of Europe. Euronext will ensure that the listing criteria for entry to the three markets are harmonized and that the requirements that have to be met by the companies on an ongoing basis are the same.

GEM—THE NEW YORK STOCK EXCHANGE'S "GLOBAL EQUITY MARKET"

GEM is the provisional name of a planned market of 10 stock exchanges that was in the early planning stages when this book went to press. The initial members are the three Euronext exchanges (Amsterdam, Brussels, and Paris), Mexico, New York, Toronto, Sao Paulo, Australia, Hong Kong, and Tokyo. GEM's goal is to create a platform for equities trading 24 hours a day in the blue chip equities listed on each of the GEM partners.

GEM is a new trading platform that will be added to each member exchange. GEM will use a *Portal Model* where investors can access the equities traded on GEM in their local time zone, quoted in their home currency. For example, a Paris investor could use his normal trading screen and see quotes for IBM in euros. At first, the 200 largest listed companies in the world will be traded on GEM. The regulations and structure of the participating exchanges will not change.

JIWAY

Jiway is a new Internet-based market launched by Sweden's OM Group and Morgan Stanley Dean Witter, whose goal is to set up a pan-European retail market for 6,000 or so listed companies. Trading on Jiway began in November 2000.

NASDAQ ALLIANCES

Nasdaq has formed several cross-border alliances with operations underway in Canada, Japan, and Hong Kong. A high priority has been to establish a European trading platform with linkages on a global basis with Nasdaq markets in the United States and Asia.

Nasdaq Europe SA/NV, a new legal entity, was created in early 2001 when Nasdaq acquired majority ownership in Easdaq. Easdaq, established in 1996, is a pan-European screen-based quote-driven market that, like Nasdaq, uses a multiple market maker system. The Easdaq acquisition allows Nasdaq to establish a presence in Europe.

The **Nasdaq Japan Market** launched its first day of trading as a section of the Osaka Stock Exchange in June 2000. Within 10 months, 46 Japanese companies were listed on the new market.

Listing regulations are closely modeled after those of the Nasdaq Stock Market. The Nasdaq Japan Market consists of the Growth Section, designed for young developing companies, and the Standard Section, for companies that have well-established operations.

In June 2000, seven Nasdaq stocks began trading on the **Stock Exchange of Hong Kong** as part of a pilot program to quote and trade Nasdaq stocks on that market. The Nasdaq shares have been admitted for trading only, and are not actually listed in Hong Kong. The stocks are quoted and traded in Hong Kong dollars. Pilot Programme issuers include Amgen, Applied Materials, Cisco Systems, Dell, Intel, Microsoft, and Starbucks.

Nasdaq Canada began operations in November 2000, with 10 securities firms initially participating in the trading of all Nasdaq-listed securities directly from Montreal. Nasdaq Canada provides Canadian investors with immediate access to both the Canadian companies listed on Nasdaq (over 40 of which were previously listed only in the United States) and other Nasdaq issues.

NEWEX

Newex is a special exchange for Eastern European companies formed by a joint venture of Deutsche Börse and Wiener Börse (Austria), announced in August 2000. Newex offers a trading and financing platform for start-ups and restructuring by Eastern companies. It is said that these companies need access to international capital, and that Austria can be a gateway market. Newex began trading in November 2000 with 10 listed companies. Dozens of companies from Poland, the Czech Republic, Hungary, and Russia are now listed on Newex. Twenty banks and trading firms from Germany, Austria, and the United Kingdom will trade on Newex.

NOREX

NOREX is a cooperative agreement of the Copenhagen, OM Stockholm, and Iceland Stock Exchanges. The Oslo Stock Exchange has signed a formal agreement to become the fourth member of the alliance, and stock exchanges of the three Baltic States have signed letters of intent.

The NOREX alliance is based on the principles of independent exchanges; cross-membership (that is, membership of all participating exchanges grants access to all listed securities), a joint trading system, and harmonized trading rules. The NOREX Alliance will not affect relations between the exchanges and their listed firms.

VIRT-X

Virt-X, the first European blue chips trading platform, is a joint venture of the SWX Swiss Exchange, Tradepoint Financial Networks PLC (a Pan-European, London-based electronic exchange), and the Tradepoint Consortium. Blue-chip shares listed on SWX moved to Virt-X, along with those listed on Tradepoint. Virt-X began operating in June 2001.

Virt-X is a London-based Recognised Investment Exchange (via Tradepoint) with a single rule book, supervised by the Financial Services Authority (FSA). Virt-x offers secondary listings only. Virt-X's informal listing procedures are based on home country listing and control.

A P P E N D I X   1 - 2

Financial Statement and Auditor's Report from Nikken Chemical Co. Ltd.'s 2000 Annual Report

CONSOLIDATED BALANCE SHEETS
Nikken Chemicals Co., Ltd. and Consolidated Subsidiary
As of March 31, 2000

ASSETS	2000 Millions of yen	2000 Thousands of U.S. dollars (Note 3)
Current assets:		
Cash and cash equivalents (Note 4)	¥ 2,139	$ 20,151
Time deposits	200	1,884
Marketable securities	1,162	10,947
Notes receivable, trade	4,865	45,831
Accounts receivable, trade	21,479	202,345
Allowances for sales rebates and loss on sales returns (Note 9)	(813)	(7,659)
Inventories (Note 6)	8,651	81,498
Deferred tax assets (Note 11)	1,080	10,174
Other current assets	320	3,015
Allowance for doubtful receivables	(103)	(970)
Total current assets	38,980	367,216
Investments:		
Marketable securities (Note 5)	1,900	17,899
Capital investments in and advances to unconsolidated subsidiaries	169	1,592
Investment securities	363	3,420
Total investments	2,432	22,911
Property, plant and equipment:		
Land	2,242	21,121
Buildings	12,798	120,565
Machinery and equipment	21,024	198,060
Construction in progress	91	857
	36,155	340,603
Accumulated depreciation (Note 7)	(21,348)	(201,112)
Total fixed assets	14,807	139,491
Other assets:		
Deferred tax assets (Note 11)	2,832	26,679
Lease guarantee deposits	814	7,669
Intangible and other assets	302	2,845
Total other assets	3,948	37,193
Total assets	¥60,167	$566,811

The accompanying notes are an integral part of these statements

(continued)

CONSOLIDATED BALANCE SHEETS (*continued*)
Nikken Chemicals Co., Ltd. and Consolidated Subsidiary
As of March 31, 2000

	2000	2000
LIABILITIES AND SHAREHOLDERS' EQUITY	Millions of yen	Thousands of U.S. dollars (Note 3)
Current liabilities:		
Bank loans (Note 8)	¥ 6,060	$ 57,089
Current portion of long-term debt (Note 8)	40	377
Notes payable, trade	755	7,113
Accounts payable, trade	11,464	107,998
Accrued taxes on income	510	4,805
Consumption tax payable	322	3,033
Other accrued expenses	262	2,468
Other current liabilities	2,194	20,669
Total current liabilities	21,607	203,552
Long-term liabilities:		
Long-term borrowings (Note 8)	140	1,319
Accrued severance indemnities (Note 10)	9,480	89,307
Total long-term liabilities	9,620	90,626
Minority shareholders' equity in consolidated subsidiary	1,270	11,964
Commitments and contingent liabilities (Note 14)		
Shareholders' equity:		
Common stock, ¥50 par value—		
Authorized—160,000,000 shares		
Issued—71,979,164 shares	6,775	63,825
Additional paid-in capital	9,061	85,360
Legal reserve (Note 12)	881	8,300
General reserves	9,708	91,455
Unappropriated retained earnings (Note 17)	1,245	11,729
Total shareholders' equity	27,670	260,669
Liabilities and shareholders' equity	¥60,167	$566,811

CONSOLIDATED STATEMENTS OF INCOME
Nikken Chemicals Co., Ltd. and Consolidated Subsidiary
For the year ended March 31, 2000

	2000	2000
	Millions of yen	Thousands of U.S. dollars (Note 3)
Net sales	¥59,793	$563,288
Cost of sales	37,063	349,157
Gross profit	22,730	214,131
Selling, general and administrative expenses (Note 13)	20,584	193,914
Operating income	2,146	20,217
Other income (expenses):		
Interest and dividend income	132	1,244
Interest expenses	(48)	(452)
Provisions for severance indemnities for prior years	(4,358)	(41,055)
Amortization of prior service costs of pensions for prior years	(724)	(6,821)
Reversal of money received attributable to warrants	1,281	12,068
Loss on disposal of fixed assets	(57)	(537)
Other, net	367	3,457
	(3,407)	(32,096)
Income before income taxes	(1,261)	(11,879)
Income taxes (Note 11):		
Current provision	1,651	15,553
Deferred benefits	(2,083)	(19,623)
	(432)	(4,070)
Loss before minority interest	(829)	(7,809)
Minority interest in income in consolidated subsidiary	116	1,093
Net loss	¥ (945)	$ (8,902)
	Yen	U.S. dollars (Note 3)
Per share of common stock:		
Net income:		
Basic	¥(12.79)	$(0.120)
Fully-diluted	(12.79)	(0.120)
Cash dividends	5.50	0.052

Pro forma amounts assuming the methods of (1) providing the methods of accruing severance indemnities and (2) amortization of prior service costs of pension are applied retroactively:

	2000	2000
	Millions of yen	Thousands of U.S. dollars (Note 3)
Net income	¥1,799	$16,948
	Yen	U.S. dollars (Note 3)
Net income per share	¥24.30	$0.229

The accompanying notes are an integral part of these statements.

CONSOLIDATED STATEMENTS OF SHAREHOLDERS' EQUITY
Nikken Chemicals Co., Ltd. and Consolidated Subsidiary
For the year ended March 31, 2000

	Number of shares issued	Common stock	Additional paid-in capital	Legal reserve	General reserves	Unappropriated retained earnings
			Millions of yen			
Balance, April 1, 1999.................................	74,259,164	¥6,775	¥10,029	¥835	¥8,981	¥1,658
2000 net income						(945)
Cash dividends...						(433)
Transfer to legal reserve				46		(46)
Transfer to general reserves...............					727	(727)
Bonuses to directors.............................						(38)
Retirement of treasury shares	(2,280,000)		(968)			
Deferred tax assets, prior years						1,776
Balance, March 31, 2000	71,979,164	¥6,775	¥ 9,061	¥881	¥9,708	¥1,245
			Thousands of U.S. dollars (Note 3)			
Balance, April 1, 1999		$63,825	$94,479	$7,867	$84,606	$15,619
2000 net income						(8,902)
Cash dividends						(4,079)
Transfer to legal reserve				433		(433)
Transfer to general reserves					6,849	(6,849)
Bonuses to directors						(358)
Retirement of treasury shares			(9,119)			
Deferred tax assets, prior years						16,731
Balance, March 31, 2000		$63,825	$85,360	$8,300	$91,455	$11,729

The accompanying notes are an integral part of these statements.

CONSOLIDATED STATEMENTS OF CASH FLOWS
Nikken Chemicals Co., Ltd. and Consolidated Subsidiary
For the year ended March 31, 2000

	2000	2000
	Millions of yen	Thousands of U.S. dollars (Note 3)
Cash flows from operating activities:		
Net loss	¥ (945)	$(8,902)
Adjustments to reconcile net income to net cash provided by operating activities—		
Depreciation and amortization	2,418	22,779
Loss on disposal of fixed assets	58	546
Provision for severance indemnities	4,452	41,941
Deferred tax assets	(2,083)	(19,623)
Realized exchange gain on bonds with warrants	1,199	11,295
Reversal of money received attributable to warrants	(1,281)	(12,068)
Write-down of securities	1	9
Dividend on company-owned group life insurance policy	(43)	(405)
Bonuses to directors	(38)	(358)
Minority interest in consolidated subsidiary	116	1,093
Changes in operating assets and liabilities—		
Trade receivables	806	7,593
Inventories	(413)	(3,891)
Other current assets	193	1,818
Trade payables	(1,154)	(10,871)
Accrued expenses and other current liabilities	(797)	(7,508)
Net cash provided by operating activities	2,489	23,448
Cash flows from investing activities:		
Acquisition of fixed assets	(4,725)	(44,512)
Disposal of fixed assets	(20)	(188)
Decrease in marketable securities	421	3,966
Refund of company-owned group life insurance policy	3,268	30,786
Other decrease in investments and other	403	3,796
Net cash used for investing activities	(653)	(6,152)
Cash flows from financing activities:		
Increase in bank loans	5,000	47,103
Borrowing of long-term bank loans	200	1,884
Repayment of long-term bank loans	(320)	(3,015)
Redemption of guaranteed bonds with warrants	(10,564)	(99,520)
Cash dividends	(433)	(4,079)
Retirement of shares acquired	(968)	(9,118)
Net cash used for financing activities	(7,085)	(66,745)
Net decrease in cash and cash equivalents	(5,249)	(49,449)
Cash and cash equivalents at:		
Beginning of period	7,388	69,600
End of period	¥ 2,139	$20,151
Supplemental information on cash flows:		
Cash paid during the period for—		
Interest	¥ 76	$ 716
Income taxes	2,821	26,576

The accompanying notes are an integral part of these statements.

NOTES TO CONSOLIDATED FINANCIAL STATEMENTS
Nikken Chemicals Co., Ltd. and Consolidated Subsidiary

1. Basis of presenting consolidated financial statements:

The Company and its subsidiaries maintain record[s] and prepare their financial statements in accordance with accounting principles generally accepted in Japan. The accompanying consolidated financial statements, which are also prepared in accordance with accounting principles generally accepted in Japan, incorporate certain modifications in format to the statutory financial statements and include statements of shareholders' equity and certain additional notes which were not contained in the statutory financial statements, so as to make the financial statements more meaningful to readers outside Japan. These modifications have no effect on net income or shareholders' equity. Up to the year ended March 31, 1999 the Company did not prepare the consolidated financial statements as there had been no significant subsidiary.

During the current year the Japanese consolidation principles was revised with respect to the definition of a subsidiary being an enterprise which is controlled by another enterprise. As a result an affiliate owned 50-percent or less voting rights may be a subsidiary if a shareholder has control (the power to govern the financial and operating policies of such affiliate so as to obtain benefits from its activities). Based on the new definition of a subsidiary Nikken Fine Chemicals Co., Ltd. mentioned below is now classified as a subsidiary, and the Company prepares the consolidated financial statements for the year ended March 31, 2000.

2. Significant accounting policies
Basis of consolidation and investments in unconsolidated subsidiaries—

The consolidated financial statements include the accounts of Nikken Chemicals Co., Ltd. and those of its 48-percent owned affiliate named Nikken Fine Chemicals Co., Ltd. (deemed subsidiary) over which the Company does have control. All significant intercompany transactions and accounts are eliminated. The other two subsidiaries are insignificant and investments therein are stated at costs.

Foreign currency securities, receivables, payables and bonds with warrants—

Marketable securities (bonds) denominated in foreign currencies are substantially covered by forward exchange contracts and are translated into yen at the forward contracted rates. Short-term receivables and payables denominated in foreign currencies are translated into yen at the exchange rate current at the end of each fiscal period. The resulting translation gains or losses are included in the determination of net income for the fiscal period.

Bonds with warrants denominated in foreign currencies are also covered by forward exchange contract and are translated into yen at the forward contracted rate. The resulting translation gain is being deducted from interest expenses on such bonds or credited to interest income over the period through each maturity date for the bonds.

Accounting for sales rebates and loss on sales returns—

Sales rebates are subsequently paid to dealers against collections of sales proceeds, and are based on various factors, including each dealer's performance against its target. The allowance for rebates is provided based on outstanding receivables at year-end applying the actual sales rebates ratio for each year. The allowance for sales rebates is not deductible for tax purposes until the rebates actually take place.

Sales returns are permitted within a specified period after delivery. An allowance for loss on sales returns is provided for gross profit and disposal of goods for potential sales returns. The potential loss arising from disposal of the goods accrued is not deductible for tax purposes until the return actually incurred and the loss realized.

Cash equivalents—

The Company considers all highly liquid investments with a remaining maturity of three months or less at the time of purchase to be cash equivalents.

Marketable securities—

Marketable securities (current and non-current), including equity securities, are stated at the amount of (i) the lower of the moving average cost or market for those having a ready market and (ii) the moving average cost for other securities.

Inventories—

Inventories are stated at the gross average cost.

Property, plant and equipment—

Property, plant and equipment is stated at cost. Depreciation is computed principally on the declining-balance method at rates based on the estimated useful lives of the assets. Maintenance and repairs, including minor renewals and betterment, are charged to income as incurred.

Investment in company-owned group life insurance policy—

In 1997, the Company purchased a company-owned group life insurance policy insuring employees' severance indemnities at their age limits. Premiums are accumulated in the policy and are accounted for as investment in company-owned group life insurance policy in the accompanying balance sheet. The investment is partially financing such severance indemnities for age limit separation. During the current year the Company surrendered such group life insurance policy.

Money received attributable to warrants—

In February 1994 the Accounting Committee of the Japanese Institute of Certified Public Accountants issued the guidance on accounting treatment on bonds with warrants effective from the fiscal period beginning on or after April 1, 1994. Such guidance is recognized as authoritative pronouncements on the generally accepted accounting principles in Japan.

The guidance requires that bonds and warrants be separately accounted for to reflect the privilege of the lower rate of interest on such bonds with warrants than that on straight bonds. The face value (or issue value) of such bonds is recorded as long-term debt and the hypothetical proceeds only attributable to the assumed straight bonds under the same level of contractual debt-servicing cost are presumed to be received by an issuing corporation, and the difference between the face value and such attributable proceeds is accounted for as "bond discount". The "bond discount" is being amortized over a period to the maturity of the bonds. The appraised value of the warrants, which is equivalent to the amount of "bond discount", is accounted for as "Money received attributable to warrants" in the current liabilities, and the proceeds thereof are included in cash together with a portion for the proceeds attributable to the assumed straight bonds as mentioned above. The balance of the "Money received attributable to warrants" is transferred to additional paid-in capital when warrantholders exercise their subscription rights and the remainder, if any, at the time of expiration of warrants is reversed to income.

During the current year the balance of the money received attributable to warrants was reversed to income as expired.

Accrued severance indemnities—

Employees whose service with the Company and its consolidated subsidiary is terminated are, under most circumstances, entitled to lump-sum severance indemnities, determined by reference to current basic rate of pay, length of service and the conditions under which the termination occurs.

The recorded liability for employees' severance indemnities at March 31, 1999 represents the present value of the amount (vested benefit) which would be required to be paid if all the eligible employees voluntarily retire at that date. During the year ended March 31, 2000 the Company and its consolidated subsidiary changed their policy to accrue severance indemnities at the full amount of the vested benefits not taking into consideration of the discount factor. Management believes that the new method of accruing severance indemnities is better measure in respect of recent employees' turnover. The resultant effect of this change was to increase accrued severance indemnities at March 31, 1999 by ¥4,358 million ($41,055 thousand) and was charged to other expenses.

The Company and its consolidated subsidiary have adopted funded pension plans, covering 30 percent of the retirement benefits for employees of the Company and 70 percent of its consolidated subsidiary. The benefits are payable either as a monthly pension or, under certain circumstances at the option of retiring employees, in a lump-sum amount. The Company and its consolidated subsidiary's contributions to the plan include amortization of prior service costs. The amortization of prior service costs of the Company is amortized over 10 years up to the years ended March 31, 1999, and amortized in fiscal 2000 over two years. Management of the Company also considers that this shortening of the year of the amortization is sound policy based on various factors including lower actuarial gains due to market and increasing ratio of involuntary separation, or age limit retirement. The effect of the addi-

tional charge as of March 31, 1999 of ¥724 million ($6,821 thousand) for two-year amortization was included in other expenses. The amortization of prior service costs of the consolidated subsidiary is made over three years.

Retirement benefits to directors and statutory auditors are also accrued at the amount of the estimated future liability in relation to service to the balance sheet date.

Income taxes—

Up to the year ended March 31, 1999 income taxes are provided based on amounts reflected in the tax returns and deferred income taxes relating to temporary differences was not recognized as interperiod income tax allocation was not practiced in Japan. Following to the dissemination of the authoritative pronouncements on interperiod tax allocation applicable to the year ended March 31, 2000 the Company and its consolidated subsidiary recorded deferred tax assets during the current year. The resultant effect for prior years at March 31, 1999 of ¥1,776 million ($16,731 thousand) was credited to unappropriated retained earnings at March 31, 1999.

Additional paid-in capital and stock splits—

Under the Japanese Commercial Code ("the Code"), the entire amount of the issue price (or conversion price) is required to be accounted for in the common stock account although a company may, by a resolution of its board of directors, account for an amount not exceeding one-half of the issue price of the shares as additional paid-in capital.

The Code provides that a "Transfer of distributable profit to the common stock account" must be approved at the general meeting of shareholders as an appropriation of unappropriated retained earnings. The Code also permits the board of directors to make a "stock split" provided (i) the aggregate par value of all issued shares after the stock split does not exceed the common stock account and (ii) the amount of aggregate net worth in the latest balance sheet divided by all issued shares after the stock split is not less than the amount of ¥50.

Dividends—

Dividends charged to unappropriated retained earnings in the accompanying statements of shareholders' equity represent (i) dividends approved at the general meeting of shareholders held during the fiscal period and paid during such period plus (ii) interim dividends paid.

Net income and dividends per share—

Basic net income per share of common stock is based on the average number of shares of common stock outstanding during each period, appropriately adjusted for stock splits. Common stock equivalents on warrants and convertible notes are not taken into consideration for the above computation. Fully-diluted net income per share of common stock is computed assuming (i) outstanding warrants at the beginning of period are all exercised at that date reflecting average market price of the common shares and (ii) outstanding convertible notes at that date are all converted to common shares after adjustment of after-tax debt servicing costs, unless antidilutive effect results. The aforementioned basic and fully-diluted net income per share computation is based on the revision of the Ruling applicable to the financial statements for public corporations, effective from the fiscal year commencing April 1, 1995 and there-after. For fiscal 2000, fully-diluted net income per common stock is considered to be the same as basic net income per common stock, since the effect of potentially dilutive securities would be antidilutive.

Cash dividends per share for each period in the accompanying statements of income represent dividends declared as applicable to the respective period, after appropriated adjustment for stock splits.

Stock and bond issue costs—

Stock and bond issue costs are charged to income as incurred.

3. U.S. dollar amounts:

The U.S. dollar amounts are included solely for convenience and have been translated as a matter of arithmetical computation only at the rate of ¥106.15 = $1, the current rate on March 31, 2000. This translation should not be construed as a representation that the yen amounts actually represent, or could be converted into, U.S. dollars.

4. Cash and cash equivalents:

Cash and cash equivalents consist of the following:

	March 31, 2000	
	Millions of yen	Thousands of U.S. dollars (Note 3)
Demand deposits with banks and minor cash on hand	¥ 625	$ 5,888
Money market funds	1,514	14,263
	¥2,139	$20,151

5. Marketable securities:

The aggregate cost and market value of marketable equity securities (non-current) of the Company are shown below:

	March 31, 2000	
At fiscal period end:	Millions of yen	Thousands of U.S. dollars (Note 3)
Aggregate cost	¥1,900	$17,899
Marketable value	2,944	27,734

6. Inventories:

Inventories comprise the following:

	March 31, 2000	
At fiscal period end:	Millions of yen	Thousands of U.S. dollars (Note 3)
Merchandise	¥2,875	$27,084
Finished products	3,954	37,249
Raw materials	701	6,604
Work in process	1,109	10,448
Supplies	12	113
	¥8,651	$81,498

7. Depreciation:

The estimated useful lives of fixed assets for computing depreciation, which are identical with the useful lives stipulated under the Japanese income tax regulations, are shown below:

	Years
Building, currently effective	3 to 50
Machinery and equipment	3 to 15

8. Bank loans:

Bank loans of ¥6,060 million ($57,089 thousand) at March 31, 2000 represent unsecured ninety-day notes payable bearing average annual interest of 1.375 percent, renewable at maturity. The unsecured long-term bank loans of ¥180 million ($1,696 thousand), including current portion of ¥40 million ($377 thousand), at March 31, 2000 bears average annual interest of 2.210 percent.

9. Allowances for sales rebates and loss on sales returns:

Allowances for sales rebates and loss on sales returns consist of the following:

	March 31, 2000	
	Millions of yen	Thousands of U.S. dollars (Note 3)
Sales rebates	¥640	$6,029
Loss on sales returns	173	1,630
	¥813	$7,659

10. Severance indemnities:

The charges to income for severance indemnities and pension benefits to employees were as follows:

	Millions of yen	Thousands of U.S. dollars (Note 3)
Year ended March 31, 2000 (including amounts applicable to prior years of ¥5,082 million − $47,876 thousand, See Note 2)	¥5,999	$56,514

The charges to income for retirement benefits to directors and statutory auditors were as follows:

	Millions of yen	Thousands of U.S. dollars (Note 3)
Year ended march 31, 2000	¥116	$1,093

Unfunded prior service cost in respect of pension benefits as of March 31, 2000 (the last valuation date of the pension fund) was ¥878 million ($8,271 thousand).

11. Income taxes:

The Company and its subsidiary are subject to a number of different income taxes which, in the aggregate, indicate a normal statutory tax rate of approximately 42 percent for the year ended March 31, 2000. the ordinary relationship between income tax expenses and pretax accounting income is distorted by a number of items, including temporary differences, various tax credits and the non-deductibility of certain expenses.

During the year ended March 31, 2000 the Company newly adopted interperiod tax allocation method and recorded deferred tax assets at March 31, 2000. The significant components of deferred tax assets and liabilities at March 31, 2000 are as shown below:

	March 31, 2000	
	Millions of yen	Thousands of U.S. dollars (Note 3)
Deferred tax assets—		
Deferred tax assets, current—		
Allowance for sales rebates	¥ 269	$ 2,534
Write-down of inventories	289	2,722
Other	522	4,918
	¥1,080	$10,174
Deferred tax assets, noncurrent—		
Accrued severance indemnities	¥2,728	$25,699
Other	176	1,658
	¥2,904	$27,357
Deferred tax liability—		
Deferred capital gain on sale of land	(72)	(678)
Deferred tax assets, noncurrent, net	¥2,832	$26,679

A reconciliation between the normal statutory tax (benefit) rate and the reported actual tax (benefit) rate is as shown below:

Reconciliation of tax rate

"Expected" income tax (benefit) rate (normal statutory tax rate)	(42)%
Entertainment expense and other expense not deductible	19
Dividend income and other income not taxable	(1)
Other	(10)
Actual income tax (benefit) rate (reported tax rate)	(34)%

12. Legal reserve:

The Code provides that an amount equal to at least 10 percent of cash outlays including each dividends and bonuses to directors be appropriated as a legal reserve. No further appropriation is required when the legal reserve equals 25 percent of the common stock account.

13. Research and development expenses:

Research and development expenses which were included in selling, general and administrative expenses were as follows:

	Millions of yen	Thousands of U.S. dollars (Note 3)
Year ended March 31, 2000	¥3,678	$34,649

14. Commitments and contingent liabilities:

Commitments outstanding as of March 31, 2000 for the purchase of property, plant and equipment were approximately ¥1,512 million ($14,244 thousand).

Rental expenses are shown below:

	Millions of yen	Thousands of U.S. dollars (Note 3)
Year ended March 31, 2000	¥1,817	$17,112

A significant portion of such rentals relates to cancelable short-term leases, many of which are renewed upon expiration. Contingent liabilities for notes discounted at March 31, 2000 amounted to ¥900 million ($8,479 thousand).

15. Derivative instrument:

Derivative instruments as of March 31, 2000 comprise mainly currency swap agreements on marketable securities denominated in U.S. dollars into yen. As described in Note 2 such marketable securities are recorded at the yen amounts receivable under such swap agreements.

16. Segment information:

Operating segment information for the year ended March 31, 2000 is shown below:

	Pharma-ceuticals	Fine Chemicals	Elimination Corporate	Consolidated total	Pharma-ceuticals	Fine Chemicals	Elimination, Corporate	Consolidated total
	Millions of yen				Thousands of U.S. dollars (Note 3)			
Sales								
External customers	¥47,976	¥11,817	¥ —	¥59,793	$451,964	$111,324	$ —	$563,288
Intersegments..........	—	325	(325)	—	—	3,062	(3,062)	—
Total	47,976	12,142	(325)	59,793	451,964	114,386	(3,062)	563,288
Operating expenses....	42,566	13,877	1,204	57,647	400,999	130,730	11,342	543,071
Operating income (loss)........................	¥ 5,410	¥(1,735)	¥(1,529)	¥ 2,146	$ 50,965	$(16,344)	$(14,404)	$ 20,217
Total assets	¥44,279	¥10,051	¥ 5,837	¥60,167	$417,136	$ 94,687	$ 54,988	$566,811
Depreciation	1,809	593	6	2,408	17,042	5,586	57	22,685
Capital expenditures ..	783	167	2	952	7,376	1,573	19	8,968

The Company and its subsidiary have no subsidiary or branch abroad nor overseas sales.

17. Subsequent events:

The following appropriations of unappropriated retained earnings of the Company for the year ended March 31, 2000 were approved at the general meeting of the shareholders held in June, 2000.

	Millions of yen	Thousands of U.S. dollars (Note 3)
Appropriations for—		
Cash dividends..	¥ 198	$1,865
Transfer to legal reserve	20	188
Unappropriated balance carried forward..	831	7,829
	¥1,049	$9,882

The above appropriations are not reflected in the accompanying financial statements (See "Dividends" in Note 2 above). The cash dividends were paid and recorded in June, 2000.

In May 2000 the Company acquired its 2,280,000 shares from the market and retired such treasury shares with a reversal of additional paid-in capital by the amount of ¥968 million ($9,119 thousand) which is equivalent to the aggregate cost of such treasury shares.

REPORT OF INDEPENDENT CERTIFIED PUBLIC ACCOUNTANTS

To the Board of Directors of
Nikken Chemicals Co., Ltd.

We have audited the accompanying consolidated balance sheet of Nikken Chemicals Co., Ltd. and its consolidated subsidiary as of March 31, 2000 and the related consolidated statement of income, shareholders' equity, and cash flows for the year then ended, stated in yen. These financial statements are the responsibility of the Company's management. Our responsibility is to express an opinion on these financial statements based on our audit.

We conducted our audit in accordance with auditing standards generally accepted in Japan. Those standards require that we plan and perform the audit to obtain reasonable assurance about whether the financial statements are free of material misstatement. An audit includes examining, on a test basis, evidence supporting the amounts and disclosures in the financial statements. An audit also includes assessing the accounting principles used and significant estimates made by management, as well as evaluating the overall financial statement presentation. We believe that our audit provides a reasonable basis for our opinion.

In our opinion, the consolidated financial statements audited by us present fairly, in all material respects, the financial position of Nikken Chemicals Co., Ltd. and its consolidated subsidiary as of March 31, 2000 and the results of their operations and their cash flows for the year then ended in conformity with accounting principles generally accepted in Japan.

As discussed in Note 2, the Company and its consolidated subsidiary changed their methods of accounting for accrued severance indemnities and amortization of prior service costs of pensions during the year ended March 31, 2000.

The United States dollar amounts in the consolidated financial statements have been translated for convenience only on the basis described in Note 3.

Tokyo, Japan
June 29, 2000

Toyo & Co.
TOYO & CO

Stock Exchange Web Sites

Country	Stock Exchange	Web Site
Argentina	Buenos Aires	www.bcba.sba.com.ar
Australia	Australia	www.asx.com.au
Austria	Vienna	www.wbag.at
Azerbaijan	Baku	www.az/bicex
Belgium	Euronext—Belgium	www.euronext.com
		www.stockexchange.be/enindex.htm
Bermuda	Bermuda	www.bsx.com
Brazil	Rio de Janeiro	www.bvrj.com.br (Portuguese only)
Brazil	Sao Paulo	www.bovespa.com.br (Portuguese only)
Canada	Montréal	www.me.org
Canada	Toronto	www.tse.com
Canada	Canadian Venture	www.cdnx.ca
Chile	Santiago	www.bolsadesantiago.com
Colombia	Bogotá	www.bolsabogata.com.co/ (Spanish only)
Colombia	Medellín	www.bolsamed.com.co (Spanish only)
Croatia	Zagreb	www.zse.hr
Czech Republic	Prague	www.pse.cz
Denmark	Copenhagen	www.xcse.dk
Finland	Helsinki	www.hex.fi
France	Paris	www.euronext.com
		www.bourse-de-paris.fr/defaultgb.htm
Germany	Deutsche Börse	deutsche-boerse.com/
Greece	Athens	www.ase.gr
Hong Kong	Hong Kong	www.hkex.com.hk
India	National Stock Exchange	www.nseindia.com
India	Surabaya	www.bes.co.id
Indonesia	Jakarta	www.jsx.co.id
Iran	Tehran	www.tse.or.ir
Israel	Tel-Aviv	hebrew.tase.co.il/www/intro.asp
Italy	Italy	www.borsaitalia.it
Japan	Osaka	www.ose.or.jp
Japan	Tokyo	www.tse.or.jp
Jordan	Amman	www.access2arabia.com/AFM/
Luxembourg	Luxembourg	www.bourse.lu
Macedonia	Macedonian	www.mse.org.mk
Malaysia	Kuala Lumpur	www.klse.com.my
Mexico	Mexico	www.bmv.com.mx

Netherlands	Euronext—Netherlands	www.euronext.com
		www.aex.nl/aex.asp?taal=en
New Zealand	New Zealand	www.nzse.co.nz
Norway	Oslo	www.ose.no
Pakistan	Lahore	www.lse.brain.net.pk
Peru	Lima	www.bvl.com.pe
Philippines	Philippines	www.pse.org.ph
Poland	Warsaw	www.gpw.com.pl
Portugal	Lisbon	www.bvl.pt
Russia	Siberian	www.sse.nsk.su (Russian only) (under construction when this book went to press)
Singapore	Singapore	www.ses.com.sg
Slovakia	Bratislava	www.bsse.sk
Slovenia	Ljubljana	www.ljse.si
South Africa	Johannesburg	www.jse.co.za
South Korea	Korea	www.kse.or.kr
Spain	Barcelona	www.borsabcn.es
Spain	Bilbao	www.bolsabilbao.es
Spain	Madrid	www.bolsamadrid.es
Sweden	Stockholm	www.xsse.se
Switzerland	Swiss	www.swx.ch
Taiwan	Taiwan	www.tse.com.tw
Thailand	Thailand	www.set.or.th
Turkey	Istanbul	www.ise.org
United Kingdom	London	www.londonstockexchange.com
United States	American (Amex)	www.amex.com
United States	Chicago	www.chicagostockex.com
United States	Nasdaq	www.nasdaq.com
		www.nasdaqnews.com
		www.nasdr.com
		www.nasdaqtrader.com
United States	New York	www.nyse.com

Note: All Web site addresses here begin with the prefix http://

Selected References

Beim, David O., and Charles W. Calomiris, *Emerging Financial Markets*, Boston: Mc-Graw-Hill Irwin, 2001.

Bloomenthal, Harold S., and Samuel Wolff, eds., *International Capital Markets and Securities Regulation—Securities Law Series*, USA: West Group, December 2000.

Euromoney Books, *The Euromoney Guide to Equity Capital Markets 2000*, London: Euromoney Institutional Investor PLC, 1999.

Federation of European Stock Exchanges (FESE), *Annual Report 2000*, Brussels: Federation of European Stock Exchanges, June 2001.

International Federation of Stock Exchanges (FIBV), *Annual Report 2000*, Paris: 2001.

Gros, Daniel, and Karel Lannoo, *The Euro Capital Market*, West Sussex, England: John Wiley & Sons Ltd., 2000.

Hodgetts, Sally, ed., *2000 International Investment Review*, England: Euromoney Institutional Investor PLC, 2000.

Lee, Ruben, *What Is an Exchange? The Automation, Management, and Regulation of Financial Markets*, Oxford, England: Oxford University Press, 1998.

Levinson, Marc, *Guide to Financial Markets*, 2d ed., London: The Economist Newspaper Ltd., 2000.

Lilja, Robert, *International Equity Markets—The Art of the Deal*, London: Euromoney Books, 1997.

Meridian Securities Markets, *World Stock Exchange Fact Book 2000*, Round Rock, TX: 2000.

PricewaterhouseCoopers LLC, *Accessing International Capital Markets*, New York: PricewaterhouseCoopers Global Capital Markets Group, 2001.

Rathborne, David, and Deborah Ritchie, eds., *The Salomon Smith Barney Guide to World Equity Markets 2000*, London: Euromoney Books and Salomon Smith Barney, 2000.

Rosen, Robert C., ed., *International Securities Regulation: Stock Exchanges of the World: Selected Rules and Regulations*, USA: Oceana Publications, 2000.

Rosen, Robert C., ed., *International Securities Regulation*, USA: Oceana Publications, 2000.

Skeete, Herbie, ed., *The Bridge Handbook of World Stock, Derivative & Commodity Exchanges 2000, Tenth Anniversary Edition*, Welwyn Garden City, Hers, U.K.: Mondo Visione, 2000.

Standard & Poor's, *Emerging Markets Factbook 2000*, New York: May 2000.

Steil, Benn, *The European Equity Markets—The State of the Union and an Agenda for the Millennium*, London: Royal Institute of International Affairs, 1996.

Valdez, Stephen, *An Introduction to Global Financial Markets*, 3d ed., London: Macmillan Press Ltd., 2000.

Young, Patrick, and Thomas Theys, *Capital Market Revolution: The Future of Markets in an Online World*, Great Britain: Pearson Education Limited, 1999.

Discussion Questions

1. Explain the term *global capital markets*. This chapter primarily discusses global equity markets. What other types of financial instruments are traded in these markets? How important are global capital markets in the world economy?

2. Some observers suggest that multinational enterprises are tightly controlled by many (and often conflicting) national laws. Others contend that no effective international law governs multinationals, and that this allows them too many freedoms and privileges. What do these two positions imply for future developments in international accounting? Answer in the form of two concise paragraphs.

3. Some have advocated that a single widely spoken language be designated as the formal international accounting language. Write a two-paragraph statement in favor of choosing English as the designated language.

4. Discuss at least three trends that clearly indicate the growing internationalization of financial markets.

5. Why have international accounting issues become more complex in recent years?

6. Accounting may be viewed as having three components: measurement, disclosure, and auditing. What are the advantages and disadvantages of this classification? Can you suggest alternative classifications that might be useful?

7. Why is the ratio of equity market capitalization divided by gross domestic product (GDP) a useful measure for comparing the development of equity markets in different countries?

8. Capital markets often are grouped into two categories: those in developed countries, and those in emerging market countries. Give your own definitions of developed and emerging market countries. Which stock exchanges shown in Exhibit 1-2 are in emerging market countries? What characteristics do they share?

9. Exhibit 1-2 shows that between 1973 and 1996, national governments in many countries sold shares in state-owned financial institutions to nongovernmental entities. Discuss how these privatizations might affect the capital markets.

10. Provide possible explanations for the low numbers of foreign listed companies in the Czech Republic, Mexico, Taiwan, and China.

11. What is a stock exchange alliance? What do the many stock exchange alliances and cooperative agreements forming around the world imply for accounting regulation and practice?

12. Refer to Exhibit 1-4. In which five countries was 1999 market capitalization the greatest? In which five countries was 1999 GDP the greatest? In which five countries was 1999 market capitalization as a percentage of GDP greatest? Compare and contrast the three lists of countries. Some equity markets are relatively large, but are small relative to their national economies. Why is this?

Exercises

1. In the second edition of this textbook (Prentice Hall, 1992) F.D.S. Choi and G. G. Mueller define international accounting as follows:

   International accounting extends general purpose, nationally oriented accounting in its broadest sense to: (1) international comparative analysis, (2) accounting measurement and reporting issues unique to multinational business transactions and the business form of the multinational enterprise, (3) accounting needs of international financial markets, and (4) harmonization of worldwide accounting and financial reporting diversity via political, organizational, professional, and standard-setting activities.

   Required: Critically evaluate the listed definition of international accounting. Propose changes to improve the definition, providing justification for any proposed changes. Alternatively, present your own definition of international accounting, and compare and contrast it with the Choi and Mueller definition.

2. The International Accounting Standards Committee (now the International Accounting Standards Board [IASB]) was founded in 1973 to promote worldwide accounting harmonization and to develop and encourage the use of International Accounting Standards (IAS).

   Required: Use your library or the World Wide Web to learn more about the IASB (The IASB's Web site is *http://www.iasb.org.uk*) What are International Accounting Standards? How do individual companies and countries around the world use them?

3. The International Federation of Accountants (IFAC) is an organization of more than 100 professional accountancy bodies that promotes international auditing harmonization.

   Required: Use your library or the World Wide Web to learn more about IFAC's history and activities (IFAC's Web site is http://www.ifac.org.) What are International Standards on Auditing (ISA)? Why have they been developed? How are they being used around the world?

4. Refer to Exhibit 1-l, which presents information on international equity offerings made by companies domiciled in North America, Europe, Africa/Middle East, Asia-Pacific, and Latin America.

   Required: Rank the five regions by total equity capital raised internationally between 1995 and 1999. Provide possible explanations for the differences in international equity capital raised. Compute mean annual rates of change in capital raised in each region. Provide possible explanations for the differences in these growth rates.

5. Examine the 1995 through 2000 growth rates in market capitalization for the 26 stock exchanges shown in Exhibit 1-3.

   Required: Identify the three stock exchanges that had the largest positive market capitalization growth rates, and the three stock exchanges that had the largest *negative* market capitalization growth rates. What are possible explanations for these growth rates?

6. Comparison of stock exchange statistics across markets and across years must be done with great caution, because exchanges use a variety of measurement approaches and revise their approaches over time.

   Required: Examine Exhibit 1-5, which presents numbers of domestic and foreign companies with shares listed on each of 26 stock exchanges as of December 31, 1995 and December 31, 2000. Do you observe any unusual changes between 1995 and 2000? Discuss possible explanations for any unusual trends you observe, as well as approaches for investigating their possible causes and making adjustments to the figures where appropriate.

7. Exhibit 1-6 presents 2000 trading volume in foreign shares for 26 stock exchanges, and Exhibit 1-5 presents the numbers of foreign companies with shares listed on each exchange as of December 31, 2000.

   Required:
   a. Compute the mean 2000 annual values of share trading per foreign issuer in each of the 26 equity markets using statistics from Exhibits 1-6 and 1-5. For example, the mean value of share trading during 2000 for foreign companies listed on the Australian equity market is US$47.9 million (US$3,639.2 million (from the top row of Exhibit 1-6) divided by 76 foreign listed companies (from the top row of Exhibit 1-5).
   b. What are the three top-ranking markets in terms of 2000 mean trade volume per foreign company? How do these three markets compare with other equity markets in terms of 2000 total foreign trading volume and numbers of foreign shares listed? What do you conclude about the attractiveness of these three markets for foreign issuers?

8. Exhibit 1-6 presents 1995 and 2000 trading volume in foreign shares for 26 stock exchanges, and Exhibit 1-5 presents the numbers of foreign companies with shares listed on each exchange as of December 31, 1995 and December 31, 2000.

Required: Compute mean share trading per foreign company in Australia, Hong Kong, Japan, and New Zealand for 2000 and 1995 using information from the exhibits. Prepare a table showing 2000 and 1995 mean trade volume per foreign company for each of the four markets. Include in your table the value of foreign share trading and numbers of listed companies for both years. Compare and contrast the four markets, and provide possible explanations for the most important differences that you observe.

9. The World Wide Web provides low-cost access to a vast amount of information about financial reporting requirements and practices worldwide.

   Required: Refer to Appendix 1-3, which provides Web site addresses for stock exchanges in more than 50 countries. Select a stock exchange and do a Web search for information about financial reporting requirements for listed companies in that market. (Many stock exchange Web sites provide information on their own financial reporting requirements (such as those related to annual and interim reporting), and links to national securities regulatory bodies.) Present a brief overview of financial reporting regulation of the stock exchange you select. (Note: The IASB Web site at www.iasb.org.uk also presents information about accounting principle requirements at stock exchanges around the world.)

10. Stock exchange Web sites vary considerably in the information they provide and their ease of use.

    Required: Select any two of the stock exchanges presented in Appendix 1-1. Explore the Web sites of each of these stock exchanges. Prepare a table that compares and contrasts the sites for types and quality of information presented, and the ease of using the Web site. Are English language press releases of listed companies available? Links to listed companies' Web sites? Listing requirements? Price and volume data for listed securities? Helpful information for investors?

11. Refer to Appendix 1-2, which presents the income tax footnote (Note 11) from Nikken Chemical Co. Ltd.'s 2000 annual report.

    Required: What information about income taxes is not disclosed by Nikken that would be disclosed by a publicly traded company in your home country?

12. Refer to Nikken Chemical Co. Ltd.'s 2000 financial statements (including notes and auditor's report) in Appendix 1-2. Also consider an annual report for a publicly traded manufacturing company in your country.

    Required: Discuss five important differences between Nikken's financial statements and those of the company in your country.

Case 1–1   e-centives, Inc.—Raising Capital in Switzerland

On October 3, 2000, e-centives, incorporated in the United States, made an initial public offering on the Swiss Stock Exchange's New Market. The company raised approximately US$40 million. e-centive's offering circular stated that no offers or sales of the company's common stock would be made in the United States, and that there would be no public market for the common stock in the United States after the offering.

THE SWISS EXCHANGE'S NEW MARKET

The Swiss Exchange launched the New Market in 1999. The New Market is designed to meet the financing needs of rapidly growing companies from Switzerland and abroad. It provides firms with a simplified means of entry to the Swiss capital markets. Listing requirements for the New Market are simple. For example, companies must have an operating track record of 12 months, the initial public listing must involve a capital increase, and to ensure market liquidity, a bank must agree to make a market in the securities.

E-CENTIVES

e-centives, Inc. is a leading online direct marketing infrastructure company. The company offers systems and technologies that enable businesses to build large, rich databases of consumer profiles and interests. In return, consumers receive a free personalized service that provides them with promotional offers based on their interests.

At the time of the public offering, e-centives maintained over 4.4 million e-centives online accounts for members. The company does not charge members a fee for its service. Instead, the company generates revenue primarily from marketers whose marketing matter is delivered to targeted groups of e-centives members.

e-centives, Inc. currently employs more than 100 people in its Bethesda, Maryland headquarters, and its offices in Redwood City, New York, and Los Angeles.

As of the offering date, the company had little revenue and had not been profitable. Revenue for the year-ended December 31, 1999 was US$740,000, with a net loss of about US$16 million. As of June 30, 2000, the company had an accumulated deficit of about US$39 million.

e-centives' growth strategy is to expand internationally. To date, the company has focused on pursing opportunities in the United States. e-centives intends to expand into Europe and other countries. The company is currently considering expanding into Switzerland, the United Kingdom, and Germany.[1]

REQUIRED

1. Refer to Exhibit 1-7, which lists factors relevant for choosing an overseas market for listing or raising capital. Which factors might have been relevant in e-centives' decision to raise capital and list on the Swiss Exchange's New Market?
2. Why do you believe e-centives chose not to raise public equity in the United States? What are the potential drawbacks related to e-centives' decision *not* to raise capital in the U.S. public markets?
3. What are the advantages and disadvantages to e-centives of using U.S. GAAP?
4. Should the SWX Swiss Exchange require e-centives to prepare its financial statements using Swiss accounting standards?
5. Learn more about the New Market at the SWX Swiss Exchange's Web site (http://www.swx.com). What are the listing requirements for the New Market? What are the financial reporting requirements? Does e-centives appear to fit the profile of the typical New Market company?

---

[1]From e-centives' offering circular dated October 2, 2000.

CHAPTER 2

DEVELOPMENT AND CLASSIFICATION

Accounting must respond to the ever-changing needs of society and reflect the cultural, economic, legal, social, and political conditions within which it operates. The history of accounting and accountants reveals continuing change. At first, accounting was little more than a recording system for certain banking services and tax collection schemes. Later it developed double-entry bookkeeping systems to meet the needs of trading ventures. Industrialization and division of labor made cost behavior analysis and managerial accounting possible. The rise of the modern corporation stimulated periodic financial reporting and auditing. More recently, accounting has found ways to measure and report environmental remediation liabilities and uncover money laundering and similar related white-collar crimes. It provides decision information for huge domestic and international public securities markets. It has extended into management consulting and incorporates ever-increasing information technology within its systems and procedures.

Why should we know how and why accounting develops? The answer is the same as it is for developmental studies in other fields. If we can identify what causes accounting to develop, we might be able to influence or anticipate its direction and rate of change. Further, we can better understand a nation's accounting by knowing the underlying factors that influence its development. Accounting clearly differs around the world, and knowledge of the developmental factors helps us see why. In other words, observable differences—as well as similarities—can be explained by these factors. Because accounting responds to its environment, different cultural, economic, legal, and political environments produce different accounting systems, and similar environments produce similar systems.

This leads us to classification. Why should we classify (compare) national or regional financial accounting systems? Classification is fundamental to understanding and analyzing why and how national accounting systems differ. We can also analyze whether these systems are converging or diverging. The goal of classification is to group countries according to the distinctive characteristics of their financial accounting systems. Classifications reveal fundamental structures that group members have in common and that distinguish the various groups from each other. By identifying similarities and differences, our understanding of accounting systems is improved. Classifications are a way of viewing the world.

Classification also has some practical benefits:[1]

1. The countries in a particular group are likely to react to new circumstances in similar ways. Countries may benefit from the experiences of other countries in the same group. For example, standard setters in Australia, Canada, New Zealand, the United Kingdom, and the United States have found it both effective and efficient to cooperate and find common solutions to certain accounting issues.[2]
2. The differences among groups are barriers to the regional and worldwide harmonization efforts discussed in Chapter 8. For these efforts to succeed, the groups involved (such as the International Accounting Standards Board at the international level and the European Union at the regional level) must understand the differences to be overcome and whether the patterns are changing over time.
3. Developing countries often lack the resources to develop their own accounting standards. These countries may be able to pattern their standards after existing standards (as China and certain countries in Eastern Europe are now doing).
4. Communication problems are likely to be more severe when a company reports to financial statement users who are unfamiliar with the company's home-country accounting standards. As a result, the company may need to provide additional information to these users. Similar problems could exist for internal communications in a multinational corporation. Accountants communicating with counterparts in another country need to be careful to *speak the same language.*

DEVELOPMENT

Every nation's accounting standards and practices result from a complex interaction of economic, historical, institutional, and cultural factors. Diversity among nations is to be expected. The factors that influence national accounting development also help explain accounting diversity among nations.

We believe the following eight factors have a significant influence on accounting development. The first seven are economic, sociohistorical, and/or institutional in nature, and they have occupied most of the attention of accounting writers. More recently, the relationship between culture (the eighth item) and accounting development has begun to be explored.

---

[1]Gary K. Meek and Shahrokh M. Saudagaran, "A Survey of Research on Financial Reporting in a Transnational Context," *Journal of Accounting Literature* 9 (1990): 154.

[2]The so-called G4 + 1 consists of the standard-setting bodies from these countries plus the International Accounting Standards Committee. For a review of the evolution and work of the G4 + 1, see D. L. Street and K. A. Shaughnessay, "The Evolution of the G4 + 1 and Its Impact on International Harmonization of Accounting," *Journal of International Accounting Auditing & Taxation* 7, no. 2 (1998): 131–161. As discussed in Chapter 8, the G4 + 1 disbanded in 2001.

1. Sources of Finance In countries with strong equity markets, such as the United States and United Kingdom, accounting focuses on how well management runs the company (profitability), and is designed to help investors assess future cash flows and the associated risks. Disclosures are extensive to meet the requirements of widespread public ownership. By contrast, in credit-based systems where banks are the dominant source of finance, accounting focuses on creditor protection through conservative accounting measurements. Because financial institutions have direct access to any information they want, extensive public disclosures are not considered necessary. Japan and Switzerland are examples.[3]

2. Legal System The legal system determines how individuals and institutions interact. The Western world has two basic orientations: legalistic (code or civil law) and non-legalistic (common or case law). Code law derives mainly from Roman law and the Code Napoléon. In code law countries, laws are an all-embracing set of requirements and procedures. Codification of accounting standards and procedures is natural and appropriate there. Thus, in code law countries, accounting rules are incorporated into national laws and tend to be highly prescriptive and procedural. By contrast, common law develops on a case-by-case basis with no attempt to cover all cases in an all-encompassing code. Of course, statute law does exist, but it tends to be less detailed and more flexible than in a code law system. This encourages experimentation and permits the exercise of judgment.[4] Common law derives from English case law. In most common law countries, accounting rules are established by private sector professional organizations. This allows them to be more adaptive and innovative. Except for broad statutory requirements, most accounting rules are not incorporated directly into statute law.[5]

3. Taxation In many countries, tax legislation effectively determines accounting standards because companies must record revenues and expenses in their accounts to claim them for tax purposes. This is the case, for example, in Germany and Sweden. In other countries, such as the Netherlands, financial and tax accounting are separate: Taxable profits are essentially financial accounting profits adjusted for differences with the tax laws. Of course, even where financial and tax accounting are separate, tax legislation may occasionally require the application of certain accounting principles. Last in, first out (LIFO) inventory valuation in the United States is an example.

---

[3]For further discussion of this point, see C. Nobes, "Towards a General Model of the Reasons for International Differences in Financial Reporting," *Abacus* (September 1998): 162–187. He points out that *outsiders* (such as individual and institutional shareholders) normally dominate ownership in strong equity countries, causing a demand for high levels of disclosure. *Insiders* (families, other companies, government, and banks) usually dominate ownership in credit-based countries, which is why low levels of disclosure are usually found there. Germany is an exception. Even though Germany is a credit-based country, German listed companies have high disclosures because of Germany's unusually large market in listed debt (p. 169).

[4]Irving Fantl, "The Case Against International Uniformity," *Management Accounting* (May 1971): 13–16.

[5]Under martial law or other national emergency situations, all aspects of the accounting function may be regulated by some central governmental court or agency. This was the case, for instance, in Nazi Germany when intensive war preparations and World War II itself required a highly uniform national accounting system for total control of all national economic activities.

4. Political and Economic Ties Accounting ideas and technologies are transferred through conquest, commerce, and similar forces. Double-entry bookkeeping, which originated in Italy in the 1400s, gradually spread across Europe along with other ideas of the Renaissance. British colonialism exported accountants and accounting concepts throughout the empire. German occupation during World War II led France to adopt its Plan Comptable (see Chapter 3). The United States forced U.S.-style accounting regulatory regimes on Japan after World War II. Many developing economies use an accounting system that was developed elsewhere, either because it was imposed on them (for example, India) or by their own choice (for example, countries of Eastern Europe now modeling their accounting systems after European Union (EU) regulations). As discussed more generally in Chapter 8, economic integration through the growth of international trade and capital flows is a powerful motivator for the harmonization of accounting standards.

5. Inflation Inflation distorts historical cost accounting and affects the tendency of a country to incorporate price changes into the accounts. Israel, Mexico, and certain countries of South America use general price-level accounting because of their experiences with hyperinflation. In the late 1970s, in response to unusually high rates of inflation, both the United States and United Kingdom experimented with reporting the effects of changing prices. Accounting responses to inflation are explored in Chapter 7.

6. Level of Economic Development This factor affects the types of business transactions conducted in an economy and determines which ones are most prevalent. The type of transactions, in turn, determines the accounting issues that are faced. For example, stock-based executive compensation or asset securitization makes little sense in economies with underdeveloped capital markets. Today, many industrial economies are becoming service economies. Accounting issues such as valuing fixed assets and recording depreciation, relevant in manufacturing, are becoming less important. New accounting challenges, such as valuing intangibles and human resources, are emerging.

7. Education Level Highly sophisticated accounting standards and practices are useless if they are misunderstood and misused. For example, a complex technical report on cost behavior variances is meaningless unless the reader understands cost accounting. Disclosures about the risks of derivative securities are not informative unless they can be read competently.

Several of these first seven variables are closely associated. For example, the common law legal system originated in Britain and was exported to such countries as Australia, Canada, and the United States. These four countries all have highly developed capital markets, which dominate the orientation of their financial reporting. Financial and tax accounting are separate. By contrast, most of Continental Europe and Japan have code law legal systems and rely on banks or the government for most of their finance. Accounting rules there generally conform to tax laws.

Establishing cause and effect is difficult. The type of legal system may predispose a country toward its system of finance. A common law legal system emphasizes shareholder rights and offers stronger investor protection than a code law system. The outcome is that strong equity markets develop in common law countries and weak ones develop in code law countries.[6] Taxation is an important function of accounting in any country with a corporate income tax. Whether it dominates the orientation of accounting may depend on whether accounting has a major competing purpose, namely, informing outside shareholders. (Tax accounting is not suitable for this purpose.) Thus, if common law results in strong equity markets, taxation will not dominate. There will be two sets of accounting rules: one for taxation and another for financial reporting. Tax rules will dominate in code law/credit-based countries, and accounting for taxation and financial reporting will be the same.[7]

Two basic orientations of accounting have evolved out of these circumstances. One is oriented toward a *fair* presentation of financial position and results of operations, while the other is designed to comply with legal requirements and tax law. The classification studies discussed later in this chapter support this dichotomy. Chapter 3 further discusses the *fair presentation* versus *legal compliance* distinction.

8. Culture Here, culture means the values and attitudes shared by a society. Cultural variables underlie nations' institutional arrangements (such as legal systems). Hofstede enunciated four national cultural dimensions (or societal values): (1) individualism, (2) power distance, (3) uncertainty avoidance, and (4) masculinity. His analysis is based on data from employees of a large U.S. multinational corporation operating in forty different countries.[8]

Briefly, *individualism* (versus *collectivism*) is a preference for a loosely knit social fabric over an interdependent, tightly knit fabric (*I* versus *we*). *Power distance* is the extent to which hierarchy and an unequal distribution of power in institutions and organizations are accepted. *Uncertainty avoidance* is the degree to which society is uncomfortable with ambiguity and an uncertain future. *Masculinity* (versus *femininity*) is the extent to which gender roles are differentiated and performance and visible achievement (traditional masculine values) are emphasized over relationships and caring (traditional feminine values). Some scholars now call this *achievement orientation.*[9]

---

[6]R. La Porta, F. Lopez-de-Silanes, A. Shleifer, and R.W. Vishny, "Legal Determinants of External Finance," *Journal of Finance* (July 1997): 1131–1150.

[7]C. Nobes, "Towards a General Model of the Reasons for International Differences in Financial Reporting," *Abacus* (September 1998): 162–187.

[8]G. Hofstede, *Culture's Consequences: International Differences in Work-Related Values,* Beverly Hills, CA: Sage Publications, 1980.

[9]Later work documents a fifth cultural dimension, called *Confucian dynamism* (or, *long-term orientation*). This later work contends that only individualism, power distance, and masculinity are universal across all cultures. Uncertainty avoidance is a unique characteristic of Western societies, whereas Confucian dynamism is unique to Eastern societies. [See G. Hofstede and M.H. Bond, "The Confucian Connection: From Cultural Roots to Economic Growth," *Organizational Dynamics* 16, no. 1 (1988): 4–21; and G. Hofstede, *Cultures and Organizations: Softwares of the Mind,* London: McGraw-Hill, 1991.] The existence of this fifth dimension has been contested. See R. Yeh and J. J. Lawrence, "Individualism and Confucian Dynamism: A Note on Hofstede's Cultural Root to Economic Growth," *Journal of International Business Studies* (third quarter 1995): 655–669. These authors note a data problem in Hofstede's subsequent work. Once an outlier is removed, Confucian dynamism no longer emerges as an independent construct; it reflects the same cultural dimension as individualism. It should also be pointed out that there are other cultural dimensions that are not considered by Hofstede. For example, religion, which extends beyond national boundaries, underlies business practices, institutional arrangements, and by extension, accounting. Language is another cultural input.

Drawing on Hofstede's analysis, Gray proposed a framework linking culture and accounting.[10] He suggests four *accounting value dimensions* that affect a nation's financial reporting practices. They are:

1. Professionalism vs. statutory control: a preference for the exercise of individual professional judgment and professional self-regulation as opposed to compliance with prescriptive legal requirements.

   A preference for independent professional judgment is consistent with a preference for a loosely knit social framework where there is more emphasis on independence, a belief in fair play and as few rules as possible, and where a variety of professional judgments will tend to be more easily tolerated. . . . [P]rofessionalism is more likely to be accepted in a small power-distance society where there is more concern for equal rights, where people at various power levels feel less threatened and more prepared to trust people, and where there is a belief in the need to justify the imposition of laws and codes.[11]

2. Uniformity vs. flexibility: a preference for uniformity and consistency over flexibility in reacting to circumstances.

   A preference for uniformity is consistent with a preference for strong uncertainty avoidance leading to a concern for law and order and rigid codes of behaviour, a need for written rules and regulations, a respect for conformity and the search for ultimate, absolute truths and values. [Uniformity] is also consistent with a preference for collectivism . . . with its tightly knit social framework, a belief in organization and order, and respect for group norms. . . . [U]niformity is more easily facilitated in a large power-distance society in that the imposition of laws and codes of a uniform character are more likely to be accepted.[12]

3. Conservatism vs. optimism: a preference for a cautious approach to measurement to cope with the uncertainty of future events instead of a more optimistic, risk-taking approach.

   A preference for more conservative measures of profits is consistent with strong uncertainty avoidance following from a concern with security and a perceived need to adopt a cautious approach to cope with uncertainty of future events. . . . [A]n emphasis on individual achievement and performance is likely to foster a less conservative approach to measurement.[13]

4. Secrecy vs. transparency: a preference for confidentiality and the restriction of business information on a need-to-know basis versus a willingness to disclose information to the public.

   A preference for secrecy is consistent with strong uncertainty avoidance following from a need to restrict information disclosures so as to avoid conflict and competition and to preserve security. . . . [H]igh power-distance societies are likely to be characterized by the restriction of information to preserve power inequalities. Secrecy is also consistent with a preference for collectivism . . . with its concern for

---

[10]S. J. Gray, "Towards a Theory of Cultural Influence on the Development of Accounting Systems Internationally," *Abacus* (March 1988): 1–15.

[11]Ibid., 9.

[12]Ibid., 9–10.

[13]Ibid., 10.

EXHIBIT 2-1 Relationships Between Gray's Accounting Values and Hofstede's Cultural Dimensions

	Accounting Values (Gray)			
Cultural Dimension (Hofstede)	*Professionalism*	*Uniformity*	*Conservatism*	*Secrecy*
Individualism	+	−	−	−
Power Distance	−	+	?	+
Uncertainty Avoidance	−	+	+	+
Masculinity	?	?	−	−

Note: "+" indicates a direct relationship between the variables; "−" indicates an inverse relationship. Question marks indicate that the nature of the relationship is indeterminate. Gray hypothesizes that individualism and uncertainty avoidance will influence accounting the most, followed by power distance, then masculinity.

Source: Adapted from Nabil Baydoun and Roger Willett, "Cultural Relevance of Western Accounting Systems to Developing Countries," *Abacus* (March 1995): 71.

those closely involved with the firm rather than external parties. . . . [S]ocieties where more emphasis is given to the quality of life, people, and the environment, will tend to be more open especially as regards socially related information.[14]

Exhibit 2-1 shows how Gray's accounting values relate to Hofstede's cultural dimensions.[15]

COMPARATIVE DEVELOPMENT PATTERNS

The following four approaches to accounting development can be observed among Western nations with market-oriented economic systems:

1. the macroeconomic pattern
2. the microeconomic pattern
3. the independent discipline approach
4. the uniform accounting approach

---

[14]Ibid., 11.

[15]An empirical test of Gray's framework may be found in S. B. Salter and F. N. Niswander, "Cultural Influence on the Development of Accounting Systems Internationally: A Test of Gray's [1988] Theory," *Journal of International Business Studies* (second quarter 1995): 379–397. Using data from 29 countries, the authors find that, while the framework has statistical support overall, specific support is rather mild. Their evidence indicates that the framework is best at explaining actual financial reporting practices and relatively weak in explaining professional and regulatory structures. Further, uncertainty avoidance is most strongly associated with Gray's accounting values. Individualism, which Gray thought would be relatively important overall, is only related to secrecy. Power distance is unrelated and masculinity is more strongly associated than Gray hypothesized. We caution that, while the study by Salter and Niswander is an important first one, single empirical studies are rarely the final word. Different data (and different countries) might produce different results.

The concepts underlying these developmental patterns were first proposed by Mueller.[16]

MACROECONOMIC PATTERN

Two central propositions in business and economics are that (1) individual firms set goals and then gear their operations toward achieving these goals, and (2) nations set national policies and adopt administrative procedures to implement these policies. Business goals are obviously narrower than national economic policy. A firm has more specific purposes to accomplish and is accountable to more identifiable interest groups. As a result, firm goals normally follow rather than lead national economic policies.

Under the macroeconomic pattern of accounting development, corporate accounting practices are derived from and designed to enhance national macroeconomic goals. The macroeconomic pattern is based on three propositions:

1. The business enterprise is the essential unit in the national economy.
2. The business enterprise accomplishes its goals best through close coordination of its activities with national economic policies.
3. Public interest is served best if business enterprise accounting is closely linked to national economic policies.

Thus, for example, a national policy of stable employment by avoiding big swings in business cycles would result in accounting practices that smooth income. Or, to promote the development of certain industries, a nation could permit rapid write-offs of capital expenditures in these industries. Sweden has followed the macroeconomic development pattern of accounting most completely.

THE MICROECONOMIC PATTERN

Under the microeconomic approach, accounting develops from the principles of microeconomics. In the microeconomic framework for accounting:

1. Individual firms are the focus of business activities.
2. The main goal of the firm is to survive.
3. A firm's best strategy for survival is economic optimization.
4. As a branch of business economics, accounting derives its concepts and applications from economic analysis.

The central accounting concept here is that the accounting process must hold the amount invested in the firm constant in real terms. This is essential for three reasons: (1) the firm cannot survive if its real capital base is depleted; (2) permanently invested capital in the firm must be central as long as the firm is the focus of business activities; and (3) an effective separation of capital and income is necessary to evaluate and control the firm's business activities.

---

[16]The concepts underlying these developmental patterns were first proposed in G. Mueller, *International Accounting*, New York: Macmillan, 1967. This pioneering work is often cited and is the basis for most of the classifications of accounting systems worldwide.

Most advocates of the microeconomic approach to accounting conclude that an accounting measurement system based on replacement costs fits this approach best, and a general managerial emphasis prevails in *all* accounting reports. Accounting in the Netherlands is the best example of the microeconomic approach.

THE INDEPENDENT DISCIPLINE APPROACH

Judgment and estimate are integral parts of business, necessary to cope with real-world complexities and ever-present uncertainties. Successful businesspeople develop intuition, and trial-and-error is often the only way to deal with constant changes in the business environment. Business produces its own concepts and methods from experience and practice. If business is the main interest served by accounting and if accounting provides an efficient and effective service to business, then accounting and business practices should follow the same pattern of development.

Thus, accounting is viewed as a service function that derives its concepts and principles from the business process it serves, not from a discipline such as economics. Accounting is an independent discipline that develops on an ad hoc, piecemeal basis from judgment and trial-and-error. The United Kingdom and the United States are countries where accounting has developed as an independent discipline.

THE UNIFORM ACCOUNTING APPROACH

Under this approach accounting is standardized and employed as a tool for administrative control by central government. Uniformity in measurement, disclosure, and presentation makes it easier to use accounting information to control all types of businesses by government planners, tax authorities, and even managers. In general, the uniform approach is used in countries with strong governmental involvement in economic planning where accounting is used to measure performance, allocate resources, collect taxes, and control prices, among other things. France, with its national uniform chart of accounts, is the leading exponent of the uniform approach.[17]

CLASSIFICATION

International accounting classification work has been done in two ways:

1. judgmental classifications
2. empirically derived classifications

Although the methods of analysis for the two approaches differ substantially, their results are generally consistent.

---

[17]European academics, such as K. Käfer (Switzerland), L. L. Illetschko (Austria), E. Schmalenbach (Germany), and A. ter Vehn (Sweden), are largely identified with generalizing accounting processes from comprehensive flow charts of accounts.

JUDGMENTAL CLASSIFICATIONS

The initial work on classifying existing accounting practices is traceable to Mueller, who asserted that 10 different sets of accounting practices can be observed. He related the 10 groupings to the distinct business environments in which they operate.[18]Mueller's classification scheme was widely used by national institutes of accountants, various international organizations, and multinational professional accounting service firms.

Later, the American Accounting Association's 1975–76 Committee on International Accounting Operations and Education classified the accounting patterns of the world into five separate "Zones of Influence." They based their conclusions on historical, cultural, and socioeconomic sources that have influenced accounting principles of financial measurement and reporting in different countries and regions.[19]

Building on these earlier efforts, Nobes suggested a classification system, depicted in Exhibit 2-2.[20] His classification considers the measurement practices in the fourteen countries depicted. Nobes's classification not only shows which countries are in different categories, but also how close or distant these categories are to one another. For example, Australian accounting, as a member of the U.K. family, is closer to U. K. accounting than it is to either Canadian or U.S. accounting. However, it is closer to these two than it is to Dutch accounting, by the subclasses involved; but closer to Dutch accounting than French and German accounting, which are entirely different classes.

Note that Nobes's two classes (*micro-based* and *macro-uniform*) roughly correspond to the two types of legal systems (common and code law, respectively) already discussed. This basis of classification suggests that, at least for the countries included in Exhibit 2-2, the legal system is the dominant factor in shaping accounting development, and is the basic point of departure for classifying their accounting methods. Accounting in common law countries is sometimes called *non-legalistic* or *Anglo-Saxon* or *Anglo-American*. Accounting in code law countries is commonly called *legalistic*. Second, note that each of Nobes's four subclasses correspond to Mueller's four comparative development patterns: "business economics, theory" is the microeconomic pattern; "business practices, pragmatic" is the independent discipline approach; "government, tax, legal" is the uniform approach; and "government, economics" is the macroeconomic pattern.[21]

---

[18]Gerhard G. Mueller, "Accounting Principles Generally Accepted in the United States Versus Those Generally Accepted Elsewhere," *International Journal of Accounting* (spring 1968): 91–103. The 10 groupings are (1) United States, Canada, The Netherlands; (2) British Commonwealth (excluding Canada); (3) Germany, Japan; (4) Continental Europe (excluding Germany, The Netherlands, and Scandinavia); (5) Scandinavia; (6) Israel, Mexico; (7) South America; (8) developing nations of the Near and Far East; (9) Africa (excluding South Africa); and (10) communist nations.

[19]American Accounting Association, "Report of the American Accounting Association Committee on International Accounting Operations and Education, 1975-1976," *Accounting Review* 52 (supplement 1977): 65–101. The five zones of influences are (1) British, (2) Franco-Spanish-Portuguese, (3) Germanic-Dutch, (4) United States, and (5) communistic.

[20]C. W. Nobes, "A Judgmental International Classification of Financial Reporting Practices," *Journal of Business Finance & Accounting* (spring 1983): 1–19. Nobes also tests and finds empirical support for his classification. For further empirical support, see T. S. Doupnik and S. B. Salter, "An Empirical Test of a Judgmental International Classification of Financial Reporting Practices," *Journal of International Business Studies* (first quarter 1993): 41–60.

[21]The dominance of the legal system in classifying accounting systems worldwide is also empirically supported in S. B. Salter and T. S. Doupnik, "The Relationship Between Legal Systems and Accounting Practices: A Classification Exercise," *Advances in International Accounting* 5 (1992): 3–22.

EXHIBIT 2-2   Nobes's Classification of Accounting Systems: 1980

A HYPOTHETICAL CLASSIFICATION OF FINANCIAL REPORTING MEASUREMENT PRACTICES IN
DEVELOPED WESTERN COUNTRIES IN 1980

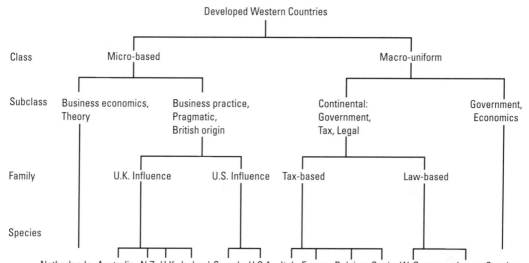

Source: Nobe's Classification of Accouting Systems 1980 from C.W. Nobes "A Judgmental International Classification of Financial Reporting Practices" *Journal of Business & Accounting*, Spring 1983, p. 7.

Gray developed a different judgmental classification scheme based on his work linking accounting and culture (see Exhibit 2-1). He classified Hofstede's 10 cultural areas according to (1) the authority and enforcement characteristics of accounting systems and (2) measurement and disclosure characteristics. Authority and enforcement concern accounting regulation: Who regulates accounting (statutory control, by the public sector; professionalism, by the private sector) and are the rules flexible or uniform? Measurement and disclosure concern accounting practice: What is the importance of conservatism and what is the degree of openness in financial reporting?

Gray's proposed mapping of accounting systems on these scales is illustrated in Exhibit 2-3. Gray's categories, like Nobes's, accommodate degrees of similarity or difference rather than being discrete. The areas within a quadrant tend to be more like each other than they are like those in other quadrants. At the same time, the distances between cultural areas suggest how similar they are according to the criteria used. Gray considers several dimensions of accounting, whereas Nobes focuses on measurement practices, and while Gray classifies regions, countries could be placed on the map instead. Note that one implication, in terms of accounting practices, is that regions with conservative measurements tend to be secretive and vice versa. (Note in the "Practice" portion of Exhibit 2-3 that only the conservatism/secrecy and the optimism/transparency quadrants are filled in.)

Nobes proposed a new classification in 1998, which is reproduced in Exhibit 2-4. Rather than focusing on countries, the 1998 classification focuses on financial reporting by companies. As discussed in Chapter 1, the 1990s witnessed phenomenal growth in global capital flows. As companies reached out to tap equity markets in other countries,

EXHIBIT 2-3 Gray's Cultural Framework for Classifying Accounting Systems

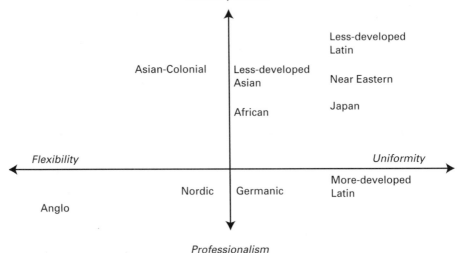

Regulation:
Authority and Enforcement

Statutory control

Asian-Colonial

Less-developed
Asian

African

Less-developed
Latin

Near Eastern

Japan

Flexibility

Uniformity

Nordic   Germanic

More-developed
Latin

Anglo

Professionalism

Practice:
Measurement and Disclosure

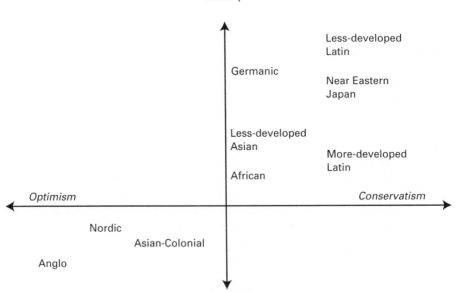

Secrecy

Germanic

Less-developed
Latin

Near Eastern
Japan

Less-developed
Asian

African

More-developed
Latin

Optimism

Conservatism

Nordic

Asian-Colonial

Anglo

Transparency

Source: Gray's Cultural Framework for Classifying Accounting Systems from S.J. Gray "Towards a Theory of Cultural Influence on the Development of Accounting Systems Internationally" *Abacus*, 24, No. 1, 1988, pp. 12-13.

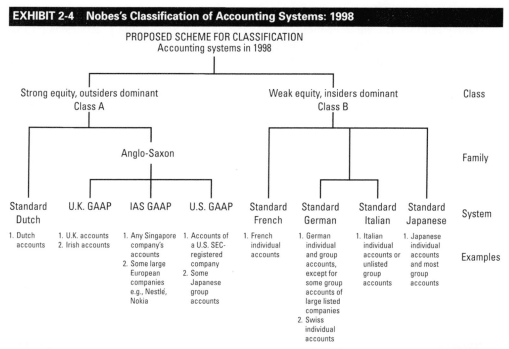

EXHIBIT 2-4   Nobes's Classification of Accounting Systems: 1998

PROPOSED SCHEME FOR CLASSIFICATION
Accounting systems in 1998

Strong equity, outsiders dominant **Class A**				Weak equity, insiders dominant **Class B**				Class
	Anglo-Saxon							Family
Standard Dutch	U.K. GAAP	IAS GAAP	U.S. GAAP	Standard French	Standard German	Standard Italian	Standard Japanese	System
1. Dutch accounts	1. U.K. accounts 2. Irish accounts	1. Any Singapore company's accounts 2. Some large European companies e.g., Nestlé, Nokia	1. Accounts of a U.S. SEC-registered company 2. Some Japanese group accounts	1. French individual accounts	1. German individual and group accounts, except for some group accounts of large listed companies 2. Swiss individual accounts	1. Italian individual accounts or unlisted group accounts	1. Japanese individual accounts and most group accounts	Examples

Sources: C. Nobes, "Towards a General Model of the Reasons for International Differences in Financial Reporting," *Abacus* (September 1998): 181; and C. Nobes and R. Parker, *Comparative International Accounting*, 6th ed., Essex: Pearson Education, 2000, 62.

many companies modified their financial reporting to suit the information needs of international capital market investors. In particular, companies from code law countries began to adopt shareholder-oriented reporting found in common law countries. Some national patterns have begun to break down. Nobes asserts that the type of finance is now more important than the legal system in classifying financial reporting systems.

EMPIRICALLY DERIVED CLASSIFICATIONS

Another way to establish a system of classification is to analyze accounting and reporting standards and/or practices actually in use. During the 1970s, a number of researchers applied factor analysis to arrive at statistically based clusters of existing accounting practices. These studies used databases of accounting principles and reporting practices prepared by Price Waterhouse International (PWI), published in three editions—1973, 1975, and 1979.[22]

An important early study is by Frank, using 1973 PWI data.[23] Four groups are empirically derived, which Franks calls *prototypes* or *accounting models:* British Commonwealth, Latin American, Continental European, and United States. Frank also

---

[22]Price Waterhouse International, *Accounting Principles and Reporting Practices—A Survey*, London: Price Waterhouse International, 1973, 1975, 1979.
[23]W. G. Frank, "An Empirical Analysis of International Accounting Principles," *Journal of Accounting Research* (autumn 1979): 593–605.

grouped the same countries by economic and social factors and found that nearly every country fell into the same groupings using the data on accounting practices as on the economic and social data. This shows that financial accounting and environmental factors are related, and it supports the proposition that accounting similarities can be expected among countries with similar environments.

A follow-up study by Nair and Frank[24] extended the Frank study in two ways. First, the 1975 PWI data were added to the 1973 data used by Frank. This allowed them to look at the stability of the groupings over time. Second, each database was separated into measurement and disclosure items, a common distinction made in accounting. Based on the 1973 measurement data, the four accounting prototypes in the Frank study emerged again; however, the disclosure groupings were different and showed no intuitive categorizations. The measurement groupings obtained from the 1975 data were nearly the same as those using 1973 data, but the disclosure groups, using the 1975 data, were different from the 1973 disclosure groups and also different from the 1975 measurement groups. Exhibit 2-5 shows the Nair and Frank classification based on measurement practices using the 1973 data.

One inference from the Nair and Frank study is that measurement practices should be distinguished from disclosure. These two aspects of accounting may very well be influenced by different factors and develop along separate lines. Another inference is that accounting measurement seems to be more stable than disclosure. This is not hard to understand considering that measurement issues are normally harder to change than disclosure issues.[25]

EXHIBIT 2-5   Nair and Frank Accounting Groups 1973 Measurement Practices

British Commonwealth	Latin American	Continental European	United States
Australia	Argentina	Belgium	Canada
Bahamas	Bolivia	France	Japan
Eire (Ireland)	Brazil	West Germany	Mexico
Fiji	Chile	Italy	Panama
Jamaica	Colombia	Spain	Philippines
Kenya	Ethiopia	Sweden	United States
Netherlands	India	Switzerland	
New Zealand	Paraguay	Venezuela	
Pakistan	Peru		
Rhodesia (Zimbabwe)	Uruguay		
Singapore			
South Africa			
Trinidad & Tobago			
United Kingdom			

Source: R. D. Nair and W. G. Frank, "The Impact of Disclosure and Measurement Practices on International Accounting Classifications," *Accounting Review* (July 1980): 429. Used with permission of *Accounting Review* and American Accounting Association.

---

[24]R. D. Nair and W. G. Frank, "The Impact of Disclosure and Measurement Practices on International Accounting Classifications," *Accounting Review* (July 1980): 426–450.

[25]The studies based on Price Waterhouse International (PWI) data have been criticized. For one, mistakes in the PWI data have been noted. For another, the data blur the distinction between accounting practices and accounting requirements. These need not be the same. Finally, the research method used by the

More recently, Doupnik and Salter classified the accounting practices of 50 countries using data they obtained from a survey of experts in these countries.[26] Their database covered a broad range of both measurement and disclosure practices as of 1990. Their statistical method enabled them to group countries into increasingly narrow clusters, consistent with Nobes's hierarchical approach. The results, displayed in Exhibit 2-6, reveal two-, six-, and nine-cluster groupings. Doupnik and Salter also examined the relationship between their accounting groupings and environmental and cultural variables. Note that the two-cluster grouping is consistent with Nobes's 1980 micro-based and macro-uniform classes. Also, a Latin American group emerges from the macro-uniform group, consistent with the studies by Nair and Frank. The micro-based group eventually splits into U.K.- and U.S.-influence groups, consistent with both Nobes (1980) and Nair and Frank.

Certain environmental factors explain the groupings. First, the two-cluster grouping indicates the dominance of a nation's legal system (code versus common law) on its accounting practices. Doupnik and Salter also find that the micro-based group relies more heavily on capital markets and is less uncertainty avoidant than the macro-uniform group. A Latin American group emerged from other macro-uniform countries due to these countries' higher inflation and generally lower level of economic development.

Doupnik and Salter also analyzed the relationship between measurement and disclosure practices. They find that countries with relatively more conservative accounting practices generally have lower levels of disclosure, and countries with less conservative accounting practices have higher levels of disclosure. This result is consistent with Gray's classification with respect to these two dimensions.

Conclusion

It is tempting to conclude that our views about classifications of accounting systems have been remarkably stable over time. This generalization is only partly true. First, it applies mainly to developed, Western nations. As discussed in Chapter 4, accounting in emerging market economies, such as the countries of Eastern Europe and China, is being significantly transformed in response to new environmental stimuli. Second, the generalization is true about *measurement* practices but not *disclosure* practices. The research discussed in this chapter focused mostly on measurement practices. In general, disclosure practices are easier to change than measurement practices. Pressure to change measurements is sometimes relieved by changing disclosures.

It is also necessary to distinguish accounting practice at the *national* level from that at the *transnational* level. Chapter 1 showed that hundreds of companies are listing their shares on stock exchanges outside their home countries. As discussed in Chapter 5, many internationally listed companies prepare dual financial reports. One set complies with local, domestic financial reporting requirements while the other uses accounting

---

authors treat all measurement and disclosure items as equally important, which they clearly are not. Trivial items may swamp important ones in the analysis. See C. W. Nobes, "An Empirical Analysis of International Accounting Principles: A Comment," *Journal of Accounting Research* (spring 1981): 268–270.

[26]T. S. Doupnik and S. B. Salter, "External Environment, Culture, and Accounting Practice: A Preliminary Test of a General Model of International Accounting Development," *International Journal of Accounting* 30, no. 3 (1995): 189–207.

EXHIBIT 2-6 Doupnik-Salter Accounting Groups

	Number of Clusters		
Country	*Two*	*Six*	*Nine*
Japan		B6	C9
Germany		B5	C8
Finland Sweden		B4	C7
Egypt Saudi Arabia Belgium UAE Liberia Thailand Panama	A2 M a c r o	B3	C6
Portugal Spain Colombia Italy Korea Denmark Norway France	u n i f o r m		C5
Argentina Mexico Brazil Chile		B2	C4
Costa Rica			C3

principles and contains disclosures aimed at international investors. The two sets of financial statements are clearly distinguishable. Moreover, this duality is now sanctioned in some code law countries, including France, Germany, and Italy. In these countries, individual company financial statements comply with national legal standards while consolidated financial statements may comply with other standards, such as International Accounting Standards or U.S. generally accepted accounting principles. In this way, consolidated statements can inform investors while individual company accounts satisfy legal requirements such as determining taxable income.

| EXHIBIT 2-6 (cont.) | | | |

Country	Number of Clusters		
	Two	Six	Nine
Malaysia			
S. Africa			
Zimbabwe			
Hong Kong			
Singapore			
Namibia			
Ireland	A1		
United Kingdom			
Zambia			C2
Australia	M		
Papua N. Guinea	i		
New Zealand	c		
Trinidad	r		
Nigeria	o	B1	
Sri Lanka			
Botswana	b		
Jamaica	a		
Philippines	s		
Taiwan	e		
Netherlands	d		
Neth. Antilles			
Luxembourg			
Bermuda			
Israel			C1
Canada			
United States			

Source: Reprinted from *Journal of Accounting,* Vol. 30, T. Doupnik and S. Salter, "External Environment, Culture and Accounting Practice" pp. 199, copyright 1995, with permission of Elsevier Science.

The classifications just discussed dominate current thinking about accounting in the world. Where are we headed? Many of the distinctions at the national level are becoming blurred. (Exhibit 2-4 reflects this.) Chapter 3 distinguishes between the *fair presentation* and *legal compliance* orientations of accounting. Countries with strong equity capital markets, like the United States and United Kingdom, already orient their accounting toward the information needs of outside shareholders. Accounting in these countries focuses on a fair presentation of financial position and results of operations. Countries with credit-based systems (weak equity markets) retain their legal compliance basis of accounting for legal entities, but are moving toward the option of fair presentation at the consolidated level in response to international capital market pressures.

We believe that the integration of the world's capital markets will be the most significant influence shaping accounting development in the future. This development permeates many of the issues covered in later chapters. For example, Chapter 3 shows how it is driving the fair presentation versus legal compliance duality in France and Germany. Chapter 5 explains how multi-listed companies often issue secondary financial statements for the benefit of investors outside their home countries. Integration of capital markets is the key driver in the international harmonization movement discussed in Chapter 8. It is also the reason, as discussed in Chapter 9, why financial statement analysis is increasingly global in scope.

Selected References

Baydoun, N., and R. Willett, "Cultural Relevance of Western Accounting Systems to Developing Countries," *Abacus* (March 1995): 67–92.

Chanchani, S., and A. MacGregor, "A Synthesis of Cultural Studies in Accounting," *Journal of Accounting Literature* 18 (1999): 1–30.

Doupnik, T. S., and S. B. Salter, "External Environment, Culture, and Accounting Practice: A Preliminary Test of a General Model of International Accounting Development," *The International Journal of Accounting* 30, no. 3 (1995): 189–207.

Gray, S. J., "Towards a Theory of Cultural Influence on the Development of Accounting Systems Internationally," *Abacus* (March 1988): 1–15.

Hamid, S., R. Craig, and F. Clark, "Religion: A Confounding Culture Element in the International Harmonization of Accounting?" *Abacus* (September 1993): 131–148.

Hofstede, G., *Culture's Consequences: International Differences in Work-Related Values*, Beverly Hills, CA: Sage Publications, 1980.

Meek, G. K., and S. M. Saudagaran,, "A Survey of Research on Financial Reporting in a Transnational Context." *Journal of Accounting Literature* 9 (1990): 145–182.

Mueller, G. G., *International Accounting*, New York: Macmillan, 1967.

Nair, R. D., and W. G. Frank, "The Impact of Disclosure and Measurement Practices on International Accounting Classifications." *Accounting Review* (July 1980): 426–450.

Nobes, C. W., "A Judgmental International Classification of Financial Reporting Practices,"

Journal of Business Finance and Accounting (spring 1983): 1–19.

Nobes, C. W., *International Accounting—General Issues and Classification*, Cheltenham: Edward Elgar Publishing, 1996.

Nobes, C., "Towards a General Model of Reasons for International Differences in Financial Reporting," *Abacus* (September 1998): 162–187.

Parker, R. H., "Importing and Exporting Accounting: The British Experience," in A. G. Hopwood, (ed.), *International Pressures for Accounting Change*, Hemel Hempstead: Prentice Hall International (U.K.), 1989, 7–29.

Perera, H., "Culture and International Accounting: Some Thoughts on Research Issues and Prospects," *Advances in International Accounting* 7 (1994): 267–285.

Porcano, T. M., and A. V. Tran, "Relationship of Tax and Financial Accounting Rules in Anglo-Saxon Countries, *The International Journal of Accounting* 33, no. 4 (1998): 433–454.

Roberts, A., "The Very Idea of Classification in International Accounting," *Accounting, Organizations and Society* 20, no. 7/8 (1995): 639–664.

Salter, S. B., and F. Niswander, "Cultural Influence on the Development of Accounting Internationally: A Test of Gray's [1988] Theory," *Journal of International Business Studies* (second quarter 1995): 379–397.

Saudagaran, S. M., and J. G. Diga, "Evaluation of the Contingency-Based Approach in

Comparative International Accounting: A Case for Alternative Research Paradigms," *Journal of Accounting Literature* 18 (1999): 57–95.

Wallace, R. S. O., and H. Gernon, "Framework for International Comparative Financial Ac-

counting," *Journal of Accounting Literature* 10 (1992): 209–263.

Zarzeski, M. T., "Spontaneous Harmonization Effects of Culture and Market Forces on Accounting Disclosure Practices," *Accounting Horizons* (March 1996): 18–37.

Discussion Questions

1. The chapter identifies seven economic, sociohistorical, and institutional factors believed to influence accounting development. Explain how each one affects accounting practice.

2. Referring to the seven factors in Question 1, rank them from most to least important as far as accounting development is concerned, then justify both the top and bottom items in your ranking.

3. Are national differences in accounting practice better explained by culture or by economic and legal factors? Why?

4. The four patterns of accounting development discussed in the chapter were originally outlined in 1967. Are these four patterns still valid today? Why or why not?

5. Why do countries that tend to have relatively conservative measurement practices also tend to be secretive in disclosure, while countries that tend to have less conservative measurement practices tend to be transparent in disclosure?

6. What is the purpose of classifying systems of accounting?

7. Three judgmental classifications of existing accounting practices were developed by Nobes (1980), Gray (1988), and Nobes (1998). How do these three classifications differ from one another? How are they consistent?

8. Compare and contrast the empirically derived classifications of existing accounting practices by Nair and Frank and Doupnik and Salter.

9. Refer to Exhibit 2-2 (Nobes's 1980 classification of accounting systems). What are the fundamental differences between accounting in micro-based countries and macro-uniform countries? Are there any similarities? How does this classification compare to Nobes's 1998 classification in Exhibit 2-4?

10. Financial reporting is broadly oriented toward a fair presentation or legal compliance. Discuss the classification studies that support this dichotomy.

11. Why does the chapter contend that many distinctions of accounting at the national level are becoming blurred? Do you agree? Why or why not?

12. What are the prospects of a convergence or harmonization of national systems of accounting and financial reporting? What factors might be influential in promoting or inhibiting change?

Exercises

1. Accounting in micro-based countries differs markedly from accounting in macro-uniform countries.

   Required: Choose one country from each of these two categories. Compare and contrast accounting in these two countries. (Hint: Many references are available.

For example, the American Institute of Certified Public Accountants publishes a *Professional Accounting in Foreign Countries* series of booklets, as do several accounting firms.)

2. The chapter identifies seven economic/legal/institutional variables that influence accounting development: sources of finance, legal system, taxation, political and economic ties, inflation, level of economic development, and education level.

   Required:
   a. Choose a country of the world other than your own and describe it on the basis of these seven dimensions. Web sites include the Encyclopaedia Britannica Online (www.eb.com) and The World Factbook (www.odci.gov/cia/publications/factbook/).
   b. Using this description, predict a general profile of financial accounting in that country.
   c. Go to the library and find a reference that describes accounting in the country that you chose. Is your prediction accurate? Why or why not?

3. Consider the following countries: (1) Belgium, (2) China, (3) Czech Republic, (4) Gambia, (5) India, (6) Mexico, (7) Senegal, and (8) Taiwan. Where would they be placed in Nobes's 1980 classification (Exhibit 2-2)? Where would they be placed in Nobes's 1998 classification (Exhibit 2-4)? Justify your answers.

4. International accounting classification work has been accomplished in two ways: (a) judgmental classifications and (b) empirically derived classifications.

   Required: Identify and discuss briefly a few pros and cons of each approach. Would you support further empirical tests of accounting classifications?

5. The text makes distinctions between four comparative accounting development patterns. Naturally, these four patterns overlap and hence are not found in completely pure forms. Within generally accepted accounting principles in the United States, LIFO inventory-pricing methods are available for financial purposes only if they are also applied in parallel fashion for tax accounting purposes. This scenario is a good example of the uniform approach to accounting development.

   Required: For each of the other three comparative accounting development patterns cited in the text, identify three specific financial accounting standards, principles, or practices in your home country that illustrates the respective pattern.

6. Refer to Exhibit 2-2 in the text. Nobes begins his classification with two broad categories: micro-based and macro-uniform. He classifies accounting in fourteen countries as follows:

Micro-based	*Micro-uniform*
Netherlands	Italy
Australia	France
New Zealand	Belgium
United Kingdom	Spain
Ireland	Germany
Canada	Japan
United States	Sweden

Required:
a. Obtain an annual report from a company headquartered in one of the seven micro-based countries and another one from one of the seven macro-uniform countries. Two sources are www.carol.co.uk and www.corporateinformation.com. (Chapter 9 lists other Web sites for company research.)
b. Compare and contrast the two annual reports along measurement and disclosure dimensions.
c. Do the similarities and differences conform to your expectations?

7. Refer to the Web sites listed in Appendix 1-3 to learn more about stock exchanges in your home country and two other countries of your choice.

Required: Prepare a table showing numbers of listed companies (if possible, broken down by foreign and domestic) for each stock exchange. Which stock exchange has the most listed companies? Discuss possible reasons for this.

8. Let us arbitrarily divide accounting development stages into a spectrum of five categories: (a) highly developed and complex; (b) well developed and mature; (c) reasonably developed, with a character of its own; (d) beginning development, mostly under outside influences; and (e) little or no measurable development.

Required: Place five different countries in each of the five accounting development categories identified. Do enough reference work to make sure that you can justify each individual country selection. Web sites include The World Factbook (www.odci.gov/cia/publications/factbook/) and Encyclopaedia Britannica Online (www.eb.com).

9. One alleged benefit of classifying accounting systems is that developing countries can save the resources that would be used to create national accounting standards by choosing a model of accounting and then emulating that type of accounting.

Required: Choose some country with an emerging market economy and find a recent article or report describing accounting there. Which type of accounting does this country seem to be following? Why is it doing so?

10. The European Union (EU)—formerly known as the European Community and at its start, the European Common Market—was formed in 1957 and now has fifteen members: Austria, Belgium, Denmark, Finland, France, Germany, Greece, Ireland, Italy, Luxembourg, the Netherlands, the United Kingdom, Spain, Sweden, and Portugal. To encourage capital movement and capital formation, the EU has issued various *Directives* designed to harmonize the generally accepted accounting principles of its member countries.

Required: Which of the factors affecting accounting development are likely to be the most serious obstacles to the EU harmonization effort? What factors indicate the EU harmonization effort can succeed?

11. Among other international agencies, the World Bank has in place a formal accounting development program for developing countries.

Required: Select any developing country and write an executive brief describing why this country would benefit substantially from some massive accounting development assistance.

12. Think ahead 10 years from now. Prepare a classification of accounting systems that you think will exist then. What factors motivate your particular classification?

Case 2–1   Are Classifications of Accounting Outmoded?

Consider the following statements by David Cairns, former Secretary-General of the International Accounting Standards Committee.[1]

> Simplistic classifications of accounting are ... of little relevance in the complex world of the 1990s; when we look at the way that countries or companies account for particular transactions and events, it is increasingly difficult to distinguish in a systematic way so-called Anglo-American accounting from Continental European accounting or American accounting from, say, German accounting.[2]

> I am increasingly persuaded ... that the distinction between Anglo-American accounting and Continental European accounting is becoming less and less relevant and more and more confused. In reaching this conclusion, I do not dispute that different economic, social and legal considerations have influenced the development of accounting in different countries. I also do not dispute the fact that there have been, and still are, differences in the means by which different countries determine accounting requirements and the form of the resulting requirements. I do believe, however, that those who continue to favour these classifications are ignoring what is happening in the world and how companies actually account for transactions and events.

> It is increasingly apparent that the different economic, social and legal considerations which have influenced national accounting do not necessarily result in different accounting and that countries are reaching the same answers irrespective of their different cultural backgrounds (or reaching different answers in spite of the similar cultural backgrounds). In fact, there are now probably far more similarities between American and German accounting than there are between American and British accounting. There are many reasons for this not least the increasing practice of standard setting bodies and other regulators to share ideas and learn from one another. They do this in the IASC, the UN, the OECD, the EU, and such groupings as G4. This cross-fertilization of ideas is not surprising because standard setting bodies in all countries are having to address the same accounting problems.[3]

REQUIRED

1. Do you agree with Mr. Cairns's assertion that classifications of accounting are simplistic and of little relevance in today's world? Are attempts to classify accounting futile and outmoded? Why or why not?

2. Some observers contend that financial reporting is becoming more and more alike among "world class" companies—the world's largest multinational corporations—and particularly those listed on the major stock exchanges such as London, New York, and Tokyo. What is the relevance of this contention for classifications of accounting and what are the factors that would cause this to happen?

---

[1] D. Cairns, "The Future Shape of Harmonization: A Reply," *European Accounting Review* 6, no. 2 (1997): 305–348.
[2] Ibid., 306.
[3] Ibid., 316.

Case 2–2   MAN AG

MAN AG, a large German industrial products and services company, adopted International Accounting Standards (IAS) for its 1998–99 fiscal year. Exhibit 2-7 is taken from MAN's 1998–99 annual report. It discusses why MAN adopted IAS and the main differences between German Commercial Code (GCC) and IAS, as they apply to MAN.

EXHIBIT 2-7   MAN AG
Notes to the Consolidated Financial Statements
Adoption of International Accounting Standards

The consolidated financial statements of MAN Aktiengesellschaft are prepared according to the International Accounting Standards (IAS) as of June 30, 1999, established by the International Accounting Standards Committee (IASC). Also applied, before the date at which their use became mandatory, for 1998/99 and for the previous financial year, were the following standards: IAS 37 (Provisions, contingent liabilities and contingent assets), as the above applies to the preparation of balance sheets and methods of valuation, IAS 17 (Leases), IAS 19 (Employee benefits), IAS 36 (Impairment of assets), as well as IAS 38 (Intangible assets).

The changeover made by the MAN Group serves to enhance the international comparability of our consolidated financial statements, and augments the comprehensibility of our financial information. The commencing of the use of cost-of-sales accounting format in our income statement and the adoption of standardized valuation methods have caused a converging of the company's internal and external accounting systems.

The standards applied accord to the EU's 7th directive. In accordance with § 292 a of Germany's Commercial Code (GCC), the compiling of the consolidated financial statements exempts the company from the obligation to publish financial statements according to German Commercial Code.

These consolidated financial statements, prepared according to IAS, are, delimited by the exceptions below, of equal value and applicability to those compiled according to GCC.

The adoption of IAS has resulted in alterations in our accounting methods. Prime among these changes:

— Tax-related special write-offs and special items are not incorporated into the consolidated financial statements.

— Plant, machinery and other equipment acquired as of July 1, 1998 and after are depreciated using the straight-line method.

— Pension accruals are valued using the projected unit credit method laid down by IAS 19, taking into account future increases in remuneration and pensions expected and the new mortality tables.

— Accruals constituted to provide for output yet to be supplied and for losses carried forward are to be valued at the cost of production, and not at full cost.

— More extensive deferring of taxes is made for tax assets.

These financial statements use accounting methods deviating in the following ways and areas from those stipulated by Germany's commercial codes:

— Construction contracts are recognized in the balance sheet according to the state of their progress.

— No accruals are constituted for the outstanding maintenance.

— Starting in 1998/99, deferred tax assets are made for tax losses carried forward.

Particulars and elucidations foreseen by Germany's commercial codes are included in our balance sheet or income statement, or in the notes.

The provisions of SIC 8 (governing the first-time application of IAS) stipulate that the adoption of IAS be accompanied by the compiling of an opening balance sheet as of July 1, 1997. The accompanying changes charged directly against retained earnings and minority interest.

Due to its foreseen sale one company included in the consolidated financial statements prepared according to GCC for 1997/98 is no longer consolidated in the accounts prepared according to IAS.

Exhibit 2-7 (*continued*)

Changes resulting in the shareholders' equity from the adoption of IAS:

in DM million	
Shareholders' equity on June 30, 1997, acc. to GCC	**4058**
cancellations of tax-related special write-offs and untaxed special items	215
reporting of construction contracts according to percentage of completion	185
revaluation of pension accruals	−591
revaluation of provisions for losses and other accruals	185
deferred taxes	132
other items	−6
Shareholders' equity on July 1, 1997, acc. to IAS	**4178**

The changeover to IAS produced the following changes in the income statement for 1997/98:

in DM million	*1997/98 acc. to GCC*	*1997/98 acc. to IAS*	*difference*
revenues from sales	24,793	24,710	−83
cost of sales and other expenditures and earnings	−23,984	−23,892	92
Income from ordinary activities	**809**	**818**	**9**
taxes on income	−197	−185	12
net income	**612**	**633**	**21**

Source: MAN Aktiengesellschaft Annual Report 1998/99, 66–67.

REQUIRED

1. Based on the information provided in the chapter, describe the basic features of German accounting. What developmental factors cause these features?
2. What differences between the accounting requirements in the GCC and IAS are highlighted in MAN's disclosure? Are the German requirements consistent with your characterizations in requirement 1?
3. Why did MAN adopt IAS?
4. What is the relevance of MAN's adoption of IAS to the classification studies discussed in the chapter?

CHAPTER 3

COMPARATIVE
ACCOUNTING I

In Chapter 2 we learned about the factors that affect the development of a nation's accounting, including its sources of finance, legal system, taxation, political and economic ties, and inflation. Chapter 2 went on to classify accounting systems according to their common elements and distinctive features.

Chapters 3 and 4 more closely examine accounting in a few selected countries. Specific knowledge of accounting in a country is needed to analyze financial statements from that country. Chapter 3 deals with six highly developed countries: France, Germany, Japan, the Netherlands, the United Kingdom, and the United States. Chapter 4 deals with four "emerging market" countries: China, the Czech Republic, Mexico, and Taiwan.

Exhibit 3-1 contains some comparative economic data about the six countries chosen for Chapter 3. Together they are home to the vast majority of the world's multinational corporations. As such, their companies are likely to be the subjects of analysis. These six countries dominate the development of international accounting today. All six were among the founders of the International Accounting Standards Committee (IASC, now International Accounting Standards Board, or IASB), and they have a major role in directing the IASB's agenda.

Accounting standards are the regulations or rules (often including laws and statutes) that govern the preparation of financial statements. *Standard setting* is the process by which accounting standards are formulated. Thus, accounting standards are the products of standard setting. However, actual practice may deviate from what the standards require. There are at least four reasons for this. First, in many countries the penalties for noncompliance with official accounting pronouncements are weak or ineffective. Second, companies may voluntarily report more information than required. Third, some countries allow companies to depart from accounting standards if doing so will better represent a company's results of operations and financial position. Finally, in some countries accounting standards apply only to individual company financial statements, not to consolidated statements. In those countries, companies are free to choose different accounting standards for their consolidated financial statements. To gain a complete picture of how accounting works in a country, we must pay attention to the

EXHIBIT 3-1 Economic Data for Selected Countries

	France	Germany	Japan	Netherlands	United Kingdom	United States
Area: sq. km.	544 thousand	358 thousand	378 thousand	42 thousand	243 thousand	9,373 thousand
Population	58.7 million	82.1 million	126.3 million	15.7 million	58.7 million	274.0 million
Gross Domestic Product	$1,465 billion	$2,180 billion	$4,089 billion	$389 billion	$1,264 billion	$7,903 billion
GDP Per Capita	$24,210	$26,570	$32,350	$24,780	$21,410	$29,240
GDP by Sector						
Agriculture	3%	1%	2%	3%	2%	2%
Industry	26%	32%	36%	27%	25%	22%
Services	71%	67%	62%	70%	73%	76%
Imports	$286.3 billion	$462.0 billion	$280.0 billion	$184.5 billion	$305.9 billion	$911.9 billion
Exports	$304.8 billion	$537.8 billion	$386.9 billion	$198.6 billion	$271.7 billion	$682.1 billion
Major Trading Partners	Germany, Italy, U.K., Spain, Belgium & Luxembourg, U.S.	France, U.S., U.K., Italy, Netherlands, Belgium & Luxembourg	U.S., China, Hong Kong, Taiwan, Germany	Germany, Belgium & Luxembourg, France, U.K., U.S.	Germany, U.S., France, Netherlands, Italy, Ireland	Canada, Japan, Mexico, Germany, U.K., China

Source: Adapted from *Pocket World in Figures 2001.* © The Economist Newspaper Group, Inc. Reprinted with permission further reproduction prohibited.

accounting standard-setting process, the resulting accounting standards, and actual practice. *Auditing* adds credibility to financial reports. Thus, we also discuss the role and purpose of auditing in the countries we examine.

BASIC CONCEPTS

Accounting standard setting normally involves a combination of private and public sector groups. The private sector includes the accounting profession and other groups affected by the financial reporting process such as users and preparers of financial statements and employees. The public sector includes such agencies as tax authorities, ministries responsible for commercial law, and securities commissions. Stock exchanges may influence the process and may be in either the private or public sector, depending on the country in question. The roles and influence of these groups in setting accounting standards differ from country to country. These differences help explain why standards vary around the world.

The relationship between accounting standards and accounting practice is complex, and does not always move in a one-way direction. In some cases, practice derives from standards; in others, standards are derived from practice. Practice can be influenced by market forces such as those related to the competition for funds in capital markets. Companies competing for funds may voluntarily provide information beyond what is required in response to the demand for information by investors and others. If the demand for such information is strong enough, standards may be changed to mandate disclosures that had been voluntary.

One key distinction in financial reporting is whether accounting is oriented toward a *fair* presentation of financial position and results of operations or toward compliance with legal requirements and tax laws. *Fairness* and *substance over form* characterize so-called Anglo-Saxon accounting. (In Exhibit 2-2, Nobes calls these countries micro-based.) Anglo-Saxon accounting systems are usually associated with a common law legal system and shareholders as the principal source of finance. Countries in this group are the United Kingdom, the United States, the Netherlands, and others strongly influenced by political and economic ties (such as British influence throughout the former British Empire and U.S. influence on Canada, Mexico, and the Philippines).

Countries whose accounting systems are oriented toward compliance with legal requirements tend to have a code law legal system and rely heavily on banks and the government as sources of finance. (In Exhibit 2-2, Nobes calls these countries macro-uniform.) This group includes most of the countries in Continental Europe, their former colonies in Africa and Southeast Asia, and Japan. They have relatively conservative measurement practices and a close linkage between financial and tax accounting. Because companies in these countries must record revenues and expenses in their accounts to claim them for tax purposes, tax laws effectively determine the amounts reported in financial statements.

The distinction between fair presentation and legal compliance countries has pervasive effects on many accounting issues such as: (1) depreciation, where the expense is determined based on the decline in an asset's usefulness over its economic useful life (fair presentation) or the amount allowed for tax purposes (legal compliance); (2) leases that are in substance a purchase of property are treated as such (fair presentation) or are treated like regular operating leases (legal compliance); and (3) pensions with costs accrued as earned by employees (fair presentation) or expensed on a pay-as-you-go basis (legal compliance). Further, the issue of deferred income taxes never arises when tax and financial accounting are the same. The distinction also applies in standard setting, in that the private sector is relatively more influential in fair presentation, common law countries, while the public sector is relatively more influential in legal compliance, code law countries.

Another issue is the use of discretionary reserves to smooth income from one period to the next. Generally, these reserves work the following way. In good years extra expenses are provided for, with the corresponding credit going to a reserve account in shareholders' equity. In lean years reserves are dissolved to boost income. This process smooths out year-to-year fluctuations in income. Because this practice jeopardizes a fair presentation, it is less common in substance-over-form countries than in legal compliance countries. Of course, if such manipulations are fully disclosed, investors can undo the effects on income. This may not be the case; reserves often are secret.

A third major issue is the use of historical cost or other valuation for tangible and intangible assets. Historical cost is universally used to value these assets when they are acquired in a transaction. However, they may be subsequently revalued on the basis of current market values or adjusted for changes in price levels. (See Chapter 7 for a related discussion of accounting for changing prices.) Further, the value of certain intangible assets, such as brand names, may be capitalized at estimated fair market value. The use of historical cost or some other measurement basis to value tangible and intangible assets also affects the amounts of depreciation and amortization expense on the income statement. A further complication is the treatment of goodwill arising from the acquisition of another business. Alternative treatments include capitalization and amortization, capitalization without amortization, or complete write-off in the year of acquisition. Income effects follow from each of these treatments.

Auditing parallels the type of legal system and the role and purpose of financial reporting. The auditing profession tends to be more developed and self-regulated in fair presentation countries, especially those influenced by the United Kingdom. Auditors also exercise more judgment when the purpose of an audit is to attest to the fair presentation of financial reports. By contrast, in code law countries the accounting profession tends to be less developed and more state regulated. In those countries, the main purpose of an audit is to ensure that the company's records and financial statements conform to legal requirements.

The trend in financial reporting is toward fair presentation, at least for consolidated financial statements. Code law countries such as France, Germany, and Japan are adapting their traditional legal compliance approach to accounting to reflect the reality of global capital markets. Chapter 8 discusses the role played by the IASB and other organizations in promoting this movement toward fair presentation consolidated financial statements.

SIX NATIONAL FINANCIAL ACCOUNTING SYSTEMS[1]

FRANCE

France is the world's leading advocate of national uniform accounting. The Ministry of National Economy approved the first formal Plan Comptable Général (national accounting code) in September 1947. A revised plan came into effect in 1957. A further revision of the

---

[1] The discussion in this section draws on the references cited at the end of the chapter.

plan was enacted in 1982 under the influence of the Fourth Directive of the European Union (EU). In 1986 the plan was extended to implement the requirements of the EU Seventh Directive on consolidated financial statements, and it was further revised in 1999.

The Plan Comptable Général provides

- objectives and principles of financial accounting and reporting
- definitions of assets, liabilities, shareholders' equity, revenues, and expenses
- recognition and valuation rules
- a standardized chart of accounts, requirements for its use, and other bookkeeping requirements
- model financial statements and rules for their presentation[2]

The mandatory use of the national uniform chart of accounts does not burden French businesses because the plan is widely accepted in practice. Moreover, various schedules required for income tax returns are based on the standardized models of the income statement and balance sheet and the state statistical office produces macroeconomic information by aggregating the financial statements of enterprises.

French accounting is so closely linked to the plan that it is possible to overlook the fact that commercial legislation (i.e., the Code de Commerce) and tax laws dictate many of France's actual financial accounting and reporting practices. Both of these predate the plan. The Code de Commerce has its roots in the 1673 and 1681 ordinances of Colbert (finance minister to Louis XIV) and was enacted by Napoleon in 1807 as a part of the legal system he created, based on written law. The first income tax law was passed in 1914, thereby linking taxation and the need to keep accounting records.

The main bases for accounting regulation in France are the 1983 Accounting Law and 1983 Accounting Decree, which made the Plan Comptable Général compulsory for all companies. Both texts are inserted in the Code de Commerce.[3] Commercial legislation in the Code de Commerce has extensive accounting and reporting provisions. Annual inventories of assets and liabilities are required. The true and fair view for financial reporting must be evidenced, and certain accounting records are granted a privileged role in specified judicial proceedings. Accounting records, which legally serve purposes of proof and verification, increasingly are considered sources of information for decision making.

Each enterprise must establish an accounting manual if it believes that this is necessary to understand and control the accounting process. At a minimum, this manual includes a detailed flow chart and explanations of the entire accounting system, descriptions of all data-processing procedures and controls, a comprehensive statement of the accounting principles underlying annual financial statements, and the procedures used in the mandatory annual counting of inventory.

Tax laws also significantly influence accounting in France. Business expenses are deductible for tax purposes only if they are fully booked and reflected in annual financial statements.

A feature of French accounting is the dichotomy between individual company financial statements and those for the consolidated group. Even though individual company accounts must follow statutory reporting requirements, the law allows French

---

[2]The Plan Comptable Général is available in French and English at www.finances.gouv.fr/CNCompta/.
[3]The legal framework for accounting includes laws passed by Parliament, government decrees dealing with the application of these laws, and ministerial orders by the Ministry of Economy and Finance.

companies to follow International Accounting Standards or even U.S. Generally Accepted Accounting Practices (GAAP) in their consolidated financial statements. The main reason for this flexibility is that when the EU Seventh Directive was implemented in 1986, many French multinationals were already preparing consolidated statements based on Anglo-Saxon principles for purposes of stock exchange listings abroad. French companies referring to IAS or U.S. GAAP often declare that their financial statements comply both with French standards and with international or U.S. standards. As European Union accounting initiatives converge with International Accounting Standards (see Chapter 8), the U.S. GAAP option will likely be eliminated.

ACCOUNTING REGULATION AND ENFORCEMENT

Five major organizations are involved in setting standards in France:[4]

1. Conseil National de la Comptabilité or CNC (National Accounting Board)
2. Comité de la Réglementation Comptable or CRC (Accounting Regulation Committee)
3. Commission des Opérations de Bourse or COB (National Securities Commission)
4. Ordre des Experts-Comptables or OEC (Institute of Public Accountants)
5. Compagnie Nationale des Commissaires aux Comptes or CNCC (National Institute of Statutory Auditors)

The CNC consists of 58 members representing the accounting profession, civil servants, and employer, trade union, and other private sector groups. Attached to the Ministry of Economy and Finance, the CNC issues rulings and recommendations on accounting issues and has major responsibility for keeping the plan current. It is consulted on accounting matters requiring regulation, but has no regulatory or enforcement powers itself. Most of the CNC's technical work is done by committees of CNC members and staff. An Urgent Issues Committee is attached to the CNC to address accounting issues needing quick resolution. Appointments to the CNC are highly prestigious and its recommendations carry much weight.

Due to a need for a flexible and expeditious means of providing regulatory authority for accounting standards, the CRC was established in 1998. The CRC converts CNC rulings and recommendations into binding regulations. Under the jurisdiction of the Ministry of Economy and Finance, it has 15 members that include representatives of different ministries, the CNC, COB, OEC, and CNCC, and judges from the two highest courts in France. CRC regulations are published in the Official Journal of the French Republic after ministerial approval. Thus, the CRC has real regulatory power.

French companies traditionally have relied less on capital markets than on other sources of finance.[5] The French equivalent of the U.S. Securities and Exchange Commission—the COB—has important but limited influence. Established in 1967, the COB supervises the new issues market and the operations of regional and national stock exchanges. The president of France appoints the chairman of the COB, and the commission reports annually to the president. This arrangement provides independence from other government departments. The COB was an early advocate of consolidation re-

---

[4]The Web site addresses are CNC and CRC: www.finances.gouv.fr/CNCompta; COB: www.cob.fr; OEC: www.experts-comptables.com; CNCC: www.cncc.fr.
[5]France has a tradition of family businesses and nationalized industries, both of which rely on debt financing.

quirements for French companies and, in general, seeks French acceptance of world-class accounting and reporting standards—at least for larger publicly listed French companies. Using its authority to issue additional rules for listed companies, the COB has pressed for better accounting and disclosure, and has successfully improved the quality of information in consolidated financial statements.

In France the accounting and auditing professions have historically been separate. French accountants and auditors are represented by two bodies, the OEC and the CNCC, despite substantial overlap in their memberships. The practice of public accounting and the right to the title *expert-comptable* is restricted to OEC members, who contract with clients to maintain and review accounting records and prepare financial statements. The OEC is under the jurisdiction of the Ministry of Economy and Finance and participates in the development of accounting standards through the CRC and the CNC. Most of its effort is devoted to professional practice issues, though before the CRC was established it issued interpretations and recommendations on the application of accounting legislation and regulations.

By contrast, the CNCC (professional association of statutory auditors, *commissaires aux comptes*) is under the jurisdiction of the Ministry of Justice. The CNCC publishes a member handbook that contains extensive professional standards. It also publishes information bulletins that provide technical assistance. Audits in France are generally similar to their counterparts elsewhere. However, French auditors must report to the state prosecutor all criminal acts that they become aware of during the audit.

With the creation of the CRC, the current role of the last three organizations in accounting standard setting has changed. The operations of the CNC also have been affected, but the CNC keeps an important role in the preparation of accounting standards.

FINANCIAL REPORTING
French companies must report the following:

1. Balance sheet
2. Income statement
3. Notes to financial statements
4. Directors' report
5. Auditor's report

Large companies also must prepare documents relating to the prevention of business bankruptcies and a social report, both of which are unique to France. There are no requirements for a statement of changes in financial position or cash flow statement. However, the CNC recommends a cash flow statement and nearly all large French companies publish one. Individual company and consolidated statements are both required, though small groups are exempt from the consolidation requirement. The Code de Commerce allows simplified financial statements for small and medium-sized companies.

To give a true and fair view (*image fidèle*), financial statements must be prepared in compliance with legislation (*régularité*) and in good faith (*sincérité*). A significant feature of French reporting is the requirement for extensive and detailed footnote disclosures, including the following items:

- Explanation of measurement rules employed (i.e., accounting policies)
- Accounting treatment of foreign currency items
- Statement of changes in fixed assets and depreciation

- Details of provisions
- Details of any revaluations
- Breakdown of receivables and liabilities by maturity
- List of subsidiaries and share holdings
- Amount of commitments for pensions and other retirement benefits
- Details of the impact of taxes on the financial statements
- Average number of employees listed by category
- Analysis of turnover by activity and geographically

The directors' report includes a review of the company's activities during the year, the company's future prospects, important post-balance sheet events, research and development activities, and a summary of the company's results for the past 5 years. The financial statements of commercial companies must be audited, except for small, limited liability companies and partnerships.

French law also contains provisions aimed at preventing bankruptcies (or mitigating their consequences). The idea is that companies with a good understanding of their internal financial affairs and that prepare sound projections can better avoid financial difficulties. Accordingly, larger companies (those with net sales in excess of FFr 120 million or more than 300 employees) prepare four documents: a statement of cash position, a statement of changes in financial position or cash flow statement, a forecast income statement, and a business plan. These documents are not audited, but are given a limited examination by the auditors. They are submitted only to the board of directors and employee representatives; they are not made available to the shareholders or the general public unless provided voluntarily (such as the cash flow statement). Thus, this information is designed as an internal early warning signal for management and workers.

A social report also is required for all companies with 300 or more employees. This report describes, analyzes, and reports on matters of training, industrial relations, health and safety conditions, wage levels and other employment benefits, and many additional relevant work environment conditions. The report is required for individual companies, not consolidated groups.

ACCOUNTING MEASUREMENTS

As noted earlier, French accounting is characterized by a duality: Individual companies must follow fixed regulations, while consolidated groups have more flexibility. Accounting for individual companies is the legal basis for distributing dividends and for calculating taxable income.

Tangible assets are normally valued at historical cost. Although revaluations are allowed, they are taxable and, therefore, are seldom found in practice. Fixed assets are depreciated according to tax provisions, normally on a straight-line or declining balance basis. Extra tax depreciation is sometimes available, in which case the additional amount taken is shown as an exceptional charge on the income statement and the corresponding credit as a tax-related provision in equity. Inventory must be valued at the lower of cost or realizable value using either First in, First Out (FIFO) or weighted-average methods.

Research and development costs are expensed as incurred, but may be capitalized in restricted circumstances. If capitalized, research and development costs must be amortized over no more than five years. Leased assets are not capitalized, and the rent paid is expensed. Pension and other retirement benefits are normally expensed when paid and future commitments are seldom recognized as liabilities. Probable losses whose amounts can be determined with reasonable accuracy are accrued. Many other risks and uncertainties may be provided for, such as those relating to litigation, restructurings, and self-insurance; these allow income-smoothing opportunities. Given the link between book and tax income, companies do not account for deferred taxes in individual company financial statements. Legal reserves must be created by appropriating 5 percent of income each year until the reserve equals 10 percent of legal capital.

French consolidated financial statements follow the fair presentation approach of reporting substance over form, for example, by capitalizing finance leases and accounting for deferred taxes. The purchase method is used to account for business combinations. Goodwill normally is capitalized and amortized to income, but no maximum amortization period is specified. Proportional consolidation is used for joint ventures and the equity method is used to account for investments in nonconsolidated entities over which significant influence is exercised. Both the temporal and closing rate methods are allowed for foreign currency translation, though the conditions for their use are not specified. It is recommended that the temporal method be used when operations are integrated with the parent and that the closing rate method be used when operations are independent of the parent. This recommendation is consistent with international and U.S. accounting standards.

GERMANY

The German accounting environment has changed continuously and remarkably since the end of World War II. At that time, business accounting emphasized national and sectional charts of account (as in France). The Commercial Code stipulated various principles of "orderly bookkeeping," and independent auditing barely survived the war.

In a major turn of events, the 1965 Corporation Law moved the German financial reporting system toward British-American ideas (but only for larger corporations). More disclosure, limited consolidation, and a corporate management report were required. The management report and additional audit requirements became legal requirements through the 1969 Corporate Publicity Law.

In the early 1970s the European Union (EU) began issuing its harmonization directives, which member countries were required to incorporate into their national laws. The Fourth, Seventh, and Eighth EU Directives all entered German law through the Comprehensive Accounting Act of December 19, 1985. This legislation is remarkable because (1) it integrates all existing German accounting, financial reporting, disclosure, and auditing requirements into a single law; (2) this single law is specified as the *third book* of the German Commercial Code (HGB), thus becoming applicable to all business entities, from limited partnerships to private and publicly held corporations; and (3) the legislation is based predominantly on European concepts and practices.

Two new laws were passed in 1998. The first added a new paragraph in the third book of the German Commercial Code allowing parent companies to use internationally accepted accounting principles in their consolidated financial statements. The second allowed the establishment of a private sector organization to set accounting standards for consolidated financial statements.

Creditor protection is a fundamental concern of German accounting as embodied in the Commercial Code. Conservative balance sheet valuations are central to creditor protection. This creates a tendency to undervalue assets and overvalue liabilities. These practices also result in a conservative income amount, which is the basis for dividends to owners. Thus, German accounting is designed to compute a prudent income amount that leaves creditors unharmed after distributions are made to owners.

Tax law also largely determines commercial accounting. The *determination principle* (*Massgeblichkeitsprinzip*) states that taxable income is determined by whatever is booked in a firm's financial records. Available tax provisions can be used only if they are fully booked. This means, among other things, that any special or highly accelerated depreciation used for tax purposes must also be booked for financial reporting purposes. The dominance of tax accounting means that no distinction is made between financial statements prepared for tax purposes and those published in financial reports.

The third fundamental characteristic of German accounting is its reliance on statutes and court decisions. Nothing else has any binding or authoritative status. Even though the EU Fourth Directive mandates application of "true and fair view" principles, its use in Germany is, at best, perfunctory.

ACCOUNTING REGULATION AND ENFORCEMENT

Before 1998, Germany had no financial accounting standard setting function, as it is understood in English-speaking countries. The German Institute provided consultation in various processes of lawmaking that affected accounting and financial reporting, but legal requirements were absolutely supreme. Similar consultation was given by the Frankfurt Stock Exchange, German trade unions, and accounting academics. The 1998 law on control and transparency (abbreviated KonTraG) introduced the requirements for the Ministry of Justice to recognize a private national standard-setting body to serve the following objectives:

- Develop recommendations for the application of accounting standards for consolidated financial statements.
- Advise the Ministry of Justice on new accounting legislation.
- Represent Germany in international accounting organizations such as the IASB.

The German Accounting Standards Committee (GASC), or in German, the *Deutsches Rechnungslegungs* Standards Committee (DRSC) was founded shortly thereafter, and duly recognized by the Ministry of Justice as the German standard-setting authority.[6]

The GASC oversees the German Accounting Standards Board (GASB), which does the technical work and issues the accounting standards. The GASB is made up of seven independent experts with a background in auditing, financial analysis, academia, and industry. Working groups are established to examine and make recommendations on the issues before the board. As a rule, these working groups have representatives from trade and industry and the auditing profession, a university professor, and a financial analyst. GASB deliberations follow a due process and meetings are open. Once issued, the standards must be approved and published by the Ministry of Justice before they become obligatory for German companies.

The new German accounting standard-setting system is broadly similar to that in the United Kingdom and the United States, as discussed later in this chapter, and to the IASB (see Chapter 8). It is important to emphasize, however, that GASB standards only

---

[6]The GASC Web site is www.drsc.de.

apply to consolidated financial statements. The GASB has the expressed intention of developing a set of German standards compatible with international accounting standards.

Certified public accountants in Germany are called *Wirtschaftsprüfer* (WPs), or enterprise examiners.[7] WPs are legally required to join the official Chamber of Accountants (*Wirtschaftsprüferkammer*), which was established in 1971 as the regulatory agency for WPs. By international standards, the German auditing (accounting) profession is small. The 1985 Accounting Act extended the audit requirement to many more companies. As a result, a second-tier body of auditors was created in the late 1980s. These individuals are Sworn Book Examiners (*Vereidigte Buchprüfer*) who are only allowed to audit small and medium-sized companies, as defined in the act. Thus, two classes of auditors are legally sanctioned to conduct independent audit examinations of companies.

FINANCIAL REPORTING

The 1985 Accounting Act specifies different accounting, auditing, and financial reporting requirements according to company size, not according to the form of business organization.[8] There are three size classes—small, medium, and large—defined in terms of balance sheet totals, annual sales totals, and numbers of employees. Companies with publicly traded securities are always classified as large. The 1985 Accounting Act specifies the content and format of financial statements, which include the following:

1. Balance sheet
2. Income statement
3. Notes
4. Management report
5. Auditor's report

Small companies are exempt from the audit requirement and may prepare an abbreviated balance sheet. Small and medium-sized companies may prepare abbreviated income statements. Small and medium-sized companies also have fewer disclosure requirements for their notes. Publicly traded companies must provide a statement of cash flows, but it is not required for other companies.

The 1985 act expanded required note disclosure. The notes section of the financial statements is usually extensive, especially for large companies. Footnote disclosures are seen as a way to achieve a true and fair view while still preparing tax-based financial statements. Disclosures include the accounting principles used, the extent to which results are affected by claiming tax benefits, unaccrued pension obligations, sales by product line and geographic markets, unaccrued contingent liabilities, and average number of employees. The management report describes the financial position and business developments during the year, important post-balance sheet events, anticipated future

---

[7] The Institute der Wirtschaftsprüfer's Web site is www.wpk.de.
[8] The three major forms of business organizations in Germany are (1) *Aktiengesellschaft* (AG), (2) *Kommanditgesellschaft auf Aktien* (KGaA), and (3) *Gesellschaft mit beschränkter Haftung* (GmbH).
  AGs are typically large corporations with two senior boards: a management board and a supervisory board. The supervisory board appoints and dismisses members of the management board, supervises the management board, and reviews and approves annual financial statements. The KGaA is a mixture of the limited partnership and the corporate form of business organization. It must have at least one shareholder who is personally liable for the company's indebtedness (the remaining shareholders are liable only to the extent of their investments in the company). KGaAs are unknown in English-speaking countries. GmbHs are privately held companies. Most medium and small businesses operate in this form.

developments, and research and development activities. Publicly traded companies must provide additional segment disclosures.

Consolidated financial statements are required for enterprises under unified management and with a majority of voting rights, dominant influence by virtue of control contracts, or the right to appoint or remove a majority of the board of directors. However, the rules are full of conditions, exceptions, and exemptions. For purposes of consolidation, all companies in the group must use identical accounting and valuation principles. However, they need not be the same as those used in individual company statements. In this way, tax-driven accounting methods in individual accounts can be eliminated in the group accounts. Consolidated accounts are not the basis for either taxation or profit distributions.

Legislation enacted in 1998 allows listed companies to use internationally accepted standards (such as IAS or U.S. GAAP) in consolidated financial statements in lieu of the German Commercial Code. The law (abbreviated KapAEG) was a concession made for the growing number of German companies forced to prepare a second set of consolidated financial statements in order to raise capital on international markets. This concession is valid until 2004, when it is anticipated that the GASC will have developed a set of German standards, compatible with IAS, for consolidated statements. By this time, the European Union's initiative on the use of IAS should also be complete (see Chapter 8).

ACCOUNTING MEASUREMENTS

Under German rules, the purchase (acquisition) method is the primary consolidation method, though pooling of interests is acceptable in limited circumstances. Two forms of the purchase method are permitted: the book value method and the revaluation method. (They essentially differ in the treatment of minority interests.[9]) Assets and liabilities of acquired enterprises are brought up to current value and any amount left over is goodwill. Goodwill can either be offset against reserves in equity or amortized systematically over its economic life. The law mentions a four-year period as the regular amortization period, but ranges up to 20 years are acceptable. The equity method must be used for nonconsolidated entities where 20 percent or more of the company is owned by another entity. Joint ventures may be accounted for using either proportional consolidation or the equity method. No requirements are in place for foreign currency translation and German companies use a number of methods. Translation differences are dealt with in many ways. As a result, special attention should be paid to the notes, where the foreign currency translation method must be described.

Historical cost is the basis for valuing tangible assets. (Germany is among the world's staunchest adherents to the historical cost principle. Strong anti-inflation attitudes have resulted from the ravages of two debilitating inflationary periods in Germany in the twentieth century.) Inventory is stated at the lower of cost or market, and FIFO, average, and LIFO are all acceptable methods of determining cost. (LIFO became acceptable for tax purposes beginning in 1990.) Depreciable fixed assets are subject to tax depreciation rates.

---

[9]Dieter Ordelheide, "Germany: Group Accounts," in *Transnational Accounting,* Dieter Ordelheide, ed., London: Macmillan Press, 1995, 1599–1602.

Research and development costs are expensed when incurred. Financial leases typically are not capitalized, but pension obligations are accrued based on their actuarially determined present value consistent with tax laws. Deferred taxes do not normally arise in individual company accounts, because these are tax determined. However, they may arise in consolidated statements if accounting methods used for consolidations are different from those used for the individual accounts. In this case deferred taxes must be set up using the liability method.

Provisions as estimates of future expenses or losses are used heavily. Provisions must be set up for deferred maintenance expenses, product guarantees, potential losses from pending transactions, and other uncertain liabilities. Optional provisions, such as those for future major repairs, are also allowed. Most companies make provisions as large as possible because legally booked expenses directly affect the determination of taxable income. Provisions give German companies many opportunities to smooth income. Portions of retained earnings often are allocated to specific reserves, including a mandated legal reserve and those resulting from the provisions just described.

As noted earlier, German companies now can choose to prepare their consolidated financial statements according to German rules described here, International Accounting Standards, or U.S. GAAP. All three choices are found in practice, and the reader of German financial statements must be careful to know which accounting standards are being followed.

JAPAN

Japanese accounting and financial reporting reflect a mixture of a number of domestic and international influences. Two separate government agencies are responsible for accounting regulations, with the further influence of Japanese corporate income tax law. In the first half of the twentieth century, accounting thinking reflected German influences; in the second half, U.S. ideas were pervasive. More recently, the effects of the International Accounting Standards have been felt. Until the late 1990s, however, external influences came to bear only gradually. In terms of what we would consider world class reporting, accounting was slow to develop in Japan.[10]

To understand Japanese accounting, one must understand Japanese culture, business practices, and history. Japan is a traditional society with strong cultural and religious roots. Group consciousness and interdependence in personal and corporate relationships in Japan contrast with independent, arm's-length relationships among individuals and groups in Western nations. Japanese companies hold equity interests in each other, and often jointly own other firms. These interlocking investments yield giant industrial conglomerates—notably the *keiretsu*. Banks are often a part of these industrial groups. The widespread use of bank credit and debt capital to finance large enterprises is unusually great from a Western perspective, and corporate managements must primarily answer to banks and other financial institutions rather than shareholders. Central government also exerts tight control on many activities in Japan, which means a strong bureaucratic control over business affairs, including accounting. Knowledge of corporate activities is primarily limited to the corporation and other insiders such as the banks and the government.

---

[10]For example, consolidated financial statements date from 1976 and requirements for segment reporting began in 1990.

This *keiretsu* business model is being transformed as the Japanese undertake structural reforms to counteract the economic stagnation of the 1990s. The financial crisis that followed the bursting of Japan's *bubble economy* also prompted a review of Japanese financial reporting standards. It became clear that many accounting practices hid how badly many Japanese companies were doing. For example:

1. Loose consolidation standards allowed Japanese companies to bury loss-making operations in affiliates. Investors could not see how profitable a company's entire operations really were.
2. Pension and severance obligations were only accrued to 40 percent of the amount owed because that was the limit of their tax deductibility. This practice led to substantial underfunding of pension obligations.
3. Securities holdings were valued at cost, not market prices. Designed to reinforce the cohesion of the *keiretsu,* these cross-holdings are vast. Companies held on to the ones with losses, but sold those with gains to prop up sagging profits.

An accounting "Big Bang" was announced in the late 1990s to make the economic health of Japanese companies more transparent and to bring Japan more in line with international standards. These accounting reforms are described later.[11]

ACCOUNTING REGULATION AND ENFORCEMENT

The national government has the most significant influence on accounting in Japan. Accounting regulation is based on three laws: the Commercial Code, the Securities and Exchange Law, and the Corporate Income Tax Law. These three laws are linked and interact with each other. A leading Japanese scholar refers to the situation as a "triangular legal system."[12]

The Commercial Code is administered by the Ministry of Justice (MOJ). It is at the center of accounting regulation in Japan and has had the most pervasive influence. Developed from German commercial law, the original code was enacted in 1890, but not implemented until 1899. Creditor and shareholder protection is its fundamental principle with an unequivocal reliance on historical cost measurements. Disclosures on credit worthiness and the availability of earnings for dividend distribution are of primary importance. All companies incorporated under the Commercial Code are required to meet its accounting provisions, which are contained in the "regulations concerning the balance sheet, income statement, business report, and supporting schedules of limited liability companies."

Publicly owned companies must meet the further requirements of the Securities and Exchange Law (SEL), administered by the Ministry of Finance.[13] The SEL is modeled after the U.S. Securities Acts and was imposed on Japan by the United States during the U.S. occupation following World War II. The main objective of the SEL is to provide information for investment decision making. Although the SEL requires the same basic

---

[11]"Japan on the Brink," *The Economist* (April 11, 1999): 15–17; "Japan Restructures, Grudgingly," *The Economist* (February 6, 1999): 63–65; "The Secrets Pour Out," *Business Week* (August 2, 1999): 50–51; "Reshaping Standards," *Accountancy* (June 2000): 110; and "Japan: Restoring Investor Confidence," *IASC Insight* (September 2000): 8.

[12]Kiyomitsu Arai, *Accounting in Japan,* Tokyo: Institute for Research in Business Administration, Waseda University, 1994, 5.

[13]The Web site is www.mof.go.jp

financial statements as the Commercial Code, the terminology, form, and content of financial statements are more precisely defined under the SEL; certain financial statement items are reclassified for presentation and additional detail is provided. Net income and shareholders' equity are, however, the same under the code and the SEL.

The Business Accounting Deliberation Council (BADC) is a special advisory body to the Ministry of Finance responsible for developing accounting standards under the SEL. The BADC is, arguably, the major source of generally accepted accounting principles in Japan today. However, the BADC cannot issue a standard at variance with commercial law (or the tax law, as discussed next). Members of the BADC are appointed by the Ministry of Finance and serve on a part-time basis. They are drawn from academic, government, and business circles as well as members of the Japanese Institute of Certified Public Accountants. (BADC members have an accounting background, in contrast to the legal backgrounds of individuals working on Commercial Code matters at the Ministry of Justice.) The BADC is supported by a research organization known as the Corporation Finance Research Institute.

Finally, the influence of the tax code is significant. Similar to France, Germany, and elsewhere, expenses can be claimed for tax purposes only if they are fully booked. Taxable income is based on the amount calculated under the Commercial Code, but if the code does not prescribe an accounting treatment, the one in the tax law is often followed.

Under the Commercial Code, the financial statements and supporting schedules of small and medium-sized companies are subject to audit only by statutory auditors. Both statutory and independent auditors must audit large corporations. Independent auditors must audit financial statements of publicly held companies in accordance with the Securities and Exchange Law. Statutory auditors do not need any particular professional qualifications and are employed by the company on a full-time basis. Statutory audits focus mainly on the managerial actions of the directors and whether they perform their duties in compliance with legal statutes. Independent audits involve examining the financial statements and records and must be performed by certified public accountants (CPAs).

The Japanese Institute of Certified Public Accountants (JICPA) is the professional organization of CPAs in Japan. All CPAs must belong to the JICPA.[14] In addition to providing guidance on the conduct of an audit, the JICPA publishes implementation guidelines on accounting matters, and consults with the BADC in developing accounting standards. Generally accepted auditing standards (similar to those in the United States) are promulgated by the BADC rather than the JICPA.

As this book goes to press, the government has proposed substantial changes to the accounting and auditing standard-setting process in Japan. These changes will shift standard-setting responsibility from the government to the accounting profession. The BADC will be replaced by an independent, private sector standard-setting body linked to the JICPA. This new accounting standards board will determine Japanese GAAP, while the JICPA will focus on auditing standards. These changes will make the standard-setting process more like that in Anglo-Saxon countries. They will also require a review of the triangular legal system. The central role of the Commercial Code and tax law as a source of accounting in Japan is diminishing.

---

[14]The Web site is www.jicpa.org.jp

FINANCIAL REPORTING

Companies incorporated under the Commercial Code are required to prepare a statutory report for approval at the annual shareholders' meeting, consisting of the following:

1. Balance sheet
2. Income statement
3. Business report
4. Proposal for appropriation of retained earnings
5. Supporting schedules

Notes accompanying the balance sheet and income statement describe the accounting policies and provide supporting details, as is typical in other countries. The business report contains an outline of the business and information about its operations, financial position, and operating results. A number of supporting schedules are also required, separate from the notes, including:

- Changes in capital stock and the statutory reserve
- Changes in bonds and other short- and long-term debt
- Changes in fixed assets and accumulated depreciation
- Collateralized assets
- Debt guarantees
- Changes in provisions
- Amounts due to and from the controlling shareholders
- Equity ownership in subsidiaries and the number of shares of the company's stock held by those subsidiaries
- Receivables due from subsidiaries
- Transactions with directors, statutory auditors, controlling shareholders and third parties that create a conflict of interest
- Remuneration paid to directors and statutory auditors

This information is prepared for a single year on a parent company basis and is audited by the statutory auditor. The Commercial Code does not require a statement of cash or funds flow.

Listed companies also must prepare financial statements under the Securities and Exchange Law, which generally requires the same basic statements as the Commercial Code plus a statement of cash flows. However, under the SEL, consolidated financial statements, not the parent company statements, are the main focus. Additional footnotes and schedules are also required.[15] Financial statements and schedules submitted under the SEL must be audited by independent auditors.

A cash flow forecast for the next 6 months is included as supplemental information in filings with the Ministry of Finance. Other forecast information is also reported such as forecasts of new capital investments and production levels and activities. Overall, the amount of corporate forecast reporting is extensive in Japan. However, this information is reported in statutory filings and rarely appears in the annual report to shareholders.

---

[15]Additional footnotes include information about such things as subsequent events and liabilities for employee retirement and severance benefits. Additional schedules detail items on the financial statements such as marketable securities, tangible and intangible assets, investments in and loans to or from affiliated companies, bonds payable and other long-term borrowings, and reserves and allowances.

ACCOUNTING MEASUREMENTS

The preparation of consolidated financial statements is based on the Securities and Exchange Law. Individual company accounts are the basis for the consolidated statements, and normally the same accounting principles are used at both levels. Subsidiaries are consolidated if a parent directly or indirectly controls their financial and operational policies. Though pooling is allowed, the purchase method of accounting for business combinations is normally used. Goodwill is measured on the basis of the fair value of the net assets acquired and is amortized over a maximum of 20 years. The equity method is used for investments in affiliated companies when the parent and subsidiaries exert significant influence over their financial and operational policies. The equity method is also used to account for joint ventures; proportional consolidation is not allowed. Under the foreign currency translation standard revised in 1999, assets and liabilities of foreign subsidiaries are translated at the current (year-end) exchange rate, revenues and expenses at the average rate, and translation adjustments are in stockholders' equity.

Inventory may be valued at cost or the lower of cost or market; cost is most often used. However, inventory must be written down to market if there is a significant and permanent decline in value. FIFO, LIFO, and average are all acceptable cost flow methods, with average the most popular. Investments in securities are valued at market. Fixed assets are valued at cost and depreciated in accordance with the tax laws. The declining-balance method is the most common depreciation method.

Research and development costs are expensed when incurred. Finance leases (those that transfer the risks and rewards of ownership to the lessee) are capitalized while lease payments on operating leases are charged to income when incurred. Deferred taxes are provided for all timing differences using the liability method. Contingent losses are provided for when they are probable and can be reasonably estimated. Pension and other employee retirement benefits are fully accrued as employees earn them and unfunded obligations are shown as a liability. Legal reserves are required: Each year a company must allocate an amount equal to at least 10 percent of cash dividends and bonuses paid to directors and statutory auditors until the legal reserve reaches 25 percent of capital stock.

Many of the accounting practices previously described were recently implemented as a result of the accounting "Big Bang" referred to earlier. These recent changes include: (1) requiring listed companies to report a statement of cash flows; (2) extending the number of subsidiaries that are consolidated based on control rather than ownership percentage; (3) extending the number of affiliates accounted for using the equity method based on significant influence rather than ownership percentage; (4) valuing investments in securities at market rather than cost; (5) full provisioning of deferred taxes; and (6) full accrual of pension and other retirement obligations. Accounting in Japan is being reshaped to bring it in line with International Accounting Standards.

THE NETHERLANDS

Dutch accounting presents several interesting paradoxes. The Dutch have relatively permissive statutory accounting and financial reporting requirements but very high professional practice standards. The Netherlands is a code law country, yet accounting is oriented toward fair presentation. Financial reporting and tax accounting are two separate activities. Further, the fairness orientation developed without a strong stock market influence. The United Kingdom and the United States have influenced Dutch accounting as much (or more) than other continental European countries, and, unlike the rest of continental Europe, the accounting profession has had a significant influence on accounting standards and regulations.[16]

Accounting in the Netherlands is considered a branch of business economics. As a result, much economic thought has been devoted to accounting topics and especially to accounting measurements. Highly respected professional accountants are often part-time professors. Thus, academic thought has a major influence upon ongoing practice.

Dutch accountants are also willing to consider foreign ideas. The Dutch were among the earliest proponents of international standards for financial accounting and reporting, and the statements of the IASB (see Chapter 8) receive substantial attention in determining acceptable practice. The Netherlands is also home to several of the largest multinational enterprises in the world, including Philips, Royal Dutch/Shell, and Unilever.[17] These enterprises have been internationally listed since the 1950s and have been influenced by foreign (particularly U.K. and U.S.) accounting. Through example, these large multinationals have influenced financial reporting of other Dutch companies. The influence of the Amsterdam Stock Exchange, however, has been minimal because it does not provide much new business capital.

ACCOUNTING REGULATION AND ENFORCEMENT

Accounting regulations in the Netherlands remained liberal until 1970, when the Act on Annual Financial Statements was enacted. The act was a part of an extensive program of changes in company legislation and was introduced partly to reflect the coming harmonization of company law within the EU. Among the major provisions of the 1970 act are the following:

- Annual financial statements shall show a fair picture of the financial position and results of the year, and all items therein must be appropriately grouped and described.
- Financial statements must be drawn up in accordance with sound business practice (i.e., accounting principles acceptable to the business community).
- The bases of stating assets and liabilities and determining results of operations must be disclosed.
- Financial statements shall be prepared on a consistent basis and material effects of changes in accounting principles properly disclosed.
- Comparative financial information for the preceding period shall be disclosed in the financial statements and accompanying footnotes.

---

[16]The idea that the business community is capable of adequate financial reporting is well entrenched in Dutch thinking. The first limited liability companies were formed in the seventeenth century without a clear legal framework on the matter. The first commercial code, introduced in the nineteenth century, viewed shareholders as responsible for management, which prompted little need for extensive accounting requirements in the law. Similar to the United Kingdom, the Dutch accounting profession emerged in the nineteenth century and has had a substantial influence on accounting. By the time an income tax on corporations was introduced (in 1940), financial reporting was already too well developed to be dominated by tax accounting. See Kees Canfferman, "The History of Financial Reporting in the Netherlands," in *European Financial Reporting: A History*, Peter Walton, ed., London: Academic Press, 1995.

[17]Royal Dutch/Shell and Unilever are binational (British and Dutch) concerns.

The 1970 act introduced the mandatory audit. It also set into motion the formation of the Tripartite Accounting Study Group (replaced in 1981 by the Council on Annual Reporting), and it gave birth to the Enterprise Chamber. The act, incorporated into the civil code in 1975, was amended by legislation in 1983 to incorporate the EU Fourth Directive, and further amended in 1988 to incorporate the EU Seventh Directive.

The Council for Annual Reporting issues guidelines on generally acceptable (not accepted) accounting principles. The council is composed of members from three different groups:

1. Preparers of financial statements (employers)
2. Users of financial statements (representatives of trade unions and financial analysts)
3. Auditors of financial statements (the Netherlands Institute of Registeraccountants, or NIvRA)[18]

The council is a private organization and is financed by grants from the business community and NIvRA. Even though the council's guidelines do not have the force of law, they are followed by most large companies and auditors.[19] The guidelines are comprehensive in scope and incorporate as far as possible the standards of the IASB. Nevertheless, the only legally enforceable accounting rules are those specified in the accounting and financial reporting provisions of the Dutch civil code.

The Enterprise Chamber, a specialist court connected with the High Court of Amsterdam, is a unique feature of the Dutch system of enforcing compliance with accounting requirements. Any interested party may complain to this chamber if it believes that a company's financial statements do not conform to applicable law. Shareholders, employees, trade unions, and even the public prosecutor (but not independent auditors) may bring proceedings to the chamber. The chamber is composed of three judges and two expert accountants, and there is no jury. Chamber decisions may lead to modifications of financial statements or various penalties. Even though the rulings apply only to defendant companies, they sometimes state general rules that may influence the reporting practices of other companies. Since its inception, the Enterprise Chamber has ruled on roughly 60 complaints.

Auditing in the Netherlands is a self-regulated profession. Its governing body is the Netherlands Institute of Registeraccountants (NIvRA), which has approximately 13,000 members.[20] It is fully autonomous in setting auditing standards and its strong professional code of conduct has statutory status.

Until 1993, only members of NIvRA could certify financial statements, but changes were made that year to incorporate the EU Eighth Directive. In the Netherlands there are two kinds of auditors: registeraccountants (RAs, or chartered accountants) and administrative accountants (AAs).[21] The 1993 changes allowed AAs to also certify financial statements, if they undergo additional training. Over time, educational and training qualifications for RAs and AAs will be standardized and the code of conduct will be the

---

[18]Neither the Amsterdam Stock Exchange nor shareholder representatives participate in the council.
[19]However, auditors can issue an unqualified opinion when there is noncompliance with a guideline, as long as the financial statements still convey a true and fair view.
[20]The NIvRA Web site is www.nivra.nl.
[21]The Nederlandse Orde van Accountants-Administratieconsultenen (NovAA) Web site is www.novaa.nl.

same in relation to audit work, the auditor's responsibilities, and independence. One set of disciplinary rules also will apply. However, NIvRA is likely to continue to dominate auditing and accounting in the Netherlands.

NIvRA is involved in everything that is accounting related in the Netherlands. It participates in the Council for Annual Reporting and in commissions charged with revising the accounting statutes of the civil code. NIvRA members serve on the Enterprise Chamber, as accounting faculty at leading Dutch universities, on the IASB, and on committees of the EU, the Organization of Economic Cooperation and Development (OECD), the UN, and the International Federation of Accountants.

FINANCIAL REPORTING

The quality of Dutch financial reporting is uniformly high. Statutory financial statements should be filed in Dutch, but English, French, and German are also acceptable. The financial statements must include the following:

1. Balance sheet
2. Income statement
3. Notes
4. Directors' report
5. Other prescribed information

A cash flow statement is not required, but is recommended by a council guideline, and most Dutch companies provide one. The notes must describe the accounting principles used in valuation and the determination of results, and the reasoning behind any accounting changes made. The directors' report reviews the financial position at the balance sheet date, and performance during the financial year. It also provides information about the expected performance during the new financial year and comments on any significant post-balance sheet events. "Other prescribed information" must include the auditor's report and profit appropriations for the year.

Annual financial reports must be presented on both a parent-company-only and a consolidated basis. The same accounting principles are used in both. Group companies for the purpose of consolidation consist of those companies that form an economic unit under common control. Consistent with EU directives, reporting requirements vary by company size. Small companies are exempt from the requirements for an audit and for consolidated financial statements, and they may file an abbreviated income statement and balance sheet. Medium-sized companies must be audited, but may publish a condensed income statement. Small, medium-sized, and large companies are defined in the civil code.

ACCOUNTING MEASUREMENTS

Even though the pooling-of-interests method of accounting for business combinations is allowed in limited circumstances, it is rarely used in the Netherlands. The purchase method is the normal practice. Goodwill is the difference between the acquisition cost and the fair value of the assets and liabilities acquired, and may be treated in the following ways:

- It may be charged against income in the year of acquisition.
- It may be charged against reserves (shareholders' equity) in the year of acquisition.

- It may be capitalized as an intangible and charged against income over the expected useful life. (If the amortization period exceeds 5 years, the length of the period must be disclosed along with the reasons for the extended useful life.)

Most companies charge goodwill to reserves. The equity method is required when the investor exercises significant influence on business and financial policy. Joint ventures may be accounted for using either the equity method or proportional consolidation. The council recommendation on foreign currency translation is consistent with International Accounting Standard 21. The balance sheet of a foreign entity that is independent of the parent is translated at the closing (year-end) rate, while the income statement is translated at the closing or average rate. Translation adjustments are charged to shareholders' equity. The temporal method is used for foreign entities that are not independent of the parent, with the translation adjustment charged to income.

The Dutch flexibility toward accounting measurements may be most evident in permitting the use of current values for tangible assets such as inventory and depreciable assets. When current values are used for these assets, their corresponding income statement amounts, cost of goods sold and depreciation are also stated at current values. Current value can be replacement value, recoverable amount, or net realizable value. Current value accounting is expected to be consistently applied; piecemeal revaluations normally are not allowed. Revaluations are offset by a revaluation reserve in shareholders' equity. Companies using current values should provide additional historical cost information in the notes. Historical cost is also acceptable. While much has been made of current value accounting in the Netherlands, few companies actually use it. Philips, arguably the most conspicuous example, started using current value accounting in 1951, but abandoned it in 1992 in the interests of international comparability. Nevertheless, current values have a place in Dutch accounting because companies that use historical cost for the balance sheet and income statement are expected to disclose supplemental current cost information in their notes.

When historical cost is used for inventory, generally it is stated at the lower of cost or market, with cost determined by FIFO, LIFO, average, or even base stock methods. Research and development costs are capitalized only when the amounts are recoverable and sufficiently certain. Leases, contingencies, and pension costs are generally measured as they are in the United Kingdom and United States, although applicable rules are significantly more general. Deferred income taxes are recognized on the basis of the comprehensive allocation concept (full provision) and measured according to the liability method. Current value accounting is not acceptable for tax purposes, so when current values are used for financial reporting, permanent rather than timing differences arise.

Because Dutch companies have flexibility in applying measurement rules, one would suspect that there are opportunities for income smoothing. In addition, certain items can bypass the income statement through direct adjustment to reserves in shareholders' equity. These include:

- Losses due to a disaster that would have been impossible or unusual to insure against
- Losses from a nationalization or similar expropriation
- The consequences of a financial restructuring

Reserves can also be used for the direct write-off of goodwill, as discussed previously, and changes in accounting principle are reflected directly in shareholders' equity reserves.

UNITED KINGDOM

Accounting in the United Kingdom developed as an independent discipline, pragmatically responding to the needs and practices of business.[22] Over time, successive companies legislation added structure and other requirements, but still allowed accountants considerable flexibility in the application of professional judgment. Since the 1970s, the most important source of development in company law has been the EU directives, most notably the Fourth and Seventh Directives. At the same time, accounting standards and the standard-setting process have become more authoritative.

The legacy of British accounting to the rest of the world is substantial. The United Kingdom was the first country in the world to develop an accountancy profession as we know it today.[23] The concept of a fair presentation of financial results and position (the true and fair view) is also of British origin. Professional accounting thinking and practice was exported to Australia, Canada, the United States, and other former British possessions including Hong Kong, India, Kenya, New Zealand, Nigeria, Singapore, and South Africa.

ACCOUNTING REGULATION AND ENFORCEMENT

The two major sources of financial accounting standards in the United Kingdom are companies law and the accounting profession. Activities of companies incorporated in the United Kingdom are broadly governed by statutes called companies acts. Companies acts have been updated, extended, and consolidated through the years. For example, in 1981 the EU Fourth Directive was implemented, adding statutory rules regarding formats, accounting principles, and basic accounting conventions. This introduced standardized formats for financial statements into Britain for the first time. Companies may choose from alternative balance sheet formats and four profit and loss account formats. The 1981 act also sets out five basic accounting principles:

1. Revenues and expenses are matched on an accrual basis.
2. Individual asset and liability items within each class of assets and liabilities are valued separately.
3. The principle of conservatism (prudence) is applied, especially in the recognition of realized income and all known liabilities and losses.
4. Consistent application of accounting policies from year to year is required.
5. The going concern principle is applicable to the entity being accounted for.

The act contains broad valuation rules in that accounts may be based on either historical or current cost.

---

[22]The United Kingdom of Great Britain and Northern Ireland is a union of England, Scotland, Wales, and Northern Ireland. Even though the United Kingdom has an integrated system of laws, monetary and fiscal policies, and social rules and regulations, important individual differences remain among these four countries. The term Britain is often used for the United Kingdom. "British, " "Anglo," and "Anglo-Saxon" are often used interchangeably to describe accounting in the United Kingdom.

[23]The first recognized accounting society was the Society of Accountants in Edinburgh, which was granted a royal charter in 1854. Similar societies were officially recognized in Glasgow in 1855 and in Aberdeen in 1867. Professional accounting began with these early professional societies.

The Companies Act 1985 consolidated and extended earlier legislation and was amended in 1989 to recognize the EU Seventh Directive. This act requires the consolidation of financial statements, although consolidation was already standard practice and consolidation techniques are left to private sector accounting standards.[24] The legal stipulations are general and allow considerable flexibility in case-by-case applications. Additional accounting recommendations are made through private sector, self-regulated professional bodies.

The following six accountancy bodies in the United Kingdom are linked through the Consultative Committee of Accountancy Bodies (CCAB), formed in 1970.[25]

1. The Institute of Chartered Accountants in England and Wales
2. The Institute of Chartered Accountants in Ireland
3. The Institute of Chartered Accountants of Scotland
4. The Association of Chartered Certified Accountants
5. The Chartered Institute of Management Accountants
6. The Chartered Institute of Public Finance and Accountancy

British standard setting evolved from recommendations on accounting principles (issued by the Institute of Chartered Accountants in England and Wales) to the 1970 formation of the Accounting Standards Steering Committee, later renamed the Accounting Standards Committee (ASC). The ASC promulgated Statements on Standard Accounting Practice (SSAPs). SSAPs were issued and enforced by the six accounting bodies, any one of which could effectively veto the standard. The veto power of these organizations often led to excessive delays and compromises in developing SSAPs. In addition, SSAPs were more in the nature of recommendations than compulsory requirements, and had little authority.

The Dearing Report, issued in 1988, expressed dissatisfaction with the existing standard-setting arrangement.[26] It recommended a new structure for setting accounting standards and enhanced authoritative support for them. The Companies Act 1989 was important not only for incorporating the EU Seventh Directive but also for enacting the recommendations of the Dearing Report. The 1989 act created a new Financial Reporting Council (FRC) with the duty of overseeing its three offshoots: the Accounting Standards Board (ASB), which replaced the ASC in 1990, an Urgent Issues Task Force (UITF), and a Financial Reporting Review Panel.[27]

The FRC sets general policy. It is an independent body whose members are drawn from the accounting profession, industry, and financial institutions. The ASB has a full-time chair, a technical director, and seven paid part-time members, and is empowered to issue accounting standards. The ASB issues Financial Reporting Standards (FRSs) after considering comments on Discussion Papers and Financial Reporting Exposure

---

[24]The Companies Act 1985 (as amended by the Companies Act 1989) applies to England, Scotland, and Wales. Similar legislation for Northern Ireland is embodied in the Companies (Northern Ireland) Order 1986.

[25]The Web site addresses are as follows: ICAEW: www.icaew.co.uk; ICAI: www.icai.ie; ICAS: www.icas.org.uk; ACCA: www.acca.co.uk; CIMA: www.cima.org.uk; and CIPFA: www.cipfa.org.uk.

[26]Sir Ron Dearing, (The Dearing Report) "The Making of Accounting Standards, Report of the Review Committee," presented to the Consultative Committee of Accountancy Bodies, 1988.

[27]Web sites are: Financial Reporting Council: www.frc.org.uk; Accounting Standards Board: www.asb.org.uk; Financial Reporting Review Panel: www.frrp.org.uk.

Drafts (FREDs). The ASB is guided by a Statement of Principles for Financial Reporting, a conceptual framework for setting accounting standards.[28] The ASB also established the UITF to respond quickly to new problems and to issue clarifications of the accounting standards and other regulations (called UITF Abstracts).

The 1989 act enacted legal sanctions for companies that do not comply with accounting standards. Both the Financial Reporting Review Panel and the Department of Trade and Industry can investigate complaints about departures from accounting standards. They can go to court to force a company to revise its financial statements. Companies must adopt accounting policies most appropriate to their particular circumstances in order to give a true and fair view, and they must regularly review their policies to ensure they remain appropriate.

Exhibit 3-2 lists the Statements of Standard Accounting Practice adopted by the ASB and the Financial Reporting Standards issued through 2000.

Auditing standards are the responsibility of the Auditing Practices Board, which the CCAB controls. The Auditing Standards Board issues Statements of Auditing Standards, which the members of the CCAB adopt automatically. Statements of Auditing Standards prescribe the basic principles and practices that an auditor is expected to follow when conducting an audit. Failure to comply with the statements causes an investigation by the relevant accountancy body, and disciplinary action may result. Of the six accountancy bodies listed earlier, only members of the first four are allowed to sign audit reports. The audit report affirms that the financial statements present a true and fair view and comply with the Companies Act 1985.

FINANCIAL REPORTING

British financial reporting is among the most comprehensive in the world. Financial statements generally include:

1. Directors' report
2. Profit and loss account and balance sheet
3. Cash flow statement
4. Statement of total recognized gains and losses[29]
5. Statement of accounting policies
6. Notes that are referenced to the financial statements
7. Auditor's report

The directors' report addresses principal business activities, review of operations and likely developments, important post-balance sheet events, recommended dividends, names of the directors and their shareholdings, and political and charitable contributions. Listed companies must include a statement on corporate governance with disclosures on directors' remuneration, audit committees and internal controls, and a declaration that the company is a going concern. Private limited companies with annual turnover (revenue) less than £350,000 and dormant companies are exempt from the annual audit requirement; all others must be audited.

Group (consolidated) financial statements are required in addition to a parent-only balance sheet. Control of subsidiary "undertakings" occurs with ownership of more

---

[28]Work on the Statement of Principles began soon after the ASB was formed and was completed in 1999.
[29]FRED22, issued December 2000, proposes to combine the statement of total recognized gains and losses and the profit and loss account into a single statement of financial performance.

EXHIBIT 3-2 U.K. Statements of Standard Accounting Practice and Financial Reporting Standards

Statements of Standard Accounting Practice

4. Accounting for government grants
5. Accounting for value added tax
9. Stocks and long-term contracts
13. Accounting for research and development
17. Accounting for post-balance sheet events
19. Accounting for investment properties
20. Foreign currency translation
21. Accounting for leases and hire purchase contracts
25. Segmental reporting

Financial Reporting Standards

1. Cash flow statements (Revised 1996)
2. Accounting for subsidiary undertakings
3. Reporting financial performance
4. Capital instruments
5. Reporting the substance of transactions
6. Acquisitions and mergers
7. Fair values in acquisition accounting
8. Related party disclosures
9. Associates and joint ventures
10. Goodwill and intangible assets
11. Impairment of fixed assets and goodwill
12. Provisions, contingent liabilities and contingent assets
13. Derivatives and other financial instruments: disclosures
14. Earnings per share
15. Tangible fixed assets
16. Current tax
17. Retirement benefits
18. Accounting policies
19. Deferred tax

than 50 percent of another company's equity capital or control of the board of directors without regard to percentage ownership. The London Stock Exchange requires that listed companies provide half-year interim reports. Listed companies must also report earnings per share, and the earnings figure used in the calculation must be after tax and extraordinary items.[30]

Another feature of U.K. financial reporting is that small and medium-sized companies are exempt from many financial reporting obligations. The Companies Act sets

---

[30]Alternative calculations of earnings per share may also be disclosed as long as they are displayed as prominently as the required figures, and a reconciliation and explanation given. The Institute of Investment Management Research has published guidelines for calculating such an alternative, "headline" earnings per share.

out size criteria. In general, small and medium-sized companies are permitted to prepare abbreviated accounts with certain minimum prescribed information. Small and medium-sized groups are exempt from preparing consolidated statements.

ACCOUNTING MEASUREMENTS

The United Kingdom allows both the acquisition and merger methods of accounting for business combinations. However, the conditions for the use of the merger method (*pooling-of-interests* in the United States) are so narrow that it is almost never used. Under the acquisition method, goodwill is calculated as the difference between the fair value of the consideration paid and the fair value of the net assets acquired. FRS 7 specifies that fair values are assigned to identifiable assets and liabilities that exist at the date of acquisition, reflecting the conditions at that time. Future operating losses and reorganization costs cannot be considered in the calculation of goodwill, but must be reflected in post-acquisition income. Goodwill is capitalized and amortized over 20 years or less; however, a longer period or an indefinite period (resulting in no amortization) is possible if goodwill is subject to an annual impairment review. Proportional consolidation is only permitted for unincorporated joint ventures. The equity method is used for *associated* undertakings (in which a company owns 20 percent or more of the voting rights and is not consolidated) and for joint ventures that are companies. SSAP 20 deals with foreign currency translation and requires the closing rate (current rate) method for independent subsidiaries and the temporal method for integrated subsidiaries. Under the former, translation differences are included in shareholders' equity reserves; under the latter, they are included in the profit and loss account. Both the closing and the average exchange rates may be used to translate the profit and loss account. The financial statements of subsidiaries operating in hyperinflationary countries must be adjusted to reflect current price levels before translation.

Assets may be valued at historical cost, current cost, or (as most companies do) using a mixture of the two. Thus, revaluations of land and buildings are permissible. Depreciation and amortization must correspond to the measurement basis used for the underlying asset. Research expenditures are written off in the year of the expenditure, and development costs may be deferred under specific circumstances. However, in practice, few British companies capitalize any development costs. Inventory (referred to as "stocks") is valued at the lower of cost or net realizable value on a FIFO or average cost basis; LIFO is not acceptable.

Leases that transfer the risks and rewards of ownership to the lessee are capitalized and the lease obligation is shown as a liability. The costs of providing pensions and other retirement benefits must be recognized systematically and rationally over the period during which the employees' services are performed. Contingent losses are accrued when they are probable and can be estimated with reasonable accuracy. Deferred taxes are calculated under the liability method, but only to the extent that it is probable that a tax asset or liability will materialize (i.e., on a partial provision basis). However, FRS 19, which companies must adopt by 2002, requires full provisioning of all timing differences. Income smoothing opportunities exist given the flexibility that exists in asset valuation and other measurement areas. Concern has been expressed in the United Kingdom over "creative accounting," and whether its use to mislead rather than inform has increased in recent years.[31] Indeed, the ASB focused much of its early attention on remedying abuses in U.K. accounting.

UNITED STATES

Accounting in the United States is regulated by a private sector body (the Financial Accounting Standards Board, or FASB), but a governmental agency (the Securities and Exchange Commission, or SEC) underpins the authority of its standards. The key link allowing this shared power system to work effectively is the 1973 SEC Accounting Series Release (ASR) No. 150. This release states:

> The Commission intends to continue its policy of looking to the private sector for leadership in establishing and improving accounting principles. For purposes of this policy, principles, standards, and practices promulgated by the FASB in its statements and interpretations, will be considered by the Commission as having substantial authoritative support, and those contrary to such FASB promulgations will be considered to have no such support.[32]

The American Institute of Certified Public Accountants (AICPA), another private sector body, sets auditing standards.[33]

ACCOUNTING REGULATION AND ENFORCEMENT

The U.S. system has no general legal requirements for publication of periodic audited financial statements. Corporations in the United States are formed under state law, not federal law. Each state has its own corporate statutes; in general, these contain minimal requirements for keeping accounting records and publishing periodic financial statements. Many of these statutes are not rigorously enforced, and reports rendered to local agencies are often unavailable to the public. Thus, annual audit and financial reporting requirements realistically exist only at the federal level as specified by the SEC. The SEC has jurisdiction over companies listed on U.S. stock exchanges and companies traded over-the-counter.[34] Other limited-liability companies have no such compulsory requirements for financial reporting, making the United States unusual by international norms.

Even though the SEC has the legal authority to prescribe accounting and reporting standards for public companies, it relies on the private sector to set them. The SEC works with the FASB and exerts pressure when it believes the FASB is moving too

---

[31]Christopher Nobes and Robert Parker, *Comparative International Accounting*, 6th ed., Harlow, U.K.: Pearson Education, 2000, 125. For an interesting case history, see A. K. Shah, "Exploring the Influences and Constraints on Creative Accounting in the United Kingdom," *European Accounting Review* 7, no. 1 (1998): 83–104.

[32]Securities and Exchange Commission, *Statement of Policy on the Establishment and Improvement of Accounting Principles and Standards*, Accounting Series Release No. 150. Reprinted in *The Development of SEC Accounting*, G. J. Previts, ed., Reading, MA: Addison-Wesley, 1981, 228.

[33]The Web sites of these three organizations are: Securities and Exchange Commission: www.sec.gov; Financial Accounting Standards Board: www.fasb.org; and American Institute of Certified Public Accountants: www.aicpa.org.

[34]Companies traded on the "pink sheets" over-the-counter market are exempt from the SEC's periodic filing requirements if they meet a minimum size test and certain other requirements.

slowly or in the wrong direction. At times, the SEC has delayed or overruled pronouncements or has imposed its own requirements.

The SEC is an independent regulatory agency, which means that Congress and the president have no direct influence over its policies. However, the five full-time SEC commissioners are appointed by the president and confirmed by the Senate, and the SEC has only those powers that Congress has granted it by statute. As part of the regulatory process, the SEC issues Accounting Series Releases, Financial Reporting Releases, and Staff Accounting Bulletins. Regulations SX and SK contain the rules for preparing financial reports that must be filed with the SEC. Annual filings by U.S. and Canadian companies are on Form 10K, while those from non-Canadian foreign companies are on Form 20F.

The FASB was established in 1973[35] and has issued 140 Statements of Financial Accounting Standards (SFASs) as of December 2000. The FASB's standards are not based on the operating needs of business managers, taxation authorities, or government policy makers. Instead, their objective is to provide information that is useful to present and potential investors, creditors, and others who make investment, credit, and similar decisions.

The FASB has seven full-time members: three from professional accounting (CPA) practice, two from industry, and one each from academia and government. Board members must sever all economic and organizational ties to prior places of employment or ownership in order to serve. The FASB's function is best described in its own mission statement, reproduced in Exhibit 3-3.

The FASB's use of a conceptual framework is a significant feature of accounting standard setting in the United States. Statements of Financial Accounting Concepts set forth fundamentals on which financial accounting and reporting standards are based.

The FASB did not seriously engage itself internationally until the 1990s. In 1991 the FASB developed its first strategic plan for international activities, and in 1994 the fourth item in the mission statement was added. The FASB is now a major cooperative international player. It focuses much of its attention on its relationship with the IASB and worked jointly with standard setters in Australia, Canada, New Zealand, and the United Kingdom (along with the IASB—the so-called G4 + 1) to develop compatible standards on issues such as disaggregated disclosures and earnings per share.

The FASB goes through lengthy due process procedures before issuing an SFAS. In developing its work agenda, it listens to individuals, professional firms, courts of law, companies, and government agencies. It also relies on an emerging issues task force and an advisory council to help identify accounting issues that need attention. Once a topic is added to the agenda, the FASB technical staff does research and analysis and an advisory task force is appointed. A Discussion Memorandum or other discussion document is disseminated for comment, and public hearings are held. The FASB considers oral and written comments in meetings open to the public. Next, an Exposure Draft is issued and further public comments are considered. An SFAS must be approved by five of the seven members. It normally takes at least 2 years to develop and finalize a new standard. The process ensures that standard setting in the United States is both political and technical.

---

[35]Two other private sector bodies established U.S. generally accepted accounting principles (GAAP) prior to the FASB. These were the Committee on Accounting Procedure (1938 to 1959) and the Accounting Principles Board (1959 to 1973).

EXHIBIT 3-3 **Mission Statement of the Financial Accounting Standards Board**

The mission of the Financial Accounting Standards Board is to establish and improve standards of financial accounting and reporting for the guidance and education of the public, including issuers, auditors, and users of financial information.

Accounting standards are essential to the efficient functioning of the economy because decisions about the allocation of resources rely heavily on credible, concise, and understandable financial information. Financial information about the operations and financial position of individual entities also is used by the public in making various other kinds of decisions.

To accomplish its mission, the FASB acts to:

1. Improve the usefulness of financial reporting by focusing on the primary characteristics of relevance and reliability and on the qualities of comparability and consistency;
2. Keep standards current to reflect changes in methods of doing business and changes in the economic environment;
3. Consider promptly any significant areas of deficiency in financial reporting that might be improved through the standard-setting process;
4. Promote the international comparability of accounting standards concurrent with improving the quality of financial reporting; and
5. Improve the common understanding of the nature and purposes of information contained in financial reports.

The FASB develops broad accounting concepts as well as standards for financial reporting. It also provides guidance on implementation of standards.

Generally accepted accounting principles (GAAP) are comprised of all financial accounting standards, rules, and regulations that must be observed in the preparation of financial reports. The SFASs are the major component of GAAP. Accounting and auditing regulations in the United States are probably more voluminous than the rest of the world combined and substantially more detailed than in any other country.

The American Institute of Certified Public Accountants (AICPA) is primarily concerned with the independent audit of financial statements by CPAs. Ten generally accepted auditing standards (GAAS) provide a general framework dealing with such issues as competence and independence in an auditor, the performance of field work, and reporting audit results. Specific auditing pronouncements are called Statements on Auditing Standards, which together with GAAS form the authoritative guidelines that CPAs must follow. The AICPA is also responsible for the Code of Professional Ethics and for administering the Uniform CPA Examination.

Financial statements are supposed to "present fairly" the financial position of the company and the results of its operations "in conformity with generally accepted accounting principles." Compliance with GAAP is the test for fair presentation. There is no subjective override, such as the "true and fair" override in the United Kingdom. The SEC also expects compliance with GAAP and will not accept an auditor's report with an "adverse" opinion.

FINANCIAL REPORTING

A typical annual financial report of a large U.S. corporation includes the following components:

1. Report of management
2. Report of independent auditors

3. Primary financial statements (income statement, balance sheet, statement of cash flows, statement of comprehensive income, and statement of stockholders' equity)
4. Management discussion and analysis of results of operations and financial condition
5. Notes to financial statements
6. Five- or ten-year comparison of selected financial data
7. Selected quarterly data

Consolidated financial statements are required, and published U.S. financial reports typically do not contain parent-company-only statements. Consolidation rules require that all controlled subsidiaries (i.e., ownership of more than 50 percent of the voting shares) be fully consolidated, including those with nonhomogeneous operations.[36] Interim (quarterly) financial reports are required for companies listed on major stock exchanges. These reports typically contain only abbreviated, unaudited financial statements and a concise management commentary.

Two further U.S. reporting practices bear mention. The first is segment reporting, which is required for all publicly traded companies. Segmental reporting requirements in the United States exceed those in most other countries. The second concerns earnings per share disclosures. Basic earnings per share is computed by dividing income available to common shareholders by the weighted-average number of common shares outstanding for the period. Diluted earnings per share reflects the potential dilution that could occur if securities or other contracts to issue common stock were exercised or converted into common stock. This treatment is substantially the same as IAS 33 (see Chapter 8).

ACCOUNTING MEASUREMENTS

Accounting measurement rules in the United States assume that a business entity will continue as a going concern. Accrual basis measurements are pervasive, and transactions and events recognition rules rely heavily on the matching concept. A consistency requirement insists on uniformity of accounting treatment of like items within each accounting period and from one period to the next. If changes in practices or procedures occur, the changes and their effects must be disclosed.

Two methods are used to account for business combinations: purchase (acquisition) and pooling-of-interests (merger). They are not alternatives: Pooling-of-interests must be used when the combination meets the criteria specified in GAAP. (Because these criteria are narrow, most business combinations are accounted for by the purchase method.) Under the purchase method, goodwill is capitalized as the difference between fair value of the consideration given in the exchange and the fair values of the underlying net assets acquired. Goodwill is amortized on a straight-line basis over a maximum of 40 years and the amortization amount is included in current period income. Under no circumstance can it be charged against shareholders' equity. (An Exposure Draft is outstanding at the time of writing that would eliminate pooling and require an impairments test for goodwill.[37]) Proportional consolidation is not practiced. Joint ventures

---

[36]The FASB has proposed extending the consolidation requirement to other entities that a company controls based on its ability to direct the entity's policies and management.

[37]The FASB Exposure Draft proposes to eliminate the pooling-of-interests method, thus requiring the purchase method for all business combinations. It also proposes that goodwill be reviewed for impairment rather than systematically amortized to income. Under the impairment approach, goodwill would only be written down and expensed to earnings in periods when its book value exceeds it fair value.

are accounted for using the equity method as are investments in nonconsolidated, 20 percent- to 50 percent-owned affiliated companies. Foreign currency translation follows the requirements of SFAS No. 52, which relies on the foreign subsidiary's functional currency to determine translation methodology.

The United States relies on historical cost to value tangible and intangible assets. Revaluations are permitted only after a business combination accounted for as a purchase. Both accelerated and straight-line depreciation methods are permissible. Estimated economic usefulness determines depreciation and amortization periods. All research and development costs are typically expensed as incurred, though there are special capitalization rules for computer software costs.

LIFO, FIFO, and average cost methods are permissible and widely used for inventory pricing. LIFO is popular because it can be used for federal income tax purposes. However, if LIFO is used for tax purposes, it must also be used for financial reporting purposes.

When financial leases are in substance the purchase of property, the value of the property is capitalized and a corresponding liability is booked. The costs of pensions and other postretirement benefits are accrued over the periods in which employees earn their benefits and unfunded obligations are reported as a liability. Contingent losses/liabilities are accrued when they are probable and the amount can be reasonably estimated. Income smoothing techniques are not allowed.

Finally, there is the issue of deferred taxes because (except for LIFO) financial and tax reporting are distinct. Income taxes are accounted for using the liability method. Deferred taxes are accrued for the tax effects of temporary differences between financial and tax accounting methods, and are measured based on the future tax rates that will apply when these items reverse. Comprehensive income tax allocation is required.

Exhibit 3-4 summarizes the significant accounting practices in the six countries surveyed in this chapter.

Selected References

Adams, C. A., P. Weetman, E. A. E. Jones, and S. J. Gray, "Reducing the Burden of U.S. GAAP Reconciliations by Foreign Companies Listed in the United States: The Key Question of Materiality," *The European Accounting Review* 8, no. 1 (1999): 1–22.

Alexander, D., and S. Archer, eds., *European Accounting Guide*, 3rd ed., San Diego: Harcourt Brace, 1998.

Ali, A., and L. S. Hwang, "Country-Specific Factors Related to Financial Reporting and the Value Relevance of Accounting Data," *Journal of Accounting Research* (spring 2000), 1–21.

Arai, K., *Accounting in Japan*, Tokyo: Waseda University Institute for Research in Business Administration, 1994.

Carmichael, D. R., S. B. Lilien, and M. Mellman, eds., *Accountants' Handbook*, 9th ed., New York: John Wiley, 1999.

Eberhartinger, E. L. E. "The Impact of Tax Rules on Financial Reporting in Germany, France, and the U.K.," *The International Journal of Accounting* 34, no. 1 (1999): 93–119.

Glaum, M., "Bridging the GAAP: The Changing Attitude of German Managers Towards Anglo-American Accounting and Accounting Harmonization," *Journal of International Financial Management and Accounting* (spring 2000): 23–47.

Harris, T. S., *Apples to Apples: Accounting for Value in World Markets*, New York: Morgan Stanley Dean Witter, 1998.

McLeay, S., ed. *Accounting Regulation in Europe*, London: Macmillan Press, 1999.

Meek, G. K., ed., *Country Studies in International Accounting—Americas and the Far East,* Cheltenham, U.K.: Edward Elger Publishing, 1996.

EXHIBIT 3-4 Summary of Significant Accounting Practices

	France	Germany	Japan	The Netherlands	United Kingdom	United States
1. Business combinations: purchase or pooling	Purchase	Purchase[1]	Purchase[1]	Purchase[1]	Purchase[1]	Both[2]
2. Goodwill	Capitalize & amortize	Capitalize & amortize or write off to reserves	Capitalize & amortize	Write off to reserves	Capitalize & amortize[3]	Capitalize & amortize[4]
3. Affiliated companies	Equity method	Equity method	Equity method[5]	Equity method	Equity method	Equity method
4. Foreign currency translation: Current rate method	Recommended for autonomous subsidiaries	No standard practice	All subsidiaries	Autonomous subsidiaries	Autonomous subsidiaries	Autonomous subsidiaries
Temporal method	Recommended for integrated subsidiaries	No standard practice	Not used	Integrated subsidiaries	Integrated subsidiaries	Integrated subsidiaries
5. Asset valuation	Historical cost	Historical cost	Historical cost	Historical & current cost	Historical & current cost	Historical cost
6. Depreciation charges	Economic based[6]	Tax based	Tax based	Economic based	Economic based	Economic based
7. LIFO inventory valuation	Not used	Not common	Not used	Not used	Not acceptable	Used
8. Finance leases	Capitalized[7]	Not capitalized	Capitalized	Capitalized	Capitalized	Capitalized
9. Deferred taxes	Accrued[8]	Accrued[8]	Accrued	Accrued	Accrued	Accrued
10. Reserves for income smoothing	Used	Used	No	Some	Some	No

[1]Pooling also allowed in narrow circumstances, but not widely used.

[2]Proposal to eliminate pooling.

[3]Nonamortization permitted if subject to annual impairment review.

[4]Proposal to base write-off on an impairments test.

[5]Used in consolidated statements; cost method used in individual company statements.

[6]In consolidated statements; tax based in individual company statements.

[7]In consolidated statements; not capitalized in individual company statements.

[8]In consolidated statements only; not accrued in individual company statements.

Nobes, C., and R. Parker, *Comparative International Accounting*, 6th ed., Harlow, U.K.: Pearson Education, 2000.

Ordelheide, D., and KPMG, eds., *Transnational Accounting*, London: Macmillan Press, 1995.

Ordre des Experts-Comptables and Compagnie Nationale des Commissaires aux Comptes, *Developments in French Accounting and Auditing 1998*, Paris: Expert Comptable Média, 1999.

Parker, R. H., and C. Nobes, *An International View of True and Fair Accounting,* London: Routledge, 1994.

Richard, J., "The Evolution of Accounting Chart Models in Europe from 1900 to 1945," *European Accounting Review* 4, no. 1 (1995): 87–124.

Walton, P., ed., *European Financial Reporting: A History*, London: Academic Press, 1995.

Walton, P., ed., *Country Studies in International Accounting—Europe.* Cheltenham, U.K.: Edward Elgar Publishing, 1996.

Walton, P., A. Haller, and B. Raffournier, eds., *International Accounting*, London: International Thompson Business Press, 1998.

Zeff, S. A., "A Perspective on the U.S. Public/Private-Sector Approach to the Regulation of Financial Reporting," *Accounting Horizons* (March 1995): 52–70.

Zeff, S. A., F. Van Der Wel, and K. Camfferman, *Company Financial Reporting: A Historical and Comparative Study of the Dutch Regulatory Process,* Amsterdam: North-Holland, 1992.

Discussion Questions

1. Financial reporting in different countries can be distinguished by an orientation toward *fair presentation* or *legal compliance.* Explain the distinction and give examples of each orientation.

2. Describe how discretionary reserves are used in some countries to smooth income from one year to the next.

3. In most countries, published financial accounting standards differ from those actually used in practice. What causes such differences and who should be concerned about them?

4. Code law countries typically have portions of their financial accounting and reporting requirements anchored in the law itself and other portions derived from professional standards or recommendations. Explain whether extensive formal legal requirements lead to high-quality levels of financial reporting.

5. Large companies often list their equity shares on different stock exchanges around the world. What accounting issues does this practice raise?

6. Consider the following statement: "Experience shows that the needs of national and international markets, for international harmonization in particular, are better served by self-regulation and development than by governmental regulation." Do you agree? Why or why not?

7. In France, financial accounting standards and practices originate primarily from three authoritative sources: (a) companies legislation (Plan Comptable Général and Code de Commerce), (b) professional opinions and recommendations (CNC, CRC, OEC, and CNCC), and (c) stock exchange regulations (COB). Which of these three has the greatest influence on day-to-day French accounting practice?

8. Consider the following statement: "The German Accounting Standards Committee has been modeled on Anglo-American and international practice." Do you agree? Why or why not?

9. Which accounting and reporting practices described in this chapter might be affected by the extensive cross-ownership among Japanese corporations? What are the likely consequences of these practices for readers of Japanese financial statements?

10. The most novel feature of the Dutch accounting scene is the Enterprise Chamber of the Court of Justice of Amsterdam. What is the mission of the Enterprise Chamber? How is this mission carried out?

11. Financial accounting and reporting in the United Kingdom is said to have lost some of its traditional Anglo roots in favor of a Euro (EU) drift. What is the reason for this change and what, if any, evidence supports it?

12. In the United States, some private and/or small public companies are exempt from compliance with certain specified SFASs. This exemption may eventually lead to different sets of GAAP for large and small companies. Is this development desirable from an international vantage point? Why or why not?

Exercises

1. This chapter provides synopses of national accounting practice systems in six developed countries.

   Required: For each country, list:
   a. the name of the national financial accounting standard-setting board or agency
   b. the name of the agency, institute, or other organization charged with supervising and enforcing financial accounting standards

2. Refer to your answer to Exercise 1.

   Required: Other than the United States, which country appears to have the most effective accounting and financial reporting supervision mechanism for companies whose securities are traded in public financial markets? Should each country that has a stock exchange (and therefore a public financial market) also have a regulatory agency that enforces accounting and financial reporting rules? Write a concise paragraph to support your answer.

3. Empirical research supports the idea that accounting diversity complicates business decision making. These complications seem particularly pronounced in multinational business operations.

   Required:
   a. From the perspective of multinational business decision making, list five distinct advantages and five distinct disadvantages of existing worldwide accounting diversity.
   b. As far as you can judge, which of the six countries has the most benign financial accounting environment in terms of multinational business operations and from the perspective of corporate management?

4. French and German companies are allowed to use International Accounting Standards or U.S. GAAP in their consolidated financial statements. Many internationally listed French and German companies take advantage of this flexibility.

   Required: Go to the Web site of the New York Stock Exchange (www.nyse.com), Nasdaq (www.nasdaq.com), or the London Stock Exchange (www.londonstockexchange.com) and identify three listed companies from either France or Germany. Refer to these companies' annual reports to document the accounting principles used. (Hint: You may link to corporate Web sites through www.corporateinformation.com and www.carol.co.uk. The NYSE and Nasdaq Web sites also have links to their listed companies.)

5. The United Kingdom and United States have a common accounting heritage and are linked by history and language. *Anglo-American* accounting is a term sometimes

used to denote their accounting styles, which are similar in orientation, purpose, and approach. Yet accounting differences still exist between these two countries.

Required:

a. Identify the major differences between U.K. and U.S. accounting that are discussed in this chapter.

b. Which country is likely to be systematically more conservative in measuring reported earnings? Why do you think so?

6. The International Federation of Accountants (IFAC) is a worldwide organization of professional accounting bodies. IFAC's Web site (www.ifac.org) has links to a number of accounting bodies around the world.

Required: Visit IFAC's Web site. List the accounting organizations discussed in this chapter that are linked to IFAC's Web site.

7. Analysts often try to restate financial statement amounts from one GAAP to another. For example, the financial statements of companies from legal compliance countries are often restated to a fair presentation basis.

Required: List the major financial statement items that you think would need to be adjusted to convert from a legal compliance to a fair presentation basis.

8. Reread Chapter 3 and its discussion questions.

Required:

a. As you go through this material, prepare a list of 20 expressions, terms, or short phrases that are unfamiliar or unusual in your home country.

b. Write a concise definition or explanation of each item.

9. In the United Kingdom and the Netherlands (as well as several other EU-member countries), different financial accounting and reporting requirements exist for small, medium-sized, and large companies.

Required:

a. What accounting and/or financial reporting concessions do small companies enjoy in the United Kingdom and the Netherlands?

b. Would you advocate a three-way company size distinction for accounting and financial reporting purposes in large countries like Japan and the United States? Why or why not?

10. Analyze the six national accounting practice systems summarized in this chapter.

Required:

a. For each of the six countries treated in this chapter, select the most important financial accounting practice or principle at variance with international norms.

b. For each selection you make, state briefly your reasons for its inclusion on your list.

11. In most countries, accounting standard setting involves a combination of private and public sector groups. The private sector includes the accounting profession and other groups affected by the financial reporting process, such as users and preparers of financial statements, and labor. The public sector includes government agencies such as tax authorities, ministries responsible for commercial law, and securities commissions. The stock market is another potential influence.

Required: Complete a matrix indicating whether each of the above groups significantly influences accounting standard setting in the six countries discussed in this chapter. List the groups across the top and the countries down the side; indicate the influence of each group with a yes or a no.

12. Listed below are certain financial ratios used by analysts:
    - *Liquidity:* current ratio; cash flow from operations to current liabilities
    - *Solvency:* debt to equity; debt to assets
    - *Profitability:* return on assets; return on equity

    Required: Assume that you are comparing the financial ratios of companies from two countries discussed in this chapter. Discuss how the accounting practices identified in Exhibit 3-4 would affect your comparison for each of the six ratios in the list.

Case 3–1   A Rose by Any Other Name

As an analyst for a securities firm, you are aware that accounting practices differ around the world. Yet you wonder whether these differences really have any material effect on companies' financial statements. You also know that the SEC in the United States requires non-U.S. registrants to reconcile key financial data from the home country GAAP basis to a U.S. GAAP basis. You obtain three such reconciliations for the 1999 reporting year.

A. GROUPE DANONE (FRANCE)

Note 2—Summary of differences between accounting principles followed by the Company and United States generally accepted accounting principles.

The accompanying financial statements have been prepared in accordance with French GAAP which differ in certain significant respects from U.S. GAAP.

DESCRIPTION OF DIFFERENCES

These differences have been reflected in the financial information given in the paragraphs below and mainly relate to the following items:

1. Brand Names Amortization Under French GAAP, the brand names that have been separately identified on the acquisition of subsidiaries are not amortized (See Note 1.C). Under U.S. GAAP, intangible assets such as brand names

must be amortized over the period estimated to be benefited, which may not exceed 40 years. For the purpose of reconciling to U.S. GAAP, brand names are amortized over a 40-year period.

2. Goodwill Relating to the Acquisition of Foreign Subsidiaries Goodwill relating to the acquisition of most foreign subsidiaries are translated in the Group's accounts using an historical exchange rate when U.S. GAAP require the use of the closing exchange rate. Under U.S. GAAP, the difference is part of the "Translation adjustments" component of stockholders' equity.

Amortization of most goodwill is computed on the basis of gross values translated at the historical exchange rate. Under U.S. GAAP, the annual amortization charge is translated at the average exchange rate during the year.

3. Stock Options The Company generally grants to the Group's eligible employees a discount from the market price for shares subscribed pursuant to share subscription or share purchase plans. Accounting for this discount is not addressed by French GAAP and these transactions have no effect on the statement of income. Under U.S. GAAP, the discount, measured at the date of grant, is considered as compensation to employees. The effect of the decrease to retained earnings and increase to stockholders' equity for the amount of compensation expense is reflected as a U.S. GAAP adjustment and shown later.

4. Available-For-Sale Securities Under French GAAP, the unrealized gains and losses on available-for-sale securities are neither recorded by companies fully integrated, nor by equity investees. Under U.S. GAAP, available-for-sale securities are carried at market value, with the unrealized result recorded directly in other comprehensive income.

5. Deferred Income Taxes on Brand Names   Deferred income taxes on brand names are not recorded. Consequently, the goodwill arising on the acquisition of the related subsidiaries is not increased by the amount of such deferred tax liability. Under U.S. GAAP, a deferred tax liability computed at the local tax rate applicable to long-term capital gains is recorded and goodwill is increased by the same amount. The deferred tax liability is reversed to profit as the related intangible asset is amortized, whereas the amortization charge of the additional goodwill matches this profit.

Had U.S. GAAP been applied, deferred income taxes (long-term liabilities) and goodwill would be increased by €381 million as of December 31, 1999 (€401 million as of December 31 1998).

Goodwill amortization, offset by an equal amount of deferred tax benefit of €13 million, €12 million, and €12 million for 1997, 1998, and 1999, respectively, would be recorded under U.S. GAAP.

6. Purchase Accounting—Fair Value   Purchase accounting applied to a less than wholly-owned subsidiary results in all of the assets and liabilities of the purchased subsidiary being recorded at fair values when the parent purchases its majority interest, and the minority interest in the subsidiary

net assets is adjusted to reflect its share of the revalued net assets (excluding goodwill).

Under U.S. GAAP, no write-up in fair value of the net assets of the subsidiary related to the minority interest should occur. Accordingly, the write-up of fair values in brand names related to the minority interest should be reversed, thus decreasing brand names and minority interest by €165 million as of December 31, 1999 (€205 million as of December 31, 1998). The remainder of the write-ups to fair value in other net assets related to the minority interest is not considered material.

7. Comprehensive Income   Comprehensive income is the term used to define all nonowner changes in shareholders' equity. Comprehensive income is a concept not addressed by French GAAP. Under U.S. GAAP, comprehensive income includes, in addition to net income:

- additional paid-in capital related to compensation costs on shares issued to employees
- net unrealized holding gains/losses arising during the period on available for sale securities
- movements in cumulative translation adjustment

RECONCILING STATEMENTS
Reconciliation of Net Income—Determination of Comprehensive Income and Reconciliation of Stockholders' Equity

The reconciliation of net income from French GAAP to U.S. GAAP, together with the reporting of U.S. GAAP comprehensive income, and a reconciliation of stockholders' equity from French GAAP to U.S. GAAP is on the following page:

(All amounts in millions of euros except per share data)	Year Ended December 31,		
	1997	*1998*	*1999*
Net income under French GAAP	559	598	682
U.S. GAAP adjustments:			
1. Brand names amortization	(46)	(45)	(46)
2. Amortization of goodwill of foreign subsidiaries	4	4	4
3. Compensation costs under stock options plans	(4)	(3)	(2)
Net income with U.S. GAAP adjustments before tax effect, and minority interests	513	554	638
Tax effect of the above adjustments	(8)	(8)	(7)
Minority interests effect of above adjustments	7	7	6
Net income under U.S. GAAP	512	553	637
Basic earnings per share under U.S. GAAP	7.22	7.85	9.11
Diluted earnings per share under U.S. GAAP	7.05	7.58	8.78
Net income under U.S. GAAP	512	553	637
Other comprehensive income, net of tax:			
Additional paid-in capital related to compensation costs on shares issued to employees	4	3	2
Change in net unrealized gains/losses on available-for-sale securities	18	39	(28)
less: Reclassification adjustment for net gains/losses included in net income	(8)	(6)	(10)
Change in cumulative translation adjustments	164	(210)	511
Other comprehensive income under U.S. GAAP	177	(174)	475
Comprehensive income under U.S. GAAP	689	379	1,112
Stockholders' equity under French GAAP	6,512	6,514	6,146
U.S. GAAP adjustments:			
1. Brand names amortization	(306)	(342)	(399)
2. Amortization of goodwill of foreign subsidiaries	(106)	(179)	19
3. Unrealized gains on available-for-sale securities	66	105	57
Tax effect of the above adjustments	(70)	(84)	(80)
Minority interests effect of above adjustments	38	43	45
Stockholders' equity under U.S. GAAP	6,134	6,057	5,788

U.S. GAAP Statement of Changes in Stockholders' Equity

(All amounts in millions of euros)	
Balance as of December 31, 1996	**5,739**
Capital stock issues	48
Dividends paid	(184)
Movements on treasury shares	(158)
Net income under U.S. GAAP for 1997	512
Other comprehensive income under U.S. GAAP for 1997	177
Balance as of December 31, 1997	**6,134**
Capital stock issues	42
Dividends paid	(203)
Conversion of debentures	64
Movements on treasury shares	(359)
Net income under U.S. GAAP for 1998	553
Other comprehensive income under U.S. GAAP for 1998	(174)
Balance as of December 31, 1998	**6,057**
Capital stock issues	73
Capital stock reduction	(1,022)
Dividends paid	(208)
Conversion of debentures	583
Movements on treasury shares	(807)
Net income under U.S. GAAP for 1999	637
Other comprehensive income under U.S. GAAP for 1999	475
Balance as of December 31, 1999	**5,788**

DESCRIPTION OF OTHER DIFFERENCES

Presentation Differences—Operating Income
Under French GAAP, operating income excludes the nonrecurring items discussed in Note 3. U.S. GAAP requires that operating income be reduced for such items.

Disclosure is made in Note 3 under French GAAP as to the after-tax effect that the nonrecurring charges had on diluted earnings per share. U.S. GAAP does not allow disclosure of the per share effects of nonrecurring charges, which do not qualify as extraordinary items, and such nonrecurring items do not qualify as extraordinary items under U.S. GAAP.

Presentation Differences—Cash Flow Statement
Under U.S. GAAP, a subtotal "Cash flows from Operations" would not be shown.

Presentation Differences—Additional Disclosures Required by SFAS 115 On December 31, 1998 and 1999, all long-term investments, other noncurrent assets and marketable securities held by the Group and categorized as available-for-sale consisted of equity securities. On December 31, 1998 and 1999, the Group had no held-to-maturity securities. On December 31, 1998 and 1999, available-for-sale securities consisted of the following on the next page:

(All amounts in millions of euros)	At December 31, 1998	1999
Securities held by consolidated companies:		
Cost	647	759
Gross unrealized gains[1]	95	56
Estimated fair value	742	815
Securities held by companies consolidated by the equity methods:		
Group's share in net unrealized gains	10	—

[1]Gross unrealized gains and losses are stated before any tax effect.

On December 31, 1998 and 1999, these investments were included in the following captions on the consolidated balance sheet.

(All amounts in millions of euros)	At December 31, 1998	1999
Long-term investments	593	639
Other noncurrent assets	63	64
Marketable securities	86	112
	742	815

For the years ended December 31, 1997, 1998, and 1999 gross realized gains and losses on available-for-sale securities were not material. The cost of securities sold is based on the average cost method.

Presentation Differences—Additional Disclosures Required by SFAS 123 SFAS 123, "Accounting for Stock-based Compensation," was adopted as of January 1, 1996. Upon the adoption of SFAS 123, the Company continues to use the measurement principles in APB 25. Had compensation cost been determined on the fair value at the grant date, net income, basic earnings per share, and diluted earnings per share would have been as follows:

(All amounts in millions of euros except per share data)	Year Ended December 31, 1997	1998	1999
Net income under U.S. GAAP	512	553	637
Additional compensation cost under SFAS 123	9	24	23
Amounts under U.S. GAAP and with the application of SFAS 123:			
Net income	503	529	614
Basic earnings per share	7.10	7.50	8.78
Diluted earnings per share	6.94	7.27	8.47

The fair values at December 31, 1998 and December 31, 1999 of the options granted were estimated for the purposes of SFAS 123 disclo-sure requirements using the Cox option-pricing model based on the following weighted average assumptions:

	1997	1998	1999
Risk-free interest rate	4.55%	3.37%	4.89%
Expected life	3.4 years	3.6 years	4.1 years
Expected volatility	30.0%	39.5%	34.5%
Expected dividend yield	2.88%	2.14%	2.43%

Unaudited Pro Forma Financial Data Disclosed

Pro forma financial data are disclosed in Note 5 to the accompanying consolidated financial state-ments, in a format that management believes is relevant to the reader to make an informed judg-ment about the accounts. The provision of such pro forma information better reflects the Group's organic growth because:

- the Group's external growth through acqui-sitions is a factor that generates additional revenues and costs every year,
- a review of businesses has been carried out over the last three years resulting in various divestitures and decreases in revenues and costs, and,
- the Company holds subsidiaries in various countries, where changes in exchange rates affect consolidated revenues and earnings reported in French francs.

The method used to determine the pro forma information disclosed in Note 5 is different from the method that is required to be used under U.S. GAAP, which provides that the ex-change rates existing in each year are used to de-termine the pro forma information as opposed to the method used in Notes 5, which results in pro forma effect given in the prior year related to ex-change rate changes that occurred in the subse-quent year.

Pro forma information on a U.S. GAAP basis would only result in providing information on the effects of acquired businesses, which are not significant so as to require pro forma disclo-sure as stipulated in APB Opinion 16 and would be determined differently.

B. PHILIPS

Application of Generally Accepted Accounting Principles in the United States of America

The accounting policies followed in the prepara-tion of the consolidated financial statements differ in some respects from those generally accepted in the United States of America.

To determine net income and stockholders' equity in accordance with generally accepted ac-counting principles in the United States of Amer-ica (U.S. GAAP), Philips has applied the following accounting principles:

- Under U.S. GAAP, divestitures that cannot be regarded as discontinued segments of business must be included in income from continuing operations. Under Dutch GAAP, prior to 1999, certain material transactions such as disposals of lines of ac-tivities, including closures of substantial production facilities, were accounted for as extraordinary items, whereas under U.S. GAAP they would have been recorded in income from operations.
- In 1999, Philips reported a credit to net in-come of EUR 62 million (versus charges of EUR 34 million in 1998 and EUR 63 mil-lion in 1997) because the excess amount of the accumulated benefit obligation over the market value of the plan assets or the exist-ing level of the pension provision in certain Company pension plans was lower than in the preceding 2 years. For U.S. GAAP pur-poses, when recording the additional mini-mum liability, a portion of this amount is capitalized as an intangible asset and the

remaining balance is charged to equity, net of applicable taxes.

- Under Dutch GAAP, certain product development and process development costs are capitalized in inventory. Under U.S. GAAP such costs must be expensed when incurred. The 1998 and 1997 figures have been adjusted to reflect this difference in accounting.
- Under Dutch GAAP, securities available for sale are valued at the lower of cost or net realizable value. Under U.S. GAAP they are valued at market price, unless such shares are restricted by contract for a period of one year or more, and unrealized holding gains or losses with respect to securities available for sale are credited or charged to stockholders' equity.
- Under Dutch GAAP, the results of foreign-exchange contracts relating to hedges of securities are deferred to stockholders' equity. Under U.S. GAAP, changes in the value of these forward exchange contracts are reported in income when sale of the securities is restricted for a period of one year or more.
- Philips reported a charge to income from operations of EUR 329 million for restructurings in its 1998 financial statements. With regard to a portion of this restructuring, EUR 40 million (EUR 23 million net of taxes), the plans had not been communicated to employees until early 1999 and, accordingly, this portion has been recorded under U.S. GAAP as a charge in 1999.
- In July 1995, Philips contributed the net assets of its cable networks, with a book value of approximately EUR 91 million, to UPC, a newly established joint venture in which Philips had acquired a 50 percent interest. Under Dutch GAAP, this transfer resulted in a gain of EUR 58 million relating to the partial disposal of its interest in these assets to the other joint venture party (UIH). For U.S. GAAP purposes, this gain was not considered realized because the consideration received by Philips principally consisted of equity and notes issued by UPC and equity in UIH. In 1997, Philips sold its 50 percent interest in this joint venture and the gain of EUR 58 million on this transaction was recognized.

- Under Dutch GAAP, majority-owned entities are consolidated. Under U.S. GAAP, consolidation of majority-owned entities is not permitted if minority interest holders have the right to participate in operating decisions of the entity. Although Philips owned 60 percent of the Philips Consumer Communications joint venture, under U.S. GAAP the venture with Lucent Technologies could not be consolidated but was accounted for under the equity method (see note 1).
- Under Dutch GAAP, catalogues of recorded music, music publishing rights, film rights and theatrical rights belonging to PolyGram (which was sold in 1998) were written down to the extent that the present value of the expected income generated by the acquired catalogues was below their book value. Under U.S. GAAP the rights were initially amortized over a maximum period of 30 years. As a result of the sale of PolyGram, the cumulative amortization has been credited to the gain on disposal in 1998 income under U.S. GAAP.
- Under Dutch GAAP, goodwill arising from acquisitions prior to 1992 was charged directly to stockholders' equity. Under U.S. GAAP, goodwill arising from acquisitions, including those prior to 1992, is capitalized and amortized over its useful life up to a maximum period of 20 years. As a result of the sale of PolyGram, the related goodwill has been fully amortized and charged to the gain on disposal in 1998 income under U.S. GAAP.
- Under Dutch GAAP, funding of NavTech's activities is accounted for as results relating to unconsolidated companies (1999: EUR 44 million, 1998: EUR 61 million, 1997: EUR 95 million) whereas under U.S. GAAP these amounts have to be included in income from operations as research and development costs.
- Under Dutch GAAP, the excess of the Company's investment over its underlying equity in the net assets of unconsolidated companies has been classified as part of intangible fixed assets, whereas under U.S. GAAP it would be included in investments in unconsolidated companies.

Reconciliation of Net Income According to Dutch GAAP Versus U.S. GAAP

	1999	*1998*	*1997*
Income from continuing operations as per the consolidated statements of income	**1,804**	541	1,231
Reclassification of extraordinary items under Dutch GAAP	—	474	1,151
	1,804	1,015	2,382
Adjustments to U.S. GAAP (net of taxes):			
Additional minimum liabilities under SFAS No. 87	**(62)**	34	63
Reversal of capitalized development costs in inventories	**(12)**	(40)	21
Reversal of provisions for restructuring	**(23)**	23	—
Reversal of gain on UPC transaction	—	—	58
Amortization of goodwill from acquisitions prior to 1992	—	—	(10)
Reversal of deferred hedge result on securities	**(90)**	—	—
Other items	**(22)**	(7)	(14)
Income from continuing operations in accordance with U.S. GAAP	1,595	1,025	2,500
Income from discontinued operations	—	210	233
Gain on disposal of discontinued operations	—	4,681	—
Extraordinary items–net	**(5)**	(16)	(43)
Net income in accordance with U.S. GAAP	1,590	5,900	2,690
Basic earnings per common share in EUR:			
Income from continuing operations	**4.63**	2.85	7.16
Income from discontinued operations	—	0.58	0.66
Gain on disposal of discontinued operations	—	13.00	—
Extraordinary items–net	**(0.02)**	(0.04)	(0.12)
Net income	**4.61**	16.39	7.70
Diluted earnings per common share in EUR:			
Income from continuing operations	**4.59**	2.82	7.02
Income from discontinued operations	—	0.58	0.65
Gain on disposal of discontinued operations	—	12.89	—
Extraordinary items–net	**(0.01)**	(0.04)	(0.12)
Net income	**4.58**	16.25	7.55

In addition to the reconciliation of net income, "comprehensive income" is required to be reported under U.S. GAAP.

Comprehensive income is defined as all changes in the equity of a business enterprise during a period, except investments by, and distributions to, equity owners. Accordingly, comprehensive income consists of net income and other items that are reflected in stockholders' equity on the balance sheet and have been excluded from the income statement. Such items of other comprehensive income include foreign currency translation adjustments, deferred gains and losses on currency transactions qualifying for hedge treatment, certain pension liability-related losses not yet recorded as pension costs, and unrealized holding gains and losses on securities available for sale.

Statement of Comprehensive Income

	1999	1998	1997
Net income in accordance with U.S. GAAP	**1,590**	5,900	2,690
Other comprehensive income (net of taxes):			
Translation differences	**419**	(152)	293
less: reclassification for translation losses included in net income	—	(42)	(38)
Deferred foreign exchange results	**(71)**	15	—
Minimum pension liability adjustment	**43**	(49)	—
Holding gains (losses) on securities available for sale	**2,131**	32	(64)
Comprehensive income in accordance with U.S. GAAP	**4,112**	5,704	2,881

Reconciliation of Stockholders' Equity According to Dutch
GAAP Versus U.S. GAAP

	1999	1998
Stockholders' equity as per the consolidated balance sheets	**14,757**	14,560
Equity adjustments that affect net income:		
Intangible assets relating to additional liabilities under SFAS No. 87	**29**	48
Reversal of capitalized development costs in inventories	**(241)**	(229)
Reversal of provisions for restructuring	—	23
Adjustment for highly inflationary countries, mainly to property, plant and equipment	—	22
Equity adjustments not affecting net income under U.S. GAAP:		
Holding gain on securities available for sale	**2,163**	32
Stockholders' equity in accordance with U.S. GAAP	**16,708**	14,456
Translation differences as included in stockholders' equity	**(991)**	(1,410)

C. CADBURY SCHWEPPES

Summary of Differences Between U.K. and U.S. Generally Accepted Accounting Principles

The financial statements are prepared in accordance with generally accepted accounting principles applicable in the United Kingdom ("U.K. GAAP"), which differ in certain significant respects from those applicable in the United States ("U.S. GAAP"). These differences relate principally to the following items and the necessary adjustments are shown in the tables set out on pages 128 to 130.

The Group has not adopted the requirements of U.S. Statement of Financial Accounting Standard (SFAS) 133 "Accounting for Derivative Instruments and Hedging Activities," which will be effective for the Group's 2001 financial statements. The Group has not quantified the impact of the standard on the U.S. GAAP amounts, however the standard could increase volatility in U.S. GAAP earnings.

(A) GOODWILL AND INTANGIBLE ASSETS

Prior to 1998, under U.K. GAAP the Group wrote off acquisition goodwill against reserves in the balance sheet in the year of acquisition. From 1998, under U.K. GAAP, acquired goodwill is capitalised and its subsequent measurement (via annual impairment review or annual amortisation charge) is determined based on the individual circumstances of each business acquired. Prior to 1998, under U.S. GAAP, goodwill was recognised on the balance sheet and amortised by charges against profit over its estimated useful life, not to exceed 40 years.

A portion of the goodwill capitalised from 1998 is not being amortised under U.K. GAAP (see Note 1); for U.S. GAAP purposes this goodwill is being amortised over a period of 20 years. Other goodwill capitalised from 1998 is being amortised over 20 years for U.K. GAAP purposes; the same estimated useful life has also been used for U.S. GAAP purposes.

Under U.K. GAAP, the cost of brands (trademarks) acquired may be capitalised and no amortisation or write-down is required unless there is an impairment in value below cost. On an annual basis, the Group reviews non-amortised goodwill and brands for possible impairment using an estimate of the related businesses' discounted cash flows in measuring whether the asset is recoverable. For U.S. GAAP purposes purchased brands are being amortised on a straight line basis over 40 years.

(B) INTEREST CAPITALISATION

Under U.K. GAAP, the capitalisation of interest is optional and the Company has only capitalised interest on major capital construction projects since 1993. Under U.S. GAAP, interest is required to be capitalised on capital construction projects and amortised over the life of the asset.

(C) FOREIGN CURRENCY HEDGES

Under U.S. GAAP, hedging of foreign currency transactions is only allowable for transactions that are firm commitments. Some of the Group's foreign currency contracts hedge forecast or budgeted transactions, which do not meet the definition of a firm commitment; gains or losses on these contracts cannot be deferred but must be recognised in net income.

Under U.K. GAAP, these gains or losses can be deferred until the hedged transaction actually occurs.

(D) DEFERRED TAXATION

Under U.K. GAAP, no provision is made for deferred taxation if there is reasonable evidence that such deferred taxation will not be payable in the foreseeable future. Under U.S. GAAP, deferred taxation is provided for all differences between the book and tax bases of assets and liabilities.

(E) REVALUATION OF PROPERTIES

Under U.K. GAAP, properties were, up to 1999, restated on the basis of appraised values in financial statements prepared in all other respects in accordance with the historical cost convention. Such restatements are not permitted under U.S. GAAP.

(F) ORDINARY DIVIDENDS

Under U.K. GAAP, final ordinary dividends are provided in the financial statements on the basis of the recommendation by the Directors, which requires subsequent approval by the shareholders to become a legal obligation of the Company. Under U.S. GAAP, dividends are only provided when the legal obligation to pay arises.

(G) PENSION COSTS

Under U.K. GAAP, the costs of providing pension benefits may be calculated by the use of any recognised actuarial method that is appropriate and whose assumptions reflect the long-term nature of the assets and liabilities involved. Under U.S. GAAP, the costs of providing these benefits are calculated using the projected unit credit method and a discount rate (being the rate of interest at which pension liabilities could be effectively settled), which reflects current market rates.

(H) CASH FLOWS

Under U.K. GAAP the Company complies with the FRS 1 "Cash Flow Statements," the objective and principles of which are similar to those set out in SFAS 95 "Statement of Cash Flows." Under FRS 1 (Revised), the Company presents its cash flows for (a) operating activities; (b) dividends from associates; (c) returns on investments and servicing of finance; (d) taxation; (e) capital expenditure and financial investments; (f) acquisitions and disposals; (g) dividends to ordinary shareholders; (h) management of liquid resources; and (i) financing activities. SFAS 95 requires only three categories of cash flow activity (a) operating; (b) investing; and (c) financing.

Cash flows arising from taxation and returns on investments and servicing of finance under FRS 1 would be included as operating activities under SFAS 95; dividend payments would be included as a financing activity under SFAS 95 and cash flows from capital expenditure, long-term investments, acquisitions and disposals would be included as investing activities under SFAS 95. In addition, under FRS 1, cash represents cash at bank and in hand less bank overdrafts; cash equivalents (liquid resources) are not included with cash. Movements of liquid resources are included under a separate heading under FRS 1.

Payments made against provisions set up on the acquisition of subsidiaries have been included in acquisitions and disposals in the cash flow statement. Under U.S. GAAP these payments would be included in determining net cash provided by operating activities.

(I) DISCONTINUED OPERATIONS

Under U.K. GAAP, the Company complies with FRS 3 "Reporting Financial Performance" in determining disposed businesses that should be classified as discontinued operations. Under U.S. GAAP the beverages units disposed in 1999 would not be considered discontinued operations as they do not constitute a separate business segment.

(J) RESTRUCTURING COSTS

The classification of costs of £11 m as restructuring in DPSUBG, the Group's U.S. bottling associate, does not meet the definition of restructuring costs under U.S. GAAP.

(K) COMPREHENSIVE INCOME STATEMENT

The requirement of FAS 130 to provide a comprehensive income statement is met by the Statement of Total Recognised Gains and Losses on page 87.

(L) EMPLOYEE TRUST

Under U.K. GAAP, own shares held by the Employee Trust are accounted for as fixed asset investments. Under U.S. GAAP, own shares are accounted for within shareholders' equity.

Effects on Profit of Differences Between U.K. and U.S. Generally Accepted Accounting Principles

	1999 £m	1998 £m	1997 £m
Profit for the Financial Year from continuing operations, net of tax (per U.K. GAAP)	**642**	348	337
U.S. GAAP adjustments:			
Amortisation of goodwill and trademarks	**(89)**	(87)	(83)
Depreciation of capitalised interest	**(6)**	(6)	(10)
Pension costs	**3**	14	(5)
Exceptional item/Disposal gain adjustment	**23**	(7)	19
Timing of recognition of foreign currency hedges	**(3)**	4	(12)
Other items	—	—	1
Taxation on above adjustments	**2**	1	7
Deferred taxation	**22**	(10)	6
Profit for the Financial Year from continuing operations, net of tax, as adjusted for U.S. GAAP	**594**	257	260
Profit from discontinued operations, net of tax, as adjusted for U.S GAAP	—	—	1
Gain on disposal of discontinued operations, net of tax, as adjusted for U.S. GAAP	—	—	356
Profit for the Financial Year as adjusted for U.S. GAAP	**594**	257	617

Earnings per ADS under U.S. GAAP	*1999* *£ per* *ADS*	*1998* *£ per* *ADS*	*1997* *£ per* *ADS*
Earnings per ADS from continuing operations:			
Basic	**1.17**	0.51	0.52
Diluted	**1.16**	0.50	0.51
Earnings per ADS from discontinued operations net of tax:			
Basic	—	—	—
Diluted	—	—	—
Gain on disposal of discontinued operations per ADS, net of tax:			
Basic	—	—	0.71
Diluted	—	—	0.70
Total earnings per ADS:			
Basic	**1.17**	0.51	1.23
Diluted	**1.16**	0.50	1.21

There is no material difference in earnings under the Basic and Diluted Earnings per ADS calculations. See Note 9 for a reconciliation of shares used in the Basic and Diluted EPS calculations.

	1999	*1998*	*1997*
Average number of ADS–Basic	**507**	508	503
Average number of ADS–Diluted	**513**	515	508

The Company applies U.S. APB Opinion 25 and related interpretations when accounting for its share option plans (see Note 29 for a summary of the plans). Had compensation cost for the Company's share option plans been determined based on the fair value at the grant date for awards under those plans consistent with the method of SFAS Statement 123 "Accounting for Stock-Based Compensation," the Company's profit and earnings per share under U.S. GAAP would have been reduced to the pro forma amounts indicated on the next page:

	1999	1998
	£m except per ADS data	
Profit for the Financial Year from continuing operations as adjusted for U.S. GAAP:		
As reported	**594**	257
Pro forma	**579**	243
Basic earnings per ADS per U.S. GAAP:		
As reported	**1.17**	0.51
Pro forma	**1.14**	0.48
Diluted earnings per ADS per U.S. GAAP:		
As reported	**1.16**	0.50
Pro forma	**1.13**	0.47

Further details regarding the fair valuation of option grants can be found in Note 29.

Cumulative Effect on Shareholders' Funds of Differences Between U.K. and U.S. Generally Accepted Accounting Principles

	1999 £m	1998 £m	1997 £m
Shareholders' Funds per U.K. GAAP	**2,240**	1,843	1,676
U.S. GAAP adjustments:			
Goodwill and intangibles	**1,011**	1,063	1,178
Pension costs	**(31)**	(30)	(45)
Interest capitalisation	**9**	15	21
Property revaluations	**(58)**	(62)	(67)
Dividends	**141**	135	127
Other items	**(4)**	—	(3)
Taxation on above adjustments	**(2)**	(5)	(6)
Deferred taxation	**(54)**	(77)	(67)
Employee Trust	**(88)**	—	—
Shareholders' Funds as adjusted for U.S. GAAP	**3,164**	2,882	2,814

The gross amounts of goodwill, brands and tangible fixed assets and the corresponding accumulated amortisation/depreciation under U.S. GAAP are as follows:

	1999 £m	1998 £m
Goodwill:		
Gross	**1,522**	1,565
Accumulated amortisation	**(295)**	(253)
	1,227	1,312
Brands:		
Gross	**1,660**	1,561
Accumulated amortisation	**(229)**	(201)
	1,431	1,360
Tangible fixed assets:		
Gross	**2,172**	2,117
Accumulated depreciation	**(1,133)**	(1,048)
	1,039	**1,069**

The analysis of cumulative exchange differences within Shareholders' Funds is as follows:

	1999 £m	1998 £m	1997 £m
Balance at beginning of year	**200**	170	137
Movement in the year:			
Translation adjustments	**6**	34	40
Tax effect	—	(4)	(7)
Balance at end of year	**206**	200	170

REQUIRED

1. Document the effects of the GAAP differences in the three 20Fs by doing the following:
   a. For the current year and for each company, calculate the percentage change for net income and for total shareholders' equity indicated by the reconciliation and using the respective non-U.S. GAAP numbers as a base.
   b. Repeat the same calculations for the preceding year. Are the percentage changes approximately the same? What is significant about your findings?
   c. For each company and for the current year, identify the two income statement items and the two balance sheet items that exhibit the relatively largest differences. Would you expect other

   multinational companies in the three countries analyzed to be subject to similar item-by-item differences?
2. Should a U.S. reader of non-U.S. financial statements find these SEC-mandated reconciliations useful?
3. Various corporate management and financing decisions are made with consequences on corporate financial statements in mind. If a given management would have had to report under a different set of GAAP, different business decisions might have been made. If we accept this assertion, then GAAP reconciliations have only limited informational value. Suggest a procedure that would represent a better solution to international financial reporting difficulties.

Case 3–2 Kiwis Cannot Fly, But at Least When Troubles Loom, They Keep Their Heads Out of the Sand.[1]

How do accounting measurement and disclosure requirements affect managerial decision making? Are such rules neutral in their effects or do "you manage what you measure?"[2] The issue affects how we think about the impacts of international accounting diversity.

Professor Louis Lowenstein writes:

> ... [G]ood financial disclosure has become a corporate governance tool of the first order—effective, timely, and (legally, at least) all but self-executing. Accountants, of course, are aware of the impact. They are the messengers who deliver to management the report cards about management's sometimes poor performance. In response, executives routinely manage today what they know *we* will measure tomorrow.[3]

Later in the same article he argues the advantages of U.S. accounting requirements over (among others) German requirements:

> One need only look at the undesignated, hidden reserves used by German corporations and others. ... Europeans like to say that these provisions or reserves are prudent or conservative, but look at the effects. Clarity and consistency of disclosure suffer; one company's earnings cease to be comparable with another's. And those reserves, which do "conservatively" understate earnings when they are created, will overstate earnings or hide losses when reversed. Daimler-Benz reversed provisions and reserves totaling DM

1.8 billion in the first half of 1993, creating a German-style "profit" at a time when its operations experienced a reality-style loss.[4]

The Daimler-Benz (now DaimlerChrysler) case was also commented on in the financial press. The following excerpts are from *The Economist*:

> Daimler now talks of "concentration on core businesses," "lean management" and other everyday slogans of global business. In Stuttgart the latest phrase is "capital efficiency," or looking for ways to make the firm's capital work harder. Daimler says it began thinking about this reexamination in 1990; but its determination to press ahead can only have been strengthened by its decision last year to become the first German company to be quoted on the New York Stock Exchange.
>
> Daimler has a lot to be embarrassed about. It invested some DM8 billion in businesses such as aerospace and white goods without thinking hard enough about the likely returns. It has billions more tied up in property, supplies and other assets.
>
> Last year, thanks to its New York listing, Daimler had to adopt American accounting practices, which tear away the veils with which German firms hide their real profits from the taxman. Although Daimler is forecasting a DM600m profit for 1993 under German accounting rules, Mr. Geiger expects it to announce a loss of DM1.7 billion under American rules.[5]

---

[1]"House of Debt: How to Encourage Fiscal Responsibility," *The Economist* (April 1, 1995), pp. 14,16.
[2]Louis Lowenstein, "Financial Transparency and Corporate Governance: You Manage What You Measure," *Columbia Law Review* (June 1996), p. 1335.
[3]Ibid., p. 1336.
[4]Ibid., p. 1341.
[5]"A Capital Suggestion," *The Economist* (April 9, 1994), p. 69.

Not until it felt the need a few years ago to list its shares in New York, in order to tap the capital available in America, did the company come under the scrutiny from shareholders that has forced it to abandon its disastrous decision of the 1980s to diversify into everything.[6]

Daimler's decision to list its shares on the New York Stock Exchange in 1993 was significant. Part of the price for that was to report its profits under accounting standards similar to America's. These have revealed hefty losses that traditional German accounts could largely have disguised, most recently of DM6 billion in 1995—the biggest peacetime loss of

any German firm. This has created pressure for dramatic changes to boost efficiency. The firm has abandoned its policy of diversifying into everything. Jürgen Schrempp, its chairman, has said that "profitability must take precedence over revenues" . . . [7]

From 1993 until 1996, Daimler-Benz prepared a reconciliation of key financial data from German to U.S. GAAP, as required by the U.S. SEC. However, in 1996, the company began preparing complete financial statements on the basis of U.S. GAAP. Exhibit 3-5, taken from the 1996 Daimler-Benz annual report, explains why the company decided to make the change.

EXHIBIT 3-5   Choice of U.S. GAAP by Daimler-Benz

With our listing on the New York Stock Exchange (NYSE) in October 1993, Daimler-Benz was the first German company to establish direct access to the world's largest and most important capital market. In so doing, we initiated a process that not only permanently affects our external reporting, but also our accounting and our internal controlling instruments. The objective of this process is to increase the transparency and efficiency of our external and internal reporting while at the same time improving the methodological basis for a corporate management attuned to the returns expected by our investors without neglecting the entitled interests of our employees, customers, and society on the whole.

Understanding Value-Based Management

The permanent and continuous expansion of our company's value is only possible when the interests of all groups that contribute to our success are given the appropriate degree of consideration. Our economic performance and satisfactory returns for our shareholders depend on motivated employees, satisfied customers, and reliable and innovative suppliers. On the other hand, only a profitable company is in a position to obtain the funds required for securing the future from the capital market at relatively favorable terms and to offer its employees secure and challenging jobs and thus earn their long-term commitment. Management at Daimler-Benz is therefore dedicated to increasing the value of the Company for the benefit of everyone involved.

The new controlling instruments in the Daimler-Benz group to support this objective include preparing the balance sheet in accordance

with American accounting principles (generally accepted accounting principles of U.S. GAAP) and reporting that is both internally and externally informative, topical, and transparent.

1996 Financial Statements Prepared Entirely in Accordance with U.S. GAAP for the First Time

Since our listing on the New York Stock Exchange we have increasingly aligned our external reporting in accordance with the information requirements of the international financial world. Important stages in the process included reconciling the result and equity capital according to German accounting principles (HGB) to conform with net income and stockholders' equity as defined by U.S. GAAP and providing additional information on the individual corporate segments. For the period between January and June 1996, we then presented the interim report

---

[6]"Hotels and Planes," *The Economist* (January 27, 1996), p. 17.
[7]"Unhappy Families," *The Economist* (February 10, 1996), p. 25.

EXHIBIT 3-5 *(cont.)*

prepared in accordance with U.S. GAAP for the first time. With our 1996 annual report, we are the first German company to present an entire year's financial statement in accordance with U.S. GAAP while at the same time complying with the provisions of the German Law to Facilitate Equity Borrowing. The report thus also conforms with EU guidelines and European accounting principles.

Improved External Disclosure

Instead of providing various figures concerning the economic performance of the Company that are derived using the HGB and U.S. GAAP but that in some instances differ significantly from each other because of the distinct accounting philosophies, we supply a complete set of figures in conformance with U.S GAAP for our shareholders, the financial analysts, and the interested public. In so doing, we fulfill accounting standards of the highest reputation worldwide, and we believe our approach more clearly and accurately reflects the economic performance, financial situation, and net worth of the Company than any other accounting system available at this time. This is not least due to the fact that U.S. accounting principles focus on investor information rather than creditor protection, which is the dominant concern under German accounting principles. Discretionary valuation is greatly limited, and the allocation of income and expenses to the individual accounting periods is based on strict economic considerations.

Advantages for All Shareholders

Using U.S. accounting principles makes it significantly easier for internationally active financial analysts or experienced institutional investors to accurately assess the financial situation and development of the Company. Moreover, it improves disclosure at Daimler-Benz as well as comparability on an international scale. This also helps promote the worldwide acceptance of our stock.

Operating Profit as a Central Value

The operating profit will be the primary focus of our performance analysis in the future. It is a key figure for measuring the operating performance

of the Company and its individual units. Based on the profit and loss statement prepared under U.S. GAAP, the operating profit is essentially made up of revenues and other income minus the cost of sales and other expenditures. The difference is adjusted to accommodate a few positions. Other important figures included in our external reporting are the net earnings per share and the liquidity statistics provided in the cash flow statement on page 55 of this report.

Internal Controlling on the Basis of Balance Sheet Values in Accordance with U.S. GAAP

The U.S. GAAP not only made Daimler-Benz more transparent from an external perspective. Because the earnings figures as derived with American accounting principles accurately reflect the economic performance of the Company, we are now able to use figures from our external reporting for the internal controlling of the Company and its individual business units rather than relying on the internal operating profit used in the past. We thus make use of the same figures both internally and externally to measure the economic performance of the Company and the business units.

Minimum Return: 12 Percent

In order to do justice to the interest requirements of the capital market, we have established a minimum return for all business units. The criterion that defines this minimum return, and at once the essential control figure for our operational business, is the operating profit, which we relate to the capital used for the operational output of goods and services. The capital employed for operational purposes is defined as the capital employed by the industrial activities on the basis of book values under U.S. GAAP minus trade accounts payable. For the financial services business, however, which is a bank-like activity, we use stockholders' equity rather than capital employed as the reference figure for the operating profit. This approach is in accordance with standard practice. The pre-tax interest rate of 12 percent that we expect from each of our business units on a medium-term basis is determined in

EXHIBIT 3-5   (cont.)

accordance with the interest requirements of the stockholders' equity and external funds tied to the capital employed. For stockholders' equity, we assume an interest requirement of 14 percent, which is in agreement with market standard returns on risk-free investments and a risk premium derived from the capital market. The average interest rate for external funds is 8 percent. In this instance, we assume that the ratio of stockholders' equity to external funds is 2:1.

Instruments for Value-Oriented Corporate Management

The activities that exceed the minimum interest requirement of 12 percent increase the value of the Company because their income exceeds the costs for the capital employed. Conversely, activities that fail to achieve the 12 percent minimum over the long term decrease the value of Daimler-Benz. The standard for measuring an activity is thus not the return generated in a single period; what is decisive is whether in the course of the entire product life cycle the return on the capital employed is adequate from a corporate and market perspective. This applies in particular to startup businesses, which cannot generate satisfactory earnings until the product begins to mature.

A return is adequate from a market perspective when it at least covers the costs of the capital employed, which is our minimum return of 12 percent. Moreover, we are committed to achieving the value that good competitors realize with comparable activities. We therefore regularly carry out benchmarks and best-practice comparisons to establish the strategic target returns for our business units. As a result, the medium- and long-term requirements for many business units are noticeably higher than the 12 percent minimum return requirement.

The operating profit in accordance with the U.S. GAAP thus forms the instrumental basis for value-oriented corporate management. In addition, we assess the longer-term earning power of a given activity on the basis of the expected cash flow and the resulting earnings value for the reporting period.

REQUIRED

1. How might managerial decision making be different under German accounting rules than under those of the United States?
2. What are Daimler-Benz's motives for choosing U.S. GAAP as a basis for financial reporting? How has the change affected how the company is managed? Why couldn't the company have been managed this way under German GAAP?
3. Does this case demonstrate the superiority of U.S. GAAP over German GAAP? Why or why not?
4. In 1998 Daimler-Benz merged with a U.S. car company, Chrysler. How did the 1996 switch to U.S. GAAP facilitate this merger? How has DaimlerChrysler performed since the 1998 merger? (DaimlerChrysler's Web site is www.daimlerchrysler.com.)

COMPARATIVE
ACCOUNTING II

Chapter 3 looked at accounting in six economically developed countries. All six have well-established mechanisms for developing accounting and auditing standards that provide comprehensive guidance for financial reporting and auditing. The four countries examined in this chapter are commonly referred to as emerging economies.[1] They are the Czech Republic, People's Republic of China (China), Republic of China (Taiwan), and Mexico.

The Czech Republic and China are converting from centrally planned economies to ones that are more market oriented. However, the extent to which they are embracing market reforms is different. The Czech Republic is moving toward a complete market economy, while China is taking a middle course in moving to a *socialist market economy,* that is, a planned economy with market adaptations. Both countries are finding it necessary to completely overhaul their accounting systems. Since the Czech Republic and China are taking different approaches to restructuring their respective economies, they are also taking different approaches to restructuring their accounting systems. Both efforts began in the 1990s and are constantly changing.

Taiwan and Mexico are capitalist countries but with traditionally heavy central government intervention and government ownership of key industries. Historically, their economies have been somewhat closed to foreign investment and international competition. This relative isolation is now changing, as both governments are privatizing their industry holdings and opening up to the global economy. Their financial accounting systems are more developed in terms of standard setting, requirements, and practices than the Czech Republic and China. Naturally, evolution in accounting is occurring in these two countries as well, but not as rapidly as in the Czech Republic and China.

---

[1]The term "emerging economies" refers loosely to newly industrialized countries (NICs) and those countries in transition from planned to free-market economies. NICs have experienced rapid industrial growth, but their economies are not yet rich in terms of per capita gross domestic product. Mexico and Taiwan are NICs and China and the Czech Republic have economies in transition.

REASONS FOR CHOOSING THESE FOUR COUNTRIES

Why did we choose these four countries to survey? China may be obvious: It is the most populous country in the world. Companies from all around the world are eager to do business with China, and its accounting developments are an important part of the structural changes in its economy.

We wanted to include a former member of the Soviet bloc. We chose the Czech Republic because accounting developments there are representative of those in other former Soviet bloc countries.

Taiwan is a so-called "Asian Tiger," one of several Asian countries experiencing rapid growth in gross domestic product in recent years, led by growth of industrial exports. Other such countries include Hong Kong (returned to China by Great Britain in 1997), South Korea, and Singapore. We think that Taiwan's historical and cultural connection to (mainland) China adds interest because of the very different directions that accounting has taken in these two economies.

Finally, we wanted to include a Latin American country. Throughout most of Latin America, a decade of free-market reforms has led to healthier economic fundamentals, such as lower inflation and faster economic growth. Protectionist barriers to imports have been dismantled for the most part, economic nationalism has been replaced by a welcoming of foreign investment, and state-owned companies are being privatized. These reforms have gone furthest in Argentina, Chile, Mexico, and Peru, and they are gathering pace in Brazil, Colombia, and Venezuela.[2] We chose Mexico because the 1994 North American Free Trade Agreement (NAFTA) created much new interest in Mexican accounting in Canada, the United States, and elsewhere. Accounting in Mexico shares many features of accounting with other Latin American countries.

SOME OBSERVATIONS ABOUT THE FOUR COUNTRIES AND THEIR ACCOUNTING

Exhibit 4-1 contains some comparative economic data about the four countries that are the focus of this chapter. China's area, population, and resulting gross domestic product (GDP) obviously dwarf the other three. However, China's imports and exports relative to GDP show how insular the Chinese economy is now. Taiwan stands in stark contrast: Trading with the rest of the world is significant to its economy. Another contrast is GDP per capita and by sector. Overall, China is significantly poorer than the other three nations and its economy is much more agricultural. Both of these are signs of significant development potential. Per capita GDP shows that Taiwan has a relatively high standard of living. The Czech Republic and Mexico are comparable, but lower. "Services" is the most important part of the economies of the Czech Republic, Taiwan, and Mexico.

The information on major trading partners reveals a pattern that is true in general, namely, that most international trade is regional in nature. This is most obvious with Mexico, where the United States accounts for more than three-fourths of Mexico's imports and exports. Most of the Czech Republic's trading is with neighboring countries,

---

[2]*The Economist*, "Back on the Pitch: A Survey of Business in Latin America," (December 6, 1997): 3–4.

EXHIBIT 4-1 Economic Data for Selected Countries

	Czech Republic	China	Taiwan	Mexico
Area in Sq.Km.	79 thousand	9.56 million	36 thousand	1.97 million
Population	10.3 million	1.26 billion	21.9 million	95.8 million
Gross Domestic Product	$53 billion	$924 billion	$262 billion	$368 billion
GDP Per Capita	$5,150	$750	$12,040	$3,840
GDP by Sector				
Agriculture	4%	18%	3%	6%
Industry	42%	49%	34%	26%
Services	54%	33%	63%	68%
Imports	$28.8 billion	$140.3 billion	$104.7 billion	$125.4 billion
Exports	$26.4 billion	$183.6 billion	$110.6 billion	$117.5 billion
Major Trading Partners	Germany, Slovakia, Austria, Russia	Japan, Hong Kong, U.S., Taiwan, S. Korea	U.S., Japan, Hong Kong	U.S., Japan

Source: Adapted from *Pocket World in Figures 2001.* © The Economist Newspaper Group, Inc. Reprinted with permission. Further reproduction prohibited.

as is much of China's. This pattern is less true with Taiwan, since the United States is Taiwan's largest trading partner.[3]

Exhibit 4-2 has other data concerning the number of Top 200 emerging market companies[4] and use of the London and New York Stock Exchanges and NASDAQ for raising capital. The number of Top 200 companies indicates that the economies and stock markets of Taiwan and Mexico are relatively more developed than those of the Czech Republic and China. The listing patterns show that Chinese and Mexican companies prefer the New York over the London Stock Exchange, while the reverse is true for companies from the Czech Republic and Taiwan. Overall, few companies from the four countries discussed in this chapter have listed on NASDAQ.

As you read about accounting in the four countries in this chapter, keep in mind the factors affecting accounting development that were discussed in Chapter 2: (1) sources of finance, (2) legal system, (3) taxation, (4) political and economic ties, (5) inflation, (6) level of economic development, (7) education level, and (8) culture. Their influence on accounting in nations with developed economies should be clear from reading Chapter 3. Do they also explain accounting in developing countries? We think so. However, the relative importance of certain factors may be quite different in developing economies than in developed ones, and the influences may appear in different ways.

To illustrate, the effect of the type of legal system is less important in the countries discussed in this chapter than the ones in Chapter 3. For example, Mexico has a civil law

---

[3]The anomaly has a historical explanation, as discussed later in this chapter in the section on Taiwan. When the Nationalists on mainland China fled to Taiwan in 1949 following the Communist victory on the mainland, the United States soon began providing substantial amounts of economic development aid to Taiwan. Trade with mainland China was out of the question, and the other countries in the region, including Japan (still recovering from World War II), were too poor and underdeveloped. The link to the United States remains to this day.

[4]Based on market capitalization expressed in U.S. dollars.

EXHIBIT 4-2 Other Data				
	Czech Republic	*China*	*Taiwan*	*Mexico*
No. of Top 200 emerging market companies[1]	1	3	34	13
No. of companies listed on London Stock Exchange[2]	4	5	13	0
No. of companies listed on New York Stock Exchange[3]	0	13	3	29
No. of companies listed on Nasdaq[4]	0	0	3	3

[1] *Source: Business Week*, (July 10, 2000): 149–150, 151.
[2] *Source:* London Stock Exchange Web site (www.londonstockexchange.com), November 30, 2000.
[3] *Source:* New York Stock Exchange, Web site (www.nyse.com), December 20, 2000.
[4] *Source:* Nasdaq Web site (www.nasdaq.com), January 30, 2001.

legal system similar to that in France and other Continental European countries, yet accounting in Mexico is oriented toward fairness, not legal compliance. Political and economic ties are arguably more important for the countries in this chapter. Mexico's substantial economic contact with the United States, which extends to accounting, explains why Mexico has fairness-oriented accounting. The United States has similar influence in Taiwan. In the Czech Republic, the effect of political and economic ties is more anticipatory than historical. European Union Directives provide the framework for the development of accounting principles, because the Czech Republic has applied for EU membership. China is basing its new accounting standards on International Accounting Standards, because it hopes to better communicate with foreign investors who are vital to its economic development plans.

FOUR NATIONAL FINANCIAL ACCOUNTING SYSTEMS[5]

CZECH REPUBLIC

The Czech Republic (CR) is located in Central Europe with Germany to the west and northwest, Austria to the south, the Slovak Republic to the east, and Poland to the north. Its territory was a part of the Austro-Hungarian Empire for nearly 300 years (from 1620 to 1918), ruled by the Austrian monarchy, the Hapsburgs. The empire collapsed at the end of World War I, and the independent nation of Czechoslovakia was formed in 1918. Between the two World Wars, Czechoslovakia was a prosperous parliamentary democracy with universal voting rights. This ended in 1938 when Britain and France allowed Nazi Germany to annex Czechoslovakia's ethnically German border territories. Within a year, Hitler controlled the rest of the nation and the Nazi occupation began. The 1946 elections and subsequent political maneuvering brought the Communist Party to power. This began the Soviet Union's domination over Czechoslovakia, which lasted

---

[5]The discussion in this section draws on the references cited at the end of the chapter.

until 1989. The internal disintegration of the Soviet regime and the collapse of the Czechoslovak Communist government in that year led to the so-called "Velvet Revolution" and the formation of a new government. In 1993 Czechoslovakia peacefully split into two nations, the Czech Republic and the Republic of Slovakia.

Accounting in the Czech Republic has changed direction several times in the twentieth century, reflecting its political history. Accounting practice and principles reflected those of the German-speaking countries of Europe until the end of World War II. Then, as a centrally planned economy was being constructed, accounting practice was based on the Soviet model. The administrative needs of various central government institutions were satisfied through such features as a uniform chart of accounts, detailed accounting methods, and uniform financial statements, obligatory for all enterprises. The focus on production and costing, based on historical costs, was emphasized over external reporting. A unified system of financial and cost accounting used the same pricing and other principles.

Of course, prices did not reflect the market forces of supply and demand. They were centrally determined and controlled, primarily on the *cost plus* basis. Losses were normally subsidized. Accounting was of limited importance in managing an enterprise. Furthermore, accounting information was considered to be secret and financial statements were not published. Although accounting information was inspected, it was not independently audited.[6]

After 1989 Czechoslovakia moved quickly toward a market-oriented economy. The government revamped its legal and administrative structure to stimulate the economy and attract foreign investments. Commercial laws and practices were adjusted to fit Western standards. Price controls were lifted. Accounting again turned westward, this time reflecting the principles embodied in the European Union Directives.

The division of Czechoslovakia did not appreciably affect this process. In 1993 the Prague Stock Exchange began regular operations. Considering the high level of economic and political development achieved in pre-1938 Czechoslovakia, these events were more a matter of returning to previously held norms than discovering new ones.[7]

Privatization of the economy involved the return of property to former owners, small privatizations in which more than 20,000 shops, restaurants, and other small businesses were sold to Czech citizens by public auction, and a series of large privatizations. A key element of the latter was an innovative coupon voucher system allowing adult Czech citizens to buy investment vouchers for a nominal price. These vouchers were used to acquire shares of newly privatized large industrial concerns. However, the privatizations have yet to cause widespread industrial restructuring. Many Czechs, with no experience as shareholders, sold their shares to investment funds owned by state-controlled Czech banks. One result was a conflict of interest for the banks, which ended up owning the same companies to whom they were lending money. The economic reforms are ongoing. Further privatizations, including the banking sector, are in the works. Among the more pressing issues are strengthening the bankruptcy laws, improving the

---

[6]Rudolf Schroll, "The New Accounting System in the Czech Republic," *European Accounting Review* 4, no. 4 (1995): 827–832; and Jan Dolezal, "The Czech Republic," in *European Accounting Guide*, 2nd ed., David Alexander and Simon Archer, eds., San Diego: Harcourt Brace Jovanovich, 1995.

[7]Willie Seal, Pat Sucher, and Ivan Zelenka, "The Changing Organization of Czech Accounting," *European Accounting Review* 4, no. 4 (1995): 667.

openness and transparency of stock market operations through tighter regulations, and restructuring enterprises.[8]

In 1995 the Czech Republic became the first post-Communist member of the OECD. The Czech Republic joined NATO in 1999 and hopes to achieve full membership in the European Union by 2003.

ACCOUNTING REGULATION AND ENFORCEMENT

The new Commercial Code was enacted by Parliament in 1991 and became effective on January 1, 1992.[9] Influenced by the Austrian roots of the old commercial code and modeled on German commercial law, it introduced a substantial amount of legislation relating to businesses. (Czech law is based on the civil code law system of Continental Europe.) This legislation includes requirements for annual financial statements, income taxes, audits, and shareholders' meetings.

The Accountancy Act that sets out the requirements for accounting was passed in 1991 and became effective on January 1, 1993. Based on the EU Fourth and Seventh Directives, the act specifies the use of a chart of accounts for record keeping and the preparation of financial statements.[10] The Ministry of Finance is responsible for accounting principles. Ministry of Finance decrees set out acceptable measurement and disclosure practices that companies must follow. Thus, accounting in the CR is influenced by the Commercial Code, the Accountancy Act, and Ministry of Finance decrees. The Stock Exchange has so far had little influence and, despite the German origins of the Commercial Code, tax legislation is not directly influential. As discussed in the following section, the *true and fair view* embodied in the Accountancy Act and taken from EU Directives is interpreted to mean that tax and financial accounts are treated differently.[11] Nevertheless, legal form takes precedence over economic substance in many cases.

Auditing is regulated by the Act on Auditors, passed in 1992. This act established the Chamber of Auditors, which oversees the registration, education, examination, and disciplining of auditors, the setting of auditing standards, and the regulation of audit practice, such as the format of the audit report. An audit of financial statements is required for all corporations (joint stock companies) and for large limited liability companies (those with prior year turnover exceeding CzK40 million or net assets exceeding

---

[8]U.S. Department of State, "Background Notes: Czech Republic" (March 1999): 10; U.S. Central Intelligence Agency, "The World Factbook 2000—Czech Republic" (2000), 6; Daniel Michaels and John Reed, "Halfway There," *Wall Street Journal Interactive Edition* (September 18, 1997): 1–6; Mark Andress, "Czech, Please!" *Accountancy* (September 2000): 60–61.

Czech capital markets are largely illiquid. In 1995 and 1996, after the initial large privatizations, there were over 1,600 Czech companies listed on the Prague Stock Exchange. However, in 1997 the exchange started delisting securities that were rarely traded. By the end of 1999, the Prague Stock Exchange had approximately 200 listed companies. See Pat Sucher, Peter Moizer, and Marcela Zarova, "The Images of the Big Six Audit Firms in the Czech Republic," *European Accounting Review* 8, no. 3 (1999): 503, 519; and *Prague Stock Exchange Factbook*, Prague: PSE, 2000, 29.

[9]In 1991 legislation was passed by the then-Czechoslovak Parliament. The Czech Republic carried forward its provisions after the division.

[10]Charts of accounts are not new to the Czech Republic because their use was required under Communism. The Czechs based their new system on the French Plan Comptable and received substantial help from the French Ministry of Finance and the French accounting profession in developing their new charts of account.

[11]Pat Sucher, Willie Seal, and Ivan Zelenka, "True and Fair View in the Czech Republic: A Note on Local Perceptions," *European Accounting Review* 5, no. 3 (1996): 551.

CzK20 million).[12] The audit is designed to assure that the accounts have been kept according to applicable legislation and decrees and that the financial statements present a true and fair view of the company's financial position and results.[13]

FINANCIAL REPORTING

The accounting period is required to be the calendar year. Financial statements must be comparative, consisting of:

1. Balance sheet
2. Profit and loss account (income statement)
3. Notes

Consistent with the requirements of EU Directives, the notes include a description of the accounting policies and other relevant information for assessing the financial statements. Examples of the latter include employee information, revenues by segment, and contingencies. The notes must also include a cash flow statement. Consolidated financial statements are required for groups with equity in excess of CzK300 million or revenues in excess of CzK600 million. Controlling interest in a subsidiary is based on either owning a majority of shares or having a direct or indirect dominant influence. In general the requirements for consolidated financial statements are the same whether or not a company is listed on the Prague Stock Exchange. However, small and other companies not subject to audit have abbreviated disclosure requirements. Financial statements are approved at the annual meeting of shareholders. Listed companies are also required to present quarterly financial statements and audited annual financial statements according to International Accounting Standards.

ACCOUNTING MEASUREMENTS

The acquisition (purchase) method is used to account for business combinations. Goodwill arising from a business combination is written off in the first year of consolidation or capitalized and amortized over 5 years. The equity method is used for associated companies (those over which the company exercises significant influence but which are not consolidated) and for joint ventures. The year-end (closing) exchange rate is used to translate both the income statement and balance sheet of foreign subsidiaries. There are no guidelines for reporting foreign currency translation adjustments.

Tangible and intangible assets are valued at cost and written off over their expected economic lives, with a 5-year maximum for intangibles. Inventory is valued at cost, and FIFO and weighted average are allowable cost flow assumptions (LIFO is not). Research and development costs may be capitalized if they relate to projects completed successfully and capable of generating future income. Leased assets are typically not capitalized, an example of form over substance. Deferred income taxes are only recognized for the difference between accounting and tax depreciation. Contingent losses are

---

[12]Corporations issue shares whereas limited liability companies do not. The latter are similar to limited partnerships.

[13]For further discussion of the development of auditing in the Czech Republic, see Pat Sucher and Ian Zelenka, "The Development of the Role of the Audit in the Czech Republic," *European Accounting Review* 7, no. 4 (1998): 723–751. The study also documents difficulties in getting Czech companies to comply with the requirements for audited financial statements. Thus, information is often unavailable to potential investors, even for publicly traded companies.

recorded when they are probable and can be reliably measured. Legal reserves are also required: Profits are appropriated annually until they reach 20 percent of equity for corporations and 10 percent for limited liability companies.

CHINA[14]

China has a quarter of the world's population, and market-oriented reforms have recently helped generate rapid economic growth. In the late 1970s, Chinese leaders began to move the economy from Soviet-style central planning to one that is more market-oriented but still under Communist Party control. To achieve this, authorities switched to a system of household responsibility in agriculture instead of the old collectivization, increased the authority of local officials and plant managers in industry, permitted a wide variety of small-scale enterprises in services and light manufacturing, and opened the economy to increased foreign trade and investment. In 1993 China's leadership approved additional long-term reforms aimed at giving more flexibility for market-oriented institutions. Central features include the share system of ownership, privatizations, the development of organized stock exchanges, and the listing of shares in Chinese companies on Western exchanges. Nevertheless, state enterprises still continue to dominate many key industries in what the Chinese call a "socialist market economy," that is, a planned economy with market adaptations.

Accounting in China has a long history. Its functioning in a stewardship role can be detected as far back as 2200 B.C. during the Hsiu Dynasty, and documents show that it was used to measure wealth and compare achievements among dukes and princes in the Xia Dynasty (2000 to 1500 B.C.). The young Confucius (551 to 479 B.C.) was a manager of warehouses and his writings mention that the job included proper accounting—keeping the records of receipts and disbursements up-to-date. Among the teachings of Confucius is the imperative to keep history, and accounting records are viewed as part of that history.

The principal characteristics of accounting in China today date from the founding of the People's Republic of China in 1949. China installed a highly centralized planned economy, reflecting Marxist principles and patterned after that of the Soviet Union. The state controlled the ownership, the right to use, and the distribution of all means of production, and enacted rigid planning and control over the economy. Production was the top priority of state-owned enterprises. Their sales and pricing were dictated by the state's planning authorities, and their financing and product costing were administered by the state's finance departments. Under this system, the purpose of accounting was to serve the needs of the state for economic planning and control. A uniform set of standardized accounts was developed to integrate information into the national economic plan. The uniform accounting system contained all-inclusive accounting rules that were mandatory for state-owned enterprises across the country.

Financial reporting was frequent and detailed. The main feature was a fund management orientation where *funds* meant the property, goods, and materials used in the

---

[14]In 1997, Great Britain ceded control of Hong Kong to China. Under the agreement between China and Britain, China has guaranteed to operate a "one country, two systems" arrangement in which Hong Kong's lifestyle will be unchanged for 50 years and basic freedoms and rights will be guaranteed by law. Accounting in Hong Kong is similar to that of the United Kingdom, described in Chapter 3. The discussion of China in this chapter refers to mainland China and excludes Hong Kong.

production process. Financial reporting emphasized the balance sheet, which reflected the source and application of funds. It focused on stewardship and accountability, or the fulfilling of production and other goals, as well as compliance with governmental policies and regulations. Accounting emphasized counting quantities and the comparison of costs and quantities. Although accounting focused more on managerial than financial objectives, its role in decision making by the managers of individual enterprises was nevertheless subordinated to the central authorities.

China's economy today is best described as a hybrid economy in which the state controls strategic commodities and industries, while other industries, as well as the commercial and private sectors, are governed by a market-oriented system. The recent economic reforms involve privatizations, including the conversion of state-owned enterprises into share-issuing corporations. New accounting rules have had to be developed for newly privatized companies and other independent limited liability companies, as well as for foreign business entities such as joint ventures. The role of the government has been changing from managing both the macro- and microeconomy to one managing at the macro level only.[15] Accounting standards were needed to reflect this new reality.

ACCOUNTING REGULATION AND ENFORCEMENT

The Accounting Law was amended in 1993 and 1999, and covers all enterprises and organizations including those not owned or controlled by the state. It outlines the general principles of accounting and defines the role of the government and the matters that require accounting procedures. The Ministry of Finance formulates accounting and auditing standards. This agency is supervised by the State Council, an executive body corresponding to a cabinet. Besides accounting and auditing matters, the ministry is responsible for a wide range of activities affecting the economy. Generally, these activities include formulating long-term economic strategies and setting the priorities for the allocation of government funds. More specifically, the ministry's responsibilities include:

- formulating and enforcing economic, tax, and other finance-related policies
- preparing the annual state budget and fiscal report
- managing state revenue and expenditure
- developing the financial management and tax system[16]

Accounting and auditing matters fall into the last category.

In 1992 the Ministry of Finance issued Accounting Standards for Business Enterprises (ASBE), a conceptual framework designed to guide the development of new ac-

---

[15]The ownership relationship between the government and state-owned enterprises has been redefined. Regulations issued by the Ministry of Finance in 1994 announced for the first time that the state is an investor in the enterprise and is responsible for the enterprise's debts limited to the amount of its capital; the enterprise has its own legal status, enjoying its own property rights and bearing independent civil responsibilities. See Zezhong Xiao and Aixiang Pan, "Developing Accounting Standards on the Basis of a Conceptual Framework by the Chinese Government," *The International Journal of Accounting* 32, no. 3 (1997): 282. For further discussion of China's reforms of state-owned enterprises, see "The Longer March," *The Economist* (September 30, 2000): 71–73.

[16]"Role of the Ministry of Finance," Ministry of Finance Web site (www.mof.gov.cn), December 16, 2000.

counting standards. These standards will eventually harmonize domestic practices and harmonize Chinese practices with international practices. Effective on July 1, 1993, the ASBE was a landmark event in China's move to a market economy. Before the ASBE, more than 40 different uniform accounting systems were in use, varying across industries and types of ownership. Even though each one of these may individually be labeled as *uniform,* they resulted in inconsistent practices overall. Thus, one motive for issuing the ASBE was to harmonize domestic accounting practices. Moreover, existing practices were incompatible with international practices and unsuited for a market-oriented economy. Harmonizing Chinese accounting to international practices serves to remove barriers of communication with foreign investors and helps meet the needs of the economic reforms already under way. Exhibit 4-3 summarizes the ASBE.

After the issuance of the ASBE, the Ministry of Finance replaced the more than 40 uniform accounting systems mentioned previously with thirteen industry-based and two ownership-based accounting systems, as listed in Exhibit 4-4. These systems are viewed as transitional until specific accounting standards can be promulgated that will apply to all enterprises operating in China.

The China Accounting Standards Committee (CASC) was established in 1998 as the authoritative body within the Ministry of Finance responsible for developing accounting standards. The standard-setting process includes assigning necessary research to task forces, the issuance of exposure drafts, and public hearings. CASC members are experts drawn from academia, accounting firms, government, professional accounting associations, and other key groups concerned with the development of accounting in China. To date, the CASC has issued 10 accounting standards on issues such as cash flow statements, debt restructuring, revenue, nonmonetary transactions, and contingencies.[17]

The China Securities Regulatory Commission (CSRC) regulates China's two stock exchanges: Shanghai, which opened in 1990, and Shenzhen, which opened in 1991. It sets regulatory guidelines, formulates and enforces market rules, and authorizes initial public offers and new shares. The CSRC also issues additional disclosure requirements for listed companies. Thus, disclosure requirements for listed companies are established by two government bodies, the Ministry of Finance and the CSRC.

Until 1995 China had two professional accounting organizations. The Chinese Institute of Certified Public Accountants (CICPA), established in 1988 under the jurisdiction of the Ministry of Finance, regulated the audit of private sector enterprises. The Chinese Association of Certified Public Auditors (CACPA) was responsible for auditing state-owned enterprises and was under the authority of a separate organization, the State Audit Administration. In 1995 CICPA and CACPA merged, keeping the name of the CICPA.

The CICPA sets the requirements for becoming a CPA, administers the CPA examination, develops auditing standards, and is responsible for the code of professional ethics. With the exception that the CICPA reports to a government agency, the regulation of public accounting practice in China may be compared to the system in the United States.

---

[17]Stephen Taylor, "Standard Bearer," *Accountancy* (August 2000): 115.

EXHIBIT 4-3   Accounting Standards for Business Enterprises

Orientation

- A uniform accounting system conforming to international standards designed to meet the needs of China's socialist market economy.
- These standards are incorporated into law.
- The accrual basis, the concept of consistency, the matching of revenue and expenses and the quality of objectivity are all required by the standards.

Assets

- The use of historical cost for assets is specified and a clear distinction between revenue expenditures and capital expenditures must be made.
- Assets should be classified into current and noncurrent categories.
- Inventories may be valued using most conventional methods, including LIFO.
- Fixed assets may be depreciated using the straight-line or the activity method. If the enterprise receives approval, accelerated depreciation may be used.
- Intangible assets, including goodwill, are recognized and are to be amortized over the period benefited.

Liabilities

- Liabilities should be classified as current or long-term.

Equity

- Equity is classified into invested capital, capital reserve, surplus reserve, and undistributed profit. Invested capital represents the face value of stock issued and government investment. Capital reserve represents stock premium, asset revaluation increments, donated capital, etc. Surplus reserve is analogous to appropriated retained earnings, and undistributed profit is analogous to unappropriated retained earnings.

Revenue/Expense/Profit

- Revenues are determined using the accrual basis including the completed contract and percentage-of-completion methods for long-term projects.
- Expenses are determined using the accrual basis and actual costs incurred. Enterprises using standard or estimated costs must adjust variances to actual at the end of the current month.
- The plan for distribution of profits must be shown in the income statement or the notes to the financial statements.

Financial Reporting and Disclosure

- Required reports consist of a balance sheet, an income statement, a statement of changes in financial position (or cash flow statement), supporting schedules, notes, and explanatory statements.
- Comparative financial statements are required.
- Consolidated financial statements are required in cases of 50% or more ownership except for enterprises not suitable for consolidation.
- Notes to financial statements must disclose accounting methods adopted, changes in accounting methods, descriptions of unusual items, and other details and explanations.

Source: Gary M. Winkle, H. Fenwick Huss, and Chen Xi-Zhu, "Accounting Standards in the People's Republic of China: Responding to Economics Reforms," *Accounting Horizons* (September 1994): 54. Used with permission of *Accounting Horizons* and American Accounting Association.

EXHIBIT 4-4   Accounting Systems in China

Industry-Based Systems

- Industrial Enterprise Accounting System
- Commercial Enterprise Accounting System
- Transportation Enterprise Accounting System
- Transportation (Railways) Enterprise Accounting System
- Transportation (Aviation) Enterprise Accounting System
- Transportation (Postal Services and Telecommunication) Enterprise Accounting System
- Hospitality Enterprise Accounting System
- Construction Enterprise Accounting System
- Real Estate Development Enterprise Accounting System
- Agricultural Enterprise Accounting System
- Financial Institution Accounting System
- Insurance Enterprise Accounting System
- Foreign Economic Cooperative Enterprise Accounting System

Ownership-Based Systems

- Foreign Investment Enterprise Accounting System
- Limited Stock Companies Accounting System

Source: Reprinted from *International Journal of Accounting,* Vol. 32, Yin Chen, Peter Jubb and Alfred Tan, "Problems of Accounting Reform in the People's Republic of China" p. 142, copyright 1997 with permission of Elsevier Science.

FINANCIAL REPORTING[18]

The accounting period is required to be the calendar year. Financial statements consist of:

1. Balance sheet
2. Income statement
3. Cash flow statement
4. Notes
5. Supporting schedules

The notes include a statement of accounting policies. As applicable, they discuss such matters as important events and related party transactions. Additionally, the notes disclose changes in capital structure, appropriations of profits, and principal taxes paid. The supporting schedules provide additional details supporting financial statement items. Financial statements must be comparative, in Chinese, and expressed in the Chinese currency, the renminbi. They are required quarterly and annually; the annual financial statements must be audited by a Chinese CPA. Consolidated financial statements are required and the annual statements must provide an overview of the enterprise's financial condition. Chinese listed companies issuing shares to foreign investors

---

[18]Different regulations apply to different types of companies such as state-owned enterprises, collectives, joint stock limited companies, and enterprises with foreign investment. As discussed earlier, China's accounting standards are evolving with the aim of developing a harmonized set of standards for all enterprises. Our discussion of financial reporting requirements and practices is limited to limited-liability companies and those with foreign investors.

(so-called B-shares) must put English and Chinese language versions of their annual reports on the CSRC Web site.[19]

ACCOUNTING MEASUREMENTS

The purchase method must be used to account for business combinations, and goodwill is written off over the period benefited. The equity method is used when the ownership of another enterprise exceeds 20 percent. When ownership exceeds 50 percent, the accounts of the subsidiary are consolidated. For overseas subsidiaries, the balance sheet is translated at the year-end exchange rate, the income statement is translated at the average-for-the-year exchange rate, and any translation difference is shown as a reserve in equity.

Although accounting measurements in China are generally aligned with international accounting practice, they differ somewhat in their emphasis. Compared to international accounting practice, reliability is stressed over relevance, historical cost is more strictly adhered to, and the principle of conservatism is practiced on a more limited basis. Tax law still has some influence, though it is declining.

Historical cost is the basis for valuing tangible assets. They are depreciated over their expected useful lives, normally on a straight-line basis. (Tax law requires straight-line depreciation and is referred to in specifying the useful lives of assets and salvage values.) FIFO, average, and LIFO are acceptable costing methods, and inventory is written down for price declines and obsolescence. Acquired intangibles are also recorded at cost and amortized over the periods benefited. Because land and much of the industrial property in China is owned by the state, companies that acquire the right to use land and industrial property rights show them as intangibles. Assets are revalued when a change in ownership takes place, such as when a state-owned enterprise is privatized. Certified asset assessment firms or CPA firms determine these valuations.

Costs associated with research and development can be capitalized in some circumstances. Finance leases are capitalized and deferred taxes are provided for. Contingent obligations are provided for when they are both probable and a reliable estimate can be made of their amount.

TAIWAN

Taiwan was originally known in the West as Formosa, a name meaning "beautiful island," given to it by Portuguese sailors in the fifteenth century. Taiwan has been predominantly Chinese since becoming a protectorate of the Chinese Empire in 1206. In 1887 Taiwan became a province of China, but from 1895 until 1945 it was a Japanese colony. At the end of World War II, Taiwan reverted to China.

The constitution of the Republic of China was written in 1946. In 1949, defeated by the Communists, the remnants of the Republic of China, led by Chiang Kai-shek, fled to Taiwan and established a provisional government there. Today, Taiwan is officially known as the Republic of China, while mainland China is known as the People's Republic of China. Each maintains claims over the other, which fosters a delicate and complex relationship between them.

Over four decades, Taiwan transformed itself from an underdeveloped, agricultural island to an economic power that is a leading producer of high-technology goods. This

---

[19]www.csrc.gov.cn.

outstanding growth has been based on the success of its manufactured products in export markets. Taiwan's economy has developed in three distinct phases since 1949. During the 1950s, agriculture and import-substituting industries dominated economic growth. The second phase began in the 1960s and focused on export expansion, propelled by the assembly of imported component parts for consumer goods and low technology, light industry. The most recent phase involves high technology and capital intensive industries. Early growth was fueled by substantial economic aid from the United States. Today Taiwan is an aid donor and major investor, especially in Asia. (In fact, Taiwan has significant investments in mainland China.[20])

Taiwan has a dynamic capitalist economy with gradually decreasing government guidance of investment and foreign trade. Small, family-owned businesses are the basis of the economy.[21] Certain strategic industries, such as military goods, petroleum refining, and public utilities were once reserved for the state, and the government had ownership positions in banks and a number of industrial firms, especially those that required large amounts of capital. However, the state is now privatizing its ownership in these firms.

Taiwan can be said to have a credit-based financial system along the lines of Germany and Japan (described in Chapter 3) rather than a capital market-based system. The Taiwan Stock Exchange opened in 1962 and has grown steadily since the second half of the 1980s. Improving the capital market is an important priority of the Taiwanese government. Although most Taiwanese companies are small and closely held by controlling families, the Taiwan Stock Exchange has the largest market capitalization of any emerging stock market.[22]

Today the United States is Taiwan's largest trading partner, taking 25 percent of its exports and supplying 17 percent of its imports.[23] The influence of the United States on accounting in Taiwan is also strong. Financial reporting, auditing, and other aspects of accounting are similar to those found in the United States.

ACCOUNTING REGULATION AND ENFORCEMENT

The Commercial Accounting Law, as amended in 1987, regulates accounting records and financial statements in Taiwan. It applies to enterprises established under the Business Regulation and Company Laws, except for small partnerships or sole proprietors. The law sets forth the accounting records that must be kept and lays out broad provisions for the financial statements, notes, and other disclosures. Requirements include accrual accounting and a calendar year fiscal period. The law also emphasizes that financial accounting is distinct from tax accounting.[24]

Accounting standards are set by the Financial Accounting Standards Committee (FASC) of the Accounting Research and Development Foundation (ARDF). The

---

[20]Since 1990, Taiwan has invested $24 billion there, and there are commitments for an additional $20 billion. See "Taiwan's Tightrope," *BusinessWeek Online*, March 20, 2000.

[21]There is one company for every 18 people, the highest density in the world. Small to medium-sized enterprises make up 98.5 percent of Taiwan's companies, 75 to 80 percent of all employment, and 47 percent of the total economy. See "In Praise of Paranoia: A Survey of Taiwan," *The Economist* (November 7, 1998): 9.

[22]*The Economist, Pocket World in Figures: 2001 Edition*, London: The Economist, 2000, 58.

[23]U.S. Department of State, "Background Notes: Taiwan," October 2000, p. 12.

[24]S. T. Chiang, "Taiwan," chap. 4 in *Financial Reporting in the West Pacific Rim*, T. E. Cooke and R. H. Parker, eds., New York: Routledge, 1994, 138.

ARDF, modeled on the Financial Accounting Foundation in the United States, was established in 1984 to upgrade the level of accounting study, advance the development of accounting and auditing standards, and help industrial and commercial enterprises improve their accounting systems. It is an endowed private institution, but is supervised by the Ministry of Finance. Its board of directors includes government officials, practicing CPAs, academics, representatives of business, and officials of the Taiwan Securities and Exchange Commission. The FASC, also established in 1984, follows a due process procedure much like the U.S. Financial Accounting Standards Board. Before it issues a standard, the FASC prepares an exposure draft, solicits opinions from parties concerned, holds public hearings if necessary, and sometimes prepares revised exposure drafts. Another committee of the ARDF, the Auditing Standards Committee, issues auditing standards, following a process much like the FASC. Accounting and auditing standards are based on national requirements, with reference to both U.S. GAAP and IAS. Companies listed on the Taiwan Stock Exchange face additional disclosure requirements of the Securities and Exchange Commission, an agency within the Ministry of Finance.[25]

The National Federation of CPA Associations (NFCPAA), an organization mandated by the CPA Law of Taiwan, represents the accounting profession. Practicing CPAs in Taiwan belong to one of the provincial or municipal CPA associations, which in turn make up the NFCPAA. The NFCPAA coordinates with government regulatory authorities on matters of concern to the profession, issues statements on professional ethics, and provides continuing professional education. Before the establishment of the ARDF, the NFCPAA also issued accounting and auditing standards.[26] The examination and licensing of CPAs is a government responsibility: The exam is administered by the Ministry of Examinations and CPA certificates are issued by the Ministry of Finance.[27]

FINANCIAL REPORTING

The Commercial Accounting Law requires the following financial statements:

1. Balance sheet
2. Income statement
3. Statement of changes in owners' equity
4. Statement of cash flows
5. Notes

The notes must disclose the following information:

- Summary of significant accounting policies
- Reasons for changes in accounting policies and their effect on the financial statements

---

[25]Young H. Chang, "Taiwan's Accounting Profession: A Response to National Economic Growth," *The International Journal of Accounting* 27, no. 1 (1992): 63–67.

[26]The NFCPAA was founded in 1946 on mainland China in the city of Nanking, and moved with the Nationalist government when it moved to Taiwan in 1949. In the 1950s, a number of American CPAs, working with the U.S. Agency for International Development, assisted in training Taiwanese government accounting personnel. American accounting textbooks are used most often for accounting education in Taiwan, so most CPAs are oriented toward U.S. standards. See S. T. Chiang, "Taiwan," chap. 4 in *Financial Reporting in the West Pacific Rim*, T. E. Cooke and R. H. Parker, eds., New York: Routledge, 1994, 140–141.

[27]Young H. Chang, "Taiwan's Accounting Profession: A Response to National Economic Growth," *The International Journal of Accounting* 27, no. 1 (1992): p. 66.

- Creditors' rights to specific assets
- Material commitments and contingent liabilities
- Limitations on the distribution of profits
- Significant events relating to owners' equity
- Significant subsequent events
- Other items that require explanation to avoid misleading impressions or that require clarification to assist in presenting the financial statements fairly[28]

Financial statements must be comparative and the fiscal period must be the calendar year. Financial statements audited by CPAs are required for publicly held companies and for nonpublic companies with capital in excess of NT$30 million or outstanding bank loans of more than NT$30 million. Banks, insurance companies, and securities firms must have their financial statements audited by CPAs.[29] State-run government enterprises are audited by government auditors. Companies listed on the stock exchange must also provide audited semiannual financial statements, quarterly financial statements reviewed by a CPA, and a monthly sales report.[30]

ACCOUNTING MEASUREMENTS

Consolidated financial statements are required when a company controls another entity, normally more than 50 percent of ownership. The purchase method is required for business combinations; the pooling of interests method is not used. Under the purchase method, assets are transferred on the basis of book values, though adjustments can be made for higher market values. Goodwill is normally capitalized and amortized over 20 years or less. The equity method is used when there is 20 percent or more ownership in another company. Foreign currency translation is consistent with International Accounting Standard 21 and the U.S. SFAS No. 52. The balance sheets of foreign entities that are independent of the parent are translated at the year-end rate and the income statement is translated at the average rate. Translation adjustments are charged to shareholders' equity. The temporal method is used for nonautonomous subsidiaries and the translation adjustment is charged to income.

Fixed assets, including land and natural resources, and intangible assets may be revalued. The government announces values for land each year, and enterprises are allowed to restate land values (annually) in accordance with the government-announced value. Other assets may be revalued in accordance with a government price index when prices rise by more than 25 percent since purchase or previous revaluation. Capital reserve accounts are credited when assets are revalued. Depreciation and amortization are calculated on the basis of estimated useful lives. The method used does not have to conform to the tax law. Intangible assets are amortized over a maximum period of 20 years. Depreciation and amortization of revalued assets are based on their carrying values after revaluation.

---

[28]Ernst & Young, *Doing Business in Taiwan*, New York: Ernst & Young International, 1994, 66–67.
[29]Publicly held companies submit their audited financial statements to the Securities and Exchange Commission and publish them in a daily newspaper. Companies with capital in excess of NT$30 million submit theirs to the Ministry of Economic Affairs, while companies with bank loans of more than $30 million submit their statements to the lending banks. Banks, insurance companies, and securities firms submit their financial statements to the Securities and Exchange Commission.
[30]Price Waterhouse, *Doing Business in Taiwan*, New York: Price Waterhouse World Firm Services BV, 1996, 100.

Inventory is stated at the lower of cost or market; FIFO, LIFO, and average are all acceptable cost flow assumptions. As with depreciation, books need not conform to tax law. Research and development costs are charged to expense when incurred. Accounting for leases, contingencies, and deferred taxes are consistent with U.S. and international approaches. Thus, finance (called *capital*) leases are capitalized and contingent losses are accrued when they are both probable and subject to a reasonable estimate. Interperiod tax allocation is required if timing differences exist; thus, deferred taxes are accrued. Taiwanese companies must also set up a legal reserve in shareholders' equity: Ten percent of net income is appropriated each year until the reserve equals the total authorized capital stock of the company.

MEXICO

Before the Spanish conquest in the 1500s, Mexico was home to several highly advanced cultures, including the Olmecs, Mayas, Toltecs, and Aztecs. Hernando Cortés conquered Mexico in 1521 and founded a Spanish colony that lasted for nearly 300 years. Mexico declared independence in 1810 and an 1821 treaty recognized Mexican independence from Spain. Except for 30 years of internal peace under General Porfirio Díaz (1877 to 1880 and 1884 to 1911), Mexico experienced political and military strife until 1929, when what is now known as the Institutional Revolutionary Party (PRI) was formed. The PRI controlled Mexico's government continuously for 70 years. The 2000 presidential election was won by the National Action Party (PAN), a center-right opposition party, thus ending the supremacy of the PRI in Mexican politics.

Mexico is the most populous Spanish-speaking country in the world and the second most populous country in Latin America (after Portuguese-speaking Brazil).[31] Mexico has a largely free market economy: Government-owned or controlled companies dominate petroleum and public utilities, but private enterprise dominates manufacturing, construction, mining, entertainment, and the service industries. In recent years, the government has also been privatizing its holdings in nonstrategic industries. Like most of Latin America, a decade of liberal reforms has helped reduce inflation, increase the rate of economic growth, and deliver healthier economic fundamentals.[32] Reforms include dismantling protectionist trade barriers, opening up to foreign investment, and signing regional trade agreements. The most important agreement for Mexico is the North American Free Trade Agreement (NAFTA), signed with Canada and the United States in 1994. The United States accounts for three-quarters of Mexico's imports, more than 80 percent of Mexico's exports, and 60 percent of all direct foreign investment.[33]

Family-controlled conglomerates dominate Mexico's private sector and, by world standards, are relatively small.[34] Although Mexico's stock market is the second largest in Latin America, it is still relatively small by international standards, as firms prefer to

---

[31]The capital, Mexico City, is the second most populous city in the world.

[32]This general trend still holds even though Mexico had a recession in 1995 when economic activity shrunk about 7 percent following the 1994 peso devaluation. The economy has since recovered (more briskly than anticipated) with average annual growth over 5 percent.

[33]*The Economist, Pocket World in Figures: 2001 Edition*, London: *The Economist,* 2000, 165; U.S. Department of Commerce, "Mexico Country Commercial Guide FY2001," chap. 10 (www2.usatrade.gov).

[34]*The Economist* notes an interesting paradox. "Capitalism has a much longer history in Latin America than in many parts of Asia. Yet whereas the largest Asian firms have grown swiftly to become household

raise capital through debt rather than equity. This is changing, however, and more and more Mexican firms are entering U.S. capital markets.

Given the dominance of family-controlled enterprises, Mexican companies traditionally guarded their information and were secretive in their financial reporting. This too is changing. Another significant feature of Mexican accounting is the use of comprehensive general price level accounting as a measurement basis.

The U.S. influence on Mexico's economy extends to accounting. "[M]any of the early leaders of the Mexican profession grew up on 'American accounting'"[35] and U.S. textbooks and professional literature (either in the original English or translated into Spanish) are used extensively in the education of accountants and as guidance on accounting issues. NAFTA accelerated a trend toward closer cooperation between professional accounting organizations in Mexico, Canada, and the United States. Today, the accounting standard-setting bodies in these three countries[36] are committed to a program of harmonization and are attempting to work in concert wherever possible. As a founding member of the International Accounting Standards Committee (now International Accounting Standards Board), Mexico is also committed to harmonization with International Accounting Standards.

ACCOUNTING REGULATION AND ENFORCEMENT

The Mexican Commercial Code and income tax laws contain requirements for keeping certain summary accounting records and preparing financial statements, but their influence on financial reporting is generally minimal. The Mexican Institute of Public Accountants (*Instituto Mexicano de Contadores Públicos*) issues accounting and auditing standards in Mexico. Accounting standards are developed by the Institute's Accounting Principles Commission; auditing standards are the responsibility of its Auditing Standards and Procedures Commission. The institute, a federation of state and other local associations of registered public accountants, is an independent nongovernmental professional association representing the overwhelming majority of public accountants. The Mexican accounting profession is mature, well organized, and highly regarded by the business community.

Despite a legal system based on civil law, accounting standard setting in Mexico takes a British-American, or Anglo-Saxon, approach rather than a Continental European one. The standard-setting process is well developed. Before standards are finalized, exposure drafts of proposed standards are issued for review and public comment. Accounting standards are recognized as authoritative by the government, in particular, by the National Banking and Securities Commission, which regulates the Mexican Stock Exchange. Mexican accounting principles do not distinguish between large and small companies, and so are applicable to all business entities. In some cases the National Banking and Securities Commission issues rules for listed companies, which generally limit certain options in generally accepted accounting principles.

---

names across the world, their Latin American counterparts have remained almost unknown outside their own region, or even their own country." (p. 7) See *The Economist*, "Back on the Pitch: A Survey of Business in Latin America" (December 6, 1997): 1–27.

[35]Stephen A. Zeff, *Forging Accounting Principles in Five Countries: A History and an Analysis of Trends,* Champaign, IL: Stipes Publishing, 1971, 96–97.

[36]The Instituto Mexicano de Contadores Públicos, Canadian Institute of Chartered Accountants, and the Financial Accounting Standards Board, respectively.

Requirements for preparing financial statements and having them audited vary by type and size of company. All companies incorporated under Mexican law (*sociedades anónimas*) must appoint at least one statutory auditor to report to the shareholders on the annual financial statements. Statutory auditors do not have to be public accountants, but when a firm uses independent auditors, a member of the auditing firm frequently acts as statutory auditor. Companies or consolidated groups that meet certain size criteria must file a tax-compliance audit report every year with the Federal Tax Audit Department of the Ministry of Finance. The report consists of audited financial statements, additional schedules, and a statement by the auditor that no irregularities were observed regarding compliance with tax laws. This audit must be done by a Mexican public accountant. Finally, companies listed on the Mexican Stock Exchange must submit annual consolidated financial statements, audited by a Mexican public accountant, to the exchange and to the National Banking and Securities Commission.

FINANCIAL REPORTING

Since 1990 the fiscal year of Mexican companies must coincide with the calendar year. Comparative consolidated financial statements must be prepared, consisting of:

1. Balance sheet
2. Income statement
3. Statement of changes in stockholders' equity
4. Statement of changes in financial position
5. Notes

Financial statements must be adjusted for inflation. The effects of the adjustment are shown in the statement of changes in stockholders' equity. The format of the statement of changes in financial position is similar to the statement of cash flows and is divided into operating, investing, and financing activities. However, because it is also prepared in constant pesos, the resulting "cash flows" do not represent cash flows as understood under historical cost accounting.

Notes are an integral part of the financial statements (covered by the auditor's report) and include the following:

- Accounting policies of the company
- Material contingencies
- Commitments for substantial purchases of assets or under lease contracts
- Details of long-term debt and foreign currency exposure
- Limitations on dividends
- Guarantees
- Employees' pension plans
- Transactions with related parties
- Income taxes[37]

---

[37]Price Waterhouse, *Doing Business in Mexico,* New York: Price Waterhouse World Firm Services BV, 1995, 125.

ACCOUNTING MEASUREMENTS[38]

Consolidated financial statements are prepared when a parent company controls another company. Control is indicated by the ability to determine operating and financial policies of a company. Control normally exists when more than 50 percent of a company's common stock is owned, but it can be obtained in other ways, including the ability to appoint management or a majority of the board of directors. The equity method is used when there is influence but not control, normally meaning an ownership level between 10 and 50 percent. Mexico has adopted International Accounting Standard No. 21 on foreign currency translation.

Both the purchase and the pooling of interests methods of accounting for business combinations may be used, depending on the circumstances. If a majority of the shareholders of the acquired company do not retain an interest in the continuing business, the purchase method is used; if they do, pooling is used. Goodwill is the excess of purchase price over the current value of the net assets acquired. It is amortized to income over the expected benefit period, which is limited to 20 years.

General price level accounting is used in Mexico. The historical costs of nonmonetary assets are restated in pesos of current purchasing power by applying factors derived from the National Consumer Price Index (NCPI). (Before 1996, current replacement cost based on appraisals or specific price indices was also acceptable. This approach was eliminated because it was viewed as less reliable and less in line with international standards based on historical cost.) The components of stockholders' equity are also restated using the NCPI. The gain or loss from holding monetary assets and liabilities is included in current period income, but the effects of other restatements are in stockholders' equity. Cost of sales and depreciation expense are expressed in constant pesos on the income statement, consistent with the treatment of inventory and fixed assets.

Research and development is expensed as incurred. Leases are classified as financing or operating. Financing leases—those transferring substantially all the benefits and risks of ownership of the asset—are capitalized, while rents from operating leases are expensed on the income statement. Contingent losses are accrued when they are likely and measurable. General contingency reserves are not acceptable under Mexican GAAP. The partial liability method is used for deferred taxes: They are only provided for timing differences whose reversal is reasonably assured within a definite period of time (generally 3 to 5 years) and will not be replaced by other timing differences of a similar nature and amount. Thus, they are normally not computed for recurring timing differences such as those arising from differences between tax and accounting depreciation. The costs of employee pensions, seniority premiums,[39] and termination pay are accrued currently when they can be reasonably estimated based on actuarial calculations. Statutory (legal) reserves are created by allocating 5 percent of income each year until the reserve equals 20 percent of the value of the outstanding capital stock.

---

[38]As noted earlier, the Mexican Institute of Public Accountants looks to the United States as well as the International Accounting Standards Board in developing generally accepted accounting principles. While the standards do not cover all areas, overall practice is fairness oriented.

[39]Seniority premiums are compensation amounts paid at the termination of employment based on how long the employee has worked. Generally, employees who voluntarily retire must work at least 15 years, but there is no minimum number years for other types of termination, such as redundancy layoffs, or if an employee dies.

EXHIBIT 4-5 Summary of Significant Accounting Practices

	Czech Republic	China	Taiwan	Mexico
1. Consolidated financial statements	Required	Required	Required	Required
2. Statement of cash flows	In notes	Required	Required	Required
3. Business combinations: purchase or pooling	Purchase	Purchase	Purchase	Both
4. Goodwill	Immediate write-off or capitalize & amortize; 5-year maximum	Capitalize & amortize	Capitalize & amortize; 20-year maximum	Capitalize & amortize; 20-year maximum
5. 20% to 50% owned affiliates	Equity method	Equity method	Equity method	Equity method[1]
6. Asset valuation	Historical cost	Historical cost	Revaluation allowed	Constant purchasing power
7. Depreciation	Economic based	Economic based[2]	Economic based	Economic based
8. LIFO inventory valuation	Not used	Acceptable	Acceptable	Acceptable[3]
9. Finance leases	Not capitalized	No guidance	Capitalized	Capitalized
10. Deferred taxes	Accrued for depreciation differences only	No guidance	Accrued	Partial liability method

[1]When ownership exceeds 10%.
[2]With reference to tax law.
[3]But with inflation accounting, not used.

Exhibit 4-5 summarizes the significant accounting practices in the four countries surveyed in this chapter.

Selected References

Canadian Institute of Chartered Accountants, *Significant Differences in GAAP in Canada, Chile, Mexico, and the United States,* 3d ed., Toronto: CICA, 2000.

Chang, Y. H., "Taiwan's Accounting Profession: A Response to National Economic Growth," *The International Journal of Accounting* 27, no. 1 (1992): 57–68.

Chen, C. J. P., F. A. Gu, and X. Su, "A Comparison of Reported Earnings under Chinese GAAP vs. IAS: Evidence from the Shanghai Stock Exchange," *Accounting Horizons* (June 1999): 91–111.

Chen, Y., P. Jubb, and A. Tran, "Problems of Accounting Reform in the People's Republic of China," *The International Journal of Accounting* 32, no. 2 (1997): 139–153.

Cooke, T. E., and R. H. Parker, eds., *Financial Reporting in the West Pacific Rim,* London: Routledge, 1994.

Davis-Friday, P. Y., and J. M. Rivera, "Inflation Accounting and 20-F Disclosures: Evidence from Mexico," *Accounting Horizons* (June 2000): 113–135.

Graham, R. C., and C. C. Wang, "Taiwan and International Accounting Standards: A Comparison," *The International Journal of Accounting* 30, no. 2 (1995): 149–167.

Hilmy, J., "Communists Among Us in a Market Economy: Accountancy in the People's Republic of China," *The International Journal of Accounting* 34, no. 4 (1999): 491–515.

Jeffrey, G., "Down Mexico Way," *Accountancy International* (March 1999): 90–02.

Jermakowicz, E., and D. D. F. Rinke, "The New Accounting Standards in the Czech Republic, Hungary, and Poland Vis-a-Vis International Accounting Standards and European Union Directives," *Journal of International Accounting & Taxation* 5, no. 1 (1996): 73–87.

Ma, R., ed., *Financial Reporting in the Pacific Asia Region*, Singapore: World Scientific Publishing, 1997.

PriceWaterhouseCoopers, *Doing Business (Czech Republic, Mexico, People's Republic of China, Taiwan)*, New York: Price Waterhouse World Firm Services BV, 1999, 1995, 1999, 1996, respectively.

PriceWaterhouseCoopers, *IAS, US GAAP and Czech GAAP: Similarities and Differences,* Prague: PWC, October 1999.

Schroll, R., "The New Accounting System in the Czech Republic," *The European Accounting Review* 4, no. 4 (1995): 827–832.

Schwartz, C. H., and M. S. Agnew, "Comparative Survey of Accounting Practices in Argentina, Brazil, Chile, Mexico, and the United States," *Bear Stearns Latin Fixed Income Corporate Credit Research* (February 4, 1997): 1–16.

Sucher, P., P. Moizer, and M. Zarova, "The Images of the Big Six Audit Firms in the Czech Republic," *European Accounting Review* 8, no. 3 (1999): 499–521.

Sucher, P., W. Seal, and I. Zelenka, "True and Fair in the Czech Republic: A Note on Local Perceptions," *The European Accounting Review* 5, no. 3 (1996): 545–557.

Xiang, B., "Institutional Factors Influencing China's Accounting Reforms and Standards," *Accounting Horizons* (June 1998): 105–119.

Xiao, Z., "Corporate Disclosures Made by Chinese Listed Companies," *The International Journal of Accounting* 34, no. 3 (1999): 349–373.

Xiao, Z., and A. Pan, "Developing Accounting Standards on the Basis of a Conceptual Framework by the Chinese Government," *The International Journal of Accounting* 32, no. 3 (1997): 279–299.

Discussion Questions

1. Level of education affects a nation's accounting development (see Chapter 2). One measure of education level is the literacy rate. *Pocket World in Figures 2001* (London: *The Economist,* 2000) gives the following literacy rates: China, 83 percent; Czech Republic, 99 percent; Mexico, 90 percent; and Taiwan, 94 percent. What do these literacy rates suggest about accounting in these four countries?

2. Exhibit 4-2 shows that 29 Mexican companies are listed on the New York Stock Exchange (as of December 2000). The 29 listings occurred as follows: 1991, 2; 1992, 3; 1993, 7; 1994, 9; 1995, 0; 1996, 2; 1997, 2; 1998, 2; 1999, 1; 2000, 1. What does the pattern of listings between 1991 and 2000 suggest?

3. The chapter states that accounting and auditing standard setting in Taiwan is patterned after that in the United States. What are the similarities and differences in standard setting in the two nations?

4. Does the development of accounting lead or lag behind the development of a nation's economy? Cite evidence from this chapter to support your answer.

5. Both China and the Czech Republic are restructuring their economies from central planning to more of a market orientation. What are the similarities and differences in the approaches each country is taking in embracing market reforms?

6. Even before Hong Kong reverted to China in 1997, China was well on the way toward developing accounting standards compatible with International Accounting Standards. How will the return of Hong Kong likely affect China's accounting standards?

7. What are the important features of accounting and financial reporting that are necessary to develop an efficient stock market with fair trading? How likely is it that the countries in this chapter will develop such a stock market? Why do you think so?

8. What is the role of tax legislation on financial accounting practices in each of the four countries treated in this chapter?

9. The Czech Republic is developing a body of accounting requirements consistent with European Union Directives. What evidence is there that Czech accounting requirements comply with these Directives? (Hint: You may want to refer to the discussion of the European Union in Chapter 8.)

10. China's aim is to develop accounting standards that are harmonized with international practices. What examples are there that Chinese accounting standards are consistent with "world class" practices?

11. What evidence is there that accounting practices in Taiwan are similar to those found in the United States?

12. Mexican companies that list their shares on the New York Stock Exchange are required by the U.S. Securities and Exchange Commission to reconcile net income and stockholders' equity from Mexican to U.S. GAAP. What are likely to be the most significant reconciliation items?

Exercises

1. This chapter provides synopses of national accounting practice systems in four emerging economies.

   Required: For each country, list:
   a. The name of the national financial accounting standard-setting board or agency.
   b. The name of the agency, institute, or other organization charged with supervising and enforcing financial accounting standards.

2. The International Federation of Accountants (IFAC) is a worldwide organization of professional accounting bodies. IFAC's Web site (www.ifac.org) has links to accounting bodies around the world.

   Required: Visit IFAC's Web site. List the accounting organizations discussed in this chapter that are linked to IFAC's Web site.

3. Reread Chapter 4 and its discussion questions.

   Required:
   a. As you go through this material, prepare a list of eight expressions, terms, or short phrases unfamiliar or unusual in your home country.
   b. Write a concise definition or explanation of each item.

4. Analyze the four national accounting practice systems summarized in the chapter.

   Required:
   a. For each of the four countries treated in the chapter, select the most important financial accounting practice or principle at variance with international norms.
   b. For each selection you make, briefly state your reasons for including it on your list.

5. Refer to Exhibit 4-2.

   Required: Discuss the factors that might explain the listing pattern observed in the table.

6. Several companies from the four countries treated in this chapter are listed on the New York Stock Exchange (NYSE), Nasdaq, and the London Stock Exchange.

   Required: Go to the NYSE Web site (www.nyse.com). Identify the companies listed on the NYSE from each of the four countries treated in this chapter and indicate the year that each company became listed. Do the same for the Nasdaq (www.nasdaq.com) and the London Stock Exchange (www.londonstockexchange.com).

7. Chapter 2 discussed certain socioeconomic and institutional factors that affect accounting development. These were (1) sources of finance, (2) legal system, (3) taxation, (4) political and economic ties, (5) inflation, (6) level of economic development, and (7) education level.

   Required:

   a. Identify the factor that you think is the most important influence on accounting in each of the four countries treated in this chapter.

   b. Explain the significance of this factor and why you think it is the most important one.

8. Refer to Exercise 7.

   Required:

   a. Identify the factor that you think is the least important influence on accounting in each of the four countries treated in this chapter.

   b. Explain why you think it is the least important one.

9. Several companies from the four countries treated in this chapter refer to International Accounting Standards in their annual reports.

   Required: Go to the Web site of the International Accounting Standards Board (www.iasb.org.uk). Identify the companies from China, the Czech Republic, Mexico, and Taiwan that refer to International Accounting Standards.

10. The role of government in developing accounting and auditing standards varies in the four countries treated in this chapter.

    Required: Compare the role of government in developing accounting and auditing standards in China, the Czech Republic, Mexico, and Taiwan.

11. Accounting standard setting in most countries involves a combination of private and public sector groups. The private sector includes the accounting profession and other groups affected by the financial reporting process, such as users and preparers of financial statements and labor. The public sector includes government agencies such as tax authorities, ministries responsible for commercial law, and securities commissions. The stock market is another potential influence.

    Required: Complete a matrix indicating whether each of these groups significantly influences accounting standard setting in the four countries discussed in this chapter. List the groups across the top and the countries down the side; indicate the influence of each group with a yes or no.

12. The following are certain financial ratios used by analysts:
    - *Liquidity:* current ratio; cash flow from operations to current liabilities
    - *Solvency:* debt to equity; debt to assets
    - *Profitability:* return on assets; return on equity

    Required: Assume that you are comparing the financial ratios of companies from two countries discussed in this chapter. Discuss how the accounting practices identified in Exhibit 4-5 would affect your comparisons for each of the six ratios listed.

Case 4–1   Does Secrecy Pay?

SIGN OF THE TIMES: TRANSPARENCY AWARDS

Prague: Czech Republic[1]

By Robert Patton

If the "ABN AMRO Signum Temporis Awards for disclosure" had been held in 1994, Seliko probably would not have walked off with a prize.

Back then, an analyst for Atlantik Financial Markets brokerage asked the managers of this Czech food producer to discuss their business plans. Sure, they said—for $200 an hour.

Several weeks of the analyst's phone calls finally wore down Seliko's top brass, which eventually met with him free of charge.

Still, the episode is a particularly appalling example of an all-too-common problem: Czech managers are notoriously tight-fisted with company information.

Through events such as the bank's Signum Temporis ("sign of the time") awards for best corporate disclosure, planned for Feb. 27 at the Prague Stock Exchange (PSE) Ball, brokers are trying to persuade executives to be more open. Award officials say some Czech companies are finally realizing that to attract more investment, they must let investors know what they're getting into.

But analysts say many Czech companies continue to frustrate investors' attempts to obtain such information. Despite the progress made so far, regional rivals Poland and Hungary have left the Czechs in the dust.

Some Czech firms simply give out as little information as possible, analysts say, and others take months to release basic financial data. Still others fail to publicize results.

A company might release new financial data, "but unless you call them, you don't know about it," said ING Barings analyst Vojtech

Kraus. "They'll just tell investors who happened to come see them that week."

Some Czech companies, particularly large conglomerates, may have good intentions but simply aren't experienced at quickly compiling and disseminating their financial data. Financial-industrial giant Skoda Plzen is good example of this, said Patria Finance analyst Ondrej Datka.

Leaving aside the shady managers with something to hide, many others simply don't believe it's important to keep investors informed.

Secretive companies often have managers with attitudes forged during the '70s and '80s, said Pavel Kohout, a portfolio manager at ING Investment Management. Under communism, secrecy—not transparency—was the watchword.

The conglomerate Chemapol is the quintessential example of a company run by old dogs who can't or simply won't learn new capitalist tricks. They've been "used to being opaque since communism," Kohout said.

Coupon privatization did little to change such attitudes. Many managers find themselves in publicly traded companies against their will.

Many Czech companies "didn't come to the stock market," said Datka. "They found themselves on the stock market as a result of privatization."

By contrast, many Polish and Hungarian firms have issued initial public offerings (IPOs) of stock and so are more concerned with investor satisfaction.

Analysts typically want a balance sheet, profit/loss statement, a cash-flow statement, and basic information about corporate outlook and goals. Legislation and PSE regulations help investors by forcing companies to divulge key financial data.

Every company with tradable securities must publish annual and semiannual reports and send them to the Finance Ministry and Czech Sta-

---

[1]Does Secrecy Pay? By Robert Patton, *The Prague Post* (February 25, 1998) www.praguepost.cz

tistical Office. And companies whose stock is traded on the PSE's primary and secondary markets must also release quarterly financial reports.

But the PSE doesn't enforce its deadlines strictly enough, said Datka. And some companies submit financial data to the PSE that is timely but "unconsolidated"—that is, it does not incorporate data for subsidiaries.

That's not very useful, because in many cases "unconsolidated data don't mean anything," Datka said, and consolidated figures often don't appear until months later.

The semiannual reports to the Ministry of Finance, too, often linger "somewhere on the table of some clerk in the Finance Ministry" for as long as two months before becoming available to the public, complained Milon Miller, project manager for the Prague branch of Consultants PlanEcon.

Investors hope capital-markets reform will stimulate foreign strategic investment into Czech companies and help make them more transparent. Strategic investors are more likely to discipline managers, said Central Europe Privatization Fund President Howard Golden.

Under such owners, secretive executives "would be more transparent or they would be out," Golden said.

The trend may have already begun. Komercni Banka, SPT Telecom and tram-maker CKD have become more generous, analysts say. In many cases, such firms are providing more information partly to attract investors.

Several analysts said the improvement is steady but incremental. Golden went so far as to say that Czech firms are "light-years ahead of where they were two to three years ago."

Is Seliko riding this wave of increasing transparency? Well, sort of.

Now that it's partly owned by the Olpran Group, Seliko wouldn't try to charge for information, Olpran spokeswoman Marie Logrova insisted.

"We wouldn't go that far, but the information we'd give out probably wouldn't be that precise," she said. "We'd have to check with the other shareholders of Seliko before providing more specific information."

And who are Seliko's other shareholders?

"I'm not authorized to answer that."

REQUIRED

1. Describe the financial reporting practices of Czech companies, as characterized in the newspaper article.
2. What are the likely causes of these practices?
3. How do these practices compare to the reporting requirements identified in the chapter?
4. What are the consequences of these practices for investors, the reporting companies, and the Prague Stock Exchange?

Case 4–2   After NAFTA

In 1992 the accounting standard-setting bodies in Canada, Mexico, and the United States (the Canadian Institute of Chartered Accountants, Instituto Mexicano de Contadores Públicos, and Financial Accounting Standards Board, respectively) did a joint study of the similarities and differences in the accounting standards of

the three countries, the underlying concepts, and the standard-setting processes. The study was a first step in spurring future cooperation for progress in accounting harmonization among the three countries. The following are certain findings taken from the joint study, published in 1994.

FINANCIAL REPORTING IN NORTH AMERICA[1]

A nation's capital markets bring together those who are seeking funds and those who have funds to lend or invest. Those who have funds to lend or invest, including individuals, investment companies, insurance companies, pension funds, banks and other thrift institutions, governments, and business corporations try to balance risks and returns.

A nation's capital markets involve both domestic and foreign consumers and providers of capital. Some capital markets are public and highly competitive, and some are private and relatively noncompetitive. In all cases, to balance risks and returns, suppliers of capital need relevant and reliable financial information about companies that are seeking capital. For that reason, accounting standards are important for capital markets.

Differences in the capital markets and economic conditions between Canada, Mexico, and the U.S. may have contributed to differences in the scope and specificity of each country's accounting standards. . . .

Of the three countries, the U.S. has, by far, the largest public capital markets. Canada's capital markets, although smaller than those of the U.S., contain many of the same characteristics—a high degree of competition, large numbers of suppliers and consumers of capital, and a wide range of debt, equity and derivative securities. Moreover, the U.S. is Canada's largest trading partner and supplier of foreign capital. It is understandable, therefore, that U.S. and Canadian accounting standards are often parallel. . . .

In contrast to Canada and the U.S., Mexico's capital market is characterized by tight control by the majority shareholders of listed companies and significant, but decreasing, participation by the Mexican government. This may be one of the reasons why Mexico's accounting standards are less specific in certain circumstances.

Economic conditions also can affect accounting standards. One example is Mexico's adoption of inflation accounting. . . . Canada and the U.S. do not include inflation adjustments in financial statements. Both, however, allow financial disclosures adjusted for either specific price changes or general inflation as supplemental information.

Despite differences in their capital markets and economic conditions, all three countries currently are experiencing certain similar economic trends:

- Growing and substantial reliance on foreign sources of capital
- Broader ownership of companies
- Growing reliance on each other as major international trading partners
- Government policies that encourage or emphasize the need for price stability.

If those trends continue, the demands of financial statement users in all three countries will become increasingly similar—suggesting the need for greater comparability and improvement in their accounting standards.

REQUIRED

1. Discuss the influence of capital market structures and economic conditions on accounting in Canada, Mexico, and the United States.
2. Based on your discussion in question 1, what features of accounting would you expect to find in these three countries? What accounting similarities and differences exist between Canada, Mexico, and the United States?
3. How likely is it that accounting in the NAFTA countries can be harmonized in the future? What factors are likely to promote such harmonization? What factors are likely to inhibit harmonization?

---

[1]Canadian Institute of Chartered Accountants, Instituto Mexicano de Contadores Públicos, and Financial Accounting Standards Board, *Financial Reporting in North America: Highlights of a Joint Study*, Norwalk: FASB, 1994, 3–5.

CHAPTER 5

REPORTING AND DISCLOSURE

In this chapter we examine the transmission of financial and nonfinancial information in an international setting. Much of our discussion addresses disclosure related to financial reporting for external users. We focus on selected topics and do not attempt to discuss every disclosure issue that applies to financial statement users, preparers, and financial professionals.

As noted in Chapter 1, the relative importance of equity markets in national economies is growing (see Exhibit 1-4), and "retail" (individual noninstitutional) investors are becoming more active in those markets. As a result, public disclosure, investor protection, shareholder value, and stock market-driven forms of corporate governance are becoming increasingly important. Thus, although disclosure practices vary substantially from country to country, they are converging. Hundreds of companies have increased their disclosures by (1) voluntarily adopting IAS or U.S. GAAP; (2) complying with domestic and overseas stock exchange and regulatory requirements; or (3) responding to various demands for information from investors and analysts.[1] However, important differences among countries will continue to affect all but the largest firms, particularly those that are not active in international capital or product markets.

Government regulators who seek to maintain or increase the credibility of their national capital markets also influence disclosure practices around the world. Stock exchanges have concluded that their continued growth and success depends on offering a high-quality market with effective investor protection. As a result, oversight by regulators and stock exchanges is increasing and disclosure requirements are becoming more stringent. The trend toward greater investor protection and enhanced disclosure will continue as stock exchanges face growing competition from each other and from less-regulated trading systems.

---

[1] For example, Schering AG, a German company, states the following in its *Annual Report 2000* "Investor Relations Activities" section: "We set great store by open communication with investors. Apart from publishing detailed interim reports every quarter, we stage regular telephone conferences and roadshows and maintain personal contacts with financial analysts and investors, all of which ensures an intense discussion on the company's development and goals."

DEVELOPMENT OF DISCLOSURE

The development of disclosure systems closely parallels the development of accounting systems discussed in Chapter 2.[2] Disclosure standards and practices are influenced by sources of finance, legal systems, political and economic ties, level of economic development, education level, culture, and other influences.

National differences in disclosure are driven largely by differences in corporate governance and finance. In the United States, the United Kingdom, and other Anglo-American countries, equity markets have provided most corporate financing and have become highly developed. In these markets, ownership tends to be spread among many shareholders, and investor protection is emphasized. Institutional investors play a growing role in these countries, demanding financial returns and increased shareholder value. Public disclosure is highly developed in response to companies' accountability to the public.

In many other countries (such as France, Germany, Japan, and numerous emerging market countries), shareholdings remain highly concentrated and banks (and/or family owners) traditionally have been the primary source of corporate financing. Structures are in place to protect incumbent management. Banks (which sometimes are both creditors and owners) and other insiders (such as corporate members of interlocking shareholder groups) provide discipline. These banks, insiders, and others are closely informed about the company's financial position and its activities. Public disclosure is less developed in these markets and large differences in the amount of information given to large shareholders and creditors vis-à-vis the public may be permitted.

VOLUNTARY DISCLOSURE

Managers have better information about their firm's current and future performance than do external parties. Several studies show that managers have incentives to disclose such information voluntarily. Benefits of enhanced disclosure may include lower transaction costs in the trading of the firm's securities, greater interest in the company by financial analysts and investors, increased share liquidity, and lower cost of capital. In one recent report[3], the Financial Accounting Standards Board (FASB) describes a FASB business reporting project that supports the view that companies can achieve capital markets benefits by enhancing their voluntary disclosure. The report includes guidance on how companies can describe and explain their investment potential to investors.

As investors around the world demand more detailed and timely information, voluntary disclosure levels are increasing in both highly developed and emerging market countries. It is widely recognized, however, that financial reporting can be an imperfect

---

[2]The terms "disclosure systems" and "accounting systems" overlap considerably. Often, as in Chapter 2 of this text, "accounting development" refers to the development of accounting standards and practices. "Disclosure development" as discussed in this chapter refers to the development of financial and nonfinancial disclosures presented in financial reports. We do not discuss disclosures made in press releases ("timely disclosure") at length, although much of the discussion in this chapter applies to this area.

[3]Financial Accounting Standards Board, *Improving Business Reporting: Insights into Enhancing Voluntary Disclosures*, as discussed in *Journal of Accountancy*, March 2001, page 8 and available at the FASB Web site at www.rutgers.edu/Accounting/raw/fasb/brrp/brrp2.html.

mechanism for communicating with outside investors when managers' incentives are not perfectly aligned with the interests of all shareholders. In one classic paper, the authors argue that managers' communication with outside investors is imperfect when: (1) managers have superior information about their firm; (2) managers' incentives are not perfectly aligned with all shareholders' interests; and (3) accounting rules and auditing are imperfect.[4] The authors state that contracting mechanisms (such as compensation linking managers' rewards to long-term share values) can reduce this conflict.

Evidence strongly indicates that corporate managers often have strong incentives to delay the disclosure of adverse news, "manage" their financial reports to convey a more positive image of the firm, and overstate their firms' financial performance and prospects. For example, executives face significant risks of being dismissed in firms whose financial or stock market performance is relatively weak. Seriously stressed firms may have a higher risk of bankruptcy, acquisition, or hostile takeover, leading to a management change. Also, the possible competitive disadvantage created when proprietary information is made public may offset the benefits of full disclosure.

Regulation (such as accounting and disclosure regulation) and third-party certification (such as auditing) can improve the functioning of markets. Accounting regulation attempts to reduce managers' ability to record economic transactions in ways that are not in shareholders' best interests. Disclosure regulation sets forth requirements to ensure that shareholders receive timely, complete, and accurate information. External auditors try to ensure that managers apply appropriate accounting policies, make reasonable accounting estimates, maintain adequate accounting records and control systems, and provide the required disclosures in a timely manner.

Although these mechanisms can strongly influence practice, managers occasionally conclude that the benefits of noncompliance with reporting requirements (e.g., a higher stock price due to inflated earnings) outweigh the costs (e.g., the risk of job loss and litigation resulting in criminal or civil penalties if the noncompliance is detected and reported). Thus, managers' disclosure choices reflect the combined effects of disclosure requirements and their incentives to disclose information voluntarily.

REGULATORY DISCLOSURE REQUIREMENTS

To protect investors, most securities exchanges (together with professional or government regulatory bodies such as the U.S. Securities and Exchange Commission and the Ministry of Finance in Japan) impose reporting and disclosure requirements on domestic and foreign companies that seek access to their markets. These exchanges want to make sure that investors have enough information to allow them to evaluate a company's performance and prospects. Nowhere is this concern more evident than in the United States, whose disclosure standards generally are considered to be the most stringent in the world.

Stock exchanges and government regulators generally require foreign listed firms to furnish almost the same financial and nonfinancial information as that required of domestic companies.[5] Foreign listed firms generally have some flexibility in the accounting

---

[4]See P. M. Healy and K. G. Palepu, "The Effect of Firms' Financial Disclosure Strategies on Stock Prices," *Accounting Horizons* 7 (March 1993), 1–11.
[5]Many countries, (e.g., the People's Republic of China and the Czech Republic) do not allow foreign companies to list their shares.

principles used and the extent of disclosure. In many countries, foreign listed firms must file with the stock exchange any information made public, distributed to shareholders, or filed with regulators in the domestic market. However, many countries do not monitor or enforce this "cross-jurisdictional conformity of disclosure" requirement.

Shareholder protection varies substantially among countries. Anglo-American countries such as Canada, the United Kingdom, and the United States provide extensive and strictly enforced shareholder protection. In contrast, shareholder protection receives less emphasis in other parts of the world. For example, while both the Shanghai and Shenzhen stock exchanges in China prohibit insider trading, they do not define this offense. Shareholder protection codes in the Czech Republic, Mexico, and many other emerging market countries also are rudimentary.[6] Even in many developed countries, the concept of investor protection is of recent origin, and many commentators argue that it still is inadequate. For example, insider trading was not a criminal offense in Germany until the enactment of the Securities Trading Act 1994.

Exhibit 5-1 presents the broad objectives of investor-oriented equity markets. As noted earlier, investor protection is a primary goal of these markets. As Exhibit 5-1

EXHIBIT 5-1 Broad Objectives for Investor-Oriented Equity Markets

Objectives: *Investor Protection*	*Market Quality*
Investors are provided with material information and are protected through monitoring and enforcement.	Markets are fair, orderly, efficient and free from abuse and misconduct.

Specifically:

1. Provide investors with material information.	1. Promote equitable access to information and trading opportunities (market fairness).
2. Monitor and enforce market rules.	2. Enhance liquidity and reduce transaction costs (market efficiency).
3. Inhibit fraud in the public offering, trading, voting and tendering of securities.	3. Contribute to freedom from abuse through monitoring and enforcement.
4. Seek comparability of financial and non-financial information (allow investors to compare companies across industries and domiciles).	4. Foster investor confidence.
	5. Facilitate capital formation.
	6. Seek conditions in which prices reflect investor perceptions of value without being arbitrary or capricious (market orderliness).

Principles:

1. *Cost Effectiveness.* The cost of market regulation should be proportionate to the benefits it secures.
2. *Market Freedom and Flexibility.* Regulation should not impede competition and market evolution.
3. *Transparent Financial Reporting and Full and Complete Disclosure.*
4. *Equal Treatment of Foreign and Domestic Firms.*

Source: Carol A. Frost and Mark Lang, "Foreign Companies and U.S. Securities Markets: Financial Reporting Policy Issues and Suggestions for Research," *Accounting Horizons* 10 (March 1996): 95–109. Used with permission of *Accounting Horizons* and American Accounting Association.

---

[6]Refer to Case 4-1, "Does Secrecy Pay?," in Chapter 4 and Case 8-2 "Accounting Quality in East Asia," in Chapter 8.

shows, this requires that investors receive timely material information and are protected through effective monitoring and enforcement. Disclosure should be sufficient to allow investors to compare companies across industries and domiciles. Implicit in Exhibit 5-1 is the idea that full and credible disclosure will enhance investor confidence, which will increase liquidity, reduce transaction costs, and improve overall market quality.

THE U.S. SEC FINANCIAL REPORTING DEBATE

The SEC generally requires foreign registrants to furnish financial information substantially similar to that required of domestic companies. However, foreign registrants' financial statements need not be prepared in accordance with U.S. GAAP if they are presented in accordance with another comprehensive body of accounting principles and are accompanied by a quantitative reconciliation to U.S. GAAP of net income, shareholders' equity, and earnings per share, if materially different.

Whether the reconciliation requirement helps or hinders the SEC in meeting its regulatory objectives is widely debated. The SEC's reporting requirements are generally consistent with the objectives of investor protection and market quality. However, stringent reporting requirements may achieve the goal of investor protection at the cost of reducing investment opportunities or imposing high transaction costs on investing.

Some commentators argue that the SEC's financial reporting requirements for foreign companies deter these companies from making their securities available in the United States.[7] As a result, it is claimed that U.S. investors are more likely to trade in markets such as the U.S. Over-the-Counter (OTC) market or overseas markets where liquidity may be relatively low, transaction costs relatively high, and investor protection less important than on the national exchanges in the United States. It then is argued that the SEC could provide U.S. investors with more investment opportunities within the regulated U.S. markets by relaxing its financial reporting requirements; this, in turn, would better balance the SEC's objectives of investor protection and market quality. It also is argued that the SEC's registration requirements actually may mislead U.S. investors by giving a false appearance of comparability to foreign financial statements that may require a significantly different interpretation than U.S. statements.

Others counter that the current accounting and disclosure system both protects investors and ensures the quality of U.S. capital markets.[8] Underlying this argument are the principles of full disclosure and equal treatment of foreign and domestic issuers. If investors in domestic securities require financial information based on U.S. GAAP to make informed decisions, then such information is just as necessary for making informed decisions about non-U.S. securities. Indeed, the competitive strength of U.S. capital markets, including their substantial liquidity and high level of investor confidence, often is attributed (at least in part) to the SEC's existing disclosure system and vigorous

---

[7]See J. L. Cochrane, "Are U.S. Regulatory Requirements for Foreign Firms Appropriate?" *Fordham International Law Journal* 17 (Symposium) 1994, S58–S67; J. L. Cochrane, J. E. Shapiro, and J. E. Tobin, "Foreign Equities and U.S. Investors: Breaking Down the Barriers Separating Supply and Demand," *Stanford Journal of Law, Business and Finance*, 1997.

[8]See Richard C. Breeden, "Foreign Companies and U.S. Securities Markets in a Time of Economic Transformation," *Fordham International Law Journal* 17 (Symposium) 1994, S77–S96; and Pat McConnell, "Practical Company Experience in Entering U.S. Markets: Significant Issues and Hurdles from the Advisor's Perspective," *Fordham International Law Journal* 17 (Symposium) 1994, S120–S128.

enforcement. It also has been argued that the SEC's reporting requirements are not the primary obstacles to foreign companies desiring to list securities in the United States.

REPORTING REQUIREMENTS FOR LISTED COMPANIES IN TEN EQUITY MARKETS

This section presents selected reporting and disclosure requirements for domestic and foreign companies listed on stock exchanges in the 10 countries discussed in Chapters 3 and 4: the People's Republic of China (China), the Czech Republic, France, Germany, Japan, Mexico, the Netherlands, the Republic of China (Taiwan), the United Kingdom, and the United States.[9]

Chapters 3 and 4 describe accounting practice and regulation in these 10 countries. This section provides additional discussion of reporting requirements established by stock exchanges and national (or regional) regulatory bodies for stock exchange-listed companies. These entities establish and enforce requirements for annual reports, interim reports, and timely disclosure, which refers to the prompt disclosure (to the public, to stock exchanges, and to regulatory agencies) of material, nonpublic information that may affect investors' decisions about the listed securities, or the prices of the listed securities. Requirements cover such areas as the contents of the financial reports, when they must be filed, whether they must be audited, and to whom they must be distributed.

In many countries, foreign (and occasionally domestic) companies are allowed (or required) to file financial statements prepared in conformity with International Accounting Standards (IAS) or sets of accounting principles other than the local (national) accounting principles. Companies listed on stock exchanges in the European Union will be required to use IAS no later than 2005, as discussed in Chapter 8.

PROSPECTUSES

Stock exchanges and regulators also promulgate requirements concerning the preparation and distribution of prospectuses (also called listing or offering documents, offering circulars, etc.) A prospectus usually is required to raise capital or list securities on organized stock exchanges. The prospectus contains information necessary to enable investors and their advisors to make an informed evaluation of the issuer, its prospects, its financial position and performance, and the securities being offered or listed. Although local requirements specify the contents of a prospectus, it usually must include at least the following:

- a history of the company;
- details of the company's operations, its markets and competitors, and its risks;

---

[9]Stock exchanges provided most of the information in this section. Also see: Meridian Securities Markets, *World Stock Exchange Fact Book 2000,* Round Rock, TX: 2000; David Rathborne and Deborah Ritchie, eds., *The Salomon Smith Barney Guide to World Equity Markets 2000,* London: Euromoney Books and Salomon Smith Barney, 2000; Robert C. Rosen, ed., *International Securities Regulation: Stock Exchanges of the World: Selected Rules and Regulations,* USA: Oceana Publications, 2000; and Herbie Skeete, ed., *The Bridge Handbook of World Stock, Derivative & Commodity Exchanges 2000, Tenth Anniversary Edition,* Welwyn Garden City, Hers, U.K.: Mondo Visione, 2000.

- information about the company's directors and senior management;
- audited historical financial information of the company; and
- details about the securities being listed.[10]

CHINA

OVERVIEW

Equity markets in China were restarted in 1978 when the Chinese government began turning to a market-oriented economy. The Chinese government has permitted the issuance of a new class of stock, called "B" shares, which are now available to both domestic and foreign investors[11]. "A" shares are reserved for domestic investors, who now also are allowed to own B shares. "H" shares have been introduced for listings by Chinese companies in Hong Kong, and "N" shares for NYSE listings.

The Chinese equity market has tremendous growth potential. As shown in Exhibit 1-4 of Chapter 1, equity market capitalization in China was only 34 percent of GDP at year-end 1998, a lower percentage than every other country shown with the exceptions of Mexico and the Czech Republic. Government investigators have recently been trying to crack down on market manipulation and other activities that have undermined confidence in Chinese equity markets. However, China remains a closed market in many respects, and foreign companies are not allowed to list there.

EQUITY MARKETS IN CHINA

Two stock exchanges operate in China: The Shanghai Securities Exchange (SHSE) and the Shenzhen Stock Exchange (SZSE).

REGULATION

The China Securities Regulatory Commission (CSRC) directly administers the SHSE and SZSE. The two exchanges now apply the same listing requirements.

ACCOUNTING PRINCIPLE REQUIREMENTS

Companies that list A shares are required to prepare their financial statements in conformance with accounting standards promulgated by the PRC Ministry of Finance. Companies that list B shares may prepare accounts adjusted to IAS. Companies that have issued H shares may follow either IAS or Hong Kong accounting standards.

---

[10]See PricewaterhouseCoopers, *Accessing International Capital Markets*, New York: Pricewaterhouse-Coopers, 2001.

[11]Ownership in B shares was restricted to foreign investors for many years. In March, 2001, Beijing began allowing Chinese investors to buy B shares as one of its initiatives to make Chinese markets more attractive to local investors. See Matt Pottinger, "Big Chinese IPOs Are Stalled for Now," *The Wall Street Journal*, March 20, 2001, page A14.

FINANCIAL REPORTING AND DISCLOSURE REQUIREMENTS

Listed companies are required to file an annual report within 4 months after the end of each fiscal year, and an interim report within 2 months after the end of the first 6 months.

Listed companies are required to report material events to the relevant authorities promptly. The Securities Law lists the events that trigger a disclosure obligation.

CZECH REPUBLIC

OVERVIEW

The Czech Republic once hampered foreign investment, but recently has been welcoming it in record amounts. The nation has been pursuing European Union membership, and privatization programs in the banking and telecommunications industries have increased investor interest in the stock market. Significant legal amendments to commercial and securities laws came into effect in 1996 with the main goals of increasing investor protection and company disclosure.

The Czech equity market is relatively small, with market capitalization at only about 25 percent of 1999 GDP (see Exhibit 1-4). There are no listed foreign companies in the Czech Republic.

EQUITY MARKETS IN THE CZECH REPUBLIC

The Prague Stock Exchange (PSE) was reestablished in 1992 after a break of over 50 years. The PSE is the only stock exchange in the Czech Republic. Securities are traded on two markets: The Main/Secondary and Free markets.

REGULATION

The State, through the Ministry of Finance, supervises the Prague Stock Exchange. The Ministry of Finance monitors business and financial results of securities issuers. The agency also appoints an exchange commissioner who operates the stock exchange. The Commercial Code, which governs contractual relationships, guarantees equal treatment under the law for foreign investors.

ACCOUNTING PRINCIPLE REQUIREMENTS

All listed companies must file audited financial statements prepared in conformance with IAS in addition to financial statements conforming to Czech accounting standards.

FINANCIAL REPORTING AND DISCLOSURE REQUIREMENTS

Companies listed on the Main Market are required to file quarterly financial information to the PSE, and Secondary Market companies are required to do so semiannually. Audited financial statements and annual reports are also required. All companies are required to report to the PSE any information that may have an effect on their securities.

The PSE does not enforce any disclosure requirements for securities listed on the Free Market.

FRANCE

OVERVIEW

France is the second largest economy in Europe (following Germany), with one of the highest per capita incomes. The French equity market ranks second in Europe and fifth in the world in terms of market capitalization. Market capitalization of domestic shares almost tripled between the 1995 and 2000 year-ends, and the value of share trading more than quadrupled in the same period.

These and other recent developments have made Euronext Paris (formerly the Paris Stock Exchange) an attractive stock exchange for foreign companies, which already account for over 15 percent of the total number of companies with securities listed in France

EQUITY MARKETS IN FRANCE

Euronext Paris includes four regulated equity markets: the Premier Marché, the Second Marché, the Nouveau Marché, and the European Depository Receipt (EDR) Market.

The Premier Marché is by far the most active securities market in France. It includes securities of large French and non-French companies. Almost all of the 164 non-French companies listed in Paris at year-end 2000 are listed on the Premier Marché.

The Second Market (Second Marché) was created in 1983 to enable medium-sized companies to obtain capital through the stock market. Criteria for listing on the Second Market are less strict than those for the Premier Marché.

The Nouveau Marché opened in March 1996 and is designed to help young, innovative companies with high-growth potential raise equity financing and give investors the ability to assume higher levels of risk.

REGULATION

The Commission des Opérations de Bourse (COB) is the French securities regulatory agency. The COB is an independent public agency closely modeled after the U.S. Securities and Exchange Commission (SEC). The COB has broad powers to undertake investigations, levy fines, and call in the French judicial authorities.

The COB recently announced plans to make rules for public offerings more stringent. Critics argue that doing an initial public offering (IPO) in France already is cumbersome, and that the new rules could deter companies from joining the Nouveau Marché, causing them to list on other European markets instead.

ACCOUNTING PRINCIPLE REQUIREMENTS

The COB requires domestic listed companies to use French GAAP as the primary accounting framework. They also can publish supplemental financial statements in accordance with IAS. Companies may follow IAS in their consolidated financial statements for domestic reporting purposes.

The COB allows foreign listed companies to use French GAAP or IAS. U.S. GAAP also may be accepted if a reconciliation table is provided.

FINANCIAL REPORTING AND DISCLOSURE REQUIREMENTS

Financial reporting rules recently were amended to ease the listing process for foreign companies. The general principle is that a foreign company listed on Euronext

Paris must provide the French public as much detailed information as it provides to the public in its home country.

Listed companies must:

- Publish, within 4 months of the close of each fiscal year, draft annual financial statements comprising a balance sheet, a profit and loss statement (with notes), and a proposed allocation of profits or losses in the Bulletin des Annonces Légales Obligatoires (BALO);
- Publish annual financial statements certified by statutory auditors in the BALO within 45 days of the annual shareholders meeting;
- File an annual reference document containing legal and business information regarding the issuer and its activity with the COB. This document can be incorporated in the issuer's annual report. For foreign issuers, this document can be prepared in English if it includes a summary in French;
- Publish a table showing turnover (sales) and pre-tax profit for the first 6 months of the current year, the first 6 months of the preceding year, and the most recent fiscal year, certified by the statutory auditors;
- Publish a report on the issuer's condition during the last 6 months and a forecast for the rest of the year; and
- Report turnover, certified by the statutory auditors, every quarter.

The COB requires (subject to certain exceptions) that the relevant company or investor publish any information that might affect the price of a share as soon as possible. Euronext Paris must be notified of all factors affecting the price of shares such as takeovers, mergers, and share capital increases.

GERMANY

OVERVIEW

The German equity market is the sixth largest in the world in market capitalization, ranking behind only London and Euronext Paris in Europe. Although Germany has been a major industrial economy for more than a century, its equity markets effectively did not exist before the 1980s. Complex ownership structures, insider trading, weak investor protection, and low risk tolerance of potential investors were among the many factors that inhibited equity market development. The German market has become more equity oriented, and tremendous equity market growth occurred during the 1990s as a result.

EQUITY MARKETS IN GERMANY

Eight stock exchanges operate in Germany, located in Berlin, Bremen, Düsseldorf, Frankfurt, Hamburg, Hanover, Munich, and Stuttgart. The Frankfurt Stock Exchange, operated by the Deutsche Börse AG (DB), accounts for more than 75 percent of total securities turnover in Germany.

Each regional stock exchange operates three market segments: the Official Market (First Segment), the Regulated Market (Second Segment), and the Regulated Unofficial

Market (Third Segment). The DB has created within the Regulated Unofficial Market a new market for growth stocks called the Neuer Markt. Neuer Markt shares must be approved for listing in the regulated market and meet additional admission criteria. The DB also has developed a high-quality segment for medium-sized companies called SMAX, with more stringent disclosure requirements than on the Official Market and the Regulated Market.[12]

REGULATION

The Deutsche Börse is supervised by its Market Supervision Board, the State Supervisory Authority, and the Federal Securities Supervisory Office (BAWe), under the German Exchange Act, the Second Financial Market Promotion Law, and other legislation. Specific rules governing the Neuer Markt have been drafted according to higher, international standards.

ACCOUNTING PRINCIPLE REQUIREMENTS

Financial reports filed by foreign listed companies need not be prepared under or reconciled to German accounting principles. Both IAS- and U.S. GAAP-based reports are allowed; however, the principal accounting policies applied must be disclosed and an indication given of how they differ from German principles.

FINANCIAL REPORTING AND DISCLOSURE REQUIREMENTS

Domestic and foreign companies that list securities on the Official List of a German exchange have periodic reporting requirements including annual reports with audited financial statements, semiannual reports, and reports of material events. Issuers whose securities are listed on the Regulated Unofficial Market are not obligated to publish semiannual reports. Copies of all reports must be publicly available and the annual report must also be sent to shareholders.

Neuer Markt–listed companies must publish quarterly financial reports. Domestic and foreign companies must publish all information necessary to enable investors to assess the financial position of the company and the rights attaching to the securities. Listed German and foreign companies must publish annual financial statements in the *Federal Gazette* and make them available to the public.

JAPAN

OVERVIEW

The Japanese economy grew steadily from the 1950s to the late 1980s. Japan has the second largest gross domestic product in the world after the United States (see Chapter 3). Japanese capital markets and personal financial assets are among the world's largest. The Tokyo Stock Exchange (TSE) is one of the three largest stock exchanges in the world based on total market value. (As discussed in Chapters 1 and 3, the 1990s were a time of stagnation in Japan.)

---

[12]The DAX® and MDAX® indices are also regarded as segments because the shares comprising these indices lead the market in terms of size and liquidity.

EQUITY MARKETS IN JAPAN

There are six stock exchanges in Japan, located in Tokyo, Osaka, Nagoya, Kyoto, Fukuoka, and Sapporo. The Tokyo Stock Exchange (TSE) is Japan's principal exchange. Domestic stocks on the TSE are assigned to either the 1ˢᵗ Section or the 2ⁿᵈ Section, while foreign stocks are assigned to the Foreign Section.

In November 1999 the TSE launched a new market called "Market Of The High-Growth and Emerging Stocks (Mothers)" for stocks of emerging companies with high growth potential, in order to foster new companies and provide investors with a wider range of investment choices.

REGULATION

Stock exchanges and the over-the-counter market in Japan are governed by the Securities and Exchange Law administered by the Ministry of Finance (MOF) and the Financial Revitalization Committee. The stock exchanges establish their own rules for the listing of securities.

ACCOUNTING PRINCIPLE REQUIREMENTS

Domestic listed companies must meet the accounting provisions of the Commercial Code and the Securities and Exchange Law, which imposes further requirements.

Financial statements submitted by a foreign company listed on the TSE must follow accounting standards as specified by the MOF:

1. A foreign issuer is allowed to submit financial statements used in the home country (known as "home country basis");
2. If the financial statements used in the home country are not sufficient in disclosure quality, the foreign issuer is allowed to submit financial statements using different accounting standards such as IAS (known as "third country basis"); and
3. If these criteria cannot be met, the MOF can specify the accounting standards used (known as the "MOF directed basis").

FINANCIAL REPORTING AND DISCLOSURE REQUIREMENTS

Domestic and foreign listed companies must promptly disclose and give the exchange notice of business results, occurrences of material facts, and many corporate decisions such as mergers, dividends and stock splits, and other required disclosure items. Domestic companies are required to file annual security reports within 6 months of the end of the fiscal year and half-yearly reports within 3 months of the end of the first 6 months.

Companies listed on Mothers also are required to prepare quarterly reports of results and to hold analysts meetings at least twice a year for the first 3 years after listing.

Many documents filed with the MOF, including the Annual Securities Report, must be in Japanese. TSE filings also should be prepared in Japanese or a Japanese translation attached.

FOREIGN SECTION OF THE TSE

An Annual Securities Report must be filed with the MOF (and without delay to the TSE) within 6 months after the end of each fiscal year, subject to certain exceptions. A semiannual report must be filed with the MOF (and without delay to the TSE) within 3 months after the end of the first 6 months of the fiscal year. Current reports must be filed with the MOF and the TSE without delay after a required disclosure item occurs; documents filed with the competent authorities in the home country and documents sent to shareholders in Japan (before submission) must be filed with the TSE.

FOREIGN COMPANIES ON MOTHERS

Annual and interim (half-year) reports must be published as soon as they are available. Quarterly business results and financial statements must be published as soon as available after the end of each quarter, and must include opinions of a certified public accountant or equivalent.

MEXICO

OVERVIEW

Mexico is the second most populous country in Latin America (after Brazil). It has a (mostly) market economy. Private enterprise dominates most industry sectors (see Chapter 4).

Although Mexico's equity market is the second largest in Latin America (ranking behind only Brazil), it is small relative to world standards. Trading has become more open, and market institutions and regulations have strengthened in recent years.

EQUITY MARKETS IN MEXICO

The Bolsa Mexicana de Valores (BMV) is the headquarters of the organized securities market in Mexico. The BVM operates the Main Market and the International Quotation System.

Although foreign instruments can be traded on the International Quotation System BMV, only four companies (all from Argentina) have taken advantage of the opportunity. In November 2000 the BMV opened its main market to foreign listings.

REGULATION

The National Banking and Securities Commission (NBSC) is a government agency under the Ministry of Finance responsible for surveillance, inspection and regulation, the central securities depository, and the stock exchange.

The BMV oversees the activities of issuers and brokerage firms, disseminates market information, and encourages the expansion and competitiveness of the Mexican securities markets. The BMV recently made comprehensive changes in its corporate structure, establishing a new set of self-regulatory responsibilities.

Securities Market Law penalties for illegal acts and fraud within financial institutions have recently been strengthened.

ACCOUNTING PRINCIPLE REQUIREMENTS

All domestic listed companies must follow Mexican accounting principles. Foreign companies quoted on the International Quotation System must file the same information they are required to provide to the local authority of their home market.

Foreign companies listed on the Main Market may prepare their financial statements in accordance with: (1) Mexican accounting principles and regulations; (2) IAS; (3) accounting principles applicable in the issuer's home country with additional disclosures about deferred taxes and financial statement restatements; or (4) U.S. GAAP.

If IAS, home country accounting principles, or U.S. GAAP are used, notes accompanying the financial statements must explain the differences between the accounting principles used and Mexican principles and regulations in sufficient detail to allow the differences between the two sets of principles to be determined.

FINANCIAL REPORTING AND DISCLOSURE REQUIREMENTS

Listed domestic companies are required to publish annual audited financial statements and unaudited quarterly financial statements, as well as other financial and operating information that might affect their share price.

Listed foreign companies are required to publish annual audited financial statements no later than June 30 of the following year, and interim financial statements having the same structure and content as the annual report.

THE NETHERLANDS

OVERVIEW

Euronext Amsterdam (formerly known as the AEX Exchange N.V.) is one of the largest stock exchanges in Europe. The average listed Dutch company had a market capitalization of about U.S.$2.7 billion at year-end 2000. The Netherlands is home to some of the largest companies in the world (for example, Royal Dutch, Unilever, and Philips), and only two other stock exchanges (the NYSE and the Swiss Exchange) have a higher average market capitalization per listed company.

The Dutch equity market is the most concentrated market in Western Europe. A few very large global companies dominate trading: At year-end 1999 the combined market capitalization of the five largest companies accounted for roughly 40 percent of total market capitalization. The Dutch equity market is widely recognized for its international focus.

EQUITY MARKETS IN THE NETHERLANDS

All equities trade either on the Official Market or on NMAX, Amsterdam's "new market" launched in 1997 for fast-growing innovative companies.

REGULATION

Euronext Amsterdam is the supervisory listing authority. The Securities Board of the Netherlands (Stichting Toezicht Effectenverkeer—STE) supervises Euronext Amsterdam.

Prospectus disclosure requirements and other listing rules recently have been tightened to restore Euronext Amsterdam's reputation and respond to investor complaints following the World Online initial public offering (IPO) scandal.[13]

---

[13]On March 17, 2000, 1 week after World Online's Amsterdam IPO, investors learned that its CEO, Nina Brink, had sold many of her shares 3 months earlier. The company's share price dropped sharply in response, and 7 months later was less than half of the offering price. Disclosures in the company's prospectus had been misleading and Goldman Sachs & Co., World Online's banker, had printed the prospectus just 2 weeks before the listing.

ACCOUNTING PRINCIPLE REQUIREMENTS

Euronext Amsterdam recommends that issuers publish financial information in accordance with International Accounting Standards and provide a reconciliation of this information with Dutch General Accounting Principles in accordance with the annual accounts. Domestic listed companies may follow Dutch GAAP, IAS, or U.K. or U.S. GAAP with reconciliation to Dutch GAAP. Foreign companies may follow either IAS or U.S. GAAP without reconciliation to Dutch GAAP.

FINANCIAL REPORTING AND DISCLOSURE REQUIREMENTS

The annual accounts, the annual report, and a half-yearly report on activities and results must be made available to the public as soon as possible, but in no event later than the period stated in the listing agreement. If the company prepares both non-consolidated and consolidated annual accounts, both sets of accounts must be made available to the public. New economy and large-scale, one-off project companies are required to publish quarterly figures.

Euronext Amsterdam advises all listed companies to publish quarterly figures in addition to the mandatory annual accounts, half-year figures, and annual report. Listed companies must inform the public immediately of any important changes in the way its securities are held or any events that may affect the price of listed shares.

TAIWAN

OVERVIEW

Taiwan has one of the largest and most active equity markets in Asia, with value of share trading in 2000 second only to that in Japan, and 1999 market capitalization at 127 percent of GDP (a relatively high level in Asia). Individual investors dominate the Taiwan stock market, accounting for over 80 percent of the value of trading in listed shares. Regulations restricting foreign investment in Taiwan are gradually being liberalized. There are no foreign companies listed in Taiwan.

EQUITY MARKETS IN TAIWAN

The Taiwan Stock Exchange (TSE) is the single stock exchange operating in Taiwan.

REGULATION

The Securities and Future Commission (SFC) is the securities authority in Taiwan and supervises all aspects of securities market operations. The TSE operates in accordance with the provisions of the Securities and Exchange Law, relevant regulations, and directions of the SFC.

ACCOUNTING REQUIREMENTS

Domestic listed companies must follow Taiwanese accounting principles. Foreign listed companies must follow their own national principles and include a reconciliation to Taiwanese GAAP.

FINANCIAL REPORTING AND DISCLOSURE REQUIREMENTS

The SFC requires all listed companies to submit audited annual and semiannual reports, quarterly financial statements that have been reviewed by public accountants, and monthly operating reports. A listed company must report any events that may have a material impact on the market for its shares within 2 days.

UNITED KINGDOM

OVERVIEW

London is a leading world capital market. More than 550 international banks and 170 global securities firms have London offices.

The London Stock Exchange (LSE) ranks behind only the United States and Japan in market capitalization and value of share trading. The LSE has more foreign listings and more active trading in foreign shares than any other stock exchange in the world. However, the LSE has had several important failed projects and strategic initiatives during the past decade. The LSE underestimated the competitive threat of Continental European stock exchanges, and has lost its leadership role in Europe.

EQUITY MARKETS IN THE UNITED KINGDOM

The LSE is the principal equity market in the United Kingdom. Over 2,900 domestic and about 500 foreign companies were listed there as of December 31, 2000.

Domestic and foreign companies list equities on the Official List (the main market) or the Alternative Investment Market (AIM), which is not part of the Official List (see Chapter 1). Technology companies joining the Official List may also be eligible to join techMARK, LSE's new market for innovative technology companies.

REGULATION

As a Recognized Investment Exchange under U.K. law, the LSE regulates listed companies on its markets, but its regulatory authority has been sharply reduced recently. The Financial Services Authority (FSA) has taken over responsibility for admission of securities to official listing, monitoring and enforcement of initial listing standards, and continuing obligations of listed companies.

The FSA is an independent nongovernmental body that exercises statutory powers under the Financial Services Act 1986, the Banking Act 1987, and certain other legislation.

The LSE has a two-stage admission process. A company's securities need to be admitted to the Official List by the U.K. Listing Authority (UKLA), a division of the Financial Services Authority, and also be admitted to trading by the exchange.

ACCOUNTING PRINCIPLE REQUIREMENTS

Accounts must be prepared in accordance with U.K. GAAP, U.S. GAAP, or IAS (with slightly different requirements for companies incorporated outside the United Kingdom). This requirement can be waived if the UKLA is satisfied that listing is in the interest of the applicant and that sufficient information is available to investors to reach an informed judgment concerning the applicant and the securities for which listing is sought.

FINANCIAL REPORTING AND DISCLOSURE REQUIREMENTS

Requirements for companies officially listed on the LSE include: (1) providing shareholders with annual audited financial statements within 6 months after the end of the fiscal year; (2) providing shareholders with unaudited interim reports, at least half yearly; and (3) notifying shareholders by circular immediately when certain transactions, such as major acquisitions and disposals, occur.

The United Kingdom has a highly developed system for ensuring complete and timely disclosure of material information. All company announcements now are published by the Regulatory News Services (RNS), operated by the LSE, and are freely available on the LSE's Web site.

CORPORATE GOVERNANCE DISCLOSURE

Listed companies must disclose, in their annual reports, the manner in which they have applied the principles of corporate governance contained in the Combined Code on Corporate Governance published in June 1998. The annual report must also contain specific information about directors' remuneration.

Foreign companies face less stringent financial reporting and disclosure requirements. The United Kingdom relies on regulation in the foreign company's home market.

UNITED STATES

OVERVIEW

The U.S. equity market long has been the world's largest and most active.[14,15] Both market capitalization of shares of domestic companies and total value of share trading in the United States have been steadily increasing as a percentage of global totals. The number of foreign companies with equities listed in the United States is increasing, in contrast to the situation in most other countries. These facts support the view that benefits to market participants of the U.S. capital market's highly developed financial reporting, disclosure, and corporate governance systems and other characteristics outweigh the competitive disadvantage of relatively high cost to companies seeking access to U.S. markets.

EQUITY MARKETS IN THE UNITED STATES

The New York Stock Exchange (NYSE), Nasdaq Stock Market, and American Stock Exchange (Amex) are the three largest of the eight stock markets operating in the United States, with 7,887 companies listed as of December 31, 2000 (see Exhibit 1-5, Chapter 1). Equities of domestic and foreign companies also are quoted on the less-regulated OTC Bulletin Board (OTCBB) and the "pink sheets" market. Companies now are required to report their current financial information to the SEC in order to meet OTCBB eligibility requirements.

---

[14]Refer to Exhibits 1-3, 1-5, and 1-6 in Chapter 1.
[15]Size measures include market capitalization of listed shares and number of companies with equity shares listed on regulated stock markets (year-end values), value of share trading, number of new listings, number of transactions, amount of capital raised by already listed companies, and amount of new capital raised by already listed companies [International Federation of Stock Exchanges (FIBV)].

REGULATION

The U.S. Securities and Exchange Commission (SEC) has statutory authority under the Securities and Exchange Act of 1934 to establish financial accounting and reporting standards for publicly held companies. The SEC administers the Securities Act 1933 and the Securities and Exchange Act of 1934, and has promulgated an extensive set of rules and regulations under each. Securities not listed on a national stock exchange or on NASDAQ but sold in over-the-counter markets also may be required to be registered under the Securities and Exchange Act of 1934.

As Self Regulatory Organizations, stock exchanges in the United States establish additional reporting and disclosure requirements for listed companies and closely review listed companies' annual reports and timely disclosures.

ACCOUNTING PRINCIPLE REQUIREMENTS

Domestic registrants are required to prepare their financial statements in conformance with U.S. GAAP. Foreign registrants may use some other comprehensive body of accounting principles, but are required to present a note reconciling income statement and balance sheet items to U.S. GAAP.

FINANCIAL REPORTING AND DISCLOSURE REQUIREMENTS

Domestic and most Canadian issuers in the United States must file annual reports on Form 10-K within 90 days of the end of the fiscal year, and quarterly reports on Form 10-Q within 45 days of the close of the first 3 quarters.

Foreign issuers on the U.S. markets must file annual reports on Form 20-F within 6 months of fiscal year-end, and interim reports when they are released in the home country. The NYSE, Amex, and NASDAQ also require foreign issuers to file interim reports with the exchanges when they release reports in the home country.

United States securities laws require or encourage timely disclosure of material nonpublic information in many situations. Stock exchanges have detailed timely disclosure rules that go beyond those imposed by the SEC and case law. Foreign issuers in the United States face the same timely disclosure rules as domestic issuers.

The SEC adopted revised disclosure requirements for foreign issuers in 1999. These standards replace most of the nonfinancial statement disclosure requirements of Form 20-F, the basic disclosure document for foreign issuers. The new international disclosure standards conform to the standards endorsed by the International Organization of Securities Commissions (IOSCO) in 1998 (see Chapter 8).

CORPORATE GOVERNANCE DISCLOSURE

The SEC requires companies to include in their annual meeting announcements (proxy statements) certain disclosures about their audit committees and reports from their audit committees containing certain disclosures. The rules are designed to improve disclosure related to the functioning of corporate audit committees.

REPORTING AND DISCLOSURE PRACTICES

What do companies around the world actually disclose in their annual reports? Annual report disclosure practices reflect managers' responses to regulatory disclosure requirements and their incentives to provide information to financial statement users voluntarily. In many parts of the world, disclosure rules mean little and monitoring and enforcement are largely absent. Insofar as disclosure rules are not enforced, the required disclosures are (in practice) voluntary, because corporate managers will not comply with disclosure rules if compliance is more costly than the expected costs of noncompliance. Therefore, it is important to clearly distinguish between disclosures that are "required" and disclosures that actually are made. It is misleading to focus on disclosure rules without also looking at actual disclosure practices.

For some types of disclosure (such as disclosures about material developments) managerial discretion plays such an important role that monitoring (and hence enforcement) is difficult. Therefore, these types of disclosure are more or less voluntary. Finally, disclosure rules vary dramatically worldwide in areas such as cash flow and changes in equity statements, related party transactions, segment reporting, fair value of financial assets and liabilities, and earnings per share.

In this section we focus on (1) disclosures of forward-looking information; (2) segment disclosures; (3) cash and funds flow statements, (4) social responsibility disclosures; (5) special disclosures for non-domestic financial statement users; (6) corporate governance disclosures; and (7) Internet business reporting and disclosure. These disclosure and reporting items are selected because of their importance to financial statement users. For example, financial analysts and regulators have emphasized the importance of corporate disclosures of forward-looking information and business segment information. One study found that major institutional investors in the United States and the United Kingdom have been concerned that most companies do not disclose sufficient forward-looking information such as that related to corporate goals and planned expenditures, and do not offer detailed information about their operating units.[16]

Cash and funds (working capital) flow information is considered highly relevant for financial statement users. For instance, the AICPA Special Committee on Financial Reporting has recommended that cash-flow statistics be reported for business segments, and accounting standards in many countries now require the presentation of cash flow statements.

DISCLOSURES OF FORWARD-LOOKING INFORMATION

Disclosures of forward-looking information are considered highly relevant in equity markets worldwide. For example, the EU's Fourth Directive states that the annual report should include an indication of the company's likely future development. As a second example, the Tokyo Stock Exchange TSE "requests" management of listed firms to provide forecasts of sales, earnings, and dividends in their annual and semiannual press releases.

Here we use the term "forward-looking information" to include: (1) forecasts of revenues, income (loss), earnings (loss) per share (eps), capital expenditures, and other financial items; (2) prospective information about future economic performance or position that is less definite than forecasts in terms of projected item, fiscal period, and

---

[16]M. R. Sesit, "Big Investors Bemoan Lack of Data on Overseas Firms," *The Wall Street Journal,* February 23, 1995, page C1.

EXHIBIT 5-2 Number of Firms Disclosing Forward-looking Information in 1993/94 Annual Reports

	France	Germany	Japan	United Kingdom	United States
Number of Sample Firms	40	40	40	40	40
Firms making no forward-looking disclosures:	3	0	5	3	0
Firms making one or more forward-looking disclosures	37	40	35	37	40
A. Firms disclosing Management's Plans or Objectives	29	28	33	25	39
B. Firms disclosing Forecasts:					
Earnings	4	11	2	2	3
Sales	7	11	1	1	2
Capital Expenditures	2	6	0	4	22
Other	2	13	0	9	18
At least one forecast	11	22	2	11	31
C. Firms disclosing "softer" prospective information	29	36	10	31	36

Source: Carol A. Frost and Kurt P. Ramin, "Corporate Financial Discussions: A Global Assessment," in Frederick D. S. Choi, ed., *International Accounting and Finance Handbook 2e.* Copyright © 1997 John Wiley & Sons. This material is used by permission of John Wiley & Sons, Inc.

projected amount;[17] and (3) statements of management's plans and objectives for future operations.

Exhibit 5-2 presents evidence on forward-looking disclosures made in the annual reports distributed by 200 large public companies, 40 each from France, Germany, Japan, the United Kingdom, and the United States.[18] Panel A shows that most of the firms in each country subsample disclosed information about management's plans and objectives. In contrast, fewer firms disclosed forecasts, ranging from a low of two firms in Japan to a high of 31 firms in the United States. Most of the U.S. forecasts involved capital expenditures, not earnings and sales, as in Germany. Finally, panel C shows that most of the firms in France, Germany, the United Kingdom, and the United States (but not Japan) also disclosed "softer" prospective information.

Exhibits 5-3 and 5-4 illustrate the types of forward-looking disclosures made by the 200 firms. Exhibit 5-3 presents forecast disclosures from the BASF AG (a German firm) Financial Report 2000. BASF forecasts annual growth in gross domestic product up to 2005, growth rates in global chemical production to 2005, sales growth in each of five

---

[17]For convenience we use the term "prospective" disclosure to refer to "softer" non-forecast disclosures.
[18]These data are from Carol A. Frost and Kurt P. Ramin, "Corporate Financial Disclosure: A Global Assessment," in *International Accounting and Finance Handbook, Second Edition,* F. D. S. Choi, ed., New York: John Wiley & Sons, 1997.

EXHIBIT 5-3   Economic, Industry, and Financial Forecast Disclosures by BASF AG

FORECAST

Economic Trends

After a period of high growth in 2000, when global gross domestic product grew by more than 4%, we expect growth in global gross domestic product to slow to approximately 3% in 2001. Up to 2005, we anticipate that the global economy will expand by a solid 3% per year, with economic fundamentals remaining attractive despite a temporary slowdown in 2001.

The main factor affecting the overall economic climate in 2001 will be the significant slowdown in the U.S. economy after eight years of strong growth. The slight weakening in Western Europe's economy will likely be offset by improved conditions in South America and Eastern Europe as well as by continued strong growth in Asia, with the exception of Japan.

Up to 2005, we forecast that on an annual basis gross domestic product will grow by 2.5% in Western Europe and 3% in North America. Japan's economy is expected to grow by just under 2%, whereas the rest of Asia is expected to regain some of the dynamic growth it achieved before the Asian crisis, with growth rates of roughly 6.5%.

Trends in the Chemical Industry

In the medium term, the chemical industry is expected to grow faster than gross national product. This positive outlook for the industry can be attributed to the innovative strength of the chemical sector, the ongoing trend worldwide of substituting conventional materials with those based on chemical substances as well as the relatively strong upsurge in demand for chemical products in regions marked by strong economic growth.

Growth in global chemical production is expected to fall just short of 4% in 2001—slightly weaker than the strong performance of 4.2% in 2000. In North America, chemical production is expected to increase by only 1.5%, whereas in Western Europe production is projected to expand by a solid 3%. In 2001, Asia will again be the growth region par excellence, with output forecast to climb 8%. From 2002 to 2005, we again expect to see a cyclical recovery, with growth rates of just over 4%.

Sales Forecast

At BASF, we are aiming to grow faster than the market in the medium term. We have set this ambitious goal in view of our product portfolio and the measures taken over the past year.

In the Chemicals segment, we are planning to achieve above-average growth in sales.

In 2001, the Plastics & Fibers segment is again expected to post the highest sales of all segments. In this segment, sales did decline in 2000, due primarily to the loss of sales from the polyolefins business after its transfer to Basell.

In the Colorants & Finishing Products segment, we intend to increase sales. The impact on sales of the transfer of our textile dyes business to DyStar will be partially offset by the acquisition of Chemdal's superabsorbents business.

The Health & Nutrition segment will change significantly following the expected sale of our pharmaceuticals activities in March 2001. Sales in the Agricultural Products division will increase substantially due to the acquisition of AHP's crop protection business, while the acquisition of Takeda's vitamins business will be the main cause for a rise in sales in the Fine Chemicals division.

In the Oil & Gas segment, we expect further growth in sales despite lower average oil prices than in 2000.

EXHIBIT 5-3 *(cont.)*

Earnings Forecast

BASF has set a financial target of increasing income from operations before special items on an average annual basis of 10% from 2000 to 2002.

We expect a significant increase in income from operations in 2001, since special charges resulting from major changes in our business portfolio burdened earnings in 2000. Furthermore, we expect that these changes will contribute to improved earnings in 2001 and the margins will improve in some of our operating divisions. In the Chemicals segment, we foresee a slight improvement in earnings. We also expect earnings to rise on a comparable basis in Plastics & Fibers, and project that earnings will improve significantly in the Colorants & Finishing Products segment due to an expected improvement in margins as well as the contribution of new acquisitions. In the Health & Nutrition segment, we also anticipate an improvement in earnings due to the contribution of AHP's crop protection activities as well as the reduction in special charge. Interest expense will be lowered substantially by using proceeds from divestitures to pay off debt.

Source: BASF AG Financial Report 2000.

segments, and income from operations for the next 2 years. Exhibit 5-4 presents sales and earnings forecasts made by Schering AG (also a German firm).

Finally, Exhibit 5-5 presents Komerci Banka AS's "Business Strategy and Overall Economic Forecast" note in its Yearly Report for 1999. Komerci Banka, a Czech company, presents a table with spaces for both 1- and 2-year ahead forecasts of costs, income (sales revenue), and profit before tax, although the company states that "it is not possible at present to provide reliable figures (for 2 years ahead)" due to the bank's preparation for privatization. The forecasts presented by BASF, Schering, and Komerci Banka illustrate the highly detailed forward-looking disclosures typical of many companies in Continental Europe (especially Germany). Financial forecasts appear less often in annual reports from the United States, the United Kingdom, and other Anglo-American countries. Many companies in these countries are deterred from disclosing forecasts due to the risk of litigation should the forecasts turn out to be inaccurate.

Exhibit 5-6 presents a "Safe Harbor for Forward-Looking Statements" disclosure included in the Annual Report 2000 of UniSource Energy Corp., a U.S. company. By providing the disclosure, UniSource Energy is able to take advantage of the safe harbor provisions (certain protections from litigation) of the Private Securities Litigation and Reform Act of 1995 for forward-looking statements. The safe harbor disclosure includes many cautionary statements. The company disclaims any obligation to update

EXHIBIT 5-4　Forecast Disclosure by Schering AG

In the 2001 financial year we will continue implementation of our growth strategy and move forward to the next goals. We will again be looking for double-digit sales growth to over 5 bn (based on last year's currency exchange rates). We expect an increase of more than 10% in net income despite the likely high marketing cost of introducing our new products.

Forecast 2001: continuing on course for growth

Source: Schering AG 2000 Annual Report, Forward by the Executive Board, p. 7.

EXHIBIT 5-5   Forecast Disclosure by Komerci Banka AS

10. Business Strategy and Overall Economic Forecast

The strategic intent of KB is to act as a dynamic universal bank, developing activities in the field of commercial as well as investment banking. The long-term objective of KB is development in accordance with the modern trends of international banking, which will ensure maximum satisfaction of the needs of target clientele, and at the same time, will be in accordance with the interests of the shareholders. The portfolio of products and services will further be developed, taking advantage of the background of the whole Financial Group of KB. The Bank intends to actively seek all-round approximation to the level required in the European Union.

In the year 2000 the major occupation of the Bank will be the preparation and realisation of its privatisation procedure. The Bank's loan portfolio will be significantly improved through the restructuring of its assets. The Bank is intent upon the close management of existing risks, which derived from the continuing difficult conditions of the economic and legal environment. KB will closely monitor its operating costs and increase productivity, which will be manifested in a further fall in the number of employees.

Forecast results for the year (IAS) in CZK billions[1])	*1999 (results achieved)*	*2000[2])*	*2001[3])*
Costs	30.2	20.2	
Income	20.4	20.3	
Profit before tax	(9.8)	0.1	

Notes:

1) According to the accounting methodology of the Czech banks (CAS) the required categories cannot be completed with final data as, following consultation with the Securities Commission, the methodology of international accounting standards (IAS) was chosen instead.

2) As a result of the uncertainties related to the future development of the Czech economy, of the financial condition of the Bank's clients and of the realisation of collateral values, the ultimate losses may be different than presently estimated and provisioned.

3) With regard to the Bank's preparation for privatisation, part of which is the ongoing transfer of loss receivables, it is not possible at present to provide reliable figures for the year 2001.

Source: Komerci Banka A.S. Yearly Report for 1999.

any forward-looking statements, and provides a detailed list of factors that might cause actual results to differ materially from the company's forward-looking statements. Cautionary disclosures such as the one shown in Exhibit 5-6 now commonly appear in annual reports of U.S. companies, non-U.S. companies listed in the United States, and in company press releases. They reflect companies' concerns about possible litigation arising in connection with their forward-looking disclosures and efforts to minimize their litigation risk by closely following the language of the applicable statute.

SEGMENT DISCLOSURES

Investor and analyst demand for information about firms' industry and geographic segment operations and financial results is significant and growing. For example, financial analysts in the United States consistently have requested financial statement data disaggregated in much greater detail than it is now. International Accounting Standards

EXHIBIT 5-6 Safe Harbor for Forward-Looking Statements Disclosure by UniSource Energy

Safe Harbor for Forward-Looking Statements

This Annual Report contains forward-looking statements as defined by the Private Securities Litigation Reform Act of 1995. UniSource Energy and TEP are including the following cautionary statements to make applicable and take advantage of the safe harbor provisions of the Private Securities Litigation Reform Act of 1995 for any forward-looking statements made by or for UniSource Energy or TEP in this Annual Report. Forward-looking statements include statements concerning plans, objectives, goals, strategies, future events or performance and underlying assumptions and other statements that are not statements of historical facts. Forward-looking statements may be identified by the use of words such as "anticipates," "estimates," "expects," "intends," "plans," "predicts," "projects," and similar expressions. From time to time, we may publish or otherwise make available forward-looking statements of this nature. All such forward-looking statements, whether written or oral, and whether made by or on behalf of UniSource Energy or TEP are expressly qualified by these cautionary statements and any other cautionary statements which may accompany the forward-looking statements. In addition, UniSource Energy and TEP disclaim any obligation to update any forward-looking statements to reflect events or circumstances after the date of this report.

Forward-looking statements involve risks and uncertainties that could cause actual results or outcomes to differ materially from those expressed in the forward-looking statements. We express our expectations, beliefs and projections in good faith and believe them to have a reasonable basis. However, we make no assurances that management's expectations, beliefs or projections will be achieved or accomplished. We have identified the following important factors that could cause actual results to differ materially from those discussed in our forward-looking statements. These may be in addition to other factors and matters discussed in other parts of this report:

1. Effects of restructuring initiatives in the electric industry and other energy-related industries.
2. Effects of competition in retail and wholesale energy markets.
3. Changes in economic conditions, demographic patterns and weather conditions in TEP's retail service area.
4. Supply and demand conditions in wholesale energy markets, including volatility in market prices and illiquidity in markets, which are affected by a variety of factors. These factors include the availability of generating capacity in the West, including hydroelectric resources, weather, natural gas prices and the impact of utility restructuring the generation divestitures in various states.
5. Changes affecting TEP's cost of providing electrical service including changes in fuel costs, generating unit-operating performance, scheduled and unscheduled plant outages, interest rates, tax laws, environmental laws, and the general rate of inflation.
6. Changes in governmental policies and regulatory actions with respect to financings and rate structures.
7. Changes affecting the cost of competing energy alternatives, including changes in available generating technologies and changes in the cost of natural gas.
8. Changes in accounting principles or the application of such principles to UniSource Energy or TEP.
9. Market conditions and technological changes affecting UniSource Energy's unregulated businesses.

Source: UniSource Energy Annual Report 2000.

EXHIBIT 5-7   Segment Disclosures by General Electric Co.

Revenues
For the years ended December 31

(In millions)	Total revenues			Intersegment revenues			External revenues		
	2000	1999	1998	2000	1999	1998	2000	1999	1998
GE									
Aircraft Engines	$ 10,779	$ 10,730	$ 10,294	$ 687	$ 477	$ 292	$ 10,092	$ 10,253	$ 10,002
Appliances	5,887	5,671	5,619	5	4	12	5,882	5,667	5,607
Industrial Products and Systems	11,848	11,555	11,222	428	530	479	11,420	11,025	10,743
NBC	6,797	5,790	5,269	—	—	—	6,797	5,790	5,269
Plastics	7,776	6,941	6,633	24	17	20	7,752	6,924	6,613
Power Systems	14,861	10,099	8,500	144	169	170	14,717	9,930	8,330
Technical Products and Services	7,915	6,863	5,323	19	15	14	7,896	6,848	5,309
Eliminations	(2,075)	(1,767)	(1,401)	(1,307)	(1,212)	(987)	(768)	(555)	(414)
Total GE segment revenues	63,788	55,882	51,459	—	—	—	63,788	55,882	51,459
Corporate items	517	619	771	—	—	—	517	619	771
GECS net earnings	5,192	4,443	3,796	—	—	—	5,192	4,443	3,796
Total GE revenues	69,497	60,944	56,026	—	—	—	69,497	60,944	56,026
GECS segment revenues	66,177	55,749	48,694	—	—	—	66,177	55,749	48,694
Eliminations	(5,821)	(5,063)	(4,521)	—	—	—	(5,821)	(5,063)	(4,251)
Consolidated revenues	$129,853	$111,630	$100,469	$ —	$ —	$ —	$129,853	$111,630	$100,469

GE revenues include income from sales of goods and services to customers and other income. Sales from one Company component to another generally are priced at equivalent commercial selling prices.

(IAS) include highly detailed segment reporting, as do accounting standards in many countries.[19]

Exhibit 5-7 presents the footnote disclosure of the geographic and industry segment financial results and position of General Electric Company. Operating segment revenues and profits are presented for 1996 through 2000, and revenues, assets, property, plant and equipment additions, and depreciation and amortization are presented for 1998 through 2000. General Electric also discloses revenues, operating profit, assets, and long-lived assets by country of origin.

Exhibit 5-8 presents segment disclosures made in the 2000 annual report of UniSource Energy Corp. Nine separate income statement items are disclosed for each segment, as well as cash flow and balance sheet items, for the company's two operating segments.

Segment disclosures from the 1999 annual report of Labinal SA (a French firm) are presented in Exhibit 5-9. Sales and net profit are the only two items disclosed for each of the company's seven operating segments (results for three of the seven segments

[19]Refer to Lee H. Radebaugh, "Segmental and Foreign Operations Disclosure," in *International Accounting and Finance Handbook, Second Edition*, F. D. S. Choi, ed., New York: John Wiley & Sons, 1997, for detailed discussion of segment and foreign operations disclosure.

EXHIBIT 5-7 *(cont.)*

(In millions)	Assets at December 31			Property, plant, and equipment additions (including equipment leased to others) For the years ended December 31			Depreciation and amortization (including goodwill and other intangibles) For the years ended December 31		
	2000	*1999*	*1998*	*2000*	*1999*	*1998*	*2000*	*1999*	*1998*
GE									
Aircraft Engines	$ **9,816**	$ 9,204	$ 9,075	$ **416**	$ 368	$ 480	$ **330**	$ 382	$ 398
Appliances	**2,775**	2,463	2,436	**213**	151	150	**142**	147	137
Industrial Products and Systems	**7,869**	6,740	6,466	**522**	423	428	**425**	433	440
NBC	**4,965**	5,243	3,264	**99**	94	105	**120**	126	127
Plastics	**9,561**	9,261	9,813	**546**	462	722	**549**	561	591
Power Systems	**11,618**	9,865	7,299	**657**	514	248	**306**	285	215
Technical Products and Services	**6,016**	5,048	3,858	**211**	164	254	**219**	230	143
Total GE segments	**52,620**	47,824	42,211	**2,664**	2,176	2,387	**2,091**	2,164	2,051
Investment in GECS	**23,022**	20,321	19,727	—	—	—	—	—	—
Corporate items and eliminations[1]	**21,123**	14,438	12,732	**55**	58	156	**157**	155	241
Total GE	**96,765**	82,583	74,670	**2,719**	2,234	2,543	**2,248**	2,319	2,292
GECS segment	**370,636**	345,018	303,297	**11,434**	15,432	8,110	**5,488**	4,372	3,568
Eliminations	**(30,395)**	(22,401)	(22,032)	—	—	—	—	—	—
Consolidated totals	**$437,006**	$405,200	$355,935	**$14,153**	$17,666	$10,653	**$7,736**	$6,691	$5,860

Additions to property, plant and equipment include amounts relating to principal business purchased.
[1]Depreciation and amortization includes $64 million of unallocated RCA goodwill amortization in 2000, 1999, and 1998 that relates to NBC.

Basis for presentation. The Company's operating businesses are organized based on the nature of products and services provided. Certain GE businesses do not meet the definition of a reportable operating segment and have been aggregated. The Industrial Products and Systems segment consists of Industrial Systems, Lighting, Transportation Systems and GE Supply. The Technical Products and Services segment consists of Medical Systems and Global eXchange Services.

Segment accounting policies are the same as policies described in note 1.

Details of segment profit by operating segment can be found on page 44 of this report. A description of operating segments for General Electric Company and consolidated affiliates is provided on the facing page.

are shown in Exhibit 5-9). Discussions of future prospects and expected sales growth are presented for each segment. Labinal does not disclose whether intersegment sales are significant, and if so, how they are treated in the segment disclosure.

CASH FLOW AND FUNDS FLOW STATEMENTS

IAS and accounting standards in the United States, the United Kingdom, and a growing number of other countries require the presentation of cash flow statements. The recent adoption of cash flow statement requirements in nations such as Japan and China reflects the growing emphasis on cash flow information by analysts and other financial statement users.

EXHIBIT 5-7 (cont.)

The table below presents data by geographic region.

Revenues and operating profit shown below are classified according to their country of origin (including exports from such areas). Revenues classified under the caption "United States" include royalty and licensing income from non-U.S. sources.

Revenues
For the years ended December 31

(In millions)	Total revenues			Intersegment revenues			External revenues		
	2000	1999	1998	2000	1999	1998	2000	1999	1998
United States	$ 90,981	$ 78,970	$ 71,799	$ 3,518	$ 2,690	$ 2,608	$ 87,463	$ 76,280	$ 69,191
Europe	24,144	22,919	21,665	1,212	1,081	837	22,932	21,838	20,828
Pacific Basin	12,921	7,879	5,166	1,218	924	951	11,703	6,955	4,215
Other (a)	8,754	7,365	6,925	999	808	690	7,755	6,557	6,235
Intercompany eliminations	(6,947)	(5,503)	(5,086)	(6,947)	(5,503)	(5,086)	—	—	—
Total	$129,853	$111,630	$100,469	$ —	$ —	$ —	$129,853	$111,630	$100,469

(In millions)	Operating profit[2]			Assets			Long-lived assets[3]		
	For the years ended December 31			At December 31			At December 31		
	2000	1999	1998	2000	1999	1998	2000	1999	1998
United States	$ 15,455	$ 13,391	$ 11,319	$277,818	$264,129	$227,311	$ 19,180	$ 21,612	$ 18,048
Europe	2,062	1,886	2,393	80,282	83,358	84,518	5,870	6,101	6,334
Pacific Basin	1,754	1,092	431	42,281	28,214	18,427	1,936	2,017	1,326
Other[1]	1,406	909	810	36,804	29,687	25,878	13,076	11,329	10,057
Intercompany eliminations	9	11	(9)	(179)	(188)	(199)	(47)	(37)	(35)
Total	$ 20,686	$ 17,289	$ 14,944	$437,006	$405,200	$355,935	$ 40,015	$ 41,022	$ 35,730

[1]Includes the Americas other than the United States and operations that cannot meaningfully be associated with specific geographic areas (for example, commercial aircraft leased by GE Capital Aviation Services).

[2]Excludes GECS income taxes of $1,912 million, $1,653 million and $1,364 million in 2000, 1999 and 1998, respectively, which are included in the measure of segment profit reported on page 44.

[3]Property, plant and equipment (including equipment leased to others).

Exhibit 5-10 presents the cash flow statement of General Electric Company. Three years of results are presented for GE Co. (consolidated), as well as for GECS (General Electric Capital Corporation) and GE (all affiliates combined other than GECS). The annual report states that cash management activities of the two segments are separate and distinct, and therefore their cash flows should be considered separately.

Exhibits 5-11 and 5-12 illustrate the variation in content and presentation format found in cash and funds flow statements around the world. Exhibit 5-11 presents the capital flow statement from the annual report of Bosch Group (Germany). Exhibit 5-12 presents cash flow information from the annual report of Southern Pacific Petroleum N.L., an Australian company. As shown in Exhibits 5-11 and 5-12, cash and funds flow disclosures provided can be far less detailed, and presented in formats much different than required by IAS.

EXHIBIT 5-8 Segment Disclosures by UniSource Energy Corp.

Note 5. Segment and Related Information

Based on the way we organize our operations and evaluate performance, we have two reportable segments. UniSource Energy's principal business segment is TEP, an electric utility business. The other reportable business segment is the unregulated energy businesses of Millennium. We describe the unregulated energy businesses of Millennium in Note 4.

As discussed in Note 1, we record our percentage share of the earnings of affiliated companies when we hold a 20% to 50% voting interest. Global Solar is consolidated. See Note 4. Our portion of the net income (loss) of the entities in which TEP and Millennium own a 20–50% interest is shown below in Net Loss from Equity Method Entities.

Intersegment revenues are not material. The only significant reconciling adjustment is for the elimination of the intercompany note between UniSource Energy and TEP as well as the related interest income and expense. All other intercompany activity and balances have been eliminated. The accounting policies of the segments are described in Note 1. We disclose selected financial data for our business segments in the following tables:

Millions of Dollars	*Segments*		*Reconciling*	*UniSource Energy*
2000	*TEP*	*Millennium*	*Adjustments*	*Consolidated*
Income Statement				
Operating Revenues	$1,028	9	(3)	1,034
Net Loss from Equity Method Entities	(2)	(2)	—	(4)
Interest Income	18	4	(8)	14
Interest Expense	166	—	—	166
Depreciation and Amortization	114	—	—	114
Income Tax (Benefit) Expense	27	(8)	(4)	15
Net Income (Loss)	51	(4)	(5)	42
Cash Flow Statement				
Capital Expenditures	(98)	(8)	—	(106)
Investments in and Loans to Equity Method Investees	(2)	(17)	—	(19)
Balance Sheet				
Total Assets	2,601	167	(97)	2,671
Investments in Equity Method Entities	9	6	—	15

SOCIAL RESPONSIBILITY DISCLOSURES

Increasingly, companies are being called upon to answer to a wide range of "stakeholders"—employees, customers, governments, and special interest groups—who have areas of concern other than a company's ability to create economic value. For many years, workers have been considered business partners in Continental Europe, with worker participation in works councils mandatory in the large companies of many countries.[20]

In economics the term *social accounting* traditionally means accounting for the economic performance of an entire nation. Here, we use the term to refer to the

---

[20]Fierce debate is now underway in the European Union concerning employees' rights to be informed and consulted via works councils. See "You're Fired," *The Economist* (April 14, 2001): 45–46.

EXHIBIT 5-8   (cont.)

Millions of Dollars 1999	Segments TEP	Millennium	Reconciling Adjustments	UniSource Energy Consolidated
Income Statement				
Operating Revenues	$804	11	—	815
Net Loss from Equity Method Entities	—	(4)	—	(4)
Interest Income	18	1	(9)	10
Gain on the Sale of New Energy	—	35	—	35
Interest Expense	123	—	—	123
Depreciation and Amortization	93	—	—	93
Income Tax (Benefit) Expense	22	12	(3)	31
Extraordinary Income—Net of Tax	23	—	—	23
Net Income (Loss)	73	11	(5)	79
Cash Flow Statement				
Capital Expenditures	(91)	(2)	—	(93)
Investments in and Loans to Equity Method Investees	—	(7)	—	(7)
Balance Sheet				
Total Assets	2,601	100	(45)	2,656
Investment in Equity Method Entities	9	24	—	33
1998				
Income Statement				
Operating Revenues	$769	2	—	771
Net Loss from Equity Method Entities	—	(14)	—	(14)
Interest Income	20	1	(9)	12
Interest Expense	118	—	—	118
Depreciation and Amortization	90	—	—	90
Income Tax (Benefit) Expense	18	(4)	(4)	10
Net Income (Loss)	42	(8)	(6)	28
Cash Flow Statement				
Capital Expenditures	(81)	—	—	(81)
Investments in and Loans to Equity Method Investees	—	(51)	—	(51)

EXHIBIT 5-9   Segment Disclosures by Labinal SA

DTM
Turbomeca Microturbo Division

Sales and income	Sales				Net profit			
	1998		1999		1998		1999	
	FF million	million	FF million	million	FF million	million	FF million	million
TURBOMECA Branch	2,911.3	443.8	3,157.5	481.3	229.4	35.0	194.7	29.7
MICROTURBO Branch	375.1	57.2	393.1	59.9	8.1	1.2	22.5	3.4
Total	3,286.4	501.0	3,550.6	541.2	237.5	36.2	217.2	33.1

Outlook

For the TURBOMECA Branch, the increase in the number of engines for delivery and the stabilizing of the support activity at a high level should be reflected by a slight increase in sales in 2000. The cuts in costs and production cycles which have already started and which will continue will lead to the necessary price reductions and increased in self-financed research.

For the MICROTURBO Branch the current developments and trials for several new products and the deadlines for the large European defense programs which they are associated with mean that an upturn in sales growth can be envisaged from 2001–2002. In the meantime, the company is counting on its international successes such as engines for the MQM 107 target drone in the U.S.A., or the APUs for the Hawk and T45 aircraft, and on the steady level of sales of spare parts and repairs to maintain business at a sufficient level for preparing for the future.

DMG
Globe Motors Division

Sales and income	Sales				Net profit			
	1998		1999		1998		1999	
	FF million	million	FF million	million	FF million	million	FF million	million
	503.0	76.7	624.2	95.2	50.6	7.7	52.7	8.0

Outlook

The outlook for the year 2000 is promising. Increased production volumes of recently launched products should be reflected by an increase in sales and results.

The Division will continue to increase its production capacity in 2000 to satisfy the expected growth in sales of innovative products with high growth potential intended for the automotive market from 2001 especially in the power assisted steering field.

EXHIBIT 5-9 *(cont.)*

DRT
Telma Retarder Division
Electromagnetic retarders for commercial vehicles and industrial applications.

| | Sales | | | | Division's contribution to the Group's net profit | | | |
| | 1998 | | 1999 | | 1998 | | 1999 | |
Sales and income	FF million	million	FF million	million	FF million	million	FF million	million
	503.0	76.7	624.2	95.2	50.6	7.7	52.7	8.0

The origin of the return to profit is the cost-savings plan carried out in 1999 and the disappearance of certain non-recurring expenses.

Outlook

The Division's business activity was steady in well-oriented markets in Europe and the United States during the first months of 2000. Sales in the heavy-duty vehicle markets in Asia and in South America continue to be depressed.

Source: Labinal Financial Report 1999.

measurement and communication of information about a firm's effects on employee welfare, the local community, and the environment. That is, *social accounting* embraces *nonfinancial* as well as financial measures of performance.

Information on employee welfare long has been of interest to labor groups. Particular areas of concern relate to working conditions, job security, and equal opportunity. Employee disclosures also are of interest to investors in that they provide useful insights about a firm's labor relations, costs, and productivity.

Information disclosure regarding number of employees has been of great interest to national governments. Number-of-employees disclosure by geographic area gives host governments information on the employment effect of multinational companies. Employee disclosure by line of business, in turn, helps identify those industries and activities that foreign direct investors find economically attractive. If there is a conflict between the behavior of the investors and the goals of the host government—for example, if investors invest in operations that employ low-skill workers while the government seeks to expand high-skill employment—an alert government could take steps to encourage foreign investment in the desired direction. When combined with geographical and/or line-of-business reporting, employee disclosure by function enables governments and labor groups to examine whether employment practices of multinational companies are consistent with local laws and norms.

Exhibits 5-13 and 5-14 present examples of social responsibility disclosures. Exhibit 5-13 shows BASF AG's annual report discussion of "Sustainable Development," a policy embraced by the company that is "a balancing act—between today's economic, ecological and social needs and the needs of future generations." Labinal SA's employment

EXHIBIT 5-10 Cash Flow Statement of General Electric Co.

For the years ended December 31 (In millions)	General Electric Company and consolidated affiliates			GE			GECS		
	2000	1999	1998	2000	1999	1998	2000	1999	1998
Cash flows—operating activities									
Net earnings	$ 12,735	$ 10,717	$ 9,296	$12,735	$10,717	$ 9,296	$ 5,192	$ 4,443	$ 3,796
Adjustments to reconcile net earnings to cash provided from operating activities									
Depreciation and amortization of property, plant and equipment	5,039	4,908	4,377	1,725	1,735	1,761	3,314	3,173	2,616
Amortization of goodwill and other intangibles	2,697	1,783	1,483	523	584	531	2,174	1,199	952
Earnings retained by GECS	—	—	—	(3,370)	(2,777)	(2,124)	—	—	—
Deferred income taxes	1,153	1,502	1,143	470	655	594	683	847	549
Decrease (increase) in GE current receivables	(537)	143	649	(550)	190	520	—	—	—
Decrease (increase) in inventories	(924)	266	150	(663)	(61)	69	(261)	327	81
Increase in accounts payable	3,297	820	1,576	845	104	199	3,047	699	1,673
Increase (decrease) in insurance liabilities and reserves	(1,009)	4,584	3,670	—	—	—	(1,009)	4,584	3,670
Provision for losses on financing receivables	2,045	1,671	1,603	—	—	—	2,045	1,671	1,603
All other operating activities	(1,806)	(1,801)	(4,587)	3,701	616	(814)	(5,901)	(2,124)	(3,985)
Cash from operating activities	22,690	24,593	19,360	15,416	11,763	10,032	9,284	14,819	10,955
Cash flows—investing activities									
Additions to property, plant and equipment	(13,967)	(15,502)	(8,982)	(2,536)	(2,036)	(2,047)	(11,431)	(13,466)	(6,935)
Dispositions of property, plant and equipment	6,767	6,262	4,043	53	—	6	6,714	6,262	4,037
Net increase in GECS financing receivables	(16,076)	(12,628)	(5,999)	—	—	—	(16,076)	(12,628)	(5,999)
Payments for principal businesses purchased	(2,332)	(11,654)	(18,610)	(1,156)	(1,594)	(1,455)	(1,176)	(10,060)	(17,155)
All other investing activities	(12,091)	(8,657)	(10,585)	(234)	(432)	477	(12,173)	(8,283)	(11,380)
Cash used for investing activities	(37,699)	(42,179)	(40,133)	(3,873)	(4,062)	(3,019)	(34,142)	(38,175)	(37,432)
Cash flows—financing activities									
Net increase (decrease) in borrowings (maturities of 90 days or less)	(8,243)	6,171	16,881	(1,331)	(1,230)	1,015	(2,121)	7,308	16,288
Newly issued debt (maturities longer than 90 days)	47,645	48,158	42,008	785	558	509	46,887	47,605	41,440
Repayments and other reductions (maturities longer than 90 days)	(32,762)	(27,539)	(32,814)	(855)	(615)	(1,787)	(31,907)	(26,924)	(31,027)
Net dispositions (purchases) of GE shares for treasury	469	(1,002)	(2,819)	469	(1,002)	(2,819)	—	—	—
Dividends paid to share owners	(5,401)	(4,587)	(3,913)	(5,401)	(4,587)	(3,913)	(1,822)	(1,666)	(1,672)
All other financing activities	12,942	622	(114)	—	—	—	12,942	622	(114)
Cash from (used for) financing activities	14,650	21,823	19,229	(6,333)	(6,876)	(6,995)	23,979	26,945	24,915
Increase (decrease) in cash and equivalents during year	(359)	4,237	(1,544)	5,210	825	18	(879)	3,589	(1,562)
Cash and equivalents at beginning of year	8,554	4,317	5,867	2,000	1,175	1,157	6,931	3,342	4,904
Cash and equivalents at end of year	$ 8,195	$ 8,554	$ 4,317	$7,210	$ 2,000	$1,175	$ 6,052	$ 6,931	$ 3,342
Supplemental disclosure of cash flows information									
Cash paid during the year for interest	$(11,617)	$(10,078)	$(9,297)	$ (388)	$ (482)	$ (620)	$(11,229)	$(9,596)	$(8,677)
Cash paid during the year for income taxes	(2,604)	(1,597)	(2,098)	(1,804)	(1,246)	(1,151)	(800)	(351)	(947)

The notes to consolidated financial statements on pages 56–76 are an integral part of this statement.

In the consolidating data on this page, "GE" means the basis of consolidation as described in note 1 to the consolidated financial statements; "GECS" means General Electric Capital Services, Inc. and all of its affiliates and associated companies. Transactions between GE and GECS have been eliminated from the "General Electric Company and consolidated affiliates" columns on page 38.

EXHIBIT 5-10 *(cont.)*

Changes in operating assets and liabilities are net of acquisitions and dispositions of principal businesses.

"Payments for principal businesses purchased" in the Statement of Cash Flows is net of cash acquired and includes debt assumed and immediately repaid in acquisitions.

"All other operating activities" in the Statement of Cash Flows consists primarily of adjustments to current and noncurrent accruals and deferrals of costs and expenses, increases and decreases in progress collections, adjustments for gains and losses on assets, increases and decreases in assets held for sale, and adjustments to assets.

Noncash transactions include the following: in 2000, the acquisition of Harmon Industries for shares of GE common stock valued at $346 million; in 1999, GE's contribution of certain media properties in exchange for a non-controlling interest in NBCi, a publicly-traded company (described in note 2); and in 1998, the acquisition of Marquette Medical Systems for shares of GE common stock valued at $829 million.

Certain supplemental information related to GE and GECS cash flows is shown below.

For the years ended December 31 (In millions)	2000	1999	1998
GE			
Purchases and sales of GE shares of treasury			
Open market purchases under share repurchase program	$ (2,226)	$ (1,866)	$ (3,646)
Other purchases	(3,116)	(5,622)	(2,829)
Dispositions (mainly to employee and dividend reinvestment plans)	5,811	6,486	3,656
	$ 469	$ (1,002)	$ (2,819)
GECS			
Financing receivables			
Increase in loans to customers	$(100,938)	$(95,201)	$(75,840)
Principal collections from customers—loans	87,432	86,379	65,573
Investment in equipment for financing leases	(15,454)	(18,173)	(20,299)
Principal collections from customers—financing leases	7,873	13,634	15,467
Net change in credit card receivables	(9,394)	(10,740)	(4,705)
Sales of financing receivables	14,405	11,473	13,805
	$ (16,076)	$(12,628)	$ (5,999)
All other investing activities			
Purchases of securities by insurance and annuity businesses	$ (35,911)	$(26,271)	$(23,897)
Dispositions and maturities of securities by insurance and annuity businesses	25,960	23,979	20,639
Proceeds from principal business dispositions	(605)	279	—
Other	(1,617)	(6,270)	(8,122)
	$ (12,173)	$ (8,283)	$(11,380)
Newly issued debt having maturities longer than 90 days			
Short-term (91 to 365 days)	$ 12,782	$ 15,799	$ 5,881
Long-term (longer than one year)	32,297	30,082	33,453
Proceeds—nonrecourse, leveraged lease debt	1,808	1,724	2,106
	$46,887	$47,605	$41,440
Repayments and other reductions of debt having maturities longer than 90 days			
Short-term (91 to 365 days)	$ (27,777)	$(21,211)	$(25,901)
Long-term (longer than one year)	(3,953)	(5,447)	(4,739)
Principal payments—nonrecourse, leveraged lease debt	(177)	(266)	(387)
	$ (31,907)	$(26,924)	$(31,027)
All other financing activities			
Proceeds from sales of investment contracts	$ 8,826	$ 7,236	$ 5,149
Redemption of investment contracts	(9,061)	(7,127)	(5,533)
Preferred stock issued by GECS affiliates—	—	513	270
Cash received upon assumption of Toho Mutual Life Insurance Company insurance liabilities	13,177	—	—
	$ 12,942	$ 622	$ (114)

EXHIBIT 5-11 Capital Flow Statement of Bosch Group Worldwide

	1999 *million DM*	*1998* *million DM*
Net income for the year	**900**	850
Depreciation of fixed assets	**3,884**	3,570
Increase of long-term accruals and accruals with valuation reserve portion	**1,588**	484
Cash flow	**6,372**	4,904
Increase in inventories and leased products	**−506**	−307
Increase in receivables	**−2,181**	−670
Change in short-term accruals	**684**	−63
Increase in liabilities	**622**	258
Additions to funds from business activities (1)	**4,991**	4,122
Additions to fixed assets	**−4,832**	−4,488
Retirements of fixed assets	**576**	242
Application of funds from investment activities (2)	**−4,970**	−2,599
Dividends 1998/1997	**−80**	−2,209
Increase in capital stock		300
Increase in capital surplus		1.735
Increase in liabilities with banks	**377**	266
Other changes in balance-sheet items	**−720**	−198
Application of funds to financial activities (3)	**−423**	−106
Change in liquidity (1) + (2) + (3)	**312**	−230
Liquidity at the beginning of the year	**7,082**	7,312
Liquidity at the end of the year	**7,394**	7,082

Source: Bosch Group 1999 Annual Report, p. 45.

disclosure from notes to its annual financial report is presented in Exhibit 5-14, which illustrates the type of information often provided in employee disclosures.[21]

SPECIAL DISCLOSURES FOR NON-DOMESTIC FINANCIAL STATEMENT USERS AND ACCOUNTING PRINCIPLES USED

Annual reports can include special disclosures to accommodate non-domestic financial statement users. Such disclosures include: (1) "convenience restatements" of financial information to a nondomestic currency; (2) limited restatements of financial results and

---

[21]Refer to Helen Gernon and Gary K. Meek, *Accounting: An International Perspective, Fifth Edition*, Boston: Irwin McGraw-Hill, 2001, and Claire B. Roberts, Sidney J. Gray, and Carol A. Adams, "Corporate Social and Environmental Disclosures," in *International Accounting and Finance Handbook, Second Edition*, F. D. S. Choi, ed., New York: John Wiley & Sons, 1997 for further discussion and illustrations. Also see Jee Hong Kim, in Ki Joo and Frederick D. S. Choi, "The Information Content of Productivity Measures: An International Comparison," *Journal of International Financial Management and Accounting* 7 (1996): 167–190.

EXHIBIT 5-12 Cash Flow Statement of Southern Pacific Petroleum N.L.

NOTE 23: CASH FLOW INFORMATION

	Note	Consolidated 2000 $000	Consolidated 1999 $000	Chief Entity 2000 $000	Chief Entity 1999 $000
Reconciliation of cash					
Cash at end of financial year as shown in the statements of cash flows are reconciled to the related items in the balance sheet as follows:					
Cash at bank		**1,088**	803	**190**	250
Deposits at call		**3,361**	3,063	**3,361**	3,063
Cash—per balance sheet		**4,449**	3,866	**3,551**	3,313
Cash account with associated company	4	**1,455**	1,194	**1,455**	1,194
Short term securities	5	**24,987**	—	**24,987**	—
		30,891	5,060	**29,993**	4,507
Reconciliation of net cash flows from operating activities to operating profit/ (loss) after tax					
Operating profit/(loss) after tax (from all activities)		**(12,622)**	(1,630)	**(10,420)**	(1,378)
Provision for repurchase of core technology expense		**443**	423	**443**	423
Depreciation of property, plant and equipment		**315**	297	**315**	297
Net loss/(gain) on disposal of property, plant and equipment		—	(514)	—	(514)
Royalty payment on research and development		**425**	420	**425**	420
Interest income on restricted deposit		**(857)**	(827)	**(857)**	(827)
Interest income and other investing activities		**(1,278)**	(1,546)	**(1,278)**	(1,546)
Net exploration and evaluation costs written off/(capitalised)		**(532)**	(3,520)	**247**	(2,033)
Provision for loans to controlled entities		—	—	**6,531**	—
Increase/(decrease) in net deferred taxes payable		**(1,878)**	(1,204)	**(1,873)**	(1,136)
Commission fee on note placement		—	750	—	750
Share of losses in associate		**2,228**	276	—	—
Loss on revaluation of land		—	30	—	—
Interest paid on convertible notes		**1,273**	—	**1,273**	—
Changes in assets and liabilities					
(Increase)/decrease in trade and other debtors		**(1)**	163	**(11)**	(131)
Decrease in inventories		**4**	4	**4**	4
Increase/(Decrease) in trade and other creditors and provision for employee entitlements		**989**	111	**(135)**	(10)
Increase in interest payable		**2**	106	**2**	106
Net cash flows from operating activities		**(11,489)**	(6,661)	**(5,334)**	(5,575)

EXHIBIT 5-12 *(cont.)*

Interest Rates

(i) Cash at bank

The weighted average interest rate for cash at bank is 5.2% (1999: 1.9%).

(ii) Deposits at call

Deposits at call are held in 11am accounts and cash management accounts. The weighted average interest rate is 6.1% (1999: 4.8%).

Non Cash Financing and Investing Activities

The consolidated entity did not have any non cash financing and investing activities during the year (1999: Nil).

Source: Southern Pacific Petroleum N.L. 2000 Annual Report.

position to a second set of accounting standards; (3) a complete set of financial statements prepared in conformance with a second set of accounting principles; and (4) discussion of differences between accounting principles used in the primary financial statements and some other set of accounting principles. Many firms in countries where English is not the primary language also translate entire annual reports from the home country language to English. Also, some firms prepare financial statements that conform to accounting standards more widely accepted than domestic standards (primarily IAS or U.S. GAAP), or that conform both to domestic standards and a second set of accounting principles.

Exhibit 5-15 illustrates one of the many dual currency statements presented in Labinal SA's annual financial report, for the convenience of readers who prefer working with financial figures in euros rather than French francs.

Exhibit 5-16 presents reconciliation disclosures and discussion of differences between U.S. and Swedish GAAP presented in the financial statements of NetCom AB, a Swedish company listed on the Nasdaq Stock Market. NetCom's disclosures are highly detailed, as are financial statement disclosures made by many non-U.S. companies that have listed equity in the United States and must comply with SEC financial reporting requirements. Chapter 9 presents further discussion and evidence on special disclosures made for nondomestic financial statement users.

CORPORATE GOVERNANCE DISCLOSURES

Companies' corporate governance practices are receiving increasing attention from regulators, investors, and analysts. The United States, United Kingdom, and Australia are among the growing number of countries that require listed companies to make specific corporate governance disclosures in their annual reports. Exhibit 5-17 presents an example of a corporate governance disclosure from the annual report of Southern Pacific Petroleum, an Australian company.

INTERNET BUSINESS REPORTING AND DISCLOSURE

The World Wide Web is increasingly being used as an information dissemination channel, with the print-based mode often playing a secondary role. Electronic information dissemination offers the advantage of often being less expensive than use of a print-

---

EXHIBIT 5-13   Social Responsibility Disclosure by BASF AG

Environment, Safety and Health: Continuous Improvement is our Aim

---

Sustainable Development is a balancing act — between today's economic, ecological and social needs and the needs of future generations. In 1992, at the United Nations Environmental Conference in Rio de Janeiro, the international community agreed on the principle of Sustainable Development, to which BASF is also committed. Last year, we made sustained profitable performance based on the principle of Sustainable Development an obligatory part of the "Values and Principles" that underlie our global activities.

Starting this year, the principle of Sustainable Development will also be reflected in our publications. This summer we will be issuing our "Environment, Safety and Health 2000" and "Social Responsibility 2000" reports. Together with the "Annual Report 2000," these documents give an account of the ecological, social and economic implications of our business.

"We act in a responsible manner and support the Responsible Care® initiatives. Economic considerations do not take priority over safety and health issues and environmental protection." This is one of the Values that underlie all decisions and actions at BASF.

But what does this actually mean for our work? Our Principles, which are closely linked to the idea of Sustainable Development, provide an answer:

- We encourage awareness of safety, health and environmental issues among our employees and strive for continuous improvements through our agreed-upon objectives.
- We produce products that are safe to manufacture, use, recycle or dispose.
- We support our customers to use our products safely and in an environmentally sound manner.
- We minimize the impact on mankind and the environment during production, storage, transportation, sale, use and disposal of our products.

When applying the Principles of BASF Group to environment, safety and health issues, appropriate consideration must be given to local circumstances. Decision-makers in individual countries are responsible for determining how to conform with BASF's Principles as well as the local legal requirements.

A High Standard Worldwide

We make sure that our strict internal regulations are put into practice. All over the world, our production plants operate to high standards. After all, only modern, safe plants and low-risk work methods are economically viable.

Source: 2000 BASF Group Annual Report.

---

based mode, and offers instantaneous communication. The Web also allows interactive information dissemination in a manner not possible in print form.[22] Securities trading using the Internet has increased the demand for Web-based business and financial reporting. Individual investors are increasingly using the Web to trade and make investment decisions, and use the Web as an important information source. For example, by January 2000, more than one-quarter of American share trades were taking place via the Internet.[23]

---

[22]See International Accounting Standards Committee, Business Reporting on the Internet, A Discussion Paper Issued by the IASC Staff, London: November, 1999, 103 pages.
[23]See *The Economist*, January 15, 2000, page 73.

EXHIBIT 5-14 Employment Disclosure by Labinal SA

4.14 Payroll Expenses and Personnel

	1999	1998	1998	99/98 Variation	98/97 Variation
Payroll expenses	4,978,832	4,550,291	3,979,985	428,541	570,306

In 1999, the payroll expenses which represented 29.7% of the production against 29.1% in 1998, increased by 9.4% compared to a production which increased by 7.3%. At a comparable perimeter and a constant exchange rate, the increase would have been 7.1% (i.e. +4% for France and +13.8% for abroad) for an average workforce which increased by 7.7% (i.e.— −0.5% for French companies and +15.7% for foreign companies).

Average number of employees
The Group's average number of employees per category of employee is broken down as follows.

	1999	1998	1997	99/98 Change
Management	2,185	2,255	2,015	−3.1%
Technicians and employees	6,753	5,923	5,193	14.0%
Workers	19,239	17,381	13,585	10.7%
Total	28,177	25,559	20,793	10.2%
Average workforce at a comparable scope of consolidation	26,761	24,857	—	7.7%

Source: Labinal Financial Report 1999, Notes to the Consolidated Accounts, p. 47.

EXHIBIT 5-15 Labinal SA French Franc-Euro Conversion Table

4.22 Euro
The significant figures for the 1997, 1998, and 1999 fiscal years have been converted into euros using the year-end exchange rate.

	In thousands of francs			In thousands of euros		
	1999	1998	1997	1999	1998	1997
Sales	16,465,960	15,371,381	12,801,081	2,510,219	2,343,352	1,951,512
Operating Income	1,173,410	1,346,633	1,017,709	178,885	205,293	155,149
Net income before tax	1,007,503	1,224,581	890,271	153,593	186,686	135,721
Net income group share	392,136	483,292	412,743	59,781	73,677	62,922
Cash flow	1,341,457	1,207,564	1,049,573	204,504	184,092	160,006
Capital	431,103	410,758	410,758	65,721	62,620	62,620
Shareholders' equity						
Group share	4,221,837	3,763,237	3,467,198	643,615	573,702	528,571
Financial debts	3,581,132	3,196,849	2,637,964	545,940	487,356	402,155
Nat securities	5,193,614	4,797,745	4,672,277	791,761	730,954	712,284
Balance Sheet total	15,099,910	13,817,707	12,444,215	2,301,966	2,106,496	1,897,108

	In francs			In euros		
Dividend per share	15.41	15.41	13.50	2.35	2.35	2.03
Net earnings per share (Group share)	47.73	58.83	50.24	7.28	8.97	7.66

Source: Labinal Financial Report 1999, Notes to the Consolidated Accounts, p. 48.

EXHIBIT 5-16   Discussion of U.S. GAAP by NetCom AB and Subsidiaries

NOTES TO THE CONSOLIDATED FINANCIAL STATEMENTS

Note 41

U.S. generally accepted accounting principles (U.S. GAAP)

The consolidated accounts were prepared based on accounting principles generally accepted in Sweden. These rules differ in certain respects from generally accepted accounting principles in the United States.

The following is a description of the adjustments based on U.S. GAAP that affect the consolidated income statement and consolidated shareholders' equity for each of the years ending December 31.

Reconciliation of net income for the year:

	Year ended December 31,			
	1997	*1998*	*1999*	*1999*
	SEK	*SEK*	*SEK*	*USD*
		(SEK/USD in thousands, except for earnings per share)		
Net income for the year based on Swedish accounting principles	48,542	66,618	3,769,129	443,166
Adjustments to comply with U.S. GAAP:				
a) Capitalized start-up costs	52,979	41,696	48,953	5,756
b) Capitalized interest expense	(2,970)	(2,970)	(2,970)	(349)
c) Transactions between companies with the same owners	20,599	20,599	20,599	2,422
d) Reporting associated companies	30,931	30,158	133,631	15,712
e) Leasing contracts	3,599	2,614	2,603	306
f) Tangible assets	826	36,697	28,847	3,392
g) Revenue recognition, prepaid cards	(4,052)	(12,135)	(15,693)	(1,845)
h) Stock options	—	—	9,242	1,087
i) Group accounting, acquisition analysis	—	—	1,574	185
j) Software development costs	—	—	(80,418)	(9,455)
k) Deferred taxes			(828,054)	(97,361)
Net adjustment	101,912	116,659	(681,686)	(80,151)
Tax effect of adjustments for U.S. GAAP	(16,736)	(20,838)	(43)	(5)
Net income for the year based on U.S. GAAP	133,718	162,439	3,087,401	363,010
Basic earnings per share, for the year	SEK 1.36	SEK 1.57	SEK 29.73	USD 3.50
Weighted avg. no. of shares outstanding	98,061,358	103,598,394	103,850,246	103,850,246
Diluted earnings per share for the year after full conversion	SEK 1.36	SEK 1.56	SEK 29.73	USD 3.50
Weighted avg. no. of shares outstanding after full conversion	103,433,579	103,850,246	103,850,246	103,850,246

EXHIBIT 5-16 *(cont.)*

Reconciliation of shareholders' equity:

	December 31,			
	1997	*1998*	*1999*	*1999*
	SEK	*SEK*	*SEK*	*USD*
			(SEK/USD in thousands)	
Shareholders' equity based on Swedish accounting principles..	3,155,259	3,268,941	7,002,314	823,317
Adjustments to comply with U.S. GAAP:				
a) Capitalized start-up costs................................	(365,778)	(322,677)	(274,955)	(32,330)
b) Capitalized interest expense...........................	26,724	23,754	20,784	2,444
c) Transactions between companies with the same owners	(112,841)	(92,242)	(71,643)	(8,424)
d) Reporting associated companies.....................	(174,165)	(133,631)	—	—
e) Leasing contracts	3,599	6,213	8,816	1,037
f) Tangible assets..	(45,314)	(8,617)	20,230	2,379
g) Revenue recognition, prepaid cards..............	(4,052)	(16,187)	(31,880)	(3,748)
h) Stock options...	—	—	9,242	1,087
i) Group accounting, acquisition analysis.........	—	—	1,574	185
j) Software development costs............................	—	—	(80,418)	(9,455)
k) Unrealized gains, available for sale securities...	—	—	2,440,996	287,007
l) Deferred taxes..			(828,054)	(97,361)
Net adjustment..	(671,827)	(543,387)	1,214,692	142,821
Tax effect of adjustments for U.S. GAAP...........	120,619	99,781	(583,741)	(68,635)
Shareholders' equity based on U.S. GAAP..	2,604,051	2,825,335	7,633,266	897,503

Extract from the consolidated balance sheets:

	Swedish GAAP		U.S. GAAP		
	1998	*1999*	*1998*	*1999*	*1999*
	SEK	*SEK*	*SEK*	*SEK*	*USD*
			(SEK/USD in thousands)		
Current assets	2,111,880	2,618,060	2,111,880	2,618,060	307,826
Fixed assets..	8,077,241	12,075,671	7,776,597	14,258,428	1,676,476
Total assets	10,189,121	14,693,731	9,888,477	16,876,488	1,984,302
Current liabilities................................	2,014,848	2,460,502	2,031,035	2,492,382	293,049
Long-term liabilities............................	4,903,793	5,229,903	5,030,568	6,749,829	793,631
Minority interest..................................	1,539	1,012	1,539	1,012	119
Total liabilities	6,920,180	7,691,417	7,063,142	9,243,223	1,086,799
Shareholders' equity	3,268,941	7,002,314	2,825,335	7,633,266	897,503

EXHIBIT 5-16 (cont.)

Restatement of reported net income and earnings per share under US GAAP

In November 1999, NetCom recognized a gain on the exchange of shares of NetCom ASA for shares of SEC (see Note 7). This gain is a non-taxable event in 1999, but may result in a taxable event in future periods. Under Swedish GAAP, a deferred tax liability is not required to be recognized. Under US GAAP, FAS 109, "Accounting for Income Taxes," would require the recognition of a deferred tax liability of SEK 828,054, which has not been previously recorded. Accordingly, the December 31, 1999 US GAAP reconciliation is restated as follows:

	Previously Reported	Additional Tax Expense	Restated
Net Income	3,915,455	(828,054)	3,087,401
Basic and diluted earnings	37.70	(7.97)	29.73

Explanation of current differences between Swedish accounting principles and U.S. GAAP

U.S. generally accepted accounting principles:

The consolidated accounts were prepared based on generally accepted accounting principles in Sweden. These rules differ in certain respects from U.S. GAAP.

The following is a description of the adjustments based on U.S. GAAP that affect consolidated net income for fiscal year ending December 31, 1997, 1998, and 1999 and the Group's consolidated shareholders' equity at December 31, 1997, 1998 and 1999. Differences between Swedish and U.S. accounting principles that are relevant to NetCom are also discussed below.

a) Capitalized start-up costs

The Group has recorded as assets start-up costs attributable to the construction of its networks to amortize over the useful life of the networks. A significant proportion of these costs are attributable to overhead incurred during the construction phase. U.S. GAAP requires such costs to be expensed; accordingly all capitalized start-up costs have been expensed as incurred for U.S. GAAP purposes and the effect of amortization has been reversed. At December 31, 1997, all start-up costs pertaining to fixed telephony in Tele2 AB had been fully amortized.

b) Capitalized interest expense

The Group has not capitalized as assets interest expenses incurred for financing constructing of certain fixed assets. Under U.S. GAAP, such interest expenses are included in the acquisition value of the fixed assets and are subsequently depreciated over the useful life of the assets. Fixed assets, depreciation and amortization were adjusted accordingly.

c) Transactions between companies with the same owners

In 1993, the Company acquired Tele2 and, in 1994, Comviq GSM AB from the Kinnevik Group. The transactions were reported based on the purchase method. Hence, the difference between the acquisition value and the market value of net assets was reported as goodwill. U.S. GAAP requires that the acquisition of operations from companies under common control be reported in a manner similar to the pooling-of-interests method. Accordingly, all reevaluations of properties, plant, equipment and other assets as well as goodwill arising at the time of establishments are eliminated in the consolidated accounts. Depreciation and amortization have been adjusted accordingly.

EXHIBIT 5-16 *(cont.)*

d) Reporting associated companies

In 1993, the Company acquired shares in the Norwegian associated company NetCom ASA from a company in the Kinnevik Group. The investment was reported based on equity accounting. In conjunction with the investment, a surplus was reported. Under U.S. GAAP, this surplus has been reversed, because it resulted from a transaction between companies under common control. Amortization was adjusted accordingly. During 1999 NetCom sold its shares and accordingly all opening balances adjustments have ben reserved.

e) Leasing contracts

The Group has certain leasing transactions, which have been treated as operating leases based on Swedish generally accepted accounting principles. U.S. GAAP classifies such contracts as financial leases.

f) Tangible assets

Certain overhead expenses that were capitalized under Swedish GAAP have been expensed for the U.S. GAAP adjustment. In addition, estimated direct payroll expenses attributable to the installation of networks have been capitalized, in accordance with U.S. GAAP.

g) Revenue recognition, prepaid cards

The Group reports revenue from the sale of prepaid cards when the cards are sold to an independent dealer. Provisions are made for anticipated future costs. Under U.S. GAAP, revenue cannot be recognized until the telephony service is being used regularly by the end-customer. For U.S. GAAP purposes an adjustment has been recorded to reflect revenue recognition over the life of the pre-paid card.

h) Stock options

Under Swedish GAAP, all options are valued using the Black-Scholes model. For U.S. GAAP purposes, the Company applies Accounting Principles Board Opinion No. 25 ("APB25") when accounting for its stock options, which requires compensation expense to be measured at the difference between the fair market value of the underlying shares and the option exercise price, recognized over the vesting period of the option. Had compensation cost for the stock options been determined based on the fair value at the grant date for awards consistent with the method of Statement of Financial Accounting Standards No. 123 "Accounting for Stock-based Compensation" ("FAS 123"), the Company's net income and earnings per share under U.S. GAAP would have been adjusted to the pro forma amounts indicated below:

	1997	*1998*	*1999*
	SEK in thousands, except earnings per share)		
Net income as adjusted for U.S. GAAP, as reported	133,718	162,439	3,087,401
Pro forma	155,362	153,187	3,080,747
Basic earnings per share for U.S. GAAP, as reported	1.36	1.57	29.73
Pro forma	1.58	1.47	29.67

i) Group accounting, acquisition analysis

Under Swedish GAAP, net assets for Ritabell AS were recorded at a higher amount than were allowed for US GAAP, due to the accounting for start up costs. Accordingly, the purchase price over the fair market value of the assets created additional goodwill for US GAAP purposes. The adjustment reflects the net effect of additional amortization of goodwill under US GAAP.

EXHIBIT 5-16 (cont.)

j) Software development costs

Under Swedish GAAP, there is no specific accounting guidance pertaining to software developed for external marketing. Under U.S. GAAP, SFAS 86, "Accounting for the Costs of Computer Software to be sold, leased or otherwise marketed," requires development costs of externally marketed software products to be expensed until technological feasibility has been established. These capitalized costs are subsequently amortized over the software life.

k) Unrealized gains, available for sale securities

Under U.S. GAAP, securities classified as available for sale are measured at fair value in the statement of financial position. Unrealized gains and losses on these investments in equity are recorded in comprehensive income, net of deferred taxes. Swedish GAAP does not provide for the marking to market of available-for-sale securities and the recognition of unrealized gains or losses. For U.S. GAAP purposes, adjustments have been made to reflect this difference.

l) Deferred taxes

Under U.S. GAAP, deferred tax amounts are required to be recognized on temporary differences, except for certain specific exemptions. Under Swedish GAAP, and in accordance the Company's tax accounting policy, the company does not provide for temporary differences related to long term strategic investments. As such, an adjustment to reflect the recognition of a deferred tax liability related to the gain on the sale of NetCom ASA shares has been made to reflect this difference.

Additional information for U.S. GAAP:

Change of accounting principle

For Swedish GAAP purposes, the Company, during 1999, implemented a change in accounting principle. This change is reflected in the Swedish financial statements as a restatement to the accounts for all periods presented. In addition, the new Swedish accounting principle, which requires goodwill relating to foreign operations to be denominated in its functional currency, was a longstanding accounting requirement under U.S. GAAP, which had not been reflected in previous reconciliations. The foreign subsidiaries' translation adjustment relating to foreign denominated assets creates an adjustment to comprehensive income under U.S. GAAP. Under U.S. GAAP, a correction of an error is reported by restating the accounts for all periods presented. Accordingly, the Swedish change in accounting principle effectively mirrored the required accounting under U.S. GAAP and no adjustment in the reconciliation was required.

Reportable segments

The Company's reportable segments are strategic business areas that offer different services. They are managed separately because each business area requires different technology and marketing strategies.

EXHIBIT 5-16 *(cont.)*

Earnings per share

Net profit/loss per share on full conversion excludes interest expense, adjusted for tax, on the outstanding convertible debentures as specified below.

	For the year ended December 31,		
	1997	1998	1999
	(SEK in thousands, except earnings per share)		
Net income for the year	133,718	162,439	3,087,401
Number of shares, weighted average	98,061,358	103,598,394	103,850,246
Basic earnings per share	SEK 1.36	SEK 1.57	SEK 29.73
Net income for the year	133,718	162,439	3,087,401
Reversal: interest for the year on the outstanding convertible debenture	14,742	—	
Reversal: 28% deferred tax on interest reversed above	(4,128)	—	—
Income for the year after full conversion	144,332	162,439	3,087,401
No. of shares outstanding after full conversion, weighted average	103,433,579	103,850,246	103,850,246
Diluted earnings per share after full conversion	SEK 1.36	SEK 1.56	SEK 29.73

Deferred tax

The following shows the estimated tax effect, related to temporary differences that is reported as deferred tax benefit in the reconciliation of accounts with U.S. GAAP.

	1998	1999
	(SEK in thousands)	
Deferred tax liability/benefit based on Swedish generally accepted accounting principles	232,715	(139,245)
Adjustments to comply with U.S. GAAP	99,781	(1,411,795)
Total deferred tax liability/benefit based on U.S. GAAP	332,496	(1,551,040)

Cash flows

The accompanying cash flow statements are prepared in a format consistent with SFAS No. 95, "Statement of Cash Flows," except that cash flow provided from operating activities is reconciled from operating income, not net income, as is required under U.S. GAAP.

EXHIBIT 5-16   (cont.)

These differences between the Swedish accounts and U.S. GAAP are described in the table below.

Cash flow from operating activities:

	Year ended December 31,		
	1997	*1998*	*1999*
	(SEK in thousands)		
Net income	48,542	66,618	3,769,129
Adjustments to reconcile net income to net cash provided by operating activities:			
Depreciation and amortization...	608,348	704,604	955,245
Minority interest..	—	(270)	(2,363)
Gain/loss of associated companies	119,282	9,929	(49,725)
Deferred income taxes..	(85,663)	165,581	411,737
Capital leases	(1,204)	(9,737)	(5,980)
Unpaid interest..	(36,209)	17,929	(32,424)
Sales of shares of associated companies	—	—	(3,227,889)
Other...	(2,941)	839	(5,635)
	650,155	955,493	1,812,095
Change in working capital, net	(239,111)	34,481	(40,974)
Cashflow provided by operating activities	411,044	989,974	1,771,121

Advertising expenses

Total advertising expenses for the year were SEK 168 million (1998: SEK 209 million; 1997: SEK 112 million).

Pensions

NetCom accounts for the valuation and disclosure of pension obligations under SFAS No. 87, "Employer's Accounting for Pensions," and SFAS No. 132, "Employers' Disclosures about pensions and other post retirement benefits." The Group provides pension benefits for all employees in Sweden through general pension plans. These Swedish pension plans are defined benefit plans but are insured with a third party. In Denmark, pension benfits are provided based on a defined contribution pension plan. Pension plans in Norway are defined benefit plans, which require U.S. GAAP valuation. However, the adjustment is not material and thus no adjustment has been made. The Group's pension costs are reported in the note "Costs of Personnel." For the year ended December 31, 1999, SEK 1.2 million (1998: SEK 1.4 million; 1997: SEK 0.5 million) was attributable to defined benefit pension plans in Norway and SEK 0.8 million (1998: SEK 0.7 million; 1997: SEK 0.0 million) was attributable to defined contribution pension plans in Denmark.

Fair value

SFAS 107, "Disclosure about Fair Values of Financial Instruments," requires the disclosure of estimated fair values for all financial instruments for which it is practicable to estimate fair value. With the exception of certain available for sale investments and certain fixed interest bearing debt, as discussed further below, all financial instruments of the Group including cash and cash equivalents, short-term investments, receivables and payables, prepaid revenues and short-term liabilities to financial institutions are deemed to approximate fair value due to short maturity. The carrying amount of the Group's long-term liabilities to financial institutions and options issued are also deemed to approximate their fair values.

EXHIBIT 5-16 *(cont.)*

Investments

The Company accounts for its investments using the Statement of Financial Accounting Standards No 115, "Accounting for Certain Investments in Debt and Equity Securities" ("SFAS 115"). This standard requires that certain debt and equity securities be adjusted to market value at the end of each accounting period. Unrealized market value gains and losses are charged to earnings if the securities are traded for short-term profit. Otherwise, such unrealized gains and losses are charged or credited to comprehensive income. Management determines the proper classifications of investments in marketable equity securities at the time of purchase and reevaluates such designations as of each balance sheet date. As of December 31, 1999 and 1998 all securities covered by SFAS 115 were designated as available for sale. Accordingly, these securities are stated at fair value, with unrealized gains and losses reported in a comprehensive income.

Available-for-sale securities:

	December 31, 1999		
	At Cost	Gross Unrealized Gain	Market Value
	(SEK in thousands)		
Société Européenne de Communication SA	3,518,004	2,440,996	5,959,000
AS Levicom Broadband	18,382	—	18,382
Suomen Kolmegee	4,699	—	4,699
SCD Invest AB	0	—	0
Brf Sundsvallshus	390	—	390
	3,541,475	2,440,996	5,982,471

Differences between cost and market of SEK 2,440,996 thousand (less deferred taxes of SEK 683,479 thousand) were credited to comprehensive income.

Fixed interest-bearing debt

The fair value of the company's fixed interest loan of nominal SEK 125 million amounts to 116 Million, based on an inputed interest of 5.13%, which management considers the currently available interest rate.

Interest cap agreements

In order to maximize the group's interest exposure, NetCom has entered into various interest cap agreements with several banks. See further note 38. The total cost for the present arrangements amounts to SEK 17.7 Million. The fair value of the interest caps arrangements amounts to SEK 27.4 Million.

Internal use software

In accordance with AICPA Statement of Position no 98-1, The company capitalizes certain direct development costs associated with internal use software, which are amortized over the economic useful life beginning when the asset is substantially ready for use. Costs incurred during the preliminary project stage, as well as maintenance and training costs, are expensed as incurred.

EXHIBIT 5-16 *(cont.)*

Financial Leasing

Minimum annual lease payments for the five year period subsequent to 1999 and in the aggregate are:

	Capitalized leases
	(SEK in thousands)
2000..	74,644
2001..	65,031
2002..	48,568
2003..	38,165
2004..	34,064
2005–2009..	93,154
2010–2014..	53,858
Total minimum lease payments......................................	407,484
Less amount representing interest	(78,526)
Present value of net minimum lease payment...........................	328,958

Nonrecurring item

Under Swedish GAAP, changes in the lag time for an equity investment earnings pick-up may be reported as a nonrecurring item. Under US GAAP, such a change would be accounted for as a change in accounting principle.

Comprehensive income

The Company accounts for Comprehensive income in accordance with SFAS No. 130 "Reporting Comprehensive Income." Comprehensive income includes net income, unrealized gains on available-for-sale securities, net of tax and foreign currency translation adjustments.

Comprehensive income:

	Year ended December 31,		
	1997	1998	1999
	(SEK in thousands)		
Net income based on U.S. GAAP..	133,718	162,439	3,087,401
Unrealized gains, available-for-sale securities, net of tax........	—	—	1,757,507
Exchange rate differences based on U.S. GAAP.....................	(4,783)	21,183	(73,475)
Comprehensive Income based on U.S. GAAP.......................	128,935	183,622	4,771,433

EXHIBIT 5-16 *(cont.)*

Accumulated Other Comprehensive Income:

	Year ended December 31,		
	1997	1998	1999
	(SEK in thousands)		
Cumulative Comprehensive Income based on U.S. GAAP, Jan 1, ...	36,145	31,362	52,545
Unrealized gains, available-for sale securities, net of tax, ...	—	—	1,757,507
Exchange rate differences based on U.S. GAAP	(4,783)	21,183	(73,475)
Cumulative Comprehensive Income based on U.S. GAAP, Dec 31, ...	31,362	52,545	1,736,587

New accounting Pronouncements

On June 15, 1998, the Financial Accounting Standards Board (FASB) issued FAS No. 133, "Accounting for Derivative Instruments and Hedging Activities," as amended by FAS No. 137, "Accounting for Derivative Instruments and Hedging Activities-Deferral of the Effective Date of FASB Statement No. 133." FAS 137 delayed the effective date of FAS 133 to be effective for fiscal years beginning after June 15, 2000. FAS 133 requires that all derivative instruments be recorded on the balance sheet at their fair value. Changes in the fair value of derivatives are recorded each period in current earnings or other comprehensive income, depending on whether or not a derivative is designated as part of a hedge transaction and, if it is, the type of hedge transaction. Management anticipates that, due to its limited use of derivative instruments, the adoption of SFAS 133 will not have a significant effect on NetCom's results of operations or its financial position based on U.S. GAAP.

In 1999, the Swedish Financial Accounting Standards Council issued Recommendation RR6:99 (effective for fiscal years beginning after January 1, 2000), "Accounting for leases," Recommendation RR9, "Accounting for taxes" (effective for fiscal years beginning after January 1, 2001), Recommendation RR11, "Revenue" (effective for fiscal years beginning after January 1, 2001), and Recommendation RR12, "Property, plant and equipment" (effective for fiscal years beginning after January 1, 2001). Management does not believe the effect of adoption of these recommendations will be material. These changes do not impact the determination of consolidated net income and consolidated shareholder's equity under U.S. GAAP.

Source: NetCom AB 1999 Financial Statements.

One important development that will facilitate Web-based business reporting is eXtensible Business Reporting Language (XBRL). XBRL is on the verge of revolutionizing financial reporting. This language will be built into nearly all future releases of accounting and financial reporting software, and most users will not need to learn how to manipulate it directly in order to enjoy its benefits.[24]

The concept of a universal financial reporting computer language emerged in 1999. Soon after, Microsoft and IBM recognized both its potential and the need to develop a single standard cooperatively rather than have each software company develop its own

---

[24]See Kurt Ramin, "Fair Values," *Business Excellence for the Intellectual Capital Investor* 1, (summer 2000): 13–16; and Stanley Zarowin and Wayne E. Harding, "Finally, Business Talks the Same Language," *Journal of Accountancy* (August 2000): 24–30.

EXHIBIT 5-17 Corporate Governance Disclosure by Southern Pacific Petroleum

Directors and management are committed to high standards of corporate governance for which the Board is ultimately responsible. The corporate governance practices set out below have operated for the whole of the year.

Board Composition and Membership

As at the date of the Directors' Report the Board is comprised of the Chairman, five executive Directors and four non-executive Directors. The Board believes that this provides an appropriate mix of qualifications, skills and experience for this stage of the company's development. The Constitution requires that one third of Directors retire each year by rotation and that no Director shall remain in office for more than three years without re-election. Directors have the ability to seek professional advice at the company's expense.

Conduct of Directors

Directors are required to conduct themselves to the highest ethical standards. Statutory requirements are required as the minimum standard to be attained. Directors must avoid any matter that may result in an actual or perceived conflict of interest and must avoid acting in a manner that is in contradiction to the interests of shareholders.

Audit Committee

Members of the Audit Committee are N. J. Paterson (non-executive Director) and V. H. Kuss (executive Director). Financial officers of the company and auditors attend by invitation. The objectives of the Committee are to:

- oversee and review audits conducted by the company's external auditors;
- maintain, by scheduling regular meetings, open lines of communication between the Board and the external auditors, exchange views and information, and confirm their respective authority and responsibilities;
- serve as an independent and objective party for the review of financial information presented in the annual report, including the related party transactions; and
- determine the adequacy and transparency of the company's administrative, operating and accounting controls.

The Committee has unlimited access to auditors and senior management, and has the ability to consult independent experts.

Corporate Governance Committee

Members of the Corporate Governance Committee are N. J. Paterson (non-executive Director), B. Davidson (non-executive Director), V. H. Kuss (executive Director) and S. L. Forbes (Manager—Finance and Administration). The responsibilities of the Committee are to:

- recommend to the Board a Statement of Corporate Governance Principles;
- prepare for and recommend on an annual basis to the Board a Corporate Governance statement to be included in the Annual Report;
- see that newly elected Directors are properly trained and inducted in their Board functions and responsibilities, and provide for ongoing professional development;
- ensure that compliance systems are in place. This includes assessing the adequacy of the company's policies and procedures; and
- act as a resource for individual Directors and the company as a whole on questions of corporate governance and corporate ethics.

The Corporate Governance Committee reports monthly to the Board and has the ability to seek professional advice at the company's expense.

EXHIBIT 5-17 (cont.)

Risk Assessment

The Board monitors operational and financial risk through a combination of departmental reporting and purpose-specific risk management committees including the Title Committee, Calls Paid Committee, Audit Committee and Corporate Governance Committee.

Code of Conduct

Employees are required to observe high ethical standards. The purpose of the company's written Code of Conduct is to encourage an awareness of these obligations and to provide guidance. The Code of Conduct covers compliance with the law, protection of company material, dealing in the company's securities, conflict of interest, occupational health and safety, record keeping, discrimination and the promotion of a positive work environment. The company has adopted Corporate Values which further develop the principles espoused in the Code of Conduct and ensure that the business of the company is conducted in an honest, open and ethical manner.

Source: Southern Pacific Petroleum N.L. Annual Report 2000.

standard, which would undermine the very idea of making the language universal. Because it has been developed cooperatively, XBRL will be free of charge to software companies that wish to use it in their software, and extensions of XBRL developed for specific industries will be available free for downloading from the Internet.

Once implemented, XBRL will automatically translate any desired item of business information—words or numbers—so that the information need be entered only once. Once entered, this information then can be used and worked with in many ways without being reformatted. Refer to Exhibits 5-18 and 5-19 for illustrations of a typical XBRL balance sheet structure (following U.S. GAAP), and a fragment of the XBRL taxonomy, respectively.

Stock exchanges, regulators, and public companies are increasingly using the Internet to provide financial statement users with immediate and low-cost access to company information. For example, more and more stock exchanges now use electronic news services to provide immediate access to all listed company announcements. These services offer an important benefit to listed companies and investors: All listed company announcements, not just those deemed "newsworthy" by the financial press, are made publicly available on a single Web site. Exhibit 5-20 presents descriptions of selected stock exchange electronic news services.

ANNUAL REPORT DISCLOSURES IN EMERGING MARKET COUNTRIES

Disclosures in annual reports of companies in emerging market countries are generally less extensive and less credible than those of companies in developed countries. For example, insufficient and misleading disclosure and lax investor protection have been cited as reasons contributing to the East Asia financial crisis of 1997.

Low disclosure levels in emerging market countries are consistent with systems of corporate governance and finance in those countries. Equity markets are not well developed, banks and insiders such as family groups supply most of the financing, and

EXHIBIT 5-18   Typical XBRL Structure of a Balance Sheet that Follows U.S. GAAP

```xml
<?xml version="1.0" encoding=?utf-8" ?>
-<schema targetNamespace=http://www.xbrl.org/us/AICPA-US-GAAP-CI-00-04-04.xsd>
  <element name="statements" type="string" /
  <element name="statements.balanceSheet" type="monetary">
  - <annotation>
      <documentation>The balance sheet as a whole is a "monetary" type because, by definition, the
      assets, liabilities and equity sum to zero.</documentation>
    </annotation>
  </element>
  - <element name="balanceSheet.title" type="string">
  - <annotation>
      <documentation>{This element is presentation related only and probably should be
      removed.}</documentation>
    </annotation>
  </element>
  - <element name="balanceSheet.date" type="string">
  - <annotation>
      <documentation>{This element is redundant with the period information already embedded in
      every item and should be removed.}</documentation>
    </annotation>
  </element>
  - <element name="balanceSheet.referenceToNotes" type="string">
  - <annotation>
      <documentation>{The intended usage of this element is so unclear that it should be
      removed.}</documentation>
```

EXHIBIT 5-19 Fragment of the Commercial and Industrial XBRL Taxonomy

XBRL US GAAP Christ&I Taxonomy 00-04-04

This list includes the "label" attribute in bold, followed by the attributes (order / type / sense / repeatable). Descriptions in italics; references in roman.

- **statements** (1 / string / none /)
  - **balance sheet** (3 / monetary / none /) *The balance sheet as a whole is a "monetary" type because, by definition, the assets, liabilities, and equity sum to zero.*
    - **title** (1 / string / none/) {*This element is presentation related only and probably should be removed*}
    - **date** (2 / string/ none/) {*This element is redundant with the period information already embedded in every item and should be removed.*}
    - **reference to notes** (3 / string / none/) {*The intended usage of this element is so unclear that it should be removed.*}
    - **assets** (1 / monetary / add /)
      - **current assets** (1 / monetary / add /)
        - **cash, cash equivalents and short term investments** (1/ monetary/add /)
          - **cash and cash equivalents** (1 / monetary / add /)
            - **cash** (1 / monetary / add /)
            - **cash equivalents** (1 / monetary / add /)
          - **short term investments** (2 / monetary / add /) *Short-term investments in debt and equity securities. {Items in the taxonomy generally have either zero children or more than one. It is unclear in this case what other children "short term investments" should have besides "marketable securities."*
            - **marketable securities** (1 / monetary / add /)
              - **available for sale** (1 / monetary / add /)
              - **held to maturity** (2 / monetary / add /)
              - **trading** (3 / monetary / add /)
        - **receivables** (3 / monetary / add /)
          - **accounts receivable-trade net** (1 / monetary / add /)
            - **accounts receivable-trade** (1 / monetary / add /)
            - **allowance for doubtful accounts** (2 / monetary / subtract /)

EXHIBIT 5-20   Stock Exchange Dissemination of Listed Company News

The Web sites of stock exchanges vary dramatically in content and ease of use. Text of some Web sites (such as the Mexican Stock Exchange) is mostly available only in the home language. Some Web sites are extremely difficult to use.

Some stock exchanges (such as Luxembourg and South Africa) refer Web site users to outside vendors for listing rules and other items. The authors' experience with these vendors has been disappointing.

Following are notes on some arbitrarily selected stock exchanges. Information is current as of April 1, 2001.

Euronext—Amsterdam (formerly Amsterdam Stock Exchange) (www.aex.nl) (www.euronext.com)

The Euronext—Amsterdam Web site contains a list of headlines (available in English) sorted by date and time. Each headline can be selected to open the full text of the announcement (in Dutch only). It appears that one year's worth of press releases is available for each listed company, along with a time series of all press releases.

Italian Exchange (Borsa Italiana) (www.borsaitalia.it)

The Italian Exchange Web site provides headlines and full text of press releases, sorted chronologically in four different categories.

Johannesburg Stock Exchange (JSE) (www.jse.co.za)

The JSE operates the Stock Exchange News Service (SENS), which resembles London's Regulatory News Service. SENS was launched and became mandatory for listed companies in 1997. The JSE Web site contains detailed guidelines for listed companies and SENS procedural requirements.

It does not appear that company press releases are available on the JSE Web site. SENS can be accessed by a direct link to the JSE through a required connection or by subscription to one of the JSE's data vendors.

Latibex (www.latibex.com)

Recently launched by the Madrid Stock Exchange, Latibex is a stock exchange based in Madrid that is designed for Latin American issuers interested in listing in Europe. The Latibex Web site contains a list of press releases headlined in chronological order with a time-stamp. "Selecting" the headline opens the full story.

London Stock Exchange (LSE) (www.londonstockexchange.com)

The LSE has operated its Regulatory News Service (RNS) for many years. Listed companies are required to submit all press releases to the LSE for publication on the RNS before or at the same time as public release.

All RNS company announcements now are freely available on the Web. The LSE Web site provides a chronological "feed" of headlines sorted by date and time. The full text of each announcement can be obtained by selecting the headline. Company announcements can be searched by name of company, keyword in headline, and time period.

Mexican Stock Exchange (BMV) (www.bmv.com.mx)

Headlines and full text (in Spanish only) of press releases are available freely on the Web site, listed chronologically.

Oslo Stock Exchange (www.ose.no)

Most Norwegian companies' announcements are in Norwegian. The Oslo SE Web site contains instructions for subscribing to an e-mail service that provides information either for selected companies or selected news stories. It may be difficult to print from this Web site.

Exhibit 5-20 *(cont.)*

PRline

This very powerful service provides free access to press release headlines, company name, date, time, and full text. Each of the four PRline Web sites provides a unique set of press releases. For example, the French Web site (**www.prline.com**) provides French press releases.

France: **www.prline.com**

Benelux (Belgium, Netherlands, Luxembourg): **www.prline.be**

Italy: **www.prline.it**

Spain: **www.prline.es**

Stock Exchange of Singapore (SGX) (www.ses.com.sg)

The SGX Web site contains press release headlines and full text sorted by date and time, also available sorted alphabetically by company name. Press releases are archived for up to 1 year.

so in general there has been less demand for credible, timely public disclosure than in more developed economies.

However, investor demand for timely and credible information about companies in emerging market countries has been growing, and regulators have responded to this demand by making disclosure requirements more stringent, and by stepping up their monitoring and enforcement efforts.

One recent study presents several types of evidence supporting the view that disclosure levels and quality are lower in emerging market countries than in developed countries.[25] For example, Exhibit 5-21 shows that 12 of the 20 countries with relatively low disclosure levels are emerging market countries. In contrast, only three of the countries with relatively high disclosure levels are emerging market countries.

Exhibit 5-22 presents information on the relative numbers of auditors in emerging markets and in developed markets. Exhibit 5-22 shows that, in general, there are more auditors per 100,000 population in developed markets than in emerging markets. Because monitoring and enforcement of sound financial reporting are enhanced by the presence of adequate numbers of accountants and auditors, Exhibit 5-22 suggests potential enforcement difficulties in the emerging markets shown there.

Empirical evidence on disclosure practices in emerging market countries has been limited until recently. However, as these countries' stock markets and listed companies seek to increase their presence, researchers are developing more evidence on what these practices are and how they differ from those in developed countries.

IMPLICATIONS FOR FINANCIAL STATEMENT USERS AND MANAGERS

Financial statement users should expect wide variation in disclosure levels and financial reporting practices. Although managers in many firms continue to be strongly influenced by the costs of disclosing proprietary information, the levels of both mandatory

---

[25]See S. M. Saudagaran and G. D. Joselito, "Financial Reporting in Emerging Capital Markets: Characteristics and Policy Issues," *Accounting Horizons* 11 (June 1997): 41–64.

EXHIBIT 5-21 Disclosure Levels of Industrial Companies in Selected Emerging Market and Developed Countries

Rank	Country	Average Score	Rank	Country	Average Score
1	United Kingdom	85	11	Spain Zimbabwe[1]	72
2	Finland Sweden	83	12	Japan Mexico[1]	71
3	Ireland	81	13	Nigeria[1]	70
4	Australia New Zealand Switzerland	80	14	Argentina[1] Belgium South Korea[1]	68
5	Malaysia[1]	79	15	Germany	67
6	Chile[1]	78	16	Italy Thailand	66
7	United States	76	17	Philippines[1]	64
8	Canada Denmark Norway	75	18	Austria	62
9	Israel Netherlands Sri Lanka[1]	74	19	Greece[1] India[1]	61
10	Hong Kong Pakistan[1]	73	20	Colombia[1] Taiwan[1] Turkey[1]	58

[1]Emerging market country

Source: Shahrokh M. Saudagaran and Joselito G. Diga, "Financial Reporting in Emerging Capital Markets: Characteristics and Policy Issues," *Accounting Horizons* 11 (June 1997), pp. 41–64, as presented in Bavishi, Vinod B., Ed., *International Accounting and Auditing Trends, 4th Edition, 1995,* Center for International Financial Analysis & Research, Inc. (Princeton, NJ: CIFAR Publications, Inc., 1995). Used with permission of *Accounting Horizons* and American Accounting Association.

and voluntary disclosure are increasing worldwide. Managers in traditionally low-disclosure countries should consider whether adopting a policy of enhanced disclosure might provide significant benefits for their firms. (The requirement to adopt IAS no later than 2005 will require many European companies outside the United Kingdom to increase their disclosures substantially.) In addition, managers who decide to provide enhanced disclosures in areas investors and analysts consider important, such as segment and reconciliation disclosures, might obtain a competitive advantage over firms with restrictive disclosure policies. Further study of the costs and benefits of enhanced disclosure in international settings should provide important evidence in this area.

Selected References

Bavishi, V. B., Ed., *International Accounting and Auditing Trends, 4th Edition, 1995,* vol. I, Princeton, NJ: CIFAR Publications, Inc., 1995.

Bayless, R., J. Cochrane, T. Harris, J. Leisenring, J. McLaughlin, and J. P. Wirtz, "International Access to U.S. Capital Markets—An AAA

EXHIBIT 5-22 Accountants and Auditors in Emerging Market and Developed Countries[1]

Emerging Markets	Number of Auditors Per 100,000 Population	Developed Markets	Number of Auditors Per 100,000 Population
Chile	87	New Zealand	550
Argentina	71	Australia	539
Malaysia	48	United Kingdom	352
South Africa	35	Canada	350
Philippines	31	Singapore	273
Taiwan	17	Ireland	262
Mexico	15	United States	168
Poland	14	Hong Kong	110
Greece	12	Italy	110
Zimbabwe	11	Denmark	106
India	9	Switzerland	53
Sri Lanka	9	Netherlands	52
Nigeria	8	France	45
South Korea	7	Sweden	41
Thailand	5	Belgium	38
Colombia	2	Germany	26
Indonesia	2	Spain	18
Pakistan	2	Finland	10
Brazil	1	Japan	10

[1]Personal communication with the International Federation of Accountants (IFAC) Secretariat, August 13, 1996.

Source: Shahrokh M. Saudagaran and Joselito G. Diga, "Financial Reporting in Emerging Capital Markets: Characteristics and Policy Issues," *Accounting Horizons* 11 (June 1997): 41–64.

Forum on Accounting Policy," *Accounting Horizons* 10 (March 1996): 75–94.

Choi, F. D. S., and R. M. Levich, "Accounting Diversity," in *The European Equity Markets: The State of the Union and an Agenda for the Millennium,* B. Steil, ed., London: European Capital Markets Institute, 1996, 259–320.

Choi, F. D. S., "Financial Reporting Requirements for Non-U.S. Registrants: International Market Perspectives," *Financial Markets, Institutions & Instruments* 6, no. 5, New York University Salomon Center, (December 1997), 23–44.

Frost, C. A., and M. Lang, "Foreign Companies and U.S. Securities Markets: Financial Reporting Policy Issues and Suggestions for Research," *Accounting Horizons* 10 (March 1996): 95–109.

Frost, C. A., and K. P. Ramin, "Corporate Financial Disclosure: A Global Assessment," in *International Accounting and Finance Handbook, Second Edition,* F. D. S. Choi, ed., New York: John Wiley & Sons, 1997.

Gernon, H., and G. K. Meek, *Accounting, An International Perspective, Fifth Edition,* Boston: Irwin McGraw-Hill, 2001.

Healy, P. M., and K. G. Palepu, "The Effect of Firms' Financial Disclosure Strategies on Stock Prices," *Accounting Horizons* 7 (March, 1993), 1–11.

International Organisation of Securities Commissions (IOSCO) Working Party No. 1, *International Disclosure Standards for Cross Border Offerings and Initial Listings by Foreign Issuers–Consultative Document,* IOSCO, August, 1997.

LaPorta, R., F. Lopez-de-Silanes, A. Shleifer, and R. Vishny, "Legal Determinants of External Finance," *The Journal of Finance* 52 (July 1997): 1131–1150.

Meek, G. K., C. B. Roberts, and S. J. Gray, "Factors Influencing Voluntary Annual Report Disclosures by U.S., U.K. and Continental European Multinational Corporations," *Journal of International Business Studies* (Third Quarter 1995): 555–572.

Nobes, C., PricewaterhouseCoopers, Arthur Andersen, BDO, Deloitte Touche Tohmatsu, Ernst & Young International, Grant Thornton, and KPMG, "GAAP 2000—A Survey of National Accounting Rules in 53 Countries," International Forum on Accountancy Development (www.ifad.net), December 2000.

Organisation for Economic Co-operation and Development (OECD), Background and Issues Paper for the OECD Symposium on the Role of Disclosure in Strengthening Corporate Governance, OECD, February 12–13, 1998.

PricewaterhouseCoopers, LLC, *Accessing International Capital Markets,* 2nd ed. New York: PricewaterhouseCoopers, 2001.

PricewaterhouseCoopers LLC, *Entering the United States Securities Markets—A Guide for Non-U.S. Companies,* New York: PricewaterhouseCoopers, 1999.

Radebaugh, L. H., "Segmental and Foreign Operations Disclosure," in *International Accounting and Finance Handbook, Second Edition,* F. D. S. Choi, ed., New York: John Wiley & Sons, 1997.

Ramin, K., "Fair Values," *Business Excellence for the Intellectual Capital Investor* 1 (summer 2000): 13–16.

Roberts, C. B., S. J. Gray, and C. A. Adams, "Corporate Social and Environmental Disclosures," in *International Accounting and Finance Handbook, Second Edition,* F. D. S. Choi, ed., New York: John Wiley & Sons, 1997.

Saudagaran, S. M. and J. G. Diga, "Financial Reporting in Emerging Capital Markets: Characteristics and Policy Issues," *Accounting Horizons* 11 (June 1997): 41–64.

Saudagaran, S. M., and G. K. Meek, "A Review of Research on Financial Reporting in International Capital Markets," *Journal of Accounting Literature,* 16 (1997): 127–159.

Discussion Questions

1. Briefly explain the distinction between accounting measurement and accounting disclosure. Which of the two reporting processes do you think promises substantial innovative advances during the next 10 years? Why?

2. Why are multinational corporations increasingly being held accountable to constituencies other than traditional investor groups?

3. Should foreign companies seeking to issue securities in the United States be required to disclose as much as U.S. companies issuing securities in the United States? Critically evaluate the arguments presented in this chapter.

4. Accounting rules in Japan, France, and Germany now require disclosure of business segment financial results. However, managers in these countries traditionally have been opposed to disclosing detailed segment information. Why have managers chosen to disclose relatively little information about the business segments of their companies, and why have accounting rules become more stringent despite their opposition?

5. What is the distinction between voluntary disclosure and mandatory disclosure? Provide at least two explanations for differences in managers' voluntary disclosure practices. Provide at least two explanations for differences in managers' mandatory disclosure practices.

6. Refer to Exhibit 5-13, which presents BASF AG's discussion of sustainable development. What is sustainable development? It is in the best interests of shareholders for BASF to adhere to the principle of sustainable development?

7. Do you expect to observe more or less voluntary disclosure by companies in emerging market countries than in developed countries? Why?

8. Do you expect to observe more or less regulatory disclosure requirements in emerging market countries than in developed countries? Why?

9. What are the two broad objectives for investor-oriented markets? Which of these do you think is the most important? Present reasons for your response.

10. From the perspective of a securities market regulator, is more required disclosure always better than less? Why or why not?

11. Why do you think that French and German annual reports contain earnings and sales forecasts more frequently than U.K. and U.S. annual reports? (Refer to Exhibit 5-2 for comparative evidence.)

12. What is corporate governance? Listed companies in some countries are required to disclose information about their corporate governance practices. Why might investors and analysts find such information useful?

Exercises

1. Exhibit 5-1 presents objectives for investor oriented equity markets. Appendix 1-3 presents stock exchange Web site addresses, and Exhibit 8-2 presents Web site addresses of securities market regulatory agencies.

   Required: Use the World Wide Web or other information sources to learn about the equity market in your home country.
   a. What types of information would help you assess whether it has the desired characteristics presented in the exhibit?
   b. Do the stock exchanges or regulatory agencies in your country provide such information?
   c. Review the exhibits in Chapter 1 and discuss what types of information they provide that are helpful in your assessment.
   d. Present your best evaluation of whether your equity market has achieved the goals of investor protection and market quality.

2. Chapter 5 presents accounting principle requirements for domestic and foreign companies listed on stock exchanges in six highly developed countries and in four emerging market countries.

   Required: Prepare a table showing the acceptability of using IAS in each country. The table should discuss requirements for both domestic and foreign listed companies. Why are accounting principle rules different sometimes for domestic and foreign companies? Do you observe an overall difference in IAS acceptability in developed versus emerging market countries? Give a possible explanation for any difference you observe.

3. Chapter 5 presents accounting principle requirements for domestic and foreign companies listed on stock exchanges in six highly developed countries and in four emerging market countries.

   Required: For each country prepare a table listing: (1) whether it has a new (equity) market (that is, a market designed for young, high-growth companies that might not meet the listing requirements of the main, primary market), (2) the name of any such market(s), and (3) any differences in accounting principle, financial reporting, or disclosure requirements for companies listed on the new market versus companies listed on the main market.

4. Chapter 5 presents accounting principle requirements for domestic and foreign companies listed on stock exchanges in six highly developed countries and in four emerging market countries. (Also refer to Exhibit 5-17, which presents a corporate governance disclosure [a requirement for listed companies in Australia] made by Southern Pacific Petroleum N.L. in its annual report.)

   Required: In which three countries are listed companies required to make corporate governance disclosures? In what respects are equity markets in these countries similar?

5. Exhibit 5-2 presents information on disclosures of forward-looking information made by firms in France, Germany, Japan, the U.K., and the U.S. Panel B of the exhibit shows the frequency with which sample firms made earnings forecasts, sales forecasts, and capital expenditure forecasts in each country.

   Required: Using evidence in the table, prepare a discussion in reasonable detail of the similarities and differences in annual report forecasting among companies in the five countries.

6. Exhibits 5-3, 5-4, and 5-5 present forecast disclosures appearing in the annual reports of BASF AG, Schering AG, and Komerci Banka AS, respectively.

   Required: Provide the following for each of the three company disclosures: (1) a list of items forecasted (e.g. sales, profits, economic growth), (2) the forecast horizon (e.g. 1 year ahead, 6 months ahead, not stated), and (3) the amount forecasted (e.g., growth of U.S.$10 million, 10 percent growth). Compare and contrast the potential usefulness of the forecasts made by the three companies. How might an investor or analyst use such forecast information?

7. Exhibit 5-6 presents a "Safe Harbor for Forward-Looking Statements" made by UniSource Energy Corp. in its Annual Report. The company is required to make the cautionary statements to qualify for certain protections from litigation connected with forward-looking disclosures.

   Required: Critically evaluate the usefulness of UniSource Energy's discussion about its forward-looking disclosures. How might the discussion influence a financial statement user's interpretation of forward-looking disclosures made by the company?

8. Exhibits 5-10, 5-11, and 5-12 present cash flow and funds flow information disclosed by companies from three different countries.

   Required:
   a. Why do cash and funds flow statements vary so dramatically from country to country?
   b. How do investors and analysts use information presented in cash and funds flow statements?
   c. Why might such statements be especially useful to nondomestic financial statement users?
   d. To the extent possible, restate the Capital Flow Statement presented in Exhibit 5-11 to the format of the Cash Flow Statement shown in Exhibit 5-10.

9. Exhibit 5-13 presents BASF AG's annual report discussion of the principle of sustainable development.

   Required: Critically evaluate the company's principle of sustainable development from each of the following perspectives: (1) investor, (2) employee, (3) customer.

10. Exhibit 5-16 presents the reconciliation disclosures made by the Swedish company NetCom AB. As discussed in the chapter, the U.S. SEC requires foreign listed

firms to present reconciliation information for material differences in net income (loss), earnings per share, and/or shareholders' equity.

Required:
a. Discuss why the SEC requires such reconciliation disclosures.
b. Specifically, how would U.S. investors use information presented in such disclosures?
c. Identify the three Swedish GAAP/U.S. GAAP accounting principle differences that have the largest impact on financial measures of NetCom AB for each of the periods shown.

11. Exhibit 5-22 presents information on accountants and auditors in emerging market and developed countries.

    Required: Use the World Wide Web or other information sources to compare and contrast the auditing profession in an emerging market country with that in a developed country. Discuss the expected effect of any observed differences on disclosure quality in companies in the two countries.

12. Assume that you are a senior executive at a large multinational company headquartered in Taiwan.

    Required: Prepare a 600-word statement outlining a proposed disclosure policy for your company.

Case 5–1   Information Access in Mexico

The following *Wall Street Journal* article discusses the limited access to information in Mexico.

"MEXICO ISN'T FREE WITH INFORMATION"

In Mexico, information is power. And just try to get your hands on any, be it mundane or profound. Everything from the number of billboards in Mexico City to the details of past presidential lives is closely guarded by government and business. The first line of defense of a Mexican secretary is the phrase *"No sabría decirle,"*—"I wouldn't know what to tell you."

This frustrates everyone from bankers to travel agents. John Donnelly, head of Chase Manhattan Bank here, says the lack of credible credit information has stymied renewed lending growth

since the 1994 peso collapse. Iris de Buendía, an agent at the Viajes Wilfer travel agency, says it is nearly impossible to get a straight answer from Mexican airlines on the timing of price promotions. "Everything is always top secret here," she says, sighing.

This vagueness has deep roots in Mexican history. The Aztecs, who commanded the central valleys of this land from the twelfth century to the fifteenth, kept their vassals in awe with a changing cast of hard-to-understand and unpredictable, but powerful, deities. The Spanish who followed were big on bureaucratic minutiae but rarely shared the details with the people they ruled. For the past 70 years, the reigning Institutional Revolutionary Party, or PRI, has worked hard to make sure inconvenient information doesn't end up in the wrong hands.

Source: The Wall Street Journal, September 10, 1998. Reprinted in *Emerging Financial Markets,* David O. Beim and Charles W. Calomiris, New York, McGraw-Hill/Irwin, 2001, p. 196.

"In Mexico, powerful people have tradition-ally kidnapped information," says historian and novelist Hector Aguilar Camin. "Part of the process of democratization is freeing it." But, he adds, "there is still a tendency to want to hold it hostage for some kind of benefit."

History, particularly when it damages the reputations of the living, is closely guarded. When researchers sought to confirm the details of a childhood shooting incident involving former president Carlos Salinas de Gortari, they found newspaper morgues purged of any reference to the event. Nor did they have better luck at the National Archives. The head of security there says a squad of government functionaries arrived to mop up Mr. Salinas's personal files when he took office in 1988.

The debate over access to information has become more explosive with the growth of a free press, the rise of opposition political parties and a big jump in the number of foreign investors do-ing business here who are demanding more transparency . . .

Lawmakers haven't had much better luck, so far, clarifying exactly what happened during the post-1994 bailout of the banking system orches-trated by President Ernesto Zedillo and his team. Finance Ministry officials say they are reluctant to give sensitive information to Congress, citing the country's bank-secrecy laws which, uniquely, protect not just data on deposits but also on loans. Lawmakers suspect the ministry is trying to pro-tect hundreds of well-connected businessmen whose bum debts ended up being bought by Mex-ico's deposit insurance fund and which will, in the end, be borne by taxpayers.

REQUIRED

1. Discuss at least five characteristics that predict relatively low disclosure levels in Mexico. Your response should be based on a review of material presented in Chapters 2 and 4 and this chapter, in addi-tion to the previous article.
2. Discuss characteristics or features that predict relatively *high* disclosure levels in Mexico. Again, refer to Chapters 2, 4, and 5 for relevant information.
3. Accounting measurement and disclosure practices are improving (from an investor protection viewpoint) in many emerging market economies. What are some of the recent improvements in these areas in Mexico? Discuss the underlying factors that help explain why the improvements are occurring.

Case 5–2   NetCom AB

Exhibit 5-16 presents Note 41 from NetCom AB's annual financial statements filed with the U.S. Securities and Exchange Commission, which in-cludes the following information: (1) reconcilia-tions of net income and shareholders' equity from a Swedish accounting principles basis to a U.S. GAAP basis; (2) explanations of current dif-ferences between Swedish accounting principles and U.S. GAAP; and (3) additional U.S. GAAP information.

REQUIRED

1. Identify the four Swedish-U.S. GAAP ac-counting principles differences that cause the largest differences in NetCom's 1999 net income prepared in conformance with the two sets of accounting principles.
2. Prepare a table showing for each of the four accounting principles differences:
   a. treatment under Swedish GAAP

b. treatment under U.S. GAAP

c. effect of the accounting principle difference on NetCom's net income in 1997, 1998, 1999

d. effect of the accounting principle difference on NetCom's shareholders' equity for 1997, 1998, 1999

e. evaluation of the two treatments (Swedish GAAP versus U.S. GAAP). Which treatment do you believe provides more useful information?

3. Does NetCom's discussion of differences between Swedish accounting principles and U.S. GAAP provide enough information for the financial statement reader to critically compare the two sets of accounting principles? Present and explanation for your response.

4. Assume that NetCom forecasts (Swedish GAAP-based) net income of 85 million SEK for the next year. Develop a forecast of NetCom's U.S. GAAP-based net income using information provided in Note 41. How reliable is your U.S. GAAP-based forecast, and how might you use the forecast?

CHAPTER 6

FOREIGN CURRENCY TRANSLATION

Foreign currency translation is one of the most vexing and controversial technical issues in accounting. It has defied theoretical and practical solutions and will continue to be of great interest due to fluctuating currency markets and the globalization of business and the world's securities markets.

Translation is the process of restating financial statement information from one currency to another. It is necessary whenever a company with operations in more than one country prepares consolidated (or group) financial statements that combine financial accounts denominated in one national currency with accounts denominated in another (i.e., the parent country's) currency. Many of its problems stem from the fact that foreign exchange rates are seldom fixed. Variable exchange rates, combined with the variety of translation methods that can be used and different treatments of translation *gains* and *losses*, make it difficult to compare financial results from one company to another, or in the same company from one period to the next. In these circumstances, it becomes a challenge for multinational enterprises to make informative disclosures of operating results and financial position. Financial analysts and others find that interpreting such information can also be quite challenging. The troubles extend to evaluating managerial performance.

REASONS FOR TRANSLATION

Companies with significant overseas operations cannot prepare consolidated financial statements unless their accounts and those of their subsidiaries are expressed in a single currency. One cannot add Mexican pesos, Japanese yen, Swiss francs, and New Zealand dollars and obtain meaningful results. The single currency traditionally is the reporting currency of the parent company. The process of restating various foreign currency balances to single currency equivalents is called *translation*.

Additional reasons for foreign currency translation are (1) recording foreign currency transactions, (2) reporting international branch and subsidiary activities, and (3) reporting the results of independent operations abroad. Just as with consolidation procedures, foreign currency transactions, such as the purchase of merchandise from China by a Canadian importer, must be translated because financial statements cannot be prepared from accounts that are expressed in more than one currency. How, for example, is one to prepare cost of goods sold when purchases are denominated in Chinese yuan, Russian rubles, and Argentine pesos? Foreign branch and subsidiary activities are another case in point. The Irish branch and its Swedish parent company are parts of a closely knit whole; it makes little sense to view the accounts of either one alone. They must be combined to present a fair and complete financial picture, and this requires foreign currency translation. While foreign subsidiaries are more independent than branches because of their separate legal existence, foreign currency translation procedures are still required for centralized planning, evaluation, coordination, and control.

Finally, the expanded scale of international investment increases the need to convey accounting information about companies domiciled in one country to users in others. This need occurs when a company wishes to list its shares on a foreign stock exchange, contemplates a foreign acquisition or joint venture, or wants to communicate its operating results and financial position to its foreign stockholders. Many Japanese companies translate their entire financial statements from Japanese yen to U.S. dollars when reporting to interested American audiences. This practice is often called a *convenience translation* and is described more fully in Chapter 9.

BACKGROUND AND TERMINOLOGY

Translation is not the same as *conversion*, which is the physical exchange of one currency for another. Translation is simply a change in monetary expression, as when a balance sheet expressed in British pounds is restated in U.S. dollar equivalents. No physical exchange occurs, and no accountable transaction takes place as it does in conversion.

Foreign currency balances are translated to domestic currency equivalents by the foreign exchange rate: the price of a unit of one currency expressed in terms of another. The currencies of major trading nations are bought and sold in global markets. Linked by sophisticated telecommunications networks, market participants include banks and other currency dealers, business enterprises, individuals, and professional traders.

By providing a venue for buyers and sellers of currencies, the foreign exchange market facilitates the transfer of international payments (e.g., from importers to exporters), allows international purchases or sales to be made on credit (e.g., bank letters of credit that permit goods to be shipped in advance of payment to an unfamiliar buyer), and provides a means for individuals or businesses to protect themselves from the risks of unstable currency values. (Chapter 11 gives a fuller discussion of exchange risk management.)

Foreign currency transactions take place in the spot, forward, or swap markets. Currency bought or sold *spot* normally must be delivered immediately, that is, within 2 business days. Thus, an American tourist departing for Geneva can purchase and immediately receive Swiss francs by paying the spot rate in dollars. Spot market rates are influenced by many factors including different inflation rates among countries, differences in national interest rates, and expectations about the direction of future rates.

Spot market exchange rates may be direct or indirect.[1] In a direct quote, the exchange rate specifies the number of domestic currency units needed to acquire a unit of

---

[1]For a daily listing of foreign exchange rates, visit www.wallstreetjournal.com.

foreign currency. For example, on a given day, the U.S. dollar price of an Indian rupee might be $0.022737. An indirect quote is the reciprocal of the direct quote: the price of a unit of the domestic currency in terms of the foreign currency. In this example, it would take approximately 43.98 rupees to acquire 1 U.S. dollar.

Translation of foreign currency balances is straightforward with either direct or indirect quotes. Domestic currency equivalents are obtained by multiplying foreign currency balances by direct exchange rate quotations or dividing foreign currency balances by indirect quotations. To illustrate, suppose that the cash balance of a U.S. subsidiary located in Bombay, India, on January 31 is Rpe1,000,000. The direct (spot) exchange rate on that date is $0.022737. The U.S. dollar equivalent of the rupee cash balance on January 31 is $22,737, calculated by translating Rpe1,000,000 in either of the following ways:

$$Rpe1,000,000 \times \$0.022737 = \$22,737 \text{ or}$$
$$Rpe1,000,000 \div Rpe43.98 = \$22,737$$

Transactions in the forward market are agreements to exchange a specified amount of one currency for another at a future date. Quotations in the forward market are expressed at either a *discount* or a *premium* from the spot rate. If spot Swiss francs are offered at $0.5368, while the 6-month forward franc is offered at $0.5433, 6-month forward Swiss francs are selling at a premium of 2.4 percent in the U.S., calculated as follows: forward premium (discount) = (forward rate − spot rate)/spot rate × 12/n, where n = number of months in the forward contract. Thus, ($0.5433 − $0.5368)/$0.5368 × 12/6 = 0.0242. Had the Swiss franc been quoted indirectly, the premium would have been determined as: forward premium (discount) = (spot rate − forward rate)/forward rate × 12/n, or (Swf1.8630 − Swf1.8407)/1.8407 × 12/6 = 0.0242.

A swap transaction involves the simultaneous spot purchase and forward sale, or spot sale and forward purchase, of a currency. Investors often use swap transactions to take advantage of higher interest rates in a foreign country while simultaneously protecting themselves against unfavorable movements in the foreign exchange rate. As an example, should interest rates in the U.S. exceed those in Switzerland, Swiss investors could purchase dollars in the spot market and invest them in higher-yielding U.S. dollar debt instruments, say 6-month U.S. Treasury notes. In doing so, however, Swiss investors would lose this yield advantage if the U.S. dollar loses value relative to the Swiss franc in the 6 months. To protect against this possibility, Swiss investors could simultaneously sell the dollars they expect to receive in 6 months at the guaranteed forward rate. Such swap transactions work well when the U.S.–Swiss interest rate differential is greater than the discount on forward dollars (i.e., the difference between spot and 6-month forward dollars). Over time, foreign currency traders will eliminate this difference, thereby creating *interest rate parity*.

Exhibit 6-1 defines the foreign currency translation terms used in this chapter.

THE PROBLEM

If foreign exchange rates were relatively stable, currency translation would be no more difficult than translating inches or feet to their metric equivalents. However, exchange rates are seldom stable. The currencies of most industrialized countries are free to find

EXHIBIT 6-1 Glossary of Foreign Currency Translation Terms

attribute. The quantifiable characteristic of an item that is measured for accounting purposes. For example, historical cost and replacement cost are attributes of an asset.

conversion. The exchange of one currency for another.

current rate. The exchange rate in effect at the relevant financial statement date.

discount. When the forward exchange rate is below the current spot rate.

exposed net asset position. The excess of assets that are measured or denominated in foreign currency and translated at the current rate over liabilities that are measured or denominated in foreign currency and translated at the current rate.

foreign currency. A currency other than the currency of the country being referred to; a currency other than the reporting currency of the enterprise being referred to.

foreign currency financial statements. Financial statements that employ foreign currency as the unit of measure.

foreign currency transactions. Transactions (for example, sales or purchases of goods or services or loans payable or receivable) whose terms are stated in a currency other than the entity's functional currency.

foreign currency translation. The process of expressing amounts denominated or measured in one currency in terms of another currency by use of the exchange rate between the two currencies.

foreign operation. An operation whose financial statements are (1) combined or consolidated with or accounted for on an equity basis in the financial statements of the reporting enterprise and (2) prepared in a currency other than the reporting currency of the reporting enterprise.

forward exchange contract. An agreement to exchange currencies of different countries at a specified rate (forward rate) at a specified future date.

functional currency. The primary currency in which an entity does business and generates and spends cash. It is usually the currency of the country where the entity is located and the currency in which the books of record are maintained.

historical rate. The foreign exchange rate that prevailed when a foreign currency asset or liability was first acquired or incurred.

local currency. Currency of a particular country being referred to; the reporting currency of a domestic or foreign operation being referred to.

monetary items. Obligations to pay or rights to receive a fixed number of currency units in the future.

reporting currency. The currency in which an enterprise prepares its financial statements.

settlement date. The date on which a payable is paid or a receivable is collected.

spot rate. The exchange rate for immediate exchange of currencies.

transaction date. The date at which a transaction (for example, a sale or purchase of merchandise or services) is recorded in a reporting entity's accounting records.

translation adjustments. Translation adjustments result from the process of translating financial statements from the entity's functional currency into the reporting currency.

unit of measure. The currency in which assets, liabilities, revenue, and expense are measured.

Source: Adapted from Statement of Financial Accounting Standard No. 52, 1981.

their own values in the currency market. Exhibit 6-2 illustrates the volatility of exchange rates of selected countries since the 1970s.

Fluctuating exchange values are particularly evident in Eastern Europe, Latin America, and certain parts of Asia. Currency fluctuations increase the number of translation rates that can be used in the translation process and create foreign exchange gains and losses. Currency movements are also closely tied to local rates of inflation, the subject of Chapter 7.

Another noteworthy feature of Exhibit 6-2 is a new currency, the *euro*. Introduced by the European Union (EU) on January 1, 1999, the euro replaces the European currency unit (ECU), a composite of the currencies of the 15 EU member states (1 ECU = 1 euro). On January 1, 2002, the euro will become the official currency of 12 EU nations that fixed their national currencies to the euro per Exhibit 6-3. Countries whose national currencies will be replaced by the euro on January 1, 2002, include Austria, Belgium, Finland, France, Germany, Greece, Ireland, Italy, Luxembourg, the Netherlands, Portugal and Spain. Before then, companies in Euroland could transact business and prepare their financial statements in their national currencies or the euro. EU members that decided not to adopt the euro are Britain, Denmark, and Sweden.[2]

As illustrated in Exhibit 6-3, euro quotes are expressed in 6 digits. Moreover, the European Commission requires that all conversions between Euroland currencies must be made through the euro. Thus the lira equivalent of 100 Austrian schillings is determined by first converting schillings to euros and then from euros to lira; that is, 100 schillings = 7.26728 euros = 14,071.4 lira.[3]

FINANCIAL STATEMENT EFFECTS OF ALTERNATIVE TRANSLATION RATES

The following three exchange rates can be used to translate foreign currency balances to domestic currency. First, the *current* rate is the exchange rate prevailing as of the financial statement date. Second, the *historical* rate is the prevailing exchange rate when a foreign currency asset is first acquired or a foreign currency liability first incurred. Finally, the *average* rate is a simple or weighted average of either current or historical exchange rates. As average rates are simply variations of current or historical rates, the following discussion focuses on the latter two.

What are the financial statement effects of using historical as opposed to current rates of exchange as foreign currency translation coefficients? Historical exchange rates generally preserve the original cost equivalent of a foreign currency item in the domestic currency statements. Suppose that a foreign subsidiary of a U.S. parent company acquires an item of inventory for 1,000 foreign currency (FC) units when the exchange rate (indirect quote) is FC2 = $1. This asset would appear in the U.S. consolidated statements at $500. Now assume that the exchange rate changes from FC2 = $1 to FC4 = $1

---

[2]Anette W. Estrada and Sander S. Wechsler, "Are You Euro-Fluent?" *Journal of Accountancy* (June 1999): 22–27.

[3]For additional information on the European Economic and Monetary Union and the euro, click on europa.eu.int/euro.

EXHIBIT 6-2 Nominal Exchange Rates (in terms of U.S. dollars)

Per. Avg	1986	1987	1988	1989	1990	1991	1992	1993	1994	1995	1996	1997	1998	1999	2000
Euro /Ecu	—	—	—	.91	.79	.81	.77	.86	.84	.77	.80	.88	.89	.94	1.1
Ger	2.17	1.80	1.76	1.88	1.62	1.66	1.56	1.65	1.62	1.43	1.50	1.73	1.76	1.84	2.16
Fra	6.92	6.01	5.96	6.38	5.44	5.64	5.29	5.66	5.54	4.99	5.11	5.83	5.90	6.16	7.24
Italy	148	129	130	137	119	124	123	157	161	162	154	170	173	181	213
	9	6	1	1	8	0	2	2	1	9	3	2	6	9	6
Spn	140	123	116	118	102	104	102	127	134	125	127	146	149	156	183
Neth	2.45	2.02	1.98	2.12	1.82	1.87	1.76	1.86	1.82	1.6	1.69	1.95	1.98	2.07	2.43
Bel	44.6	37.3	36.7	9.4	33.4	34.2	32.1	34.6	33.4	29.5	30.9	35.8	36.3	37.9	44.5
Aus	15.3	12.6	12.3	13.2	11.4	11.7	10.9	11.6	11.4	10.1	10.6	12.2	12.4	12.9	15.2
Por	149	141	144	157	143	145	135	161	166	150	154	175	180	188	221
Fin	5.1	4.4	4.2	4.3	3.8	4.1	4.5	5.7	5.2	4.4	4.6	5.2	5.3	5.6	6.6
Ire	.75	.67	.66	.71	.60	.62	.59	.68	.67	.62	.63	.66	.70	.74	.87
Swz	1.80	1.49	1.46	1.64	1.39	1.43	1.41	1.48	1.37	1.18	1.24	1.45	1.45	1.50	1.72
UK	.68	.61	.56	.61	.56	.57	.57	.67	.65	.63	.64	.61	.60	.62	.66
Swn	7.1	6.3	6.1	6.5	5.9	6.1	5.8	7.8	7.7	7.1	6.7	7.6	7.9	8.3	9.1
Nor	7.4	6.7	6.5	6.9	6.3	6.5	6.2	7.1	7.0	6.3	6.5	7.1	7.6	7.8	9.1
Gre	139	135	142	163	158	182	190	229	242	232	241	273	295	306	371
Cze	15.0	13.7	14.4	14.6	17.8	29.1	28.3	29.2	28.8	26.5	27.1	31.7	32.2	34.6	40.3
Hun	46.3	47.4	51.2	60.5	63.0	74.7	79.0	91.8	105	124	149	187	214	238	286
Pol	.02	.03	.05	.24	.94	1.06	1.36	1.81	2.27	2.42	2.70	3.28	3.49	3.97	4.49
Isrl	1.49	1.59	1.60	1.92	2.01	2.28	2.46	2.83	3.01	3.01	3.19	3.45	3.80	4.14	4.14
Rus	.00	.00	.00	.00	.00	.00	.22	.93	2.18	4.56	5.13	5.79	10.1	24.9	28.3
Tur	.7	.8	1.4	2.1	2.6	4.2	6.9	11.1	30.4	46.0	81.9	153	262	422	617
Afr	2.29	2.04	2.27	2.62	2.59	2.76	2.85	3.27	3.55	3.63	4.30	4.61	5.54	6.11	7.03
USA	1.00	1.00	1.00	1.00	1.00	1.00	1.00	1.00	1.00	1.00	1.00	1.00	1.00	1.00	1.00
Can	1.39	1.33	1.23	1.18	1.17	1.15	1.21	1.29	1.37	1.37	1.36	1.38	1.48	1.49	1.50
Mex	.64	1.41	2.28	2.49	2.84	3.01	3.04	3.11	3.38	6.42	7.60	7.92	9.15	9.55	9.51
Arg	0.0	0.0	0.0	.04	.48	.95	.99	1.0	1.0	1.0	1.0	1.0	1.0	1.0	1.0
Bra	0.0	0.0	0.0	0.0	0.0	0.0	0.0	.03	.64	.92	1.0	1.08	1.16	1.82	1.83

Chle	191	218	247	261	304	350	366	407	420	397	412	419	460	509	522
Col	193	242	298	381	494	607	639	814	826	914	1036	1142	1428	1759	2058
Ecua	.1	.2	.3	.53	.80	1.06	1.52	1.86	2.10	2.56	3.19	3.99	5.45	11.8	25.0
Peru	0.0	0.0	0.0	0.0	.06	.76	1.23	1.98	2.19	2.25	2.45	2.66	2.93	:3.38	3.50
Ven	19.8	27.8	33.4	38.6	47.0	55.0	66.6	91.3	149	184	464	488	548	606	679
Japa	168	145	128	138	145	135	127	111	102	94	109	121	131	114	108
Chin	3.4	3.7	3.7	3.7	4.8	5.3	5.5	5.8	8.6	8.4	8.3	8.3	8.3	8.3	8.3
HK	7.8	7.8	7.8	7.8	7.8	7.8	7.7	7.7	7.7	7.7	7.7	7.7	7.8	:7.8	:7.8
Indo	1.3	1.6	1.7	1.8	1.8	1.9	2.0	2.1	2.2	2.2	2.3	2.9	10.2	7.8	8.3
Indi	12.5	B:12.9	13.9	16.1	17.5	22.7	28.0	31.1	31.4	32.4	35.4	36.3	41.3	43.1	44.0
Kor	881	822	731	672	707	733	781	802	804	771	805	956	1399	1189	1120
Mal	2.6	2.5	2.6	2.7	2.7	2.8	2.6	2.6	2.6	2.5	2.5	2.8	4.2	4.45	3.8
Phil	19.9	20.1	20.4	21.0	23.4	26.6	24.7	26.6	26.4	25.7	26.2	29.7	40.9	39.1	41.9
Sing	2.2	2.1	2.0	1.9	1.8	1.7	1.6	1.6	1.5	1.4	1.4	1.5	1.6	1.7	1.7
Thai	26.0	25.5	25.2	25.6	25.5	25.5	25.4	25.3	25.1	24.9	25.3	31.4	41.3	37.8	38.9
Taiw	37.8	31.8	28.6	26.4	26.9	26.8	25.2	26.4	26.5	26.5	27.5	28.7	33.5	32.3	30.7
Aust	1.50	1.43	1.28	1.27	1.28	1.28	1.36	1.47	1.37	1.35	1.28	1.35	1.59	1.55	1.73
NZ	1.91	1.69	1.53	1.67	1.68	1.73	1.86	1.85	1.69	1.52	1.45	1.51	1.87	1.89	2.13

Source: Goldman Sachs, *The Global Currency Analyst*, New York: Goldman Sachs, 2000.

EXHIBIT 6-3	Fixed Euro Conversion Rates
Country	*Rate*
EU euro	1.0
Austrian schilling	13.7603
Belgian franc	40.3399
Finnish markka	5.94573
French franc	6.55957
German mark	1.95583
Irish punt	.787564
Italian lira	1936.27
Luxembourg franc	40.3399
Dutch guilder	2.20371
Portuguese escudo	200.482
Spanish peseta	166.386

by the next financial statement date and that the inventory item is still on hand. Will the U.S. dollar equivalent of the inventory now change to $250? Of course not. As long as we translate the original FC1,000 cost at the rate that prevailed when the asset was acquired (historical rate), it will appear in the U.S. financial statements at $500, its historical cost expressed in U.S. dollars. *Use of historical exchange rates shields financial statements from foreign currency translation gains or losses*, that is, from increases or decreases in the dollar equivalents of foreign currency balances due to fluctuations in the translation rate between reporting periods. *The use of current rates causes translation gains or losses*. Thus, in the previous example, translating the FC1,000 piece of inventory at the current rate (FC4 = $1) would yield a translation loss of $250 (FC1,000 ÷ 2 − FC1,000 ÷ 4).

Here we must distinguish between *translation* gains and losses and *transaction* gains and losses, both of which fall under the label *exchange gains and losses*. Foreign currency transactions occur whenever an enterprise purchases or sells goods for which payment is made in a foreign currency or when it borrows or lends foreign currency. Translation is necessary to maintain the accounting records in the currency of the reporting enterprise.

Of the two types of transaction adjustments, the first, *gains and losses on settled transactions*, arises whenever the exchange rate used to book the original transaction differs from the rate used at settlement. Thus, if a U.S. parent company borrows FC1,000 when the exchange rate is FC2 = $1 and then converts the proceeds to dollars, it will receive $500 and record a $500 liability on its books. If the foreign exchange rate rises to FC1 = $1 when the loan is repaid, the U.S. company will have to pay out $1,000 to discharge its FC1,000 debt. The company has suffered a $500 conversion loss.

The second type of transaction adjustment, *gains or losses on unsettled transactions*, arises whenever financial statements are prepared before a transaction is settled. In the preceding example, assume that the FC1,000 is borrowed during year 1 and repaid during year 2. If the exchange rate prevailing at the financial statement date is FC1.5 = $1, the dollar equivalent of the FC1,000 loan will be $667, creating an exchange loss of $167.

Until the foreign currency debt is actually repaid, however, this *unrealized* exchange loss is similar in nature to a translation loss as it results from a restatement process.

Exhibit 6-4 lays out the distinction between transaction and translation gains and losses. Differences in exchange rates in effect at the various dates shown cause the various types of exchange adjustments.

When considering exchange gains and losses, it is critical to distinguish between transaction gains and losses and translation gains and losses. A realized (or settled) transaction creates a real gain or loss. Accountants generally agree that such a gain or loss should be reflected immediately in income. In contrast, translation adjustments (including gains or losses on unsettled transactions) are *unrealized* or *paper* items. The appropriate accounting treatment of these gains or losses is less obvious.

Fluctuating exchange rates cause several major issues in accounting for foreign currency translation:

1. Which exchange rate should be used to translate foreign currency balances to domestic currency?
2. Which foreign currency assets and liabilities are exposed to exchange rate changes?
3. How should translation gains and losses be accounted for?

These issues are treated in the balance of this chapter. Chapter 11 covers the accounting treatment of foreign currency transactions.

FIGURE 6-4   Types of Exchange Adjustments

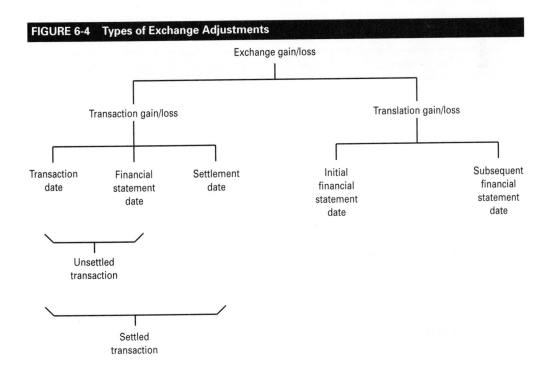

FOREIGN CURRENCY TRANSLATION

Companies operating internationally use a variety of methods to express, in terms of their domestic currency, the assets, liabilities, revenues, and expenses that are stated in a foreign currency. These translation methods can be classified into two types: those that use a *single* translation rate to restate foreign balances to their domestic currency equivalents and those that use *multiple* rates. Exhibit 6-5 summarizes the treatment of specific balance sheet items under these translation methods.

SINGLE RATE METHOD

The single rate method, long popular in Europe, applies a single exchange rate, the current or closing rate, to all foreign currency assets and liabilities. Foreign currency revenues and expenses are generally translated at exchange rates prevailing when these items are recognized.

For convenience, however, these items are typically translated by an appropriately weighted average of current exchange rates for the period. Under this method, the financial statements of a foreign operation (viewed by the parent as an autonomous entity) have their own reporting domicile: the local currency environment in which the foreign affiliate does business.

Under the current rate method, the consolidated statements preserve the original financial statement relationships (such as financial ratios) of the individual entities as all foreign currency financial statement items are translated by a single rate. That is, consolidated results reflect the currency perspectives of each entity whose results go into

EXHIBIT 6-5	Exchange Rates Employed in Different Translation Methods for Specific Balance Sheet Items			
	Current	*Current-Noncurrent*	*Monetary-Nonmonetary*	*Temporal*
Cash	C	C	C	C
Accounts receivable	C	C	C	C
Inventories				
Cost	C	C	H	H
Market	C	C	H	C
Investments				
Cost	C	H	H	H
Market	C	H	H	C
Fixed assets	C	H	H	H
Other assets	C	H	H	H
Accounts payable	C	C	C	C
Long-term debt	C	H	C	C
Common stock	H	H	H	H
Retained earnings	*	*	*	*

Note: C = current rate: H = historical rate; and * = residual, balancing figure representing a composite of successive current rates.

the consolidated totals, not the single-currency perspective of the parent company. Some people fault this method on the grounds that using multiple currency perspectives violates the basic purpose of consolidated financial statements.

For accounting purposes, a foreign currency asset or liability is said to be *exposed* to exchange rate risk if a change in the exchange rate causes its parent currency equivalent to change. Given this definition, the current rate method presumes that all local currency assets are exposed to exchange risk as the current (versus the historical) rate changes the parent currency equivalent of a foreign currency balance every time exchange rates change. This seldom happens, however, as inventory and fixed asset values are generally supported by local inflation.

Consider the following example. Suppose that a foreign affiliate of a U.S. multinational corporation (MNC) buys a tract of land at the beginning of the period for FC1,000,000. The exchange rate (historical rate) was FC1 = $1. Thus, the historical cost of the investment in dollars is $1,000,000 (= FC1,000,000 ÷ FC1). Due to inflation, the land rises in value to FC1,500,000 (unrecognized under U.S. GAAP) while the exchange rate declines to FC1.4 = $1 by period's end. If this foreign currency asset were translated to U.S. dollars using the current rate, its original dollar value of $1,000,000 would now be recorded at $714,286 (= FC1,000,000 ÷ FC1.4) implying an exchange loss of $285,714. Yet the increase in the fair market value of the land indicates that its current value in U.S. dollars is really $1,071,285 (FC1,500,000 ÷ FC1.4) This suggests that translated asset values make little sense without making local price level adjustments first. Also, translation of a historical cost number by a current market-determined exchange rate (e.g., FC1,000,000 ÷ FC1.4 = $714,286) produces a result that resembles neither historical cost ($1,000,000) nor current market value ($1,071,285).

Finally, translating all foreign currency balances by the current rate creates translation gains and losses every time exchange rates change. Reflecting such exchange adjustments in current income could significantly distort reported measures of performance. Many of these gains and losses may never be fully realized, as changes in exchange rates often reverse direction.

MULTIPLE RATE METHODS

Multiple rate methods combine the current and historical exchange rates in the translation process.

CURRENT-NONCURRENT METHOD

Under the current-noncurrent method, a foreign subsidiary's current assets and current liabilities are translated into their parent company's reporting currency at the current rate. Noncurrent assets and liabilities are translated at historical rates. Income statement items (except for depreciation and amortization charges) are translated at average rates applicable to each month of operation or on the basis of weighted averages covering the whole period being reported. Depreciation and amortization charges are translated at the historical rates in effect when the related assets were acquired.

Unfortunately, this method makes little economic sense. Using the year-end rate to translate current assets implies that foreign currency cash, receivables, and inventories are equally exposed to exchange risk. This is simply not true. For example, if the local price of inventory can be increased after a devaluation, its value is protected from currency exchange risk. On the other hand, translation of long-term debt at the historical rate shifts the impact of fluctuating currencies to the year of settlement. Many consider this to be at odds with reality. Moreover, current and noncurrent definitions are merely a classification scheme, not a conceptual justification of which rates to use in translation.

MONETARY-NONMONETARY METHOD[4]

The monetary-nonmonetary method also uses a balance sheet classification scheme to determine appropriate translation rates. *Monetary* assets and liabilities are translated at the current rate. *Nonmonetary* items—fixed assets, long-term investments, and inventories—are translated at historical rates. Income statement items are translated under procedures similar to those described for the current-noncurrent framework.

Unlike the current-noncurrent method, this method views monetary assets and liabilities as exposed to exchange rate risk. Since monetary items are settled in cash, use of the current rate to translate these items produces domestic currency equivalents that reflect their realizable or settlement values. It also reflects changes in the domestic currency equivalent of long-term debt in the period in which they occur, producing a more timely indicator of exchange rate effects.

Note, however, that the monetary-nonmonetary method relies on a classification scheme to determine appropriate translation rates. This may lead to inappropriate results. For example, this method translates all nonmonetary assets at historical rates, which is not reasonable for assets stated at current market values (such as investment securities and inventory and fixed assets written down to market). Multiplying the current market value of a nonmonetary asset by a historical exchange rate yields an amount in the domestic currency that is neither the item's current equivalent nor its historical cost. This method also distorts profit margins by matching sales at current prices and translation rates against cost of sales measured at historical costs and translation rates.

TEMPORAL METHOD[5]

With the temporal method, currency translation is a measurement conversion process or a restatement of a given value. It does not change the *attribute* of an item being measured; it only changes the unit of measure. Translation of foreign balances restates the currency denomination of these items, but not their actual valuation. Under U.S. GAAP, cash is measured in terms of the amount owned at the balance sheet date. Receivables and payables are stated at amounts expected to be received or paid when due. Other assets and liabilities are measured at money prices that prevailed when the items were acquired or incurred (historical prices). Some, however, are measured at prices prevailing as of the financial statement date (current prices), such as inventories under the lower of cost or market rule. In short, a time dimension is associated with these money values.

In the temporal method, monetary items such as cash, receivables, and payables are translated at the current rate. Nonmonetary items are translated at rates that preserve their original measurement bases. Specifically, assets carried on the foreign currency statements at historical cost are translated at the historical rate. Why? Because *historical* cost in foreign currency translated by a *historical* exchange rate yields *historical* cost in domestic currency. Similarly, nonmonetary items carried abroad at current values are

---

[4]This method was originally proposed in Samuel R. Hepworth, *Reporting Foreign Operations,* Ann Arbor, MI: University of Michigan, 1956.
[5]This method was originally proposed in Leonard Lorensen, "Reporting Foreign Operations of U.S. Companies in U.S. Dollars," *Accounting Research Study No. 12,* New York: American Institute of Certified Public Accountants, 1972.

translated at the current rate because *current* value in foreign currency translated by a *current* exchange rate produces *current* value in domestic currency. Revenue and expense items are translated at rates that prevailed when the underlying transactions took place, although average rates are suggested when revenue or expense transactions are voluminous.

When nonmonetary items abroad are valued at historical cost, the translation procedures resulting from the temporal method are virtually identical to those produced by the monetary-nonmonetary method. The two translation methods differ only if other asset valuation bases are employed, such as replacement cost, market values, or discounted cash flows.

Because it is similar to the monetary-nonmonetary method, the temporal method shares most of its advantages and disadvantages. In deliberately ignoring local inflation, this method shares a limitation with the other translation methods discussed. (Of course, historical cost accounting ignores inflation as well!).

All four methods just described have been used in the United States at one time or another and can be found today in various countries. In general, they produce noticeably different foreign currency translation results. The first three methods (i.e., the current rate, current-noncurrent, and monetary-nonmonetary) are predicated on identifying which assets and liabilities are exposed to, or sheltered from, currency exchange risk. The translation methodology is then applied consistent with this distinction. The current rate method presumes that the entire foreign operation is exposed to exchange rate risk since all assets and liabilities are translated at the year-end exchange rate. The current-noncurrent rate method presumes that only the current assets and liabilities are so exposed, while the monetary-nonmonetary method presumes that monetary assets and liabilities are exposed. In contrast, the temporal method is designed to preserve the underlying theoretical basis of accounting measurement used in preparing the financial statements being translated.

FINANCIAL STATEMENT EFFECTS

Exhibits 6-6 and 6-7 highlight the financial statement effects of the major translation methods described. The balance sheet of a hypothetical Mexican subsidiary of a U.S.-based multinational enterprise appears in pesos in the first column of Exhibit 6-6. The second column depicts the U.S. dollar equivalents of the Mexican peso (P) balances when the exchange rate was P1 = $0.13. Should the peso depreciate to P1 = $0.10, several different accounting results are possible.

Under the current rate method, exchange rate changes affect the dollar equivalents of the Mexican subsidiary's *total* foreign currency assets (TA) and liabilities (TL) in the current period. Since their dollar values are affected by changes in the current rate, they are said to be *exposed* (in an *accounting* sense) to foreign exchange risk. Accordingly, under the current rate method, an exposed net asset position (TA > TL) results in a translation loss if the Mexican peso loses value, and an exchange gain if the peso gains value. An exposed peso net liability position (TA < TL) produces a translation gain if the Mexican peso loses value and a loss if the peso gains value. In our example, current rate translation yields a $450 translation loss, since the dollar equivalent of the Mexican subsidiary's net asset position *after* the peso depreciation is $1,500 (P15,000 × $0.10), whereas the dollar equivalent *before* the depreciation was $1,950 (P15,000 × $0.13).

EXHIBIT 6-6 Mexican Subsidiary Balance Sheet

	Pesos	U.S. Dollars Before Peso Devaluation ($0.13 = P1)	U.S. Dollars After Peso Depreciation ($0.10 = P1)			
			Current Rate	Current-Noncurrent	Monetary-Nonmonetary	Temporal
Assets						
Cash	P 3,000	$ 390	$ 300	$ 300	$ 300	$ 300
Accounts Receivable	6,000	780	600	600	600	600
Inventories	9,000	1,170	900	900	1,170	900[1]
Fixed assets (net)	18,000	2,340	1,800	2,340	2,340	2,340
Total	P 36,000	$4,680	$ 3,600	$4,140	4,410	$4,140
Liabilities & Owners' Equity						
Short-term payables	P 9,000	$1,170	$ 900	$ 900	$ 900	$ 900
Long-term debt	12,000	1,560	1,200	1,560	1,200	1,200
Stockholders' equity	15,000	1,950	1,500	1,680	2,310	2,040
Total	P 36,000	$4,680	$ 3,600	$4,140	$ 4,410	$4,140
Accounting exposure (P)			15,000	9,000	(12,000)	(3,000)
Translation gain (loss)($)			(450)	(270)	360	90

Note: If the exchange rate remained unchanged over time, the translated statements would be the same under all translation methods.

[1] Assume inventories are carried at lower of cost or market. If they were carried at historical cost, the temporal balance sheet would be identical to the monetary-nonmonetary method.

220

EXHIBIT 6-7 Mexican Subsidiary Income Statement (in thousands)

	Pesos	U.S. Dollars Before Peso Devaluation ($0.13 = P1)	U.S. Dollars After Peso Depreciation ($0.10 = P1)			
			Current Rate	Current-Noncurrent	Monetary-Nonmonetary	Temporal
Sales	P 40,000	$5,200	$4,000	$4,000	$4,000	$4,000
Cost of sales	20,000	2,600	2,000	2,000	2,600	2,600[1]
Depreciation[2]	1,800	234	180	234	234	234
All other expenses	8,000	1,040	800	800	800	800
Income before tax	10,200	1,326	1,020	966	366	366
Income tax (30%)	3,060	(398)	(306)	(306)	(306)	(306)
Translation gain (loss)[3]	—		(450)	(270)	360	(90)
Net income (loss)	P 7,140	928	$ 264	$ 390	$ 420	$ (30)

Note: This example assumes that the income statement is prepared the day after devaluation.

[1] Assumes that inventories were written down to market at period's end.

[2] Estimated life of fixed assets is assumed to be 10 years.

[3] This example reflects what reported earnings would look like if all translation gains or losses were immediately reflected in current income.

Under the current-noncurrent method, the U.S. company's accounting exposure is measured by its peso net current asset or liability position (a positive P9,000 in our example). Under the monetary-nonmonetary method, exposure is measured by its net peso monetary asset or liability position (a negative P12,000). Accounting *exposure* under the temporal principle depends on whether the Mexican subsidiary's inventories or other nonmonetary assets are valued at historical cost (and therefore not exposed) or some other valuation basis (a negative P3,000 in our example).

To summarize, the different translation methods in our example give a wide array of accounting results, ranging from a $450 loss under the current rate method to a $360 gain under the monetary-nonmonetary method. This difference is large given that all the results are based on the same facts. What is more, operations reporting respectable profits before currency translation may well report losses or much lower earnings after translation (the converse is also true). To protect themselves against the financial statement effects of currency swings, financial managers may execute protective maneuvers known as *hedging strategies*. Chapter 11 covers hedging options and foreign exchange risk management in greater detail.

WHICH IS BEST?

We reject the traditional assumption that a single translation method can be appropriate for all circumstances in which translations occur and for all purposes that translation serves. Circumstances underlying foreign exchange translation differ widely. Translating accounts from a stable to an unstable currency is not the same as translating accounts from an unstable currency to a stable one. Likewise, there is little similarity between translations involving import- or export-type transactions and those involving a permanently established affiliate or subsidiary company in another country that reinvests its local earnings and does not intend to repatriate any funds to the parent company in the near future.

Second, translations are made for different purposes. Translating the accounts of a foreign subsidiary to consolidate those accounts with those of the parent company has very little in common with translating the accounts of an independent company mainly for the convenience of various foreign audiences-of-interest.

We therefore pose three questions:

1. Is it reasonable to use more than one translation method?
2. If so, what should be the acceptable methods and under what conditions should they be applied?
3. Are there situations in which translations should not be done at all?

As to the first question, it is clear that a single translation method cannot equally serve translations occurring under different conditions and for different purposes. More than one translation method is needed.

Regarding the second question, we think that three different translation approaches can be accepted: (1) the historical method, (2) the current method, and (3) no translation at all. Financial accounts of foreign entities can be translated either from a parent company perspective or from a local perspective. Under the parent company perspective, foreign operations are extensions of parent company operations and are, in large measure, sources of domestic currency cash flows. Accordingly, the object of translation is to change the unit of measure for financial statements of foreign subsidiaries to the domestic currency, and to make the foreign statements conform to accounting principles generally accepted in the country of the parent company. We think these objectives are best achieved by translation methods that use historical rates of exchange. We prefer the temporal principle, as it generally maintains the accounting principles used to measure assets and liabilities originally expressed in foreign currency units.[6] Because foreign statements under a parent company perspective are first adjusted to reflect parent company accounting principles (*before* translation), the temporal principle is appropriate, as it changes a measurement in foreign currency into a measurement in domestic currency without changing the basis of measurement.

The temporal translation method is easily adapted to processes that make accounting adjustments during the translation. When this is so, adjustments for differences between two or more sets of accounting concepts and practices are made along with the translation of currency amounts. For example, inventories or certain liabilities may be restated according to accounting practices different from those originally used. The temporal principle can accommodate any asset valuation framework, be it historical cost, current replacement price, or net realizable values.

The current rate method of translation is a straightforward translation (restatement) from one *currency language* to another. There is no change in the nature of the accounts; only their particular form of expression is changed. The current rate method is appropriate when the translated accounts of foreign subsidiaries keep the local currency as the unit of measure; that is, when foreign entities are viewed from a local (as opposed to a parent) company perspective. Translation at the current rate does not change any of the initial relationships (e.g., financial ratios) in the foreign currency statements, as all account balances are simply multiplied by a constant. This approach is also useful when the accounts of an independent company are translated for the convenience of foreign stockholders or other external user groups.

A second use of the current rate method happens when price-level-adjusted accounts are to be translated to another currency. If reliable price level adjustments are made in a given set of accounts and if domestic price level changes for the currency are reflected closely in related foreign exchange rate movements, the current rate translation of price-level-adjusted data yields results that are comparable to translating historical cost accounts under the historical rate translation method.[7] This topic is covered in Chapter 7.

Are there situations in which translations should not be done at all? We think so. No translation is appropriate between highly unstable and highly stable currencies. Translation of one into the other will not produce meaningful information using any translation method. No translation also means non-consolidation of financial statements. We think this is reasonable. If a currency is unstable enough to put account

---

[6]See Frederick D. S. Choi and Gerhard G. Mueller, *An Introduction to Multinational Accounting,* Upper Saddle River, NJ: Prentice Hall, 1978.
[7]Alas, empirical evidence suggests that exchange rate changes and differential inflation are seldom perfectly negatively correlated. For recent evidence on the distortions caused by this market anomaly, see David A. Ziebart and Jong-Hag Choi, "The Difficulty of Achieving Economic Reality Through Foreign Currency Translation," *International Journal of Accounting* 33, no. 4 (1998): 403–414.

translations out of the question, financial statement consolidation should also be out of the question. No translation is necessary when financial statements of independent companies are issued for purely informational purposes to residents in another country that is in a comparable stage of economic development and has a comparable national currency situation. Finally, certain special management reports should not be translated. Effective international managers should be able to evaluate situations and reach decisions in terms of more than one currency unit. Some internal company reports may have several different columns of monetary amounts, each in a different currency unit. Translation may be impossible for certain other reports (such as those on a possible international acquisition) because historical foreign exchange rate information may not be available. Still other types of reports may translate current or monetary items only and leave other items untranslated.

APPROPRIATE CURRENT RATE

Thus far we have referred to rates of exchange used in translation methods as either *historical* or *current*. Average rates are often used in income statements for expediency. The choice of an appropriate exchange rate is not clear-cut because several exchange rates are in effect for any currency at any time. There are buying rates and selling rates, spot rates and forward rates, official rates and free-market rates, and many rate differentials in between. We believe that an appropriate translation rate should reflect economic and business reality as closely as possible. The free-market rate quoted for spot transactions in the country where the accounts to be translated originate is the only rate that appropriately measures current transaction values.

Sometimes a country applies different exchange rates to different transactions. In these situations, one must choose among several existing rates. Several possibilities have been suggested: (1) dividend remittance rates, (2) free-market rates, and (3) any applicable penalty or preference rates, such as those associated with imports or exports. Your authors believe that free-market rates are preferable, with one exception: Where specific exchange controls are in effect (i.e., when certain funds are definitely earmarked for specific transactions to which specific foreign exchange rates apply), the applicable rates should be used. For instance, if a Latin American subsidiary of a U.S. parent has received permission to import certain goods from the United States at a favorable rate and has set aside certain funds to do so, the earmarked funds should be translated to dollars at the special preference rate. The current year-end free-market rate should then be applied to the balance of the foreign cash account. This procedure translates portions of a foreign currency cash account at two or more different translation rates. That is fine as long as it properly and fully reflects economic reality.

TRANSLATION GAINS AND LOSSES

Exhibit 6-6 illustrated four translation adjustments resulting from applying various translation methods to foreign currency financial statements. Internationally, accounting treatments of these adjustments are as diverse as the translation procedures. Approaches to accounting for translation adjustments range from *deferral* to *no deferral* with hybrid approaches in between.[8]

DEFERRAL

Exclusion of translation adjustments in current income is generally advocated because these adjustments merely result from a restatement process. Changes in the domestic currency equivalents of a foreign subsidiary's net assets are unrealized and have no effect on the local currency cash flows generated by the foreign entity. Therefore, it would be misleading to include such adjustments in current income. Under these circumstances, translation adjustments should be accumulated separately as a part of consolidated equity. Parkinson offers additional reasons to support deferral:

> It can be argued that the gain or loss relates to a very long-term investment — perhaps even a permanent investment — of a . . . parent in a foreign subsidiary; that the gain or loss will not become realized until the foreign operation is closed down and all the net assets are distributed to the parent; that at or before such time the change in the exchange rate may have reversed — i.e., that no gain or loss will ever be realized. It can also be argued that operating results recorded in the periods following the currency revaluation (and translated at the then current exchange rate) will indicate the increased or decreased worth of the foreign operation and that in these circumstances there is no need to record a one-time translation gain or loss in the income statement — that in fact the recording of such a gain or loss might be misleading.[9]

Deferral may be opposed on the grounds that exchange rates may not reverse themselves. Even if they do, deferral of exchange adjustments is premised on predicting exchange rates, a most difficult task. Some argue that deferring translation gains or losses masks the behavior of exchange rate changes; that is, rate changes are historical facts and financial statement users are best served if the effects of exchange rate fluctuations are accounted for when they occur. According to FAS No. 8 (par. 199), "Exchange rates fluctuate; accounting should not give the impression that rates are stable."

DEFERRAL AND AMORTIZATION

Some favor deferring translation gains or losses and amortizing these adjustments over the life of related balance sheet items. As an example, assume that the acquisition of a fixed asset is financed by issuing debt. It can be argued that principal and interest payments on the debt are *covered* by cash flows generated from using the fixed asset. Here, the translation gain or loss associated with the debt would be deferred and amortized over the life of the related fixed asset, that is, released to income in a manner compatible with depreciation expense. Alternatively, the translation gain or loss arising from

---

[8]For additional treatment of the issues discussed here, see Financial Accounting Standards Board, "An Analysis of Issues Related to Accounting for Foreign Currency Translation," *FASB Discussion Memorandum,* Stamford, CT: FASB, February 21, 1974, 79–102.

[9]MacDonald R. Parkinson, *Translation of Foreign Currencies,* Toronto: Canadian Institute of Chartered Accountants, 1972, 101–102.

the debt could be deferred and amortized over the remaining life of the debt as an adjustment to interest expense.

Such approaches can be criticized on theoretical and practical grounds. For example, finance theory tells us that capital budgeting decisions about fixed asset investments are independent of decisions about how to finance them. Linking the two looks more like a device to smooth income. Adjusting interest expense is also suspect. Domestic borrowing costs are not adjusted to reflect changes in market interest rates or the fair value of the debt. Why should fluctuations in currency values have such an effect?

PARTIAL DEFERRAL

A third option in accounting for translation gains and losses is to recognize losses as soon as they occur, but to recognize gains only as they are realized. Although conservative, deferring a translation gain solely because it is a gain denies that a rate change has occurred. Moreover, deferral of translation gains while recognizing translation losses is logically inconsistent. This approach also lacks any explicit criteria to determine when to realize a translation gain. Also, those who favor deferral of translation gains are at a loss to determine how much to defer. In the past, companies have netted current gains against prior losses and deferred the difference. This implies that translation gains or losses are not period items and will "wash out" in the long run. If this were so, deferrals would be a questionable practice.

NO DEFERRAL

A final option is to recognize translation gains and losses in the income statement immediately. This option views deferral of any type as artificial and misleading. Deferral criteria are often attacked as internally inconsistent and impossible to implement. However, including translation gains and losses in current income introduces a random element to earnings that could result in significant earning fluctuations whenever exchange rates change. Moreover, including such paper gains and losses in reported earnings can mislead statement readers, because these adjustments do not always provide information compatible with the expected economic effects of rate changes on an enterprise's cash flows.

WHERE ARE WE?

The objectives of translation have an important bearing on the nature of any potential translation adjustment. If a local currency perspective is maintained (local company perspective), reflecting a translation adjustment in current income is unwarranted. Recall that a local company perspective requires the current rate translation method in order to preserve relationships existing in the foreign currency statements. In our opinion, including translation gains or losses in income distorts original financial relationships and may mislead users of the information. Translation gains or losses should be treated from a local currency perspective as adjustments to the owners' equity.

If the reporting currency of the parent company is the unit of measure for the translated financial statements (parent company perspective), it is advisable to recognize translation gains or losses in income immediately. The parent company perspective views a foreign subsidiary as an extension of the parent. Translation gains and losses reflect increases or decreases in the domestic currency equity of the foreign investment and should be recognized.

TRANSLATION ACCOUNTING DEBATES

Translation accounting practices have changed in response to the increasing complexity of multinational operations and changes in the international monetary system. Responses by the United States to the evolving translation problem are representative of the approaches developed elsewhere. Therefore, we present a brief history of U.S. foreign currency accounting.

PRE-1965

Before 1965 the translation practices of many U.S. companies were guided by *Accounting Research Bulletin No. 4* (ARB No. 4),[10] later reissued as Chapter 12 of ARB No. 43.[11] This statement advocated the current-noncurrent method. Transaction gains or losses were taken directly to income. Translation gains or losses were netted during the period. Net translation losses were recognized in current income, while net translation gains were deferred in a balance sheet suspense account and used to offset translation losses in future periods.

1965–1975

Chapter 12 of ARB No. 43 allowed certain exceptions to the current-noncurrent method. Under special circumstances, inventory could be translated at historical rates. Long-term debt incurred to acquire long-term assets could be restated at the current rate when there was a large (presumably permanent) change in the exchange rate. Any accounting difference caused by debt restatement was treated as part of the asset's cost. Translating *all* foreign currency payables and receivables at the current rate was allowed after *Accounting Principles Board Opinion No. 6* was issued in 1965.[12] This change to ARB No. 43 gave companies another translation option.

1975–1981

To end the variety of treatments allowed under previous translation standards, the FASB issued the controversial FAS No. 8 in 1975.[13] This statement significantly changed U.S. practice and that of foreign companies subscribing to U.S. GAAP by requiring the temporal method of translation. Equally important, deferral of translation gains and losses was no longer permitted. Translation and transaction exchange gains and losses had to be recognized in income during the period of the rate change.

---

[10]American Institute of Certified Public Accountants, Committee on Accounting Procedure, "Foreign Operations and Foreign Exchange," *Accounting Research Bulletin No. 4,* New York: AICPA, 1939.

[11]American Institute of Certified Public Accountants, Committee on Accounting Procedure, "Restatement and Revision of Accounting Research Bulletins," *Accounting Research Bulletin No. 43,* New York: AICPA, 1953.

[12]American Institute of Certified Public Accountants, "Status of Accounting Research Bulletins," *Accounting Principles Board Opinion No. 6,* New York: AICPA, 1965.

[13]Financial Accounting Standards Board, "Accounting for the Translation of Foreign Currency Transactions and Foreign Currency Financial Statements," *Statement of Financial Accounting Standards No. 8,* Stamford, CT: FASB, 1975.

Corporate reaction to FAS No. 8 was mixed. While some applauded it for its theoretical merits, many condemned it for the distortions it caused in reported corporate earnings. FAS No. 8 was criticized for producing accounting results not in accord with economic reality. The yo-yo effect of FAS No. 8 on corporate earnings also caused concern among executives of multinational companies. They worried that their companies' reported earnings would appear more volatile than those of domestic companies, and thereby depress their stock prices. Despite evidence that this concern was misguided,[14] FAS No. 8 had a significant effect on corporate management practices. Studies on its economic impact[15] found that many management groups spent corporate cash to minimize noncash (translation) adjustments. Managing translation adjustments also diverted time from ordinary operating problems.

1981–PRESENT

In May 1978, the FASB invited public comment on its first twelve pronouncements. Most of the 200 letters received related to FAS No. 8, urging that it be changed. Responding to the dissatisfaction, the FASB reconsidered FAS No. 8 and, after many public meetings and two exposure drafts, issued *Statement of Financial Accounting Standards No. 52* in 1981.[16]

FEATURES OF STANDARD NO. 52

The objectives of translation under FAS No. 52 differ substantially from those of FAS No. 8. FAS No. 8 adopted a parent company perspective by requiring that foreign currency financial statements be presented as if all transactions had taken place in U.S. dollars. Standard No. 52 recognizes that both the parent company and the local company perspectives are valid reporting frameworks. Its translation rules are thus designed to

1. Reflect, in consolidated statements, the financial results and relationships measured in the primary currency in which each consolidated entity does business (its *functional currency*).
2. Provide information that is generally compatible with the expected economic effects of an exchange rate change on an enterprise's cash flows and equity.

These objectives are based on the concept of a *functional currency*. The functional currency of an entity is defined as the currency of the primary economic environment in which it operates and generates cash flows. If a foreign subsidiary's operation is relatively self-contained and integrated within the foreign country (i.e., one that manufactures a product for local distribution), it will normally generate and spend its home

---

[14]Roland Dukes, *An Empirical Investigation of the Effects of Statement of Financial Accounting Standards No. 8 on Security Return Behavior,* Stamford, CT: FASB, December 1978.

[15]For example, T. G. Evans, W. R. Folks, and M. Jilling, *The Impact of Financial Accounting Standards No. 8 on the Foreign Exchange Risk Management Practices of American Multinationals: An Economic Impact Study,* Stamford, CT: FASB, 1978; J. K. Shank, J. F. Dillard, and R. J. Murdock, *Assessing the Economic Impact of FASB 8,* New York: Financial Executives Research Foundation, 1979; and F. D. S. Choi, H. D. Lowe, and R. G. Worthley, "Accountors, Accountants, and Standard No. 8," *Journal of International Business Studies,* fall 1978.

[16]Financial Accounting Standards Board, "Foreign Currency Translation," *Statement of Financial Accounting Standards No. 52,* Stamford, CT: FASB, 1981.

country's currency. Hence, the home currency (e.g., francs for the Belgian subsidiary of a U.S. parent) is its functional currency. If a foreign entity keeps its accounts in a currency other than the functional currency (e.g., the Indian accounts of a U.S. subsidiary whose functional currency is really British pounds, rather than Indian rupees), its functional currency is the third-country currency (pounds). If a foreign entity is merely an extension of a U.S. parent company (e.g., a Mexican assembly operation that receives components from its U.S. parent and ships the assembled product back to the United States), its functional currency is the U.S. dollar. Exhibit 6-8 identifies circumstances justifying use of either the local or parent currency as the functional currency. Determining the functional currency thus determines the choice of translation method and the disposition of exchange gains and losses.

TRANSLATION WHEN LOCAL CURRENCY IS THE FUNCTIONAL CURRENCY

If the functional currency is the foreign currency in which the foreign entity's records are kept, its financial statements are *translated* to dollars using the current rate method. Resulting translation gains or losses are disclosed in a separate component of consolidated equity. This preserves the financial statement ratios as calculated from the local currency statements. The following current rate procedures are used:

1. All foreign currency assets and liabilities are translated to dollars using the exchange rate prevailing as of the balance sheet date; capital accounts are translated at historical rates.
2. Revenues and expenses are translated using the exchange rate prevailing on the transaction date, although weighted average rates can be used for expediency.

EXHIBIT 6-8	Functional Currency Criteria	
Economic Factors	*Circumstances Favoring Local Currency as Functional Currency*	*Circumstances Favoring Parent Currency as Functional Currency*
Cash Flows	Primarily in the local currency and do not impact parent's cash flows	Directly impact parent's cash flows and are currently remittable to the parent
Sales price	Largely irresponsive to exchange rate changes and governed primarily by local competition	Responsive to changes in exchange rates and determined by worldwide competition
Sales market	Largely in the host country and denominated in local currency	Largely in the parent country and denominated in parent currency
Expenses	Incurred primarily in the local environment	Primarily related to productive factors imported from the parent company
Financing	Primarily denominated in local currency and serviced by local operations	Primarily from the parent or reliance on parent company to meet debt obligations
Intercompany transactions	Infrequent, not extensive	Frequent and extensive

Source: Financial Accounting Standards Board, *Statement of Financial Accounting Standards No. 52,* Stamford, CT: FASB, 1981, Appendix A.

3. Translation gains and losses are reported in a separate component of consolidated stockholders' equity. These exchange adjustments do not go into the income statement until the foreign operation is sold or the investment is judged to have permanently lost value.

TRANSLATION WHEN THE U.S. DOLLAR IS THE FUNCTIONAL CURRENCY

When the U.S. dollar is a foreign entity's functional currency, its foreign currency financial statements are remeasured to dollars using the temporal method prescribed by FAS No. 8. All translation gains and losses resulting from the translation process are included in determining current period income. Specifically:

1. Monetary assets and liabilities and nonmonetary assets valued at current market prices are translated using the rate prevailing as of the financial statement date; other nonmonetary items and capital accounts are translated at historical rates.
2. Revenues and expenses are translated using average exchange rates for the period except those items related to nonmonetary items (e.g., cost of sales and depreciation expense), which are translated using historical rates.
3. Translation gains and losses are reflected in current income.

TRANSLATION WHEN FOREIGN CURRENCY IS THE FUNCTIONAL CURRENCY

A foreign entity may keep its records in one foreign currency when its functional currency is another foreign currency. In this situation, the financial statements are first remeasured from the local currency into the functional currency (temporal method) and then translated into U.S. dollars using the current rate method.

Exhibit 6-9 charts the translation procedures described here, and the appendix to this chapter demonstrates the mechanics of foreign currency translation.

An exception to the current rate method is required for subsidiaries located in places where the cumulative rate of inflation during the preceding 3 years exceeds 100 percent. In such hyperinflationary conditions, the dollar (the stronger currency) is considered the functional currency, requiring use of the temporal translation method.

Where an entity has more than one distinct and separable operation (e.g., a branch or division), each operation may be considered as a separate entity with its own functional currency. Thus, a U.S. parent might have a self-contained manufacturing operation in Mexico designed to serve the Latin American market and a separate sales outlet for the parent company's exported products. Under these circumstances, financial statements of the manufacturing operation would be translated to dollars using the current rate method. The peso statements of the Mexican sales outlet would be remeasured in dollars using the temporal method.

Once the functional currency for a foreign entity is determined, FAS No. 52 requires that it be used consistently unless changes in economic circumstances clearly indicate that the functional currency has changed. If a reporting enterprise can justify the change in conformity with Accounting Principles Board Opinion No. 20, "Accounting Changes," the accounting change need not be accounted for retroactively.

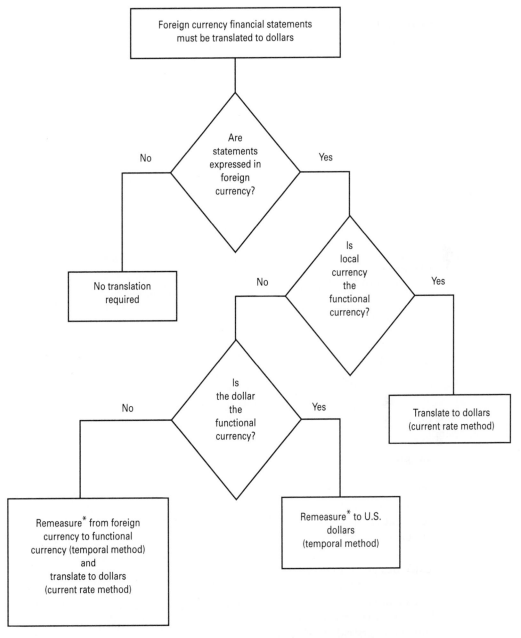

*The term *remeasure* means to translate so as to change the unit of measure from a foreign currency to the functional currency.

FIGURE 6-9   Translation Procedure Flow Chart

THE DEBATE CONTINUES

FAS No. 52 was designed to quiet many of the criticisms leveled at FAS No. 8.[17] Recent empirical evidence also lends support to FAS No. 52.[18] New issues stir new controversies,[19] and the following sections discuss several of them.

REPORTING PERSPECTIVE

In adopting the notion of functional currency, FAS No. 52 accommodates both local and parent company reporting perspectives in the consolidated financial statements. Several questions may be posed. First, are financial statement readers better served by incorporating two different reporting perspectives and, therefore, two different currency frameworks in a single set of consolidated financial statements? Is a translation adjustment produced under the temporal method any different in substance from that produced under the current rate method? If not, is any useful purpose served by disclosing some translation adjustments in income and others in stockholders' equity? Is FAS No. 8's concept of a single unit of measure (the parent company's reporting currency) the lesser of two evils? Should we stop translating foreign currency financial statements altogether? Doing so would avoid many of the pitfalls associated with current translation methods, including the problem of incorporating more than one perspective in the translated results.[20]

It has also been suggested that FAS No. 52 is inconsistent with the theory of consolidation, which is to show the statements of a parent company and its subsidiaries as if the group were operating as a single company. Yet subsidiaries whose functional currency is the local currency operate relatively independently of the parent. If the multinational doesn't operate as a single company, then why consolidate those parts that are independent?[21]

---

[17]For evidence of market reactions to FAS No. 52 versus FAS No. 8, see David A. Ziebart and David H. Kim, "An Examination of the Market Reactions Associated with SFAS No. 8 and SFAS No. 52," *Accounting Review* (April 1987): 343–357; Zabihollah Rezaee, "Capital Market Reactions to Accounting Policy Deliberations: An Empirical Study of Accounting for Foreign Currency Translation 1974–1982," *Journal of Business Finance and Accounting* (winter 1990): 635–648; and Zabihollah Rezaee, R. Phillip Malone, and Russell Briner, "Capital Market Response to SFAS No. 8 and 52: Professional Adaptation," *Journal of Accounting, Auditing, and Finance* (summer 1993): 313–332.

[18]As examples, Ziebart and Kim found significant share price and volume reactions upon the release of FAS 52, David A. Ziebart, " An Investigation of the Price and Trading Reactions to the Issuance of SFAS No. 52," *Journal of Accounting, Auditing and Finance* (winter 1991): 35–47. Bartov finds that FAS 52 produces a better accounting measure for economic exposure than FAS No. 8, Eli Bartov "Foreign Currency Exposure of Multinational Firms: Accounting Measures and Market Valuation," *Contemporary Accounting Research* (winter 1997): 623–652. Ayres and Rodgers show that reliance on FAS 52 improves analysts' earnings forecasts, Frances L. Ayres and Jacci L. Rodgers, "Further Evidence on the Impact of SFAS 52 on Analysts' Earnings Forecasts," *Journal of International Financial Management and Accounting* (June 1994): 120–141.

[19]A recent opinion survey rated FAS No. 52 as one of the best and worst American accounting standards issued to date! Cheri L. Reither, " What Are the Best and the Worst Accounting Standards?" *Accounting Horizon* 12, no. 3 (1998): 283–292.

[20]Paul Rosenfield, "Accounting for Foreign Operations," *Journal of Accountancy* (August 1987): 112.

[21]C. W. Nobes, "An Analysis of the Use of 'Theory' in the UK and US Currency Translation Standards," reprinted in C. W. Nobes, *Issues in International Accounting,* New York: Garland, 1986, 129–130.

WHAT HAPPENED TO HISTORICAL COST?

As noted earlier in the chapter, translating a balance measured under historical cost at the current exchange rate produces an amount in U.S. dollars that is neither the item's historical cost nor its current value equivalent. Such a translated amount defies theoretical description. Historical cost is the basis of U.S. GAAP and most overseas assets of most multinationals will have historical cost measurements. Yet the current rate method is used for translation whenever a local currency is deemed to be the functional currency. Even if financial statement users can still make sense of the consolidated amounts, the theoretical incoherence remains.

CONCEPT OF INCOME

Under FAS No. 52, adjustments arising from the translation of foreign currency financial statements and certain transactions are made directly to shareholders' equity, thus bypassing the income statement. The apparent intention of this was to give statement readers more accurate and less confusing income numbers. Some, however, dislike the idea of burying translation adjustments that were previously disclosed. They fear readers may be confused as to the effects of fluctuating exchange rates on a company's worth.[22]

MANAGED EARNINGS

FAS No. 52 provides opportunities to manage earnings. Consider the choice of functional currencies. An examination of the functional currency criteria shown in Exhibit 6-7 suggests that the choice of a functional currency is not straightforward. A foreign subsidiary's operations could satisfy opposing criteria. For example, a foreign subsidiary may incur its expenses primarily in the local country and make its sales primarily in the local environment and denominated in local currency. These circumstances would favor selection of the local currency as the functional currency. Yet the same operation may be financed entirely by the parent company with cash flows remitted to the parent. Therefore, the parent currency could be selected as the functional currency. The different possible outcomes involved in selecting functional currencies may be one reason why Exxon-Mobil Oil chooses the local currency as the functional currency for most of its foreign operations, while Chevron, Texaco, and Unocal choose the dollar. When choice criteria conflict and the choice can significantly affect reporting outcomes, there are opportunities for earnings management.

Research to date is inconclusive as to whether managers manipulate income (and other financial statement amounts) by the choice of functional currency.[23] Some evidence of earnings management appears when one looks at when companies chose to

---

[22]Of course there are other equity adjustments, namely unrealized gains and losses on certain debt and equity securities and minimum pension liability adjustments. Under FAS No. 130 (effective for fiscal years beginning after December 15, 1997), U.S. companies must report these amounts in *comprehensive income* as an adjustment to net income.

[23]For example, see J. H. Amernic and B. J. B. Galvin, "Implementing the New Foreign Currency Rules in Canada and the United States: A Challenge to Professional Judgement," *International Journal of Accounting* (spring 1984): 165–180; Thomas G. Evans and Timothy S. Doupnik, *Determining the Functional Currency Under Statement 52,* Stamford, CT: FASB, 1986, 11–12; Dileep R. Mehta and Samanta B. Thapa, "FAS 52, Functional Currency, and the Non-comparability of Financial Reports," *International Journal of Accounting* 26, no. 2 (1991): 71–84; and Robert J. Kirsch and Thomas G. Evans, "The Implementation of

adopt FAS No. 52 (they had three choices: 1981, 1982, or 1983). Evidence shows that companies chose the adoption date in part based on when the effects on income were the most favorable.[24] Such motives as these reduce the credibility of multinationals' consolidated financial statements.

FOREIGN CURRENCY TRANSLATION AND INFLATION

An inverse relationship between a country's rate of inflation and its currency's external value has been empirically demonstrated.[25] Consequently, use of the current rate to translate the cost of nonmonetary assets located in inflationary environments will eventually produce domestic currency equivalents far below their original measurement bases. At the same time, translated earnings would be greater because of correspondingly lower depreciation charges. Such translated results could easily mislead rather than inform. Lower dollar valuations would usually understate the actual earning power of foreign assets supported by local inflation, and inflated return on investment ratios of foreign operations could create false expectations of future profitability.

The FASB decided against inflation adjustments before translation, believing such adjustments to be inconsistent with the historical cost valuation framework used in basic U.S. statements. As a solution, FAS No. 52 requires use of the U.S. dollar as the functional currency for foreign operations domiciled in hyperinflationary environments (those countries where the cumulative rate of inflation exceeds 100 percent over a 3-year period). This procedure would hold constant the dollar equivalents of foreign currency assets, as they would be translated at the historical rate (by the temporal method).

This method has its limitations. First, translation at the historical rate is meaningful only if differential rates of inflation between the subsidiary's host country and parent country are perfectly negatively correlated with exchange rates. If not, the dollar equivalents of foreign currency assets in inflationary environments will be misleading. Should inflation rates in the hyperinflationary economy fall below 100 percent in a future 3-year period, switching to the current rate method (because local currency would become the functional currency) could produce a significant translation adjustment to consolidated equity, as exchange rates may change significantly during the interim. Under these circumstances, charging stockholders' equity with translation losses on foreign currency fixed assets could have a significant effect on financial ratios with stockholders' equity

FAS 52: Did the Foreign Currency Approach Prevail?" *International Journal of Accounting* 29, no. 1 (1994): 20–33.

[24]For evidence of earnings motivation for switching currency translation methods, see Dahli Gray, "Corporate Preferences for Foreign Currency Accounting Standards," *Journal of Accounting Research*, Autumn 1984, pp. 760–64; James J. Benjamin, Steven Grossman, and Casper Wiggins, "The Impact of Foreign Currency Translation on Reporting During the Phase-in of SFAS No. 52," *Journal of Accounting, Auditing, and Finance*, Volume 1, No. 3, 1996, pp. 174–84; Frances L. Ayres, "Characteristics of Firms Electing Early Adoption of SFAS 52," *Journal of Accounting and Economics*, June 1986, pp. 143–58; and Robert W. Rutledge, "Does Management Engage in the Manipulation of Earnings?" *Journal of International Accounting, Auditing, and Taxation*, Volume 4, No. 1, 1995, pp. 69–86.

[25]B. Balassa, "The Purchasing Power Parity Doctrine: A Reappraisal," *Journal of Political Economy*, 1964, pp. 145–54; R. Z. Aliber and C. P. Stickney, "Accounting Measures of Foreign Exchange Exposure: The Long and Short of It," *Accounting Review*, January 1975, pp. 44–57; and W. Beaver and M. Wolfson, "Foreign Currency Translation in Perfect and Complete Markets," *Journal of Accounting Research*, Autumn 1982, pp. 528–60.

in the denominator. The issue of foreign currency translation cannot be separated from the issue of accounting for foreign inflation, which is treated at greater length in the next chapter.

FOREIGN CURRENCY TRANSLATION ELSEWHERE

We now look briefly at foreign currency translation in other parts of the world. FAS No. 52 has become the basis for similar standards elsewhere. The Canadian Institute of Chartered Accountants (CICA), the U.K.'s Accounting Standards Committee (now, board) and the International Accounting Standards Committee all participated in the deliberations that led to FAS No. 52. It is not surprising to find that their corresponding standards are largely compatible with it.[26]

The main difference between the Canadian standard (CICA 1650) and FAS No. 52 concerns foreign long-term debt. In Canada, gains and losses from translation are deferred and amortized; in the U.S. they are recognized in income immediately. Canada has issued a second exposure draft proposing to eliminate its defer and amortize approach. While the exposure draft is still under consideration, withdrawal of the first exposure draft reflected concerns over the earnings impact of nondeferral.[27]

There are two major differences between the U.K. and U.S. standards. The U.K. standard permits the income statement of self-contained subsidiaries to be translated at either the current or average-for-the-year exchange rate; the latter must be used in the United States. The second difference relates to self-contained subsidiaries in hyperinflationary countries. In the United Kingdom, financial statements must first be adjusted to current price levels and then translated using the current rate; in the United States, the temporal method is used.

Finally, there is an important distinction between IAS 21 (as revised) and FAS No. 52. Under IAS 21, the financial statements of subsidiaries in highly inflationary environments must be adjusted to reflect changes in the general price level before translation, a treatment like that in the U.K. standard.

Australia and New Zealand issued standards in 1988. Compared to FAS No. 52, the Australian standard calls for revaluing noncurrent, nonmonetary assets for subsidiaries in high inflation countries prior to translation. The New Zealand standard is silent on the issue. The New Zealand standard also calls for the monetary-nonmonetary method of translation for subsidiaries with operations integrated with the parent. Since this produces results very similar to the temporal method, this difference with FAS No. 52 has little practical effect.

The foreign currency translation standards discussed here are broadly comparable with FAS No. 52. Nevertheless, multinationals following these standards could still

---

[26]All three standards were issued in 1983, roughly eighteen months after FAS No. 52. The Canadian standard is Accounting Recommendation 1650 and the British standard is Statement of Standard Accounting Practice 20; both are titled "Foreign Currency Translation." The original International Accounting Standard 21 was modified in 1993 and is now called, "The Effects of Changes in Foreign Exchange Rates."
[27]Rotenberg provides evidence suggesting that the impact of the proposed changes on reported leverage and profitability of Canadian companies would be significant. W. Rotenberg, "Harmonization of Foreign Currency Translation Practices: Canadian Treatment of Long Term Monetary Items," *International Journal of Accounting* 33, no. 4 (1998): 415–431.

produce differing consolidated financial statements, depending on their circumstances. This inconsistency would, in turn, inhibit comparison and complicate decision making.[28]

Practice elsewhere is more diverse. Japan recently changed its standard to require the current rate method in all circumstances, with translation adjustments shown on the balance sheet in stockholders' equity. The EU Fourth and Seventh Directives (see Chapter 8) have no provisions on foreign currency translation. Most Continental EU countries, including France and Germany, have no standards. As a result, practice is up to the companies. A survey of six German chemical companies found that two used the temporal method, two based their approach on the principle of functional currency, and two used the closing rate method.[29] However, some German and a number of French multinationals follow IAS (see Chapters 5 and 8) in preparing consolidated financial statements. They probably comply with IAS 21. Generally, practice is fluid in countries without standards.

CURRENT TRENDS

We conclude with our opening comment: Foreign currency translation is one of the most vexing and controversial technical issues in accounting, and is far from resolution. Where are we headed internationally? Will we ever reach closure? We think that the answer depends on how the harmonization activities of the IASB unfold. Chapter 8 discusses this effort, and its likelihood for success, extensively. An increasing number of internationally listed companies are following IAS and (as discussed in Chapter 8) the world's stock exchanges are under increasing pressure to allow IAS in lieu of domestic standards for foreign company listings. (Many stock exchanges already do this.) In the United States, foreign companies are allowed to follow the international standard (IAS 21) instead of the U.S. standard (FAS No. 52) in foreign currency translation. In time, the FASB may resolve the differences between FAS No. 52 and IAS 21 in favor of the international standard. We think this would encourage other standards setters to do likewise in resolving their differences with IAS 21.

APPENDIX: TRANSLATION AND REMEASUREMENT UNDER FAS NO. 52

Exhibit 6-10 presents comparative foreign currency balance sheets at December 31, 20X1 and 20X2, and a statement of income for the year ended December 31, 20X2 for C&M Corporation, a wholly owned foreign subsidiary of a U.S. company. The statements conform with U.S. generally accepted accounting principles before translation to U.S. dollars.

---

[28]Robert J. Kirsch and Dawn Becker-Dermer, "Proposed Revisions of International Accounting Standard No. 21 and Their Implications for Translation Accounting in Selected English-Speaking Countries," *International Journal of Accounting* 30, no. 1 (1995): 1–24.

[29]Peter Fiege, "How 'Uniform' Is Financial Reporting in Germany? — The Example of Foreign Currency Translation," *European Accounting Review* 6, no. 1 (1997): 109–122.

EXHIBIT 6-10   Financial Statements of C&M Corporation

Balance Sheet	12/31/X1	12/31/X2
Cash	FC 300	FC 500
Accounts receivable (net)	1,300	1,000
Inventories (lower of FIFO cost or market)	1,200	1,500
Fixed assets (net)	9,000	8,000
Total assets	FC 11,800	FC 11,000
Accounts payable	FC 2,200	FC 2,400
Long-term debt	4,400	3,000
Capital stock	2,000	2,000
Retained earnings	3,200	3,600
Total liabilities and owners' equity	FC 11,800	FC 11,000

Income Statement		Year Ended 12/31/X2
Sales		FC 10,000
Expenses		
Cost of sales	5,950	
Depreciation (straight-line)	1,000	
Other	1,493	8,443
Operating income		FC 1,557
Income taxes		467
Net income		FC 1,090

Capital stock was issued and fixed assets acquired when the exchange rate was FC1 = $.17. Inventories at January 1, 20X2, were acquired during the fourth quarter of 20X1. Purchases (FC6, 250), sales, other expenses, and dividends (FC690) occurred evenly during 20X2. Retained earnings in U.S. dollars at December 31, 20X1, under the temporal method were $316. Exchange rates for calendar 20X2 were as follows:

January 1, 20X2	FC1 = $.23
December 31, 20X2	FC1 = $.18
Average during 20X2	FC1 = $.22
Average during fourth quarter, 20X1	FC1 = $.23
Average during fourth quarter, 20X2	FC1 = $.19

CURRENT RATE METHOD

Translation adjustments under the current rate method arise whenever (1) year-end foreign currency balances are translated at a current rate that differs from that used to translate ending balances of the previous period, and (2) foreign currency financial statements are translated at a current rate that differs from exchange rates used during the period. The translation adjustment is calculated by (1) multiplying the beginning foreign currency net asset balance by the change in the current rate during the period and (2) multiplying the increase or decrease in net assets during the period by the difference between the average exchange rate and the end-of-period exchange rate. Exhibit 6-11 depicts how the FAS No. 52 translation process applies to these figures.

As can be seen, translation procedures under the current rate method are straightforward. However, the derivation of the beginning cumulative translation adjustment merits some explanation. Assume that calendar 20X2 is the first year in which the current rate method is adopted (e.g., the previous translation method was the temporal method, as the U.S. dollar was considered functional before 20X2). Under this scenario, a one-time translation adjustment would be calculated as of January 1, 20X2. This figure approximates the amount by which beginning stockholders' equity would differ in light of the switch from the temporal to the current rate method. It is calculated by

---

EXHIBIT 6-11 Current Rate Method of Translation (Local Currency Is Functional Currency)

	Foreign Currency	Exchange Rate	Dollar Equivalents
Balance Sheet Accounts			
Assets			
Cash	FC 500	$.18	$ 90
Accounts receivable	1,000	.18	180
Inventories	1,500	.18	270
Fixed assets	8,000	.18	1,440
Total	FC 11,000		$1,980
Liabilities and Stockholders' Equity			
Accounts payable	FC 2,400	.18	$ 432
Long-term debt	3,000	.18	540
Capital stock	2,000	.17	340
Retained earnings	3,600	1	404
Translation adjustment (cumulative)		2	264
Total	11,000		$1,980
Income Statement Accounts			
Sales	FC 10,000	.22	$2,200
Cost of sales	(5,950)	.22	(1,309)
Depreciation	(1,000)	.22	(220)
Other expenses	(1,493)	.22	(328)
Income before income taxes	FC 1,557		$ 343
Income taxes	(467)	.22	(103)
Net income	FC 1,090		$ 240
Retained earnings, 12/31/X1	3,200		316
Less: dividends	(690)	.22	(152)
Retained earnings, 12/31/X2	FC 3,600		$ 404

[1]See statement of income and retained earnings.

[2]The cumulative translation adjustment of $264 is comprised of two parts: (1) the cumulative translation adjustment at the beginning of the year, and (2) the translation adjustment for the current year.

translating C&M Corporation's January 1, 20X2, foreign currency net asset position at the current rate prevailing on that date. (This result simulates what C&M's beginning net asset position would be had it used the current rate method all along.) The difference between this amount and the amount of net assets under the temporal method constitutes C&M Corporation's beginning-of-period cumulative translation adjustment, as illustrated here.

Net assets, 12/31/X1 (1/1/X2)		FC 5,200
Multiplied by exchange rate as of 1/1/X2 (FC1 = $.23)		× $.23
Less: As reported stockholders' equity, 12/31/X1:		1,196
Capital stock	$340	
Retained earnings (per temporal method)	316	656
Cumulative translation adjustment, 1/1/X2		$540

Given this information, the following steps yield a translation adjustment of $(276) for calendar 20X2.

1. Net assets, 12/31/X1 (1/1/X2)		FC 5,200	
Multiplied by change in current rate:			
Rate, 12/31/X1 (1/1/X2)	FC1 = $.23		
Rate, 12/31/X2	FC1 = $.18	× $(.05)	$(260)
2. Change in net assets during year (net income less dividends)		FC 400	
Multiplied by difference between average and year-end rate:			
Average rate	FC1 = $.22		
Year-end rate	FC1 = $.18	× $(.04)	$ (16)
Total			$(276)

The final cumulative translation adjustment for 20X2 of $264 is reached by adding the $(276) translation adjustment for 20X2 to the beginning balance of $540.

TEMPORAL METHOD

Exhibit 6-12 illustrates the FAS No. 52 remeasurement process when the dollar is the functional currency. In contrast to the current rate method, the temporal method translates foreign currency balances using historical as well as current exchange rates. Calculation of the exchange adjustment, which aggregates both transaction and translation gains and losses, also differs. In this example, the first component of the translation

EXHIBIT 6-12   Temporal Method of Translation (U.S. Dollar Is Functional Currency)

	Foreign Currency	Exchange Rate	Dollar Equivalents
Balance Sheet Accounts			
Assets			
Cash	FC 500	$.18	$ 90
Accounts receivable	1,000	.18	180
Inventories	1,500	.19	285
Fixed assets	8,000	.17	1,360
Total	FC 11,000		$1,915
Liabilities and Stockholders' Equity			
Accounts payable	FC 2,400	.18	$ 432
Long-term debt	3,000	.18	540
Capital stock	2,000	.17	340
Retained earnings	3,600	1	603
Translation adjustment	----	2	----
Total	11,000		$1,915
Income Statement Accounts			
Sales	FC 10,000	.22	$2,200
Cost of sales	(5,950)	3	(1,366)
Depreciation	(1,000)	.17	(170)
Other expenses	(1,493)	.22	(328)
Aggregate exchange gain (loss)	----	4	206
Income taxes	467	.22	(103)
Net income	FC 1,090		$ 439
Retained earnings, 12/31/X1	3,200		316
Dividends	(690)	.22	(152)
Retained earnings, 12/31/X2	FC 3,600		$ 603

[1]See statement of income and retained earnings.

[2]Under the temporal method, translation adjustments ("gains and losses") appear directly in consolidated income as opposed to stockholders' equity.

[3]The dollar equivalent of cost of sales is derived by translating the components of cost of sales—namely, purchases or cost of production plus beginning and ending inventories by appropriate exchange rates as follows:

Beginning inventories	FC 1,200 at $.23 =	$ 276
Purchases	FC 6,250 at $.22 =	$1,375
Cost of goods available for sale		$1,651
Ending inventories	FC 1,500 at $.19 =	$ 285
Cost of sales		$1,366

[4]The aggregate exchange gain or loss figure combines both transaction and translation gains and losses.

adjustment is found by multiplying the beginning net monetary asset position by the change in the current rate during the year. Thus:

(12/31/X1 Monetary assets − monetary liabilities) × change in current rate
= (FC1,600 − FC6,600) × ($.18 − $.23)
= $250

The second component is found by first identifying the variables (i.e., sources and uses of monetary items) that caused the foreign subsidiary's net monetary asset position (exposure) to change, and then multiplying these items by the difference between the year-end exchange rate and the rates that pertain to them. This is illustrated here.

Change in net monetary asset position:

12/31//X1	FC (5,000)
12/31/X2	FC (3,900)
	FC 1,100

Composition of change:
Sources of monetary items multiplied by difference between year-end and average rate:

Net income	FC 1,090
Depreciation	FC 1,000
	2,090 × (.18 − .22) = $ (84)

Uses of monetary items multiplied by difference between year-end and average rate:

Increase in inventories	FC 300
Dividends	FC 690
	900 × (.18 − .22) = $40

The aggregate exchange adjustment is the sum of any transaction gain or loss together with the individual translation components derived, that is, $250 + ($84) + $40 = $206.

Selected References

Accounting Standards Committee, "Foreign Currency Translation," *Statement of Standard Accounting Practice No. 20*, London, U.K.: ASC, 1983.

Ayres, Frances L., "Characteristics of Firms Electing Early Adoption of SFAS 52," *Journal of Accounting and Economics* (June 1986): 143–158.

Ayres, Frances L., and Jacci L. Rodgers, "Further Evidence on the Impact of SFAS 52 on Analysts' Earnings Forecasts," *Journal of International Financial Management and Accounting* (June 1994): 120–141.

Bartov, Eli, "Foreign Currency Exposure of Multinational Firms: Accounting Measures and Market Valuation," *Contemporary Accounting Research* (winter 1997): 623–652.

Beaver, William, and Mark Wolfson, "Foreign Currency Translation and Changing Prices in Perfect and Complete Markets," *Journal of Accounting Research* (fall 1982): 528–550.

Collins, Daniel W., and William K. Salatka, "Noisy Accounting Earnings Signals and Earnings Response Coefficients: The Case of Foreign Currency Accounting," *Contemporary Accounting Research* (fall 1993) 119–159.

Estrada, Anette W., and Sander S. Wechsler, "Are You Euro-Fluent?" *Journal of Accountancy* (June 1999): 22–27.

Financial Accounting Standards Board, "Accounting for the Translation of Foreign Currency Transactions and Foreign Currency Financial Statements," *Statement of Financial*

Accounting Standards No. 8, Stamford, CT: FASB, October 1975.

Financial Accounting Standards Board, "Foreign Currency Translation," *Statement of Financial Accounting Standards No. 52*, Stamford, CT: FASB, December 1981.

Goldberg, Stephen R., and Joseph H. Godwin, "Foreign Currency Translation Under Two Cases—Integrated and Isolated Economies," *Journal of International Financial Management and Accounting* (June 1994): 97–119.

Goldman Sachs, *The Global Currency Analyst*, New York: Goldman Sachs Global Currency Research, June 2000.

Granger, C. J., "Accounting for Foreign Operations—19th Century Contributions to the Accounting Literature," *British Accounting Review* (June 1993): 151–176.

Griffin, Paul A., "Management's Preferences for FASB Statement No. 52: Predictive Ability Results," *Abacu* (December 1983): 130–138.

Harris, Trevor S., "Foreign Currency Translation: A Primer," in *Apples to Apples*, New York: Morgan Stanley Dean Witter, March 18, 1999, 28–45.

Houston, Carol Olson, "Foreign Currency Translation Research: A Review and Synthe-sis," *Journal of Accounting Literature* 8 (1989): 25–48.

International Accounting Standards Committee, "The Effects of Changes in Foreign Exchange Rates," *International Accounting Standard 21* (revised), London, U.K.: IASC, 1993.

Kirsch, Robert J., and Dawn Becker-Dermer, "Proposed Revisions of International Accounting Standard No. 21 and their Implications for Translation Accounting in Selected English-Speaking Countries," *International Journal of Accounting* 30, no. 1 (1995): 1–24.

Rotenberg, W., "Harmonization of Foreign Currency Translation Practices: Canadian Treatment of Long Term Monetary Items," *International Journal of Accounting* 33, no. 4 (1998): 415–431.

Soo, Billy S., and Lisa Gilbert Soo, "Accounting for the Multinational Firm: Is the Translation Process Valued by the Stock Market?" *Accounting Review* (October 1994): 617–637.

Ziebart, David A., and Jong-Hag Choi, "The Difficulty of Achieving Economic Reality Through Foreign Currency Translation," *International Journal of Accounting* 33, no. 4 (1998): 403–414.

Discussion Questions

1. Because currency translation simply involves multiplying or dividing a foreign currency balance by the appropriate exchange rate, why is it so controversial?

2. What is the difference between the *spot, forward,* and *swap* markets? Illustrate each description with an example.

3. What do *current, historical,* and *average* exchange rates mean in the context of foreign currency translation? Explain which cause(s) translation gains and losses, and which do(es) not?

4. Briefly explain the nature of foreign currency translation as (a) a *restatement process* and (b) a *remeasurement process.*

5. Compare and contrast features of the major foreign currency translation methods introduced in this chapter. Which method do you think is best? Why?

6. What is the rationale for including translation gains and losses in current income? Explain the rationale for deferral.

7. Why is the current rate method of translation inconsistent with historical cost? Give an example.

8. Do you agree with the definition of foreign exchange exposure presented in this chapter? Why or why not?

9. Describe the conceptual underpinnings of "functional currency," a key concept in FAS No. 52.

10. How does the treatment of translation gains and losses differ between the current and temporal translation methods under FAS No. 52, and what is the rationale for the differing accounting treatments?

11. What lessons, if any, can be learned from examining the history of foreign currency translation in the United States?

12. FAS No. 52 can be viewed as a practical compromise to the foreign currency translation problem. Do you think FAS No. 52 will end the foreign currency translation debate?

Exercises

1. Assume that your Spanish affiliate reports sales revenue of 250,000 pesetas. Referring to Exhibit 6-1, translate this revenue figure to U.S. dollars using the average indirect quote for pesetas. Do the same using a direct quote.

2. Refer to Exhibit 6-3 in this chapter. Using the information provided, determine the *cross rate* (i.e., a rate computed from two other exchange rates) between the Luxembourg franc and the Dutch guilder, using the methodology required by the European Commission.

3. Company X is headquartered in Country A and reports in the currency unit of Country A, the A$. Company Y is headquartered in Country B and reports in the currency unit of Country B, the Bkr. Company X and Company Y hold identical assets, A$100 and Bkr100, at the beginning and at the end of the year. At the beginning of the year, the exchange rate is A$1 = Bkr1.25. At the end of the year, the exchange rate is A$1 = Bkr2. No transactions occur during the year.

   Required:
   a. Calculate total assets reported by Company X and Company Y at the beginning and at the end of the year. Which company has a gain and which has a loss for the year?

   b. Does your answer to Question 3a make sense? Would it matter if Companies X and Y intended to repatriate their respective foreign assets rather than keep them invested permanently?

   c. What is the lesson from all of this? Is it all a shell game?

4. For more than a decade, *The Economist* has published a "Big Mac" index as a guide to whether currencies are at their "correct" level. It is based on the theory of purchasing-power parity (PPP): the idea that a dollar should buy the same amount in all countries. The Big Mac PPP is the exchange rate at which a "Big Mac" would cost the same in America as abroad. Comparing actual exchange rates with PPP gives one indication of whether a currency is under- or overvalued, and it is a way to predict exchange rate movements. Exhibit 6-13 is reproduced from the April 3, 1999 issue.

   The first column in Exhibit 6-13 shows the local-currency price of a Big Mac; the second one converts it into dollars. The third column calculates Big Mac PPPs which, when compared to actual exchange rates on April 3, 1999, indicates the degree to which the local currency is under- or overvalued (the final column).

   Required:
   a. According to Exhibit 6-13, which five currencies are the most undervalued and which five are the most overvalued, compared to the U.S. dollar?

   b. Using Exhibit 6-2, how well did the Big Mac index predict the direction of these ten exchange rates through May 2000?

EXHIBIT 6-13 The Hamburger Standard

	Big Mac Prices		Implied PPP[1] of the Dollar	Actual $ Exchange Rate 7/4/97	Under (−)/ Over (+) Valuation Against the Dollar %
	In Local Currency	In Dollars			
United States[2]	$2.43	2.43	—	—	—
Argentina	Peso2.50	2.50	1.03	1.00	+3
Australia	A$2.65	1.94	1.03	1.29	−20
Austria	Sch34.00	2.82	14.0	12.0	+17
Brazil	Real2.95	1.71	1.21	1.73	−30
Britain	£1.90	3.07	1.28HH	1.61HH	+26
Canada	C$2.99	1.98	1.23	1.51	−19
Chile	Peso1.25	2.60	518	484	+7
China	Yuan9.90	1.20	4.07	8.28	−51
Denmark	DKr24.75	3.58	10.19	6.19	+47
Euro Area	Euro 2.52	2.71	.97[3]	1.08[3]	+11
France	FFr8.50	2.87	7.20	6.10	+18
Germany	DM4.95	2.72	2.04	1.82	+12
Hong Kong	HK$10.2	1.32	4.20	7.75	−46
Hungary	Forint299	1.26	123	237	−48
Indonesia	Rupiah14,500	1.66	5,967	8,725	−32
Israel	Shekel13.9	3.44	5.72	4.04	+42
Italy	Lire4,500	2.50	1,852	1,799	+3
Netherlands	Fl5.45	2.66	2.24	2.05	+10
Spain	Pta375	2.43	154	155	0
Japan	¥294	2.44	121	120	0
Malaysia	M$4.52	1.19	1.86	3.80	−51
Mexico	Peso19.9	2.09	8.19	9.54	−14
New Zealand	NZ$3.40	1.82	1.40	1.87	−25
Poland	Zloty5.50	1.38	2.26	3.98	−43
Russia	Rouble33.5	1.35	13.79	24.7	−44
Singapore	S$3.20	1.85	1.32	1.73	−24
South Africa	Rand8.60	1.38	3.54	6.22	−43
South Korea	Won3,000	2.46	1,235	1,218	+1
Sweden	SKr24.0	2.88	9.88	8.32	+19
Switzerland	SFr5.90	3.97	2.43	1.48	+64
Taiwan	NT$70.0	2.11	28.8	33.2	−13
Thailand	Baht52.0	1.38	21.4	37.6	−43

[1]Purchasing-power; local price divided by price in the United States.

[2]Average of New York, Chicago, San Francisco, and Atlanta

HH dollars per pound

[3]Dollars per euro

Source: The Economist (April 3, 1999): 66. © *The Economist* Newspaper Group, Inc. Reprinted with permission. Further reproduction prohibited.

5. On January 20X3, the wholly owned Mexican affiliate of a Canadian parent company acquired an inventory of computer hard drives for its assembly operation. The cost incurred was 15,000,000 pesos when the exchange rate was 15 pesos = C$1. By year-end, the Mexican affiliate had used three-fourths of the acquired hard drives. Due to advances in hardware technology, the remaining inventory was marked down to its net realizable value of 1,750,000 pesos. The year-end exchange rate was 17 pesos = C$1. The average rate during the year was 16 pesos = C$1.

Required:

a. Translate the ending inventory to Canadian dollars assuming the Mexican affiliate's functional currency is the Mexican peso.

b. Would your answer change if the functional currency were the Canadian dollar? Please explain.

6. Dragon Corporation, the Taiwanese affiliate of a U.S. manufacturer, has the balance sheet shown in Exhibit 6-14. The current exchange rate is $.035 = NT$ 1 (29 Taiwanese dollars to the U.S. dollar).

Required:

a. Translate the Taiwanese dollar balance sheet of Dragon Corporation into U.S. dollars at the current exchange rate of $.035 = NT$ 1. All monetary accounts in Dragon's balance sheet are denominated in Taiwanese dollars.

b. Assume the Taiwan dollar revalues from $.035 = NT$ 1 to $.045 = NT$1. What would be the translation effect if Dragon's balance sheet is translated by the current-noncurrent method? By the monetary-nonmonetary method?

c. Assume instead that the Taiwan dollar weakens from $.035 = NT$ 1 to $.027 = NT$ 1. What would be the translation effect under each of the two translation methods?

7. Use the information provided in Exercise 6.

Required:

a. What would be the translation effect if Dragon Corporation's balance sheet were translated by the temporal method assuming the Taiwanese dollar appreciates by 25 percent? By the current rate method?

b. If the Taiwanese dollar depreciates by 25 percent, what would be the translation effects under each of the two methods in requirement a?

c. Based on your previous calculations and in Exercise 6, which translation method—current-noncurrent, monetary-nonmonetary, temporal, or current—gives statement readers the most meaningful information?

EXHIBIT 6-14 **Balance Sheet of Dragon Corporation (000,000's)**			
Assets		*Liabilities*	
Cash	NT$ 5,000	Accounts payable	NT$21,000
Accounts receivable	14,000	Long-term debt	27,000
Inventories[1]			
(cost = 24,000)	22,000		
Fixed assets, net	39,000	Stockholders' equity	32,000
Total assets	NT$80,000	Total Liabilities	NT$80,000

[1]Inventories are carried at the lower of cost or market.

8. A 100 percent–owned foreign subsidiary's trial balance consists of the accounts listed as follows. Which exchange rate—current, historical, or average—would be used to translate these accounts to dollars assuming that the foreign currency is the functional currency? Which rates would be used if the U.S. dollar were the functional currency?

Trial Balance Accounts

Cash	Common stock
Marketable securities (cost)	Premium on common stock
Accounts receivable	Retained earnings
Inventory (market)	Sales
Equipment	Purchases
Accumulated depreciation	Cost of sales
Prepaid expenses	General and administrative expenses
Goodwill	Selling expenses
Accounts payable	Depreciation
Due to parent (denominated in dollars)	Amortization of goodwill
Bonds payable	Income tax expense
Income taxes payable	Intercompany interest expense
Deferred income taxes	

---

9. U.S. Multinational Corporation's subsidiary in Bangkok has on its books fixed assets valued at 7,500,000 baht. One-third of the assets were acquired 2 years ago when the exchange rate was B40 = $1. The other fixed assets were acquired last year when the exchange rate was B38 = $1. Each layer of fixed assets is being depreciated straight-line with an estimated useful life of 20 years. Relevant exchange rates for the current year are:

$$\text{Year-end rate: } B36 = \$1$$
$$\text{Average rate: } B37 = \$1$$

Required:
a. Calculate the Thai subsidiary's depreciation expense for the current year, assuming the baht is the functional currency.
b. Repeat requirement a. assuming instead that the U.S. dollar is the functional currency.

10. Trojan Corporation USA borrowed 1,000,000 German marks at the beginning of the calendar year when the exchange rate was $.54 = DM 1. Before repaying this one-year loan, Trojan Corporation learns that the mark has depreciated to $.46 = DM 1. It also discovers that its German subsidiary has an exposed net asset position of DM 3,000,000, which will produce a translation loss upon consolidation. What is the exchange gain or loss that will be reported in consolidated income if
a. The dollar is the foreign operation's functional currency?
b. The German mark is the foreign operation's functional currency?

11. On December 15, A. C. Corporation acquires 100 percent of the net assets of the Sando Company based in Tokyo, Japan, for ¥60,000,000. At the time, the exchange

rate was $1.00 = ¥105. The acquisition price is traceable to the following identifiable assets:

Cash	¥ 6,450,000
Inventory	16,000,000
Fixed Assets	37,550,000

As a calendar-year company, A. C. Corporation prepares consolidated financial statements every December 31. However, by the consolidation date, the Japanese yen depreciates such that the new spot rate is $1.00 = ¥115.

Required:
a. Assuming no transactions took place before consolidation, what would be the translation gain or loss if Sando's balance sheet were translated to dollars by the temporal rate method?
b. How does the translation adjustment affect A. C. Corporation's cash flows?

12. MJM Corporation operates a subsidiary in hyperinflationary country X. A fixed asset was purchased 1 year ago for LC (local currency) 1,000,000 when the exchange rate was LC82 = $1.00. At year-end, the exchange rate is LC147 = $1.00. Inflation was 51 percent over the same period.

Required:
a. Translate the value of the fixed asset into U.S. dollars according to FAS No. 52.
b. Translate the value of the fixed asset into U.S. dollars according to International Accounting Standard 21.

Case 6-1 Regents Corporation

Regents Corporation is a recently acquired U.S. manufacturing subsidiary located on the outskirts of London. Its products are marketed principally in the United Kingdom with sales invoiced in pounds and prices determined by local competitive conditions. Expenses (labor, materials, and other production costs) are mostly local, although a significant quantity of components is now imported from the U.S. parent. Financing is primarily in U.S. dollars provided by the parent.

Headquarters management must decide on the functional currency for its London operation:

Should it be the U.S. dollar or the British pound? You are asked to advise management on the appropriate currency designation and its relative financial statement effects. Prepare a report that supports your recommendations and identify any policy issues your analysis uncovers.

Exhibit 6-15 presents comparative balance sheets for Regents Corporation at December 31, 20X3 and 20X4, and a statement of income for the year ended December 31, 20X4. The statements conform with U.S. generally accepted accounting principles prior to translation to dollars.

EXHIBIT 6-15 **Regents Corporation Financial Statements**

Balance Sheet	12/31/X3	12/31/X4
Assets		
Cash	£ 1,060	£ 1,150
Accounts receivable	2,890	3,100
Inventory (FIFO)	3,040	3,430
Fixed assets	4,400	4,900
− Accumulated depreciation	(420)	(720)
Intangible asset (patent)		70
Total	£10,970	£11,930
Liabilities and Stockholders' Equity		
Accounts payable	£ 1,610	£ 1,385
Due to parent	1,800	1,310
Long-term debt	4,500	4,000
Deferred taxes	80	120
Common stock	1,500	1,500
Retained earnings	1,480	3,615
Total	£10,970	£11,930

Case 6-2   Managing Offshore Investments: Whose Currency?[1]

The Offshore Investment Fund (OIF) was incorporated in Fairfield, Connecticut, for the sole purpose of allowing U.S. shareholders to invest in Spanish securities. The fund is listed on the New York Stock Exchange. The fund custodian is the Shady Rest Bank and Trust Company of Connecticut ("Shady Rest"), which keeps the fund's accounts. The question of which currency to use in keeping the fund's books arose at once. Shady Rest prepared the fund's books in Spanish pesetas, since the fund was a country fund that invested solely in securities listed on the Madrid Stock Exchange. Subsequently, the fund's auditors stated that, in their opinion, the functional currency should be the U.S. dollar.

EFFECTS OF THE DECISION

The decision to possibly adopt the U.S. dollar as the functional currency for the fund created considerable managerial headaches. For one thing, the work of rewriting and reworking the accounting transactions was a monumental task that delayed the publication of the annual accounts. The concept of the functional currency was a foreign concept in Spain, and the effects of the functional currency choice were not made clear to the managers. Consequently, they continued to manage the fund until late in November without appreciating the impact the currency choice had on the fund's results.

---

[1]This case is based on an actual occurrence. The names have been changed to ensure anonymity.

EXHIBIT 6-15 *(cont.)*		
Income Statement		*Year Ended 12/31/X4*
Sales		£16,700
Expenses		
Cost of sales	£11,300	
General and administrative	1,600	
Depreciation	300	
Interest	480	13,680
Operating income		£ 3,020
Transaction gain (loss)		125
Income before taxes		£ 3,145
Income taxes		
Current	£ 670	
Deferred	40	710
Net income		£ 2,435
Retained earnings at 12/31/X8		1,480
		3,915
Dividends		300
Retained earnings at 12/31/X9		£ 3,615

Exchange rate information and additional data:

1. Exchange rates:

December 31, 20X3	$1.50 = £1
December 31, 20X4	$1.60 = £1
Average during 20X4	$1.56 = £1
Average during fourth quarter 20X3	$1.48 = £1
Average during fourth quarter 20X4	$1.58 = £1

2. Common stock was acquired, long-term debt issued, and original fixed assets purchased when the exchange rate was $1.40 = £1.

3. **Due to parent** account is denominated in U.S. dollars.

4. Exchange rate prevailing when the intangible asset (patent) was acquired and additional fixed assets purchased was $1.52 = £1.

5. Purchases and dividends occurred evenly during 20X4.

6. Of the £300 depreciation expense for 20X4, £20 relates to fixed assets purchased during 20X4.

7. Deferred taxes are translated at the current rate.

8. Inventory represents approximately 3 months of production.

Additional difficulties caused by the functional currency choice were:

a. Shady Rest, with some $300 billion in various funds under management, still had not developed an adequate multi-currency accounting system. Whereas accounting for a security acquisition would normally be recorded in a simple bookkeeping entry, three entries were now required. In addition, payment for the purchase itself could impact the income statement in the current period.

b. More serious problems related to day-to-day operations. When a transaction was initiated, the fund manager had no idea of its ultimate financial effect. As an example, during the first year of operations, the Fund manager was certain that his portfolio sales had generated a profit of more than $1 million. When the sales finally showed up in the accounts, the transaction gain was offset by currency losses of some $7 million!

REASONS GIVEN FOR CHOOSING THE DOLLAR AS FUNCTIONAL

The auditors gave the following reasons for choosing the dollar as the fund's functional currency:

    a. Incorporation in the United States

    b. Funded with U.S. shareholder capital

    c. Dividends determined and paid in U.S. dollars

    d. Financial reporting under U.S. GAAP and in U.S. dollars

    e. Administration and advisory fees calculated on U.S. net assets and paid in U.S. dollars

    f. Most expenses incurred and paid in U.S. dollars

    g. Accounting records kept in U.S. dollars

    h. Subject to U.S. tax, S.E.C., and 1940 Exchange Act regulations

Since the fund was set up to invest in Spain, it is assumed that U.S. shareholders are interested in the impact of an exchange rate change on the fund's cash flows and equity; that is, the shareholders do not invest in Spanish securities only because of attractive yields, but also are making a currency play that directly affects the measurement of cash flow and equity.

MANAGEMENT'S VIEWPOINT

Management disagreed with the auditors. Following is its rebuttal:

    a. *Incorporation in the United States with U.S. shareholders.* FAS 52 clearly states that the functional currency should be determined by "the primary economic environment in which that entity operates rather than by the technical detail of incorporation." Similarly, nowhere does FAS 52 state that the facts that the company has U.S. shareholders and pays dividends in U.S. dollars are relevant. In fact, FAS 52 concerns itself

throughout with the firm and its management rather that its shareholders.

    b. *Financial reporting in U.S. dollars under U.S. GAAP.* The auditors fail to differentiate between reporting currency and functional currency. It is clear that the U.S. dollar should be the reporting currency, but that alone does not mean that the U.S. dollar is the functional currency.

    c. *Payment of certain expenses in dollars.* The payment of expenses in U.S. dollars is no reason to make the dollar the functional currency. While expenses of some $8 million for calendar year 20X3 were incurred in U.S. dollars, income of over $100 million was earned in Spanish pesetas.

    d. *U.S. tax and S.E.C. regulations.* These considerations are relevant for the reporting currency, not the functional currency.

The decisive argument against identifying the dollar as the functional currency is that doing so does not provide information that is, in the words of FAS 52, "generally compatible with the expected economic effect of a rate change on an enterprise's cash flow and equity." Specifically, the operating cash flow of the Fund is located entirely in Spain once the initial transfer of funds raised by the issue of capital is made. The Fund buys and sells investments in Spain, and receives all its income from Spain. If the functional currency is Spanish pesetas, then realized currency fluctuations are recognized only when money is repatriated to the U.S. The present practice of "realizing" an exchange profit or loss when, for example, cash in Spain is exchanged for an investment purchased in Spain is wrong and misleading.

Consider an example. Suppose that the fund deposits P100,000,000 in a Spanish bank when the exchange rate is P1 = $0.005682. One week later, when the exchange rate is P1 = $0.005618, the fund purchases and pays for an investment of P100,000,000, which it sells for cash on the same day, having decided the investment was unwise. Ignoring transaction costs, the fund has P100,000,000 in cash in Madrid at both the beginning and the end of the week. If the functional currency is Spanish pesetas, there is no realized gain or loss. However, translation to dollars generates an unrealized currency loss of $6,400, which would be realized only when the amount in question is repatriated to the United States. This is analogous to the purchase of a stock whose price later falls. If the U.S. dollar is the functional currency, the transaction in question would result in a realized loss on exchange of $6,400. This result is absurd in terms of any common sense view of cash flow; indeed, it highlights that, given the fund's purpose, the effect on the reporting of income of adopting the U.S. dollar as the functional currency is equally absurd.

The net asset value of the fund is determined each week in U.S. dollars, and reported to stockholders in U.S. dollars. This is entirely consistent with having the U.S. dollar as the appropriate reporting currency. Using the dollar as the functional currency implies that there is a realistic and practical option on each transaction of moving between the dollar and the Spanish peseta. This assumption is patently wrong; the fund will only repatriate its base capital under two circumstances: (1) liquidation; or (2) as a temporary expedient if Spanish yields fall below U.S. yields.

GENERAL THRUST OF FAS 52

The language of FAS 52 indicates that its authors did not write it with direct reference to a situation such as that of the Offshore Investment Fund, that is, a company that raises money for the single purpose of investing it in a foreign country. FAS 52 seems rather to be written from the viewpoint of an operating holding company owning a separate, distinct foreign operating subsidiary.

FAS 52 defines the functional currency of an entity as the currency of the primary economic environment in which that entity operates. Had the fund been incorporated in Malta and, as a separate entity, borrowed the funds from its U.S. parent, use of the local currency would have been automatic. If substance is to prevail over form, one must conclude that the Spanish pesetas should still be used.

Paragraph 6 of FAS 52 states, "for an entity with operations that are relatively self-contained and integrated within a particular country, the functional currency generally would be the currency of that country." This statement reinforces the operational aspect that governs the choice of the functional currency; it is surely wrong to argue that the operations of the fund are conducted anywhere but in Spain.

Paragraph 8 reinforces the contention that "management's judgment will be required to determine the functional currency in which financial results and relationships are measured with the greatest degree of relevance and reliability."

Finally, paragraphs 80 and 81 draw a very clear distinction that reinforces our (management's) contention. Paragraph 80 reads:

> In the first class are foreign operations that are relatively self-contained and integrated within a particular country or economic environment. The day-to-day operations are not dependent upon the economic environment of the parent's functional currency; the foreign operation primarily generates and expends foreign currency. The foreign currency net cash flows that it generates may be reinvested and converted and distributed to the parent. For this class, the foreign currency is the functional currency.

This definition should be contrasted with paragraph 81, which states:

> In the second class . . . the day-to-day operations are dependent on the economic environment of the parent's currency, and the changes in the foreign entity's individual assets and liabilities impact directly on the cash flows of the parent company in the parent's currency. For this class, the U.S. dollar is the functional currency.

Since the purpose of single country funds is to create entities of the first rather than the second class, Paragraph 80 precisely describes the operations of the Overseas Investment Fund.

REQUIRED

Based on the arguments presented, what do you think should be the functional currency in this case?

CHAPTER 7

ACCOUNTING FOR CHANGING PRICES

Fluctuating currency values and changes in money prices of goods and services today are integral features of international business. First, we must distinguish between general and specific price movements. A *general price level change* occurs when, on average, the prices of *all* goods and services in an economy change. The monetary unit gains or loses purchasing power. An overall increase in prices is called *inflation;* a decrease, *deflation.* A *specific price change,* on the other hand, refers to a change in the price of a specific good or service caused by changes in demand and supply. Thus, the annual rate of inflation in a country may average 5 percent while the specific price of one-bedroom apartments may rise by 50 percent during the same period.

Exhibit 7-1 defines additional terminology used in this chapter.

As consumers, we are well aware of inflation's effects on our material standard of living. We immediately feel its impact on our pocketbooks when the price of oil (and hence, gasoline) or a Big Mac increases. Businesses also feel inflation's effects when the prices of their factor inputs rise.

While changing prices occur worldwide, their business and financial reporting effects vary from country to country. Europe and North America, for instance, have had relatively modest general price level increases, averaging less than 3 percent per year during the last decade. By contrast, Eastern Europe and Latin America have had much higher inflation rates. In the mid-1990s, annual rates of inflation were as high as 106 percent in Turkey, 198 percent in Russia, and 2,076 percent in Brazil![1]

Local inflation affects exchange rates used to translate foreign currency balances to their domestic currency equivalents. As we shall see, it is hard to separate foreign currency translation from inflation when accounting for foreign operations.

---

[1]Goldman Sachs, *The Global Currency Analyst*, New York: Goldman Sachs, June 2000, 36.

EXHIBIT 7-1   Glossary of Inflation Accounting Terms

attribute. The quantifiable characteristic of an item that is measured for accounting purposes. For example, historical cost and replacement cost are attributes of an asset.

current cost adjustments. Adjusting asset values for changes in specific prices.

disposable wealth. The amount of a firm's net assets that could be withdrawn without reducing its beginning level of net assets.

gearing adjustment. The benefit to shareholders' purchasing power gain, from debt financing and signals that the firm need not recognize the additional replacement cost of operating assets to the extent they are financed by debt. The U.S. expression for gearing is leverage.

general purchasing power equivalents. Currency amounts that have been adjusted for changes in the general level of prices.

general purchasing gains and losses. *See* **monetary gains and losses.**

historical cost-constant currency. *See* **general purchasing power equivalents.**

holding gain. Increase in the current cost of a nonmonetary asset.

hyperinflation. An excessive rate of inflation as when the general level of prices in an economy increases by more than 25 percent per annum.

inflation. Increase in the general level of prices of all goods and services in an economy.

monetary asset. A claim to a fixed amount of currency in the future, like cash or accounts receivable.

monetary gains. Increases in general purchasing power that occur when monetary liabilities are held during a period of inflation.

monetary liability. An obligation to pay a fixed amount of currency in the future such as an account payable or debt that bears a fixed rate of interest.

monetary losses. Decreases in general purchasing power that occur when monetary assets are held during a period of inflation.

monetary working capital adjustment. The effect of specific price changes on the total amount of working capital used by the business in its operations.

nominal amounts. Currency amounts that have not been adjusted for changing prices.

nonmonetary asset. An asset that does not represent a fixed claim to cash, such as inventory or plant and equipment.

nonmonetary liability. A debt that does not require the payment of a fixed sum of cash in the future such as a customer advance. Here the obligation is to provide the customer a good or service whose value may change because of inflation.

parity adjustment. An adjustment that reflects the difference in inflation between the parent and host countries.

permanent assets. A Brazilian term for fixed assets, buildings, investments, deferred charges and their respective depreciation, and depletion or amortization amounts.

price index. A cost ratio where the numerator is the cost of a representative "basket" of goods and services in the current year and the denominator is the cost of the same basket of goods and services in a benchmark year.

purchasing power. The general ability of a monetary unit to command goods and services.

real profit. Net income that has been adjusted for changing prices.

replacement cost. The current cost of replacing the service potential of an asset in the normal course of business.

reporting currency. The currency in which an entity prepares its financial statements.

restate-translate method. Used when a parent company consolidates the accounts of a foreign subsidiary located in an inflationary environment. With this method, first the subsidiary's accounts are restated for local inflation, and then are translated to parent currency.

specific price change. The change in the price of a specific commodity, such as inventory or equipment.

translate-restate method. A consolidation method that first translates a foreign subsidiary's accounts to parent currency and then restates the translated amounts for parent country inflation.

WHY ARE FINANCIAL STATEMENTS POTENTIALLY MISLEADING DURING PERIODS OF CHANGING PRICES?

During a period of inflation, asset values recorded at their original acquisition costs seldom reflect their current (higher) value. Understated asset values result in understated expenses and overstated income. From a managerial perspective, these measurement inaccuracies distort (1) financial projections based on unadjusted historical time series data, (2) budgets against which results are measured, and (3) performance data that fail to isolate the uncontrollable effects of inflation.[2] Overstated earnings may in turn lead to:

- Increases in proportionate taxation
- Requests by shareholders for more dividends
- Demands for higher wages by workers
- Disadvantageous actions by host governments (e.g., imposition of excess profit taxes)

Should a firm distribute all of its overstated earnings (in the form of higher taxes, dividends, wages, and the like), it may not keep enough resources to replace specific assets whose prices have risen, such as inventories and plant and equipment.

Failure to adjust corporate financial data for changes in the purchasing power of the monetary unit also makes it hard for financial statement readers to interpret and compare reported operating performances of companies.[3] In an inflationary period, revenues are typically expressed in currency with a lower general purchasing power (i.e., purchasing power of the current period) than applies to the related expenses. Expenses are expressed in currency with a higher general purchasing power because typically they reflect the consumption of resources that were acquired when the monetary unit had more purchasing power. Subtracting expenses based on historical purchasing power from revenues based on current purchasing power results in an inaccurate measure of income. Conventional accounting procedures also ignore purchasing power gains and losses that arise from holding cash (or equivalents) during an inflationary period. If you held cash during a year in which the inflation rate was 100 percent, it would take twice as much cash at the end of the year to have the same purchasing power as your original cash balance. This further distorts business performance comparisons for financial statement readers.

Therefore, it is useful to recognize inflation's effects explicitly for several reasons:

1. The effects of changing prices depend partially on the transactions and circumstances of an enterprise. Users do not have detailed information about these factors.
2. Managing the problems caused by changing prices depends on an accurate understanding of the problems. An accurate understanding requires that business performance be reported in terms that allow for the effects of changing prices.

---

[2]For additional managerial implications of inflation, see Chapter 10.
[3]For a recent example of the information content of inflation-adjusted numbers, see Paquita Y. Davis-Friday and Juan Rivera, "Inflation Accounting and 20-F Disclosures: Evidence from Mexico," *Accounting Horizons* (June 2000): 113–135.

3. Statements by managers about the problems caused by changing prices are easier to believe when businesses publish financial information that addresses those problems.[4]

Even when inflation rates slow, accounting for changing prices is useful because the cumulative effect of low inflation over time can be significant. As examples, the cumulative inflation rate in the United States from 1991 to 2000 was 28 percent; it was 17.5 percent for Singapore and 36.8 percent for Italy for the same time period. The distorting effects of prior inflation can also persist for many years, given the long lives of many assets. And, as mentioned earlier, specific price changes may be significant even when the general price level does not change much.

TYPES OF INFLATION ADJUSTMENTS

Statistical series that measure changes in both general and specific prices do not generally move in parallel. Each type of price change has a different effect on measures of a firm's financial position and operating performance and is accounted for with different objectives in mind. Hereafter, accounting for the financial statement effects of general price level changes is called the *historical cost-constant purchasing power* model. Accounting for specific price changes is referred to as the *current cost* model.

GENERAL PRICE LEVEL ADJUSTMENTS

Currency amounts adjusted for general price level (purchasing power) changes are called *historical cost-constant currency* or *general purchasing power equivalents*. Currency amounts that have not been so adjusted are called *nominal amounts*. For example, during a period of rising prices, a long-lived asset that is on the balance sheet at its original acquisition cost is expressed in *nominal* currency. When its historical cost is allocated to the current period's income (in the form of depreciation expense), revenues, which reflect current purchasing power, are matched with costs that reflect the (higher) purchasing power of the earlier period when the asset was bought. Therefore, nominal amounts must be adjusted for changes in the general purchasing power of money to match them appropriately with current transactions.

PRICE INDEXES

General price level changes are measured by a price level index of the form $\Sigma p_1 q_1 / \Sigma p_0 q_0$, where p = price of a given commodity, and q = quantity consumed. A price index is a cost ratio. For example, if a family of four spends \$20,000 to buy a representative basket of goods and services at the end of 1 (base) year and \$22,000 to buy that same basket a year later, the year-end price index for the next year is \$22,000/\$20,000 or 1.100. This figure implies a 10 percent rate of inflation during the year. Similarly, if the basket in question costs our family of four \$23,500 2 years later, the general price

[4]Financial Accounting Standards Board, "Financial Reporting and Changing Prices," *Statement of Financial Accounting Standards No. 33* Stamford, CT: FASB, September 1979.

level index would be $23,500/$20,000, or 1.175, implying 17.5 percent inflation since the base year. The index for the base year is $20,000/$20,000 or 1.000.

USE OF PRICE INDEXES

Price index numbers are used to translate sums of money paid in past periods to their end-of-period purchasing power equivalents (i.e., historical cost-constant purchasing power). The method used is as follows:

$$GPL_c/GPL_{td} \times \text{Nominal amount}_{td} = PPE_c$$

where

GPL = general price index
c = current period
td = transaction date
PPE = general purchasing power equivalent

For example, suppose that $500 is spent at the end of the base year and $700 1 year later. To restate these expenditures at their year 3 purchasing power equivalents, using price index numbers from our example, we would do the following:

	Nominal Expenditure	Adjustment Factor	Year 3 Purchasing Power Equivalent
Year 1	$500	1.175/1.000	$587.50
Year 2	$700	1.175/1.100	$747.73

It would take $587.50 at the end of year 2 to buy (in general) what $500 would have bought at the end of year 1. Similarly, it would take $747.73 at the end of year 3 to buy (in general) what $700 would have bought a year earlier.

Price level adjusted figures do not represent the current cost of the items in question. They are still historical cost numbers. The historical cost numbers are merely restated in a new unit of measure—general purchasing power at the end of the period.

When transactions occur uniformly throughout a period (such as revenues from the sale of goods or services), a shortcut price level adjustment can be used. In expressing revenues as end-of-period purchasing power equivalents, rather than price level adjusting each day's revenues (365 calculations!), one could multiply total annual revenues by the ratio of the year-end index to the average general price level index (such as a monthly weighted average) for the year. Thus:

$$GPL_c/GPL_{avg} \times \text{Total revenues} = PPE_c$$

OBJECT OF GENERAL PRICE LEVEL ADJUSTMENTS

Let us briefly review the conventional notion of enterprise income. Traditionally, income (disposable wealth) is that portion of a firm's wealth (i.e., net assets) that the firm can withdraw during an accounting period without reducing its wealth beneath its original level. Assuming no additional owner investments or withdrawals during the period, if a firm's beginning net assets were £30,000 and its ending net assets increased to £45,000 due to profitable operations, its income would be £15,000. If it paid a dividend of £15,000, the firm's end of period wealth would be exactly what it was at the beginning. Hence, conventional accounting measures income as the maximum amount that can be withdrawn from the firm without reducing its original money capital.

If we cannot assume stable prices, the conventional measure of income may not accurately measure a firm's disposable wealth. Assume that the general price level rises by 21 percent during a year. To keep up with inflation, a firm that begins the year with $100 would want its original investment to grow to at least $121, because it would take that much at year's-end to buy what $100 would have bought at the beginning. Suppose that, using conventional accounting, the firm earns $50 (after tax). Withdrawing $50 would reduce the firm's nominal end-of-period wealth to the original $100, less than it needs to keep up with inflation ($121). The historical cost-constant purchasing power model takes this discrepancy into account by measuring income so that the firm could pay out its entire income as dividends while having as much purchasing power at the end of the period as at the beginning.

To illustrate, suppose that an Argentine merchandiser begins the calendar year with AP 100,000 in cash (no debt), which is immediately converted into salable inventory (e.g., 10,000 compact discs of an Argentinian rock star at a unit cost of 10 pesos). The firm sells the entire inventory uniformly during the year at a 50 percent markup. Assuming no inflation, enterprise income would be AP 50,000, the difference between ending and beginning net assets ($150,000 − $100,000), or as revenue minus expenses (cost of CDs sold). Withdrawal of AP 50,000 would leave the firm with AP 100,000, as much money capital as at the start of the year, maintaining its original investment.

Suppose instead that the period had a 21 percent inflation rate with the general price level (1.21 at year-end) averaging 1.10 during the year. Inflation-adjusted income would be measured (in thousands) as follows:

	Nominal Pesos	Adjustment Factor	Constant Pesos
Revenues	AP150	1.21/1.10	AP165
− Expenses	100	1.21/1.00	121
Operating income	AP 50		AP 44
− Monetary loss	—		15
Net income	AP 50		AP 29

In these calculations, sales took place at the same rate throughout the year, so they are adjusted by the ratio of the end-of-year index to the year's average price index. Because the inventory sold during the year was bought at the beginning of the year, cost of sales is adjusted by the ratio of the year-end index to the beginning-of-year index.

Where did the monetary loss come from? During inflation, firms will have changes in wealth that are unrelated to operating activities. These arise from *monetary assets or liabilities,* claims to or obligations to pay a fixed amount of currency in the future. Monetary assets include cash and accounts receivable, which generally lose purchasing power during periods of inflation. Monetary liabilities include most payables, which generally create purchasing power gains during inflation. In our example, the firm received and held cash during a period when cash lost purchasing power. As inventory was sold for cash, cash was received uniformly throughout the year. The firm's cash balance at the end of the year is only AP 150,000, resulting in a AP 15,000 loss in general purchasing power (a monetary loss) despite AP 165,000 in revenue.

In contrast to conventional accounting, income using the historical cost-constant purchasing power model is only $29,000. However, withdrawing AP 29,000 makes the firm's end-of-period wealth AP 121,000 (AP 150,000 − AP 29,000), giving it as much purchasing power at the end of the period as at the beginning.

Mexico's inflation accounting pronouncement B-10 is consistent with the historical cost-constant purchasing power model. Exhibit 7-2 contrasts Mexico's reporting requirements for the income statement with those for U.S. GAAP. Exhibit 7-3 summarizes inflation reporting requirements for Mexican balance sheets.

CURRENT COST ADJUSTMENTS

The current cost model differs from conventional accounting in two major respects. First, assets are valued at their current cost rather than their historical cost. Second, income is the amount of resources that the firm can distribute during a period (not counting tax considerations) while maintaining its productive capacity or physical capital. One way to maintain capital is to adjust a firm's original net asset position (using appropriate specific price indexes or direct pricing) to reflect changes in the asset's current cost equivalent during the period. Continuing our previous example, the transactions of our hypothetical merchandiser under the current costing framework can be illustrated using the accounting equation as our analytical framework (figures given in thousands):

	Assets		=	Liabilities	+	Owners' Equity
	Cash	Inventory				Capital
1.	100					100
2.	(100)	100				
3.	150					150 rev.
4.		40				40 OE reval.
5.		(140)				(140) exp.

Line 1 depicts the financial statement effects of the initial 100,000 investment into the firm. Line 2 depicts the exchange of cash for inventory. Assuming a 50 percent mark-up, line 3 shows the sale of inventory for cash, which increases owners' equity by the same amount. To reflect the current cost of the sale, the merchandiser increases the carrying value of inventories by 40 percent, as depicted in line 4. The offset to the 40 percent write-up of inventory is an AP 40 increase in an owners' equity revaluation account. This adjustment does two things. The owners' equity revaluation amount tells statement readers that the firm must keep an additional AP 40 in the business to enable it to replace inventories whose replacement costs have risen. The inventory revaluation, in

EXHIBIT 7-2 Comparison Between Mexican B-10 and U.S. GAAP

B-10	*FASB (U.S. GAAP)*
Sales	Sales
−GPL Cost of goods sold	**−Historical Cost of goods sold**
−Revalued depreciation	**−Historical depreciation**
Gross profit	Gross profit
−Selling, general, and administrative costs	−Selling, general, and administrative costs
Operating profit	Operating profit
−Net interest expense	−Net interest expense
−Net foreign exchange loss	−Net foreign exchange loss
+Monetary gain or loss	
Pre-tax income	Pre-tax income
−Taxes	−Translation gain or loss[1]
	−Taxes
Net income	Net income

[1]Assuming U.S. dollar is the functional currency.

turn, increases the cost of resources consumed (cost of sales), line 5. Thus, current revenues are matched against the current economic cost (not the historical cost) incurred to generate those revenues. In our example, current cost-based net income is measured as AP 150,000 − (AP 100,000 × 140/100) = AP 10,000. The current cost profit of AP 10,000 is the amount the firm could spend without reducing its business operations. Thus, the current cost model attempts to preserve a firm's physical capital or productive capacity. An instructive example of current cost reporting provided by a Swedish manufacturer appears in Exhibit 7-4.

EXHIBIT 7-3 B-10 Balance Sheet Requirements

Inventories	→	Must be restated using general price indexes
Fixed assets		Recognition of write-up on nonmonetary
Other nonmonetary assets		assets disclosed in shareholders' equity
Accumulated depreciation		
Depreciation expense		
Cost of goods sold		
Monetary gains/losses	→	Calculated by applying price index to net monetary position (i.e., monetary assets − monetary liabilities); recognized in the income statement
Components of shareholders' equity	→	Restated by applying price index
Foreign exchange gains/losses	→	All are assumed to be realized; must flow through the income statement
Constant currency restatement	→	Legislation B-12 requires that all financial statements presented must be restated in general purchasing power at the date of the balance sheet presented.

EXHIBIT 7-4 Current Cost Accounting Example

Current Cost Income Statement

	20X2	*20X1*
Invoiced sales	25,121	24,454
Current cost of goods sold	−21,488	−21,126
Current cost depreciation	−982	−856
Operating profit after depreciation	2,651	2,472
Price changes, inventory	74	65
Price changes, fixed assets	−35	110
Operating profit before financial items	2,690	2,647
Financial items	139	175
Purchasing power adjustment, equity	0	−221
Real profit after financial items	2,829	2,601
Taxes	−1,107	−990
Minority interest	−25	−27
Net profit	1,697	1,584

Current Cost Balance Sheet

Assets	*20X2*	*20X1*
Cash, bank and short-term investments	2,485	1,886
Receivables	6,031	6,021
Inventories	5,102	5,136
Fixed assets	10,474	10,221
Total assets	24,092	23,264

Liabilities and Shareholders' Equity		
Current liabilities	7,311	7,853
Long-term liabilities	4,086	3,852
Unrealized price changes	844	1,085
Shareholders' equity	11,851	10,474
Total liabilities and shareholders' equity	24,092	23,264

Reconciliation Between Traditional and Current Cost Accounting

Profit after net financial items according to traditional accounting			3,070
Change, unrealized price changes:			
Price change, goods sold	−69		
Price change, depreciation	−211	−280	
Price change for the year:			
Inventory	74		
Fixed assets	−35	39	−241
Adjustment for inflation			0
Real profit after financial items			2,829

WHICH METHOD IS BEST?

Proponents of the historical cost-constant purchasing power model argue that the current cost model violates the historical cost measurement framework because it is not based on original acquisition costs. They also claim it is based on hypothetical expected costs and, therefore, is too subjective and too hard to implement in practice. Ignoring changes in the general purchasing power of money makes interperiod comparisons hard to interpret and also fails to consider gains and losses from holding monetary items such as debt. Those who favor current cost adjustments argue that businesses are not affected by general inflation, but rather by increases in specific operating costs and plant expenditures. Often, it could be misleading to record purchasing power gains from holding debt during inflation. Highly leveraged firms could show large monetary gains while on the brink of bankruptcy.[5] In some countries it is possible that general price indexes could be politicized.

The *current cost-constant purchasing power* model combines the features of both the historical cost-constant purchasing power and the current cost models. This hybrid framework recognizes increases in an asset's current value as a gain in wealth, and in so doing facilitates comparisons between current income and income in prior periods. The firm is considered to be better off only if the asset appreciates more than the general rate of inflation.[6] Thus, if a stock investment increases in value from $100 to $150 while the general price level increases from 100 to 130, the real gain from this investment is only $20 ($150 − $100 × 130/100). Monetary gains or losses, which the current cost model generally ignores, are part of the measurement. In general, this hybrid model has advantages and drawbacks similar to the other two models we have considered.

INTERNATIONAL PERSPECTIVE ON INFLATION ACCOUNTING

Several countries have experimented with different inflation accounting methods. Actual practices have also reflected pragmatic considerations such as the severity of national inflation and the views of those directly affected by inflation accounting numbers. Examining several different inflation accounting methods is valuable in assessing the current state of the art.

UNITED STATES

In 1979 the FASB issued *Statement of Financial Accounting Standards (SFAS) No. 33*. Entitled "Financial Reporting and Changing Prices," this statement required U.S. enterprises with inventories and property, plant, and equipment (before deducting accumulated depreciation) of more than $125 million, or total assets of more than $1 billion (after deducting accumulated depreciation), to experiment for 5 years with disclosing *both* historical cost-constant purchasing power and current cost-constant purchasing power. These disclosures were to supplement rather than replace historical cost as the basic measurement framework for primary financial statements.[7]

---

[5]R. Vancil, "Inflation Accounting—The Great Controversy," *Harvard Business Review* (March–April 1976): 58–67.

[6]Robert R. Sterling, "Relevant Financial Reporting in an Age of Price Changes," *Journal of Accountancy*, (February 1975): 42–51.

[7]Financial Accounting Standards Board, "Financial Reporting and Changing Prices," *Statement of Financial Accounting Standards No. 33*, Stamford, CT: FASB, 1979.

Many users and preparers of financial information that complied with SFAS No. 33 found that (1) the dual disclosures required by the FASB were confusing, (2) the cost of preparing the dual disclosures was excessive, and (3) historical cost-constant purchasing power disclosures were less useful than current cost data. Since then, the FASB has decided to encourage, but no longer require, U.S. reporting entities to disclose either historical cost-constant purchasing power or current cost-constant purchasing power information.[8] The FASB published guidelines (SFAS 89) to assist enterprises that report the statement effects of changing prices and to be a starting point for any future inflation accounting standard.[9]

Reporting enterprises are encouraged to disclose the following information for each of the 5 most recent years:

- Net sales and other operating revenues
- Income from continuing operations on a current cost basis[10]
- Purchasing power (monetary) gains or losses on net monetary items
- Increases or decreases in the current cost or lower recoverable amount (i.e., the net amount of cash expected to be recoverable from use or sale) of inventory or property, plant and equipment, net of inflation (general price level changes)
- Any aggregate foreign currency translation adjustment, on a current cost basis, that arises from the consolidation process
- Net assets at year-end on a current cost basis
- Earnings per share (from continuing operations) on a current cost basis
- Dividends per share of common stock
- Year-end market price per share of common stock
- Level of the Consumer Price Index (CPI) used to measure income from continuing operations

To increase the comparability of this data, information may be presented either in (1) average (or year-end) purchasing power equivalents, or (2) base period (1967) dollars used in calculating the CPI. Whenever income on a current cost-constant purchasing power basis differs significantly from historical cost income, firms are asked to provide more data.

FOREIGN OPERATIONS

SFAS No. 89 disclosure guidelines also cover foreign operations included in the consolidated statements of U.S. parent companies. Enterprises that adopt the dollar as the functional currency for measuring their foreign operations view these operations from a parent currency perspective. Accordingly, their accounts should be translated to dollars, then adjusted for U.S. inflation (the translate-restate method). Multinational enterprises adopting the local currency as functional for most of their foreign operations adopt a local currency perspective. The FASB allows companies to use either the translate-restate method, or adjust for foreign inflation and then translate to U.S. dollars (the restate-translate method). (Appendix 7-1 illustrates this methodology.) Ac-

---

[8]Financial Accounting Standards Board, "Financial Reporting and Changing Prices," *Statement of Financial Accounting Standards No. 89*, Stamford, CT: FASB, December 1986.
[9]Ibid., pars. 7–62.
[10]After-tax income excluding the results of discontinued operations, extraordinary items, cumulative effects of accounting changes, translation adjustments, monetary gains and losses, and holding gains (i.e., increases or decreases in the current cost or lower recoverable amount of nonmonetary assets and liabilities).

cordingly, adjustments to current cost data to reflect inflation may be based on either the U.S. *or* the foreign general price level index. Exhibit 7-5 summarizes these provisions.

UNITED KINGDOM

The U.K. Accounting Standards Committee (ASC) issued *Statement of Standard Accounting Practice No. 16* (SSAP No. 16), "Current Cost Accounting," on a 3-year experimental basis in March 1980. Although SSAP No. 16 was withdrawn in 1988, its methodology is recommended for companies that voluntarily produce inflation-adjusted accounts.[11]

SSAP No. 16 differs from SFAS No. 33 in two major respects. First, whereas the U.S. standard required both constant dollar and current cost accounting, SSAP No. 16 adopted only the current cost method for external reporting. Second, whereas the U.S. inflation adjustment focused on the income statement, the U.K. current cost statement required both a current cost income statement and a balance sheet, with explanatory notes. The U.K. standard allowed three reporting options:

1. Presenting current cost accounts as the basic statements with supplementary historical cost accounts.

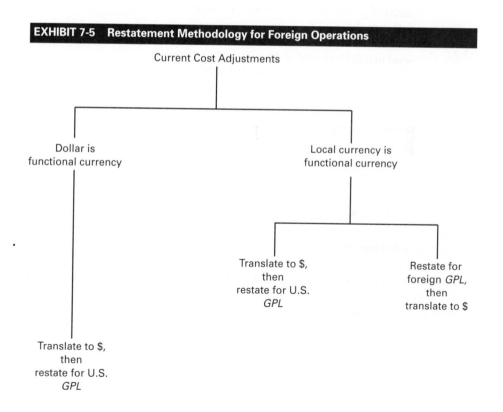

EXHIBIT 7-5   Restatement Methodology for Foreign Operations

Current Cost Adjustments

Dollar is functional currency

Local currency is functional currency

Translate to $, then restate for U.S. GPL

Restate for foreign *GPL,* then translate to $

Translate to $, then restate for U.S. GPL

---

[11]Accounting Standards Committee, *Handbook on Accounting for the Effects of Changing Prices,* London, U.K.: Chartac Books, 1986.

2. Presenting historical cost accounts as the basic statements with supplementary current cost accounts.
3. Presenting current cost accounts as the only accounts accompanied by adequate historical cost information.

In its treatment of gains and losses related to monetary items, FAS No. 33 required separate disclosure of a single figure. SSAP No. 16 required two figures, both reflecting the effects of *specific* price changes. The first, called a *monetary working capital adjustment* (MWCA), recognized the effect of specific price changes on the total amount of working capital used by businesses in their operations. The second, called the *gearing adjustment,* allowed for the impact of specific price changes on a firm's nonmonetary assets (e.g., depreciation, cost of sales, and monetary working capital). As a formula, the gearing adjustment equals:

$$[(TL - CA)/(FA + I + MWC)](CC \text{ Dep. Adj.} + CC \text{ Sales Adj.} + MWCA)$$

where

$$
\begin{aligned}
TL &= \text{total liabilities other than trade payables} \\
CA &= \text{current assets other than trade receivables} \\
FA &= \text{fixed assets including investments} \\
I &= \text{inventory} \\
MWC &= \text{monetary working capital} \\
CC \text{ Dep. Adj.} &= \text{current cost depreciation adjustment} \\
CC \text{ Sales Adj.} &= \text{current cost of sales adjustment} \\
MWCA &= \text{monetary working capital adjustment}
\end{aligned}
$$

The gearing adjustment acknowledges that the income statement need not recognize the additional replacement cost of operating assets so far as they are financed by debt.

BRAZIL

Inflation is often an accepted part of the business scene in Latin America, Eastern Europe, and Southeast Asia. Brazil's past experience with hyperinflation makes its inflation accounting initiatives instructive.

Although no longer required,[12] recommended inflation accounting in Brazil today reflects two sets of reporting options—Brazilian Corporate Law and the Brazil Securities and Exchange Commission.[13] Inflation adjustments complying with corporate law restate permanent assets and stockholders' equity accounts using a price index recognized by the federal government for measuring devaluation of the local currency.[14] Permanent assets include fixed assets, buildings, investments, deferred charges and their respective depreciation, and amortization or depletion accounts (including any related provisions for losses).[15] Stockholders' equity accounts comprise capital, reve-

---

[12]Financial analysts and Brazilian financial executives we have interviewed continue to adjust Brazilian accounts for changing prices to facilitate their analyses. Should significant inflation recur in Brazil, the inflation adjustments we describe will likely be reinstated.
[13]Coopers & Lybrand, *1993 International Accounting Summaries,* New York: John Wiley & Sons, 1993, B-25.
[14]Ibid., B-27.
[15]Permanent assets do not include inventories, which is a conceptual shortcoming of this inflation accounting model.

nue reserves, revaluation reserves, retained earnings, and a capital reserves account used to record the price level adjustment to capital. The latter results from revaluing fixed assets to their current replacement costs less a provision for technical and physical depreciation.

Inflation adjustments to permanent assets and stockholders' equity are netted with the excess being disclosed separately in current earnings as a monetary correction gain or loss. Exhibit 7-6 contains an illustration of this inflation accounting methodology.

The price level adjustment to stockholders' equity (R$275) is the amount by which the shareholders' beginning-of-period investment must grow to keep up with inflation. A permanent asset adjustment that is less than the equity adjustment causes a purchasing power loss reflecting the firm's exposure on its net monetary assets (i.e., working capital). To illustrate, let:

M = monetary assets
N = nonmonetary assets
L = liabilities
E = equity
i = inflation rate

Then

$$M + N = L + E \tag{7.1}$$

Multiplying both sides of Equation (7.1) by $(1 + i)$ quantifies the impact of inflation on the firm's financial position. Thus

$$M(1 + i) + N(1 + i) = L(1 + i) + E(1 + i) \tag{7.2}$$

Equation (7.2) can be reexpressed as

$$M + Mi + N + Ni = L + Li + E + Ei \tag{7.3}$$

Regrouping Equation (7.3) as:

$$M + \underbrace{N + Ni}_{\substack{\text{permanent} \\ \text{asset} \\ \text{adjustment}}} = L + \underbrace{E + Ei}_{\substack{\text{owners'} \\ \text{equity} \\ \text{adjustment}}} + \underbrace{(L - M)i}_{\substack{\text{monetary} \\ \text{gain or loss}}} \tag{7.4}$$

Since $M + N = L + E$:

$$Ni = Ei + (L - M)i \tag{7.5}$$

Or

$$\underbrace{Ni}_{\substack{\text{inflation} \\ \text{adjustment} \\ \text{to nonmonetary} \\ \text{(permanent)} \\ \text{assets}}} - \underbrace{Ei}_{\substack{\text{inflation} \\ \text{adjustment} \\ \text{to owners'} \\ \text{equity}}} = \underbrace{(L - M)i}_{\substack{\text{monetary} \\ \text{gain or loss}}} \tag{7.6}$$

Conversely, a permanent asset adjustment greater than the equity adjustment produces a purchasing power gain, suggesting that some of the assets have been financed

EXHIBIT 7-6   Inflation Adjustments Brazilian Style

Historical Amounts			Inflation-Corrected Amounts Assuming a 25% Rate of Inflation		
Balance Sheet	*1/1/X5*	*12/31/X5*			*12/31/X5*
Current assets	R$ 150	R$ 450	Current assets		R$ 450
Permanent assets	1,600	1,600	Permanent assets		2,000[1]
Provision for depreciation	(200)	(300)	Provision for		
			Depreciation	(300)	
			Monetary correction	(75)[2]	
			Correction of historical charge to P&L	(25)[3]	(400)
Total	R$1,550	R$1,750	Total		R$2,050
Current liabilities	R$ 50	R$ 50	Current liabilities		R$ 50
Long-term debt	400	400	Long-tern debt		400
Equity:			Equity:		
Capital	800	800	Capital		800
			Capital reserve		200[4]
Reserves	300	300	Reserves		375[5]
Profit of period		200	Profit of period		225
Total	1,550	1,750	Total		R$2,050

Income Statement Year Ended 12/31/X5			*Year Ended 12/31/X5*		
Operating profit		R$ 500	Operating profit		R$ 500
Depreciation of period (historical)		100	Depreciation of period	100	
			Correction of depreciation	25	125
Trading profit		400	Trading profit		375
			Inflationary loss:		
Exchange loss on foreign debt		(100)	Exchange loss on foreign debt	(100)	
Monetary correction on local debt		(100)	Monetary correction – local debt	(100)	
			Gain on correction of balance sheet	50[6]	(150)
Net profit		R$ 200	Net profit		R$ 225

[1]Represents the original R$1,600 plus a 25 percent(R$400) adjustment.

[2]25 percent of the original R$300.

[3]25 percent of the period's depreciation expense (typically based on the average value of fixed assets).

[4]25 percent of the original capital balance of R$800.

[5]Represents the original R$300 plus a 25 percent (R$75) adjustment.

[6]Gain on correction of the balance sheet:

Correction of permanent assets	R$400	
Correction of depreciation allowance	75	325
Correction of capital	200	
Correction of reserves	75	275
		50

by borrowing. For example, suppose that a firm's financial position before monetary correction is

Permanent assets	1,000	Liabilities	500
		Owners' equity	500

With an annual inflation rate of 30 percent, a price level adjusted balance sheet would show:

Permanent assets	1,300	Liabilities	500
		Capital	500
		Capital reserve	150
		Monetary gain	150[1]

[1]This analysis (monetary gain) assumes that liabilities are of the fixed rate variety or are floating rate obligations where the actual rate of inflation exceeds the expected rate that is incorporated into the terms of the original borrowing.

The Brazilian Securities Exchange Commission requires another inflation accounting method for publicly traded companies.[16] Listed companies must remeasure all transactions during the period using their functional currency. At the end of the period, the prevailing general price level index converts units of general purchasing power into units of nominal local currency. Also:

- Inventory is included as a nonmonetary asset and is remeasured with the functional currency.
- Noninterest-bearing monetary items with maturities exceeding 90 days are discounted to their present values to allocate resulting inflationary gains and losses to appropriate accounting periods (e.g., the discount on trade receivables is treated as a reduction of sales, the discount on accounts payable reduces purchases, and so forth).
- Balance sheet adjustments are similarly reclassified to appropriate line items in the income statement (e.g., the balance sheet adjustment to accounts receivable is reclassified as a reduction of sales).

To relieve Brazilian firms from having to present two sets of financial statements in their annual reports, the Securities Exchange Commission blended features of the corporate law methodology into its price level accounting methodology.

INTERNATIONAL ACCOUNTING STANDARDS COMMITTEE

In November 1981 the International Accounting Standards Committee issued IAS No. 15, "Information Reflecting the Effects of Changing Prices." IAS 15 recommends that large publicly traded enterprises disclose the following information, typically in supplementary form, using any method that adjusts for changing prices:

1. The amount of the adjustment to, or the adjusted amount of, depreciation of property, plant and equipment
2. The amount of the adjustment to, or the adjusted amount of, cost of sales

[16]Coopers & Lybrand, *1993 International Accounting Summaries*, New York: John Wiley & Sons, 1993, B-32–B-33.

3. A financing adjustment(s), if such adjustment(s) is generally part of the method adopted for reporting information on changing prices
4. The enterprise results recomputed to reflect the effects of the items described in (1) and (2) and, where appropriate, (3), and any other items separately disclosed that the method adopted requires

If a current cost method is adopted, the current cost of inventories and of property, plant, and equipment should be disclosed. Disclosure of methods used to compute the inflation adjustments is also required.[17]

Because inflation rates have fallen in many countries recently, the IASC decided that enterprises need not disclose information on changing prices. In keeping with recent developments in the United States and United Kingdom, the IASC encourages enterprises to present information reflecting the effects of changing prices and urges those that do to disclose the items required by IAS 15.

The IASC has concluded that reports of financial position and operating performance in local currency are not meaningful in a hyperinflationary environment. Therefore, it issued IAS 29, "Financial Reporting in Hyperinflationary Economies," which requires (rather than recommends) the restatement of primary financial statement information. Specifically, financial statements of an enterprise that reports in a currency of a hyperinflationary economy, whether based on a historical or current cost valuation framework, should be reexpressed in terms of constant purchasing power as of the balance sheet date. This rule also applies to corresponding figures for the preceding period. Purchasing power gains or losses related to a net monetary liability or asset position are to be included in current income. Reporting enterprises should also disclose

1. The fact that restatement for changes in the general purchasing power of the measuring unit has been made
2. The asset valuation framework employed in the primary statements (i.e., historical or current cost valuation)
3. The identity and level of the price index at the balance sheet date, together with its movement during the reporting period
4. The net monetary gain or loss during the period[18]

INFLATION ISSUES

Four inflation accounting issues are especially troublesome. They are (1) whether constant dollars or current costs better measure the effects of inflation, (2) the accounting treatment of inflation gains and losses, (3) accounting for foreign inflation, and (4) avoiding the *double-dip* phenomenon. We discuss issue 1 together with issue 3.

---

[17]International Accounting Standards Committee, "Accounting Responses to Changing Prices," *International Standard No. 6*, London: IASC, 1977, par. 17.
[18]International Accounting Standards Committee, "Financial Reporting in Hyperinflationary Economies," *International Accounting Standard No. 29*, London: IASC, 1989.

INFLATION GAINS AND LOSSES

Treatment of gains and losses on monetary items (i.e., cash, receivables, and payables) is controversial. Our survey of various country practices reveals important variations in this respect.

Gains or losses on monetary items in the United States are determined by restating, in constant dollars, the beginning and ending balance of, and transactions in, all monetary assets and liabilities (including long-term debt). The resulting figure is disclosed as a separate item. This treatment views gains and losses in monetary items as different in nature from other types of earnings.

In the United Kingdom, gains and losses on monetary items are partitioned into monetary working capital and a gearing adjustment. Both figures are determined in relation to specific (not general) price changes. The gearing adjustment indicates the benefit (or cost) to shareholders from debt financing during a period of changing prices. This figure is added (deducted) to (from) current cost operating profit to yield a disposable wealth measure called "Current Cost Profit Attributable to Shareholders."

The Brazilian approach, no longer required, does not adjust current assets and liabilities explicitly, as these amounts are expressed in terms of realizable values.[19] However, as Exhibit 7-6 shows, the adjustment from netting price level-adjusted permanent assets and owners' equity represents the general purchasing power gain or loss in financing working capital from debt or equity. A permanent asset adjustment that exceeds an equity adjustment represents that portion of permanent assets being financed by debt, creating a purchasing power gain. Conversely, an equity adjustment greater than the permanent asset adjustment denotes the portion of working capital financed by equity. A purchasing power loss is recognized for this portion during an inflationary period.

SSAP No. 16 has great merit in dealing with the effects of inflation. Along with inventories and plant and equipment, an enterprise needs to increase its net nominal monetary working capital to maintain its operating capability with increasing prices. It also benefits from using debt during inflation. However, the magnitude of these phenomena should not be measured in general purchasing power terms because a firm rarely, if ever, invests in an economy's market basket. We believe that the purpose of inflation accounting is to measure the performance of an enterprise and enable anyone interested to assess the amounts, timing, and likelihood of future cash flows.[20]

A firm can measure its command over specific goods and services by using an index to calculate its monetary gains and losses.[21] Because not all enterprises can construct firm-specific purchasing power indexes, the British approach is a good practical alternative. However, rather than disclose the gearing adjustment (or some equivalent), we prefer to treat it as a reduction of the current cost adjustments for depreciation, cost of sales, and monetary working capital. We think that current cost charges from restating historical cost income during inflation are offset by the reduced burden of servicing debt used to finance those operating items. (See Exhibit 7-7 for an illustration.)

---

[19]Price Waterhouse, *Doing Business in Brazil*, New York: Price Waterhouse World Firm Limited, 1994.
[20]Financial Accounting Standards Board, "Objectives of Financial Reporting by Business Enterprises," *Statement of Financial Accounting Concepts No. 1*, Stamford, CT: FASB, November 1978, par. 37.
[21]Frederick D. S. Choi, "Foreign Inflation and Management Decisions," *Management Accounting* (June 1977), pp. 21–27.

EXHIBIT 7-7 Alternative Current Cost Monetary Disclosures

SSAP No. 16 (ALT. 1)			SSAP No. 16 (Alt. 2)			Suggested Method		
Historical cost-based operating income		2,900	Historical cost-based operating income		2,900	Historical cost-based operating income		2,900
Less: Current cost adjustments			Less: Current cost adjustments			Less: Current cost adjustments		
Cost of sales	(460)		Cost of sales	(460)		Cost of sales	(460)	
Monetary working capital	(100)		Monetary working capital	(100)		Depreciation	(950)	
Working capital	(560)		Working capital	(560)		Monetary working capital	(100)	
Depreciation	(950)	(1,510)	Depreciation	(950)	(1,510)	Gearing adjustment	166	(1,344)
Current cost operating income		1,390	Current cost operating income		1,390	Current cost-based operating income		1,556
Gearing adjustment	166		Interest payable less receivable		(200)	Interest payable less receivable		(200)
Interest payable less receivable	(200)	(34)			1,190			
Current cost profit before taxation		1,356	Taxation		(730)	Current cost-based net income before taxes		1,356
			Current cost profit after interest and taxation		460			
Taxation		(730)				Taxes		(730)
Current cost profit attributable to shareholders		626	Gearing adjustment		166	Current cost-based net income		626
			Current cost profit attributable to shareholders		626			

HOLDING GAINS AND LOSSES

Current value accounting divides total earnings into two parts: (1) operating income (the difference between current revenues and the current cost of resources consumed) and (2) unrealized gains that result from the possession of nonmonetary assets whose replacement value rises with inflation. Even though the measurement of holding gains is straightforward, their accounting treatment is not. Should portions of raw materials inventory gains be realized in periods when the respective inventories are turned into finished goods and sold? Are there ever unrealized adjustment gains or losses that should be deferred? Or should all such gains or losses be lumped together and disclosed in a special new section within stockholders' equity?

We think that increases in the replacement cost of operating assets (e.g., higher pro-jected cash outflows to replace equipment) are not gains, realized or not. Whereas current cost-based income measures a firm's approximate disposable wealth, changes in the current cost of inventory, plant, equipment, and other operating assets are revaluations of owners' equity, which is the portion of earnings that the business must keep to preserve its physical capital (or productive capacity). Assets held for speculation, such as vacant land or marketable securities, do not need to be replaced to maintain productive capacity. Hence, if current cost adjustments include these items, increases or decreases in their current cost (value) equivalents (up to their realizable values) should be stated directly in income.

ACCOUNTING FOR FOREIGN INFLATION

We have not yet decided which inflation accounting approach is best. In the United States, the FASB tried to cope with inflation by requiring large reporting entities to experiment with both historical cost-constant purchasing power and current cost disclosures. FAS No. 89, which encourages (but no longer requires) companies to account for changing prices, leaves the issue unresolved at two levels. First, companies may continue to maintain the value of their nonmonetary assets at historical cost (restated for general price level changes) or restate them to their current cost equivalents. Second, companies that elect to provide supplementary current cost data for foreign operations have a choice of two methods for translating and restating foreign accounts in U.S. dollars. How do we choose between these two methods? We can choose with a decision-oriented framework.

Investors care about a firm's dividend-generating potential, since their investment's value ultimately depends on future dividends. A firm's dividend-generating potential is directly related to its capacity to produce goods and services. Only when a firm preserves its productive capacity (and thus its earning power) will there be future dividends to consider.

Therefore, investors need specific, not general price-level-adjusted statements. Why? Because specific price level adjustments (our current cost model) determine the maximum amount that the firm can pay as dividends (disposable wealth) without reducing its productive capacity.

This conclusion implies that the restate-translate versus translate-restate issue is trivial. Both methods are based on a valuation framework that has little to recommend it—historical cost. Neither method changes that framework. No matter how it's adjusted, the historical cost model is still the historical cost model!

We favor the following price level adjustment procedure:

1. Restate the financial statements of all subsidiaries, both domestic and foreign, and the statements of the parent, to reflect changes in specific prices (e.g., current costs).
2. Translate the accounts of all foreign subsidiaries into domestic currency equivalents using a constant (e.g., the current or a base-year foreign exchange rate).
3. Use specific price indexes that are relevant to what the firm consumes in calculating monetary gains or losses. A parent company perspective requires domestic price indexes; a local company perspective requires local price indexes.

Restating both foreign and domestic accounts to their specific current price equivalents produces decision-relevant information. This information provides investors the greatest possible amount of information concerning future dividends. It would be much easier to compare and evaluate the consolidated results of all firms than it is now. This reporting philosophy was stated by Dewey R. Borst, comptroller of Inland Steel Company:

> Management seeks the best current information to monitor how they have done in the past, and to guide them in their current decision making. Outsiders value financial statements for the same general purpose of determining how the firm has done in the past and how it is likely to perform in the future. Therefore, there is no legitimate need to have two distinct sets of data and methods of presentation of financial information. The same data now available through the development of managerial accounting is also suitable for outsiders.[22]

AVOIDING THE DOUBLE-DIP

When restating foreign accounts for foreign inflation, care must be taken to avoid the *double-dip*. This problem exists because local inflation directly affects the exchange rates used in translation. While economic theory assumes an inverse relationship between a country's internal rate of inflation and the external value of its currency, evidence suggests that this relationship seldom holds (at least in the short run).[23] Accordingly, the size of the resulting adjustment to eliminate the double-dip will vary depending on to what degree exchange rates and differential inflation are negatively correlated.

As noted before, inflation adjustments to cost of sale or depreciation expense are designed to reduce "as reported" earnings to avoid overstating income. However, due to the inverse relationship between local inflation and currency values, changes in the exchange rate between successive financial statements, generally caused by inflation (at least over a period of time), will make at least part of the impact of inflation (i.e., currency translation adjustments) affect a company's "as reported" results. Thus, to avoid adjusting for the effects of inflation twice, the inflation adjustment should take into account the translation loss already reflected in a firm's "as reported" results.

This adjustment is relevant to U.S.-based multinational enterprises (MNEs) that have adopted the dollar as the functional currency for their foreign operations under FAS No. 52 and that translate inventories using the current exchange rate. It is also germane to non-U.S.-based MNEs that recognize translation gains and losses in current income. It is especially pertinent to European MNEs in view of currently used currency translation methods. A survey of foreign currency translation practices in Denmark, France, Germany, the Netherlands, Sweden, Switzerland, and the United Kingdom, showed that companies there tend to use the current rate method of translation.[24] Even though many companies reported currency translation gains and losses in balance sheet

---

[22]"Accounting vs. Reality: How Wide Is the 'GAAP,'" *The Week in Review* (July 13, 1982): 1.
[23]Michael Adler and Bernard Dumans, "International Portfolio and Corporation Finance: A Synthesis," *Journal of Finance* (June 1983): 925–984.
[24]For example, see David Alexander and Simon Archer, eds., *European Accounting Guide*, 4th edition, New York: Aspen Law and Business, 2001.

reserves, a significant number—particularly in Germany, the Netherlands, and Sweden—reflected such gains and losses directly in current earnings. Absent any offsetting adjustments, such companies could reduce or increase earnings twice when accounting for foreign inflation.

The following inventory accounting example shows the relationship between inflation and foreign currency translation. The company in question uses the FIFO inventory-costing method and translates inventory to dollars at the current exchange rate. We assume the following:

- Local country inflation was 20 percent in the year just ended. U.S. inflation was 6 percent during the year.
- The opening exchange rate on January 1 was LC1 = $1.00.
- The closing exchange rate on December 31 was LC1 = $0.88.
- Currency devaluation during the year to maintain purchasing power parity was 12 percent.
- Local currency inventory was LC200 on January 1 and LC240 on December 31.
- No change occurred in the physical quantity of inventory during the year.

The dollar equivalent of beginning and ending inventory is calculated as follows:

	LC Amount	*Exchange Rate*	*$ Amount*
Jan. 1 FIFO inventory	200	LC = $1.00	$200
Dec. 31 FIFO inventory	240	LC = $0.88	$211

"As reported" income will reflect a translation loss of $29 (assuming that the currency was devalued at year-end), the difference between translating LC240 inventory on December 31 at $0.88 versus $1.00.

During the next inventory turnover period, "as reported" cost of sales will, therefore, be LC240 in local currency, $211 in dollars.

If cost of sales were adjusted for inflation by the restate-translate method, this company might do as follows:

- Remove the year's 20 percent inflation from December 31 local currency inventory (240/1.20), reducing it to LC 200—the same as it was on January 1 (before inflation).
- The local currency cost of sales adjustment would then be LC40, the amount required to change December 31 inventory from LC240 to LC200.
- Next, translate the local currency cost of sales adjustment (LC40) to dollars at $1.00, making a $40 cost of sales adjustment (LC40 × $1.00 = $40).

Note that on an inflation-adjusted basis, this company has reduced earnings by a $29 translation loss and a $40 cost of sales inflation adjustment—a total of $69, or 34 percent of what began as $200 of inventory on January 1. Yet inflation was only 20 percent! Double dipping caused this difference. The dollar calculations include a partial overlap between the currency devaluation loss, which *results* from inflation, and the cost of sales adjustment for inflation, which is *a root cause* of the currency devaluation. The restate-translate cost of sales inflation adjustment alone was enough. It would offset not only the U.S. inflation rate (6 percent in this example) but also the 12 percent inflation differential between this country's 20 percent rate and the U.S. 6 percent rate—which led to the 12 percent devaluation. We conclude that if cost of sales is adjusted to remove local country inflation, it is necessary to reverse any inventory translation loss that was reflected in "as reported" earnings. Appendix B provides a case analysis.

A P P E N D I X   7 - 1

Supplementary Current Cost Disclosures

Here we illustrate how to prepare supplementary current cost information for a foreign subsidiary located in Italy whose functional currency is the euro. Exhibit 7-8 presents comparative financial statements for our hypothetical subsidiary, Bocconi Corporation. Exhibit 7-9 gives exchange rate and general price level information. To simplify the illustration, we assume that Bocconi Corpo-

ration has equipment but no inventory. The equipment was acquired at the beginning of 20X0 and is being depreciated in straight-line fashion with a useful life of 10 years and no salvage value. No equipment was acquired or disposed of during the year. The current cost of the equipment at year-end is as follows:

	20X0	
20X1		
Current cost (in thousands)	Euro 8,000	Euro 11,000
Accumulated depreciation	(800)	(2,200)
Net current cost	Euro 7,200	Euro 8,800

EXHIBIT 7-8	Historical Cost Financial Statements of Bocconi Corporation (in Thousands)	
	20X0	**20X1**
Balance Sheet		
Cash	Euro 2,500	Euro 5,100
Equipment, net	4,000	3,500
Total assets	Euro 6,500	Euro 8,600
Current Liabilities	Euro 1,000	Euro 1,200
Long-term debt	3,000	4,000
Owner's equity	2,500	3,400
Total equities	Euro 6,500	Euro 8,600
Income Statement		
Revenue		Euro 10,000
Operating expenses	Euro 7,700	
Depreciation	500	
Other	900	9,100
Net income		900
Owners' equity: 19X0		2,500
Owners' equity: 19X1		Euro 3,400

EXHIBIT 7-9 Hypothetical Price Data

Exchange Rates:

12/31/X0	Euro 1.800 = $1
Average for 19X1	Euro 1.875 = $1
12/31/X1	Euro 1.950 = $1

General Price Level Indexes:

	Italy	*United States*
12/31/X0	200	130
Average for 19X1	215	134
12/31/X1	230	138

Management has determined that the equipment's recoverable amount exceeds its net current cost.

THE TRANSLATE-RESTATE METHOD

First, we translate current cost accounts (denominated in euros) to dollars. Then we convert these amounts to current cost-constant dollar equivalents by restating them for changes in the U.S. general price level.

Current cost depreciation of the equipment is calculated as follows (in millions):

Current cost: 12/31/X0	Euro	8,000
Current cost: 12/31/X1		11,000
		19,000
		÷2
Average current cost	Euro	9,500
		×10%
Current cost depreciation	Euro	950

Then, this current cost depreciation is translated to dollars and restated for U.S. inflation. Restatement is simplified if current cost (in euro) is translated to average-for-the-year dollars. This is done by translating the current cost depreciation (in euro) to dollars using an average exchange rate. Here, current cost depreciation in average-for-the-year dollars (which simulates *average* rather than *year-end* purchasing power equivalents) is $506,667 (Euro 950,000 × 1/1.875).

Adding back historical cost depreciation (Euro 500,000) to reported earnings (Euro 900,000) and subtracting the current cost equivalent computed previously (Euro 950,000) yields current cost-based income from continuing operations of Euro 450,000. Current cost-based income in constant dollars is $240,000 (Lit 450,000 × 1/1.875).

Next we calculate increases in the current cost of equipment (net of general inflation). The effect of exchange rate changes during the period must be held constant. To handle rate changes, we translate beginning-of-period and end-of-period current cost balances to dollars at the average exchange rate, then restate these dollar equivalents to average purchasing power (i.e., constant dollar) equivalents. This procedure is illustrated below:

	Current Cost (in Thousands Euro)		*Translate (Avg. Rate)*		*Current Cost ($1,000s)*		*Restate (U.S. GPL)*		*Current Cost/ Constant $ (in 1,000s)*
Current cost, net 12/31/X0	Euro 7,200	×	1/1.875	=	$3,840	×	134/130	=	$3,958
Depreciation	(800)	×	1/1.875	=	(533)			=	(533)
Current cost, net 12/31/X1	8,800	×	1/1.875	=	4,693	×	134/138	=	4,557
	Euro 2,400				$1,386				$1,132

Because depreciation is measured in constant euros, we assume it is expressed in constant dollars upon translation at the average exchange rate. Here, the difference between the nominal dollar ($1,386) and constant dollar equivalent ($1,132), or $254, is the inflation component of the equipment's current cost increase.

As Bocconi Corporation maintained a net monetary liability position during the year (see Exhibit 7-8), it gained purchasing power. We calculate this monetary gain as follows:

	Euro (in Thousands)	Avg. Exchange Rate	Dollars (in Thousands)	Restate	Constant Dollars (in Thousands)
Net monetary liabilities 12/31/X0	Euro (1,500) ×	1/1.875 =	$(800)	× 134/130 =	$(825)
Decrease during year	1,400 ×	1/1.875 =	747		747
Net monetary liabilities 12/31/X1	Euro 100 ×	1/1.875 =	$ (53)	× 134/138 =	52
Monetary gain					$ 26

Translation of euro balances to U.S. dollars when exchange rates have changed causes a translation adjustment. This translation adjustment is the amount necessary to reconcile beginning owners' equity on a current cost basis with current cost-based ending owners' equity in constant dollars. Current cost equity in nominal euros at the beginning and end of 20X0 is computed

by adding net monetary items and equipment net of depreciation at current cost. Current cost equity in nominal dollars is determined by translating the nominal euro balances by the average exchange rate (see Exhibit 7-10).

The translation adjustment is calculated as follows:

Owners' equity, 12/31/X0 (in avg. 20X1 constant dollars):		
$3,166 × 134/130 =	$3,263	
+ Current cost-based income	$ 240	
+ Purchasing power gain		26
+ Increase in current cost of equipment, net of inflation	1,132	1,398
		4,661
− Translation adjustment		(328)
= Owners' equity − 12/31/X1(in avg. 20X1 constant dollars):		
$4,462 × 134/138 =		$4,333

THE RESTATE-TRANSLATE METHOD

We follow procedures similar to the translate-restate method. The major difference is that we

adjust for general inflation in Italy using an Italian general price level index before translating to U.S. dollars.

Current cost depreciation in lira and operating income are determined as before. For

EXHIBIT 7-10 Current Cost Equity in Nominal Euro (in Thousands) and Dollars (in Thousands)

		December 31				
		20X0			20X1	
	Euro	*Exchange Rate*	*$*	*Euro*	*Exchange Rate*	*$*
Cash	2,500	1/1.900	389	5,100	1/1.950	2,615
Current liability	(1,000)	1/1.800	(556)	(1,200)	1/1.950	(615)
Long-term debt	(3,000)	1/1.800	(1,667)	(4,000)	1/1.950	(2,051)
Net monetary liability	(1,500)		(834)	(100)		(51)
Equipment, net	7,200	1/1,200	4,000	8,800	1/1.950	4,513
Current cost-based equity	5,700		3,166	8,700		4,462

Bocconi Corporation, these amounts are Euro 950,000 and Euro 450,000, respectively. The increase in the current cost of equipment, net of inflation, is determined by restating both the beginning-of-year and end-of-year equipment current cost balances using appropriate Italian general price level indexes. Thus:

	Nominal Euro (in Thousands)	Restate for Italy's GPL	Constant Euro (in Thousands)
Current cost, net 12/31/X0	Euro 7,200 ×	215/200 =	Euro 7,740
Depreciation	(800)		(800)
Current cost, net 12/31/X1	8,800 ×	215/230 =	8,226
	Euro 2,400		Euro 1,286

Boconni Corporation's monetary gain, expressed in constant euros, is calculated as follows:

	Nominal Euros (in Thousands)	Restate for Italy's GPL	Constant Euros (in Thousands)
Net monetary liability 12/31/X0	Euro 1,500 ×	215/200 =	Euro 1,612
Decrease during year	(1,400)		(1,400)
Net monetary liability	100 ×	215/230 =	(93)
Purchasing power gain			Euro 119

Translation of current cost/constant euro balances to U.S. dollars using the restate-

translate method causes the following translation adjustment:

	Constant Euro (in Thousands)	Translate	Constant Euro in Dollars (in Thousands)
Owners' equity, 12/31/X0 (in avg. 20X1 constant euro):			
Lit 5,700 × 215/200 =	Lit 6,251	× 1/1.800 =	$3,473
+ Current cost-based income	450	× 1/1.875 =	240
+ Monetary gain	119	× 1/1.875 =	64
+ Current cost increase, net of inflation	1,286	× 1/1.875 =	686
Subtotal			4,463
– Translation adjustment			(292)
Owners' equity-12/31/X1 (in avg. 20X1 constant lira):			
Euro 8,700 × 215/230 =	Euro 8,133	× 1/1.950 =	$4,171

PARITY ADJUSTMENT

The restate-translate method requires a *parity adjustment* in addition to the translation adjustment. Why? The restate-translate method produces current cost/constant euro performance measures expressed in U.S. dollar equivalents. When these numbers are part of the 5-year supplementary current costs disclosures, they must be expressed in constant dollars to enable trend analysis. Thus, expressing current cost/constant euro balances in terms of constant dollars results in a restate-*translate-restate* procedure. The parity adjustment reflects the differences in infla-

tion between the parent and host country in restating beginning and ending owners' equity to average currency units and reconciles the restate-translate disclosures (had the latter approach been employed instead).

In our example, the increase in owners' equity (per the translate-restate method) is $1,070 ($4,333 – $3,263). Under the restate-translate method, the increase in the *dollar equivalents* of owners' equity expressed in average *constant euros* is $698 ($4,171 – $3,473). The difference between these two amounts, $372 ($1,070 – $698), is the parity adjustment.

A P P E N D I X   7 - 2

Accounting for Foreign Inflation: A Case Analysis

The following case study highlights how a leading U.S.-based MNE, the General Electric Company (GE), accounts for foreign inflation. Most of our discussion will be limited to inventory and cost of sales, as well as monetary gains and losses. The procedures for inventories and cost of sales also apply to fixed assets and their related cost expirations when these accounts are translated using the current rate.[1]

GE uses the temporal method of foreign currency translation because the U.S. dollar is its functional currency for most of its foreign operations. Inventories are generally translated at the current rate to signal that they are exposed to exchange-rate risk. GE management believes that it needs the restate-translate method of accounting for inflation, using specific local price indexes for fixed assets and inventory, to properly measure its foreign operations on an inflation-adjusted basis. Accordingly, GE adjusts the local currency cost of foreign fixed assets and inventory for local specific price changes and then translates at the current exchange rate. Restatement of fixed assets, from which restated depreciation expense is derived, uses generally understood practices (i.e., restate for current cost and then translate to dollars) and is not repeated here. For inventory, however, the cost of sales inflation adjustment cannot be derived from the restated balance sheet inventory value. Therefore, we will explain these two inflation adjustments separately.

CURRENT COST INVENTORY ADJUSTMENT

For FIFO inventories that are not material in amount or that turn over very frequently, GE assumes that current cost and FIFO book cost are

essentially equivalent. Accordingly, the historical book cost is reported as current cost.

With LIFO inventories, and FIFO inventories not excluded by the previous criteria, GE restates ending inventories to their current cost equivalents using local specific price indexes before translation to dollars at the current rate. If the inventory input rate is relatively constant, the current cost inventory adjustment is approximated by applying one-half of the local inflation rate during the inventory accumulation period. Thus, assuming a 4-month accumulation period, an annual inflation rate of 30 percent, an ending inventory balance of LC1,000,000, and an ending exchange rate of LC1 = $0.40, the dollar FIFO inventory value restated to a current cost basis would be:

$$30\%/12 \text{ mos.} = (2.5\%/\text{mo.} \times 4 \text{ mos.})/2$$
$$\times \text{ LC1,000,000} = \text{LC50,000}$$
$$\text{LC1,000,000} + \text{LC50,000} = \text{LC1,050,000}$$
$$\times \$0.40 = \$420,000$$

If the foreign subsidiary carries its inventories on a LIFO basis, its restated FIFO value is calculated in the same manner, using its LIFO cost index as the inflation rate.

CURRENT COST OF SALES ADJUSTMENT: SIMULATED LIFO

When a foreign operation uses LIFO accounting for its "as reported" results, the cost of sales is close to market. Therefore, no cost of sales inflation adjustment is made. For foreign operations that use FIFO accounting, GE's inflation adjustment simulates what would have been charged to cost of sales under LIFO accounting. However, to

---

[1]The following discussion is excerpted from Frederick D. S. Choi, "Resolving the Inflation/Currency Translation Dilemma," *Management International Review 27*, no. 2 (1987), pp. 28–33.

avoid the double-dip effect, the company also takes into account any inventory translation loss that is already reflected in "as reported" results. To illustrate, suppose that the December 31 FIFO inventory balance is LC5,000, that the year's inflation rate was 30 percent (January 1 index 100, December 31 index 130), and that the currency devalued by 20 percent from LC1 = $0.50 at January 1 to LC1 = $0.40 at December 31.

The following sequential analysis shows how the double-counting phenomenon is minimized. Steps 1 through 3 illustrate how the current cost of sales adjustment is derived in local currency. Step 4 expresses this inflation adjustment in parent currency (i.e., U.S. dollars). Step 5 identifies the translation loss that has already been booked as a result of having translated inventories to dollars at a current rate that fell during the year. Finally, step 6 subtracts the translation loss already reflected in "as reported" results from the current cost of sales adjustment.

1. December 31 FIFO inventory subject to simulated LIFO charge   LC5,000

2. Restate line 1 to January 1 cost level (LC5,000 × 100/130)   LC3,846

3. Difference between line 1 and line 2 inventory values represents current year local currency FIFO inventory inflation   LC1,154

4. Translate line 3 to dollars at the *January 1* exchange rate (LC1,154 × $0.50). The result is simulated *dollar* LIFO expense for the current year $ 577

5. Calculate the translation loss on FIFO inventory (line 1)that was already reflected in "as reported" results:

   a. Translate line 1 to January 1 exchange rate (LC5,000 × $0.50) $2,500

   b. Translate line 1 at December 31 exchange rate (LC5,000 x $0.40) $2,000

   c. The difference is inventory translation loss already reflected in "as reported" results $ (500)

6. The net of line 4 and 5c is the cost of sales adjustment in dollars:

   a. Simulated dollar LIFO expense from line 4 $ 577

   b. Less: Inventory translation loss already reflected in "as reported" results (from line 5c) $ (500)

   c. The difference is the net dollar current cost of sales adjustment $ 77

Usually, when inflation outpaces devaluation, the dollar current cost of sales adjustment will be positive (i.e., a deduction from "as reported" earnings). However, if devaluation outpaces inflation, the adjustment will be negative (i.e., the dollar cost of sales adjustment would be subtracted from, rather than added to, "as reported" dollar cost of sales).

CURRENT COST MONETARY ADJUSTMENT

The final inflation adjustment described here relates to the fact that debtors typically gain during inflation because typically they repay fixed monetary obligations in currencies of reduced purchasing power. Accordingly, if a foreign affiliate has used debt to finance part of its fixed assets and inventory, its inflation-adjusted data include a monetary adjustment (i.e., a purchasing power gain). However, because GE limits its inflation adjustments to inventories, fixed assets, and their related cost expirations, it limits the monetary adjustment to that portion of liabilities used to finance fixed assets and inventories—hereafter known as *applied liabilities.* As a *debtor's gain,* the monetary adjustment recognizes that the interest expense being paid on applied liabilities includes compensation to the lender for the eroding purchasing power of the funds loaned. It also partly offsets income-reducing inflation adjustments for depreciation expense and cost of sales due to the impact of inflation on fixed assets and inventory replacement costs.

Calculation of the monetary adjustment involves two steps, because local inflation impacts exchange rates used to translate local currency liabilities to their dollar equivalents. Thus, the purchasing power gain on local currency liabilities used to finance fixed assets and inventories during an inflationary period is partly or fully offset by a reversal of any translation gains (or losses) on these liabilities already reflected in "as reported" results. These gains result from having translated monetary liabilities by an exchange rate that fell during the period.

In the following illustration, assume that a foreign subsidiary's local currency cost of fixed assets and FIFO inventory add up to LC10,600, that its net worth is LC7,500, that differential inflation between the parent and host country is 30 percent, and that the local currency devalued by 20 percent from LC1 = $0.50 at January 1 to LC1 = $0.40 at December 31. The current cost monetary adjustment is calculated as follows. Steps 1 through 5 identify the portion of monetary liabilities employed to finance assets whose values have been adjusted for inflation. Steps 6 and 7 calculate the monetary gains on these applied liabilities in local currency. Step 8 reexpresses this gain in U.S. dollars. Step 9 identifies the translation gain resulting from having translated monetary liabilities to dollars by an exchange rate (the current rate) that depreciated during the year. Finally, step 10 subtracts the translation gain on the monetary liabilities from the purchasing power gain on the same accounts to yield (in this example) a net monetary gain from changing prices.

1. Local currency cost fixed assets at December 31 — LC 5,600
2. FIFO inventory at December 31 — LC 5,000
3. Total of lines 1 and 2 — LC10,600
4. Subtract net worth at December 31 — LC (7,500)
5. The balance represents "applied liabilities" — LC 3,100

6. Restate December 31 applied liabilities to their January 1 purchasing power equivalent (i.e., multiply LC 3,100 by 100/130) — LC 2,385
7. The difference between lines 5 and 6 is the purchasing power gain on applied liabilities — LC 715
8. Translate line 7 to dollars at the *January 1* exchange rate. The result is the debtor's gain from inflation in *dollars* (LC 715 × $0.50) — $ 358
9. Calculate the year's translation gain (loss) on applied LC liabilities already reflected in "as reported" results:
    a. Line 5 times January 1 exchange rate (LC 3,100 × $0.50) — $1,550
    b. Line 5 times December 31 exchange rate (LC 3,100) × $0.40) — $1,240
    c. The difference is the translation gain — $ 310
10. The difference between line 8 and line 9c. is the dollar current cost monetary adjustment:
    a. Line 8 (debtor's gain from inflation) — $358 cr.
    b. If line 9c. is a translation gain, show it as a debit to reverse it and, vice versa — $(310) dr.
    c. Add lines 10(a) and 10(b). If the sum is a credit, treat it as an addition to "as reported" income and, vice versa — $ 48

Selected References

Accounting Standards Committee, Handbook on Accounting for the Effects of Changing Prices, London: ASC, 1986.

Archambault, Jeffrey J., and Marie E. Archambault, "A Cross-National Test of Determinants of Inflation Accounting Practices," *International Journal of Accounting* 34, no. 2 (1999): 189–207.

Barniv, Ran, "The Value Relevance of Inflation-Adjusted and Historical Cost Earnings During Hyperinflation," *Journal of International Accounting, Auditing and Taxation* 8, no. 2 (1999): 269–287.

Beaver, W. H., and M. A. Wolfson, "Foreign Currency Translation and Changing Prices in Perfect and Complete Markets," *Journal of Accounting Research* (autumn 1982): 528–550.

Callard, C. G., and D. C. Kleinman, "Inflation-Adjusted Accounting: Does It Matter?" *Financial Analysts Journal* (May–June 1985): 51–59.

Chasteen, L., " A Taxonomy of Price Change Models," *The Accounting Review* (July 1984): 515–520.

Choi, F. D. S., "Resolving the Inflation/Currency Translation Dilemma," *Management International Review* 27, no. 2 (1987): 26–34.

Choi, F. D. S., and R. R. Gunn, "Hyperinflation Reporting and Performance Assessment," *Journal of Financial Statement Analysis* (summer 1997), 30–38.

Coopers & Lybrand, *1993 International Accounting Summaries*, New York: John Wiley & Sons, 1993.

Cotrim, J., "Inflation Accounting South American Style," *World Accounting Report* (April 1985).

Davis-Friday, Paquita Y., and Juan M. Rivera, "Inflation Accounting and 20-F Disclosures: Evidence from Mexico," *Accounting Horizons* (June 2000): 113–135.

Epstein, Barry J., and Abbas Ali Mirza, IAS 2000: Interpretation and Application of International Accounting Standards, New York: John Wiley & Sons, 2000.

Financial Accounting Standards Board, "Financial Reporting and Changing Prices," Statement of Financial Accounting Standards No. 33, Stamford, CT: FASB, September 1979.

Financial Accounting Standards Board, "Financial Reporting and Changing Prices," Statement of Financial Accounting Standards No. 89, Stamford, CT: FASB, December 1986.

Goldman Sachs, The Global Currency Analyst, New York: Goldman Sachs, June 2000.

International Accounting Standards Committee, "Information Reflecting the Effects of Changing Prices," *International Accounting Standard 15*, London: IASC, November 1981.

International Accounting Standards Committee, "Financial Reporting in Hyperinflationary Economies," *International Accounting Standard 29*, London: IASC, 1989.

Price Waterhouse, *Indexation in Brazilian Accounting*, Sao Paulo: Price Waterhouse Auditores Independentes, 1984.

Sale, T. J., and R. W. Scapens, "Accounting for the Effects of Changing Prices," *Journal of Accountancy* (July 1980): 82–87.

Wyman, H. E. "Accounting for the Effects of Inflation," in *International Accounting and Finance Handbook*, F. D. S. Choi, ed., New York: John Wiley & Sons, 1997, 29.

Discussion Questions

1. Consider the statement: "The object of accounting for changing prices is to assure that a company is able to maintain its operating capability." How accurate is it?
2. From a user's perspective, what is the inherent problem in attempting to analyze historical cost-based financial statements of a company domiciled in an inflationary, devaluation-prone country?
3. What is a general price level index and of what use is it for financial statement readers?

4. Following are the remarks of a prominent American Congressman. Explain why you agree or disagree with them.

> The plain fact of the matter is that inflation accounting is a premature, imprecise, and underdeveloped method of recording basic business facts. To insist that any system of inflation accounting can afford the accuracy and fairness needed for the efficient operation of our tax system is simply foolish. My years on the Ways and Means Committee have exposed me to the many appeals of business—from corporate tax "reform" to the need for capital formation—which have served as a guise for reducing the tax contributions of American business. In this respect, I see inflation accounting as another in a long line of attempts to minimize corporate taxation through backdoor gimmickry.

5. Professional accountancy bodies the world over generally agree that inflation may become so great that conventional financial statements lose much of their significance and price-level-adjusted statements become more meaningful. Since domestic rates of inflation vary significantly from country to country, at what point do price-level-adjusted financial statements become more meaningful? How does one determine whether the benefits of price-level-adjusted accounting information exceed its costs?

6. Briefly describe the nature of the historical cost-constant purchasing power and current cost models. How are they similar? How do they differ?

7. Refer to Exhibit 7-4, which contains the current costing disclosure format used by Atlas Copco. Can you explain how the income statement items *Price changes, inventory* and *Price changes, fixed assets* were derived? What do these numbers mean? Do you agree that they should be included in reported earnings?

8. What might explain the reluctance of accounting standard setters (primarily those in the highly industrialized countries) to require the disclosure of changing prices information in general purpose financial statements? Can you identify any problems associated with such a policy? Can you identify any advantages?

9. As a potential investor in the shares of multinational enterprises, which inflation method—restate-translate or translate-restate—would give you consolidated information most relevant to your decision needs? Which information set is best from the viewpoint of the foreign subsidiary's shareholders?

10. What is a *gearing adjustment* and on what ideas is it based?

11. How does accounting for foreign inflation differ from accounting for domestic inflation?

12. What does *double-dipping* mean in accounting for foreign inflation?

Exercises

1. Zonolia Enterprises has equipment on its books that it acquired 2 years ago. The equipment is being depreciated in straight-line fashion over a 10-year period and has no salvage value. The current cost of this equipment at the end of year 2 was 8,000,000,000 zonos (Z). During year 3, the specific price index for equipment increased from 100 to 137.5.

   Required: Based on this information, calculate the equipment's net current cost (i.e., current cost less accumulated depreciation) at the end of year 3.

2. General price level index information for the country of Zonolia is as follows:

12/31/X2	30,000
Average	32,900
12/31/X3	36,000

Required: Using this information and the information in exercise 1, calculate the increase in the current cost of Zonolia Enterprise's equipment, net of inflation?

3. Now assume that Zonolia Enterprises is a foreign subsidiary of a U.S.-based multinational corporation and that its financial statements are consolidated with those of its U.S. parent. Relevant exchange rate and general price level information for the year are given here (general price level information for Zonolia are provided in exercise 2):

Exchange rate:

12/31/X2	Z 4,400 = $1
Average 19X3	Z 4,800 = $1
12/31/X3	Z 5,290 = $1

Required: What would be the increase in the current cost of Zonolia Enterprise's equipment, net of inflation, when expressed in U.S. dollars under the restate-translate methodology? Under the translate-restate method?

4. Assume that Zonolia Enterprise's comparative balance sheets (at historical cost) for 19X2 and 19X3 are as follows:

Balance Sheet	19X2	19X3
Cash	Z 2,500	Z 5,100
Equipment, net	4,000	3,500
Total assets	Z 6,500	Z 8,600
Current liabilities	Z 1,000	Z 1,200
Long-term debt	3,000	4,000
Owners' equity	2,500	3,400
Total	Z 6,500	Z 8,600

Required: What was the change in Zonolia's net monetary asset or liability position?

5. Calculate Zonolia Enterprise's net monetary gain or loss in local currency for 19X3 based on the general price level information provided in exercise 2.

6. Based on the price information provided in previous exercises, calculate Zonolia Enterprise's net monetary gain in dollars under the restate-translate method and under the translate-restate method.

7. Sobrero Corporation, a Mexican affiliate of a major U.S.-based hotel chain, starts the calendar year with 1 billion pesos (P) cash equity investment. It immediately acquires a refurbished hotel in Acapulco for P 900 million. Owing to a favorable tourist season, Sobrero Corporation's rental revenues were P 144 million for the year. Operating expenses of P 86,400,000 together with rental revenues were incurred uniformly throughout the year. The building, comprising 80 percent of the original purchase price (balance attributed to land), has an estimated useful life of 20 years and is being depreciated in straight-line fashion. By year-end, the Mexican consumer price index rose to 420 from an initial level of 263, averaging 340 during the year.

Required:

a. Prepare financial statements for Sobrero Corporation's first year of operations in terms of the historical cost model and the historical cost-constant dollar model.

b. Compare and evaluate the information content of rate-of-return statistics computed using each of these models.

8. Based on the operating information provided in exercise 7, now assume that Mexico's construction cost index increased by 80 percent during the year while the price of vacant properties adjacent to Sobrero Corporation's hotel increased in value by 90 percent.

Required: Using this information to restate the value of the company's non-monetary assets, what would Sobrero Corporation's financial statements look like under the current cost model?

9. The balance sheet of Rackett & Ball plc., a U.K.-based sporting goods manufacturer, is presented here. Figures are stated in millions of pounds (£m). During the year, the producers' price index increased from 100 to 120, averaging 110. The aggregate current cost of sales, depreciation, and monetary working capital adjustment is assumed to be £216m.

	20X1 £m	20X2 £m
Fixed Assets:		
Intangible assets	56	150
Tangible assets	260	318
Investments	4	5
	320	479
Current Assets:		
Inventory	175	220
Trade receivable	242	270
Marketable securities	30	50
Cash	25	25
	472	565
Current Liabilities:		
Trade payables	(170)	(160)
Net current assets	302	405
Total assets less current liabilities	622	884
Long-term liabilities	85	128
Total net assets	237	356
Owner's Equity:		
Common stock	42	42
Premium on common stock	87	87
Retained earnings	108	227
Total owner's equity	237	356

Required: Assuming that changes in the producers price index are a satisfactory measure of the change in R&B's purchasing power calculate, as best as you can, R&B's monetary working capital adjustment and its gearing adjustment.

10. Aztec Corporation, a U.S. subsidiary in Mexico City, begins and ends its calendar year with an inventory balance of P 500 million. The dollar/peso exchange rate on January 1 was $0.02 = P 1. During the year, the U.S. general price level advances from 180 to 198 while the Mexican general price level doubles. The exchange rate on December 31 was $0.015 = P 1.

Required:

a. Using the temporal method of translation, calculate the dollar equivalent of the inventory balance by first restating for foreign inflation, then translating to U.S. dollars.

b. Repeat part (a), but translate the nominal peso balances to dollars before restating for U.S. inflation.

c. Which dollar figure do you think provides the more useful information?

d. If you are dissatisfied with either result, suggest a method that would provide more useful information than those in parts (a) or (b).

11. Cappucino Enterprises, S.A., a U.S. subsidiary domiciled in Italy, accounts for its inventories on a FIFO basis. The company translates its inventories to dollars at the current rate. Year-end inventories are recorded at 10,920,000 lira (L). During the year, the replacement cost of inventories increases by 20 percent. Inflation and exchange rate information are as follows:

> January 1: Specific price index = 100; $1 = L1,300
> December 31: Specific price index = 120; $1 = L1,690

Required: Based on this information, calculate the dollar current cost adjustment for cost of sales while avoiding a double charge for inflation.

12. The year-end balance sheet of Helsinki Corporation, a wholly owned British affiliate in Finland, is reproduced here. Relevant exchange rate and inflation information is also provided.

Balance Sheet	20X3			
Cash	FIM 2,000		Short-term debt	FIM 8,000
Inventory	8,000		Long-term debt	25,000
Plant & equipment, net	20,000			
Other assets	5,000		Owners' equity	2,000
Total	FIM 35,000			FIM 35,000

Exchange rate and price information:

January 1:	General price index = 300
	FIM 7.2 = £1
December 31:	General price index = 390
	FIM 9.0 = £1

Required: Using this information, calculate the monetary adjustment without double counting for the effects of foreign inflation (assume that the U.K inflation rate is negligible).

Case 7–1 Kashmir Enterprises

Kashmir Enterprises, an Indian carpet manufacturer, begins the calendar year with the following Indian rupee (Rpe) balances:

Cash	**920,000**	**Accounts payable**	**420,000**
Inventory	640,000	Owners' equity	1,140,000
	$1,560,000		$1,560,000

During the first week in January, the company acquires additional manufacturing supplies costing Rpe 2,400,000 on account and a warehouse for Rpe 3,200,000 paying Rpe 800,000 down and signing a 20-year, 10 percent note for the balance. The warehouse (assume no salvage value) is depreciated straight-line over the period of the note. Cash sales were Rpe 6,000,000 for the year, selling and administrative expenses, including office rent, were Rpe 1,200,000. Payments on account totaled Rpe 2,200,000 while inventory on hand at year-end was Rpe 80,000. Except for interest expense paid on December 31, all other cash receipts and payments took place uniformly throughout the year.

On January 1, the U.S. dollar/rupee exchange rate was $.025 = Rpe 1; at year-end it was $.02 = Rpe 1. The average exchange rate during the year was $.022. The Indian consumer price index rose from 128 to 160 by December 31, averaging 144 during the year. At the new financial statement date, the cost to replace supplies had increased by 30 percent; the cost to rebuild a comparable warehouse (based on the construction cost index) was approximately Rpe 480,000.

REQUIRED

1. Assuming beginning inventories were acquired when the general price index level was 128, prepare Kashmir Enterprises' financial statements (i.e., income statement and balance sheet) under the (a) conventional original transactions cost model, (b) historical cost-constant rupee model, and (c) current cost model.

2. Comment on which financial statement set gives Indian readers the most useful performance and wealth measures.

3. Now assume that Kashmir Enterprises' U.S. headquarters management wants to see the Indian rupee statements in U.S. dollars. Two price level foreign currency translation procedures are requested. The first is to translate Kashmir's unadjusted rupee statements to dollars (use the current rate method) and then restate the resulting dollar amounts accounting for U.S. inflation (the U.S. general price level at the financial statement date was 108, up 8 percent from the previous year). The second is to restate the Indian rupee statements accounting for inflation (using the historical cost-constant franc model), then translate the adjusted amounts to dollars using the current rate. Comment on which of the two resulting sets of dollar statements you prefer for use by American readers. (The U.S. general price level averaged 104 during the year).

Case 7–2   Icelandic Enterprises, Inc.

In 1993 Icelandic Enterprises was incorporated in Reykjavik to manufacture and distribute women's cosmetics in Iceland. All of its outstanding stock was acquired at the beginning of 2001 by International Cosmetics, Ltd. (IC), a U.S.-based MNE headquartered in Sandy Hook, Connecticut.

Competition with major cosmetics manufacturers both within and outside Iceland was very keen. As a result, Icelandic Enterprises (now a wholly-owned subsidiary of International Cosmetics), was under constant pressure to expand its product offerings. This required frequent investment in new equipment. Competition also affected the company's pricing flexibility. As the demand for cosmetics was price elastic, Icelandic lost market share every time it raised its prices. Accordingly, when Icelandic increased selling prices, it did so in small amounts while increasing its advertising and promotional efforts to minimize the adverse effects of the price increase on sales volume.

International Cosmetic's financial policies with respect to Icelandic were dictated by two major considerations: the continued inflation and devaluation of the Icelandic kronur (Ikr). To counter these, headquarters management was eager to recoup its dollar investment in Icelandic Enterprises through dollar dividends. If dividends were not possible, subsidiary managers were instructed to preserve IC's original equity investment in Icelandic kronur. Due to the unstable kronur, all financial management analyses were made in dollars.

International Cosmetics designated the dollar as Icelandic Enterprise's functional currency. Accordingly, it adopted the temporal method when translating Icelandic's kronur accounts to their dollar equivalents. All monetary assets and liabilities were translated to dollars using the current exchange rate. All nonmonetary items, except those assets that were carried at current values, were translated using historical rates. Income and expense accounts were translated at average exchange rates prevailing during the year, except depreciation and amortization charges that were related to assets translated at historical exchange rates. Translation gains and losses were taken directly to consolidated earnings.

Adjusting Icelandic's accounts for inflation was not attempted. Management believed that such restatements were too costly and subjective. IC's management also claimed that translating Icelandic's accounts to dollars automatically approximated the impact of inflation.

The following is a comparative balance sheet and income statement for Icelandic Enterprises, along with relevant foreign exchange and general price level indexes.

REQUIRED

1. Comment on International Cosmetic's policies on the basis of "as reported" earnings.
2. Is management correct in stating that by translating their financial reports into dollars they "automatically approximate the impact of inflation"?
3. What revised actions/policies would you recommend based on inflation-adjusted figures?

| Balance Sheet | 2001 | | 2002 | |
(000's)	Dollars	Kronur	Dollars	Kronur
Cash	7,715	221,176	9,086	368,414
Accts. receivable	18,000	516,078	21,202	859,633
Inventory	118,706	2,949,017	154,988	4,912,187
PP&E, net[1]	283,252	1,493,250	265,706	2,032,050
Other assets	22,022	272,013	28,838	716,426
Total	449,695	5,451,534	479,820	8,888,710
Current liab's	94,748	2,716,438	82,673	3,351,980
Due to parent	50,000	1,433,500	50,000	2,027,250
Capital stock[2]	98,758	713,430	98,758	713,430
Retained earnings	206,189	588,166	248,389	2,796,050
Total	449,695	5,451,534	479,820	8,888,710

| Income Statement | 2001 | | 2002 | |
	Dollars	Kronur	Dollars	Kronur
Net sales	328,805	8,168,500	462,248	14,650,500
Cost of sales	150,012	3,726,750	199,874	6,334,800
Gross margin	178,793	4,341,750	262,354	8,315,700
Selling expenses	78,493	1,950,000	110,841	3,513,000
Gen. & adm. exp.	28,680	712,500	49,647	1,573,500
Depreciation	44,056	221,250	47,002	305,700
Operating income	27,564	1,458,000	54,864	2,923,500
Interest expense	7,064	175,500	11,453	363,000
Income before taxes[3]	20,500	1,282,500	43,411	2,560,500

National Inflation and Exchange Rates[4]

	1997	1998	1999	2000	2001	2002
Consumer price index:						
Iceland	63.1	100.0	150.6	224.7	418.2	547.0
United States	88.1	100.0	110.4	117.1	120.9	126.1
Kronur per dollar:						
Year-end	3.949	6.239	8.173	16.625	28.670	40.545
Average	3.526	4.798	7.224	12.352	24.843	31.694

[1]Plant and equipment were acquired at the beginning of each period as follows: 1998, Ikr 1,250,000; 1999, Ikr 427,500; 2000, Ikr 375,000; 2001, Ikr 160,000; 2002, Ikr 844,500. Depreciation is calculated at 10 percent per annum. A full year's depreciation is charged in the year of acquisition. Assume there were no disposals during any of the years.

[2]Common stock was acquired when the exchange rate was Ikr 7.224 = $1.

[3]Inclusive of translation gains and losses.

[4]The inflation and exchange rate relationships used here are based on actual data for an earlier period.

CHAPTER 8

INTERNATIONAL ACCOUNTING HARMONIZATION

INTRODUCTION

"Harmonization" is a process of increasing the compatibility of accounting practices by setting limits on how much they can vary. Harmonized standards are free of logical conflicts, and should improve the comparability of financial information from different countries.

Efforts to harmonize accounting standards began even before the creation of the International Accounting Standards Committee (IASC) in 1973.[1] More recently, companies seeking capital outside of their home markets and investors attempting to diversify their investments internationally faced increasing problems resulting from national differences in accounting measurement, disclosure, and auditing. In response, harmonization efforts accelerated during the 1990s. International accounting harmonization now is one of the most important issues facing securities regulators, stock exchanges, and those who prepare or use financial statements.

People occasionally use the terms *harmonization* and *standardization* interchangeably, but in contrast to harmonization, standardization generally means the imposition of a rigid and narrow set of rules, and may even apply a single standard or rule to all situations. Standardization does not accommodate national differences and, therefore, is more difficult to implement internationally. Harmonization is much more flexible and open; it does not take a one-size-fits-all approach, but accommodates national differences and has made a great deal of progress internationally in recent years.

The European Union's Fourth Company Law Directive illustrates the concept of harmonization. The directive (discussed in more detail later in this chapter) specifies many accounting measurement and disclosure requirements. By narrowing the range of accounting alternatives, but at the same time allowing more than one basis for measuring costs, the directive *harmonizes* accounting for valuing long-term tangible assets. In

---

[1]The IASC is the predecessor body to the International Accounting Standards Board (IASB).

valuing long-term tangible assets, the directive permits historical cost, price-level-adjusted historical cost, and current cost measurements.[2]

Comparability of financial information is a more clear-cut concept than is *harmonization*. Financial information produced under different accounting, disclosure, and/or auditing systems is comparable if it is similar in enough ways that financial statement users can compare it (at least along some dimensions) without needing to be intimately familiar with more than one system. The substantial differences in financial reporting requirements and practices around the world, and the increasing need of financial statement users to compare information from different countries, have been the driving forces behind the movement to harmonize accounting.

Accounting harmonization includes the harmonization of (1) accounting standards (which deal with measurement and disclosure); (2) disclosures made by publicly traded companies in connection with securities offerings and stock exchange listings; and (3) auditing standards.[3]

Efforts to achieve international accounting harmonization have been marked by sharp debates. Should accounting standards be harmonized, standardized, or left alone? Should all enterprises, large and small, in all industries be subject to the same standards? Is it reasonable that less-developed countries adopt the same accounting standards as those used in highly developed countries?

A SURVEY OF INTERNATIONAL HARMONIZATION

ADVANTAGES OF INTERNATIONAL HARMONIZATION

Proponents of international harmonization claim that harmonization (or even standardization) has many advantages. Sir Bryan Carsberg, former Secretary General of the IASC, wrote the following in September 2000:

> A thoughtful approach to assessing the desirability of international harmonisation recognises that the costs and benefits vary from case to case. Those of us who have English as their mother tongue probably feel fortunate that English is becoming a widely used second language throughout the world. But, even if it were feasible, we would stop short of seeking agreement that English or some other common language should replace the 6,800 or so languages currently in use. We would recognise that language is an indispensable vehicle for culture and that the elimination of different languages would entail enormous losses in literature and other expressions of culture.
>
> What about the harmonisation of taxation and social security systems? Businesses would experience considerable benefits in planning, systems costs, training and so on from harmonisation. But this case shows us another disadvantage of harmonisation. Taxation and social security systems have powerful

---

[2]In contrast, "standardization" would apply a single valuation basis. For example, in the United States a historical transaction cost-based measurement rule is applied to all long-term tangible assets.

[3]This is just a partial listing. Harmonization also is concerned with such diverse areas as offering and listing requirements, auditor education, and immediate public disclosure of material information, to name a few. In this chapter, the term "accounting" often refers to accounting standards, which deal with both measurement and disclosure.

influences on economic efficiency. Different systems have different effects. The ability to compare the working of different approaches in different countries enables countries to make improvements to their systems. Countries are in competition and the competition forces them to adopt efficient systems through the operation of a kind of market force. Agreement on a unified system of taxation would be like the establishment of a cartel and would deprive us of the benefits of competition among countries.

The case for harmonisation in accounting standards is a particularly strong one. Accounting has relatively low cultural value. Competition among different accounting approaches, while not without merit, probably is better left to optional extras in reporting rather than the basic reporting systems; and the potential cost savings and other benefits are very great. . . .

The accounting profession really is becoming global. But perhaps that term is better avoided. Perhaps we should raise our sights and look for universal accounting standards.[4]

Others have argued that financial statement users have difficulty interpreting information produced under nondomestic accounting systems. They claim that harmonization will make it more likely that users will interpret the information correctly, and thus make better decisions based on that information.

CRITICISMS OF INTERNATIONAL STANDARDS

The internationalization of accounting standards has had many critics. As early as 1971 (before the IASC was formed), some said that international standards setting was too simple a solution for a complex problem. It was claimed that accounting, as a social science, has built-in flexibility and that its ability to adapt to widely different situations is one of its most important values. It was doubted that international standards could be flexible enough to handle differences in national backgrounds, traditions, and economic environments, and some thought that it would be a politically unacceptable challenge to national sovereignty.

Other observers have argued that international accounting standard setting is essentially a tactic of the large international accounting service firms to expand their markets. Multinational accounting firms are indispensable, it is said, to apply international standards in national environments where those standards might seem distant and complex. Also, as international financial institutions and international markets insist on the use of international standards, only large international accounting firms can meet this demand.

Moreover, it has been feared that adoption of international standards may create "standards overload." Corporations must respond to an ever-growing array of national, social, political, and economic pressures and are hard put to comply with additional complex and costly international requirements. A related argument is that national political concerns frequently intrude on accounting standards and that international political influences would compromise accounting standards unacceptably.

---

[4]Sir Bryan Carsberg, "Raising Our Sights," *Accountancy* (September 2000): 1.

Still others argue that there is now a well-developed international capital market that has grown rapidly in recent years without "global GAAP." One commentator states:

> Harmonization of international accounting principles is unlikely to come about. Too many different national groups have vested interests in maintaining their own standards and practices which have developed from widely different perspectives and histories. There is not a single powerful champion of the proposal for harmonization. There is no authoritative body with the ability to mandate the adoption of Global GAAP. . . . I have argued that Global GAAP is unlikely to be achieved due to the institutional impediments in the standard setting process and because there is no demonstrated need in order to fuel the growth of robust international capital markets.[5]

Events since Mr. Goeltz's article have not been in line with this statement. International harmonization has moved forward with increasing speed, and many of the "different national groups" have been prominent in this effort.

RECONCILIATION AND MUTUAL RECOGNITION

As international equity issuance and trading grow, problems related to distributing financial statements in nondomestic jurisdictions become more important. Some supporters argue that international harmonization will help resolve problems associated with filings of cross-border financial statements.

Two other approaches have been advanced as possible solutions to problems related to cross-border financial statement filings: (1) reconciliation; and (2) mutual recognition (also known as "reciprocity").[6] With reconciliation, foreign firms can prepare financial statements using home country accounting standards, but also must provide a reconciliation between critical accounting measures (such as net income and shareholders' equity) of the home country and the country where the financial statements are being filed. For example, the U.S. Securities and Exchange Commission (SEC) permits foreign registrants to use accounting principles other than U.S. GAAP as the basis for financial statements they file. However, the SEC also requires reconciliation disclosures (see Chapter 5).

Reconciliations are less costly than preparing a full set of financial statements under a different set of accounting principles. However, they only provide a summary, not the full picture of the enterprise.

Mutual recognition exists when regulators outside the home country accept a foreign firm's financial statements based on home country principles. For example, the London Stock Exchange accepts U.S. GAAP-based financial statements in filings made by foreign companies. Reciprocity does not improve the cross-country comparability of financial statements, and can create an "unlevel playing field" in that it may allow foreign companies to apply less rigorous standards than apply to domestic companies.

---

[5]Richard K. Goeltz, "International Accounting Harmonization: The Impossible (And Unnecessary?) Dream," *Accounting Horizons* (March 1991): 85–88.
[6]See Carrie Bloomer, ed., *The IASC-U.S. Comparison Project: A Report on the Similarities and Differences Between IASC Standards and U.S. GAAP, Second Edition,* Norwalk, CT: Financial Accounting Standards Board, 1999.

EVALUATION

The harmonization debate may never be completely settled. Some arguments against harmonization have merit. However, increasing evidence shows that the goal of international harmonization of accounting, disclosure, and auditing has been so widely accepted that the trend towards international harmonization will continue or accelerate. Harmonization debates aside, all dimensions of accounting *are* becoming harmonized worldwide. Growing numbers of companies are voluntarily adopting International Accounting Standards (IAS). Many countries have adopted IAS in their entirety, base their national standards on IAS, or allow the use of IAS. Leading international organizations and standard-setting bodies throughout the world (European Commission, World Trade Organization, Organization for Economic Cooperation and Development, among others) strongly support the goals of the International Accounting Standards Board (IASB). Progress in harmonizing disclosure and auditing has been impressive.

Finally, national differences in the underlying factors that lead to variation in accounting, disclosure, and auditing practice are narrowing as capital and product markets become more international. Many companies have voluntarily adopted IAS. These companies see economic benefits in adopting accounting and disclosure standards that are credible internationally. Also, as discussed in Chapter 5, companies are voluntarily expanding their disclosures in line with IAS in response to demand from institutional investors and other financial statement users. The success of recent harmonization efforts by international organizations may demonstrate that harmonization is happening as a natural response to economic forces.

APPLICABILITY OF INTERNATIONAL STANDARDS

International accounting standards are used as a result of (a) international or political agreement, (b) voluntary (or professionally encouraged) compliance, or (c) decisions by national accounting standard setters. The application of the EU accounting-related directives results from an international political agreement. Increasing numbers of companies are deciding that the use of IAS is in their interest even if it is not required. Many countries now allow companies to base their financial statements on IAS, and some require it.

When accounting standards are applied through political, legal, or regulatory procedures, statutory rules typically govern the process. Interested parties determine what the rules are and how they should be implemented. Legal and regulatory cases flesh out the details. The EU is the only instance to date where a form of internationalization of accounting standards is broadly applicable and legally enforceable.

All other international standards efforts in accounting are voluntary in nature. Their acceptance depends on those who use accounting standards. There is no problem when an international standard and a national standard are the same, but when national and international standards differ, national standards usually come first (take primacy). For example, multinational companies may use international accounting standards and also accept and use national standards. When companies adopt more than one set of accounting standards, the result is often that they must issue one set of reports for each set of accounting standards they adopt. This multiple approach to financial reporting by multinational corporations is likely to increase.

SOME SIGNIFICANT EVENTS IN THE HISTORY OF INTERNATIONAL ACCOUNTING STANDARD SETTING

1959—Jacob Kraayenhof, founding partner of a major European firm of independent accountants, urges that work on international accounting standards begin.

1961—Groupe d'Etudes, consisting of practicing accounting professionals, is established in Europe to advise European Union authorities on matters concerning accounting.

1966—Accountants International Study Group is formed by professional institutes in Canada, the United Kingdom and the United States.

1973—International Accounting Standards Committee (IASC) is created.

1976—Organization for Economic Cooperation and Development (OECD) issues its Declaration on Investment in Multinational Enterprises containing guidelines on "Disclosure of Information."

1977—International Federation of Accountants (IFAC) is founded.

1977—Group of Experts appointed by United Nations Economic and Social Council issues four-part report on *International Standards of Accounting and Reporting for Transnational Corporations*.

1978—Commission of the European Community issues Fourth Directive as first move toward European accounting harmonization.

1981—IASC establishes consultative group of nonmember organizations to widen the input to international standard setting.

1984—London Stock Exchange states that it expects listed companies not incorporated within the United Kingdom or Ireland to comply with international accounting standards.

1987—The International Organization of Securities Commissions (IOSCO) resolves at its annual conference to promote the use of common standards in accounting and auditing practices.

1989—IASC issues Exposure Draft 32 on comparability of financial statements. *Framework for the Preparation and Presentation of Financial Statements* is published by IASC.

1995—IASC Board and IOSCO Technical Committee agree on a work plan whose successful completion will result in IAS forming a comprehensive core set of standards. Successful completion of these standards will allow the IOSCO Technical Committee to recommend endorsement of IAS for cross-border capital raising and listing purposes in all global markets.

1995—European Commission adopts a new approach to accounting harmonization that would allow the use of IAS by companies listing on international capital markets.

1996—U.S. Securities and Exchange Commission (SEC) announces that it ". . . supports the IASC's objective to develop, as expeditiously as possible, accounting standards that could be used for preparing financial statements that could be used in cross-border offerings."

1998—IOSCO publishes the report "International Disclosure Standards for Cross Border Offerings and Initial Listings by Foreign Issuers."

1999 — International Forum on Accountancy Development (IFAD) meets for the first time in June.

2000 — IOSCO accepts, in toto, all 40 core standards prepared by the IASC in response to IOSCO's 1993 wish list.

2001 — In February the European Commission proposed a regulation that would require all EU companies listed on a regulated market to prepare consolidated accounts in accordance with IAS by 2005.

2001 — International Accounting Standards Board (IASB) succeeded the IASC and assumed its responsibilities on April 1.

OVERVIEW OF MAJOR INTERNATIONAL ORGANIZATIONS PROMOTING ACCOUNTING HARMONIZATION

Six organizations have been key players in setting international accounting standards and in promoting international accounting harmonization:

1. International Accounting Standards Board (IASB)
2. Commission of the European Union (EU)
3. International Organization of Securities Commissions (IOSCO)
4. International Federation of Accountants (IFAC)
5. United Nations Intergovernmental Working Group of Experts on International Standards of Accounting and Reporting (ISAR), part of United Nations Conference on Trade and Development (UNCTAD)
6. Organization for Economic Cooperation and Development Working Group on Accounting Standards (OECD Working Group)

The IASB represents private sector interests and organizations. The EU Commission, referred to as the European Commission (EC), the OECD Working Group, and the ISAR are political entities that derive their powers from international agreements. IFAC's main activities include issuing technical and professional guidance and promoting the adoption of IFAC and IASB pronouncements. IOSCO promotes high standards of regulation, including harmonized accounting and disclosure standards for cross-border capital raising and trading.

The International Forum on Accountancy Development (IFAD) had its first meeting in June 1999. Its stated purpose is to raise accounting and standards worldwide to at least the level of IAS, but in an orderly way that will allow countries to prepare the necessary foundation for them to adopt IAS successfully. IFAC, the World Bank, the seven largest accounting firms (as of 1999), and many other organizations were instrumental in organizing IFAD.

Also important is the International Federation of Stock Exchanges (FIBV), the trade organization for regulated securities and derivative markets worldwide. The FIBV promotes the professional business development of financial markets. One of the FIBV's goals is to establish harmonized standards for business processes (including financial reporting and disclosure) in cross-border trading in securities, including cross-border public offerings.

Many regional accounting organizations (such as the ASEAN Federation of Accountants and the Nordic Federation of Accountants) participate in some cross-country standard setting within their respective regions. The Fédération des Experts Comptables Européens (FEE) (Federation of European Accountants) represents national accounting bodies in Europe. Other regional organizations include the Fédération des Bourses Européennes (FESE), or Federation of European Stock Exchanges, and The Forum of European Securities Commissions (FESCO), created in December 1997 and consisting of 17 securities regulators from 17 European nations.

Refer to Exhibit 8-1 for Web sites offering information about major international organizations and accounting harmonization activities. Exhibit 8-2 presents the Web site addresses of national regulatory and accountancy organizations, many of which are actively involved in accounting harmonization activities.

INTERNATIONAL ACCOUNTING STANDARDS BOARD

The International Accounting Standards Board (IASB), formerly the IASC, is an independent private sector standards-setting body founded in 1973 by professional accounting organizations in nine countries and restructured in 2001. (The reorganization made IASC into an umbrella organization under which the IASB carries out its work.) Before the restructuring, the IASC issued 41 International Accounting Standards (IAS) and a Framework for the Preparation and Presentation of Financial Statements. The IASB's objectives are:

1. to develop, in the public interest, a single set of high quality, understandable and enforceable global accounting standards that require high quality, transparent and comparable information in financial statements and other financial reporting to help participants in the world's capital markets and other users make economic decisions;
2. to promote the use and rigorous application of those standards; and
3. to bring about convergence of national accounting standards and International Accounting Standards to high quality solutions.[7]

The IASB represents over 120 accounting organizations from 91 countries. With a remarkably broad base of support, IASB is the driving force in international accounting standard setting. Exhibit 8-3 lists the current IASB Standards (as of April 2001). IASB Standards are closely compatible with accounting standards promulgated in the United States, Canada, the United Kingdom, and other countries that use Anglo-Saxon accounting. Thus, IASB standards follow the principles of fair presentation and full disclosure (see Chapter 2). The IASB Web site (www.iasb.org.uk) presents a detailed summary of the 34 current IASB standards.

During the first decade of the IASC, international accounting standards were more descriptive than prescriptive. These early standards codified similar national practices

---

[7]See the IASB Web site (http://www.iasb.org.uk).

EXHIBIT 8-1   Web Sites Offering Information about Major International Organizations and Accounting Harmonization Activities
(Note: All Web Site Addresses Begin with "http://")

Organization	*Web Site Address*
Bank for International Settlements	www.bis.org
Confederation of Asian & Pacific Accountants (CAPA)	capa.com.my
Deloitte Touche Tohmatsu IAS Plus Web site	www.iasplus.com
European Union (EU)	europa.eu.int
European Commission—Internal Market and Financial Services	europa.eu.int/comm./internal_market/en/index.htm
Fédération des Experts Comptables Européens (FEE) a/k/a European Federation of Accountants	www.fee.be
FEE *Euro Information Service*	www.euro.fee.be
Federation of European Securities Exchanges a/k/a Fédération des Bourses Européennes (FESE)	www.fese.be
International Accounting Standards Board (ISAB)	www.iasb.org.uk
International Association of Insurance Supervisors (IAIS)	www.iaisweb.org
International Center for Accounting Reform (Russia) (ICAR)	www.icar.ru
International Federation of Accountants (IFAC)	www.ifac.org
International Federation of Stock Exchanges (FIBV)	www.fibv.com
International Finance & Commodities Institute (IFCI) a/k/a International Financial Risk Institute	risk.ifci.ch
International Forum on Accountancy Development (IFAD)	www.ifad.net
International Monetary Fund (IMF)	www.imf.org
International Organization of Securities Commissions (IOSCO)	www.iosco.org
Organization for Economic Co-Operation and Development (OECD)	www.oecd.org
United Nations Conference on Trade and Development (UNCTAD)	www.unctad.org
World Bank	www.worldbank.org
World Trade Organization (WTO)	www.wto.org/

Note: This listing was correct when this book went to press. Web site addresses often change, and occasionally are discontinued. Active Web sites are sometimes temporarily inaccessible due to technical problems.

EXHIBIT 8-2	Web Site Addresses of Selected Regulatory and Accountancy Organizations (All Addresses Begin with the Prefix http://www)
Organization	*Web Site Address*

Government and Regulatory Organizations

Organization	Web Site Address
U.K. Financial Services Authority (FSA)	fsa.gov.uk
U.S. Securities and Exchange Commission (SEC)	sec.gov
U.S. Securities and Exchange Commission (SEC) Edgar Database	sec.gov/edgar.shtml
Search Edgar Database via FreeEdgar	freeedgar.com
French Commission des Operations de Bourse (COB) (in French or English)	cob.fr

National Professional Accountancy Organizations

Organization	Web Site Address
Argentina—Federación Argentina de Consejos Profesionales de Ciencias Económicas	facpce.com.ar
Barbados—The Institute of Chartered Accountants of Barbados	Icab.bb
Belgium—Institut des Experts Comptables	Accountancy.be
Belgium—Institut des Réviseurs d'Entreprises	accountancy.be
Canada—CMA Canada	Cma-canada.org
Canada—Canadian Institute of Chartered Accountants	Cica.ca
Canada—Certified General Accountants' Association of Canada	cga-canada.org
Cyprus—The Institute of Certified Public Accountants of Cyprus	Icpac.org.cy
France—Conseil Supérieur de l'Ordre des Experts-Comptables	Experts-comptables.com
Georgia—Georgian Federation of Professional Accountants and Auditors	Gfpaa.kheta.ge
Germany—Institut der Wirtschaftsprufer in Deutschland (English-language home page under development)	idw.de
Hong Kong—Hong Kong Society of Accountants	Hksa.org.hk
Hong Kong—Hong Kong Association of Accounting Technicians	hkaat.org.hk
India—Institute of Chartered Accountants of India	icai.org
Ireland—Institute of Chartered Accountants in Ireland	icai.ie
Japan—Japanese Institute of Certified Public Accountants	Jicpa.or.jp/n_eng/index.html
Jordan—Arab Society of Certified Accountants	Ascasociety.org
Kenya—Institute of Certified Public Accountants of Kenya	Icpak.com
Korea—Korean Institute of Certified Public Accountants	Kicpa.or.kr
Malaysia—The Malaysian Institute of Accountants	mia.org.my
Malta—The Malta Institute of Accountants	Miamalta.org
Nepal—Institute of Chartered Accountants of Nepal	Ican.org.np
Netherlands—Koninklijk Nederlands Instituut van Registeraccountants	Nivra.nl
New Zealand—Institute of Chartered Accountants of New Zealand	Icanz.co.nz
Nigeria—Institute of Chartered Accountants of Nigeria	Ican.org.ng
Norway—Den norske Revisorforening (DnR)	Revisornett.no

EXHIBIT 8-2 *(cont.)*

Organization	*Web Site Address*
Pakistan—Institute of Cost and Management Accountants of Pakistan	Icmap.com.pk
Pakistan—The Institute of Chartered Accountants of Pakistan	Icpa.org.pk
Philippines—Philippine Institute of Certified Public Accountants	Picpa.com.ph
Romania—Corpul Expertilor Contabili si Contabililor Autorizati din Romania	Ceccar.ro
Singapore—Institute of Certified Public Accountants of Singapore	Accountants.org.sg
South Africa—The South African Institute of Chartered Accountants (SAICA)	Saica.co.za
South Africa—Institute of Commercial and Financial Accountants of Southern Africa	cfa-sa.co.za
Sri Lanka—The Institute of Chartered Accountants of Sri Lanka	Lanka.net/ica
Sweden—Föreningen Auktoriserade Revisorer	far.se
Turkey—Union of Chambers of Certified Public Accountants of Turkey	Turmob.org.tr
U.K.—The Institute of Chartered Accountants in England & Wales	Icaew.co.uk
U.K.—Chartered Institute of Management Accountants	Cimaglobal.com
U.K.—The Association of Chartered Certified Accountants	Acca.org.uk
U.K.—The Chartered Institute of Public Finance and Accountancy	Cipfa.org.uk
U.K.—The Institute of Chartered Accountants of Scotland	Icas.org.uk
U.K.—Association of Accounting Technicians	aat.co.uk
U.S.—American Institute of CPAs	Aicpa.org
U.S.—National Association of State Boards of Accountancy	Nasba.org
U.S.—Public Oversight Board Panel on Audit Effectiveness	Pobauditpanel.org
U.S.—Institute of Management Accountants	imanet.org
U.S.—The Institute of Internal Auditors	Theiia.org
Zimbabwe—The Institute of Chartered Accountants of Zimbabwe	Icaz.org.zw

Accounting Standard Setting Bodies

Australian Accounting Standards Board (AASB)	Aasb.com.au
Canadian Accounting Standards Board (ASB)	Cica.ca/cica/cicawebsite.nsf/public/ SGAccountingStandards
German Accounting Standards Board (GASB)-English	Drsc.de/eng/index.html
New Zealand Accounting Standards Board (go to this site, then click Advocacy Guidance & Standards button)	Icanz.co.nz/ScriptContent/index.cfm
United Kingdom Accounting Standards Board (ASB)	asb.org.uk
U.S. Financial Accounting Standards Board (FASB)	Fasb.org
U.S. Federal Government Accounting Standards Advisory Board (FASAB)	Financenet.gov/fasab.htm

Note: This listing was correct when this book went to press. Web site addresses often change and occasionally are discontinued. Active Web sites are sometimes temporarily inaccessible due to technical problems

EXHIBIT 8-3   Current IASB Standards

Standard	Effective Date	Description
IAS 1	July 1, 1998	Presentation of Financial Statements (replaces IAS 1, Disclosure of Accounting Policies)
IAS 2		No longer effective. Replaced by IAS 27.
IAS 3		No longer effective. Replaced by IAS 27 and IAS 28.
IAS 4		No longer effective. Replaced by IAS 16 and IAS 38.
IAS 5		No longer effective. Replaced by IAS 1.
IAS 6		No longer effective. Replaced by IAS 15.
IAS 7	January 1, 1979	Cash Flow Statements
IAS 8	January 1, 1979	Profit or Loss for the Period, Fundamental Errors and Changes in Accounting Policies
IAS 9		No longer effective. Replaced by IAS 38.
IAS 10	January 1, 2000	Events Occurring after the Balance Sheet Date (In 1998, the portion of IAS 10 dealing with contingencies was replaced by IAS 37.)
IAS 11	January 1, 1980	Construction Contracts
IAS 12	January 1, 1998	Income Taxes (Replaces IAS 12, Accounting for Taxes on Income.)
IAS 13		No longer effective. Superseded by IAS 1.
IAS 14	July 1, 1998	Segment Reporting (Replaces IAS 14, Reporting Financial Information by Segment.)
IAS 15	January 1, 1983	Information Reflecting the Effects of Changing Prices
IAS 16	January 1, 1983	Property, Plant and Equipment
IAS 17	January 1, 1999	Leases (Replaces IAS 17, Accounting for Leases.)
IAS 18	January 1, 1984	Revenue
IAS 19	January 1, 1985	Employee Benefits
IAS 20	January 1, 1984	Accounting for Government Grants and Disclosure of Government Assistance
IAS 21	January 1, 1985	The Effects of Changes in Foreign Exchange Rates
IAS 22	January 1, 1985	Business Combinations
IAS 23	January 1, 1986	Borrowing Costs
IAS 24	January 1, 1986	Related Party Disclosures
IAS 25		No longer effective. Replaced by IAS 39 and IAS 40 effective January 1, 2001.
IAS 26	January 1, 1988	Accounting and Reporting by Retirement Benefit Plans
IAS 27	January 1, 1990	Consolidated Financial Statements and Accounting for Investments in Subsidiaries
IAS 28	January 1, 1990	Accounting for Investments in Associates
IAS 29	January 1, 1990	Financial Reporting in Hyperinflationary Economies
IAS 30	January 1, 1991	Disclosures in the Financial Statements of Banks and Similar Financial Institutions
IAS 31	January 1, 1992	Financial Reporting of Interests in Joint Ventures
IAS 32	January 1, 1996	Financial Instruments: Disclosures and Presentation
IAS 33	January 1, 1998	Earnings Per Share
IAS 34	January 1, 1999	Interim Financial Reporting
IAS 35	January 1, 1999	Discontinuing Operations
IAS 36	July 1, 1999	Impairment of Assets
IAS 37	July 1, 1999	Provisions, Contingent Liabilities and Contingent Assets
IAS 38	July 1, 1999	Intangible Assets
IAS 39	January 1, 2001	Financial Instruments: Recognition and Measurement
IAS 40	January 1, 2001	Investment Property
IAS 41	January 1, 2003	Agriculture

Source: IASB Web site http://www.iasb.org.uk, April 9, 2001.

and excluded *outlier* practices. The IASC started to address more difficult issues during its second 10 years and responded to concerns that its standards included too many alternative accounting treatments and were not rigorous enough.

IASC's Core Standards and the IOSCO Agreement

The IASB (and the former IASC) has been striving to develop accounting standards that will be accepted by securities regulators around the world. As part of that effort, the IASC adopted a work plan to produce a comprehensive core set of high-quality standards. In July 1995 the IOSCO Technical Committee stated its agreement with the work plan, as follows:

> The [IASC] Board has developed a work plan that the Technical Committee agrees will result, upon successful completion, in IAS comprising a comprehensive core set of standards. Completion of comprehensive core standards that are acceptable to the [IOSCO] Technical Committee will allow the Technical Committee to recommend endorsement of IAS for cross border capital raising and listing purposes in all global markets. IOSCO has already endorsed IAS 7, Cash Flow Statements, and has indicated to the IASC that 14 of the existing International Accounting Standards do not require additional improvement, providing that the other core standards are successfully completed.[8]

Refer to Exhibit 8-4 for a list of the 40 core standards.

The Core Standards were completed with the approval of IAS 39 (Financial Instruments: Recognition and Measurement) in December 1998. IOSCO's review of the Core Standards began in 1999, and in 2000 it endorsed the use of IASB Standards for cross-border offerings and listings.

The New IASB Structure

The IASC board formed a Strategy Working Party (SWP) to consider what IASC's strategy and structure should be after completion of the core standards work program. In December 1998, the SWP approved a discussion paper, "Shaping IASC for the Future," to encourage and focus discussion. In November 1999 the IASC board unanimously approved a resolution supporting a proposed new structure with the following main features: (1) IASC would be established as an independent organization; (2) the organization would have two main bodies, the trustees and the board, as well as a Standing Interpretations Committee and Standards Advisory Council; and (3) the trustees would appoint the board members, exercise oversight, and raise the funds needed, whereas the board would have sole responsibility for setting accounting standards.

The restructured IASB met for the first time in April 2001. The IASB, as reorganized, includes the following bodies.[9]

---

[8]In October 1993, Working Party I of IOSCO's Technical Committee agreed to a set of accounting issues that would have to be addressed in a core set of international accounting standards appropriate for use in cross-border offerings and multiple listings.

[9]Much of this section is based on information published on the IASB Web site (http://iasb.org.uk).

EXHIBIT 8-4   IOSCO Core Standards and Corresponding IAS

"Core Standards" as Set Forth in IOSCO's 1993 Wish List	Current IAS (last revision)
General	
1 Disclosure of accounting policies	IAS 1 (1997)
2 Changes in accounting policies	IAS 8 (1993)
3 Information disclosed in financial statements	IAS 1 (1997)
Income Statement	
4 Revenue recognition	IAS 18 (1993)
5 Construction contracts	IAS 11 (1993)
6 Production and purchase costs	IAS 2 (1993)
7 Depreciation	IAS 4 (1976) and IAS 16 (1998)
8 Impairment	IAS 16 (1998)
9 Taxes	IAS 12 (2000)
10 Extraordinary items	IAS 8 (1993)
11 Government grants	IAS 20 (1983)
12 Retirement benefits	IAS 19 (2000)
13 Other employee benefits	IAS 19 (2000)
14 Research and development	IAS 38 (1998)
15 Interest	IAS 23 (1993)
16 Hedging	IAS 39 (2000)
Balance Sheet	
17 Property, plant and equipment	IAS 16 (1998)
18 Leases	IAS 17 (1997)
19 Inventories	IAS 2 (1993)
20 Deferred taxes	IAS 12 (2000)
21 Foreign currency	IAS 21 (1993)
22 Investments	IAS 39 (2000) and IAS 40 (2000)
23 Financial instruments/off balance sheet items	IAS 32 (2000)
24 Joint ventures	IAS 31 (2000)
25 Contingencies	IAS 37 (1998)
26 Events occurring after the balance sheet date	IAS 10 (1999)
27 Current assets and current liabilities	IAS 1 (1997)
28 Business combinations (including goodwill)	IAS 22 (1998)
29 Intangibles other than R&D and goodwill	IAS 38 (1998)
Cash Flow Statement	
30 Cash flow statements	IAS 7 (1992)

EXHIBIT 8-4 *(cont.)*	
"Core Standards" as Set Forth in *IOSCO's 1993 Wish List*	*Current IAS (last revision)*
Other Standards	
31 Consolidated financial statements	IAS 27 (2000)
32 Subsidiaries in hyperinflationary economies	IAS 21 (1993) and IAS 29 (1989)
33 Associates and equity financing	IAS 28 (2000)
34 Segment reporting	IAS 14 (1997)
35 Interim reporting	IAS 34 (1998)
36 Earnings per share	IAS 33 (1997)
37 Related party disclosures	IAS 24 (1984)
38 Discontinuing operations	IAS 35 (1998)
39 Fundamental errors	IAS 8 (1993)
40 Changes in estimates	IAS 8 (1993)

1. **Trustees.** The IASB has 19 trustees: 6 from North America, 6 from Europe, 4 from the Asia/Pacific region, and 3 from any area ("subject to establishing overall geographic balance").[10] The trustees appoint the members of the board; the Standing Interpretations Committee and the Standards Advisory Council are responsible for raising funds, and supervise and review the priorities and operations of the IASB.

2. **IASB Board.** The board establishes and improves standards of financial accounting and reporting for businesses. Its responsibilities include "complete responsibility for all IASB technical matters including the preparation and issuing of international Accounting Standards and Exposure Drafts . . . and final interpretations by the Standing Interpretations Committee," and approving project proposals and methods and procedures for developing standards. The board consists of 14 members, appointed by the trustees to provide "the best available combination of technical skills and background experience of relevant international business and market conditions." All board members are paid IASB employees; 12 are to be full-time and 2 may be part-time. Members are appointed for a 5-year term, renewable once.

3. **Standards Advisory Council.** The Standards Advisory Council, appointed by the trustees, is made up of "about thirty members, having a diversity of geographic and professional backgrounds, appointed for renewable terms of three years." The Standards Advisory Council normally meets 3 times each year. Its responsibilities are to give the board advice on its agenda and priorities, to inform the board of the views "or the organizations and individuals on the council on major standard setting project," and to give "other advice" to the board or the trustees.

4. **Standing Interpretations Committee (SIC).** The SIC consists of 12 members appointed by the trustees. The SIC interprets "the application of International Accounting Standards, in the context of IASB's framework," publishes draft interpretations and reviews public comments on them, and obtains board approval for final interpretations.

---

[10] All direct quotations in this section are from the IASB Constitution as of April 9, 2001, found on its Web site (http://www.iasb.org.uk).

The IASB follows due process in setting accounting standards. For each standard, the board may publish a "Draft Statement of Principles" or other discussion document that sets out the various possible requirements for the standard and the arguments for and against each one. Subsequently, the board publishes an "Exposure Draft" for public comment, and it then examines the arguments put forward in the comment process before deciding on the final form of the standard. An Exposure Draft and final standard can be issued only when 8 members of the board have voted in favor of doing so.[11]

RECOGNITION AND SUPPORT FOR THE IASB

International Accounting Standards are now widely accepted around the world. For example, they are (1) used by many countries as the basis for national accounting requirements; (2) used as an international benchmark in many major industrialized countries and emerging market countries that develop their own standards; (3) accepted by many stock exchanges and regulators that allow foreign or domestic companies to file financial statements prepared in conformance with IAS; and (4) recognized by the EC and other supranational bodies. In 1995, the EC endorsed IAS, stating:

> Rather than amend existing Directives, the proposal is to improve the present situation by associating the EU with the efforts undertaken by IASC and IOSCO towards a broader international harmonisation of accounting standards.

In 2001, the EC announced plans to require all EU companies listed on recognized stock exchanges to use IASB in preparing consolidated financial statements no later than 2005.

Many large European companies (e.g., Bayer, Schering, and Roche) have switched to IAS in response to investor and analyst demand for enhanced disclosure and improved financial reporting quality. For example, Bayer's chairman stated that use of IAS would "provide our stockholders, lenders, and the general public with more comprehensive information. It also improves the international comparability of our figures."[12]

Many companies now refer to their use of IAS in annual reports. As Exhibit 8-5 shows, IASB lists 168 companies in April 2001 that use IAS. For a company to be included on the IASB list, the auditor's report and summary of accounting policies, or footnotes, must state that the financial statements conform to IAS without qualification.

Exhibit 8-5 shows that German and Swiss companies form the largest national groups of companies that use IAS. This suggests that these companies believe that financial statements based on IAS will give them more credibility than financial statements based on national accounting requirements. This is not surprising, because low levels of disclosure and a great degree of accounting flexibility have characterized both German and Swiss accounting.

U.S. SECURITIES AND EXCHANGE COMMISSION RESPONSE TO IAS

The SEC does not accept IAS as a basis for financial statements filed by companies listing on U.S. stock exchanges. However, the SEC is under increasing pressure to make U.S. capital markets more accessible to non-U.S. issuers. It is impossible to predict whether

---

[11]Source: IASB Web site (http://www.iasb.org.uk) April 9, 2001.
[12]Daren Nickel Anhalt, "Accounting Move Aids Growth," *Pensions & Investments* (June 12, 1995): 14, 17.

EXHIBIT 8-5 Companies Referring to Their Use of International Accounting Standards in 2001	
Country	*Number of Companies*
Austria	9
Bahrain	6
China	2
Cyprus	2
Czech Republic	2
Denmark	11
Finland	3
France	1
Germany	61
Hong Kong	5
Hungary	3
Kuwait	1
Latvia	1
South Africa	3
Sweden	1
Switzerland	50
Turkey	2
United Arab Emirates	4
Zimbabwe	1
Total	**168**

Source: This information is tabulated from "Companies Referring to Their Use of IAS" on the IASB Web site (http://www.iasb.org.uk) as of April 9, 2001. This list does not claim to be complete.

the SEC will ever accept financial statements prepared in conformance with IAS in filings by non-U.S. registrants. In 1996 the SEC expressed support for the IASB's objective to develop accounting standards for use in financial statements used in cross-border offerings. However, the SEC also stated that three conditions must be met for it to accept IASB standards. By stating these conditions (in following list), the SEC has given itself great flexibility as to how far it will accept the use of IAS by foreign registrants.[13]

1. The standards must include a core set of accounting pronouncements that constitutes a comprehensive, generally accepted basis of accounting;
2. The standards must be of high quality—they must result in comparability and transparency, and they must provide for full disclosure; and
3. The standards must be rigorously interpreted and applied.

COMPARISONS BETWEEN IAS AND OTHER COMPREHENSIVE BODIES OF ACCOUNTING PRINCIPLES

Numerous analyses have compared IAS to other bodies of accounting principles. There are several motivations for these analyses. Regulators and standard setters in many

---

[13]U.S. Securities and Exchange Commission, "News Release—SEC Statement Regarding International Accounting Standards," Washington D.C.: U.S. Securities and Exchange Commission, April 11, 1996.

nations want to be aware of the degree of conformity between home principles and IAS, the extent to which home principles have to be revised to be in conformance with IAS, or the acceptability of IAS using home country standards as a benchmark.

The Financial Accounting Standards Board (FASB) began a major project comparing IAS and U.S. standards in 1995, and published detailed reports in 1996 and 1999.[14] The IASC-U.S. GAAP Comparison Project was part of FASB's plan for international activities, which includes promotion of international comparability of accounting standards. A key goal of the study was to provide information for assessing the acceptability of IAS for securities listings in the United States.

The FASB analysis was structured around five categories of similarities and differences: recognition differences; measurement differences; alternatives; lack of requirements or guidance; and other differences. For example, an IAS and U.S. standard might use similar recognition criteria but use different measurement approaches, or perhaps one set of standards addresses a topic not explicitly addressed by the other. One standard might provide requirements or guidance for a particular topic not covered by its counterpart, or permit a choice between two or more alternative accounting methods for a similar transaction, where its counterpart uses a single method.

David Cairns, former Secretary-General of the IASC, prepared a highly useful analysis of the key differences and similarities between IAS and U.S. GAAP, based primarily on the FASB study.[15] Cairns emphasizes that determining whether IAS require or allow the same accounting treatments as are required by U.S. GAAP (or vice versa) is not straightforward, and he presents examples of the complexities and ambiguities involved. Although it is possible for U.S. GAAP companies to report compliance with IAS and vice versa, recent changes to both IAS and U.S. GAAP make such disclosures difficult to interrupt.

EUROPEAN UNION (EU)

The Treaty of Rome established the EU in 1957, with the goal of harmonizing the legal and economic systems of its member states. The EU presently comprises 15 member countries (Austria, Belgium, Denmark, Finland, France, Germany, Greece, Ireland, Italy, Luxembourg, The Netherlands, Portugal, Spain, Sweden, and the United Kingdom), and is preparing to expand in eastern and southern Europe. In contrast to the IASB, which has no authority to require implementation of its accounting standards, the EC (the governing body of the EU) has full enforcement powers for its accounting directives throughout the member states.

The EC embarked on a major program of company law harmonization soon after it was formed.[16] EC directives now cover all aspects of company law. Several have a di-

---

[14]Bloomer, Carrie, Ed., *The IASC-U.S. Comparison Project: A Report on the Similarities and Differences between IASC Standards and U.S. GAAP*, Norwalk, CT: Financial Accounting Standards Board, 1996; and Bloomer, Carrie, Ed., *The IASC-U.S. Comparison Project: A Report on the Similarities and Differences between IASC Standards and U.S. GAAP, Second Edition*, Norwalk, CT: Financial Accounting Standards Board, 1999.

[15]David Cairns, "Waving a Different Flag," *Accountancy* (September 2000): 104–106.

[16]EU directives become law of member states through a complex, lengthy process. Preliminary work leads to the issuance of a draft directive (i.e., exposure draft) by the EU. When a draft directive is broadly

rect bearing on accounting. Of these, many consider the Fourth, Seventh, and Eighth Directives to be historically and substantively the most important.

In June 2000, the commission adopted a financial reporting strategy that will include modernizing the Fourth and Seventh Directives during 2001 and 2002. The commission will also work to create stronger enforcement, based on "a high quality statutory audit as well as a strengthened coordination among European securities regulators to ensure a proper enforcement of accounting standards."[17]

FOURTH DIRECTIVE

The EU's Fourth Directive, issued in 1978, is the broadest and most comprehensive set of accounting rules within the EU framework. Both public and private companies must comply.

Fourth Directive requirements include the following:[18]

1. *Format* rules for the balance sheet (Articles 9 and 10) and the profit and loss account (Articles 23–26). These reflect the French and German traditions of detailed statutory prescriptions of format, but include options to meet the needs of different national regulations and practices.
2. *Disclosure* requirements (Article 43) average existing practice among EU member states, with options where there can be serious conflict.
3. *Valuation* rules (Articles 31–42) based upon historical cost but with alternative rules allowing current values. Standard-setters in the United Kingdom, Ireland, and the Netherlands were actively encouraging the adoption of current cost accounting when the directive was issued.
4. *The true and fair view* (Article 2) prevails over specific provisions where circumstances justify it. These circumstances are exceptional and may be defined by individual member states in the context of their own accounting systems.

The overriding requirement—that companies must give a true and fair view—holds true for footnote disclosures, just as it does for financial statements. Therefore, companies may have to make disclosures beyond those specifically required, which are:

- A description of major accounting policies.
- A list of affiliates in which a company holds 20 percent or more of shares.
- Details of changes in shareholders' equity and the number of shares in each class of stock outstanding. (Note that a statement of changes in shareholders' equity is not required.)
- Details of long-term and secured debt.
- Details of commitments and contingencies, including separate disclosure of pension obligations.

---

acceptable (after hearings and other evaluation procedures), it is submitted to the member states for ratification after approval from the European Council. After the EU adopts a directive, each member state adopts and implements it. Directives are binding on member states, but the method of implementation is left to the discretion of national authorities.

[17]"International Accounting Standards: Mandatory for Listed Companies by 2005." *Single Market News,* no. 25 (March 2001): 18–19.

[18]Per Thorell and Geoffrey Whittington, "The Harmonization of Accounting Within the European Union—Problems, Perspectives and Strategies," *The European Accounting Review* 3 (1994): 218.

- Segment information, including sales by type of product and by geographical area. A company may omit this information if it is "seriously prejudicial" to its activities.
- The average number of employees and total personnel cost—for example, wages, social security, and pensions by category of employees.
- Directors' compensation, loans, and advances.
- Differences between income taxes currently payable and the amount charged to operations, and the extent to which operating results have been affected by special income tax incentives.

Financial statement elements must be stated in accordance with certain fundamental accounting concepts including historical cost, going concern, prudence, accrual accounting, and consistency. The directive also requires the following specific practices and alternatives:

1. *Property, plant and equipment*—Fixed assets with a limited useful economic life must be depreciated by systematic annual charges to operations. If a member country allows any special tax incentives that result in excessive depreciation charges to income for any period, companies must disclose the nature and amount of the charge.
2. *Intercorporate investments*—All holdings in affiliated enterprises should be valued at cost. However, member countries may allow use of the equity method, provided there is full disclosure of all changes in intercorporate investment accounts. Unrealized equity method income from affiliates must be shown as a nondistributable item in owners' equity.[19]
3. *Intangible assets*—Amounts capitalized, such as goodwill, formation and start-up expenses, and research and development costs should be amortized over a period no longer than 5 years. If they wish, member countries may authorize a longer period of amortization for research and development costs and for goodwill, but the period may not exceed the asset's economic useful life.
4. *Inventories*—Stated amounts must be valued at the lower of cost or market. Member countries may allow actual cost, FIFO, LIFO, weighted average, or a similar cost method. Or they may allow more than one of these methods. If there is a material difference between replacement cost and the stated amount at the balance sheet date, as happens with LIFO, companies must disclose the difference.
5. *Current assets*—Individual items should be valued at the lower of cost (purchase price or production cost) or market.
6. *Liabilities*—All foreseeable liabilities and potential losses must be provided for, even if they become apparent after year-end.
7. *Long-term debt*—If long-term debt is issued at a discount, a *reasonable amount* of amortization is required each year and the total must be completely written off no later than the time when the debt is repaid.
8. *Organization expenses*—While subject to the same amortization rules as other intangible assets, there is a dividends limitation rule regarding organization expenses. No dividends are to be paid until unrestricted retail earnings are at least equal in amount to any unamortized organization expenses.

---

[19]The Seventh Directive requires that the equity method be used in consolidated financial statements.

9. *Inflation accounting*—As noted previously, member countries may either permit or require companies to present primary or supplementary inflation-adjusted financial statements. The member country's legislation should specify, in detail, the methods companies must follow in arriving at reported amounts. The directive lists the following possible bases for this accounting:

- Revaluation of tangible fixed assets (i.e., property, plant, and equipment) and financial fixed assets such as investments or loans.
- Replacement cost for plant, equipment, and inventories.
- Valuation of all financial statement items by a method designed to recognize the effects of inflation.[20]

The implementation options allowed to member countries were utilized differentially. For instance, Article 2 (5) allows member states to define "exceptional circumstances" that would require departures from any provision of the Fourth Directive in order to give a "true and fair view." No member state has utilized this option. On the other hand, Article 47 (2)(a)(b) allows member countries the option to permit preparation and publication of only abridged balance sheets and abridged notes thereto. All EC member states have used this option in whole or in part. Article 45 allows the option of omitting disclosure of sales and geographical locations of business segments. All member countries authorize such omission. Thus, it is of utmost importance that the implementation status of each directive in each member country be accorded as much attention as the directive itself.[21]

SEVENTH DIRECTIVE

Another major accounting directive addresses the issue of consolidated financial statements. The Seventh Directive was issued on June 13, 1983, after its initial proposal in 1976. The provisions of the Seventh Directive continue to be controversial because consolidated financial statements were the exception rather than the rule in most EU countries at the time of the Seventh Directive's passage. Because of the newness of consolidations as a legal requirement, member states were given wide latitude and many options for the incorporation of the Seventh Directive into their individual national company law.

Fundamentally, the Seventh Directive requires consolidation where either the parent or a subsidiary company is a limited liability company, regardless of the location of its registered office. The principle of legal power of control determines the consolidation obligation. Such control is deemed to exist if the parent company has:

1. the majority of voting rights; or
2. the right to appoint a majority of the board of directors; or
3. the right to exercise dominant influence over a limited liability company pursuant to a control contract; or
4. control over a majority of voting rights, pursuant to agreements with other shareholders.

---

[20]Reprinted from Ernst & Whinney, *Fourth Directive—European Company Law,* New York: E & W International Series, 1980, 4–6.
[21]Based on G. G. Mueller, "1992 and Harmonization Efforts in the EC," *Handbook of International Accounting,* F. D. S. Choi, ed., New York: John Wiley, 1992.

These conditions illustrate that the scope of consolidations under the Seventh Directive is broader than the corresponding scope of traditional British-American consolidation methods.

Article 13 of the Seventh Directive specifies conditions allowing exclusion from the EC consolidation obligation. Specifically mentioned grounds for exclusion are:

1. An undertaking is of negligible importance from the perspective of true and fair view financial reporting, that is, the amounts involved are immaterial.
2. Severe long-term restrictions exist, as may be the case for foreign subsidiaries subject to severe foreign currency restrictions.
3. Disproportionate expense or undue delay are unavoidable with regard to the information necessary to prepare consolidated financial statements in accordance with the directive.
4. Shares of another enterprise are held exclusively for subsequent resale; that is, the controlled relationship is likely to be temporary.

Article 14 of the Seventh Directive also allows exclusion from consolidation if demonstrably dissimilar activities prevail. Because the definition of "dissimilar" was likely to be interpreted differently from member country to member country, the Seventh Directive qualifies this exclusion possibility by stating that a diversified group providing different products and services is not, per se, reason for exclusion.[22]

EIGHTH DIRECTIVE

The Eighth Directive of April 10, 1984, addresses various aspects of the qualifications of professionals authorized to carry out legally required (statutory) audits. Essentially, this directive lays down minimum qualifications of auditors. The Eighth Directive does not deal with mutual recognition of auditors from one EC country to another. It also does not encompass freedom of professional establishment among the EC countries. However, Article II of this directive states that member states may approve professionals who have obtained all or part of their qualifications in another EC country on the condition that these qualifications can be considered equivalent and that the professionals concerned furnish proof of sufficient knowledge about local law.

Required training must be completed under the supervision of an approved auditor. Independence is required, but the Eighth Directive gives discretionary power to EC countries to determine conditions of independence. Thus, professional independence requirements for auditors still vary greatly among the EC member countries.[23]

HAVE EU HARMONIZATION EFFORTS BEEN SUCCESSFUL?

The success of EU harmonization efforts has been debated. Karel van Hulle, head of Financial-Information-Accounting Standards at the European Commission, described some of the difficulties in this manner:[24]

---

[22]See endnote 21.

[23]See Arnold Schilder, "Research Opportunities in Auditing in the European Union," *Accounting Horizons* 10 (December 1996): 98–108.

[24]Karel van Hulle, "International Harmonisation of Accounting Principles: A European Perspective," *Wirtschaftsprüferkammer—Mitteilungen*, special edition (June 1997): 44–50.

It must be admitted that the comparability achieved through the harmonisation process is far from perfect. First of all, the Accounting Directives contain primarily minimum rules. They are *not* dealing with a number of important accounting issues. Secondly, the provisions of the Directives are not always interpreted in the same way by Member States. A number of questions relating to the interpretation of the Directives have been dealt with by the Contact Committee on the Accounting Directives.[25] Other questions have remained on the table. It has been difficult to arrive at an agreed position on these questions because the text of the Directives often leaves much scope for interpretation and Member States were not prepared to compromise on the interpretation. The general wording of some of the provisions in the Accounting Directives has been an important reason why the Commission has not brought some of these questions before the European Court of Justice for a final ruling.[26]

THE EU's NEW APPROACH AND THE INTEGRATION OF EUROPEAN FINANCIAL MARKETS

One of the EU's goals is to achieve integration of European financial markets. Toward this end, the commission has introduced directives and undertaken major new initiatives to achieve a single market for:

- raising capital on an EU-wide basis;
- establishing a common legal framework for integrated securities and derivatives markets; and
- achieving a single set of accounting standards for listed companies.

In November 1995 the European Commission (EC) adopted a new approach to accounting harmonization, referred to as the New Accounting Strategy. The commission announced that the EU needs to move promptly in order to give a clear signal that companies seeking listings in the United States and other world markets will be able to remain within the EU accounting framework.[27] The EC also stressed that the EU needs to strengthen its commitment to the international standard-setting process, which offers the most efficient and rapid solution for the problems of companies operating on an international scale.

In June 2000, the commission adopted a new financial reporting strategy. The cornerstone of this strategy is a proposed regulation that would require all EU companies listed on regulated markets, including banks, insurance companies, and SMEs (Small- and Medium-Sized companies), to prepare consolidated accounts in accordance with IAS. (Unlisted SMEs will not be covered, but may find it in their interest to adopt IAS

---

[25]European Commission Contact Committee on the Accounting Directives, The Accounting Harmonisation in the European Community, *Problems of Applying the Fourth Directive on the Annual Accounts of Limited Companies,* Luxembourg: Office for Official Publications of the European Communities, 1990.

[26]Also see Bindon, Kathleen R., and Helen Gernon, "The European Union: Regulation Moves Financial Reporting Toward Comparability," *Research in Accounting Regulation* 9 (1995): 23–48; Van Hulle, K., and K.U. Leuven, "Harmonization of Accounting Standards—A View from the European Community," *The European Accounting Review* 1 (May 1992): 161–172.

[27]See the EC's communication "Accounting Harmonisation: A New Strategy vis-à-vis International Harmonisation," COM 95 (508) final of November 14, 1995.

voluntarily, especially if they seek international capital.) This regulation will affect some 7,000 listed EU companies, as compared with 275 listed EU companies that used IAS as of April 2001. It is designed "to encourage cross-border trade in financial services and so create a fully-integrated market, by helping to make financial information more transparent and easily comparable." Also due to be announced in spring 2001 are proposals to modernize the existing directives on prospectuses and to secure access to securities markets through a common registration system based on comparable market information, including one set of accounting standards.[28]

The EU member states have adopted the key EU directives to a large extent, and an integrated European securities market is gradually taking shape. However, although EU members' listing requirements are broadly similar, the establishment of a true "Single European Market" is a long way off. Many of the requirements are ambiguous in practice, and member states have flexibility in interpreting and applying them. The proposed regulation requiring the use of IAS by all EU-listed companies no later than 2005 is expected to be a major step toward overcoming these difficulties.

The purpose of the directives is to simplify and harmonize the process of marketing securities within the EU, while ensuring that there is sufficient disclosure of relevant information to properly protect potential investors in an issue of securities. Some of the key requirements of the directives are outlined in the following sections.

PUBLIC OFFERS DIRECTIVE

This directive deals with the preparation, approval, and distribution of the prospectus to be published when securities are offered to the public, but are not to be listed on a stock exchange of a member state. Whereas the Admission and Disclosure Directive sets out the information to be published when securities are admitted to listing, the Public Offers Directive requires a prospectus when securities are first offered to the public in a member state, whether or not those securities are to be listed.

The directive also provides the framework for prospectuses to be mutually recognized throughout the EU. If applications for listing are made simultaneously or within a short interval in more than one member state, then, subject to translation and the addition of local information (for example, taxation and publication of notices), the listing particulars approved by one member state must be accepted in other member states without additional information being required for further approval.

INVESTMENT SERVICES DIRECTIVE

The Investment Services Directive (ISD) is the cornerstone of the EU legislative framework for investment firms and securities markets. It has eliminated a first set of legal obstacles to the single market for securities with the *single passport* conferred on authorized investment firms now in wide use. The ISD has liberalized access to regulated markets and stock exchanges. Pan-European dealing in nationally listed securities has been facilitated.

Prior to the ISD, statutory safeguards and supervisory practices differed widely across the EU. Important provisions of the ISD lay down requirements for national

---

[28] *Single Market News*, no. 25, op. cit.

competent authorities, and assign responsibilities and obligations for supervising regulatory provisions laid down in the directive. A wide-ranging overhaul of the ISD is underway to overcome difficulties that have limited its effectiveness.

EU ADMISSION AND DISCLOSURE DIRECTIVE

The EC recently proposed a new directive that combines and codifies requirements from several existing directives and amendments in order to simplify and clarify EU law related to the admission of securities to official stock exchange listing, the preparation and distribution of listing particulars (often referred to as a prospectus), interim reporting, and certain other disclosures. Contents of the superceded directives are fully preserved. Key topics covered in this legislative codification include the following.

Admission to Listing: Companies seeking a listing of their securities must comply with the minimum requirements and conditions for admission to official listing on any stock exchange within the EU. Requirements are related to areas such as the legal status of the company and its shares, the minimum size of the company, and the negotiability of the shares. All member states must designate a national authority (competent authority) competent to decide on the admission of securities to official listing.

Listing Particulars: Listing particulars must be published prior to the listing of a document. The listing particulars document must contain information that will "enable investors and their investment advisors to make an informed assessment of the asset and liabilities, financial position, profits and losses, and prospects of the issuer and of the rights attaching to such securities." Requirements imposed by the directive include the need for:

- information about the company, its share capital, and loan capital;
- details on the company's principal activities, place of business, and employees; and
- financial information on the company or group (as appropriate) including balance sheets, profit and loss accounts, and statements of cash flows (or equivalent) for the last 3 years with notes for the last financial year.

Interim Reports: Companies admitted to listing are required to publish certain types of information on a regular basis. For instance, they must publish half-yearly reports on their activities, and profits and losses during the first 6 months of each financial year. This report is to be published within 4 months of the end of the relevant 6-month period and must contain certain basic information specified in the directive.

INTERNATIONAL ORGANIZATION OF SECURITIES COMMISSIONS (IOSCO)

The International Organization of Securities Commissions (IOSCO) consists of securities regulators from more than 80 countries. IOSCO's goals are to develop international consensus, exchange information, establish adequate standards of investor protection, and provide mutual assistance for effective surveillance and enforcement.

IOSCO has worked extensively on international disclosure and accounting standards to facilitate the ability of companies to raise capital efficiently in global securities markets. In 1998 IOSCO published a set of nonfinancial disclosure standards that may eventually enable companies to use a single prospectus to offer or list shares on any of the world's major capital markets. Securities regulators worldwide are increasingly adopting these standards.[29]

Working Party No. 1 focuses on multinational disclosure and accounting. Its main objective is to facilitate the process whereby world class issuers can raise capital in the most effective and efficient way on all capital markets where investor demand exists. A working party study completed in 1989 presented recommendations for facilitating multinational equity offerings. The report recommended "that regulators be encouraged, where consistent with their legal mandate and the goal of investor protection, to facilitate the use of single disclosure documents, whether by harmonisation of standards, reciprocity or otherwise."

Exhibit 8-6 presents a brief summary of the 10 disclosure standards. The summary is important because it indicates the comprehensiveness proposed by Working Party No. 1. The disclosure standards proposed are also highly detailed.

INTERNATIONAL FEDERATION OF ACCOUNTANTS (IFAC)

The IFAC is a worldwide organization with 128 member organizations in 91 countries, representing more than 2 million accountants. Organized in 1977, its stated goal is "to develop the profession and harmonize its standards worldwide to enable accountants to provide services of consistently high quality in the public interest."[30]

The IFAC Assembly, which meets every 2.5 years, has one representative from each of IFAC's member organizations. The assembly elects a council, which is made up of individuals from 18 countries elected for 2.5-year terms. The council, which meets twice a year, sets IFAC policy and supervises its operations. Day-to-day administration is provided by the IFAC Secretariat located in New York, which is staffed by accounting professionals from around the world.

Much of IFAC's professional work is done through standing committees. At this writing, the standing committees were:

1. International Auditing Practices
2. Ethics
3. Education
4. Financial and Management Accounting
5. Information Technology
6. Public Sector
7. Membership

IFAC's council occasionally appoints special task forces to address important issues. At the end of March 1998 there were six task forces:

- Anti-Corruption
- GATS (General Agreement on Trade in Services)
- Legal Liability

---

[29]See International Organization of Securities Commissions Annual Report 1997, Montreal.
[30]From the IFAC Web site (http:www.ifac.org/FactsAndFigures/index.html), April 1, 1998.

EXHIBIT 8-6   Summary of International Disclosure Standards for Cross-Border Offerings and Initial Listings by Foreign Issuers (Published by International Organization of Securities Commissions, 1998)

1. Identity of Directors, Senior Management and Advisers and Responsibility Statement

This standard identifies the company representatives and other individuals involved in the company's listing or registration and indicates the persons responsible. The definition of the persons covered by this standard may vary in each country and would be determined by host country law.

2. Offer Statistics and Expected Timetable

This standard provides key information regarding the conduct of any offering and the identification of important dates relating to the offering. It is understood that listings do not always involve offerings.

3. Key Information

This standard summarizes key information about the company's financial condition, capitalization and risk factors.

4. Information on the Company

This standard provides information about the company's business operations, the products it makes or the services it provides, and the factors that affect the business.

5. Operating and Financial Review and Prospects

This standard provides management's explanation of factors that have affected the company's financial condition and results of operations, and management's assessment of factors and trends which are anticipated to have a material effect on the company's financial condition and results of operations in future periods. In some countries a forecast or statement of the company's prospects for the current year and/or other future periods may be required.

6. Directors and Officers

This standard provides information concerning the company's directors and managers that will allow investors to assess such individuals' experience, qualifications and levels of compensation, as well as their relationship with the company. The definition of the persons covered by this disclosure standard may vary in each country and would be determined by host country law. Information is also required concerning the company's employees.

7. Major Shareholders and Related Party Transactions

This standard provides information regarding the major shareholders and others that control or may control the company. The standard also provides information regarding transactions the company has entered into with persons affiliated with the company and whether the terms of such transactions are fair to the company.

8. Financial Information

This standard specifies which financial statements must be included in the document, as well as the periods to be covered, the age of the financial statements and other information of a financial nature. The country in which the company is listed (or is applying for listing) will determine the comprehensive bodies of accounting and auditing principles that will be accepted for use in preparation and audit of the financial statements.

9. The Offer

This standard provides information regarding the offer of securities, the plan for distribution of the securities and related matters.

10. Additional Information

This standard provides information, most of which is of a statutory nature, which is not covered elsewhere in the document.

Source: International Organization of Securities Commissions (IOSCO), *International Disclosure Standards for Cross Border Offerings and Initial Listings by Foreign Issuers,* 1998.

- Quality Assurance
- Small and Medium Enterprise
- Structure and Organization

IFAC's International Accounting Practices Committee issues International Standards on Auditing (ISA), which are organized into the following groups:

- Introductory Matters
- Responsibilities
- Planning
- Audit Evidence
- Using Work of Others
- Audit Conclusions and Reporting
- Specialized Areas
- Related Services (RSs)

IFAC has close ties with other international organizations such as IASB and IOSCO. The financial statements of an increasing number of companies are being audited in conformity with IFAC's International Standards on Auditing. For example, see the auditor's report for Shanghai Tyre & Rubber Co., Ltd. in Appendix 8-2.

UNITED NATIONS INTERGOVERNMENTAL WORKING GROUP OF EXPERTS ON INTERNATIONAL STANDARDS OF ACCOUNTING AND REPORTING (ISAR)

ISAR was created in 1982 and is the only intergovernmental working group devoted to accounting and auditing at the corporate level. Its specific mandate is to promote the harmonization of national accounting standards for enterprises. ISAR accomplishes its mandate by discussing and promulgating best practices, including those recommended by IASB. In recent years, ISAR focused on important topics that other organizations were not yet ready to address, such as environmental accounting. It has also conducted technical assistance projects in a number of areas such as accounting reform and retraining in the Russian Federation, Azerbaijan and Uzbekistan, and designing and developing a long-distance learning program in accountancy for French-speaking Africa.[31]

ORGANIZATION FOR ECONOMIC COOPERATION AND DEVELOPMENT (OECD)

OECD is the international organization of the industrialized, market economy countries. It functions through its governing body, the OECD Council, and its network of about 200 committees and working groups. Its publication *Financial Market Trends*, issued 3 times each year, assesses trends and prospects in the international and major domestic financial markets of the OECD area. Description and analysis of the structure

---

[31]From Background Paper, "The Intergovernmental Working Group of Experts on International Standards of Accounting and Reporting (ISAR)—UNCTAD," December 1997.

and regulation of securities markets is often published either as an OECD publication or as a special feature in *Financial Market Trends*. With its membership consisting of larger, industrialized countries, the OECD is often a counterweight to other bodies (such as the United Nations and the International Confederation of Free Trade Unions) that have built-in tendencies to act contrary to the interests of its members.[32]

CONCLUSION

In recent years, many people have come to believe that international harmonization is a necessary step in reducing the regulatory barriers to cross-border, capital-raising efforts. The current debate is increasingly becoming not *whether* to harmonize, but *how* to harmonize. Although national differences in environmental factors (such as systems of corporate governance and finance) that affect accounting development will persist for some time, financial reporting systems are slowly converging as international capital markets become more investor oriented. These days it is impossible to address capital market and stock exchange regulatory issues without considering international harmonization of accounting principles, disclosure, and/or auditing.

---

[32]From the OECD Web site (www.oecdwash.org), April 1, 1998.

Comparison of IASB, U.S. and U.K. Standards

Subject	IAS	U.S. GAAP	U.K. GAAP
Financial Statements—General Requirements			
Contents of financial statements	Two years' balance sheets, income, recognized gains and losses, and cash flow statements.	Comparable to IAS, except SEC requires 3 years for all statements except balance sheet.	Comparable to IAS.
True and fair view override	In very rare cases, override standards where essential to give "true and fair view."	No override of standards permitted.	Comparable to IAS.
Accounting convention	Historical cost, but increasingly assets may be revalued.	No revaluations except some securities and derivatives at fair value.	Comparable to IAS.
Changes in accounting policies	Either restate comparatives and prior year opening retained earnings or include effect in current year income.	Generally include effect in current year income statement.	Restate comparatives and prior year opening retained earnings.
Correction of fundamental errors	Either restate comparatives or include effect in current year income.	Restate comparatives.	Comparable to U.S. GAAP.
Changes in accounting estimates	Account for in income in the current and future periods, as appropriate.	Comparable to IAS.	Comparable to IAS.
Group Reporting			
Definition of subsidiary	Based on voting control.	Controlling interest through majority of voting shares or by contract. Recent proposals comparable to IAS.	Comparable to IAS.
Exclusion of subsidiaries from consolidation	Only if severe long-term restrictions are acquired and held for resale in the near future. Dissimilar activities are not a justification.	Comparable to IAS.	Comparable to IAS.
Definition of associate	Based on significant influence presumed if 20% interest of participation in entity's affairs.	Broadly comparable to IAS.	Requires evidence of exercise of significant influence.
Presentation of associate results	Use equity method. Show share of profits and losses.	Use equity method. Show share of post-tax result.	Use expanded equity method. Share of operating profit, exceptional items, and tax shown separately.
Disclosures about significant associates	Minimal	Give detailed information on significant associates' assets, liabilities, and results.	Comparable to U.S. GAAP.
Equity method or proportional consolidation for joint ventures	Both proportional consolidation and equity method permitted. Consolidate own assets/liabilities in limited circumstances such as oil and gas joint operations.	Predominantly use equity method. Use proportional consolidation in limited circumstances, such as oil and gas ventures.	Generally use gross equity method. Consolidate own assets/liabilities in limited circumstances such as oil and gas joint arrangements.

Subject	IAS	U.S. GAAP	U.K. GAAP
Foreign Currency Translation			
Individual company	Translate at rate on date of transaction; monetary assets/liabilities at balance sheet rate; nonmonetary items at historical rate.	Comparable to IAS.	Comparable to IAS.
Foreign entities within consolidated financial statements	Use closing rate for balance sheets; average rate for income statements. Take exchange differences to equity and include in gain on disposal of subsidiary.	Comparable to IAS.	Use closing rate for balance sheets; either average or closing rate for income statements. Take exchange differences to statement of recognized gains/losses (STRGL). Not included in gains on disposal.
Hyperinflation—foreign entity	Adjust local statements of foreign entity to current price levels prior to translation.	Remeasure local currency statements using the reporting currency as the functional currency.	Either adopt IAS or U.S. GAAP method.
Business Combinations			
Purchase method—fair values on acquisition.	Fair value assets and liabilities of acquired entity.	Broadly comparable to IAS, but specific rules for acquired in-process research and development.	Comparable to IAS.
	Some plant closure and restructuring liabilities relating to the acquired entity may be provided in fair value exercise if specific criteria met.	Broadly comparable to IAS.	Few acquisition provisions allowed.
Purchase method—subsequent adjustments to fair values	Fair values can be corrected against goodwill up to the end of the year after acquisition if additional evidence of values becomes available. Record subsequent adjustments in income statement.	In practice, broadly comparable to IAS.	Broadly comparable to IAS, except investigation of values must have been ongoing.
	Reversals of acquisition provisions always adjust goodwill.	Comparable to IAS.	Few acquisition provisions allowed.
Purchase method—contingent consideration	Estimated at acquisition then subsequently corrected against goodwill.	Not recognized until the contingency is resolved or the amount is determinable.	Comparable to IAS.
Purchase method—minority interests at acquisition	State at share of fair value of net assets or at share of preacquisition carrying value of net assets.	Usually state at share of preacquisition carrying value of net assets.	State at share of fair value of net assets.
Purchase method—disclosure	Disclosures include names and descriptions of combining entities, method of accounting for acquisition, date of acquisition, and impact on results and financial position of acquirer.	Broadly comparable to IAS, but also must present pro forma income statement information as if acquisition occurred at start of comparative period.	Broadly comparable to IAS, but also must present table showing book values, fair value adjustments, and fair values of acquired assets and liabilities.

(continued)

Subject	IAS	U.S. GAAP	U.K. GAAP
Purchase method—goodwill	Capitalize and amortize over useful life, normally not longer than 20 years.	Capitalize and amortize over useful life, with maximum of 40 years. (*note: The FASB has issued an exposure draft that would require an impairments test.*)	Comparable to IAS, although indefinite life may be used in certain circumstances.
Purchase method—negative goodwill	If relates to expected future losses/costs recognize in income when these occur; otherwise record as negative asset and recognize over useful lives of identifiable, nonmonetary assets. Any excess over the fair values of such assets is recognized in income immediately.	Reduce proportionally the fair values assigned to noncurrent assets (except marketable securities). Record any excess as deferred income and recognize in income over no longer than 40 years. Recent proposals similar, but any excess is recognized in income immediately.	Record as negative asset and recognize in income to match depreciation of nonmonetary assets; any excess over the fair values of such assets is recognized in income over period likely to benefit.
Pooling of interests method	Severely restricted to "true mergers of equals." Rules focus on lack of identification of an acquirer.	Rules focus predominately on attributes of combining entities and manner of transaction. U.S. poolings more common in practice than under IAS or U.K. GAAP. The FASB has issued an exposure draft that would prohibit this method.	Restrictions similar to IAS. Criteria include size of entities and low-level limits on non-share consideration.

Main Accounting Principles

Subject	IAS	U.S. GAAP	U.K. GAAP
Intangible assets	Capitalize if recognition criteria met; intangible assets must be amortized over useful life, normally no longer than 20 years. Revaluations are permitted in rare circumstances.	Capitalize purchased intangible assets and amortize over useful life, no longer than 40 years. Revaluations are not permitted. Recent proposals for useful lives similar to U.K. GAAP.	Broadly comparable to IAS, although may use indefinite life in certain circumstances.
Research and development costs	Expense research costs as incurred. Capitalize and amortize development costs only if stringent criteria are met.	Expense both research and development costs as incurred. Some software development costs must be capitalized.	Comparable to IAS except optional to capitalize and amortize development costs if criteria met.
Property, plant, and equipment	Use historical cost or revalued amounts. Frequent valuations of entire classes of assets necessary when revalued amounts used.	Revaluations not permitted.	Comparable to IAS.
Investment properties	Either treat as investment or property, plant, and equipment. Recent proposal to measure at historical cost or fair value and recognize changes in fair value in income statement.	Treat as for other properties (use historical cost).	Carry at open market value without depreciation.

Subject	IAS	U.S. GAAP	U.K. GAAP
Impairment of assets	If impairment indicated, write down assets to higher of net selling price and value in use based on discounted cash flows. If no loss arises, reconsider useful lives of those assets. Reversals of losses permitted in certain circumstances.	Impairment trigger based on undiscounted cash flows. If less than carrying amount, measure impairment loss using market value of discounted cash flows. If no loss arises, reconsider useful lives of those assets. Reversals of losses prohibited.	Comparable to IAS.
Capitalization of borrowing costs	Permitted for qualifying assets.	Compulsory when relates to construction of certain assets.	Comparable to IAS.
Leases—classification	Finance lease if substantially all risks and rewards of ownership transferred. Substance rather than form is important.	Similar to IAS but considerably more extensive form-driven requirements.	Comparable to IAS.
Leases—lessee accounting	Record finance leases as asset and obligation for future rentals. Normally depreciate over useful life of asset. Apportion rental payments to give constant interest rate on outstanding obligation. Generally charge operating lease rentals on straight-line basis.	Comparable to IAS.	Comparable to IAS.
Leases—lessor accounting	Record amounts due under finance leases as a receivable. Allocate gross earnings to give constant rate of return based on (pretax) net investment method.	Comparable to IAS but specific rules for leveraged leases.	Presentation comparable to IAS but measurement basis differs: Use (post-tax) net cash investment method for allocating gross earnings.
Leases—sale and lease-back transactions	Defer and amortize profit arising on sale and finance leaseback. If an operating lease arises then profit recognition depends on sale proceeds compared to fair value of the asset.	Defer and amortize profits up to certain limits. Immediately recognize losses. Consider specific strict criteria if a real estate transaction.	Broadly comparable to IAS.
Investments	Depends on classification of investment—if held to maturity then carry at amortized cost, otherwise at fair value. Unrealized gains/losses on trading securities go to income statement and on available-for-sale investments can go either to equity or income.	Comparable to IAS except unrealized gains/losses on available-for-sale securities go to other comprehensive income.	Carry long-term investments at cost, market value, or other appropriate basis such as net asset value. Carry current asset investments at lower of cost and net realizable value (NRV) or at current cost.

(continued)

Subject	IAS	U.S. GAAP	U.K. GAAP
Inventories and long-term contracts	Carry at lower cost and NRV. Use FIFO, LIFO, or weighted average method to determine cost. Recognize long-term contract revenues and profits using percentage of completion method.	Broadly comparable to IAS—more common use of LIFO. Use completed contract method for long-term contract accounting in limited circumstances.	Comparable to IAS except that LIFO method not permitted.
Revenue recognition	Recognize revenue if meets specific criteria.	Broadly comparable to IAS. Numerous accounting standards for specific industries and situations.	No detailed standard on revenue recognition but practice similar to IAS.
Derecognition of financial assets	Recognize and derecognize assets based on control.	Comparable to IAS. Legal isolation of assets even in bankruptcy necessary for derecognition.	Recognize and derecognize assets based on risks and rewards, focusing in part on substance rather than just legal form.
Provisions—general	Record provisions relating to present obligations from past events if probable outflow of resources can be estimated reliably.	Comparable to IAS, with rules for specific situations (employee termination costs, environmental liabilities, loss contingencies, etc.).	Comparable to IAS.
Provisions—restructuring	Make restructuring provisions if detailed formal plan announced or implementation effectively begun.	Comparable to IAS.	Comparable to IAS.
Contingencies	Disclose unrecognized possible losses and probable gains.	Comparable to IAS.	Comparable to IAS.
Employee benefits—pension costs; defined benefit plans	Must use projected unit credit method to determine benefit obligation. Use current market high-quality bond rate to discount benefit obligation. Value assets at fair value or using discounted cash flows if market prices unavailable. Actuarial gains/losses outside a 10% corridor are amortized over the average remaining service lives of participating employees. Faster recognition permitted using any systematic method (including immediate recognition) if consistently applied. Extensive disclosures.	Broadly comparable to IAS, although several minor differences.	Wider choice of actuarial methods than IAS, but recent proposals comparable to IAS. Discount benefit obligation at long-term risk-adjusted rate. Recent exposure draft proposals comparable to IAS. Value assets on actuarial basis. Recent exposure draft comparable to IAS. Recognize actuarial gains and losses over average remaining service lives of current employees—no corridor approach. Recent exposure draft proposes detailed rules on the recognition of all actuarial gains and losses immediately in the STRGL. Fewer disclosures than IAS, although exposure draft proposes more extensive disclosure.

Subject	IAS	U.S. GAAP	U.K. GAAP
Employee benefits—other	Account for postretirement benefits as pensions. Rules also given for termination benefits arising from redundancies and other post-employment and long-term employee benefits. Account for termination indemnity plans as pensions.	Comparable to IAS for postretirement benefits. Accrue for post-employment costs if criteria met. Choice of measurement methods for termination indemnity plans.	Comparable to IAS for postretirement benefits. Other benefits not covered by standards, but practice generally comparable to IAS. Recent exposure draft covers other employee benefits.
Employee stock compensation	Disclosures required but no standard or proposals on measurement.	Two alternative methods available for cost: intrinsic value (market price at measurement date less any employee contribution or exercise price) or fair value using option pricing model. Charge cost of share awards or options over period of employee's performance.	Cost is based on intrinsic value (market value at date of grant less any employee contribution or exercise price). Charge cost of share awards or options immediately unless there are future performance conditions.
Employee share option plans (ESOP)—presentation in balance sheet of sponsor	No standard and no proposals.	Classify ESOP shares as deduction from equity. Include debt of ESOP on balance sheet.	Classify ESOP shares as assets ("own shares"). Include debt of ESOP on balance sheet.
Government grants	Recognize as deferred income and amortize. May offset capital grants against asset values.	Comparable to IAS.	Comparable to IAS except may not offset capital grants against asset values.
Deferred income taxes	Use full provision method, driven by balance sheet temporary differences. Recognize deferred tax assets if recovery is probable.	Comparable to IAS, but recognize all deferred tax assets and then provide valuation allowance if recovery is less than 50% likely.	(*note: Effective 2002, full provisioning of all timing differences will be required.*) Use partial provision method, driven by future income statement aggregate timing differences. Recognize deferred tax assets if recoverable without replacement by equivalent timing differences. Full asset recognizable for deferred tax relating to pension costs.
Capital instruments—categorization of shares	Classify capital instruments depending on substance of obligations of the issuer. Mandatorily redeemable preference shares generally are liabilities, not equity.	Analyze shareholders' equity between common stock and other categories. Redeemable preference shares normally mezzanine category (between debt and equity).	Present all shares within shareholders' funds; analyze between equity and non-equity interests. All preference shares are shown as non-equity within shareholders' funds.
Capital instruments—purchase of own shares	Show as deduction from equity.	Comparable to IAS.	By law, cancel directly purchased shares (unless held in a trust); create capital redemption reserve.

(*continued*)

Subject	IAS	U.S. GAAP	U.K. GAAP
Capital instruments— convertible debt	Account for convertible debt on split basis, allocating proceeds between equity and debt.	Convertible debt usually is a liability.	Comparable to U.S. GAAP.
Derivatives and other financial instruments— measurement of hedges of foreign entity investments	Gains/losses on hedges of foreign entity investments recorded in equity including hedge ineffectiveness on nonderivatives. For derivatives, record hedge ineffectiveness in the income statement. Gains/losses held in equity must be transferred to income statement on disposal of investment.	Broadly comparable to IAS except all hedge ineffectiveness recorded in the income statement.	Broadly comparable to U.S. GAAP, except no transfer to income statement of exchange gains/losses previously recorded in equity.
Derivatives and other financial instruments— measurement of financial instruments and hedging activities	Measure derivatives and hedges at fair value; take changes in fair value to income statement except for effective cash flow hedges where they are taken to equity until effect of transaction goes through income, then transferred to income statement. Deferred amount recognized in initial measurement of asset/liability for cash flow hedges of future transactions (basis adjustment).	Comparable to IAS except no "basis adjustment" on cash flow hedges of future transactions. Hedges of firm commitments are fair value hedges (cash flow hedges under IAS).	No comprehensive guidance currently. Financial liabilities measured at amortized net proceeds, with gains and losses from premature settlements taken to income statements. Also see "Investments."
Derivatives and other financial instruments— proposals for the future	Participating in long-term project with Joint Work Group—preferred approaches are to measure all financial assets and liabilities at fair value; recognize nearly all gains and losses from changes in fair value in current period income; and preclude special accounting for financial instruments used for hedges.	Participating in long-term project with Joint Working Group.	Participating in long-term project with Joint Working Group.

Other Accounting and Reporting Issues

Subject	IAS	U.S. GAAP	U.K. GAAP
Related party transactions—definition	Determine by level of direct or indirect control and significant influence of one party over another, or common control of both parties.	Broadly comparable to IAS.	Broadly comparable to IAS.

Subject	IAS	U.S. GAAP	U.K. GAAP
Related party transactions—disclosures	Disclose name of related party and nature of relationship and types of transactions. For control relationships, give disclosures regardless of whether transactions occur.	Broadly comparable to IAS.	Broadly comparable to IAS.
	Some exemptions available for separate financial statements of subsidiaries.	Exemptions are narrower than under IAS.	Exemptions are more widely available than under IAS.
Post balance sheet events	Adjust financial statements for subsequent events, providing evidence of conditions at blance sheet date and materially affecting amounts in financial statements. Disclose non-adjusting events.	Comparable to IAS.	Comparable to IAS.
Discontinuing/ discontinued operations— measurement	Make provisions for some costs if considered a restructuring and criteria for recognizing a provision met.	Accrue at measurement date for estimated operating loss in wind-down period and on disposal.	Comparable to IAS.
	Write down assets to higher of net selling price and value in use based on discounted cash flows.	Carry assets at lower of carrying amount and net realizable value.	
Discontinuing/ discontinued operations— presentation and main disclosures	Give details of discontinuing operation. Disclose (on face of income statement) pretax gain or loss from discontinuance.	Report discontinued operations as a separate line item on face of income statement (net of tax and below-net income from continuing operations).	Disclose (on face of income statement) components of operating profit relating to discontinued operations.
Earnings per share (EPS)—diluted	Use weighted average potential dilutive shares as denominator for diluted EPS. Use "treasury stock" method for share options/warrants.	Comparable to IAS.	Comparable to IAS.
Extraordinary and exceptional items	Extraordinary items limited to a few events outside control of company. Exceptional items usually shown in the notes.	Broadly comparable to IAS. Do not show subtotals of income from operations before exceptional items.	Extraordinary items do not exist. Must disclose certain exceptional items on face of income statement.
Segment reporting— scope and basis of formats	Public entities. Report primary and secondary segment formats based on risks and returns and internal reporting structure.	Public entities. Report based on internal operating segments.	Public and very large private entities. Report based on classes of business and geographical areas.

(continued)

Subject	IAS	U.S. GAAP	U.K. GAAP
Segment reporting—accounting policies	Use consolidated GAAP accounting policies.	Use internal financial reporting policies (even if accounting policies may differ from consolidated GAAP).	Comparable to IAS.
Segment reporting—disclosures	Disclosures for primary segment format include revenues, results, capex, total assets, and liabilities. For secondary segment format, report revenues, total assets, and capex.	Similar disclosures to IAS except liabilities and geographical capex not required. Depreciation, amortization, tax, interest and exceptional/extraordinary items disclosed if reported internally.	Disclose revenue, results, and net assets. Equal prominence to disclosures by class of business and geographically.
Cash flow statements—format and method	Standard headings, but flexibility of contents. Use direct or indirect method.	Similar headings to IAS but more specific guidance given for items to include in each. Use direct or indirect method.	Many standard headings and required contents of each. Use direct or indirect method.
Cash flow statements—definition of cash and cash equivalents	Cash includes overdrafts and cash equivalents with short-term maturities (less than 3 months).	Cash excludes overdrafts but includes cash equivalents with short-term maturities.	Cash includes overdrafts but excludes cash equivalents.
Cash flow statements—exemptions	No exemptions available.	Limited exemptions for certain investment enterprises.	Limited exemptions for certain subsidiaries and mutual funds.
Statement of recognized gains and losses/comprehensive income	Give statement of recognized gains and losses either as separate primary statement or separately highlighted in primary statement of movements in equity.	Disclose total comprehensive income, either combined with income statement or as under IAS. Also track and disclose cumulative amounts.	Give primary statement of total recognized gains and losses.
Operating and financial review	No mandatory standards—suggested features include analytical discussion of business and financial information.	Public entities must prepare Management's Discussion and Analysis (MD&A) with SEC mandating the contents, focusing on liquidity, capital resources, and results of operations.	Not mandatory, but given in practice by major listed companies. Contents broadly comparable to IAS.
Interim financial reporting	Not mandatory to prepare interim statements but must use standard if prepared. Basis should be consistent with full year statements and include comparatives.	If issued, the contents of interim statements are prescribed and basis should be consistent with full year statements. Quarterly reporting also necessary for SEC registrants (domestic U.S. enterprises only).	Mandatory for listed entities (half-yearly); minimal contents specified by the London Stock Exchange. ASB nonmandatory statement is similar to IAS.

Source: PricewaterhouseCoopers, *International Accounting Standards—Similarities and Differences IAS, U.S. GAAP and U.K. GAAP,* London: PricewaterhouseCoopers, February 2000.

Shanghai Tyre & Rubber Co., Ltd. and Subsidiaries Notes to Consolidated Financial Statements

AUDITORS' REPORT

TO THE SHAREHOLDERS OF
  SHANGHAI TYRE & RUBBER CO., LTD.
(Incorporated in the People's Republic of China (the "PRC") with limited liability)

We have audited the consolidated balance sheets of Shanghai Tyre & Rubber Co., Ltd. (the "Company") and its subsidiaries (hereinafter together with the Company referred to as the "Group") as of December 31, 1999 and 1998, and the related consolidated statements of income, changes in shareholders' equity and cash flows for the years then ended. These consolidated financial statements are the responsibility of the Company's management. Our responsibility is to express an opinion on these consolidated financial statements based on our audits.

We conducted our audits in accordance with International Standards on Auditing issued by the International Federation of Accountants. Those Standards require that we plan and perform the audit to obtain reasonable assurance about whether the consolidated financial statements are free of material misstatement. An audit includes examining, on a test basis, evidence supporting the amounts and disclosures in the financial statements. An audit also includes assessing the accounting principles used and significant estimates made by management, as well as evaluating the overall consolidated financial statement presentation. We believe that our audits provide a reasonable basis for our opinion.

In our opinion, the consolidated financial statements referred to above present fairly, in all material respects, the consolidated financial position of the Group as of December 31, 1999 and 1998, and the consolidated results of its operations and its cash flows for the years then ended in accordance with International Accounting Standards issued by the International Accounting Standards Committee.

Hong Kong, PRC
April 24, 2000

The accompanying notes are an integral part of these consolidated financial statements.

SHANGHAI TYRE & RUBBER CO., LTD. AND SUBSIDIARIES
NOTES TO CONSOLIDATED FINANCIAL STATEMENTS
DECEMBER 31, 1999 AND 1998

(Amounts expressed in thousands of Renminbi Yuan ("RMB") unless otherwise stated)

1. ORGANISATION AND OPERATIONS

Shanghai Tyre & Rubber Co., Ltd. ("the Company") was incorporated on July 11, 1982 as a result of the reorganisation of a state-owned enterprise into a joint stock company limited by shares. The Company's listed shares included in ordinary shares ("A shares") and domestically listed foreign investment shares ("B shares") are traded on the Shanghai Stock Exchange.

The Company's principal activity is the manufacture of various types of rubber tyres (primarily bias tyres and radial tyres), other rubber products and machinery for production of rubber products for industrial and commercial use.

The parent company and ultimate parent company of the Company is Shanghai Hua Yi (Group) Company ("Hua Yi").

2. BASIS OF PRESENTATION

During the year ended December 31, 1999, the Group incurred a net loss of approximately RMB 257 million and has an accumulated deficit of approximately RMB 237 million. As of the same date, its current liabilities exceed its current assets by approximately RMB 527 million.

The Group's consolidated financial statements as of December 31, 1999 have been prepared based on the going concern assumption. The Group's ability to continue as a going concern, realise the carrying value of its assets and repay its liabilities as they fall due is dependent on the success of its future operations and the ongoing financial support of its bankers and the parent company, Hua Yi. Hua Yi has provided the Group with an undertaking to provide funds to enable the Group to meet its liabilities as they fall due and to finance its continuing operations.

3. PRINCIPAL ACCOUNTING POLICIES

The consolidated financial statements include the financial statements of the Company and its consolidated subsidiaries. Please refer to Note 3 (f) for details of consolidated subsidiaries.

The consolidated financial statements were prepared in conformity with International Accounting Standards ("IAS") as if those standards had been applied consistently throughout the years. This basis of accounting differs from that used in the accounts of the Company, prepared in accordance with accounting standards and regulations applicable to joint stock limited companies in the PRC ("Statutory Accounts").

The impact of the IAS adjustments on the Statutory Accounts is shown in Note 12.

The following accounting policies were adopted in the preparation of the accompanying consolidated financial statements:

(a) Fixed assets and depreciation

Fixed assets are stated at cost less accumulated depreciation. The cost of an asset comprises its purchase price and any directly attributable costs of bringing the asset to its working condition and location for its intended use.

Expenditure incurred after the fixed assets have been put into operation, is recognized as an expense in the period in which it is incurred. In situations where it is probable that the expenditure has resulted in an increase in the future economic benefits expected to be obtained from the use of the asset, the expenditure is capitalized as an additional cost of the fixed asset.

Depreciation is calculated using the straight-line method to write off the cost, after taking into account the estimated residual value at 3%–10% of cost over its expected useful life. The expected useful lives are as follows:

Buildings	20 years
Machinery and equipment	10 years
Motor vehicles	5 years
Furniture, fixtures and office equipment	5 years

When assets are sold or retired, their cost and accumulated depreciation are eliminated from the accounts and any gain or loss resulting from their disposals is included in the statements of income.

(b) Construction-in-progress

Construction-in-progress represents buildings under construction and machinery and equipment under installation and is stated at cost. This includes costs of construction and machinery and equipment, other direct costs plus borrowing costs which include interest charges attributable to borrowings used to finance these projects during the construction or installation period.

No provision for depreciation is provided on construction-in-progress until the relevant assets are completed and put into use.

(c) Borrowing costs

Borrowing costs are expensed as incurred except that borrowing costs directly attributable to the construction of buildings and machinery and equipment that require a substantial period of time to bring them to their intended use are capitalized as cost of the buildings and machinery and equipment at rates based on the actual cost of the specific borrowings.

(d) Deferred expenditures

Deferred expenditures include molds, utility capacity expansion charges, trial-run costs, project design fees, and staff quarters and are amortized on a straight-line basis over their estimated beneficial periods ranging from three to ten years.

(e) Intangible assets

(i) Land use right

Land use right is stated at cost less accumulated amortization. Amortization is calculated using the straight-line method over the life of the land use right.

(ii) Trademark

Trademarks are stated at acquisition cost less accumulated amortization. Amortization is calculated using the straight-line method to write off the cost over the expected future economic life of ten years.

(f) Subsidiaries

A subsidiary is a company in which the Company has the power to govern its financial and operating policies so as to obtain benefits from its activities.

Details of the Company's consolidated subsidiaries as of December 31, 1999 are as follows:

Name of subsidiary	Principal activities	Location	Percentage of ownership
Shanghai Tyre & Rubber Real Estate Management Company ("REMC") (indirectly held)	Property development	Shanghai	100%
Shanghai Tyre & Rubber Trading Company	Trading of rubber tyres and rubber products	Shanghai	100% (90% directly and 10% indirectly held)
Shanghai Tyre & Rubber Co., Ltd. Si Jin Rubber Factory	Production of inner tubes	Shanghai	70% (directly held)
Shanghai Dong Hai Rubber Factory	Production of rubber tyres	Shanghai	65% (directly held)
Haikou Hai Hua Tyre and Rubber Co., Ltd. ("Hai Hua")	Production and sale of rubber tyres	Haikou	100% (90% directly and 10% indirectly held)
Shanghai Tai Feng Industry and Trade Company	Trading of rubber tyres, building materials and automobile parts	Shanghai	100% (indirectly held)
Shanghai Hua Lun Economic Development Company	Trading of rubber tyres	Shanghai	90% (indirectly held)
Xuzhou Hai Peng Tyre Co., Ltd. ("Hai Peng")	Production of rubber tyres	Jiangsu	76.62% (directly held)
Shanghai Da Fu Rubber Co., Ltd. previously Shanghai Da Fu Rubber Factory ("Da Fu Factory")	Production and sale of rubber tyres	Shanghai	100% (90% directly and 10% indirectly held)
Luoyang Hai Hong Tyre Co., Ltd. ("Hai Hong")	Production and sale of of rubber tyres	Luoyang	53% (1998: 60%) (directly held)
Huikou Fu Hua Tyre Trading Co., Ltd.	Trading of rubber tyres and rubber products	Haikou	100% (90% directly and 10% indirectly held)
Shanghai Lun Xing Trading Co., Ltd.	Trading of rubber tyres and rubber products	Shanghai	100% (90% directly and 10% indirectly held)

All material intra-group transactions and balances are eliminated on consolidation.

The statements of income and net assets of the other subsidiaries are not consolidated because they are not material to the consolidated statements of income and net assets of the Group as a whole.

Investment in unconsolidated subsidiaries are accounted for using the equity method of accounting, provision for permanent diminution in value will be recorded as a reduction of the carrying amount, if any.

(g) Associated companies

An associated company is a company, not being a subsidiary or a joint venture, in which the Company holds, directly or indirectly, not less than 20% nor more than 50% of the equity interest as a long-term investment and is able to exercise significant influence on this company.

Investments in the principal associated companies are accounted for using the equity method of accounting: while the investments in associated companies with statements of income and net assets not material to the Group as a whole are accounted for at cost less provision for permanent diminution in value, if any.

(h) Contractual joint ventures

A contractual joint venture is a company which is held for long-term purposes and is jointly managed by the Company and its joint venture partner.

Investments in contractual joint ventures are accounted for using the equity method of accounting.

(i) Other long-term investments

Other long-term investments held for long-term purposes are stated at cost less provision for permanent diminution in value, if any. Income derived from such investments is accounted for to the extent of dividends received and receivable.

Upon disposal of a long-term investment, the difference between net disposal proceeds and the carrying amount is charged or credited to the statements of income.

(j) Inventories

Inventories are stated at the lower of cost and net realisable value. Cost includes costs of raw materials computed using the weighted average method of costing and, in the case of work-in-process and finished goods, direct labour and an appropriate proportion of production overheads. Net realisable value is determined on the basis of estimated selling prices less further costs expected to be incurred to completion and the related direct selling and distribution expenses. Provision is made for obsolete, slow-moving and defective items where appropriate.

Properties for sale are stated at the lower of cost and net realisable value. Cost of properties comprises land cost and other direct costs attributable to such properties using the weighted average method of costing. Net realisable value is determined on the basis of estimated selling price less further cost expected to be incurred to completion of properties and the related direct selling and distribution expenses.

(k) Provision for doubtful debts

Provision for doubtful debts is provided based on the collectibility of the receivables.

(l) Cash and cash equivalents

Cash represents cash in hand and deposits with any banks or other financial institutions which are re-payable on demand.

Cash equivalents represent short-term, highly liquid investments which are readily convertible into known amounts of cash and which are within three months of maturity when acquired, less advances from banks repayable within three months from dates of the advances.

(m) Negative goodwill

Any excess, as at the date of the transaction, of the acquirer's interest in the fair values of the identifiable assets and liabilities acquired over the cost of the acquisition is recognized as negative goodwill.

The amount of negative goodwill is recognized as income on a systematic basis over the remaining weighted average useful life of the identifiable acquired depreciable/amortisable assets.

(n) Revenue recognition

Revenue is recognized on the following basis:

(i) Sales of goods

Turnover represents sales at invoiced value (excluding Value-Added Tax) of goods supplied to customers, net of returns, business tax, consumption tax and surtaxes.

Revenue is recognized when the significant risks and rewards of ownership of goods have been transferred to the buyers.

(ii) Sales of properties

Sale of properties sale is recognized upon the signing of the sale agreements and the titles of the properties have been transferred to the buyers.

(iii) Interest income

Interest income is recognized on a time proportion basis that take into account the effective yield on the assets.

(iv) Dividend income

Dividend income is recognized when the right to receive dividend is established.

(o) Operating leases

Leases where substantially all the rewards and risks of ownership of assets remain with the leasing company are accounted for as operating leases. Rental payments under operating leases are charged to the income statement on a straight-line basis over the period of the relevant leases.

(p) Staff welfare and retirement benefits

The Group is required to provide certain staff welfare and retirement benefits to its employees under the existing PRC legislation. The Group's obligation, including a contribution to a defined contribution retirement plan administered by a government agency, is usually determined based on a certain percentage of the basic salary of the employees. The Group accounts for these benefits on an accrual basis.

(q) Related parties

Parties are considered to be related if one party has the ability, directly or indirectly, to control the other party, or exercise significant influence over the other party in making financial and operating decisions. Parties are also considered to be related if they are subject to common control or common significant influence.

(r) Taxation

Individual companies within the Group provide for income tax on the basis of their profit for financial reporting purposes, adjusted for income and expense items which are not assessable or deductible for income tax purposes.

Deferred taxation is provided under the balance sheet liability method in respect of significant temporary differences arising from differences between the carrying amount of an asset and liability for financial reporting purposes and the amount used for income tax purposes. Deferred tax assets are recognized to the extent that it is probable that sufficient taxable profit will be available against which the deductible temporary differences can be utilized.

(s) Foreign currency translation

Individual companies in the Group maintain their books and accounting records in RMB, which is not a freely convertible currency. Foreign currency transactions are translated into RMB at the rates of exchange prevailing at the time of the transactions. Monetary assets and liabilities denominated in foreign currencies at the balance sheet date are translated into RMB at the rates of exchange prevailing at that date; non-monetary assets and liabilities denominated in foreign currencies are translated at historical rates.

Exchange differences attributable to the translation of foreign currency borrowings used to finance the construction of buildings and installation of machinery and equipment, for periods prior to their being in a condition to enter service, are included in the cost of construction-in-progress or the related fixed assets.

Other exchange differences are dealt with in the statements of income.

12. IMPACT OF IAS ADJUSTMENTS ON NET (LOSS) PROFIT/NET ASSETS

	Net (loss) profit for the years ended December 31,		Net assets as of December 31,	
	1999 *RMB' 000*	*1998* *RMB' 000*	*1999* *RMB' 000*	*1998* *RMB' 000*
As reported in the Statutory Accounts of the Group	2,596	124,906	2,300,343	2,560,001
Restatement of prior year results due to changes in statutory accounting policies	—	(123,614)	—	(269,140)
As reported in the restated Statutory Accounts of the Group	2,596	1,292	2,300,343	2,290,861
Impact of adjustments				
reversal of (increase in) depreciation and amortization expense	20,496	25,995	(118,438)	(138,934)
reversal (write-off) of over-capitalized interest expense and exchange differences	159	5,291	(126,183)	(126,342)
provision for or write-off of doubtful debts	(108,553)	76,425	21,100	129,653
restatement of inventories at the lower of cost or net realizable value and adjustment of over inventoried expenses for idle capacity	(44,054)	20,576	(35,411)	8,643
write-down of idle fixed-assets	(10,746)	1,254	(13,253)	(2,507)
revaluation of assets purchased in foreign currencies before January 1, 1994	(7,660)	(18,548)	75,324	82,984
deferred foreign currency exchange differences	—	(14,117)	—	—
recognition of investment in unconsolidated subsidiaries and associated companies using equity method of accounting	—	(4,222)	—	—
goodwill arising from acquisition of Shanghai Steel Wire Factory	(68,279)	—	(68,279)	—
deferred tax	18,637	7,891	72,429	53,792
others	(59,246)	15,918	(101,622)	(47,560)
As restated to conform to IAS for the Group	(256,650)	117,765	2,006,010	2,250,590

Selected References

Arthur Andersen, BDO, Deloitte Touche Tohmatsu, Ernst & Young International, Grant Thornton, KPMG, and PricewaterhouseCoopers, *GAAP 2000 — A Survey of National Accounting Rules in 53 Countries,* December 2001.

Bloomer, Carrie, ed., *The IASC-U.S. Comparison Project: A Report on the Similarities and Differences between IASC Standards and U.S. GAAP, Second Edition*, Norwalk, CT: Financial Accounting Standards Board, 1999.

Buijink, Willem, Steven Maijoor, Roger Meuwissen, and Argen van Witteloostuijn, *Final Report of a Study on The Role, Position and Liability of the Statutory Auditor Within the European Union* (commissioned by DG XV of the Ueropean Commission), Brussels-Luxembourg: Office for Official Publications of the European Communities, 1996.

Coopers & Lybrand LLP, *Understanding IAS — Analysis and Interpretation*, Great Britain: Coopers & Lybrand (United Kingdom), September 1996.

European Commission Contact Committee on the Accounting Directives, *An Examination of the Conformity Between the International Accounting Standards and the European Accounting Directives*, Brussels, ECSC-EC-EAEC, 1996.

Federation of European Stock Exchanges (FESE), *Annual Report 1999*, Brussels: FESE, June 2000.

Fédération des Experts Comptables Europeens, FEE, *The Role, Position and Liability of the Statutory Auditor in the European Union*, Brussels: FEE, January 1996.

Gruner, John W., and Stephen Salter, "Building a Cohesive Accountancy Profession," in *International Accounting and Finance Handbook*, F. D. S. Choi, ed., New York: John Wiley & Sons, 1997.

Guy, Dan M., and D. R. Carmichael, *Guide to International Standards on Auditing and Related Services 2000,* Fort Worth Texas: Practitioners Publishing Company, 1999.

International Accounting Standards Committee (IASC). *International Accounting Standards 2000*, London: IASC, 2000.

International Accounting Standards Committee. *International Accounting Standards Explained,* New York: John Wiley & Sons, 2000.

International Federation of Accountants (IFAC), *IFAC Handbook 2000 — Technical Pronouncements*, New York: IFAC, 2000.

International Federation of Stock Exchanges (FIBV), *Annual Report 2000,* Paris: FIBV, 2001.

International Organization of Securities Commissions (IOSCO), *Report on International Disclosure Standards for Cross-Border Offerings and Initial Listings by Foreign Issuers,* September 1998.

International Organization of Securities Commissions (IOSCO), *IASC Standards — Report of the Technical Committee of the International Organization of Securities Commissions*, www.iosco.org, May 2000.

Mueller, Gerhard G., "Harmonization Efforts in the European Union," in *International Accounting and Finance Handbook*, F. D. S., ed., New York: John Wiley & Sons, 1997.

PricewaterhouseCoopers, *International Accounting Standards — Similarities and Differences IAS, US GAAP and UK GAAP*, London: PricewaterhouseCoopers, February 2000.

PricewaterhouseCoopers, *International Accounting Standards in Europe 2005 or Now? The Views of Over 700 Chief Financial Officers*, London: PricewaterhouseCoopers, November 2000.

United Nations Conference on Trade and Development (UNCTAD), The Intergovernmental Working Group of Experts on International Standards of Accounting and Reporting, *United Nations Conference on Trade and Development Conclusions on Accounting and Reporting by Transnational Corporations*, New York and Geneva: United Nations, http://www.unicc.org/unctad/en/pressref/tncacc.htm, 1994.

Wyatt, Arthur R. "International Accounting Standards and Organizations: Quo Vadis?" in *International Accounting and Finance Handbook*, F. D. S., ed., New York: John Wiley & Sons, 1997.

Discussion Questions

1. From a financial statement user's viewpoint, what is the most important source of accounting difference: measurement or disclosure? For which area is it most important to achieve international accounting harmonization?

2. What evidence is there that International Accounting Standards (IAS) are becoming widely accepted around the world? What are at least four different ways that national accounting standard setters use IAS in setting their own standards?

3. What are at least five similarities and at least five differences between IASB standards and those of your home country?

4. Is the growing use of International Accounting Standards around the world an example of accounting harmonization or accounting standardization? Discuss.

5. Compare and contrast the following proposed approaches for dealing with international differences in accounting, disclosure, and auditing standards: (1) reciprocity; (2) reconciliation; (3) international standards.

6. What are the key rationales that support the development and widespread application of International Accounting Standards?

7. What are the key rationales *against* the development and widespread application of International Accounting Standards?

8. What is the purpose of accounting harmonization in the European Union (EU)? Describe each of the following EU directives: the Fourth Directive, the Seventh Directive, and the Eighth Directive.

9. What are three significant differences (if any) between requirements of the EU directives and accounting principles in your home country?

10. Sir Bryan Carsberg states that "The case for harmonisation in accounting standards is a particularly strong one. Accounting has relatively low cultural value." Critically evaluate these statements.

11. Why is the concept of auditing harmonization important? Will international harmonization of auditing standards be more or less difficult to achieve than international harmonization of accounting principles?

12. Describe IOSCO's work on harmonizing disclosure standards for cross-border offerings and initial listings by foreign issuers. Why is this work important to securities regulators around the world?

Exercises

1. Three solutions have been proposed for resolving the problems associated with filing financial statements across national borders: (1) reciprocity (also known as mutual recognition); (2) reconciliation; and (3) use of international standards.

   Required: Present a complete but concise evaluation of each of the three approaches. What do you expect is the preferred approach from the perspective of each of the following groups: (1) investors; (2) company management; (3) regulatory authorities; (4) stock exchanges; and (5) professional associations? Discuss your reasons for each response. Which approach do you predict will eventually dominate?

2. Exhibit 8-1 presents Web site addresses of many major international organizations involved in international accounting harmonization.

   Required:
   a. From among these member organizations, select three that interest you.

    b. For each of the three organizations you select, describe its membership, its organizational focus, and why it is concerned with international financial accounting standard setting.

3. Exhibit 8-2 presents Web site addresses of national accountancy organizations, many of which are involved in international accounting standard-setting and harmonization activities.

    Required: Select one of the accounting organizations and search its Web site for information about its involvement in international accounting standard-setting and harmonization. Prepare a detailed description of the organization's activities in these areas.

4. The text discusses the many organizations involved with international harmonization activities including the IASC, EU, and IFAC.

    Required:
    a. Compare and contrast these three organizations in terms of their standard setting procedures.
    b. At what types and sizes of enterprises are their standards *primarily* directed?
    c. Briefly critique the following statement: "Acceptance of international accounting standards (accounting principles, disclosures, and auditing), as far as it has come and is likely to come in the near future, is significantly centered in companies operating in multiple countries."

5. The chapter contains a chronology of some significant events in the history of international accounting standard setting.

    Required: Select one of the events identified, consult some literature references about it, and prepare a 300-word essay describing the event and indicating why it is deemed significant.

6. Exhibit 8-3 identifies 34 effective IASB standards and their respective titles.

    Required: Using information on the IASB Web site (www.iasb.org.uk), or other available information, prepare an updated list of IASB standards and exposure drafts.

7. Many large global companies specifically state in their annual reports that their financial statements are prepared in accordance with IAS. Exhibit 8-5 shows the distribution of these companies by home country.

    Required: Discuss why most of the companies are based in Continental Europe. Identify other geographic regions that are represented and those that are not represented in Exhibit 8-5. Provide possible explanations for your findings.

8. Appendix 8-1 presents a summary of similarities and differences among IAS, U.S. GAAP, and U.K. GAAP. One section of the summary presents a comparison of 29 main accounting principles.

    Required: Identify at most 5 accounting principle differences between IAS and U.K. GAAP, and at most 5 differences between IAS and U.S. GAAP that potentially have the largest effect on financial statements. Provide a rationale for each of your choices.

9. The IASB Web site (www.iasb.org.uk) summarizes each of the 34 current International Accounting Standards.

    Required: Identify the standards that permit the use of alternative accounting treatments. For each, briefly describe the benchmark treatment and the allowed alternative treatment. To what extent might companies' use of these different treatments reduce the comparability of the resulting financial statements?

10. The IASB Web site (www.iasb.org.uk) summarizes each of the 34 current International Accounting Standards.

   Required: Answer each of the following questions.

   a. In measuring inventories at the lower of cost or net realizable value, does net realizable value mean:
      i. estimated replacement cost, or
      ii. estimated selling price less estimated costs to complete and sell the iinventory?

   b. Under International Accounting Standards, which of the following methods is (or are) acceptable to account for an investment in a joint venture?
      i. cost method
      ii. equity method
      iii. proportionate consolidation
      iv. consolidation

   c. A company has borrowed money by issuing 1-year notes payable with various maturity dates. When such notes become due, the company has consistently refinanced them with new 1-year notes. May these borrowings and repayments be netted in reporting financing activities in the cash flow statement? Yes or No?

   d. A company leases a retail store under a finance lease and, therefore, must recognize the leased asset and the related lease liability in its balance sheet. Is the recognition of the leased asset and related lease liability at inception of the lease:
      i. reported as both an investing activity and a financing activity in the cash flow statement, or
      ii. not reported in the cash flow statement.

   e. Which of the following would be classified as an extraordinary item?
      i. gain resulting from receiving insurance proceeds in excess of the carrying amount of a factory building destroyed by fire
      ii. loss from settlement of a product liability lawsuit
      iii. claims paid by an airline as a result of a plane crash
      iv. destruction of a communications satellite during launch

11. The IASB Web site (www.iasb.org.uk) summarizes each of the 34 current International Accounting Standards.

   Required: Answer each of the following questions.

   a. In Year 1, an enterprise accrued its warranty obligation based on its best estimate of the expected cost to repair defective products during the 3-year warranty coverage period. During Year 2, warranty claims were significantly more than expected due to unrecognized quality control problems in Year 1. Is it appropriate to restate the financial statements for Year 1 to reflect the revised estimate of the warranty obligation?

   b. True or false: An enterprise with a 31 December year-end declares a dividend on its common shares on 5 January. The dividend is recognized as a liability at year-end.

   c. After initial recognition, which of the following financial assets are not remeasured at fair value?
      i. options on unquoted equity securities
      ii. marketable securities (equities)
      iii. derivative financial instruments that are financial assets
      iv. fixed maturity instruments the enterprise intends to hold to maturity

   d. An earthquake in January of Year 2 causes substantial uninsured damage to a company's major factory building. The company's financial statements for the year ended 31 December Year 1 have not yet been published. Is the damage loss recorded in the income statement for:

   i. Year 1
   ii. Year 2

e. A company has 1,000 ordinary shares outstanding and 100 preferred shares. Each preferred share receives a dividend of 1 each year and is convertible into 2 ordinary shares. In Year 1, the company's net income is 1,000 before deducting the preferred dividend. Quantify:

   i. basic earnings per share
   ii. diluted earnings per share

12. Appendix 8-1 summarizes each of the 34 current International Accounting Standards (Refer to IASB Web site, www.iasb.org.uk, for the complete summaries).

Required: Answer each of the following questions.

a. Which of the following is true? An enterprise that follows the policy of revaluing its property, plant, and equipment may apply that policy:

   i. to all assets within a single country on a country-by-country basis
   ii. to all assets within a single broad class, such as to land and buildings but not to machinery and equipment
   iii. to all assets of a certain age, such as all assets 10 years old or older.

b. True or false: Interest cost on funds borrowed by an enterprise to finance the construction of a new building must be capitalized as part of the cost of the building.

c. An enterprise makes a small investment in the ordinary shares of Company X. A year later, how will the investment be carried in the enterprise's balance sheet under International Accounting Standards?

   i. at cost
   ii. at fair value
   iii. at lower of cost and fair value determined on a portfolio basis

d. An enterprise has an asset with a carrying amount of 1,000 that is destroyed. Under the terms of an insurance policy it receives a replacement asset with a fair value of 4,000. How is this transaction recorded?

e. A mining company operates in a country that does not require a mine operator to rehabilitate and restore mining sites once the site has been worked. However, the company has a publicly announced policy of restoring all of its sites. It expects that 90 percent of the eventual cost will relate to the extraction of mineral reserves and 10 percent to the initial development of the mine. What, if any provision for site restoration should it recognize, and when?

Case 8–1   Shanghai Tyre & Rubber Co., Ltd.

Shanghai Tyre & Rubber Co., Ltd. manufactures various automobile and motorcycle tires and rubber-making machinery. The company is headquartered in Shanghai, China and has 6 core factories, 18 wholly owned subsidiaries, 12 jointly owned subsidiaries, and 18 contractual companies. Shanghai Tyre employs 11,800 full-time workers and has a market capitalization of

U.S.$343 million. The company has shares listed on the Shanghai Stock Exchange.

You are an equity research analyst and have been asked to prepare a research report on Shanghai Tyre & Rubber Co. Your business strategy analysis indicates that Shanghai Tyre's sales growth and strong financial performance can probably be sustained. However, although your qualitative analysis has yielded promising results, you are concerned that your financial analysis will be difficult due to accounting and audit quality issues and your unfamiliarity with Chinese accounting standards.

You start your analysis by becoming familiar with the accounting principles used to prepare Shanghai Tyre's 1996 financial statements. You are encouraged that the company states that its financial statements conform to IASB standards, but realize that how accounting standards are applied is as important as the standards themselves.

REQUIRED

Examine Shanghai Tyre's Note 2, "Principal Accounting Policies" in Appendix 8-2, and read about IASB Standards on the IASB Web site (http://www.iasb.org.uk).

1. As much as possible, assess the extent to which Shanghai Tyre's accounting principles conform to IASC standards.
2. How reliable is your assessment?
3. What further information would help your assessment?
4. Does the auditor's report (presented in Appendix 8-2) provide information useful in your assessment? Explain.
5. Refer to Note 10. (also in Appendix 8-2) which presents information on the impact of IAS adjustments on Shanghai Tyre's net profit (loss). Does Note 10 provide information useful to you? In what respects does the reconciliation disclosure in Note 10 differ from Netcom AB's reconciliation disclosure presented in Chapter 5? What financial statement user groups benefit the most from Shanghai Tyre's and Netcom's reconciliation disclosures, respectively?

Case 8–2   Accounting Quality in East Asia

"KOREAN MURK"[1]

For all the salutary shock of Asia's financial crisis, South Korean companies can still cook their books. After the crisis hit South Korea in 1997, the government watchdog for accounting standards tightened up the existing lax rules, but there is still a long way to go. Over the past three years, one in every three companies the watchdog has selected at random turns out to have violated the rules. A study recently published by PricewaterhouseCoopers, an international accounting firm, finds that South Korea has the most opaque standards of accounting and corporate governance of the 35 countries it surveyed.

Opacity may have long been evident, but its effects can still shock. In July 1999, when Daewoo, an industrial giant, collapsed with debts of $80 billion, everybody was taken by surprise. At the end of 1998 it had hugely inflated assets and hidden debts that totaled some $34 billion. Against the inflated assets, the conglomerate borrowed about $7.5 billion from banks, while $20 billion was illegally channeled to a secret account in London, or so claims the state prosecution agency. Now 27 people have been charged, in-

[1]"Asian Corporate Governance: Korean Murk" *The Economist* 358, no. 8215 (March 31, 2001): 69–70. © *The Economist* Newspaper Group, Inc. Reprinted with permission. Further reproduction prohibited.

cluding former senior managers of Daewoo and its auditors. Daewoo's founder, Kim Woo Choong, remains in hiding after fleeing abroad.

Alarmed by the Daewoo collapse, the national assembly passed a law promising harsh punishment to accountants who fail in their duties. Under the law, which takes effect on April 1, the finance minister can fine firms up to 100m won ($380,000), and individuals up to 50m won if they fail to discover that the books they are auditing have been cooked. Accountants also face criminal charges and, if convicted, up to three years in prison.

Such severe punishments may not, however, swiftly bring an end to creative accounting at South Korean companies. For a start, the accounting rules that the government introduced in the wake of the financial crisis still fall far short of international standards. For instance, South Korean companies can count as assets payments that are not due for a year or more.

Another problem is a shortage of qualified auditors. There are about 8,000 companies, including all of South Korea's listed firms, that are required by law to produce financial statements audited by independent accountants. Although some 4,000 accountants are certified to audit financial statements, most of these are tax specialists. Moreover, because almost all companies close their books at the same time, at the end of the calendar year, that creates a sudden increase in the workload.

One way to discourage companies from creative accounting is to introduce a law that would allow minority shareholders to file class-action suits. That is a cause championed by Ha Seung Soo of the People's Solidarity for Participatory Democracy, a civic group that campaigns for the rights of minority shareholders. The finance ministry plans to draft a law which, if passed, would make it possible to bring suits against companies with assets of more than 2 trillion won. Mr. Ha points out that only a dozen or so firms would be affected.

REQUIRED

1. This article states that accounting standards in South Korea "fall far short of international standards." Would the adoption of IAS improve financial reporting quality in Korea?

2. Is it fair to say that this article suggests that formal accounting standards mean relatively little if there is not a general consensus in a country's business culture that these standards be followed and enforced? What changes would need to occur in South Korea for real progress in financial reporting and corporate governance to occur? What are the implications for the prospects for successful accounting harmonization?

3. Many experts say that companies will make credible financial disclosures only if there is a strong investor demand for them. Can improvements in corporate financial reporting and governance be forced in absence of investor demand? What good are regulations in the absence of an underlying demand? Discuss.

CHAPTER 9

INTERNATIONAL FINANCIAL STATEMENT ANALYSIS

INTRODUCTION

Investors, equity research analysts, bankers, and other financial statement users have a growing need to read and analyze nondomestic financial statements and make cross-border financial comparisons. As discussed in Chapter 1, there has been tremendous growth in international capital issuance and trading in recent years due to privatizations, economic growth, relaxation of capital controls, and many other causes.

The need to understand and use nondomestic financial statements has also increased as merger and acquisition activities have become more international. The value of cross-border mergers grew steadily during the 1990s. Measured as a share of world GDP, cross-border mergers rose in value from 0.5 percent in 1987 to over 2 percent in 1999. Most of these deals involved developed countries.[1]

Finally, as business becomes more global, financial statements become more important than ever as a basis for competitive analysis, credit decisions, and business negotiations. Continued reduction in national trade barriers, the emergence of Europe as a unified market, convergence of consumer tastes and preferences, and a growing sophistication of business firms in penetrating nondomestic markets have significantly intensified multinational business competition. All this creates a further need for international financial statement analysis and valuation.

This chapter synthesizes information presented in Chapters 1 through 8 by examining several opportunities and challenges encountered in analyzing foreign financial statements, and provides suggestions for the analyst. The business analysis framework presented in Palepu, Bernard, & Healy[2] provides a useful structure for discussion.

---

[1] *The Economist*, "Emerging-Market Indicators," October 7, 2000, p. 124.
[2] Palepu, Krishna G., Victor L. Bernard, and Paul M. Healy, *Business Analysis and Valuation Using Financial Statements,* Cincinnati, Ohio: South-Western College Publishing, 1996, 685 pp.

CHALLENGES AND OPPORTUNITIES
IN CROSS-BORDER ANALYSIS

Cross-border financial analysis involves multiple jurisdictions; for example, where the analyst is studying companies outside of the home country or comparing companies from two or more countries. Unique challenges face those doing international analysis.

Most important, nations vary dramatically in their accounting practices, disclosure quality, legal and regulatory systems, types and extent of business risk, and numerous other characteristics. This variation means that analysis tools that are effective in one jurisdiction might be ineffective in a different jurisdiction. The analyst often faces daunting challenges in obtaining credible information, and in many emerging market economies, many analyses will have limited reliability.

International financial analysis and valuation are characterized by many contradictions. On one hand, the rapid pace of harmonization of accounting standards is leading to enhanced comparability of financial information worldwide. However, vast differences in financial reporting practices remain, and some analysts question the extent to which greater uniformity in accounting standards will actually result in the provision of comparable information by leading companies in an industry.[3]

As discussed in Chapter 5, companies around the world are disclosing more information, and more credible information. However, in many countries there continues to be a great gulf between expectations based on these advances and reality. For example, many countries including Japan, Korea, and the Czech Republic are striving to improve the availability and quality of information about public companies. Access to freely available information relevant for financial analysis is growing dramatically with dissemination of company information on the Internet. However, at the same time, financial analysts are frustrated in their attempts to gather information (for example, see Cases 4-1 and 8-2 in this text, that deal with difficulties in obtaining company information in the Czech Republic and South Korea, respectively). Many governments continue to publish highly suspect information.

Finally, accounting quality and disclosure credibility have recently been criticized by senior regulators in countries such as the United States, with traditions of full disclosure, "quality" financial reporting, and relatively stringent regulation. In a warning to foreign corporations eager to raise monies in the U.S. capital markets, former U.S. Securities and Exchange Commission chairman, Arthur Levitt Jr., states, "If you want to play with U.S. investors and raise capital in U.S. markets, then you have to play by tougher rules. We're not going to embrace any standard that isn't as good as our own."[4]

However, the barriers to international financial analysis and valuation are falling, and the overall trend for the analyst is positive. The globalization of capital markets, advances in information technology, and increasing competition by national governments, stock exchanges, and companies for investors and trading activity are creating incentives for companies to voluntarily improve their external financial reporting practices.

With continuing globalization and improvements in international accounting and disclosure, the distinctions between cross-border and within-border financial analysis

---

[3]For example, see Trevor Pijper, "More Uniformity, Please—Might Nestlé and Unilever One Day Present Similar Information Similarly?" *Accountancy*, July, 2000, p. 103.
[4]Nanette Byrns, "Needed: Accounting the World Can Trust," *Business Week*, October 12, 1998, p. 46.

will blur. For example, since the implementation of the euro, portfolio diversification strategies in Europe are increasingly based on industry sectors rather than countries. Rather than balancing stock picks among strong and weak currency countries, portfolio managers can focus on picking the best companies in an industry regardless of country of origin.

Globalization also means that strictly domestic analysis becomes less relevant. Interdependencies are growing and no company is insulated from events happening worldwide. Thus, international dimensions of financial analysis are becoming more tractable, yet at the same time, less easy to avoid.

BUSINESS ANALYSIS FRAMEWORK

Palepu, Bernard, and Healy introduce and develop a framework for business analysis and valuation using financial statement data. The framework's four stages of analysis (discussed in more detail in the following pages) are: (1) business strategy analysis; (2) accounting analysis; (3) financial analysis (ratio analysis and cash flow analysis); and (4) prospective analysis (forecasting and valuation). The relative importance of each stage depends on the purpose of the analysis. The business analysis framework can be applied to many decision contexts including securities analysis, credit analysis, and merger and acquisition analysis.

INTERNATIONAL BUSINESS STRATEGY ANALYSIS

Business strategy analysis is a necessary first step in financial statement analysis. It provides a qualitative understanding of a company, its competitors, and its economic environment that ensures that quantitative analysis is based on reality. By identifying key profit drivers and business risks, business strategy analysis helps the analyst make realistic forecasts.[5] Standard procedures for gathering information for business strategy analysis include examining annual reports and other company publications, and speaking with company staff, analysts, and other financial professionals. The use of additional information sources, such as the World Wide Web, trade groups, competitors, customers, reporters, lobbyists, regulators, and the trade press is becoming more common. The accuracy, reliability, and relevance of each type of information gathered also needs to be evaluated.[6]

Business strategy analysis is often complex and difficult in an international setting. As noted previously, key profit drivers and type of business risk vary among countries, and understanding them can be daunting. Business and legal environments and corporate objectives vary around the world. Many risks (such as regulatory risk, foreign exchange risk, and credit risk, among others) need to be evaluated and brought together coherently.[7] In some countries, sources of information are limited and may not be accurate.

---

[5]"Profit drivers" are principal financial and operating elements that affect a firm's profitability.
[6]Financial analysts are increasingly using techniques developed in the fast-growing business discipline of "Competitive Intelligence" (CI). See Peter Bartram, "Spies Like Us." *Accountancy*, July, 2000, pp. 44,45.
[7]Refer to Chapter 11 for detailed discussion of financial risk management.

INFORMATION AVAILABILITY

Business strategy analysis is especially difficult in some countries due to a lack of reliable information about macroeconomic developments, industry conditions, and the companies under analysis. Governments in developed countries are sometimes accused of publishing faulty or misleading economic statistics, and the situation is much worse in many emerging economies. For example, one reason the 1994/95 Mexican currency crisis was a surprise was that the government concealed information about its shrinking foreign reserves and exploding money supply. Some countries delay publishing statistics when the numbers are unfavorable, or even falsify their economic figures.[8]

Obtaining industry and company information is also difficult in many countries. Investors frequently complain about a lack of data on overseas companies. The availability and quality of company information varies greatly across countries, and has been strikingly low in many (particularly developing economies).[9] Recently, many large companies that list and raise capital in overseas markets have been expanding their disclosures and have voluntarily switched to globally recognized accounting principles such as International Accounting Standards.[10]

RECOMMENDATIONS FOR ANALYSIS

It is often difficult to do an adequate business analysis in an international setting by using traditional research methods. More frequently, travel is necessary to learn about local business climates and how industries and companies actually operate, especially in emerging market countries. Fortunately, barriers to visiting many emerging market countries have been falling. The World Wide Web also offers quick access to information that recently was difficult or impossible to obtain. Exhibit 9-1 presents a sampling of freely available Web resources that can be used to learn about country risks and travel conditions.

Country information can also be found in "international briefings" publications distributed by large accounting firms, banks, and brokerages.[11] The International Federation of Stock Exchanges (FIBV, http://www.fibv.com) and the Federation of European Stock Exchanges (FESE, http://www.fese.be) publish highly informative international newsletters, and *Accountancy, The Economist, Financial Analysts Journal,* and *Euromoney* magazines provide many articles highly relevant for international financial analysis.

Finally, it is important to remember that enormous risks may follow when an adequate business strategy analysis is not done. Consider the recent financial crisis in East Asia (see Chapter 1). Some commentators have argued that one important cause of the

---

[8]See *The Economist*, "The Insatiable in Pursuit of the Unquantifiable." March 4, 1995: pp. 71,72. for an analysis of the quality of economic statistics in 24 emerging markets.

[9]See Chapter 5, "International Financial Reporting and Disclosure," for further discussion. Also see: Sesit, M.R., "Big Investors Bemoan Lack of Data on Overseas Firms." *The Wall Street Journal*, February 23, 1995, p. C1; *The Economist*, "Asia's Stockmarket Nightmare," December 20, 1997, pp. 107–108; Dwyer, Paula, "Shareholder Revolt," *Business Week* (September 18, 1995), pp. 60–64; "Saudagaran, S. M., and J. G. Diga, "Financial Reporting in Emerging Capital Markets: Characteristics and Policy Issues," *Accounting Horizons*, June, 1997, pp. 41–64.

[10]Refer to Chapter 5 for discussion of other voluntary financial reporting practices companies use to accommodate international financial statement users.

[11]For example, PricewaterhouseCoopers LLC publishes *International Briefings* every month, which reports on notable business, political and economic developments worldwide.

EXHIBIT 9-1	Country Information Freely Available on the Internet	
Organization	*Web Site Address*	*Description*
Political and Economic Risk Consultancy, Ltd. (PERC)	http://www.asiarisk.com/	Country outlooks; connection to other WWW sites
U.S. State Department	http://travel.state.gov/	Travel warnings
Financial Times	http://ft.com	Country reports (also industry reports, company news and financial information)
Canada Department of Foreign Affairs and International Trade	http://www.dfait-maeci.gc.ca/ english/menu.htm	Market information
World Tourism Organization	http://www.world-tourism.org	Newsletters Press releases

crisis was that foreign investors eagerly invested in companies that did not provide complete or credible disclosures, and in markets about which they knew little and in which financial reporting rules were not strictly enforced.[12]

ACCOUNTING ANALYSIS

The purpose of accounting analysis is to assess the extent to which a firm's accounting amounts reflect economic reality. The analyst needs to evaluate the firm's accounting policies and estimates, and assess the nature and extent of a firm's accounting *flexibility*.[13] To reach reliable conclusions, the analyst must adjust reported accounting amounts to remove distortions caused by the use of accounting methods the analyst may judge to be inappropriate. (For example, the analyst might believe that a company's revaluations of fixed assets result in unreasonably high asset carrying amounts.)

Corporate managers are allowed to make many accounting-related judgments because they know the most about their firm's operations and financial condition. Flexibility in financial reporting is important because it allows managers to use the most appropriate methods and estimates for their firm. However, managers have incentives to use accounting discretion to manipulate reported profits, because profits are often used to evaluate managerial performance.[14]

Within their framework, Healy, Bernard, and Palepu suggest the following sequence for evaluating a firm's accounting quality:

1. Identify key accounting policies
2. Assess accounting flexibility

---

[12]See, for example, *The Economist,* "Asia's Stockmarket Nightmare" (December 20, 1997, p. 107); and *Fortune* "Asia: What Went Wrong" (March 2, 1998).

[13]Accounting "flexibility" refers to managerial discretion in choosing which accounting policies and estimates to apply to a particular accounting event.

[14]Healy, Bernard and Palepu list the following systematic influences on corporate managers' accounting decisions: (1) Accounting-based debt covenants; (2) Management compensation; (3) Corporate control contests; (4) Tax considerations; (5) Regulatory considerations; (6) Capital market considerations; (7) Stakeholder considerations; (8) Competitive considerations.

3. Evaluate accounting strategy
4. Evaluate the quality of disclosure
5. Identify potential red flags (e.g. unusually large asset write-offs, unexplained transactions that boost profits, or an increasing gap between a company's reported income and its cash flow from operations)
6. Adjust for accounting distortions[15]

Two unique issues confront those doing accounting analysis in an international setting. The first is cross-country variation in accounting measurement quality, disclosure quality, and audit quality; the second concerns the difficulty in obtaining information needed to conduct accounting analysis.

Cross-country variation in quality of accounting measurement, disclosure, and auditing is dramatic. National characteristics that cause this variation include required and generally accepted practices, monitoring and enforcement, and extent of managerial discretion in financial reporting.[16] Exhibits 3-4 and 4-5 of this text present summaries of significant accounting practices in six highly developed countries and four emerging countries, respectively. The exhibits, which summarize only a subset of major accounting topics, show that significant managerial discretion may be used in many countries including France, Germany, China, and Taiwan.

Consider accounting practices in Germany. As discussed in Chapter 3, German financial accounting is closely aligned with tax reporting, and creditor protection is a second goal of financial reporting. As a result, financial reports are prepared with a creditor focus rather than an investor focus. The resulting conservative reporting bias may generate accounting amounts that do not reflect economic reality. German managers have great discretion in their use of reserves and in implementing many accounting policies. Even where specific procedures are mandated, monitoring and enforcement of compliance with reporting requirements is far short of what investors can expect in the United States.[17]

Disclosure quality and the level of audit assurance must also be closely scrutinized when analyzing a German company's financial statements. Footnote disclosure of accounting policies is quite limited in some German annual reports. Identifying the components of large financial statement items (such as reserve accounts) can be difficult. Also, the German auditing environment is dramatically different from countries such as the United States and the United Kingdom. Auditor independence rules in Germany are much less comprehensive and intricate than in the United States and the United

---

[15]For example, evaluating the accounting quality of Océ NV, a Dutch Company, could include questions under each of the points listed in this paragraph such as (1) Does Océ NV periodically revalue its fixed assets? (2) What options do Dutch GAAP allow for fixed asset valuation? (3) Has Océ adopted a conservative or aggressive approach in valuing balance sheet items? (4) Does Océ disclose enough information for the financial statement user to "undo" its conservative (or aggressive) valuation strategy? (5) Has Océ made unusually large asset write-offs, reported unexplained transactions that boost profits, or do comparable financial statements reveal an increasing gap between Océ's reported income and its cash flows from operations? and (6) Remove the financial statement effects (if any) of Océ's highly conservative (or aggressive) depreciation policies.

[16]See Khalaf, Roula, "Buyer Beware," *Forbes*, June 29, 1994: 204; *Euromoney* Capital Markets Report, "Equity? Was ist das?" July, 1994, p. 82; Henriques, Diana B., "In World Markets, Loose Regulation," *New York Times*, July 23, 1991, pp. D1, D6.

[17]For example, the Deutsche Börse's Neuer Markt has faced continuing problems with high profile occurrences of fraud and other financial reporting inadequacies.

Kingdom, and German managers might consider it inappropriate for auditors to question their oral statements. German auditors are also more hesitant to accept responsibility for detecting irregularities than their U.S. or U.K. counterparts.[18]

External auditors play a key role in assuring that accounting standards are followed. Legal systems provide enforcement mechanisms for ensuring that auditors remain as independent a practicable. However, audit environments are not uniform around the world. Exhibit 9-2 presents cross-country differences in auditor liability by country and audit firm, and shows that auditor litigation has been rare in Germany.[19]

Financial reporting in China provides a second example of how accounting measurement, disclosure, and audit quality can vary dramatically from accounting practices in Anglo-American countries. Although China is implementing major accounting reform as part of its transition from a planned economy to a controlled market economy, until recently it did not have financial reporting and external auditing in forms that would be familiar to Westerners.[20] Private investors and creditors were virtually nonexistent for 3 decades after the People's Republic was founded in 1948, and The Accounting Law, which sets forth accounting and reporting requirements, was adopted only in 1985. Accounting Standards for Business Enterprises, which specifies that such

EXHIBIT 9-2   Recent Auditor's Liability Cases by Country and Audit Firm

Country	Arthur Andersen	Coopers & Lybrand	Deloitte Touche	Ernst and Young	KPMG	Price Waterhouse	Others	Total
United States	7	8	7	3	5	1	4	35
United Kingdom	1	3	3	2	5	1	2	17
Australia	1	1	4	—	3	3	2	14
Canada	—	3	1	2	1	—	3	10
Italy	1	—	—	1	2	2	1	7
Spain	1	1	—	1	—	2	—	5
New Zealand	—	—	—	1	1	—	1	3
Germany	—	—	—	1	—	1	—	2
Hong Kong	—	—	1	—	—	1	—	2
Ireland	—	—	—	1	—	—	1	2
Sweden	—	—	—	—	1	1	—	2
Netherlands	—	—	—	1	—	—	—	1
Total	**11**	**16**	**16**	**13**	**18**	**12**	**14**	**100**

Source: Bavishi, Vinod B., ed., and Center for International Financial Analysis & Research, Inc., *International Accounting and Auditing Trends*, 4ᵗʰ Edition, 1995, Vol. II, Princeton, NJ: CIFAR Publications, Inc., 1995, 81.

---

[18]See Frost, Carol A. and Kurt P. Ramin, "International Auditing Differences," *Journal of Accountancy*, April 1996, p. 62–67; Frost, Carol A. and Kurt P. Ramin, "Corporate Financial Disclosure: A Global Assessment," in Frederick D. S. Choi, Ed., *International Accounting and Finance Handbook*, New York: John Wiley & Sons, Inc., 1997: 18.1–18.33; Coopers & Lybrand Deutsche Revision AG, *Accounting and Auditing in Germany, Third Edition*, January, 1991.

[19]Refer to Chapter 3 for further discussion of financial reporting in Germany.

[20]For further discussion, see Chapter 4; Ajay Adhikari, and Shawn Z. Wang, "Accounting for China," *Management Accounting*, April, 1995: 27–32; *The Economist*, "Asia's Stockmarket Nightmare, December 20, 1997: 107–108; and David Cairns, "When East Meets West," *Accountancy—International Edition*.

basic accounting practices as double-entry bookkeeping and the accrual basis should be used, became effective in 1993. The auditing profession is also very new in China.[21]

SUGGESTIONS FOR THE ANALYST

Especially when analyzing companies in emerging market countries, the analyst should meet often with management to evaluate their financial reporting incentives and accounting policies. Many companies in emerging market countries are closely held, and managers may not have strong incentives for full and credible disclosure. Accounting policies in some countries may be similar or identical to IAS (or other widely accepted standards), but managers often have great discretion in how those policies are applied.

For example, one portfolio manager described his analysis of Siam Cement, the leader in Thailand's cement industry, and a recently established competitor.[22] Siam Cement depreciated parts of its cement plant over 5 years. This aggressive strategy was designed to minimize tax payments because financial records must conform to tax records in Thailand. In contrast, the competitor used a depreciation period of 20 years to maximize reported earnings (which meant that it paid more tax than necessary).

It is critical for the analyst to remember that the level of credibility and rigor of financial reporting in Anglo-American countries is generally much higher than that found elsewhere. In fact, financial reporting quality can be surprisingly low in both developed and emerging market countries.[23]

Finally, as noted earlier, new communications technology (including the World Wide Web) is having a great impact on all stages of financial research. Many companies and countries now have Web sites that make it much easier for anyone interested to gather information. Refer to the section entitled "Information Access" later in this chapter for a discussion of useful information sources for accounting analysis.

INTERNATIONAL FINANCIAL ANALYSIS

The goal of financial analysis is to evaluate a firm's current and past performance, and to judge whether its performance can be sustained. Ratio analysis and cash flow analysis are important tools in financial analysis. Ratio analysis involves comparison of ratios between the firm and other firms in the same industry, comparison of a firm's ratios across years or other fiscal periods, and/or comparison of ratios to some absolute benchmark.[24] It provides insights on the comparative and relative significance of financial statement items. Palepu, Bernard, and Healy point out that ratio analysis can

---

[21]See Sarah Gray, Ed., "World Watch—Will China's Firms Conquer the World?" *Accountancy-International Edition,* September 1997, page 6.

[22]See Denning, Mark E., "The Essentials of Emerging Markets Research," in *Investing Worldwide VII— Focus on Emerging Markets,* Charlottesville, Virginia: Association for Investment Management and Research (AIMR), September 1996, 72 pp.; and Dean LeBaron, "Emerging Markets Research—Must You Be There?" in *Investing Worldwide VII—Focus on Emerging Markets,* Charlottesville, Virginia: Association for Investment Management and Research (AIMR), September 1996, 72 pp.

[23]For example, see "Asia's Stock Market Nightmare" in *The Economist,* December 20, 1997, page 107.

[24]See Palepu, Bernard and Healy (1996); Stickney, Clyde P. and Paul R. Brown, *Financial Reporting and Statement Analysis* (Fort Worth, The Dryden Press, 1998); and White, Sondhi and Fried (1998) for further discussion.

help evaluate the effectiveness of managers' policies in (1) operating management, (2) investment management, (3) financing strategy, and (4) dividend policies. A summary of commonly used financial ratios appears in Exhibit 9-3.

Cash flow analysis focuses on the cash flow statement, which provides information about a firm's cash inflows and outflows, classified among operating, investing, and financing activities, and disclosures about periodic noncash investing and financing activities. Analysts can use cash flow analysis to address many questions about the firm's performance and management. For example, has the firm generated positive cash flows from operations? How have cash flow components changed across time? What have been the cash flow consequences of management decisions about financial policy, dividend policy, and investment?[25]

RATIO ANALYSIS

Two issues must be addressed in analyzing ratios in an international setting. First, do cross-country differences in accounting principles cause significant variation in financial statement amounts of companies from different countries? Second, how do differences in local culture and economic and competitive conditions affect the interpretation of accounting measures and financial ratios, even if accounting measurements from different countries are restated to achieve "accounting comparability"?

Extensive evidence reveals substantial cross-country differences in profitability, leverage, and other financial statement ratios and amounts that result from both accounting and non-accounting factors. (The next section discusses cross-country differences in two *valuation* ratios, the price-to-earnings and price-to-book ratios.) For example, Exhibit 9-4 compares sales revenue, net income, and leverage (total debt/shareholders' equity) from 400 firms, 80 each domiciled in France, Germany, Japan, the United Kingdom, and the United States.[26] The five 80-firm country samples were matched according to size (market value of equity), and all firms belong to the manufacturing industry group (SIC codes 20 through 39). Exhibit 9-4 shows that all three financial measures vary substantially among the country samples. For example, median net income is much greater in the United Kingdom and the United States than in Germany and Japan. Variation in net income is partially explained by accounting principle differences because financial reporting is generally less conservative in the United Kingdom and the United States than in Germany and Japan. Non-accounting factors also affect reported net income. For example, the creditor focus in France, Germany, and Japan may result in lower net income than in the United States and the United Kingdom because there is less pressure on managers in those countries to report steadily increasing net income.

Exhibit 9-4 also shows that median leverage in the United Kingdom and the United States is lower than in Germany and Japan, partially because conservative accounting in Germany and Japan results in lower reported shareholders' equity than in the United Kingdom and the United States. Higher leverage in Germany, Japan (and France) also

---

[25]See Palepu, Bernard and Healy (1996), Stickney and Brown (1998) and White, Sondhi and Fried (1998) for further discussion.

[26]See Carol A. Frost, "Characteristics and Information Value of Corporate Disclosures of Forward-Looking Information in Global Equity Markets," Dartmouth College Working Paper, February 1998, 43 pp.

EXHIBIT 9-3 Summary of Financial Ratios

Ratio	*Formula for Computation*
I. Liquidity	
1. Current ratio	$\dfrac{\text{Current assets}}{\text{Current liabilities}}$
2. Quick or acid-test ratio	$\dfrac{\text{Cash, marketable securities \& receivables}}{\text{Current liabilities}}$
3. Current cash debt ratio	$\dfrac{\text{Net cash provided by operating activities}}{\text{Average current liabilities}}$
II. Efficiency	
4. Receivables turnover	$\dfrac{\text{Net sales}}{\text{Average trade receivables (net)}}$
5. Inventory turnover	$\dfrac{\text{Cost of goods sold}}{\text{Average inventory}}$
6. Asset turnover	$\dfrac{\text{Net sales}}{\text{Average total assets}}$
III. Profitability	
7. Profit margin on sales	$\dfrac{\text{Net income}}{\text{Net sales}}$
8. Rate of return on assets	$\dfrac{\text{Net income}}{\text{Average total assets}}$
9. Rate of return on common stock equity	$\dfrac{\text{Net income minus preferred dividends}}{\text{Average common stockholders' equity}}$
10. Earnings per share	$\dfrac{\text{Net income minus preferred dividends}}{\text{Weighted shares outstanding}}$
11. Payout ratio	$\dfrac{\text{Cash dividends}}{\text{Net income}}$
IV. Coverage	
12. Debt to total assets ratio	$\dfrac{\text{Debt}}{\text{Total assets or equities}}$
13. Times interest earned	$\dfrac{\text{Income before interest charges and taxes}}{\text{Interest charges}}$
14. Cash debt coverage ratio	$\dfrac{\text{Net cash provided by operating activities}}{\text{Average total liabilities}}$
15. Book value per share	$\dfrac{\text{Common stockholders' equity}}{\text{Outstanding shares}}$

Source: Donald E. Kleso and Jerry J. Weygendt, *Intermediate Accounting, 9e* (New York: John Wiley & Sons, Inc., 1998) p. 1384. This material is used by permission of John Wiley & Sons, Inc.

EXHIBIT 9-4 **Financial Characteristics and Major Shareholdings of 400 Firms Domiciled in France, Germany, Japan, the United Kingdom, and the United States During 1993[1]**

		France	Germany	Japan	United Kingdom	United States
Number of Firms in Sample		80	80	80	80	80
Sales[2] ($U.S. millions)	Mean (Median)	2,262.293 (617.039)	3,571.104 (760.686)	2,053.024 (405.415)	1,310.285 (289.887)	1,645.58 (426.98)
Net Income[2] ($U.S. millions)	Mean (Median)	41.289 (8.296)	−21.884 (1.808)	−15.522 (0.894)	67.098 (19.688)	50.413 (13.188)
Leverage[2] (Total debt/ shareholders' equity)	Mean (Median)	1.007 (0.665)	1.116 (0.560)	2.032 (1.282)	0.852 (0.330)	0.514 (0.400)
Major Shareholdings[3] as Percentage of Total Outstanding Shares	Mean (Median)	0.597 (0.589)	0.595 (0.600)	0.445 (0.403)	0.233 (0.149)	0.336 (0.304)

[1]This table presents summary statistics for 400 sample firms, 80 each domiciled in France, Germany, Japan, the United Kingdom, and the United States, matched on market value of equity (as of late calendar 1993), and all drawn from the manufacturing industry group (SIC codes 20–39).

[2]Financial and equity data are from *Compact Disclosure* for the 80 U.S. sample firms, and from *Worldscope* for the 320 non-U.S. firms. Sales revenue and net income are for fiscal 1993, where fiscal 1993 includes fiscal years ending July 1, 1993 through June 30, 1994. Leverage (total debt to book value of shareholders' equity) is as of the fiscal 1993 balance sheet date.

[3]Major shareholdings are from *Compact Disclosure* ("shares held by 5% shareholders") for U.S. firms, and from *Worldscope* for non-U.S. firms. The major shareholding measures are not strictly comparable, because of variation in major shareholding disclosure thresholds in the five countries.

Source: Carol A. Frost, "Characteristics and Information Value of Corporate Disclosures of Forward-Looking Information in Global Equity Markets," Dartmouth College Working Paper, February 1998.

results from more debt in the capital structure, reflecting the heavy dependence on bank financing in those countries.[27]

How large are the differences in financial statement items caused by differences among national accounting principles? Hundreds of non-U.S. companies listed on U.S. stock exchanges give footnote reconciliation disclosures that provide evidence on this question, at least in the context of differences between U.S. GAAP-based and non-U.S. GAAP-based accounting amounts.

A survey of financial statement reconciliations by foreign registrants prepared by the U.S. SEC[28] provides a detailed discussion of the principal income statement reconciling differences disclosed in registration statements or annual reports filed by non-U.S. registrants during the period of 1991 through 1993. Exhibit 9-5 shows that 84 of the

[27]For example, see Raghuram G. Rajan and Luigi Zingales, "What Do We Know about Capital Structure? Some Evidence from International Data," *The Journal of Finance*, 50 (December 1995), pp. 1421–1460; R. Jacobson and D. Aaker, "Myopic Management Behavior with Efficient, But Imperfect, Financial Markets," *Journal of Accounting and Economics* 19 (October 1993), pp. 383–405; S. H. Hanke and A. Walters, "Governance," *Forbes* (April 11, 1994), p. 87; and *Euromoney*, "Equity, Was ist das?" (July 1994), pp. 82, 84–85.

[28]U.S. Securities and Exchange Commission, Division of Corporation Finance, *Survey of Financial Statement Reconciliations by Foreign Registrants*, May 1, 1993, 54 pp.

528 registrants surveyed used U.S. GAAP. Two hundred and eighty-six of the remaining 444 registrants disclosed material differences between net income as reported in their financial statements and U.S. GAAP-based net income. The exhibit also shows that the five types of financial statement differences disclosed by the largest number of registrants are (in descending order): (1) depreciation and amortization, (2) deferred or capitalized costs, (3) deferred taxes, (4) pensions, and (5) foreign currency translation.

Exhibit 9-6 presents further results from the SEC study, and shows that more than two-thirds of the registrants that disclosed material differences in net income reported that income under U.S. GAAP was lower than under foreign GAAP. Nearly half of them reported income differences greater than 25 percent. Twenty-five of the 87 registrants that reported that income under U.S. GAAP was *greater* than under foreign

EXHIBIT 9-5 Frequency of Income Statement Reconciling Differences Disclosed by Foreign Registrants in the United States During 1991–1993[1]	
Total Registrants Surveyed	528
Registrants Reporting No Material Differences	158
Registrants Reporting Reconciling Items	286
Registrants Using U.S. GAAP	84

Differences:[2]	Number of Registrants
Depreciation and Amortization	137
Deferred or Capitalized Costs	117
Deferred Taxes	114
Pensions	66
Foreign Currency Translation	62
Gain/Loss on Disposed Assets	48
Business Combinations	37
Extraordinary Items, Discontinued Operations and Changes in Accounting	37
Compensation	26
Equity Method	23
Investments	19
Full Cost Write-down	18
Research and Development	14
Preferred Dividends	7
Other[3]	103

[1]Categorization of balance sheet reconciliation differences is not included. Such differences were attributable to the same general categories as the income statement differences.

[2]General categories of reconciling differences were identified to permit aggregation of similar items. A registrant may have differences in more than one category. Reconciling differences identified in the survey relate only to the fiscal year included in the survey and may not be indicative of future or prior periods.

[3]This category is an aggregation of dissimilar reconciling differences that occurred more frequently such as early retirement, revenue recognition, contingencies, minority interests, and leases.

Source: U.S. Securities and Exchange Commission, Division of Corporation Finance, *Survey of Financial Statement Reconciliations by Foreign Registrants,* Washington, D.C.: U.S. Securities and Exchange Commission, May 1, 1993.

EXHIBIT 9-6 Reconciliation Variances

Panel A—Income

Income Under U.S. GAAP Versus Income Under Foreign GAAP	Number of Registrants
Positive Reconciliation Variances:	
(U.S. GAAP Greater)	
More than 100%	8
50.01% to 100%	8
25.01% to 50%	9
10.01% to 25%	15
0.01% to 10%	47
	87
Negative Reconciliation Variances:	
(U.S. GAAP Less)	
More than 100%	33
50.01% to 100%	23
25.01% to 50%	26
10.01% to 25%	44
0.01% to 10%	60
	186
Reported No Material Differences	158

Panel B—Equity

Equity Under U.S. GAAP Versus Equity Under Foreign GAAP	Number of Registrants
Positive Reconciliation Variances:	
(U.S. GAAP Greater)	
More than 100%	20
50.01% to 100%	9
25.01% to 50%	8
10.01% to 25%	17
0.01% to 10%	31
	85
Negative Reconciliation Variances:	
(U.S. GAAP Less)	
More than 100%	11
50.01% to 100%	19
25.01% to 50%	23
10.01% to 25%	41
0.01% to 10%	65
	159
Reported No Material Differences	162

Source: U.S. Securities and Exchange Commission, Division of Corporation Finance, *Survey of Financial Statement Reconciliations by Foreign Registrants,* Washington, D.C.: U.S. Securities and Exchange Commission, May 1, 1993.

GAAP reported differences greater than 25 percent. Panel B of Exhibit 9-6 reports similar results for reconciliations of shareholders' equity. Overall, the evidence in the SEC study shows that financial statement differences under U.S. versus non-U.S. GAAP are highly material for many companies, and that U.S. GAAP tend to result in lower net income and higher shareholders' equity than non-U.S. GAAP.

Evidence from SEC registrants' reconciliation disclosures therefore indicates that GAAP differences can cause significant variation in financial statement numbers. The analyst will often choose to make financial statements more comparable by making accounting principle adjustments to the financial statements being analyzed. Appendix 9-1 illustrates the restatement of an income and balance sheet from Japan GAAP to U.S. GAAP.

Even after financial statement amounts are made reasonably comparable (by adjusting for accounting principle differences), interpretation of those amounts must consider cross-country differences in economic, competitive, and other conditions. Analysis of Japanese companies provides a good illustration. For example, Brown and Stickney argue that the relation between financial and tax reporting, the importance in Japan of operating through corporate groups (*keiretsu*), and the tolerance in Japan for heavy use of short-term financial leverage must all be considered when analyzing the profitability and risk of Japanese companies.[29] For example, Japanese reported earnings tend to be lower than earnings reported in Anglo-American countries, even after adjusting for GAAP differences. The close linkage between tax and financial reporting gives Japanese companies an incentive to be conservative in determining their income. Also, because high intercorporate stock holdings reduce the percentage of shares held by outsiders, Japanese companies are under less pressure to report ever-increasing earnings than are companies in the United States and other Anglo-American countries.[30]

Refer to Appendix 9-2 for further detailed discussion of international ratio analysis. The appendix focuses on comparison of Japanese and U.S. financial ratios and their interpretation.

CASH FLOW ANALYSIS

As discussed earlier, cash flow analysis provides insights about a company's cash flows and management. Highly detailed cash flow statements are required under U.S. GAAP, U.K. GAAP, IAS, and accounting standards in a growing number of other countries.[31] Cash flow-related measures are especially useful in international analysis because they are less affected by accounting principle differences than are earnings-based measures.

When cash flow statements are not presented, it is often difficult to compute cash flows from operations and other cash flow measures by adjusting accrual-based earnings. Many companies simply do not disclose the information needed to make the

---

[29]Brown, Paul R. and Clyde P. Stickney. Instructional Case: Tanaguchi Corporation, *Issues in Accounting Education* 7 (Spring, 1992): 57–68.

[30]McKinnon (Jill L. McKinnon, "Application of Anglo-American Principles of Consolidation to Corporate Financial Disclosure in Japan," in *ABACUS* 20 (1984): 16–33) provides further detail on corporate groups in Japan versus those in Anglo-American countries. She argues that the Anglo-American consolidation methods adopted by Japan in 1977 may reflect international pressure for accounting conformity more than the inherent desirability of those methods. She implies that as a result, Japanese consolidated financial statements are less useful than they might be otherwise. The McKinnon study provides an important illustration that knowing what accounting principles are used is only the first step in interpreting financial statements from different countries.

[31]Refer to Chapters 3 and 4 of this text.

adjustments. As one example, German balance sheets often contain surprisingly large reserve accounts that reflect many different types of accrual. Few (if any) details are presented that might allow the financial statement user to assess the implications for operating, investment, and financing cash flows.

COPING MECHANISMS

How do financial statement users cope with cross-country accounting principle differences? Several approaches are used. Some analysts restate foreign accounting measures to an internationally recognized set of principles, or to some other common basis. Others develop a detailed understanding of accounting practices in a limited set of countries and restrict their analysis to firms located in those countries.

Brown, Soybel, and Stickney illustrate the use of a restatement algorithm to enhance cross-border comparisons of financial performance.[32] They restate the operating performance of U.S. and Japanese companies to a similar reporting basis. Rather than convert U.S. data to a Japanese financial reporting basis, or Japanese data to a U.S. financial reporting basis, they adjust (as necessary) both U.S. and Japanese data to achieve uniform accounting principles.[33]

Speidell and Bavishi analyzed over 100 companies from 12 countries and, using a spreadsheet template, made adjustments to standardize accounting for depreciation, non-equity and discretionary reserves, goodwill, consolidation, valuation of investment, asset revaluation, inventory adjustments, intercompany transactions, foreign currency translation, extraordinary items, and deferred taxes.[34] Speidell and Bavishi discuss different approaches that can be used in restatement. For example, when two companies are compared, their financial items can be adjusted to a common basis. Another approach is to assume a company's operating structure is similar to other multinational companies in the same industry and use (for example) average depreciation expenses of those companies. Speidell and Bavishi report highly significant restatement adjustments in net income, operating income, and book value for companies in many of the countries analyzed.

Appendix 9-1 illustrates a third approach, in which the financial statements of a hypothetical Japanese business (Nis-Son Enterprises Inc.) are restated from a Japan GAAP basis to a U.S. GAAP basis. The restatement algorithm used in Appendix 9-1 involves a detailed analysis of numerous financial statement items.

Relatively simple restatement algorithms can be effective. One approach is to focus on a few of the most material financial statement differences for which enough information is available to make reliable adjustments. For example Brown, Soybel, and Stickney summarize many differences between Japan and U.S. GAAP, but their restatement algorithm focuses on only four accounting principle differences: (1) inven-

---

[32]Paul R. Brown, Virginia E. Soybel and Clyde P. Stickney, "Comparing U.S. and Japanese Corporate-Level Operating Performance Using Financial Statement Data," *Strategic Management Journal,* February 1994.

[33]Brown, Paul R., Virginia E. Soybel, and Clyde P. Stickney, "Achieving Comparability of U.S. and Japanese Price-Earnings Ratios," in Choi, Frederick D. S., Ed., *International Accounting and Finance Handbook, Second Edition* (New York: John Wiley & Sons, Inc., 1997), pp. 7.1–7.18.

[34]Lawrence S. Speidell and Vinod B. Bavishi, "GAAP Arbitrage: Valuation Opportunities in International Accounting Standards," *Financial Analysts Journal* (Nov.-Dec. 1992): pp. 58–66.

tory cost assumptions, (2) depreciation method, (3) bonuses to directors and statutory auditors, and (4) deferred taxes and special tax reserves.[35]

However, even simple restatement approaches involve a lot of work. It is, therefore, no surprise that analysts who work with many companies increasingly rely on financial statement amounts that commercial vendors have restated to a common accounting basis.

Choi and Levich contrast the restatement approach with one that removes the need to conduct cross-market financial analysis and valuation.[36] With their approach, each country or multiple country region is followed by an analyst who adopts a local perspective and becomes a specialist for that geographic area. Institutional investors who follow this approach can be said to have developed a *multiple principles capability* (MPC). This approach is possible because international investment firms tend to be organized along geographic lines, with individual analysts or analyst groups following a single country or region.

In an earlier study, Choi and Levich conducted in-depth interviews with institutional investors, corporate issuers, investment underwriters, and other market participants in Japan, Switzerland, the United Kingdom, the United States, and Germany.[37] Approximately one-half of those interviewed said that their capital market decisions were affected by accounting diversity. More than half of the investors interviewed said that accounting differences hindered the measurement of their decision variables and ultimately affected their investment decisions.

Many investors coped by restating foreign accounting amounts in the reporting principles of their home country or in an internationally recognized set of accounting principles. However, restatement did not eliminate the problem of accounting diversity. This suggests that (at least for some financial statement users) existing restatement algorithms are not optimal, are being applied improperly, or cannot produce meaningful information.

In 1996 Choi and Levich analyzed accounting and disclosure diversity in Europe to assess whether variation in national norms create significant barriers to financial statement users, thus discouraging investment in particular national markets.[38] They argue that differences in international accounting principles are so significant that cross-country comparisons based on publicly reported accounting data might not be meaningful, and note that "top-down" investment approaches might be affected by this problem. With a top-down investment approach, investors first decide on an asset allocation across countries based on macroeconomic variables. The resulting portfolio consists of companies from different *country* groups rather than *industry* groups. Because each country has a fixed weight within the portfolio, investors can then select the best stocks in each country, rather than compare companies in a single industry but in different countries.

A few investors surveyed by Choi and Levich relied on original accounting statements and a well-developed knowledge of foreign accounting practices and financial

---

[35]See Brown, Paul R., Virginia E. Soybel, and Clyde P. Stickney, "Achieving Comparability of U.S. and Japanese Price-Earnings Ratios," in Choi, Frederick D. S., Ed., *International Accounting and Finance Handbook, Second Edition* (New York: John Wiley & Sons, Inc., 1997), pp. 7.1–7.18

[36]See Choi, Frederick D. S., and Richard M. Levich, "Accounting Diversity," in Steil, Benn, Ed., *The European Equity Markets: The State of the Union and an Agenda for the Millennium* (London: European Capital Markets Institute, 1996), pp. 259–320.

[37]Choi, Frederick D. S. and Richard M. Levich, *The Capital Market Effects of International Accounting Diversity* (Homewood, IL: Dow Jones-Irwin, 1990).

[38]Choi and Levich (1996), op. cit.

market conditions. These investors reported no decision problems or capital market effects.

Special coping mechanisms are needed for financial analysis of companies in countries such as Japan, which are characterized by low disclosure levels and a culture of secrecy (especially vis-à-vis foreigners). One response by pension funds and other institutions investing in Japan has been to use Japanese fund managers who, as natives, have better access to information about Japanese companies.[39]

INTERNATIONAL PROSPECTIVE ANALYSIS

Prospective analysis involves predicting a company's future, and is the final step in Palepu, Bernard, and Healy's business analysis framework. Forecasting and valuation are the two main steps in prospective analysis.

In forecasting, analysts make explicit forecasts to communicate their assessments of firms' prospects. Palepu, Bernard, and Healy point out that forecasting is not a separate activity, but rather a way to summarize the results of business strategy analysis, accounting analysis, and financial analysis. For example, how will a company's change in business strategy affect future sales volume and profits? Has the company recently adopted new accounting policies that will make current earnings appear stronger, perhaps at the cost of lower earnings next year? Will financial ratio trends identified in financial analysis continue into future periods?

In valuation, the second step of prospective analysis, analysts convert quantitative forecasts into an estimate of a firm's value. Valuation is used implicitly or explicitly in many business decisions. For example, valuation is the basis of equity analysts' investment recommendations. In analyzing a possible merger, the potential acquirer will estimate the value of the target firm. Many different valuation approaches are used in practice, ranging from complex methods such as discounted cash flow analysis to simpler techniques based on price-based multiples.[40]

Experts in international valuation give this warning to those doing international prospective analysis: "Any rules you've learned in your home country will fall apart overseas." Exchange rate fluctuations, accounting differences, different business practices and customs, capital market differences, and many other factors will have major effects on international forecasting and valuation.

Here we very briefly discuss the use of price-based (valuation) multiples in an international setting. Our goal is to illustrate a few of the issues facing those who do in-

---

[39]For further discussion and evidence on how financial professionals cope with accounting diversity, see Frederick D. S. Choi and Richard M. Levich, "International Accounting Diversity and Capital Market Decisions," in Choi, Frederick D. S., Ed., *International Accounting and Finance Handbook, Second Edition* (New York: John Wiley & Sons, Inc., 1997), pp. 6.1–6.26. For further discussion of international financial analysis, see Frederick D. S. Choi, Ed., *International Accounting and Finance Handbook*, Second Edition, (New York: John Wiley & Sons, Inc., 1997), 39 Chapters; Choi and Levich (1990, 1996, 1997); the many publications of the Association for Investment Management and Research that include papers on a variety of international financial and business analysis subjects. Also see Jan R. Squires, Ed. *ICFA Continuing Education: Finding Reality in Reported Earnings* (Charlottesville, Virginia, AIMR, May, 1997), 68 pages, Katrina F. Sherrerd, Ed., *Investing Worldwide VII: Focus on Emerging Markets* (Charlottesville, Virginia, AIMR, Sept., 1996), 72 pages; and Elizabeth A. Collins, Ed., *Investing Worldwide VI* (Charlottesville, Virginia, AIMR, January, 1996), 78 pages; Vinod B. Bavishi, Ed., *International Accounting and Auditing Trends, 4th Edition, 1995* (Chapters 3 and 4), and other selected references at the end of the chapter.
[40]See Palepu, Bernard, & Healy (1996) for further discussion.

ternational prospective analysis. We do not discuss more complex valuation issues and approaches that are beyond the scope of this text.[41]

Valuation multiples such as price-to-earnings (P/E) and price-to-book (P/B) ratios are often used to estimate a firm's value. One common approach is to calculate the desired multiple for a group of comparable firms (such as other firms in the same industry), and then apply the multiple to the firm being valued to get a reasonable price. For example, if the price-to-earnings ratio of the industry group is 15, and the firm's earnings are forecast to be $1.75/share, then $20.00 per share is a reasonable price for the firm being analyzed. One might use the valuation multiples approach to determine the bid price for an acquisition candidate. If the candidate is a European company, comparable firms might be chosen from selected European countries.

Reliance on valuation multiples assumes that market prices reflect future prospects and that pricing of firms with similar operating and financial characteristics (such as firms in the same industry) is applicable to the firm being analyzed because of its similarity to those firms. Application of price multiples in a cross-border setting is challenging because it requires that the determinants of each multiple, and reasons why multiples vary across firms, be thoroughly understood.

National differences in accounting principles are one source of cross-country variation in these ratios. For example, such differences cause P/E ratios in Japan to generally be higher than those in the United States (recall that reported earnings in Japan are lower than in the United States for comparable companies with similar financial performance). However, even after adjusting for accounting differences, P/E ratios in Japan are still much higher than in the United States.

French and Poterba examined disparities between Japanese and U.S. P/E ratios and the steep increase in Japanese P/E ratios during the late 1980s.[42] They made several accounting adjustments to the Japanese data and found that their adjustments reduced but did not eliminate the difference between Japanese and U.S. P/E ratios. French and Poterba concluded that accounting differences explain about half of the long-term differences between U.S. and Japanese P/E ratios.

Brown, Soybel, and Stickney also investigated why Japanese P/E ratios are higher than U.S. P/E ratios.[43] They found that adjusting for different accounting principles explains only a small part of the difference. A comparison of their study with French and Poterba's shows how different approaches and assumptions can lead to very different conclusions about valuation ratios.[44]

---

[41]For further discussion of international forecasting and valuation issues, see Tom Copeland, Tim Koller, and Jack Murrin, *Valuation: Measuring and Managing the Value of Companies, Second Edition* (New York, John Wiley & Sons, Inc., 1994), Chapters 12 and 13; W. Carl Kester and Julia Morley, *Note on Cross-Border Valuation*, Harvard Business School Case 9-292-084 Rev. 7/6/1992 (Boston, MA, President and Fellows of Harvard College, 1992), 24 pages; and numerous publications issued by the Association for Investment Management and Research, such as the *Investing Worldwide* series.

[42]French, Kenneth R., and James M. Poterba, "Were Japanese Stock Prices Too High?" *Journal of Financial Economics* 29 (1991), pp. 337–362.

[43]Brown, Paul R., Virginia E. Soybel, and Clyde P. Stickney, "Achieving Comparability of U.S. and Japanese Price-Earnings Ratios," op. cit.

[44]See Brown, Soybel and Stickney, "Achieving Comparability of U.S. and Japanese Price-Earnings Ratios," op. cit. for a review of comparative analyses of Japanese and U.S. P/E ratios. For further comparative evidence on cross-country differences in P/E and P/B ratios, see Speidell and Bavishi, op. cit., and Peter Joos and Mark Lang, "The Effects of Accounting Diversity: Evidence from the European Union," *Journal of Accounting Research* 32 (Supplement, 1994) pp. 141–175.

Exhibit 9-7 presents P/E ratios (Panel A) and dividend yields (Panel B) in 1990, 1996, and 1999 for public companies in 12 markets. The exhibit shows that these measures vary dramatically across countries, and across time within a single country. For example, the mean P/E ratio in France increased by about 150 percent from 1990 to 1999. In contrast, German P/E ratios quintupled, and Nasdaq (United States) P/E ratios increased from an average of 11 at year-end 1990 to 205 at year-end 1999.

The substantial variation in valuation ratios shown in Exhibit 9-7 reflects changes in financial performance and in market prices across time and countries. As discussed previously, even French and Poterba's rigorous analysis of the changes in P/E ratios in Japan during the late 1980s yielded only partial answers. Thus, it is probably impossible to fully understand differences among P/E ratios in different countries and over time. The complexity of analyzing P/E ratios suggests that other valuation approaches will also be complex in an international context.

FURTHER ISSUES

All four stages of business analysis (business strategy, accounting, financial analysis, and prospective analysis) may be affected by the following factors: (1) information access, (2) timeliness of information, (3) language and terminology barriers, (4) foreign currency issues, and (5) differences in types and formats of financial statements.

INFORMATION ACCESS

Information about thousands of companies from around the world has become more widely available in recent years. Countless information sources are appearing on the World Wide Web. Companies around the world now have Web sites, and their annual reports are available free of charge from various Internet and other sources. Refer to Exhibit 9-8 for 38 Web sites that provide information highly relevant for company research.

Many companies also respond to written and telephone requests for their annual reports and other financial documents. For example, in one recent study more than 70 percent of a sample of 160 large public companies contacted in France, Germany, the United Kingdom, and the United States responded to written requests for their annual reports.[45] However, only 15 (37.5 percent) of the 40 large Japanese companies contacted responded. Thus, the amount of company information available varies considerably from country to country.

Exhibit 9-9 presents evidence on availability of annual reports of the 20 largest companies in each of four emerging economies: China, Czech Republic, Mexico, and Taiwan. The exhibit shows that only about half of the companies in Taiwan published English language annual reports.

Many commercial databases provide access to financial and stock market data for tens of thousands of companies around the world. Companies covered by commercial databases tend to be large companies that are of the most interest to financial statement users and investors. It is striking that even in emerging market countries such as China and the Czech Republic, data for many firms are now available.

---

[45]See Carol A. Frost and Kurt Ramin, "Corporate Financial Reporting and Disclosure: A Global Assessment" in Choi, F. D. S., ed. *Handbook of International Accounting and Finance, Second Edition*, New York: John Wiley & Sons, April 1997.

EXHIBIT 9-7 Price/Earnings and Dividend Yield Ratios

Panel A—Mean Price/Earnings

Country	1990	1996	1999
China (PRC)	N/A	27.80	48.20
Czech Republic	N/A	12.69	15.94
France	10.20	38.30	24.60
Germany	11.60	20.70	55.00
Japan	39.80	79.30	N/A
Mexico	11.89	13.48	17.20
Netherlands	8.90	17.70	27.50
Taiwan	31.11	29.01	47.73
U.K.	10.60	15.90	30.50
U.S. (Amex)	6.10	20.10	36.20
U.S. (Nasdaq)	11.13	26.30	205.50
U.S. (NYSE)	14.80	20.60	31.26

Panel B—Mean Dividend Yield (%)

Country	1990	1996	1999
China (PRC)	N/A	0.80	0.80
Czech Republic	N/A	1.43	0.62
France	3.94	2.70	1.46
Germany	3.78	1.80	2.60
Japan	0.49	0.72	0.99
Mexico	3.40	1.40	0.80
Netherlands	4.86	2.61	1.80
Taiwan	3.70	3.94	2.68
U.K.	5.60	3.90	2.00
U.S. (Amex)	2.40	1.50	N/A
U.S. (Nasdaq)	N/A	N/A	N/A
U.S. (NYSE)	3.70	2.10	1.10

Sources: World Stock Exchange Fact Book 2000, Round Rock TX: Meridian Securities Markets LLC, except as follows: 1996 and 1999 data for France, and 1999 data for U.S. (Amex) and U.S. (Nasdaq) are from David Rathborne and Deborah Ritchie, eds., *The Salomon Smith Barney Guide to World Equity Markets 2000* (London: Euromoney Books and Salomon Smith Barney, 2000); 1999 data for China (PRC) are from *Emerging Markets Factbook 2000* (New York, Standard and Poor's: May, 2000).

N/A—not available

The *World Stock Exchange Fact Book 2000* defines ratios as follows: P/E Ratio = Total market value of all stocks/Total net earnings of all stocks ina given period; Dividend Yield = Total annualized gross dividends of all stocks/Total market value of all stocks.

EXHIBIT 9-8 **Freely Available Web Sites for Company Research (All Web sites begin with the prefix http://www.)**

Name of Web Site	Web Site Address	What It Provides
Accessing annual reports and accounts	carol.co.uk	Access to annual reports.
Annual Reports Library, The	zpub.com/sf/arl/	Alphabetical listing of U.S. corporations with links to home pages and annual reports that can be downloaded free of charge with Adobe Acrobat Reader.
Annual Report Gallery	reportgallery.com/bigaz.htm	Access to annual reports.
Asian Business Watch	asianbusinesswatch.com	Company and stock market news for Japan and Asia.
Babel	babel.altavista.com	Translates text files; only does first few pages of long documents.
Bank of England	bank of england.co.uk/	United Kingdom monetary and financial statistics, working papers and other publications, information on the bank's structure and functions, and much more.
BFA-NET: Bureau of Financial Analysis Network	bfanet.com	South African company and stock market information; check out "Little Facts."
Bloomberg News Service	bloomberg.com/	Highlights from the Bloomberg news service.
Businessjeeves.com	businessjeeves.com	Good starting place; many links.
Business Week Online	businessweek.com	Current issue, archives, and an assortment of worthwhile data.
CAROL: Company Annual Reports Online	carol.co.uk	Online annual reports for some European companies.
Cross Border Capital	liquidity.com/	Reports on equity, fixed income, and currency markets in over 70 developed and emerging markets. Reports over 6 months old available for free (with registration).
Daiwa Securities	dir.co.jp/Reception/research.html	Research reports and forecasts on the Japanese economy.
Edgar—U.S. Securities & Exchange Commission	sec.gov/edgar.shtml	Most SEC filings since 1996.
Emerging Markets Companion (The)	emgmkts.com/	Many useful links and resources on Asia, Latin America, Africa, and Europe.
EnterWeb: The Enterprise Development Web site	enterweb.org/welcome.htm	Meta-index to business and finance globalization, and more. "The focus is on micro, small and medium enterprise development both in developed and developing countries."
Europages—European Business Directory	europages.com/	Lists 500,000 companies in 30 countries; includes some manufacturer's catalogs.
FEE Euro Information Service	euro.fee.be	Information on the transition to the euro in the European Union; requires registration (free).
Financial Times of London	ft.com/	Online edition of the Financial Times; current articles, market information, and more.
FT Interactive Data	turboguide.com/data2/cdprod1/doc/cdrom.frame/002/686.pub.FT.Excel.html	Good sampling from FT Excel databases; must register

EXHIBIT 9-8 *(cont.)*

Name of Web Site	*Web Site Address*	*What It Provides*
Hong Kong Securities and Futures Commission	hksfc.org.hk	Information on Hong Kong securities markets.
Hoover's Online	hoovers.com	Some information, such as press releases, is free. Links to company home pages and other information. Includes more than 800 of the most important non-U.S. companies.
INO Global Market	ino.com/	Information for traders in futures and options markets worldwide.
International Business Resources on the WWW (Michigan State University Center for International Business Education and Research)	ciber.bus.msu.edu/busres.htm	Links to good investment and macro sites.
International Monetary Fund	imf.org/	IMF news, publications, and more.
Internet Corruption Rankings	gwdg.de/~uwvw/icr_serv.htm	Provides the TI-Corruption Perception Index, a comparative assessment of the integrity of many countries, along with many other links and services.
National Corporate Services, Inc. International Investing	natcorp.com/	Excellent start point; many links to sites providing free financial information.
NIRI Useful Investor Relations Sites	niri.org	Links to interesting Web sites.
Public Register's Annual Report, The	prars.com	Annual reports, prospectuses or 10-K's on over 32,000 U.S. companies.
Rutgers Accounting Network (RAW)	rutgers.edu/Accounting/raw.html	Excellent starting place.
Stewart Mayhew's Directory of Worldwide Securities Exchanges	voltaire.is.tcu.edu/~vmihov/exchanges/xlinks.htm	Links to official home pages of stock markets and derivatives exchanges around the world.
Stock City	stockcity.com	ADR profiles, organized by sector, region, and country. Profiles require Adobe Acrobat Reader.
Streetlink Investor Information Center	streetlink.com	Financial reports available online; U.S. companies only.
United Nations System	unsystem.org	Spotty coverage of companies and accounting information; good information on communications and country background.
USA Today Money	usatoday.com/money/mfront.htm	Comprehensive assortment of news and data.
VIBES: Virtual International Business and Economic Sources—Comprehensive Sources	uncc.edu/lis/library/reference/intbus/vibehome.htm	Great for linking to regional sites; excellent starting place, especially good for macro data.
Wright Investor' Service	profiles.wisi.com	Can search alphabetically, by country, or by industry.
Yahoo! Finance	quote.yahoo.com	Extensive data, news, and stock quotes.

Sources: Sarah Buckingham, Reference Librarian, Feldberg Library, Amos Tuck School of Business, and the authors.

EXHIBIT 9-9	Annual Reports and Whether Listed or Traded				
	No. of Companies with Annual Reports Available for 1999		No. of Companies Listed or Traded		
Country	Home Language	English	London	U.S. Amex, Nasdaq, NYSE	U.S. OTC
China	14	10	2	1	0
Czech Republic	11	11	4	0	1
Mexico	11	10	0	5	1
Taiwan	14	6	3	3	1

Other valuable information sources include (1) government publications, (2) economic research organizations, (3) international organizations such as the United Nations, and (4) accounting, auditing, and securities market organizations. Web site addresses appear throughout this text and are only a starting point for gathering information.

TIMELINESS OF INFORMATION

The timeliness of annual reports, regulatory filings, and accounting-related press releases varies dramatically by country. For example, Exhibit 9-10 gives the average number of days between fiscal year-end and audit report dates for a sample of more than 5,000 companies from 40 countries.[46] Exhibit 9-10 shows that more than 90 days pass between the fiscal year-end and the audit report date in 12 of the countries examined including France, Germany, and Hong Kong. This is a contrast to countries such as the United States, Mexico, and Taiwan, where the number of days averages less than 60.

In one study,[47] Carol Frost reports that the timeliness of earnings-related press releases varies internationally. In this study of 400 firms from the same five countries, she reports the disclosure lags in Exhibit 9-11 (where the lag is the number of days between the fiscal year-end and the date of the press release).

This evidence shows that financial information in most countries (including the United Kingdom) is publicly available much later than in the United States.[48]

---

[46]The audit report date is often considered to be a reasonable indication of when corporate financial information first becomes publicly available.

[47]Carol A. Frost, "Characteristics and Information Value of Corporate Disclosures of Forward-Looking Information in Global Equity Markets," Dartmouth College Working Paper, February 1998.

[48]For further information on the timeliness of disclosures, see Carol A. Frost and Grace Pownall, "Accounting Disclosure Practices in the United States and the United Kingdom," *Journal of Accounting Research* (Spring 1994), pp. 75–102; Carol A. Frost and William R. Kinney, Jr., "Disclosure Choices of Foreign Registrants in the United States," *Journal of Accounting Research* (Spring, 1996); Andrew Alford, Jennifer Jones, Richard Leftwich, and Mark Zmijewski, "The Relative Informativeness of Accounting Disclosures in Different Countries," *Journal of Accounting Research* 31 (Supplement 1993): 183–223; and Christine Botosan and Carol A. Frost, "Regulation, Disclosure and Market Liquidity: An Examination of Foreign Issuers in Regulated versus Less Regulated U.S. Equity Markets" (October 1997), Washington University and Dartmouth College working paper.

EXHIBIT 9-10 Average Number of Days Elapsed Between Fiscal Year-End Date and Date of Auditors' Report[1]

Average Number of Days Elapsed	Countries	Number of Observations
1–30		
31–60	Brazil	40
	Canada	294
	Chile	28
	Colombia	14
	Mexico	28
	Philippines	16
	South Korea	28
	Taiwan	10
	Thailand	34
	United States	2,201
61–90	Argentina	20
	Australia	111
	Denmark	56
	Finland	55
	Ireland	21
	Israel	12
	Japan	1,232
	Netherlands	98
	New Zealand	22
	Norway	31
	Portugal	34
	Singapore	76
	South Africa	128
	Spain	33
	Sweden	83
	Switzerland	73
	United Kingdom	1,091
	Zimbabwe	16
91–120	Austria	30
	Belgium	39
	France	182
	Germany	258
	Greece	18
	Hong Kong	112
	India	238
	Italy	60
	Malaysia	86
	Nigeria	26
	Sri Lanka	24
121 and over	Pakistan	54

[1]This table was prepared using data presented in Bavishi, Vinod B., Ed., *International Accounting and Auditing Trends, 4th Edition, 1995,* Vol. II, Center for International Financial Analysis & Research, Inc., Princeton, NJ: CIFAR Publications, Inc., 1995.

EXHIBIT 9-11	Disclosure Lags	
Country	*Mean Lag (days)*	*Median Lag (days)*
France	73	66
Germany	82	73
Japan	46	49
United Kingdom	72	68
United States	26	23

FOREIGN CURRENCY CONSIDERATIONS

Accounts denominated in foreign currency present financial analysts with two types of problems. The first relates to reader convenience; the second to information content.

The vast majority of companies around the world denominate their financial accounts in the currency of their domicile. To a U.S. reader accustomed to dealing in dollars, analysis of accounts expressed in Dutch guilders may be confusing. A normal inclination is to translate foreign currency balances to domestic currency. However, foreign currency reports are, for the most part, troublesome in appearance only. Financial ratios that transform nominal (interval) measurements to percentage relationships are independent of currency. A current ratio computed from a Dutch balance sheet expressed in guilders is the same as one computed from the same financial statement translated into dollars. Consider the year-end balance sheet accounts of a British company, as found in Exhibit 9-12.

Assuming year-end dollar/pound exchanges rates of $2.10, $2.20, and $1.60 for 20X1, 20X2, and 20X3, respectively, the current ratio will be 1.5 to 1 for 20X1, 1.6 to 1 for 20X2, and 1.6 to 1 for 20X3, whether expressed in British pounds or U.S. dollars. Local currency (e.g., pound) balances are especially appropriate when analyzing financial trends.

Readers who prefer a domestic currency framework when analyzing foreign currency accounts may apply a *convenience translation* using year-end exchange rates. One must be careful, however, when analyzing translated trend data. Use of convenience rates to translate foreign currency accounts can distort underlying financial patterns in local currency. To illustrate, assume the 3-year sales revenue patterns for our British concern found in Exhibit 9-13.

Convenience translations using the year-end exchange rates employed earlier (i.e., $2.10 for 20X1, $2.20 for 20X2, and $1.60 for 20X3) yield a U.S. dollar sales increase of 7.5 percent [($53,056–$49,350) / $49,350] over the 3-year period. The sales gain in pounds, however, is 41 percent [(£33,160–£23,500) / £23,500].

An alternative approach is to translate foreign currency data to domestic currency using a single base year's exchange rate. But which base-year exchange rate should be used? In our example, should the sales figures be translated using the 20X1 exchange rate, the 20X2 exchange rate, or the 20X3 exchange rate?

EXHIBIT 9-12	Year-End Balance Sheets—British Company		
	20X1	*20X2*	*20X3*
Current assets	£12,500	£12,200	£12,800
Current liabilities	£ 8,333	£ 7,625	£ 8,000

EXHIBIT 9-13	Three-Year Sales Revenue—British Company		
	20X1	*20X2*	*20X3*
Sales revenue	£23,500	£28,650	£33,160

Although we prefer to analyze foreign statements in local currency, we favor the use of the most recent year's exchange rate as a convenience translator for readers who prefer domestic currency statistics. An exception is warranted, however, if the foreign currency financial statements have been adjusted for changes in the general purchasing power of the foreign currency unit (see Chapter 7 for a discussion of this treatment). If foreign currency balances are expressed in base-year purchasing power equivalents, year-end exchange rates associated with the given base year should be employed. In our example, if sales revenues were expressed in pounds of 20X1 general purchasing power, the 20X1 exchange rate would have been an appropriate translation rate.

While translated statements give readers the convenience of viewing foreign currency accounts in a familiar currency, they may give a distorted picture. Specifically, exchange rate changes and accounting procedures together often produce domestic currency equivalents that conflict with underlying events. We illustrate this problem using the statement of cash flows as an example.

Recall from Chapter 6 that consolidated financial statements allow a multinational company to report the results of its worldwide operations in a single currency. Also recall that a variety of currency translation methods are in use internationally. Regardless of the currency translation method employed, it is not always clear to readers of consolidated funds flow statements, whether reported fund sources or uses reflect the results of an operational decision or simply an exchange rate change.

To illustrate, the translated statements of earnings, financial position, and cash flows for the Danish affiliate of a U.S.-based multinational company appear in Exhibit 9-14. The parent company employs the current rate method and defines the krone as its functional currency for consolidation purposes.

A cursory examination of the translated statement of cash flows shows that major sources of cash were operations (net income plus depreciation), the issuance of long-term debt, and a translation adjustment. In turn, cash was used to increase the company's investment in fixed assets.

The pattern of cash flow shown in Exhibit 9-14 differs from that experienced by a purely domestic company due to the presence of an aggregate translation adjustment. However, examination of this component of the translated funds statement reveals that it does not really constitute a *source* or *use* of cash. The translation adjustment is calculated by multiplying the beginning foreign currency net asset balance by the change in the current rate during the period and, second, by multiplying the increase or decrease in net assets during the period by the difference between the average exchange rate and end-of-period exchange rate. This procedure, together with the dual nature of the accounting equation, suggests that most components of the translated funds statement are a mix of translation effects and actual cash flows. In our current example, a statement reader needs to figure out whether the increase of long-term debt in the amount of $1,584,000 is an indication of the Danish affiliate's financing activities or is largely an accounting adjustment. Similar considerations apply to the purported $2,695,000 investment in fixed assets.

EXHIBIT 9-14 **Translated Financial Statements of Danish Subsidiary**
Translated Balance Sheet as of 12/31/X1 and 12/31/X2

	December 31	
	20X1	*20X2*
Assets (000's)		
Cash	$ 2,400	$ 3,990
Net fixed assets	8,500	10,640
Total assets	$10,900	$14,630
Liabilities and Owners' Equity		
U.S. $500 payable	$ 500	$ 500
Long-term franc debt	4,800	6,384
Capital stock	3,818	3,818
Retained earnings	1,782	2,030
Translation adjustment	—	1,898
Total liabilities and stockholders' equity	$10,900	$14,630

Translated Statement of Income
for the Year 20X2 (000's)

Sales		$ 1,332
Expenses		
Operating costs	$ 666	
Depreciation	555	
Foreign exchange gain	(139)	1,082
Net income		$ 250

Translated Statement of Cash Flows
(000's)

Sources		
Net income	$ 250	
Depreciation	555	
Increase in long-term debt	1,584	
Translation adjustment	1,898	$ 4,287
Uses		
Increase in fixed assets		2,695
Net increase in cash (approximate due to rounding)		$ 1,590

Assume that the translated statements appearing in Exhibit 9-14 are based on the Danish krone balances appearing in Exhibit 9-15 and that the relevant exchange rate information is as stated.

A cash flow comparison between the functional currency (krone) and the reporting currency (dollars) yields some striking contrasts. While the cash flow statement generated from the translated balance sheet and income statement (Exhibit 9-14) shows long-term debt as a source of funds, the krone statement (Exhibit 9-15) suggests that this was not the case. Likewise, what appears to be an investment in fixed assets from a dollar perspective turns out to be a pure translation phenomenon.

| EXHIBIT 9-15 | **Financial Statements for Wholly Owned Danish Subsidiary** |

Local Currency Balance Sheet as of 12/31/X1 and 12/31/X2

	December 31	
	20X1	*20X2*
Assets		
Cash	Dkr 24,000	Dkr 30,000
Net fixed assets	85,000	80,000
Total assets	Dkr109,000	Dkr110,000
Liabilities and Owners' Equity		
U.S. $500 payable	Dkr 5,000	Dkr 3,750
Long-term krone debt	48,000	48,000
Capital stock	46,000	46,000
Retained earnings	10,000	12,250
Total liabilities and owners' equity	Dkr109,000	Dkr110,000

Statement of Cash Flows

Sources	
Net income	Dkr 2,250
Depreciation	5,000
Less: Krone foreign-exchange gain	1,250
Uses:	
None	
Net increase in cash	Dkr 6,000

Relevant Exchange Rates

December 31, 20X1	Dkr1 = $.100
Average during 20X2	Dkr1 = $.111
December 31, 20X2	Dkr1 = $.113

Closer analysis provides insight into the magnitude of the translation effects. An analysis of the fixed asset account reveals that there was no purchase, sale, or retirement of fixed assets during the year. Thus, the year-end balance should have been the beginning book value, $8,500,000 (Dkr 85,000,000), less depreciation of $555,000 (Dkr 5,000,000), or $7,945,000. The actual ending balance was $10,640,000, suggesting that the entire increase in fixed assets ($10,640,000–$7,945,000) was due to an exchange rate effect. Similarly, there was no change in Danish Krone long-term debt during the year. Because this monetary liability was translated by an exchange rate that revalued during the year, the entire increase in long-term debt ($6,384,000–$4,800,000) also arose from a translation adjustment. Similar transactional analyses account for additional translation effects related to the Danish subsidiary's working capital accounts. These effects are summarized in Exhibit 9-16.

Note that the sum of all the translation effects appearing in Exhibit 9-14 equals the aggregate translation adjustment appearing in the shareholders' equity section of the translated balance sheet. An informed reader can better determine the influence of

EXHIBIT 9-16 Analysis of Exchange Rate Effects		
	Debit	*Credit*
Cash	$ 924	
Fixed assets	2,695	
Intercompany payable		$ 138
Long-term debt		1,584
	$3,619	$1,722
Aggregate translation adjustment		1,897
	$3,619	$3,619

exchange rate changes from a firm's financing and investing activities using the foregoing analysis.

DIFFERENCES IN STATEMENT FORMAT

Balance sheet and income statement formats vary from country to country. For example, in contrast to the United States, where most companies adopt the balance sheet account format with assets appearing on the left and equity claims on the right, the format is often the reverse in the United Kingdom. As a second example, in contrast to U.S. balance sheets, which display assets in decreasing order of liquidity, and liabilities in increasing order of maturity, in many countries the most liquid assets and the shortest-term liabilities appear at the foot of the balance sheet.

Classification differences also abound internationally. For example, accumulated depreciation is reported as a contra-asset account in the United States. In Germany, depreciable assets are usually reported net of accumulated depreciation, but all current period changes in long-term asset accounts are shown directly in the balance sheet. In most countries, the distinction between a current and noncurrent liability is 1 year. In Germany it is often 4 years. Handbooks like the AICPA's *Professional Accounting Series*[49] may be consulted for a detailed treatment of other classification differences prevailing in individual countries.

Financial statement format differences, while troublesome, are seldom critical because the underlying structure of financial statements is quite similar around the world. Accordingly, most format differences can usually be reconciled with a little effort.

LANGUAGE AND TERMINOLOGY BARRIERS

Language differences among countries can present information barriers to financial statement users. Most companies domiciled in non-English-speaking countries publish their annual reports in the home country language. However, growing numbers of the relatively large companies in developed economies provide English-language versions of their annual reports, as shown in Exhibit 9-17.

---

[49]For example, see American Institute of Certified Public Accountants, *The Accounting Profession in France* (New York: AICPA, 1992). Also see Spicer & Oppenheim, *The Spicer & Oppenheim Guide to Financial Statements Around the World* (New York: John Wiley & Sons, 1989).

EXHIBIT 9-17	**Accounting Principles and Annual Report Availability in Five Highly Developed Countries**				
	France	*Germany*	*Japan*	*United Kingdom*	*United States*
Number of Firms	40	40	40	40	40
A. Accounting Principles Used[1]					
Local Standards	27	40	40	40	40
International Accounting Standards (IAS)[2]	9	0	0	0	0
U.S. Standards[3]	5	0	0	0	N.A.[4]
B. France, Germany, and Japan Firms:					
Firms that Distribute an English Language Annual Report	32	35	26	N.A.[4]	N.A.[4]
C. Firms that Provide a Convenience Restatement to Nondomestic Currency	5	2	25	3	0
D. Firms that Provide Limited Restatement to Nondomestic GAAP	0	1	0	3	0
E. Firms that Provide a Second Set of Financial Statements in Nondomestic GAAP	0	0	0	0	0

[1]Analysis assumes domestic accounting principles are used if no disclosures of accounting principles are made. Analysis of accounting principles used in these firms' 1994/95 annual reports indicates that one German firm changed from local standards to IAS between 1993/94 and 1994/95.

[2]Includes firms disclosing that their financial statements conform to both local standards and IAS.

[3]Includes firms disclosing that their financial statements conform to both local standards and U.S. standards, and to local standards, IAS, and U.S. standards.

[4]N.A.: Not Applicable

Source: Carol A. Frost and Kurt P. Ramin, "Corporate Financial Disclosure: A Global Assessment," in F. D. S. Choi, ed., *International Accounting and Finance Handbook, Second Edition,* Copyright © 1997, John Wiley & Sons. This material is used by permission of John Wiley & Sons, Inc. Information is from analysis of 1993/94 annual reports of 200 relatively large (average market value = U.S. $2.5 billion) publicly traded firms, 40 each domiciled in France, Germany, Japan, the United Kingdom, and the United States.

Accounting terminology differences can also cause difficulty. For example, U.S. readers associate the term *stock* with certificates of corporate ownership. Readers in the United Kingdom, on the other hand, associate the term with a firm's inventory of unsold goods. Other examples of terminology differences between the United Kingdom and the United States include turnover (sales revenue), and debtors and creditors (accounts receivable and payable).

In summary, many substantial issues confront the user of international financial statements. Perhaps the most difficult issues concern foreign currency and the availability and credibility of financial information. Difficulties with foreign currency will probably have a pervasive influence on international accounting for some time. In contrast, problems related to information availability and credibility are gradually decreasing as more and more companies, regulatory authorities, and stock exchanges recognize the importance of improving investors' access to timely and credible information.

Illustration of Restatement of Japanese GAAP Financial Statements to a U.S. GAAP Basis

In this appendix we show how GAAP restatements might be used to reduce the effects of accounting diversity. Exhibit 9-21 contains the year-end financial statements of Nis-Son Enterprises Inc. (Japan) and Lincoln Corporation (United States), with relevant notes. To aid comparison with Lincoln, we will restate Nis-Son's statements to a U.S. GAAP basis.

Based on the information provided and examining the notes in sequence, the following adjustments are required:

1. Inventories are adjusted to reflect differences in costing methods. Adjustments would increase inventories and decrease cost of sales by ¥198,000.

2. The difference between straight-line and sum-of-the-year's-digits depreciation for the current year yields an adjustment to cost of sales and net plant and equipment of ¥46,750. The difference in depreciation for the preceding year is ¥140,250. Based on a marginal tax rate of 35 percent, the ¥140,250 increase in reported pretax earnings would create ¥49,088 in deferred taxes with the balance credited to retained earnings.

3. Under U.S. GAAP the lease transaction would be capitalized. Discounting the stream of ¥40,000,000 rental payments for 5 years at 8 percent yields a present value of ¥159,600,000 attributed to both a leased asset and a lease obligation. Based on this amount, we can break down the ¥40,000,000 lease payment into an interest payment of ¥12,768,000 and a ¥27,232,000 reduction of the lease obligation. Straight-line depreciation would yield an expense of ¥31,920,000.

4. Under SFAS No. 52 the translation gain would be removed from long-term debt and included in income.

5. Compared to U.S. GAAP, the goodwill amortization expense is ¥10,800,000 larger. We would make an adjusting entry to recognize an asset and reduce operating expenses.

6. As the United States does not permit discretionary reserves, these reserves would be removed and included in income.

7. These adjustments, which Exhibit 9-22 summarizes in spreadsheet form, increase Nis-Son's restated earnings by ¥328,062,000. Of this, ¥20,000,000 relating to the translation gain is not recognized for tax purposes. All this yields a tax expense of ¥114,822,000, deferred taxes of ¥7,000,000, and a balance of ¥107,822,000 currently payable in taxes.

If accounting principle differences were the only differences among countries, a simple conversion (similar to converting distances from miles to kilometers) would be enough to enable anyone to understand accounting reports and interpret them without ambiguity.[1] Unfortunately, major economic and cultural differences among countries often make such an approach impossible, even when comparing accounting figures prepared in two countries but using the same accounting principles. If economic and cultural differences are major, a simple restatement of foreign accounting reports using domestic principles may not be enough for domestic readers to analyze the reports properly. Appendix 9-2 amplifies this important point.

---

[1] Of course, we assume that the statement user has enough information on hand to make the adjustments.

EXHIBIT 9-22   Nis-Son Enterprises—Solution

	Unadjusted	Adjustments		Adjusted	Dollars
Sales	¥1,400,000			¥1,400,000	$10,000
Operating expenses:					
Cost of sales	1,120,000	3)	(198,000)		
		4a)	(46,750)		
		5)	31,920	907,170	6,480
Selling and administrative	100,000			100,000	714
Other operating	114,200	5)	(40,000)		
		7)	(10,800)		
		8)	(26,400)		
		9)	(30,800)	6,200	44
Losses (gains)	—	6)	20,000	(20,000)	(143)
Interest	28,000	5)	12,768	40,768	291
Taxes	23,800	9)	114,822	138,622	990
Net income	¥ 14,000	10)	213,240	¥227,240	$ 1,624
Cash	¥ 124,500			¥124,500	$ 889
Accounts receivable	510,000			510,000	3,643
Marketable securities	45,000			45,000	321
Inventory	390,000	3)	198,000	588,000	4,200
Investments	150,000			150,000	1,071
Plant & equipment, net	280,500	4a)	46,750		
		4b)	140,250		
		5)	127,680	595,180	4,251
Goodwill		7)	10,800	10,800	77
Total assets	¥1,500,000			¥2,023,480	$14,452
Short-term payables	¥165,000			¥165,000	$ 1,178
Short-term debt	525,000			525,000	3,750
Deferred taxes	—	4b)	49,088		
		9)	7,000	56,088	401
Other current liabilities	90,000	9)	107,822	197,822	1,413
Long-term debt	520,000	6)	(20,000)		
		5)	132,368	632,368	4,517
Reserves	90,000	8)	26,400		
		8)	30,800	32,800	234
Capital stock	75,000			75,000	536
Retained earnings	35,000	4b)	91,162		
		10)	213,240	339,402	2,414
Total liabilities and owners' equity	¥1,500,000			¥2,023,480	$14,453

International Ratio Analysis[1]

Financial ratio analysis is a well-established tool for financial performance evaluation, credit analysis, and security analysis. While financial ratios may correctly measure liquidity, efficiency, and profitability in within-country comparisons, they are often misused when applied to cross-border financial comparisons, due in part to accounting principle differences. A more serious problem is that investors may misinterpret these ratios because they do not understand a foreign environment, even when financial statements are based on U.S. GAAP.

Consider Japan. An initial comparison of aggregate financial ratios for Japanese and U.S. firms reveals striking differences. Japanese companies generally appear less liquid, less solvent, less efficient, and less profitable than their U.S. counterparts. However, after Japanese ratios are adjusted for differences between Japanese and U.S. GAAP, they are still very different from ratios found in comparable U.S. companies.

ENVIRONMENTAL CONSIDERATIONS

Japanese companies appear to have very high leverage. For example, in the analysis shown in Exhibit 9-6 mean leverage (total debt/shareholders' equity) in the Japan sample is 2.032, compared with 0.514 in the U.S. sample. However, high debt ratios traditionally have not been major sources of concern in Japan. Part of the reason is historical.

When the Japanese government (under pressure from the United States) ended 200 years

of isolation in the mid-nineteenth century, it made rapid economic growth and development a major national goal. To achieve this goal, the government established an extensive banking infrastructure to supply industry with most of its financing. The dependence of industrial companies on the banking system increased after World War II. Large new industrial groupings called *keiretsu* evolved with major commercial banks at their core. Linked through business and personal ties, banks and their associated companies are very close. When loans become delinquent, banks (often) extend the terms of repayment or (occasionally) refinance the loan. A bank might even install a key bank official as president or board member of a troubled company to help it out. Other companies in the *keiretsu* can prepay receivables owed to the distressed firm and allow longer periods for that firm to repay its receivables. With this ability to manipulate and postpone interest and principal payments, long-term debt in Japan works more like equity in the United States.[2]

Because long-term debt in Japan has many of the characteristics of preferred stock, interest payments in Japan can be likened to dividends. Accordingly, interest coverage ratios, which are generally much lower in Japan than in the United States, are not viewed with much concern. Earnings in Japan beyond those needed to make loan payments benefit the bank little. When loans are negotiated, the borrower makes (and seldom discloses) a general agreement to give the bank collateral or guarantees upon the bank's request. Also at the bank's request, borrowing companies must submit their year-end proposed appropria-

---

[1]The following discussion is taken from a three-nation study by Frederick D.S. Choi and collaborators in Japan, Korea, and the United States. We gratefully acknowledge the cooperation of Messers. Hisaaki Hino of Morgan Guaranty Trust Company, Junichi Ujiie of Nomura Securities Company, Ltd., Professors Sang Kee Min and Sang Oh Nam of Seoul National University, and Professor Arthur I. Stonehill of Oregon State University.

[2]The gradual liberalization of Japan's financial system is eroding the keiretsu system. See *The Economist*, "Japan Inc. Frays at the Edges," June 3, 1995, page 67.

tion of revenue (including dividends) to the bank before it can be submitted to shareholders for approval. Banks customarily insist on compensating balances even though they are illegal, with 20 to 50 percent of company borrowings reportedly kept with the bank as time (or other) deposits. Under these conditions, low interest coverage usually does not mean a high risk of default.

Institutional and cultural factors also affect liquidity ratios without necessarily changing the financial risk that the ratios are designed to measure. For example, an American reader who sees the relatively low current ratios of Japanese companies (resulting from relatively high short-term debt) might conclude that Japanese companies have a relatively lower ability to cover their short-term debt. In Japan, however, high short-term debt seldom indicates a lack of liquidity. Short-term debt is attractive to companies because short-term obligations typically have lower interest rates than long-term obligations. Moreover, short-term borrowings in Japan are seldom repaid but normally are renewed or *rolled over*. Banks are happy to renew these loans as this allows them to adjust their interest rates to changing market conditions. Thus, short-term debt in Japan works like long-term debt elsewhere. In fact, the use of short-term debt to finance long-term assets appears to be the rule, not the exception, in Japan.

Longer average collection periods also reflect differences in business customs. Purchases in Japan are rarely made in cash. Postdated checks with maturities ranging between 60 and 90 days are common. The Japanese tradition of lifetime employment has some influence on collection policies. Companies often go to great lengths to accommodate their commercial customers. During business downturns, companies extend repayment terms to avoid placing their customers in a financial bind that might force them to discharge employees. In return, continued patronage ensures stability in employment (and other respects) for the selling company. In-ventory turnover numbers are similarly affected. During slack periods, manufacturing companies prefer to continue production and build inventories rather than idle workers.

Japanese managers are not as concerned with short-term profits as their U.S. counterparts. They have more job security than prevails in the United States. Equity shares in Japanese companies are largely held by related commercial banks, suppliers, and customers. These shareholders are more interested in maintaining their close business ties than in stock market gains, and will hold shares on a long-term basis regardless of short-term market performance.

Corporate managers in Japan believe that increased market share will assure long-run profits. For this reason, sales growth is their main objective. Growing sales contribute to higher employment and greater job security, and as such are consistent with the tradition of lifetime employment. Because all Japanese enterprises seek sales growth, price competition is intense, resulting in low profit margin and profitability statistics. This is especially so for large companies that usually sell heavily in extremely competitive export markets.

So, are Japanese companies truly more risky, less efficient, and less profitable than their U.S. counterparts? Not necessarily.

In Europe, national characteristics also appear to strongly influence profit measurement. Large companies in France and Germany tend to be more conservative in measuring profits than large companies in the United Kingdom. Also important are tax laws and reliance on lenders rather than investors for capital.

Thus, when analyzing foreign financial statements, readers must be careful to determine whether observed differences in firm performance result from: (a) accounting measurement differences; (b) economic, cultural, or institutional differences; or (c) real differences in the attributes being measured.

Selected References

American Institute of Certified Public Accountants. *The Accounting Profession in Country Series,* New York: AICPA, 1988 to date.

Bavishi, Vinod B., ed. *International Accounting and Auditing Trends, 4th Edition, 1995,* Vols. I and II, Princeton, NJ: CIFAR Publications, Inc., 1995.

Beim, David O., and Charles W. Calomiris, *Emerging Financial Markets*, Boston: McGraw-Hill, 2001.

Bindon, Kathleen, and Tracy Smith, "Corporate Financial Data for International Investment Decisions," in *International Accounting and Finance Handbook, Second Edition,* F. D. S. Choi, ed., New York: John Wiley & Sons, 1997, 9.1–9.34.

Brown, Paul R., Virginia E. Soybel, and Clyde P. Stickney, "Achieving Comparability of U.S. and Japanese Price-Earnings Ratios," in *International Accounting and Finance Handbook, Second Edition,* F. D. S. Choi, ed., New York: John Wiley & Sons, 1997, 7.1–7.18.

Choi, Frederick D. S., and Richard M. Levich, *The Capital Market Effects of International Accounting Diversity*, Homewood, IL: Dow Jones-Irwin, 1990.

Choi, Frederick D. S., and Richard M. Levich, "Accounting Diversity," in *The European Equity Markets: The State of the Union and an Agenda for the Millennium,* Benn Steil, ed., London: European Capital Markets Institute, 1996, 259–320.

Choi, Frederick D. S., and Richard M. Levich, "International Accounting Diversity and Capital Market Decisions," in *International Accounting and Finance Handbook, Second Edition,* F. D. S. Choi, ed., New York: John Wiley & Sons, 1997, 6.1–6.26.

Copeland, Tom, Tim Koller, and Jack Murrin, "Valuing Foreign Subsidiaries" and "Valuation Outside of the United States," in *Valuation: Measuring and Managing the Value of Companies, Second Edition,* New York: John Wiley & Sons, 1994.

Decker, William E., Jr., and Paul Brunner, "A Summary of Accounting Principle Differences Around the World," in *International Accounting and Finance Handbook,* F. D. S. Choi, ed., New York, John Wiley & Sons, 1997.

Erb, Claude B., Campbell R. Harvey, and Tadas E. Viskanta, *Country Risk in Global Financial Management,* Charlottesville, VA: Association for Investment Management and Research, 1998.

Kester, Carl W., and Julia Morley, *Note on Cross-Border Valuation,* Boston: Harvard Business School 9-292-084, Rev. July 6, 1992.

"Of Prophets and Profits—Beware Attempts to Forecast Company Profits," *The Economist,* (April 7, 2001): 84.

Palepu, Krishna G., Victor L. Bernard, and Paul M. Healy. *Business Analysis and Valuation Using Financial Statements,* Cincinnati, OH: South-Western College Publishing, 1996.

PricewaterhouseCoopers, *The Opacity Index January 2001—Launching a New Measure of the Effects of Opacity on the Cost and Availability of Capital in Countries World-Wide,* A Project of the PricewaterhouseCoopers Endowment for the Study of Transparency and Sustainability, (www.opacityindex.com), January 2001.

Sherman, Ronald, and Rebecca Todd, "International Financial Statement Analysis," in *International Accounting and Finance Handbook, Second Edition,* F. D. S. Choi, ed., New York: John Wiley & Sons, 1997, 8.1–8.61.

Squires, Jan R., ed., *ICFA Continuing Education—Finding Reality in Reported Earnings,* Charlottesville, VA: Association for Investment Management and Research, 1997.

Stickney, Clyde P., and Paul R. Brown, *Financial Reporting and Statement Analysis: A Strategic Perspective, Fourth Edition,* Fort Worth, TX: Harcourt Brace & Company, 1998.

U.S. Securities and Exchange Commission, Division of Corporation Finance, *Survey of Financial Statement Reconciliations by Foreign Registrants,* Washington, D.C.: U.S. Securities and Exchange Commission, May 1, 1993

White, Gerald I., Ashwinpaul C. Sondhi, and Dov Fried, *The Analysis and Use of Financial Statements, Second Edition,* New York, John Wiley & Sons, Inc., 1998.

Discussion Questions

1. What are the four main steps in doing a business analysis using financial statements? Why, at each step, is analysis in a cross-border context more difficult than a single-country analysis?

2. What are the information needs of four user groups that rely on foreign financial statements for their financial decisions? Are the four main steps in financial statement analysis equally important to your four groups? If not, what are the differences?

3. One interpretation of the popular efficient markets hypothesis is that the market fully impounds all public information as soon as it becomes available. Thus, it is supposedly not possible to beat the market if fundamental financial analysis techniques are applied to publicly available information such as a firm's published accounts. Why might this hypothesis be more tenable in the United States than in other international capital markets?

4. While English-language translations of foreign annual reports appear with increasing frequency, it is sometimes necessary to analyze a foreign report stated in the language and reporting terminology of the reporting company's domicile. What are some ways to deal with this problem? State your answer in one or two well-written paragraphs.

5. How does the translation of foreign currency financial statements differ from the foreign currency translation process described in Chapter 6?

6. If you were asked to provide the five most important recommendations you could think of to others analyzing nondomestic financial statements, what would they be?

7. In what country(ies) is accounting information most timely, detailed, and credible? Why?

8. What are several factors that must be taken into account when comparing the reported profitability of companies in different countries?

9. Choi and Levich found that investors cope with accounting principles differences in two fundamentally different ways. What are these coping mechanisms and which of the two do you favor?

10. Non-U.S. companies listed on U.S. stock exchanges are not required to base their financial statements on U.S. GAAP. However, these companies *are* generally required to provide reconciliation disclosures that quantify any material differences between their reported net income and what their net income would be under U.S. GAAP. What are the most frequently disclosed types of material differences? Is U.S. GAAP net income usually larger or smaller than net income as reported under home country GAAP? Why?

11. The quick (or acid test) ratio is frequently used to assess the short-term debt-paying ability of a business enterprise. As a rule of thumb, U.S. commercial lenders often consider a ratio of at least 1 to 1 to be satisfactory. Why might it be inappropriate to apply this standard when evaluating the liquidity of a non-U.S. company?

12. ABC Company, a U.S.-based MNC, uses the temporal translation method (see Chapter 6) in consolidating the results of its foreign operations. Translation gains or losses incurred upon consolidation are reflected immediately in reported earnings. Company XYZ, a Dutch MNC, employs the current rate method with translation gains and losses going into owners' equity. What financial ratios are most likely to be affected by these different accounting principles, and what are the implications for security analysts?

Exercises

1. Condensed comparative income statements of Señorina Panchos, a Mexican restaurant chain, for the years 20X3 through 20X5 are presented in Exhibit 9-18 (000,000's pesos).

EXHIBIT 9-18 Comparative Income Statements: Señorina Panchos			
	20X3	*20X4*	*20X5*
Sales	91,600	114,300	138,900
Gross margin	15,500	20,500	27,700
Net income	8,500	10,800	15,900

You are interested in gauging the past trend in dividends paid by Señorina Panchos from a dollar perspective. The company's payout ratio (ratio of dividends paid to reported earnings) has averaged 30 percent. Foreign exchange rates during the 3-year period are found in Exhibit 9-19.

EXHIBIT 9-19 Foreign Exchange Rates			
	20X3	*20X4*	*20X5*
Year-end rates	$1 = P 2,112	$1 = P 2,640	$1 = P 3,000

Required: Prepare a trend analysis of dividends paid by Señorina Panchos from a U.S. perspective assuming (a) there are no restrictions on the payment of dividends to U.S. investors and (b) Señorina Panchos' accounting practices are similar to those in the United States.

2. Based on the balance sheet and income statement data contained in Exhibit 9-14, and using the suggested work sheet format Shown in Exhibit 9-20 or one of your own choosing, show how the statement of cash flows appearing in Exhibit 9-14 was derived.

EXHIBIT 9-20 Statement of Cash Flows Work Sheet			
	Beginning Balance	*Debit*	*Credit*	*Ending Balance*
Balance sheet items (detailed)				
		Sources of Funds	Uses of Funds	
Net change in cash				

3. Refer again to Exhibits 9-14 and 9-15. Show how you would modify the consolidated funds statement appearing in Exhibit 9-14 to enable an investor to get a better feel for the actual investing and financing activities of the Danish subsidiary.

4. Read the financial statements (including notes) for Nikken Chemicals Co., Ltd., in Appendix 1-2 of Chapter 1. Also review an annual report of a company of your choice domiciled in your home country, using the World Wide Web or your library.
   Required: List at least five differences in the types of information disclosed by Nikken Chemicals and the information disclosed by the company you selected. Does Nikken Chemicals disclose more or less information, overall, than the company you selected? What other sources, if any, might be used to obtain additional information about Nikken Chemicals?

5. Read Appendix 9-1. Referring to Exhibit 9-21 and related notes, assume instead that Nis-Son's inventories were costed using the FIFO method and that Lincoln Corporation employed the LIFO method. Provide the adjusting journal entries to restate Nis-Son's inventories to a LIFO basis, assuming that ending inventories would have been ¥250 million lower under the LIFO method.

EXHIBIT 9-21   Year-End Financial Statements and Related Notes

	Nis-Son Enterprises (¥ Thousands)	Lincoln Enterprises ($Thousands)
Income Statements		
Sales	¥1,400,000	$12,000
Operating expenses:		
Cost of sales	1,120,000	10,044
Selling and administrative	100,000	575
Other operating	114,200	319
Goodwill amortization		10
Operating income	¥65,800	$1,052
Gains (losses)	—	—
Interest expenses	28,000	130
Income before taxes	37,800	922
Income taxes	23,800	258
Income after taxes	14,000	664
Equity in earnings of unconsolidated subsidiaries	—	116
Net income	¥ 14,000	$780
Balance Sheets		
Cash	¥ 124,500	$1,920
Accounts receivable net	510,000	1,660
Marketable securities	45,000	500
Inventory	390,000	1,680
Investments	150,000	1,000
Plant & equipment, net	280,600	5,160
Goodwill	—	80
Total assets	¥1,500,000	$12,000
Short-term payables	¥ 165,000	$1,800
Short-term debt	525,000	2,160
Deferred taxes	—	—
Other current liabilities	90,000	—
Long-term debt	520,000	2,400

EXHIBIT 9-21 *(cont.)*

	Enterprises (¥ Thousands)	Nis-Son Lincoln Enterprises ($Thousands)
Reserves	90,000	—
Capital stock	75,000	960
Retained earnings	35,000	4,680
Total liabilities and owners' equity	¥1,500,000	$12,000

Notes to Nis-Son's Financial Statements:

1. The balance sheet and income statement were prepared in accordance with the Japanese Commercial Code and related regulations.

2. Investments in subsidiaries and affiliated companies are stated at cost.

3. Inventories are stated at average cost. Ending inventories restated to a FIFO basis would have been ¥198 million higher.

4. Plant and equipment are carried at cost. Depreciation, with minor exceptions, is computed by the sum-of-the-years-digits method. Plant and equipment, purchased 2 years ago, have an estimated life of 4 years.

5. Operating expenses include lease rental payments of ¥40 million. The average term of the lease contracts is 4 years. All leases transfer ownership to the lessor at the end of the least term. Lincoln Enterprise's cost of capital is estimated to be 8 percent.

6. A translation gain of ¥20 million relating to consolidation of foreign operations with a net monetary liability position is being deferred under long-term debt.

7. Purchased goodwill, the premium paid in a merger or acquisition transaction, was ¥12 million for the year and is included under other operating expenses. Under U.S. generally accepted accounting principles (GAAP), it would have been amortized to expense over a 10-year period.

8. Nis-Son Enterprise is allowed to set up special purpose reserves (i.e., government-sanctioned charges against earnings) equal to a certain percentage of total export revenues. This year's charge (including in other operating expenses) was ¥26,400,000. Similarly, this year's addition to Nis-Son's general purpose reserves was ¥30,800,000.

9. Deferred taxes are not provided in Japan for book-tax purposes.

10. The ¥/$ exchange rate at year-end was ¥140 = $1.

11. Nis-Son Enterprise's marginal income tax rate is 35 percent.

Notes to Lincoln Enterprises' financial statements:

1. The balance sheet and income statement are based on U.S. GAAP.

2. Inventories are carried at FIFO cost.

3. Plant and equipment are depreciated in straight-line fashion.

4. Foreign operations are consolidated with those of the parent using the temporal method of currency translation as Lincoln adopts the U.S. dollar as its functional currency.

6. Using traditional financial ratio analysis and the original account balances appearing in Exhibit 9-5, compare the profitability, solvency, and liquidity of Nis-Son and Lincoln Enterprises.

7. Recompute the profitability, solvency, and liquidity ratios calculated in Exercise 6 based on Nis-Son's restated numbers (i.e., Nis-Son's U.S. GAAP numbers). Based on the restated numbers, together with the material presented in this chapter, which of the two companies (Nis-Son or Lincoln Enterprises) appears to be better for investment? State specific reasons for your decision.

8. Refer to Exhibit 9-7. This exhibit presents P/E ratios for public companies in 10 countries.

Required: For both 1990 and 1996 (panels A and B of the exhibit), rank order the P/E ratios for China, Germany, NYSE (United States), and Nasdaq (United States). Discuss why the mean P/E ratio for each of the four countries changed between 1990 and 1996. Specifically: Why did China's P/E ratio decrease? Why did P/E ratios in Germany and on NYSE and Nasdaq in the United States increase? Why did Nasdaq's P/E ratio increase so much more than NYSE's P/E ratio? What explains the *differences* in P/E ratio trends among the four countries?

9. Examine the financial information presented in Appendix 1-1 of Chapter 1 for Nikken Chemicals Co., Ltd.

Required: Referring to the accounting policy footnotes and auditors' report, list the accounting standards used and the auditing standards used. Discuss which of these sources of cross-country accounting differences is the most important in a financial analysis of Nikken Chemicals. Least important? Why?

10. Refer to Exhibit 9-2, which presents recent auditor's liability cases by country and audit firm.

Required: Does the incidence of liability cases vary more by country or by auditor? In what countries is auditor litigation most frequent? Least frequent? Why? What are the implications for doing financial analysis in the 12 countries presented? Are relatively high levels of auditor litigation good or bad for financial statement users? Present reasons for your answer.

11. Refer to Exhibit 9-7 and compute an average of the combined P/E ratios for France, Germany, and the Netherlands for the years 1996 and 1999, respectively. Do the same for China, the Czech Republic and Mexico. Based on what you have learned in this and earlier chapters, explain any differences that you observe between these two sets of country groupings and the implications of your analysis for investors.

12. Identify three to four criteria that you would personally use to judge the merits of any corporate database. Use these criteria to rate the information content of each Web site appearing in Exhibit 9-8 as excellent, fair or poor.

Case 9–1   Accounting Quality Analysis

Accounting quality varies substantially among countries. Companies' financial statements, notes, and auditor reports often yield important clues about accounting quality.

REQUIRED

1. Based on general information given in the text about financial reporting and eco-

nomic and business environments in Japan, what is your overall assessment of accounting quality in that country?

2. Study the financial statements, notes, and auditor's report of Nikken Chemicals Co., Ltd., presented in Appendix 1-2 of Chapter 1. Is the accounting quality reflected in these materials consistent with your expectations (based on your knowledge of Japan)? Critically evaluate

the accounting quality of Nikken Chemicals, including a discussion of factors that led to your conclusions.

3. If you could, what further evidence would you gather to more completely assess accounting quality for Nikken Chemicals?

Case 9–2   Restatement of International Accounting Standards to U.S. GAAP

Refer to Appendix 1-2 of Chapter 1, which presents the financial statements (including notes) and auditor's report for Nikken Chemicals Co., Ltd. Refer to Study Note 2, Significant Accounting Policies, which presents the basis of financial statement presentation for this company.

2. Discuss whether your restatement provides sufficient information for a comparison between Nikken Chemicals' financial performance and condition with a manufacturer of chemicals in your home company.

REQUIRED

1. Restate the income statement and balance sheet to a U.S. GAAP basis, using one of the approaches discussed in the text.

CHAPTER 10

MANAGERIAL PLANNING AND CONTROL

The globalization of business and continued advances in information technology are changing the world of management accounting. Global competition, foreign exchange risk, governmental restrictions on fund remittances across national borders, tax laws, national interest rate differentials, and the effects of changing commodity and equity prices on enterprise assets, earnings, and capital costs are among the variables that complicate management decisions. At the same time, developments such as video conferencing, the Internet, and electronic data interchange are changing the economics of production, distribution, and financing. Production is increasingly awarded to the company in the world that does it best. Cooperative global links based on strategic alliances are replacing arms-length relationships among manufacturers, suppliers, and customers, and an increasing emphasis is being placed on financial management and individuals with strong analytic and presentation skills.[1]

Global competition and the speed of knowledge dissemination support the narrowing of national variations in management accounting practices around the world.[2] In addition, common forces such as market and technology changes, cost and performance pressures, and the coordination of global operations are driving management of multinational companies not only to adopt similar internal accounting techniques, but to use these techniques in similar fashion.[3] Managerial accounting issues discussed in this book fall into three broad areas: financial planning and control systems (this chapter), international risk management (Chapter 11), and international taxation and transfer pricing (Chapter 12). Specific subtopics in this chapter include business modeling,

[1] Mike Anastas, "The Changing World of Management Accounting and Financial Management," *Management Accounting* (October 1997): 48–51.

[2] A. Bhimani, ed., *Management Accounting: European Perspectives,* Oxford: Oxford University Press, 1996; Michael D. Shields, "Management Accounting Practices in Europe: A Perspective from the States," *Management Accounting Research* 9 (1998): 501–513; and Chris Guilding, Karen S. Cravens, and Mike Tayles, "An International Comparison of Strategic Management Accounting Practices," *Management Accounting Research* 9 (2000): 113–135.

[3] T. Sheridan, "Management Accounting in Global European Corporations: Anglophone and Continental Viewpoints," *Management Accounting Research* 6 (1995): 287–294.

strategic costing, capital and operational budgeting, management information systems and control, profitability analysis, and internal performance evaluation.

BUSINESS MODELING

A recent survey finds that management accountants are spending more time on strategic planning issues than ever before.[4] Business modeling is *big picture*, and it consists of formulating, implementing, and evaluating a firm's long-range business plan.[5] It involves four critical dimensions:[6]

1. Identifying key factors relevant to the future progress of the company
2. Formulating appropriate techniques to forecast future developments and assess the company's ability to adapt to or exploit these developments
3. Developing data sources to support strategic choices
4. Translating selected options into specific courses of action

Research has established an association between corporate success and factors such as market share, market growth, and capital intensity.[7] Relative product quality and employee productivity are also critical performance factors. Accordingly, corporate models that focus on optimizing these factors are likely to succeed.

PLANNING TOOLS

It is helpful for a company to scan its external and internal environments to identify threats and opportunities. Systems can be set in place to gather information on competitors and market conditions. Both competitors and market conditions are analyzed for their impact on a company's competitive status and profitability. Insights gleaned from this analysis are used to plan measures to maintain or enlarge market share, or to identify and exploit new product and market opportunities.

One such tool is the WOTS-UP analysis. Concerned with corporate strengths and weaknesses in relation to a firm's operating environment, this technique helps management generate a set of feasible strategies. (However, the WOTS-UP analysis is limited in that it fails to identify a *best* strategy.) Exhibit 10-1 shows a WOTS-UP analysis done by the German automaker, Daimler Benz (now DaimlerChrysler). For example, extending Daimler's distribution and service network in Eastern Europe is a promising strategy, given the company's strengths in product quality, truck sales, lower breakeven point, and synergistic potential. The low value of the U.S. dollar, rising foreign competition in Germany, and the perceived advantages of strengthening basic research in new

---

[4]Institute of Management Accountants, "Role Changing for Management Accountants," *Journal of Accountancy* (November 1999): 17, 20.

[5]Evidence suggests that nationality may influence the extent to which the executive suite embraces planning on a long-range basis. See George S. Yip, Johny K. Johansson, and Johan Roos, "Effects of Nationality on Global Strategy," *Management International Review* (1997): 365–385.

[6]Kiyohiko Ito and Klaus R. Macharzina, "Strategic Planning Systems," in F. D. S. Choi, ed., *International Accounting and Finance Handbook*, 2d ed., New York: John Wiley & Sons, 1997.

[7]C. T. Marshall and R. D. Buzzell, "PIMS and the FTC Line-of-Business Data: A Comparison," *Strategic Management Journal* 2, no. 4 (1990): 269–82.

EXHIBIT 10-1 WOTS-UP Analysis of Daimler Benz AG

Strengths (S)	*Weaknesses (W)*
1. Product quality improved 20% from previous year	1. Acquisition of high-tech firms leads to coordination problems
2. R & D potential higher than other automobile producers	2. High wage level (most of the production is located in Germany)
3. 50% percent share of comfort limousine market	3. Fewer joint ventures (international alliances) than Japanese automobile producers
4. Daimler Benz trucks lead industry	
5. Breakeven point decreased from 1.0 to 0.7 million vehicles	
6. Several acquisitions (e.g., AEG, Dornier, MBB) improved the synergistic potential of Daimler Benz	
7. Excellent financial situation of Daimler Benz	
8. High economies of scope	

Opportunities (O)	*SO-Strategies*	*WO-Strategies*
1. High-tech industries (microelectronics, aerospace) growing 20% per year	1. Acquire automobile producers in Eastern Germany (03/S7)	1. Expand transfer of managers between headquarters and subsidiaries (03/W1)
2. Consumers' disposable income increasing 6% per year	2. Extend the distribution and service net in Eastern Europe (03/S7)	2. Produce cars in the eastern part of Germany (03/W2)
3. Liberalization of Eastern European Countries	3. Develop several versions of the "Baby Benz" (02, 03/S5, S7)	3. Intensify HR development on each level (01/W2)
4. Image and service problems of Japanese automobile firms	4. Use production capacity for civil products (03/S6, S8)	4. Form international aerospace joint venture company (01/W3)

Threats (T)	*Short-Term Strategies*	*Long-Term Strategies*
1. Low value of the dollar	1. Place selective advertising; boost advertising expenditures 30% (T3, T5/S1, S3)	1. Build strategic alliances (strategic networks) to reduce cost of R & D investment and to solve ecological problems (T6/W3)
2. Rising interest rate		
3. Foreign imports, esp. luxury cars, gaining market share	2. Strengthen basic research in new fields of technology (solar energy, biotechnology, computing and robotics; electrical car engines) (T4, T6/S7. S8)	2. Improve productivity and quality (in production, administration, distribution and services) (T1, T3/W2)
4. Gulf crisis leads to increasing gas prices		
5. BMW has an excellent new line of cars		
6. Rising ecological problems throughout the world		
7. Military (defense) markets may break off due to peace movement		

Source: K. Ito and K. R. Macharzina, "Strategic Planning Systems," in F. D. S. Choi, ed., *International Accounting and Finance Handbook, 2e.* Copyright © 1997 John Wiley & Sons. This material is used by permission of John Wiley & Sons, Inc.

technologies by building strategic alliances may explain Daimler's acquisition of the Chrysler Corporation in the United States.

Decision tools currently used in strategic planning systems all depend on the quality of information regarding a firm's internal and external environment. Accountants can help corporate planners obtain data useful in strategic planning decisions; however, much of the required information comes from sources other than accounting records.

STRATEGIC COSTING

While traditional product and standard costing systems continue to fill a role in cost control, certain Japanese companies use management accounting systems that support and reinforce their manufacturing strategies, thus establishing a direct link between management accounting practices and corporate goals.[8] Rather than design products to better use existing technologies and work flows, many Japanese companies design and build products at prices intended to assure market success.[9] Consider the Daihatsu Motor Company. Its product development cycle (which normally lasts 3 years) begins with the production manager instructing Daihatsu's departments to submit design and performance specifications that they believe the car should meet. This is followed by a cost estimate based not on what it will cost to build the car, but rather on an allowable cost per car. This *allowable cost* is based on subtracting a target profit margin that reflects the company's strategic plans and financial projections from a target sales price the company believes the market will accept. While used as a target, the allowable cost is not static. During production, allowable cost is reduced every month by a cost reduction rate based on short-term profit objectives. In later years, actual costs of the previous year are the starting point for further reductions, thus assuring ongoing cost cutting for as long as the car is in production.[10]

This market-driven system, known as *Kaizen costing*, significantly reduces the reliance on traditional standard costing systems. Standard costing systems seek to minimize variances between budgeted and actual costs. *Kaizen* costing emphasizes doing what is necessary to achieve a desired performance level under competitive market conditions.

Another example of strategic costing is *behavioral costing*.[11] In a process costing system, overhead is applied to goods or routine services using an overhead application rate. From a traditional cost accounting perspective, manufacturing overhead is allocated to products on a cause-and-effect basis. Despite the capital intensity of many Japanese manufacturers, the use of direct labor as an allocation base for assigning overhead costs has continued. This practice encourages production managers to reduce

---

[8]Hema Wijewardena and Anura De Zoysa, "A Comparative Analysis of Management Accounting Practices in Australia and Japan: An Empirical Investigation," *International Journal of Accounting* 34, no. 1 (1999): 49–70.

[9]M. Sakurai, "Target Costing and How to Use It," *Journal of Cost and Management* (summer 1989): 39–50.

[10]The following discussion is taken from T. Hiromoto, "Japanese Management Accounting," *Harvard Business Review* (July–August 1988): 22–26.

[11]Ibid.

rather than just accumulate costs (i.e., encourage automation). A production manager wishing to reduce his overhead burden is motivated to substitute capital for labor.

Exhibit 10-2 summarizes the major differences between standard and *kaizen* costing concepts.

CAPITAL BUDGETING

The decision to invest abroad is a critical element in the global strategy of a multinational company. Direct foreign investment typically involves large sums of capital and uncertain prospects. Investment risk is compounded by an unfamiliar, complex, constantly changing international environment. Formal planning is imperative and normally is done within a capital budgeting framework that compares the benefits and costs of the proposed investment. Capital budgeting analysis helps ensure that strategic plans are financially feasible and advantageous.

Sophisticated approaches to investment decisions are available. Procedures exist to determine a firm's optimum capital structure, measure a firm's cost of capital, and evaluate investment alternatives under conditions of uncertainty. Decision rules for investment choice typically call for discounting an investment's risk-adjusted cash flows at an appropriate interest rate: the firm's weighted average cost of capital. Normally, a firm increases the wealth of its owners by making investments that promise positive net present values. When considering mutually exclusive options, a rational company will select the option that promises the maximum net present value.

In the international arena, investment planning quickly becomes even more complicated. Different tax laws and accounting measurement rules, different rates of inflation, risks of expropriation, fluctuating exchange rates, exchange controls, restrictions on the transferability of foreign earnings, and language and intercultural differences all introduce complexity not usually found domestically. The difficulty of quantifying such data makes the problem that much worse.

EXHIBIT 10-2   Standard Versus *Kaizen* Costing Concepts

Standard Cost Concepts	*Kaizen Cost Concepts*
Cost Control	Cost Reduction
Predicated on existing manufacturing conditions	Predicated on continuous manufacturing improvement
Objective: Compliance with performance standards	Objective: Achieve cost reduction targets
Standards set annually	Cost reduction targets set monthly
	Continuous improvement in manufacturing methods to attain target costs
Variance analysis based on actual vs. standard	Variance analysis based on constant cost reduction
Investigate when standards not met	Investigate when target costs not achieved

Source: Reprinted with permission from Yasuhiro Monden and John Y. Lee, "How a Japanese Auto Maker Reduces Costs," *Management Accounting* (Now *Strategic Finance*) August 1993, pp. 22–26, published by the IMA, Montvale, New Jersey, www.ima.org.

Multinational adaptations of traditional investment planning models have been made in three major areas: (1) determination of the relevant return from a multinational investment, (2) measurement of expected cash flows, and (3) calculation of the multinational cost of capital.

FINANCIAL RETURN PERSPECTIVES

A manager must determine the *relevant return* to assess a foreign investment opportunity. Should the international financial manager evaluate expected investment returns from the perspective of the foreign project or that of the parent company?[12] Returns from the two perspectives could differ significantly due to (1) government restrictions on repatriation of earnings and capital, (2) license fees, royalties, and other payments that provide income to the parent but are expenses to the subsidiary, (3) differential rates of national inflation, (4) changing foreign currency values, and (5) differential taxes, to name a few.

One might argue that the return and risk of a foreign investment should be evaluated from the point of view of the parent company's domestic stockholders. However, it also can be argued that such an approach is no longer appropriate. First, investors in the parent company increasingly come from a worldwide community. Investment objectives should reflect the interests of all shareholders, not just the domestic ones. Observation also suggests that many multinational companies have long-run (as opposed to short-run) investment horizons. Funds generated abroad tend to be reinvested abroad rather than repatriated to the parent company. Under these circumstances, it may be appropriate to evaluate returns from a host country perspective. Emphasis on local project returns is consistent with the goal of maximizing consolidated group earnings.[13]

An appealing solution is to recognize that financial managers must meet many goals, responding to investor and noninvestor groups in the organization and its environment.[14] The host country government is one such group for a foreign investment. Compatibility between the goals of the multinational investor and the host government can be gauged through two financial return calculations: one from the host country perspective, the other from the parent country perspective. The host country perspective assumes that a profitable foreign investment (including the local opportunity cost of capital) does not misallocate the host country's scarce resources.[15] Evaluating an investment opportunity from a local perspective also gives the parent company useful information. If a foreign investment does not promise a risk-adjusted return higher than the returns of local competitors, parent company shareholders would be better off investing directly in the local companies.

---

[12]This issue parallels, in many respects, the problem of currency perspectives associated with foreign currency translation discussed in Chapter 6.

[13]As mentioned in Chapter 6, earnings of majority-owned affiliates are generally consolidated with those of the parent. Earnings of less than majority-owned affiliates are typically accounted for under either the equity or cost methods.

[14]David K. Eiteman, Arthur I. Stonehill, and Michael Moffett, *Multinational Business Finance*, 9th ed., Reading, MA: Addison-Wesley, 2000.

[15]For example, a country would probably look favorably on a proposed investment promising a 21 percent return on assets employed when investments of comparable risk elsewhere in the country yield 18 percent.

At first glance, the accounting implications of multiple rate-of-return calculations appear straightforward. Nothing could be less true. In an earlier discussion, we assumed that project rate-of-return calculations were a proxy for host country evaluation of a foreign investment. In practice, the analysis is much more complicated. Do project rate-of-return calculations really reflect a host country's opportunity costs? Are the expected returns from a foreign investment limited to projected cash flows, or must other externalities be considered? How are any additional benefits measured? Does a foreign investment require any special overhead spending by the host government? What is the risk from a host country viewpoint, and how can it be measured? Questions such as these call for a massive increase in the amount and complexity of the information needed to calculate rates of return.

MEASURING EXPECTED RETURNS

It is challenging to measure the expected cash flows of a foreign investment. Assume, for purposes of discussion, that a U.S. multinational corporation is considering purchasing 100 percent ownership of a manufacturing facility in Russia. The U.S. parent will finance one-half of the investment in the form of cash and equipment; the balance will be financed by local bank borrowing at market rates. The Russian facility would import one-half of its raw materials and components from the U.S. parent and export one-half of its output to Hungary. To repatriate funds to the parent company, the Russian facility would pay the U.S. parent a licensing fee, royalties for use of parent company patents, and technical service fees for management services rendered. Earnings of the Russian facility would be remitted to the parent as dividends. Exhibit 10-3 provides a diagram of prospective cash flows that need to be measured.[16]

The basic methods for estimating projected cash flows associated with the Russian facility are similar to those used for a domestic company. Expected receipts are based on sales projections and anticipated collection experience. Operating expenses (converted to their cash equivalents) and local taxes are similarly forecast. Additional complexities must be considered, however. They include:

1. Project versus parent cash flows
2. Parent cash flows tied to financing
3. Subsidized financing
4. Political risk

This process also must consider the impact of changing prices and fluctuating currency values on expected foreign currency returns. If local currency cash flows were fixed (for example, if the Russian venture was in the form of a bond investment), it would be straightforward to measure exchange rate effects. Here, depreciation of the Russian ruble relative to the U.S. dollar reduces the dollar equivalent of future interest income. When an ongoing manufacturing enterprise generates foreign currency income, the analysis is more complicated, as exchange rate changes influence net operating cash

---

[16]For an extended discussion of this subject, see David K. Eiteman, "Foreign Investment Analysis," in F. D. S. Choi, ed., *International Accounting and Finance Handbook*, New York: John Wiley & Sons, 1997, 28.1–28.19 and *2001 Cumulative Supplement*, 28.1–28.2.

EXHIBIT 10-3 Cash Flow Components

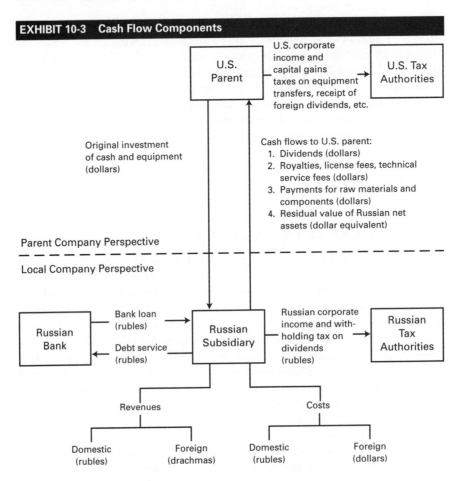

flows. Accordingly, accounting measurements of exchange rate effects for each type of activity (such as domestic versus export sales, domestic versus imported costs, and their cumulative effects on projected cash flows) are necessary.

The following example illustrates the effects of changing prices and currency values on expected returns for the first two years of a 6-year investment project. The Russian facility's cash flows, as shown in Exhibit 10-4, are determined under the following assumptions.

1. The Russian facility is expected to sell 100,000 units of its manufactured product in the local market at an initial unit price of 2,020 Russian rubles (R). Another 100,000 units will be exported to Hungary and priced in forints (F) reflecting the ruble base price.
2. Changes in local selling prices are tied to annual rates of inflation in Russia and Hungary, which are expected to average 20 percent and 10 percent, respectively.
3. Domestic and foreign unit sales are expected to increase each year by 10 percent.
4. The ruble is forecast to depreciate relative to the forint by 10 percent per year.

EXHIBIT 10-4 Cash Flows from Russian Subsidiary		
	Year 1	*Year 2*
Sales (units)		
Domestic	100,000	110,000
Foreign	100,000	110,000
Price (per unit)		
Domestic	R2,020	R2,424
Foreign	R2,020	R2,444
	(F20,200)	(F22,220)
Gross Revenues		
Domestic	R202,000,000	R266,640,000
Foreign	R202,000,000	R268,849,000
	(F2,020,000,000)	(F2,444,000,000)
Total	R404,000,000	R535,480,000
Raw Materials (cost per unit)		
Domestic	R400	R480
Foreign	R400	R462
	($20)	($22)
Labor (cost per unit)	R200	R240
Variable cost (per unit)	R1,000	R1,182
Total variable costs	R200,000,000	R260,040,000
Licensing fees, royalties, etc.	R 40,400,000	R 53,548,000
Depreciation expense	R 60,000,000	R 60,000,000
Selling & administrative expense	R 48,000,000	R 55,200,000
Total	R348,400,000	R428,788,000
Net operating income	R 55,600,000	R106,692,000
Corporate income tax(40%)	R 22,240,000	R 42,676,000
Net income	R 33,360,000	R 64,016,000
+Depreciation	R 60,000,000	R 60,000,000
Net cash flow(rubles)	R 93,360,000	R124,016,000
Net cash flow(dollars)	$4,668,000	$5,905,000

Exchange Rates:

R0.1 = D1   R0.11 = D1

R20 = $1   R21 = $1

5. Variable costs of production (raw materials and labor) also reflect local inflation rates.

6. Because 50 percent of the Russian manufacturer's raw materials are imported from the United States, imported raw material prices are expected to increase by 10 percent each year in line with anticipated U.S. and Russian inflation.

7. Anticipated depreciation of the ruble relative to the U.S. dollar is 5 percent.

8. Licensing and other fees are expected to average 10 percent of gross revenues.

9. Selling and administrative expenses are expected to increase by 15 percent each year from an initial level of R 48,000,000.

10. Depreciation expense is R 60,000,000 a year.
11. The Russian corporate tax rate is 40 percent.
12. Projected annual cash flows will increase from R 93,360,000 to R 124,016,000 in local currency. Measured in U.S. dollars, net cash flows increase from $4,668,000 to $5,905,000.

In this example, a depreciating local currency had increased projected local cash flows due to the structure of the foreign operation's product and factor markets.

When a parent company perspective is used, cash flows to the parent company seldom mirror those of its overseas affiliate. The only relevant cash flows are those with direct consequences for the parent.

Major sources of parent cash flows include debt service on loans by the parent, dividends, licensing fees, overhead charges, royalties, transfer prices on purchases from or sales to the parent (see Chapter 12 for a further discussion of this managerial topic), and the estimated terminal value of the project. Measurement of these cash flows requires an understanding of national accounting differences, governmental repatriation policies, potential future inflation and exchange rates, and differential taxes.

Differences in accounting principles are relevant to the extent that financial managers rely on locally based pro forma financial statements in estimating future cash flows. Where the underlying measurement rules used in preparing these accounts differ from those of the parent country, differences in cash flow estimates could arise. As examples, depreciation based on replacement values rather than historical costs (as practiced by certain large multinationals in the Netherlands and Italy) could affect corporate income taxes and consequently cash flow. Differences in inventory costing methods could influence cash flow measures and the timing of total cash flow.

Balance of payment considerations may lead host governments to limit the repatriation of dividends or other cash payments to the parent company. For example, some countries limit the repatriation of dividends to a certain proportion of a company's capital base that has been formally registered with the host government. Others do not allow repatriation of cash flows made possible by tax-deductible expenses, as these are not part of reported earnings from which dividends are declared. This consideration alone would reduce the cash flows that could be repatriated in our previous Russian example by 66 and 50 percent, respectively, for the 2 years examined.

A parent company naturally cares about the value of foreign cash flows measured in parent currency. Accordingly, it needs estimates of future inflation and its impact on future exchange rates used to convert foreign cash flows to parent currency. Finally, provisions relating to the taxation of foreign source income must be considered. For instance, in the United States the receipt of a royalty payment on which a foreign withholding tax has been assessed gives rise to a foreign tax credit designed to minimize the double taxation of foreign source income. (International tax considerations are detailed in Chapter 12.)

MULTINATIONAL COST OF CAPITAL

If foreign investments are evaluated with this discounted cash flow model, an appropriate discount rate must be developed. Capital budgeting theory typically uses a firm's cost of capital as its discount rate; that is, a project must yield a return at least equal to a firm's capital costs to be accepted.[17] This *hurdle rate* is related to the proportions of debt and equity in a firm's financial structure as follows where:

k_a = weighted average (after tax) of capital
k_e = cost of equity
k_i = cost of debt before tax
E = value of a firm's equity
D = value of a firm's debt
S = value of a firm's capital structure $(E + D)$
t = marginal tax rate

It is not easy to measure a multinational company's cost of capital. The cost of equity capital may be calculated in several ways. One popular method combines the expected dividend yield with the expected dividend growth rate. Letting D_i = expected dividends per share at period's end, P_0 = the current market price of the stock at the beginning of the period, and g = expected growth rate in dividends, the cost of equity, k_e, is calculated as $k_e = D_i/P_0 + g$. Even though it is easy to measure current stock prices, in most countries where a multinational firm's shares are listed, it is often troublesome to measure D and g. First, D_i is an expectation. Expected dividends depend on the operating cash flows of the company as a whole. Measuring these cash flows is complicated by environmental considerations such as those mentioned in our Russian example. Moreover, measurement of the dividend growth rate, which is itself a function of expected future cash flows, is complicated by exchange controls and other government restrictions on cross-border funds transfers.

Similar problems relate to the measurement of the debt component of the average cost of capital. In a single nation, the cost of debt is the effective interest rate multiplied by $(1 - t)$ because interest is generally a tax-deductible expense. When a multinational company borrows foreign currencies, however, additional factors enter the picture. The effective after-tax interest cost now includes foreign exchange gains or losses that arise whenever foreign exchange rates fluctuate between the transaction and settlement dates (see Chapter 11). Suppose that a U.S. multinational borrows 100,000 Israeli shekels for 1 year at 8 percent interest when the dollar/shekel exchange rate is $0.24 = Shk 1. Should the shekel appreciate to $0.264 = Shk 1 before repayment, the borrowing company will incur a transaction loss of Shk 108,000 × ($ 0.264 − $0.240) = $2.592. This additional cost of debt financing would be tax deductible. Assuming a corporate tax rate of 40 percent, the after-tax cost of debt would be .18 (1 − .40), or 10.8 percent, as opposed to 4 percent in a purely domestic transaction.

Additional tax considerations apply when a multinational borrows funds in several foreign capital markets. Current and prospective tax rates in each foreign market over the life of the loan must be considered. The tax-deductibe status of interest payments must be checked, because not all national taxing authorities recognize interest deductions (particularly if the associated loan is between related entities). Moreover, recognition of deferred taxes, which arise whenever income for tax purposes differs from

---

[17]For an examination of the relationship between corporate strategy and finance, see Lars Oxelheim, Arthus Stonehill, Trond Randoy, Kaisa Vikkula, Kare B. Dullum, and Karl-Markus Moden, *Corporate Strategies to Internationalize the Cost of Capital*, Handelsshojskolens Forlag: Copenhagen Business School Press, 1998.

income for external reporting purposes, is becoming a generally accepted practice in many industrialized countries where MNCs operate. Because deferred taxes are considered a liability on which no interest is paid, one can ask whether they are really an interest-free source of financing and should be included in determining the cost of capital. Although this idea merits consideration, we do not believe that the cost of capital calculation should include deferred taxes.[18]

It is not always straightforward to implement international capital budgeting theory in practice. All of the capital budgeting approaches we have examined assume that the required information is readily available. Unfortunately, in actual practice, the most difficult and critical aspect of the entire capital budgeting process is obtaining accurate and timely information, especially in the international sphere, where different climates, culture, languages, and information technologies complicate matters.

MANAGEMENT INFORMATION SYSTEMS AND CONTROL

Once questions of strategy have been decided, attention generally focuses on the equally important areas of financial control and performance evaluation. These considerations are especially important as they enable financial managers to

1. Implement the global financial strategy of the MNE
2. Evaluate the degree to which the chosen strategies contribute to achieving enterprise goals
3. Motivate management and employees to achieve the enterprise's financial goals as effectively and efficiently as possible

INFORMATION AND INFORMATION SYSTEMS

Multinational managers typically require a greater volume of sophisticated information than their domestic counterparts. A multinational framework is inherently more complex than a single-country framework; many environmental complexities impede the simple, effective flow of business information.

As an example, the information requirements of regional or corporate financial planners concern both operating and environmental data. Information demanded from managerial accountants in the field depends on how much decision-making power local managers have. The greater the authority of local managers, the less information is passed on to headquarters. Exhibit 10-5 details four major classes of information that managerial accountants prepare for central corporate management.[19] For each set of data transmitted, corporate management must determine the relevant time period of the reports, the level of accuracy required, the frequency of reporting, and the costs and benefits of timely preparation and transmission. Exhibit 10-6 sets forth some environmental factors that complicate information flow.

---

[18]As discussed in Chapter 6, deferred taxes under the current rate method are translated at the current rate with any translation gains and losses taken to owners' equity and held in suspense until realized. Under the temporal method, they are translated at the historical rate. Because current earnings are not burdened with exchange rate effects under either treatment, neither should the costs of capital be relieved by what is, in effect, an interest-free loan from a government.

[19]John B. Giannotti and Richard W. Smith, *Treasury Management*, New York: John Wiley, 1981.

EXHIBIT 10-5 Corporate/Regional Data Requirements for Financial Managers			
Collections	*Liquidity*	*Operating Expenses*	*Disbursements*
Credit control	Borrowings outstanding	Forecast of receipts and disbursements by currency	Order placement
Major accounts outstanding, with history and credit limits	Investments made	Forecast of exports and imports by country	Raw material inventory levels
	All investment/borrowing facilities available with rates applied		Payments
Accounts receivable		Histogram data for all major currencies affecting the operating company	Amounts paid in the period by currency
Aging report, including intercompany	Forecast of range of cash positions		Projected disbursements by currency
Major delinquent accounts	Forecast of interest rate developments	Summary of all exposed positions and hedging actions taken	Variance analysis of previous projections
Summary of days outstanding	Variance analysis of previous projections	Variance analysis of previous projections	
Receipts			
Amounts collected in the period by currency			
Projected collections by currency			
Variance analysis of previous projections			

Source: John B. Gianotti and Richard W. Smith, *Treasury Management* (New York: John Wiley & Sons © 1981) p. 415. This material is used by permission of John Wiley & Sons, Inc.

Distance is an obvious complication. Due to geographic circumstances, formal information communications generally substitute for personal contacts between local operating managers and headquarters management.[20] Developments in information technology should reduce, but will not entirely eliminate, this complication.[21]

Other important environmental factors affecting information flows are the many legal, political, social, and cultural factors that bear upon multinational financial decisions. For example, secrecy is much more prevalent in business dealings abroad than in the United States. Consequently, U.S. headquarters management often must rely on internal auditors to monitor foreign subsidiaries. Economic considerations, such as competitive conditions, international tax developments, transnational financing possibilities, foreign inflation, and fluctuating currency values, also must be considered.

Information feedback requirements must also be considered. It is easy to neglect an operation located halfway around the world. All units of a multinational system must constantly receive timely and relevant information. It is impossible to coordinate group activities without effective dissemination of information.

---

[20]Schweikart has shown empirically that formal accounting communications are considered more helpful in some countries, while informal discussion as a form of information is considered more helpful in others. See James A. Schweikart, "The Relevance of Managerial Accounting Information: A Multinational Analysis," *Accounting Organizations and Society* 11, no. 6 (1986): 541–554.

[21]Caroline Dorsa, "Drawing Data from the Same Well," *Financial Executive* (September/October 1996): 35–38.

EXHIBIT 10-6   Framework for Multinational Control

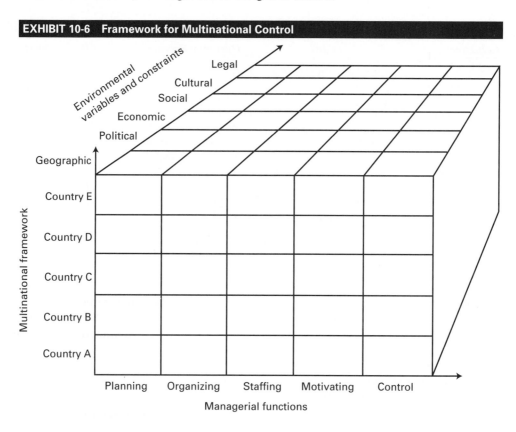

Designers of business information flows traditionally assume that information moves up and down traditional management hierarchies. Such a design may be appropriate where individual corporate units have little to do with one another. However, when corporate units interact frequently, as often happens internationally, lateral information flows—such as between Far Eastern subsidiaries of a European multinational—may be as important as the flow of information to and from headquarters.

For all of these reasons, international managers care about (1) the type and quantity of information they receive and (2) the systems through which such information is generated and transmitted to information users. The information itself must not be confused with the system through which it flows.

INFORMATION ISSUES

Cross-cultural studies have convincingly shown that managers in different environments have different ways of analyzing and resolving problems, different decision time frames, and different information needs on which to base business decisions.[22] Hence,

---

[22]G. Harrison and J. McKinnon, "Cross-Cultural Research in Management Control Systems Design: A Review of the Current State," *Accounting, Organizations and Society,* forthcoming, and Sam Beldona, Andrew C. Inkpen, and Arvind Phatak, "Are Japanese Managers More Long-Term Oriented Than United States Managers?" *Management International Review* (3rd quarter 1998): 239–256.

we have a fundamental problem for the multinational enterprise. Local managers are likely to want different decision information than headquarters management. Deliberate redundancy is often the only way to meet different but parallel information needs. We shall return to this point shortly.

A second major information problem is the question of translation. For example, in evaluating operations, U.S. managers generally prefer reports stated in U.S. dollars. Accordingly, reports from foreign operations of U.S. multinationals are typically translated to their U.S. dollar equivalents in order for U.S. headquarters managers to evaluate their dollar investments. However, does translating foreign currency amounts for managerial review purposes preserve the data without distortions?

A special feature of consolidated reports is that financial statements prepared according to foreign accounting principles are usually first restated to parent country accounting principles before being consolidated. Does this restatement somehow alter the information content of the accounts that go into a group consolidation?

SYSTEMS ISSUES

Perhaps the biggest challenge facing systems specialists is designing corporate information systems that allow financial managers to respond appropriately to the phenomenon of global competition. Conditions are changing. Owing to deregulation of markets and reduction of tariff barriers, firms are increasingly able to access foreign markets either directly or indirectly through joint ventures, strategic alliances, and other cooperative arrangements. This more open access has led to more intense global competition where competitors adopt strategies to (1) protect market share at home, (2) penetrate competitors' home markets to deny them market share and revenues, and (3) generate significant market share in key third-country markets.

In an era of global competition, CEOs need information systems that enable them to plan, coordinate, and control effective worldwide production, marketing, and financial strategies. To facilitate this objective, software information developers in the United States have created a new computer language, XBRL. XBRL stands for *extensible business reporting language* and is a standard computer programming enhancement that is being included in all accounting and financial reporting software in the United States. Once added to the software, XBRL automatically translates all numbers and words so that each data segment is identified in a standard way when viewed by a Web browser or sent to a particular spreadsheet application.[23] Useful for all enterprises regardless of industry or size, XBRL will also reduce information processing, calculating, and formatting costs because financial data only needs to be created and formatted once regardless of intended use. Software giants Microsoft and IBM have joined the business community in this important effort to develop a common business reporting language. Not only will it make the distribution of financial information fast and easy, it will also

---

[23]XBRL tags each segment of computerized business information with an identification marker that remains with the data when moved or changed. No matter how an application software formats or rearranges the information, the markers remain with the data. Thus a number identified as an asset or a liability, for instance, will always be recognized in this manner. For more information on the technical aspects of XBRL, go to www.xbrl.com.

eliminate the need for rewriting financial reports to accommodate incompatible accounting systems. Parallel efforts are reportedly underway in other countries along with involvement of the International Accounting Standards Committee.[24]

ISSUES IN FINANCIAL CONTROL

Management control systems aim at accomplishing enterprise objectives in the most effective and efficient manner. Financial control systems, in turn, are quantitative measurement and communication systems that facilitate control through (1) communicating financial goals as appropriate within the organization, (2) specifying criteria and standards for evaluating performance, (3) monitoring performance, and (4) communicating deviations between actual and planned performance to those responsible.

A sound financial control system enables top management to focus the activities of its subsidiaries toward common objectives. A control system consists of operational and financial policies, internal reporting structures, operating budgets, and procedure manuals consistent with top management's goals. Suboptimal behavior, which occurs when a subunit strives to achieve its own ends at the expense of the whole organization, thus is minimized. A timely reporting system that constantly monitors each unit is a good motivator. An efficient control system also enables headquarters management to evaluate the strategic plans of the company and to revise them when needed. Management's strategic planning tasks are aided by an information system that informs management of environmental changes that might significantly impact the company. Finally, a good control system enables top management to properly evaluate the performance of subordinates by ensuring that subordinates are held accountable only for events they can control.

If a well-designed control system is useful to a uninational company, it is invaluable to its multinational counterpart. As we have repeatedly observed, conditions that impact on management decisions abroad are not only different but constantly changing.

DOMESTIC VERSUS MULTINATIONAL CONTROL SYSTEM

How should a well-functioning control system be designed in a multinational company? Should a parent company use its domestic control system, unaltered, in its foreign operations? Studies show that the systems used by many multinational enterprises to control their foreign operations are identical, in many respects, to those used domestically. System items commonly exported include financial and budgetary control and the tendency to apply the same standards developed to evaluate domestic operations. In a now classic paper, David Hawkins offers four basic reasonsfor this:

1. Financial control considerations are seldom critical in the early stages of establishing a foreign operation.
2. It is normally cheaper to transplant the domestic system than to create from scratch an entire system designed for the foreign operation.

---

[24]Stanley Zarowin and Wayne E. Harding, "Finally, Business Talks the Same Language," *Journal of Accountancy* (August 2000): 25–30.

3. To simplify preparing and analyzing consolidated financial statements, the corporate controller's office insists that all operating subsidiaries use similar forms and schedules to record and transmit financial and operating data.

4. Former domestic executives working in the foreign operation and their corporate superiors are more comfortable if they can continue to use as much of the domestic control system as possible, largely because they reached the highest levels of management by mastering the domestic system.[25]

Some writers argue that financial control systems abroad should be the same as those used at home. We disagree. It is difficult to believe that a central controller's staff could design a single and effective worldwide control system given that the multinational operating environment is so diverse. A look back to the many elements in Exhibit 10-6 illustrates this point.

Environmental diversity has an unlimited potential impact on the financial control process. Earlier we observed that geographical distances often impede traditional methods of communicating between affiliates and company headquarters. Although better technology might overcome geographical distance, cultural distance is harder to overcome. Culture and the business environment interact to create unique sets of managerial values in a country.[26] Language difficulties, cross-cultural differences in attitude toward risk and authority, differences in need-achievement levels, and other cultural attributes often result in bad consequences including (1) misunderstood directives, (2) lower tolerance of criticism, (3) unwillingness to discuss business problems openly or to seek assistance, (4) loss of confidence among foreign managers, (5) unwillingness to delegate authority, and (6) reluctance to assume responsibility.

Managers of multinational companies face many tough issues, especially when senior management steeped in one culture must operate in another. Should there be a separate communications system for foreign nationals? Should performance standards for foreign nationals differ from those for their domestic counterparts? Should motivational techniques used overseas differ from those used domestically? Distribution channels, credit terms, industrial policies, financial institutions, and business practices all vary from country to country. These diverse business practices require international financial managers to adapt.

Consider *business gratuities*. Direct or indirect payments to secure a business favor violate the Foreign Corrupt Practices Act (FCPA) in the United States. In many parts of the world, however, business gratuities are a part of everyday business affairs. Government officials often have the power to cripple local operations if the expected gratuities are not paid. Unofficial payments to mail carriers are often a prerequisite for timely delivery of mail. Apart from the ethical issues, business gratuities give financial managers of U.S. multinational enterprises a major problem. If the formal financial control system monitors and acknowledges such payments, a U.S. parent company may expose itself to liability and possible embarrassment at home. If such payments are concealed from the control system through bogus documentation and contrived accounting transactions, the entire control system quickly breaks down.

---

[25]David F. Hawkins, "Controlling Foreign Operations," *Financial Executive* (February 1965): 25–32.
[26]David A. Ralston, David J. Gustafson, Kenny M. Cheung, and Robert H. Terpstra, "Differences in Managerial Values: A Study of U.S., Hong Kong and PRC Managers, *Journal of International Business Studies* (second quarter 1993): 249–275.

Sexual harassment is another issue. Insensitivity to gender differences and politically correct behavior can be expensive. Executives of Mitsubishi in the United States recently learned this the hard way.[27]

Companies with foreign operations must also adapt to unfamiliar governmental regulations and restrictions. Exchange controls, restrictions on capital flows, joint ownership requirements, and many other specific business regulations are examples.

The environmental considerations related to the strength of a nation's currency may be the most important for the design of overseas control systems of all those shown in Exhibit 10-6. Internal rates of inflation and fluctuating currency values are critical, and corporate control systems must allow for them. Applying financial controls designed for a stable environment to one that is less stable is a recipe for failure.[28]

OPERATIONAL BUDGETING

Having established its strategic goals and capital budget, management next focuses on short-range planning. Short-range planning involves creating operational budgets or profit plans where needed in the organization. These profit plans are the basis for cash management forecasts, operating decisions, and management compensation schemes.

Budgeted income statements of foreign affiliates are first converted to parent country accounting principles and translated from the local currency (FC) to the parent currency (PC). Periodic comparisons of actual and budgeted profit performance in parent currency require appropriate variance analyses to ensure that deviations from budget are correctly diagnosed for managerial action. While variance analysis is, in principle, the same internationally as domestically, currency fluctuations make it more complex.

The financial performance of a foreign operation can be measured in local currency, home country currency, or both. The currency used can have a significant impact in judging the performance of a foreign unit and its manager. Fluctuating currency values can turn profits (measured in local currency) into losses (expressed in home country currency).

Some favor a local currency perspective because foreign transactions take place in a foreign environment and are done in foreign currency. Foreign currency translation gains and losses are not considered when operations are evaluated in local currency.[29] One executive holding this view said:

> We evaluate our foreign operations primarily based on their local currency results. It is our belief that over the long run, the ability to achieve good performance in local currency terms will result in good performance in dollar terms. Good performance in local currency terms can only be achieved if prices are raised in line with local inflation, which over a period of time compensates for changes in the exchange rate.[30]

---

[27]Paul A. Samuelson, "Economic and Cultural Aspects of Tomorrow's Multinational Firms," *Japan and the World Economy* (December 2000): 393–394.

[28]Hassel found foreign subsidiary managers to be especially sensitive to the relevance of accounting-based performance measures if these measures are not sensitized to the dynamics of the local operating environment. See L. G. Hassel, "Performance Evaluation in a Multinational Environment," *Journal of International Financial Management and Accounting* 3, no. 2 (1991) 17–38.

[29]Helen G. Morsicato, *Currency Translation and Performance Evaluation in Multinationals*, Ann Arbor, MI: UMI Research Press, 1980.

[30]Business International, Assessing Foreign Subsidiary Performance, p. 31.

Those who favor a parent currency perspective argue that ultimately, home country shareholders care about domestic currency returns. Because they judge headquarters management by domestic currency returns, foreign managers should be judged by the same standard. In the words of a corporate controller:

> We are a dollar-based company. We're concerned with dollar results, not francs or pounds. We want our subsidiary managers to run their operations with that in mind. Furthermore, converting results into dollars makes it easier to evaluate and compare our subsidiaries.[31]

Problems remain even if parent currency is considered a better measure of performance than local currency. In theory, the exchange rate between two countries should move in proportion to changes in their differential inflation rates. Thus, if the rate of inflation is 10 percent in Italy and 30 percent in Turkey, the Turkish lira should lose approximately 20 percent of its value relative to the Italian lira. In practice, changes in currency exchange values that lag behind foreign rates of inflation can distort performance measures. Local currency earnings and their dollar equivalents increase during excessive inflation. In the following period, when the foreign currency loses value, the dollar value of local earnings falls, even if local currency earnings increase. Under these circumstances, measuring with parent currency introduces random elements in measuring the performance of foreign operations if changes in foreign exchange rates do not *track* differences in inflation rates.

In the long run, one must judge a foreign unit's value as an investment in terms of home country currency. A parent currency perspective is appropriate for strategic planning and long-term investment decisions, but the currency framework used in evaluating managerial performance must depend on who is held accountable for exchange risk. (This issue is separate from who is *responsible* for exchange risks.) If corporate treasury manages exchange risks, then it is logical to measure foreign performance in local currency. Parent currency measures are just as valid if exchange gains and losses are removed in evaluating foreign managers. If local managers have the necessary tools to manage exchange gains and losses, measuring their performance in parent currency is justifiable.

Consider some aspects of the budgetary process. Control over a network of domestic and foreign operations requires that foreign currency budgets be expressed in parent currency for comparison.

When parent currency figures are used, a change in exchange rates used to establish the budget and to monitor performance causes a variance beyond that due to other changes. Three possible rates can be used in drafting the beginning-of-period operating budget:

1. The spot rate in effect when the budget is established
2. A rate that is expected to prevail at the end of the budget period (projected rate)
3. The rate at the end of the period if the budget is updated whenever exchange rates change (ending rate)[32]

[31]Ibid., p. 31.
[32]Donald R. Lessard and Peter Lorange, "Currency Changes and Management Control: Resolving the Centralization/Decentralization Dilemma," *Accounting Review* (July 1977): 628–37.

Comparable rates can be used to track performance relative to budget. If different exchange rate combinations are used to set the budget and to track performance, this creates different allocations of responsibilities for exchange rate changes and leads to different possible managerial responses. Let us consider some possibilities.

1. *Budget and track performance at initial spot rate.* Exchange rate changes have no effect on the evaluation of the foreign manager's performance. Local managers have little incentive to incorporate anticipated exchange rate changes into their operating decisions.
2. *Budget at ending (updated) rate and track at ending rate.* This combination produces similar results. Local management need not consider exchange rates because the same rate is used for budgeting and evaluation.
3. *Budgeting at initial rate and track at ending rate.* Local managers have full responsibility for exchange rate changes. Potential negative consequences include padding of budgets by local managers or hedging that may not be optimal for the corporation.
4. *Budget and track performance using projected exchange rates.* This system reflects a local currency perspective. Local managers are encouraged to incorporate expected exchange rate changes into their operating plans but are not held responsible for unexpected rate changes, which the parent company absorbs.
5. *Budget at projected rate and track at ending rate.* This exchange rate combination does not hold the local manager accountable for expected rate changes. Managers are responsible for (and thereby encouraged to hedge) unanticipated exchange rate changes.

Which option is best for evaluating managerial performance? All five are found in practice. We focus on the last two, the most common.

As an illustration, assume the following (LC = local currency):

Projected rate of exchange:	$0.50 = LC 1	Actual end-of-period rate:	$0.25 = LC 1
Budgeted earnings in LC:	800,000	Actual earnings in LC:	1,000,000
Budget earnings in $:	400,000	Actual earnings in $:	250,000

If the projected rate is used in monitoring performance, the dollar result is $500,000 (LC1,000,000 × $0.50), or $100,000 above budget. The manager appears to have done well. But, if the actual end-of-period rate is used, the result is $250,000 (LC1,000,000 × $0.25), or $150,000 below budget. The manager appears to have done poorly. Which rate should be used?

Most discussions of this problem favor option 4. Using the projected exchange rate in budgeting encourages managers to include expected exchange rate movements in their operating decisions. Use of the projected rate to monitor performance, in turn, shields local managers from unanticipated exchange rate changes they cannot control. Also, protection against exchange risk can be coordinated on a company-wide basis.

We think that use of a projected exchange rate for budgeting and the actual ending rate for tracking performance (option 5) also has merit. Like option 4, this approach encourages managers to include anticipated exchange rate changes in their plans for the budget period. Unlike option 4, holding local and corporate managers accountable for unexpected rate changes encourages them to respond to exchange rate movements.[33] Option 5 is especially useful when local operating plans can be changed to accommodate unanticipated currency developments. Where any remaining variances between actual and projected rates are ignored when evaluating local managers (i.e., the remaining variance is regarded as a forecasting error, which is the responsibility of corporate headquarters), this system offers additional benefits over option 4.

When responsibility for exchange variances is divided between various levels in management, budget variances need to be analyzed by responsibility level. In our previous example, the foreign subsidiary's operating variance and exchange rate variance would be analyzed as shown in Exhibit 10-7.

The total budget variance of $-\$150,000$ (LC800,000 × $0.50 − LC1,000,000 × $0.25) would consist of a positive variance of $100,000 attributed to the foreign manager (LC800,000 × $0.50 − LC1,000,000 × $0.50) and a negative variance of $-\$250,000$ attributed to corporate headquarters (LC1,000,000 × $0.50 − LC1,000,000 × $0.25).

Exhibit 10-8 illustrates a framework for analyzing budget variances when the responsibility for exchange variances is divided between local management, an international division's operating management (parent currency variation) and corporate treasury (variance from budget rates). Here, the international division is responsible for hedging unexpected exchange rate changes while corporate treasury is responsible for accurate rate forecasts.

ANALYSIS OF EXCHANGE RATE CHANGES

We now provide a more comprehensive example of an exchange rate variance analysis.[34] Exhibit 10-9 shows the budgeted and actual condensed income statements for FC Company at the start and end of the 20X1 budget year. The profit plan for the year (expressed in parent company GAAP) is translated to parent currency at the beginning-of-period exchange rate of FC1 = PC1. The foreign currency devalues by 20 percent by year-end.

EXHIBIT 10-7   Analysis of Exchange Rate Variances

		Computation		
Responsibility		*Operating Item*	*Exchange Rate*	*Variance*
Local currency operations (Foreign management)	−	LC Budget × LC Actual ×	Budget Budget	= Local-currency operating variance
Parent currency operations (Headquarters' management)	−	LC Actual × LC Actual ×	Budget Actual	= Parent-currency exchange variance

---

[33]Imagine what would happen if a foreign manager, projecting a 30 percent local currency devaluation, actually gets a 70 percent devaluation and does nothing to offset the larger than expected devaluation because his performance is measured using the projected rate.

[34]Gerald F. Lewis, "Multinational Budgeting and Control Systems," in *International Accounting and Finance Handbook*, 2nd ed., F. D. S. Choi, New York: John Wiley & Sons, Inc., 1997, 26.1–26.22.

EXHIBIT 10-8 Three-Way Analysis of Exchange Rate Variance

| | Computation | | |
| | | | |
Responsibility	*Operating Item*	*Exchange Rate*	*Variance*
Local currency operations (Local management)	LC Budget $\times$ Budget $-$ LC Actual $\times$ Budget $=$		Local-currency operating variance
Parent-currency operations (International division)	LC Actual $\times$ Budget $-$ LC Actual $\times$ Actual $=$		Parent-currency operating variance
Foreign exchange variance from budget (Treasury)	LC Budget $\times$ Budget $-$ LC Budget $\times$ Actual $=$		Exchange rate variance from budget

Source: John B. Gianotti and Richard W. Smith, *Treasury Management* (New York: John Wiley & Sons © 1981) p. 415. This material is used by permission of John Wiley & Sons, Inc.

A performance report breaking out price-, volume- and exchange-rate-induced variances appears in Exhibit 10-10.

From the perspective of the foreign affiliate, performance variances are measured in local currency and reflect the difference between budget and actual figures for each item in the income statement. These performance variances are detailed in column (7) of Exhibit 10-10. Variances for sales revenues and cost of sales can be broken down into price (cost) and volume variances. The sale volume variance of FC1,000 is determined by multiplying the change in unit sales volume, 200 units, by the budgeted selling price of FC5. Applying a similar methodology to cost of sales produces a volume variance of 200 units $\times$ FC3 = FC600. Thus, the net volume variance affecting gross margin and operating income column (9), is FC1,000 $-$ FC600 = FC400. Variances in sales revenues and cost of sales attributed to price (cost) changes during the budget period are found by multiplying the actual number of units sold by the change in selling price (production cost). This calculation yields a negative price variance of 1,200 units $\times$ $-$FC0.25 = $-$FC300 for sales revenue, and a positive cost variance of 1,200 units $\times$ $-$FC0.60 = FC720 for cost of sales—see column (10). Differences between budgeted and actual expenses are shown as nominal variances in column (11).

EXHIBIT 10-9 Income Statement for Exchange Rate Variance Analysis

		Budget		*Actual*
Revenues		FC5,000		FC5,700[1]
Cost of goods sold		3,000[2]		2,880
Gross margin		FC2,000		FC2,820
Operating expenses	750		825	
Depreciation	500		500	
Interest	250	1,500	300	1,625
Operating income		FC 500		FC1,195

[1]The company employs the FIFO costing method and production equaled sales during the year. Unit production costs dropped from a planned FC3.00 to FC2.40 per unit.

[2]Actual sales increased by 200 units during the year at a price of FC4.75, FC.25 lower than expected.

EXHIBIT 10-10 Performance Report FC Company (For the Budget Period Ending 12/31/X1)

	(1)	(2)	(3)	(4)	(5)	(6)	(7)	(8)	(9)	(10)	(11)	(12)
	Budget			Actual			Total		Variance Analysis			
	FC	FX	PC	FC	FX	PC	FC	PC	Vol.	Price/(Cost)	Reported	Exch. Rate
Revenue	5,000	1.0	5,000	5,700	.8	4,560	700	(440)	1,000	(300)		(1,140)
Beg. inventory	(3,000)	1.0	(3,000)	(2,800)	1.0	(2,800)	200	200				
Production	(3,000)	1.0	(3,000)	(2,880)	.8	(2,304)	120	696				
Goods available	(6,000)		(6,000)	(5,680)		(5,104)	320	896				
End. inventory	3,000	1.0	3,000	2,800	.8	2,240	(200)	(1,760)				
Cost of sales	(3,000)		(3,000)	(2,880)		(2,864)	120	136	(600)	720		16
Gross margin	2,000		2,000	2,820		1,696	820	(304)	400	420		(1,124)
Operating exp.	(750)	1.0	(750)	(825)	.8	(660)	(75)	90			(75)	165
Depreciation	(500)	1.0	(500)	(500)	1.0	(500)	–	–				–
Interest	(250)	1.0	(250)	(300)	.8	(240)	(50)	10			(50)	60
Operating income	500		500	1,195		296	695	(204)	400	420	(125)	(899)

407

Based on this analysis, we can see that the improvement in FC Company's operating income of FC695 (Column 7) is attributable to the following factors:

Higher volume (Column 9)	FC400
Lower selling price (Column 10)	(300)
Lower production cost (Column 10)	720
Higher expenses (Column 11)	(125)
Increase in operating income (Column 7)	FC695

When FC Company's performance is evaluated from the parent company perspective, first its local currency results are translated to parent currency. Let us assume that Parent Company designates the parent currency as its functional currency. Accordingly, FC Company's budgeted income statement is translated to parent currency using the temporal translation method. Had the local currency been designated as functional, the current rate translation method would have been used. (See Chapter 6 for a detailed description of these methods.)

To simplify our analysis, Parent Company will analyze FC Company's budget variances using the exchange rate prevailing at the budget date (FC1.00 = PC1.00).[35]

With this approach, price and volume variances for sales and cost of sales will mirror those calculated under a local company perspective. The effect of exchange rate changes is calculated by multiplying actual results reported in parent currency by the change in the exchange rate during the budget period. The total variance for sales revenues in parent currency, PC5,000 − PC4,560 = PC440, would be broken down into the following volume, price, and exchange rate variances:

$$\text{Volume variance in col.(9)} = 200 \text{ units} \times FC5 = FC1{,}000 \times 1.0 = PC1{,}000$$

$$\text{Price variance in col. (10)} = 1{,}200 \text{ units} \times -FC0.25$$
$$= FC(300) \times 1.0 = PC(300)$$

$$\text{Exchange rate variance in col. (12)} = FC5{,}700 \times -PC0.2 = PC(1{,}140)$$

Similarly, the total variance for cost of sales can be broken down as follows:

$$\text{Volume variance} = 200 \text{ units} \times FC3 = FC600 \times 1.0 = PC(600)$$

$$\text{Cost variance} = 1{,}200 \text{ units} \times -FC0.60 = FC(720) \times 1.0 = PC720$$

Exchange rate variance is computed by multiplying each component of cost of goods sold by the exchange rate change in column (12):

Beginning inventory	FC2,800	×	-0-	=	0
Production	FC2,880	×	−PC.2	=	576
Ending inventory	FC2,800	×	−PC.2	=	(560)
					16

---

[35] Alternative exchange rate benchmarks and their implications for performance evaluation of foreign operations are considered in a later section of this chapter.

Exchange rate variances for operating expenses and depreciation are computed by multiplying the actual figures in local currency by the exchange rate change during the period. This yields an exchange variance for operating expenses FC825 × −PC0.2 = PC165 and an exchange variance of FC(300) × −PC0.2 = PC60 for interest.

In evaluating FC Company's performance in parent currency, the shortfall of −PC124 in operating earnings can be attributed to the following factors:

Higher sales volume	PC+400
Lower selling price	(300)
Lower production cost	+720
Higher operating expenses	(75)
Higher interest expenses	(50)
Exchange rate changes (column 12)	(899)
Decrease in parent currency operating earnings (column 8)	PC(204)

A currency translation phenomenon caused by a weakening of the local currency relative to the reporting currency is a major cause of the poor operating result. The following section discusses the proper evaluation of this currency effect.

PERFORMANCE EVALUATION OF FOREIGN OPERATIONS

Evaluating performance is central to an effective control system. A properly designed performance evaluation system allows top management to (1) judge the profitability of existing operations, (2) spot areas that are not performing as planned, (3) allocate limited corporate resources productively, and (4) evaluate managerial performance.

Developing an effective performance evaluation system is as much an art as a science. Its complexity increases with overseas operations. Performance evaluation of foreign operations must deal with such complications as exchange rate volatility, foreign inflation, transfer pricing, and a host of other environmental effects. If these factors are ignored, headquarters risks receiving distorted measures of operating results. Inappropriate standards of performance may motivate overseas managers to take actions not in line with corporate goals. Direct consequences are reduced corporate efficiency and (possibly) reduced competitiveness.

The remaining sections of this chapter examine some major issues associated with the performance evaluation of foreign operations, describe how leading MNCs evaluate performance, and offer some general policy guidelines.

CONSISTENCY

Survey results show that a principal goal of performance evaluation is to ensure profitability.[36] There is a potential conflict, however, when the performance evaluation

---

[36]William Persen and Van Lessing, *Evaluating the Financial Performance of Overseas Operations,* New York: Financial Executives Research Foundation, 1979, 16.

system does not suit the specific nature of a foreign operation that may have purposes other than short-run profit.[37]

Given the uniqueness of each foreign subsidiary's mission, performance evaluation systems must allow for how the subsidiary's objectives fit in with overall corporate goals. For example, if a foreign subsidiary's purpose is to produce components for other units in the system, it should be evaluated in terms of how its prices, production, quality, and delivery timetables compare to other sources of supply. Subsidiary managers should participate fully in establishing their objectives. Their participation helps to ensure that they will be evaluated within a framework that is sensitive to local operating conditions and consistent with overall corporate goals. Companies should be sure not to sacrifice long-term objectives because subsidiary managers are preoccupied with short-term results. This adherence to long-term goals can be accomplished by making sure that short-term performance goals and management incentives fit within the company's strategic plans.

UNIT VERSUS MANAGERIAL PERFORMANCE

> *Controller A:* I think generally we would look upon the manager's and unit's performance as about one and the same. The operation of the foreign unit is the responsibility of the manager and how the unit does is pretty much tied in with his evaluation.[38]

> *Controller B:* In terms of evaluating the manager, it is very much related to how he is doing against his budget because he did present his budget which was approved by the executive office and this was his plan of action for the coming year. Now in terms of evaluating whether his unit is one that we want to continue or invest in or whether we should be looking at other alternatives, the return on investment becomes the significant factor.[39]

Should we distinguish between the performance of the unit and the performance of its manager in evaluating a foreign operation? Although some may believe there is no distinction, this position can be held only under limited conditions.

The actions of several parties, each with a different stake in the outcome, may affect the performance of a foreign operation. These parties include (but are not limited to) local management, headquarters management, the host government, and the parent company's government.

Local managers obviously influence reported earnings through their operating decisions. Decisions made at corporate headquarters also affect foreign earnings. For ex-

---

[37]MNCs establish foreign operations for many reasons. Companies that depend on a steady supply of raw materials generally expand overseas to secure their supplies. Others invest abroad to lower production costs by obtaining less costly labor, power, or auxiliary services. When a company can no longer profitably export to a market because of increased tariffs, often it will establish a local operation there. Other reasons for expanding abroad include the need to (1) avoid losing a foreign market to major competitors, (2) create markets for components and related products, (3) diversify business risks, (4) search for new markets, (5) satisfy government regulations, and (6) spread overhead costs among more producing units. Many of these objectives are strategic rather than tactical in nature.

[38]Paul A. Samuelson, "Economic and Cultural Aspects of Tomorrow's Multinational Firms," *Japan and the World Economy* (December 2000): 393–394.

[39]Ibid., p. 26.

ample, to protect the value of assets located in devaluation-prone countries, corporate treasury will often instruct foreign units to transfer funds to subsidiaries located in strong-currency countries.

Host government actions and policies also directly affect the reported results of a foreign subsidiary. Required minimum capitalization ratios in various countries often enlarge the investment base against which earnings are compared. Foreign exchange controls that limit the availability of foreign currency to pay for needed imports will often depress a subsidiary's performance. Wage and price controls can also damage the reported performance of local managers.

These considerations make it clear that a distinction must be made between managerial and unit performance. Local managers should be evaluated only on those balance sheet and income statement items they can influence. This specific evaluation can be done in practice by dividing each balance sheet and income statement item into controllable and noncontrollable components, as illustrated in Exhibit 10-11.

Under this framework, for example, a manager of a U.S. affiliate in Italy would not be held accountable for effective interest charges incurred in connection with a Swiss franc borrowing mandated by corporate treasury. Because the borrowing decision was made at headquarters, headquarters management is responsible for the interest cost (i.e., the nominal interest rate in Switzerland plus the exchange risk). Because the affiliate derives some benefit from the loan proceeds, it should pay an equitable interest charge. This related charge is called a *capital charge* and is based on the cost that would have been incurred had the Italian manager borrowed locally or from the parent.

PERFORMANCE CRITERIA

A single criterion is unlikely to capture all factors of performance of interest to headquarters management. Two of the more widely used financial performance criteria used by MNCs for evaluating their foreign operations are return on investment (ROI) and budgeted performance. ROI relates enterprise income to a specified investment base;

EXHIBIT 10-11 Partitioned Financial Statements (Local Currency)		
	Locally Controllable	*Locally Noncontrollable*
Balance Sheet		
Assets (detailed)	xx	xx
Liabilities (detailed)	xx	xx
Owners' equity (detailed)	xx	xx
Income Statement		
Revenues	xx	xx
Operating expenses	xx	xx
Interest	xx	xx
"Other"	xx	xx
Taxes	xx	xx
Net Income	xx	xx

budgeted performance compares operating performance to a budget. Budgetary control means that any difference between budget and actual performance can be traced to the manager or unit responsible. One classic study demonstrated that budgetary control is better than ROI comparisons for evaluating managerial performance.[40] ROI measures may be more appropriate for measuring unit performance, while budget comparisons may be more useful in evaluating managers.

Many companies do not confine their performance criteria to financial considerations. Nonfinancial criteria reinforce financial measures by focusing on actions that may significantly affect long-term performance. These criteria are especially important in distinguishing between managerial and unit performance.

Important nonfinancial measures include market share, product and process innovation, personnel development (gauged in terms of number of people promoted in relation to the number of promotable employees), employee morale (ascertained by in-house opinion surveys), and productivity measurements. No less significant is performance in social responsibility and host government relations. Such nonfinancial factors are vital to ensure continued success abroad.

Additional issues concern identifying relevant components of ROI and budget indicators and measuring them. Variations in ROI and budget comparisons relate to appropriate elements of income and the investment base. Thus, should income be the difference between revenues and expenses as they appear in a subsidiary's conventional income statement, or should it incorporate other dimensions? While conventional income measures may reflect a firm's results better than a strictly cash flow measure, they can be misleading in an international setting. To begin, net income may include allocated corporate expenses that the unit manager cannot control. It may not reflect the strategic nature of the foreign unit's mission. A subsidiary's reported results rarely reflect its total contribution.

To remedy these shortcomings, corporate accountants need to specify, as accurately as they can, the returns specifically attributable to the foreign subsidiary's existence. To report profits, therefore, they should *add back* things such as (1) royalty payments, service fees, and corporate allocations charged to the foreign subsidiary and (2) profits on intracorporate sales to the subsidiary. If sales to the subsidiary are not made at arm's-length prices, the foreign subsidiary's profits should be adjusted for transfer pricing subsidies (transfer prices are discussed more fully in Chapter 12). Income amounts used for managerial evaluations should preferably include only those elements of revenues and expense that unit managers can control.

What about the ROI denominator? Should it consist of shareholders' equity? Should it incorporate shareholders' equity plus total interest-bearing debt (alternatively, fixed assets plus net working capital)? Should it be total assets? If so, should assets include nonproductive resources that are carried because of local environmental constraints? Should it include assets that are allocated by corporate headquarters, such as those corporate treasury controls?

As with income, we believe that a distinction should be made. For managers, the investment base should consist of the resources they can control. Thus, excess inventories (stockpiled because of host government exchange control policies), should be elimi-

---

[40]Sidney M. Robbins and Robert B. Stobaugh, "The Bent Measuring Stick in Foreign Subsidiaries," *Harvard Business Review* (September–October 1973): 80–88.

nated, as should intracorporate receivables and cash balances over whose levels the local managers have little influence. For the subsidiary, the investment base should include all capital employed in accomplishing its stated objectives.

Assume, as an example, that a foreign unit ends the year with the following foreign currency (FC) financial position. (Current liabilities exclude any interest-paying debt including the current portion of long-term debt.)

Cash	FC 500	Current liabilities	FC	300
Accounts receivable	200	Long-term debt		800
Inventory	300			
Fixed assets	1,000	Owners' equity		900
	FC 2,000		FC 2,000	

Assume further that earnings before interest and taxes (EBIT) are FC200. Local interest rates average 12 percent.

Many companies in the United Kingdom and the United States compute ROI by relating EBIT to fixed assets plus net working capital. In our example, this investment base yields an ROI statistic of 11.7 percent (FC200/FC1,700). The comparable figure for many Netherlands-based MNCs, however, is closer to 16.7 percent, because Dutch companies typically remove the ending cash balance from the definition of capital employed. (Cash on hand is considered a nonearning asset in the Netherlands).[41]

MEASUREMENT ISSUES AND CHANGING PRICES IN EVALUATION

The designer of an evaluation system for foreign operations must also face the issue of accounting measurements. Should local currency asset values be adjusted for changing prices where inflation is a significant force?[42] Such restatements directly affect measures of various ROI components and performance statistics for budgeting and performance evaluation. For example, failure to account for inflation generally overstates return on investment measures. As a result, corporate resources may not be directed to their most promising use within the corporation.

In Chapter 7 we said that an internal information system, sensitive to the effects of changing prices, provides a foundation for an inflation management strategy.[43] For a closer look at such issues, we begin by examining the performance evaluation practices of ICI, the U.K. chemical giant.

---

[41]On the other hand, Dutch companies use cash on hand as a standard of comparison. Return on assets employed should at least exceed the return that would have been earned had cash been invested in the local capital market, 12 percent in our example.

[42]Even in countries where rates of inflation are low, the cumulative effect of changing prices on long-lived assets can be significant. This is especially true of a capital-intensive multibusiness with older fixed assets.

[43]For an excellent discussion on managing inflation risk, see T. R. Collins, "Risk Management in Hyperinflationary Environments," in *Handbook of International Accounting,* D. S. Choi, ed., New York: John Wiley, 1991.

PERFORMANCE EVALUATION PRACTICES: ICI

During the oil embargo of the early 1970s, the price of oil, one of ICI's major raw materials, shot up by a factor of 5 in 1 year. As a result, top management was informed that even a 50 percent rate of return was inadequate![44]

An examination of the impact of inflation on historical accounts disclosed six adverse consequences: (1) cost of goods sold was understated compared with current sales, (2) capital employed was understated in relation to its current value, (3) as a result of (1) and (2), returns on capital were doubly overstated, (4) comparisons of divisional performance based on similar assets of different ages were spurious, (5) intercountry comparisons of subsidiary performance were meaningless, and (6) performance comparisons over time were invalid.

To eliminate these distortions, ICI incorporated current cost adjustments (CCA) in its internal reporting system. According to a company spokesperson, "It provided a vitally needed management tool."[45]

ICI divides its performance measures into two categories: long-term (at least 1 year) and short-term. Cash flow generation by product and ROI are the principal long-term measures. With its cash flow measure, ICI seeks to determine whether a product will earn enough money to pay for replacing its plant, its share of corporate costs, and return enough profit to finance realistic growth. In modeling its operations, ICI discovered that the required rate of CCA return differed by country. For example, its operations in Germany needed twice the U.K. rate of return to finance the same rate of growth, primarily due to tax factors.

ICI's measure of ROI is the ratio of current cost operating profit (before interest, taxes, and dividends) to current cost fixed assets plus net working capital. Assets are valued at replacement cost net of depreciation for large businesses, and at gross for smaller product lines to eliminate distortions due to the age of the assets (i.e., the denominator would decrease over time simply due to depreciation, thus raising the rate of return).

In Western Europe, profit is measured before interest and taxes because these expenses are the responsibility of headquarters, and it is difficult to relate a loan to a particular project or determine the actual tax paid when a product is made in one country and sold in several others. Where performance is evaluated on a subsidiary basis, (e.g., Brazil and Australia), profit is measured after interest and tax. ICI does this because these subsidiaries do their own borrowing, and investment decisions there are influenced by local taxes and tax incentives.

By using a current cost ROI as opposed to a historical cost return, ICI has largely insulated its measure of return from local taxes, tax incentives, and inflation. As a result, ICI can compare businesses in different countries and at different times.

While ICI mainly uses cash flow generation and ROI to assess long-term performance, its principal short-term performance measure is to compare actual results against budget, with particular interest in financial ratios such as gross profit margin (i.e., profit before corporate costs). The company has a 3-year plan: The plan's first year is that period's operating budget. Performance is tracked monthly and quarterly. Quarterly results are considered more significant.

---

[44]Business International, *Assessing Foreign Subsidiary Performance*, p. 124.
[45]Ibid., 45.

Like most MNCs, ICI incorporates inflationary expectations in budgeting local selling prices and operating costs such as expected labor costs. ICI prefers to incorporate current values in its budgeting system and forecasts a replacement value for cost of goods sold and depreciation.

ICI states that the reason for this approach is

> to force management's attention to the fact that if a company is in a volatile cost setup, as we are when the price of oil and derivatives can go up or down very fast, it has to use the cost it will incur to replace raw materials and factor that into its selling price. If it uses historic cost, the profit may not be adequate to continue purchasing oil at today's cost.[46]

Thus performance is tracked using the actual cost of goods incurred each month. The unit's manager is held accountable for the variance (if any), because unexpected (i.e., greater than forecasted) increases in cost can be countered by raising prices.[47]

The budget also includes a forecasted depreciation expense based on local indexes reflecting the asset's replacement cost. The local manager is not responsible for any variance (calculated quarterly) between forecasted and actual depreciation because it is not feasible to discern and react to a change in forecasted depreciation, but the product manager is expected to make budgeted profit after actual depreciation.

ICI also includes a forecasted monetary working capital adjustment (MWCA) in its budget. (See Chapter 7 for a discussion of this concept.) ICI does not find the difference between forecasted and actual MWCA to be very meaningful because it is invariably due to changes in costs and selling prices and it shows up elsewhere in the profit and loss account.[48]

ICI's solution to inflation reporting largely focuses on aggregate balance sheets and income statements. We next offer an internal reporting system that allows management to examine reported numbers in more disaggregated fashion.

INFLATION AND PERFORMANCE MEASUREMENT

FAS No. 52 mandates use of the temporal translation method described in Chapter 6 in consolidating the accounts of foreign affiliates domiciled in high-inflation environments. Even though FAS No. 52 and similar national pronouncements provide useful guidelines in preparing hard currency statements, they do not meet the information needs of firms operating in high-inflation countries.[49] In high-inflation environments, financial reports prepared in conformity with FAS No. 52 tend to distort reality by

- Overstating or understating revenues and expenses
- Reporting large translation gains or losses that are difficult to interpret
- Distorting performance comparisons over time

---

[46]Ibid., 126.

[47]This assumes that competitors suffered the same cost increases, which may not always be true due to exchange rate factors.

[48]The gearing adjustment on net, nontrading monetary liabilities (a form of purchasing power gain) is not incorporated into budgeting because raising funds is headquarters' responsibility.

[49]Coopers & Lybrand, *Reporting Reality from High-Inflation Countries,* New York: Author, 1989, 5–6.

Our reporting framework overcomes these limitations and is based on the following assumptions:[50]

1. Management's objective of maximizing the value of the firm is framed in terms of a currency that holds its value (i.e., a hard currency). Accordingly, the best way to measure the performance of an affiliate located in a high-inflation environment is in terms of hard currency.[51]

2. Our model also implicitly assumes that inflation rates, exchange rates, and interest rates are interrelated. (This assumption is not critical to the proposal.)

A common reporting convention in accounting for foreign currency transactions is to record revenues and expenses at exchange rates prevailing at the financial statement date. (Use of average rates is also common.) A better option is to report local currency transactions at the exchange rate prevailing on the payment date. Recording a transaction at any other date muddles the measurement process by introducing gains or losses in the purchasing power of money—or, alternatively, implicit interest—into the exchange transaction.

In a perfectly competitive market, all local currency transactions would be in cash. With inflation, it is advantageous for buyers to delay payment for as long as possible and for sellers to accelerate collections. The payment date is determined by the competitive strengths of the contracting parties. Our recommended reporting treatment produces reported numbers that are reliable, economically interpretable, and symmetric in the sense that economically similar transactions produce similar financial statement numbers when translated into a common currency.[52] One could say that the model uses accrual accounting with a cash accounting mentality.

An example will highlight the translation gains and losses generated by FAS No. 52 reporting. While many would attribute gains or losses in our example to foreign exchange risk, they are really due to improper accounting for events that occurred "above the line."

Following are our working assumptions:

- Inflation and Turkish lira (TL) devaluation is 30 percent per month or 1.2 percent per workday.
- The general price level at selected intervals for the months 1 and 2 are:

1/1	100.0
1/10	109.6
1/20	119.6
1/30	130.0
2/10	141.6
2/20	154.5
2/30	169.0

---

[50]Frederick D. S. Choi and Ronald R. Gunn, "Hyperinflation Reporting and Performance Assessment," *Journal of Financial Statement Analysis* (summer 1997): 30–38.

[51]Interviews with financial executives of U.S.-based multinationals as well as subsidiary managers suggest that this assumption is consistent with corporate practices at the micro level. It also appears consistent with practices at the macro level. Witness the recent trend of more and more Latin American countries pegging their currencies to the U.S. dollar. Matt Moffett and Jonathan Friedland, "Mexican Peso Collapse Presents Stark Choices to Latin Economies," *Wall Street Journal*, January 6, 1995, A1.

[52]The notion of economic interpretability and symmetry are discussed more rigorously in William H. Beaver and Mark A. Wolfson, "Foreign Currency Translation and Changing Prices in Perfect and Complete Markets," *Journal of Accounting Research* (autumn 1992): 528–550.

The real rate of interest is 1 1/2 percent per month or 20 per cent per year.
- Cash balances are kept in hard currency (U.S. dollars).
- Month-end rates are used to record expense transactions.

SALES REVENUE

Suppose that the firm sells TL 2,000,000 worth of merchandise in month 1, with varying invoice dates and payment terms. Assuming that financial statements are prepared monthly, the conventional practice is to record the sales transaction at the month-end exchange rate regardless of when the sale is invoiced or when payment is received. Sales reported using the month-end exchange rate are TL 2,000,000/130 = $15,385.

First assume that the sale is invoiced on day 1 of month 1, with payment received immediately in cash = TL 2,000,000/TL 100 = $20,000. Conventional treatment measures the transaction at month's end rather than when cash is received, but the economic basis of the transaction is the cash that is actually received on the invoice date. Here revenues are understated by 30 percent or $4,615 determined as follows:

Actual	$20,000
Reported	15,385
Variance	$ 4,615

In keeping with the temporal translation method, this $4,615 understatement of sales is offset by an equivalent nonoperating translation gain appearing below the line.[53]

Next, assume instead that the sale is invoiced on day 5, and that the client receives 25 days payment terms. In our model, the transaction is booked on the same day that payment is received. From an economic point of view, there is no variance and no nonoperating translation gain or loss.

Actual	$15,385
Reported	$15,385
Variance	$ -0-

From a control perspective, management should be able to learn from the salesperson what the expected profit margin is on the day of sale. The salesperson does not have to wait until the books are closed to have this information, which is already at hand as invoices in hyperinflationary environments clearly state the payment due date.

In the following example, assume that the client is invoiced on day 30 with payment required a month later. From an economic point of view, the firm collects $11,834 (= TL 2,000,000/TL 169). The accounting system reports $15,385 resulting in a variance of $3,551.

---

[53] Assume that the firm in question begins the period with a $10,000 equity investment and immediately converts this cash balance to saleable inventories. The goods are marked up 100 percent over cost and sold for cash the next day. In this case, the aggregate exchange adjustment would be $4,615, determined either as a plug when preparing the end of period translated balance sheet, or as a positive aggregate translation adjustment comprising the gain on the hard currency cash balance.

Actual	$11,834
Reported	15,385
Variance	$ 3,551

Here, the conventional reporting system overstates sales by 23.1 percent with the positive variance offset by an equivalent nonoperating translation loss below the line.

Exhibit 10-12 shows the magnitude of the distortions associated with differing invoicing and payment terms. Depending on sales terms, sales can be overstated or understated by significant amounts.

Why do we care about these distortions? The traditional reporting system has a bad effect on the behavior of the sales force. For example, it gives the company's sales force no motivation to improve payment terms. If sales are recorded at the end of month rate, sales personnel do not care whether they are paid in cash or in 30 or 60 days. It is important to have a system that encourages the sales force to act in the company's best interests.

In addition, traditional reporting systems do not motivate the sales force to invoice and ship earlier in the month. When sales are recorded at end-of-month rates, the sales force does not care about the time of delivery. Yet, even one day's delay in shipment could be costly; 1.5 percent in lost interest in our example. Another glance at Exhibit 10-12 shows that bonuses and commission payments are based on inflated sales values whenever payment terms carry over to the following period.

Perhaps the most serious shortcoming of traditional reporting systems is that they encourage manipulation of results. Assume now that exchange rates at the end of each of the next 3 months are as follows:

End-of-month 1	130 = $1
End-of-month 2	169 = $1
End-of-month 3	220 = $1

Suppose that a salesperson arranges the following with a favored customer: deliver and invoice TL 2,000,000 of a product on day 30 of month 1 at TL 2,500,000 with 60-day payment terms instead of invoicing at TL 2,000,000 on the same date with 30-day payment terms. The attractiveness of this arrangement is easy to figure out. Under conventional reporting methods the revised sales value is TL 2,500,000/TL 130 = $19,231

EXHIBIT 10-12 Distortions in Invoice and Payment Dates (TL 2,000,000 Sales in Month 1)

Invoice Day	Payment Terms	Today's Number	Proposed Number	Diff.	%
1	Cash	15,385	20,000	4,615	30.0%
5	5 days	15,385	18,248	2,863	18.6%
5	15 days	15,385	16,722	1,337	8.7%
5	25 days	15,385	15,385	0.000	0.0%
10	30 days	15,385	14,124	−1,261	−8.2%
20	30 days	15,385	12,945	−2,440	−15.9%
30	30 days	15,385	11,834	−3,551	−23.1%

versus TL 2,000,000/TL 130 = $15,385 under traditional measurements, an additional sales gain of almost $4,000 or 25 percent. From the customer's point of view, the actual cost of the purchase is only TL 2,500,000/TL 220 = $11,364 versus TL 2,000,000/ TL 169 = $11,834, a savings that is hard to resist. Under these circumstances, the *customer* is likely to initiate such a proposal.

Under our proposed reporting system the incentives for such arrangements are reduced. When the sales transaction is reported at the exchange rate prevailing on the payment date, the transaction is recorded at $11,364 rather than $11,834. From the selling firm's perspective, it would be better to invoice the sale at TL 2,000,000 with 30-day payment terms. Our proposed reporting system gives the salesperson an incentive to do so.

Our model thus uses the actual or forecasted exchange rate prevailing on the day of payment to record local currency transactions. Because those dates are generally in the accounts receivable system (i.e., on sales invoices) this system is readily implemented. The idea is to use accrual accounting while maintaining a cash accounting mentality. Some have correctly argued that sales and expenses in hyperinflationary environments have a built-in implicit interest rate. (Hence, the need to discount local currency transactions to their present values before translation.) Our model emphasizes the difference in the exchange rate between the invoice date and the collection date, and thereby automatically incorporates the implicit interest differential (i.e., the International Fisher Effect[54]). Under our reporting framework, there is no need to think about what the interest rate is or worry about how to calculate an appropriate discount. After all, operating management cares about the exchange rate difference.

What happens if the customer delays payment beyond the promised date? In our reporting framework, normal payment conditions are shown in reported sales and gross margins. Thus, if a customer agrees to pay on a certain date, the transaction is booked at the exchange rate prevailing on the agreed payment date. If payment takes place after the promised date, the loss in dollars is reported below the line as a translation loss attributed to the applicable line of business or sales segment. That loss is offset by interest income as original sales terms include an explicit interest cost for delayed payments, which would appear as additional interest income below the line.

To summarize, our transactions-based reporting model

- Allocates translation gains and losses to specific revenues and expenses to which they are related
- Provides both headquarters and subsidiary management with numbers that will support better decisions
- Eliminates the need for parallel controls
- Facilitates performance comparisons over time
- Can be implemented on a cost effective basis

---

[54]Under a freely floating system of exchange rates, spot rates of exchange are theoretically determined by the interrelationships between national rates of inflation, interest rates, and forward rates of exchange, usually expressed as premiums or discounts from the spot rate. If the forecasted rate of inflation in Brazil 1 month ahead is 30 percent higher than in the United States, the cruzeiro can be forecast to decline in value by 30 percent relative to the dollar. By the same token, interest rates for maturities of comparable risk can be expected to be 30 percent higher on Brazilian securities than on comparable U.S. securities. For an extended discussion of these relationships, see David K. Eiteman, Arthur I. Stonehill, and Michael H. Moffett, *Multinational Business Finance*, 7th ed., Reading, Mass: Addison-Wesley Publishing, 1995, 50–62; and Ian H. Giddy, "Exchange Risk: Whose Views?" *Financial Management* (summer 1977): 22–33.

FOREIGN CURRENCY TRANSLATION

The foreign exchange variance analysis earlier in the chapter assumes that local managers are responsible for domestic operating results. Ideally, the local manager's responsibility for exchange variances should be in line with the ability to react to exchange rate changes.

The economic impact of changes in exchange rates on performance can be more profound than can be seen through accounting measures alone. To more fully assess the impact of inflation and currency volatility, and gauge their own ability to react, companies need to analyze their competitive market position and the impact of currency changes on their costs and revenues and those of their competition. To shed more light on this issue, we return to ICI's handling of exchange rates and budgetary control.

Like many MNCs, ICI uses a forecasted rate of exchange to set budgets and the actual end-of-period rate to measure performance. Unlike many MNCs, ICI believes that the variance that results when the actual exchange rate differs from the budget rate is not meaningful by itself. For example, the company may have budgeted a rate for the euro for its subsidiary in France and the end-of-the-month exchange rate turns out to be identical to the forecasted rate. There is no arithmetic variance, but ICI may have lost some sales volume in France. The reason may be that its competitors are exporters from Canada and the Canadian dollar has weakened against the euro. As a result the Canadians may have a margin advantage against ICI and can lower their prices in euros to maintain the same level of profits when converting to Canadian dollars.

Thus, ICI believes that exchange rate changes have more impact than accounting measures convey. It finds that further analysis is necessary to determine the real impact of currency fluctuations on performance, to arrive at effective reactions, and to determine how far the local manager is to be held accountable for protecting his budgeted profit in pounds sterling.

To achieve these objectives, ICI looks at the currencies in which its costs and revenues arise in relation to those of its competitors. Here is a view from within the company:

> We buy oil and oil related products, which are basically dollar denominated, and we are not a price-maker but are in competition with other producers in Europe. Our oil costs are dollar denominated and our revenues are denominated in other European currencies. If the pound appreciates against all other currencies, then revenues arising from foreign sales, and even those from U.K. sales subject to competitive pressures, will be reduced. As partial compensation, raw material costs (dollar-denominated oil) will be lower, but on balance ICI is worse off because the decrease in raw material costs is less than the decrease in sales revenue in absolute terms. The figure can be significant because ICI is the U.K.'s largest single exporter. Currency movements in the opposite direction are, of course, possible and in fact have recently occurred. An appreciation of the U.S. dollar against all other currencies puts the same raw material cost pressures on our European competitors as on U.K. manufacturing operations so we will not suffer a comparative disadvantage. The comparative disadvantage would arise if there was a depreciation of the pound versus the dollar coupled with a depreciation of other European cur-

rencies against the pound, which happened in 1980. This would both reduce our income and increase our costs.[55]

This approach to analyzing the economic impact of currency movements affects ICI's evaluation of its managers, whose freedom to react to such external circumstances is limited. In measuring the manager's performance, the company takes into account the extent to which he has been affected by factors beyond his control and also his reaction to them.

PERFORMANCE STANDARDS

Once questions of measurement are resolved, companies must develop meaningful standards with which to evaluate performance. But what standards are appropriate for a company with operations all over the world? Let's look at some possibilities.

A company may have certain corporate-wide standards, such as a minimum required ROI, that it applies to individual subsidiaries or product lines; or it may set different ROI levels or other benchmarks (such as gross margin) for different subsidiaries or product lines. These standards may be incorporated into budgets and can later be compared with results. Performance can also be measured over time. Companies may require stated improvement in specific ratios or income. Past performance is usually significant in developing the next period's budget. Finally, firms can compare their own overseas performance with that of competitors or compare its own units with one another.

Comparing the performance of foreign units against that of their competitors can be useful. At the same time, these comparisons have many pitfalls. (See Chapter 9 for a more extensive discussion of problems involved in analyzing foreign financial statements.) For example, when competitors are local firms, the problem of data availability and adequacy may be considerable, especially if competitors are privately held. When data is available, comparisons might be difficult. Competitors' transfer pricing policies and accounting principles may be impossible to determine. Cross-border comparisons compound these problems even further.

Comparing subsidiaries with other units of the parent company, either at home or abroad, must also be done cautiously as questions of comparability again arise. Differences in subsidiary objectives will automatically bias performance comparisons unless directly accounted for. Even if subsidiary objectives are the same, differences in country risk profiles must be considered. If higher levels of risk are to be offset by higher levels of return, it is reasonable to expect higher profitability from operations in riskier countries. To date, however, no single agreed-upon formula guides how to incorporate these country risks in assessing subsidiary performance.

Many firms require a shorter payback period, adjust cash flow projections for risk, or raise the required rate of return when considering investments in riskier countries.[56] ROI is readily adjusted for political risk because one can set a desired ROI to include

[55]Ibid., 127.

[56]For an analysis of the impact of political risk on the cost of capital, see Kirt C. Butler and Domingo Castelo Joaquin, "A Note on Political Risk and the Required Return on Foreign Direct Investment," *Journal of International Business Studies* 29, no. 3 (1998): 599–608.

a premium in line with risk in a given country (offset to some extent by lower risk that results from geographical diversification of a firm's portfolio of foreign operations.)[57]

Applying risk premiums to an ROI goal is unavoidably subjective, but the process can be made systematic. One approach is to adjust the corporate-wide ROI by a numerical risk index developed for each country. For example, assume that a country-by-country risk assessment service, such as Business International, assigns a total score of 65 out of 100 possible points to Country Y. (A higher number indicates a lower country risk.) If a company's worldwide target ROI is 15 percent, Country Y's risk-adjusted target ROI is about 23 percent (15 divided by 65 percent). If Country Z's risk index is 75, its target ROI will be 20 percent (15 divided by 75 percent). Under this system, differences between a subsidiary's actual ROI and its budgeted ROI are calculated and used to compare the performance of subsidiaries in different countries. In this example, if one subsidiary's actual ROI in Country Y was 23.5 percent and the ROI of another subsidiary in Country Z was 21 percent, the subsidiary in Country Z will have performed better, as its variance from budgeted ROI was a positive 1 percent versus .5 percent for the subsidiary in Country Y.

An overall risk index may not reflect the risk to which a particular foreign subsidiary is exposed. For example, the risk exposure of an oil company's subsidiary may differ from that of a consumer goods manufacturer in the same country. Thus, the risk index should be modified to reflect the specific risk to each unit. A more critical issue, however, is whether a company-wide ROI standard should be applied at all.

Performance evaluations based on a single company-wide standard are generally unsatisfactory. A performance budget is a more useful standard of comparison for multinational operations. Realistic budgets enable performance targets to incorporate considerations that are unique to a particular unit. Comparisons of actual performance to a budget also enables headquarters management to distinguish those results for which subsidiary managers can be held responsible from those that are beyond their control.

Following are seven caveats that may be useful guidelines for those who evaluate the results of foreign operations:

1. Foreign subsidiaries should not be evaluated as independent profit centers when they are really strategic components of a multinational system.
2. Company-wide return on investment criteria should be supplemented by performance measures tailored to the specific objectives and environments of each foreign unit.
3. Specific goals that consider each subsidiary's internal and external environment should be incorporated in performance budgets.
4. A subsidiary's performance should be evaluated in terms of departures from these objectives, the reasons for those departures, and managerial responses to unforeseen developments.
5. Subsidiary managers should not be held responsible for results that are beyond their control (at home and abroad).
6. Subsidiary managers whose performance is being measured should participate fully in setting the goals by which they will be judged.
7. Multiple measures of performance, financial and nonfinancial, should be used in evaluating foreign operations.

---

[57]Tamir Agmon and Donald Lessard suggest that investors value the international diversification provided by MNCs.

A Multinational Comparison

To provide an international perspective on performance evaluation of foreign operations, we briefly describe the practices of 88 leading MNCs in the United States and abroad (including the United Kingdom, Sweden, Switzerland, France, Germany, and Japan). Survey findings are based on a multinational questionnaire survey, personal interviews, and executive roundtables with senior executives sponsored by Business International Corporation.[58]

System Objectives

Both U.S. and non-U.S. survey respondents indicated that the primary purpose of their performance evaluation system was to ensure adequate profitability. The ability to identify possible problems (deviations from plan) and facilitate resource allocation decisions was also considered important. Evaluating the subsidiary manager was not as important. This result may indicate that unit performance is an important part of managerial evaluation.

Performance Criteria

Financial criteria tend to dominate performance evaluation systems. Both U.S. and non-U.S. MNCs stated that the most important financial criterion used to evaluate the performance of overseas units is budgeted versus actual profit, followed by ROI. This information contrasts with earlier studies that found ROI to be the sole performance criterion used by U.S. MNCs to judge their foreign subsidiaries.[59] Also considered somewhat important were budget versus actual sales, return on sales, return on assets, budget versus actual return on investment, and operating cash flows. As for cash flows, however, U.S.-based multinationals tended to stress cash flows to the parent, whereas non-U.S. multinationals preferred cash flows to the foreign subsidiary. Interestingly, both groups gave little importance to the notion of residual income recommended in the literature.

Despite difficulties in measurement, some nonfinancial criteria were considered important. Market share was considered most important, followed by productivity improvement, relationships with host governments, quality control, and employee development and safety. Responses here were similar for U.S. and non-U.S. firms.

A noteworthy finding was the similarity in financial *and* nonfinancial criteria used by U.S. and European multinationals to evaluate managerial and unit performance. The similarity included domestic and foreign operations.[60] Although many companies were aware of the importance of evaluating the manager independent of the unit, it appears that some companies blurred this distinction.

---

[58]Business International Corporation, *New Directions in Managing Currency Risks: Changing Corporate Strategies and Systems Under FAS No. 52.* New York: BI, 1982.

[59]Robbins and Stobaugh's discussion of the "bent measuring stick" was apparently influential!

[60]This finding is corroborated by Susan Borkowski in her study, "International Managerial Performance Evaluation: A Five Country Comparison," *Journal of International Business Studies* (3rd quarter 1999): 533–55. She finds that the multinational companies surveyed in Canada, Germany, Japan, the United Kingdom, and United States employ the same criteria to evaluate managers at home and abroad. She also posits that technical and product innovation, as a nonfinancial performance criterion, tends to be more important to European than to Asian or North American-based MNCs.

Despite the similarities in performance criteria employed internationally, measures of these criteria varied. Whereas U.S. companies were divided over using before-tax or after-tax numbers in computing ROI ratios, non-U.S. companies generally chose before-tax calculations. U.S. multinationals were also split over deducting headquarters expenses and foreign exchange adjustments from the reports of foreign subsidiaries. Non-U.S. MNCs tended to exclude them. The reason many companies gave for not including certain expenses in their evaluations was that the manager often could not control them. Other companies said that some expenses could not be attributed to a particular unit.

CURRENCY VOLATILITY

Both U.S. and non-U.S. multinationals treated transaction gains and losses consistently. These currency adjustments are generally included in the performance measures of both the foreign unit and its manager. For both respondent groups, the unit manager's accountability for transaction gains and losses was generally in line with his or her authority to hedge them.

United States companies using the temporal method of translation tended to include translation gains and losses mainly in measuring the performance of the foreign unit (56 percent) and the corporate treasury (56 percent). A minority also held foreign managers accountable for this item. Non-U.S. MNCs, on the other hand, generally did not hold either the unit or its manager accountable for exchange adjustments, but placed the responsibility higher in the corporation.

Survey results showed that most firms (both U.S. and non-U.S.) used projected exchange rates to establish budgets and end-of-period rates to track performance. In most cases, variances due to the use of these different exchange rates were regarded as forecasting errors and not held against either the unit or the manager. Those that held subsidiary managers accountable for these variances believed that local managers had the authority and the means to achieve their targeted results.

INFLATION AND PERFORMANCE EVALUATION

When asked whether they formally incorporated inflation adjustments into their performance evaluation systems, the overwhelming majority of U.S. multinationals stated that they did not.[61] When U.S. firms made internal adjustments for inflation, the process was largely confined to budgeting. As with foreign exchange adjustments, these companies incorporated an anticipated inflation rate into the budget and then used the actual rate at the period's end to monitor performance.

In marked contrast, the consensus among European multinationals (particularly those based in the United Kingdom and Sweden) was that inflation adjustments—no matter how crude—gave more useful performance measures than unadjusted cost figures. More than half adjusted their foreign units' assets for inflation and based depreciation and cost of goods sold on the restated amounts. These firms generally believe

---

[61]Even in Brazil, where government-supplied indexes are available for revaluing assets and inflation adjustments are made for local reporting purposes, most U.S. companies surveyed continued to use historical cost to assess the performance of their Brazilian operations.

that in preparing consolidated accounts, foreign statements should first be restated for local inflation and then translated to the parent company currency.

OTHER ENVIRONMENTAL PROBLEMS

Price controls, required minimum capitalization ratios, and differences in local business practices also were cited as affecting the evaluation of foreign operations generally. Other problems found in less-industrialized environments included time delays in producing information, a shortage of local accounting expertise, and different concepts of control. Asked whether these and other socioeconomic and political considerations were taken into account when evaluating foreign operations, both MNC groups generally said no.

PERFORMANCE STANDARDS

In ranking various performance evaluation standards, both U.S. and non-U.S. firms ranked performance relative to plan or budget first. Historical comparisons of a unit's performance over time were also considered useful. Both MNC groups gave less importance to performance comparisons with competitors in the same country and with related units in the corporate system. Only 40 percent of both survey groups adjusted their performance standards for country risk. Those doing so tended to require a higher rate of return for riskier countries. However, U.S.-based MNCs were more likely to incorporate country risk into the budgeting process.

SATISFACTION WITH EXISTING SYSTEMS

Most multinationals surveyed were satisfied with their existing systems. Only a minority of companies (14 percent for U.S. and 21 percent for non-U.S. companies) believed that their evaluation systems might induce foreign managers to act contrary to the company's overall interest. Approximately one-fourth of the U.S. and one-third of the non-U.S. MNCs anticipated a need for future changes in their performance evaluation systems.

Selected References

Baber, William, Yuji Ijiri, and Sok-Hyon Kang, "Profit-Volume-Exchange Rate Analysis for Planning International Operations," *Journal of International Financial Management and Accounting* (summer 1996): 85–101.

Bhimani, A. (ed.), Management Accounting: European Perspectives, Oxford: Oxford University Press, 1996.

Bartov, Eli and G. M. Bodner, "Firm Valuation, Earnings Expectations and the Exchange Rate Exposure Effect," *Journal of Finance* (December 1994): 1775–1785.

Beaver, William H. and Mark A. Wolfson, "Foreign Currency Translation and Changing Prices in Perfect and Complete Markets," *Journal of Accounting Research* (autumn 1992) 528–550.

Choi, Frederick D. S. and Ronald R. Gunn, "Hyperinflation Reporting and Performance Assessment," *Journal of Financial Statement Analysis* (summer 1997): 30–38.

Collins, T. R., "Risk Management in Hyperinflationary Environments," in *International Accounting and Finance Handbook*, 2nd ed., F. D. S. Choi, New York: John Wiley & Sons, Inc., 1997.

Coopers & Lybrand, *Reporting Reality from High-Inflation Countries,* New York: Coopers & Lybrand, 1989.

Deans, P. C. and M. Kane, *International Dimensions of Information Systems and*

Technology, Boston: PWS-Kent Publishing Company, 1992.

Eiteman, D. K., Arthur I. Stonehill, and Michael H. Moffett, *Multinational Business Finance,* Addison Wesley, 2000.

Haka, Susan F., "International Managerial Accounting Research: Framework and Opportunities," in *Research Priorities in International Accounting for the 1990s,*" Cheryl Fulkerson, ed., Sarasota, FL: American Accounting Association, 1996.

G. Harrison and J. McKinnon, "Cross-Cultural Research in Management Control Systems Design: A Review of the Current State," *Accounting, Organizations and Society.* Forthcoming.

Hassel, L. G., "Performance Evaluation in a Multinational Environment," *Journal of International Financial Management and Accounting* 3, no. 1 (1991): 17–38.

Logue, D. E. and G. S. Oldfield, "Managing Foreign Assets When Foreign Exchange Markets Are Efficient," *Financial Management* (summer 1997): 16–22.

Ito, Kiyohiko and Klaus R. Macharzina, "Strategic Planning Systems," in *International Accounting and Finance Handbook, 2001 Cumulative Supplement,* F. D. S. Choi, New York: John Wiley & Sons, 2001.

Jacque, L. L., *Management and Control of Foreign Exchange Risk,* Norwell, MA: Kluwer Academic Publishers, 1996.

Kawada, Makato and Daniel F. Johnson, "Strategic Management Accounting: Why and How," *Management Accounting* (August 1993): 34.

Nonaka, I. and H. Takeuchi, *The Knowledge Creating Company: How Japanese Companies Create the Dynamics of Innovation,* New York: Oxford University Press, 1995.

Yip, George S., Johny K. Johansson, and Johan Roos, "Effects of Nationality on Global Strategy," *Management International Review* (April 1997): 365–385.

Zarowin, Stanley and Wayne E. Harding, "Finally, Business Talks the Same Language," *Journal of Accountancy* (August 2000): 25–30.

Discussion Questions

1. This chapter identifies four dimensions of the strategic planning process. How does Daihatsu's management accounting system, described in this chapter, conform with that process?

2. Companies must decide whose rate of return (i.e., local versus parent currency returns) to use when evaluating foreign direct investment opportunities. Discuss the internal reporting dimensions of this decision in a paragraph or two.

3. As an employee on the financial staff of Multinational Enterprises, you are assigned to a 3-person team that is assigned to examine the financial feasibility of establishing a wholly owned manufacturing subsidiary in the Czech Republic. You are to compute an appropriate hurdle (discount) rate with which to conduct a discounted cash flow analysis. List all the parameters you would consider in measuring your company's cost of capital (discount rate).

4. Chapter 2 briefly described how culture influences external reporting principles. Can the same be said for internal reporting systems?

5. What impact, if any, does global competition have on the design of management information systems?

6. WOTS-UP analysis fails to identify a best strategy. Refer to Exhibit 10-1 and examine the strategies Daimler Benz identified in its two-by-two matrix. What other strategies would you have considered?

7. Why is it better to record sales transacted in a high-inflation country and denominated in foreign currency at the expected spot rate on the date the transaction is settled, instead of the average or month-end spot rate prescribed by conventional accounting.

8. Make a three-by-three matrix corresponding to the three possible exchange rates that could be used to establish a foreign currency budget and track performance, namely, initial spot, projected, and ending rates. Identify which cells of your matrix make operational sense and which do not. For the cells that make sense, identify the effects that each exchange rate combination would likely have on the behavior of the foreign manager responsible for budgeted results.

9. Foreign exchange rates are used to establish budgets and track actual performance. Of the various exchange rate combinations mentioned in this chapter, which do you favor? Why? Is your view the same when you add local inflation to the budgeting process?

10. List six arguments that support a parent company's use of its domestic control systems for its foreign operations, and six arguments against this practice.

11. The financial vice-president of your company's overseas operations is responsible for achieving a dollar profit before taxes, but after foreign currency translation and conversion gains and losses. As an independent outside director, draft a short discussion memorandum to the CEO evaluating this policy.

12. The chapter text gives examples of counterproductive performance evaluation practices used by multinational companies. Take two of the examples and suggest how to improve the procedures. Hint: The seven caveats near the end of the chapter are a good start for your discussion.

Exercises

1. Glasgow Corporation manufactures a product that is marketed in North America, Europe and Asia. Its total manufacturing cost to produce 100 units of good × is $2,250, detailed as follows:

Raw materials	$ 500
Direct labor	1,000
Overhead	750
Total	$2,250

The company bases its selling price on a cost-plus formula.

Required: What would be Glasgow Corporation's selling price per unit if it wants a gross profit of 10 percent above cost?

2. Glasgow Corporation (in Exercise 1) wants to be price competitive on an international basis. To accomplish this it must be able to price its product no higher than $21.50. Using the target costing methodology described in this chapter, what would be Glasgow Corporation's allowable costs? Assume that the company still wants a profit margin of 10 percent of its allowable costs. What does your calculation imply about its manufacturing costs?

3. Review the operating data incorporated in Exhibit 10-3 for the Russian subsidiary of the U.S. parent company.

Required: Using Exhibit 10-3 as a guide, prepare a cash flow report from a parent currency perspective identifying the components of the expected returns from the Russian investment for the first two years of its operations. The U.S. parent company is only allowed to receive 70 percent of its affiliate's reported net income, after Russian corporate income taxes, as dividends. However, U.S. tax law provides a credit against U.S. taxes for any foreign income taxes paid.

4. Assume that management is considering whether to make the foreign direct investment described in Exercise 3. Investment will require $8,000,000 in equity capital. Cash flows to the parent are expected to increase by 5 percent over the previous year for each year after year 2 (through year 6). Exchange rate forecasts are as follows:

Year	Rate
1	R 20 = $1
2	R 21 = $1
3	R 23 = $1
4–6	R 25 = $1

Management insists on a risk premium of 10 percent when evaluating foreign projects.

Required: Assuming a weighted average cost of capital of 10 percent and no expected changes in differential tax rates, evaluate the desirability of the Russian investment using a traditional discounted cash flow analysis.

5. Do a WOTS-UP analysis for your school or firm relative to its major competitor. Based on your analysis, suggest several countermeasures your dean or CEO might consider to maintain or improve your organization's competitive standing.

6. Assume the following:
   - Inflation and Turkish lira (TL) devaluation is 30 percent per month or 1.2 percent per workday.
   - The general price levels at selected intervals for the current month are:

1/1	100.0
1/10	109.6
1/20	119.6
1/30	130.0

   - The real rate of interest is 1.5 percent per month or 20 percent per year.
   - Cash balances are kept in hard currency (dollars).
   - Month-end rates are used to record expense transactions.

   Required: Based on these assumptions, prepare a table showing the distortions that can occur when the following expense transactions are recorded using conventional measurement rules (i.e., month-end rates in this example) instead of the internal reporting structure recommended in this chapter.
   Transactions:

Invoice Date	Payment Terms
1	Cash
5	15 days
5	25 days

7. Exhibit 10-6, "Framework for Multinational Control," provides a way of thinking about the financial control process in a multinational setting. Assume that a parent company domiciled in your country is comparing the performance statistics (for instance, return on equity) of two wholly owned affiliates: one in Mexico, the other in Japan. Try to identify how each of the variables and constraints identified

in the matrix might affect the numerator and/or denominator of the ROI statistic and its interpretation.

8. Global Enterprises, Inc. uses a number of performance criteria to evaluate its overseas operations, including return on investment. Compagnie de Calais, its French subsidiary, submits the performance report shown in Exhibit 10-13 for the current fiscal year (translated to U.S. dollar equivalents). Included in sales are $250,000 worth of components sold by Compagnie de Calais to its sister subsidiary in Brussels at a transfer price set by corporate headquarters at 40 percent above an arm's-length price. Cost of goods sold includes excess labor costs of $75,000 owing to local labor laws. Administrative expenses include $25,000 of head-quarters expenses, which are allocated by Global Enterprises to its French affili-ate. The parent company holds all of its subsidiaries responsible for their fair share of corporate expenses. Local financing decisions are centralized at corporate trea-sury, as are all matters related to tax planning. At the same time, Global Enter-prises thinks that all subsidiaries should be able to cover reasonable financing costs. Moreover, it thinks that foreign managers should be motivated to use local resources as efficiently as possible. Hence, Compagnie de Calais is assessed a capital charge based on its net assets and the parent company's average cost of capital. This figure, which amounts of $60,000, is included in the $81,000 interest expense figure. One-half of the exchange gains and losses figure is attributed to transactions losses resulting from the French subsidiary's export activities. The bal-ance is due to translating the French accounts to U.S. dollars for consolidation pur-poses. Exchange risk management is also centralized at corporate treasury.

Required: Based on the foregoing information, prepare a performance report that isolates those elements that should be included in performance appraisals of the foreign unit.

9. In evaluating the performance of a foreign manager, a parent company should never penalize a manager for things the manager cannot control. Given the infor-mation provided in Exercise 8, prepare a performance report identifying the rele-vant elements for evaluating the manager of Compagnie de Calais.

10. To encourage its foreign managers to incorporate expected exchange rate changes into their operating decisions, Vancouver Enterprises requires that all foreign cur-rency budgets be set in Canadian dollars using exchange rates projected for the

EXHIBIT 10-13 Compagnie de Calais Performance Report		
Sales		$2,100,000
Other income		60,000
		$2,160,000
Costs and Expenses		
Cost of sales	$1,600,000	
Selling and administrative	165,000	
Depreciation	80,000	
Interest	81,000	
Exchange losses	184,000	2,110,000
Income before taxes		$ 50,000
Income taxes		21,000
Net income		$ 30,600

end of the budget period. To further motivate its local managers to react to unexpected rate changes, operating results at period's end are translated to dollars at the actual spot rate prevailing at that time. Deviations between actual and budgeted exchange rates are discarded in judging the manager's performance.

At the start of the 19X4 fiscal year, budgeted results for a Mexican affiliate, the Cuernavaca Corporation, were as follows (amounts in thousands):

Sales	P8,000,000	C$2,560
Expenses	6,400,000	2,048
Income	P1,600,000	C$ 512

Actual results for the year in dollars were: sales, C$2,160,000; expenses, C$1,680,000; and net income, C$480,000. Relevant exchange rates for the peso during the year were as follows:

Jan. 1 19X4 spot rate:	$.00040
Global Enterprise's one-year forecast	$.00032
Dec. 31, 19/X4 spot rate	$.00024

Required: Based on the foregoing information, did the Mexican manager perform well? Support your answer using the variance analysis suggested in the chapter. (Refer to Exhibit 10-7.)

11. Exhibit 10-10 contains a performance report that breaks out various operating variances of a foreign affiliate, assuming the parent currency is the functional currency under FAS No. 52. Using the information in Exhibit 10-10, repeat the variance analysis, assuming instead that the parent company defines the local currency as its functional currency.

12. Parent Company establishes three wholly owned affiliates in countries X, Y, and Z. Its total investment in each of the respective affiliates at the beginning of the year, together with year-end returns in parent currency (PC) appear here:

Subsidiary	Total Assets	Returns
X	PC1,000,000	PC250,000
Y	PC3,000,000	PC900,000
Z	PC1,500,000	PC600,000

Parent Company requires a return on its domestic investments of 10 percent and is evaluating the annual performance of its three foreign affiliates. To establish an appropriate performance benchmark, Parent Company subscribes to a country risk evaluation service that compiles an unweighted risk index for various countries around the world. The risk scores for each of the n countries are:

Country	Risk Score (out of 60)
X	30
Y	21
Z	15

Other things being equal, the higher the score, the lower the country's risk.
Required: Prepare an analysis for Parent Company's management indicating which affiliate performed best.

Case 10–1

Foreign Operations Disclosures: A Tangled Affair

You have recently been hired as a junior analyst at a major investment bank in New York City. One of your first assignments is to analyze the foreign operations performance statistics of MBI Corporation, a large multinational company in the computer industry. Foreign operations disclosures for the years 2000, 1999, and 1998 are reproduced in Exhibit 10-14.

EXHIBIT 10-14 MBI Data on Non-U.S. Operations			
Non-U.S. Operations *(Dollars in Millions)*	*2000*	*1999*	*1998*
At year-end:			
Net assets employed:			
Current assets	$ 24,337	$ 20,361	$ 20,005
Current liabilities	15,917	12,124	11,481
Working capital	$ 8,420	$ 8,237	$ 8,524
Plant and equipment, net	11,628	9,879	9,354
Investments and other assets	9,077	6,822	5,251
	$ 29,125	$ 24,938	$ 23,129
Long-term debt	$ 5,060	$ 3,358	$ 2,340
Other liabilities	2,699	2,607	2,505
Deferred taxes	2,381	1,184	1,580
	$ 10,140	$ 7,779	$ 6,425
Net assets employed	$ 18,985	$ 17,159	$ 16,704
Number of employees	168,283	167,291	163,904
For the year:			
Revenue	$ 41,886	$ 36,965	$ 34,361
Earnings before income taxes	$ 7,844	$ 7,496	$ 7,088
Provision for income taxes	3,270	3,388	3,009
Net earnings	$ 4,574	$ 4,108	$ 4,079

Notes: Non-U.S. subsidiaries that operate in a local currency environment account for approximately 90 percent of the company's non-U.S. revenue. The remaining 10 percent of the company's non-U.S. revenue is from subsidiaries and branches that operate in U.S. dollars or whose economic environments are highly inflationary.

As the value of the dollar weakens, net assets recorded in local currencies translate into more U.S. dollars than they would have at the previous year's rates. Conversely, as the dollar becomes stronger, net assets recorded in local currencies translate into fewer U.S. dollars than they would have at the previous year's rates. The translation adjustments, resulting from the translation of net assets, amounted to $3,266 million at December 31, 2000, $1,698 million at December 31, 1999, and $1,917 million at December 31, 1998. The changes in translation adjustments since the end of 1998 are a reflection of the strengthening of the dollar in 1999 and the weakening of the dollar in 2000.

EXHIBIT 10-15 Dollar's Trade-Weighted Exchange Index, 1998–2000 (1983 = 100)	
December 31	*Index*
1998	92.8
1999	93.7
2000	83.7
Average Rates for Years, 1990–2000	
1990	87.4
1991	103.4
1992	116.6
1993	125.3
1994	138.2
1995	143.0
1996	112.2
1997	96.9
1998	92.7
1999	98.6
2000	89.1

You observe a healthy increase in net assets, revenues, and pretax earnings in the year 2000 compared with that for 1999. The text accompanying MBI's foreign operations disclosures, however, suggests that foreign currencies fluctuated during the period under study. Hence, you are wondering whether the reported numbers actually mirror the performance of foreign operations in local currencies.

Unfortunately, MBI does not disclose indexes explaining the movement of the major currencies in which it conducts its business. Given MBI's scale of operations, you decide to use a trade-weighted index provided by the U.S. government as a proxy (see Exhibit 10-15).

REQUIRED

On the basis of the information provided, are your suspicions confirmed?

Case 10–2   Assessing Foreign Subsidiary Performance in a World of Floating Exchange Rates

General Electric Company's worldwide performance evaluation system is based on a policy of decentralization. The policy reflects its conviction that managers will become more responsible and their business will be better managed if they are given the authority and necessary tools to budget and achieve a targeted net income—in dollar terms. Moreover, decentralization permits the company to overcome the difficulty of centrally exercising detailed control over its large and diverse operations. Foreign affiliate managers, like their domestic counterparts, are accountable for dollar income—a practice not followed by many MNCs.

In the words of one financial executive, "Although many U.S. corporations are decentralized in their U.S. operations, they seem to be less so with regard to their foreign operations. One reason may be the concern as to whether foreign managers are sufficiently trained in some aspects of international finance, such as foreign exchange exposure management. We feel this is essential training, and our people get that training."[1]

General Electric does not have any rigid standards for comparing the performance of its affiliates. Strategic and operating plans are agreed upon for each business, including financial targets. Like most other companies, GE generally requires a higher rate of return from investment proposals in riskier countries and has a system of ranking countries according to relative risk. A proposed investment in a high-risk area will have more difficulty being approved and will generally require a higher ROI, but approval depends on both the forecasted ROI and the company's total strategic objectives in each country.

The system of budgeting and forecasting extends five years into the future. The first year of the long-range forecast becomes a preliminary budget for the year ahead. A year later the budget is revised, a comparison is made between it and the original forecast, and changes are accounted for.

Measurement of an affiliated company's performance is related to the objectives of its strategic plan and the annual budgets that are derived from the plan. The primary financial measure is success in achieving the affiliates' committed dollar net income. Other measurements include ROI (calculated as the sum of reported net income plus after-tax interest expense, divided by the sum of net worth plus borrowings), net income to sales ratios, market share, inventory and receivable turnover rates, and currency exposure.

While the performance of both an affiliate and its manager are measured primarily on bottom-line results, the review of the manager includes other measurements. Assessments include how well the manager has dealt with government relations, the progress made toward achieving certain targets such as increasing market share, and success in maintaining good employee relationships. These measurements are based on the strategic plan and targets that were established between the manager and parent company supervisor at the start of a period.

GE conducts periodic operating reviews where each manager is reviewed by the level above. The focus is on planning, results, and most recent estimates. This evaluation process provides corporate management with an opportunity to determine whether short-term actions are being taken at the expense of long-range goals.

To minimize currency exposure, GE finances fixed assets with equity and holds the affiliate responsible for maintaining a balanced position on working capital. The policy is modified as necessary for varying circumstances.

Unlike MNCs that have centralized the financing and exposure management functions at the head office, GE makes exposure management a responsibility of its local managers, overseen by sector and corporate personnel. To avoid the transaction costs of having, for example, a French affiliate hedge its position by buying French francs forward, GE has provisions for internal hedging arrangements. Corporate treasury obtains currency exposure data from all affiliates and provides needed information on offsets. Therefore, units can execute a hedging agreement between themselves without going to outside sources.

In setting the budget, the affiliate's manager uses the exchange rate he expects to prevail. General Electric believes that, although predicting rates of exchange is not an exact science, the managers of its foreign businesses have the necessary authority and tools to take those actions that will enable them to achieve their budgeted income. These tools include hedging and pricing decisions. The manager can not only raise prices, cut costs, lead payments, lag receivables,

---

[1]Czechowicz et al., Assessing Foreign Subsidiary Performance, p. 104.

borrow locally, and remit dividends quickly, but he can also take out forward contracts if they are available.

The affiliate manager has the responsibility and authority to protect the unit against currency fluctuations and, therefore, is accountable for dollar profits regardless of exchange rate changes. According to a company spokesperson:

> If an unexpected devaluation occurs, the affiliate's performance is still measured in terms of dollar income vis-à-vis budget. GE considers changes in the rate of exchange in the same way as other risks that occur in a country. For example, if an affiliate's sales are less than those budgeted for, because of a recession in that economy, countermeasures are available to the affiliate. If one contends that these things are not controllable, how does one manage a company? We're not saying it's controllable in the sense that it can be prevented from happening, but it is susceptible to the countermeasures—some before and some after the event occurs.[2]

REQUIRED

1. Compare GE's approach to performance evaluation with that of ICI (mentioned in the chapter).
2. Critically evaluate the strengths and weaknesses of each company's approach to the performance evaluation of its foreign managers as it relates to the problem of fluctuating currency values.
3. Which approach to performance evaluation do you support and why?

---

[2]Ibid., 106.

CHAPTER 11

FINANCIAL RISK MANAGEMENT

Corporate treasurers around the world have sought new and imaginative ways to hedge their exposures to the increasing volatility of foreign exchange rates, interest rates, and commodity and equity prices. The financial services industry has responded by offering a plethora of financial products, including currency swaps, interest rate swaps, and options. These financial instruments have developed very rapidly and global accounting standard setters are currently working on appropriate measurement and reporting principles. Because many of these financial instruments are treated as off-balance-sheet items, the real risks inherent in their use are often masked. We now examine some of the internal reporting and control issues associated with this fascinating area.

ESSENTIALS

The main goal of financial risk management is to minimize the risk of loss arising from unexpected changes in the prices of currencies, interest rates, commodities, and equities. The exposure to such price changes is known as *market risk*. For example, a corporation in Sweden that issues new stock to Swedish investors might view market risk as exposure to rising stock prices. An unexpected rise in stock prices is undesirable if the issuer could have issued fewer shares for the same amount of cash by waiting. A Swedish investor, on the other hand, would view risk as the possibility of a fall in equity prices. If stock prices were to fall significantly in the near future, the investor would rather wait before buying.

Market participants tend to be risk averse. Many will trade some potential profits for protection from adverse price changes. Financial intermediaries and market makers have responded by creating financial products that enable a market participant to transfer the risk of unexpected price changes to someone else—a *counterparty*. For example, a financial intermediary might sell a corporate issuer an option (i.e., the right but not the obligation) to buy stock and the investor (the counterparty) an option to sell the stock short.

Market risk has many dimensions. Although we will focus on price or rate risk, risk management needs to consider other risks.[1] *Liquidity risk* exists because not all financial risk management products can be freely traded. Highly illiquid markets include real estate and small capitalization stocks.[2] *Market discontinuities* refer to the risk that markets may not always produce gradual price changes. The stock market break of October 1987 is a case in point. *Credit risk* is the likelihood that a counterparty to a risk management contract will not meet its obligations. For example, a counterparty agreeing to exchange French euros for Canadian dollars may fail to deliver euros on the promised date. *Regulatory risk* is the risk that a public authority may prevent a financial product from being used for its intended purpose. For example, the Kuala Lumpur stock exchange does not permit the use of short sales as a hedge against equity price risk. *Tax risk* is the risk that certain hedge transactions will not receive the desired tax treatment. An example is the treatment of foreign exchange losses as capital gains when ordinary income is preferred. *Accounting risk* is the risk that a hedge transaction will not be accounted for as part of the transaction it is intended to hedge. An example of this is when the gain on the hedge of a purchase commitment is treated as "other income" instead of a reduction of the cost of the purchase.

WHY MANAGE FINANCIAL RISKS?

The rapid growth of risk management services suggests that management often can increase firm value by controlling financial risks. Moreover, investors and other stakeholders increasingly expect financial managers to identify and actively manage market risk exposures.[3] If the value of the firm equals the present value of its future cash flows, active exposure management is justified on several grounds.

First, exposure management helps stabilize a firm's expected cash flows. A more stable cash flow stream helps minimize earnings surprises, thereby increasing the present value of expected cash flows.[4] Stable earnings also reduce the likelihood of default and bankruptcy risk, or the risk that earnings may not cover contractual debt service payments.

Active exposure management enables firms to concentrate on their primary business risks. Thus, a manufacturer can hedge its interest rate and currency risks and concentrate on production and marketing. Similar benefits are available to financial institutions.[5]

Debt holders, employees, and customers also gain from exposure management. As debt holders generally have a lower risk tolerance than shareholders, limiting the firm's risk exposure helps align the interests of shareholders and bondholders. Derivative products allow employer-administered pension funds to enjoy higher returns by permitting them to invest in certain instruments without having to actually buy or sell the

---

[1] Gary L. Gastineau, *Dictionary of Financial Risk Management*, Chicago: Probus Publishing Company, 1992, 5–11.

[2] Recent financial innovations such as real estate investment trusts have improved liquidity in many of these previously illiquid markets.

[3] Peter Coy, "Perils of the Hedge Highwire," *Business Week* (October 26, 1998): 74, 76–77.

[4] For some recent empirical evidence on the use of derivatives for earnings management purposes, see Jan Barton, "Does the Use of Financial Derivatives Affect Earnings Management Decisions? *Accounting Review* 76, no. 1 (January 2001): 1–26.

[5] Elijah Brewer, Bernadette Minton, and James Moser, "The Effect of Bank-Held Derivatives on Credit Accessibility," Federal Reserve Bank of Chicago, Working Paper 94–5, April 1994.

underlying instruments. Finally, because losses caused by certain price and rate risks are passed on to customers in the form of higher prices, exposure management limits customers' exposure to these risks.[6]

ROLE OF ACCOUNTING

Management accountants play an important role in the risk management process. They identify exposures to market risks, measure the benefits and costs of risk protection, and account for specific hedge products.

IDENTIFYING MARKET RISKS

J. P. Morgan has devised a useful framework for identifying a firm's exposure to various types of market risks. Called the *exposure management cube*, this framework examines the relationship of various market risks on the value drivers of a firm and its competitors. Exhibit 11-1 gives an adaptation of this framework.

EXHIBIT 11-1   Exposure Management Cube

Competitor Z
Competitor Y
Your company

Value drivers	Market risks				
	Foreign exchange	Interest rates	Commodity prices	Equity prices	Other
Revenue					
Cost of sales					
Operating expenses					
Taxes					
Current assets					
Current liabilities					
Fixed assets					
Other					

Source: J. P. Morgan et al., "The J. P. Morgan/Arthur Andersen Guide to Corporate Exposure Management," *Risk Magazine,* 1994, 19.

[6] J. P. Morgan & Co., Inc., Arthur Andersen & Co., SC, and Financial Engineering Limited, "The J. P. Morgan/Arthur Andersen Guide to Corporate Exposure Management," *Risk Magazine* (1994).

The term *value drivers* in Exhibit 11-1 refers to the principal financial condition and operating performance items that impact the firm's value. Market risks refer to foreign exchange and interest rate risk, as well as commodity and equity price risks. The third dimension of the exposure management cube examines the relationship of market risks and value drivers for each of the firm's principal competitors.

To illustrate, let us examine the first row of the exposure management cube. Interest rate risk may affect the revenue of the firm in the following manner. Credit sales are normally collected after a certain period, depending on the credit terms offered the client (e.g., 30, 60, or 90 days). The firm usually relies on short-term loans to finance current operations, such as wages and other operating expenses. Rising interest rates before the receivables are collected would reduce the firm's return from sales. Credit sales denominated in foreign currency would yield less than expected parent currency should the foreign currency lose value before collection. Fluctuating commodity prices can have a significant impact on revenues. For example, the sugar industry in Hawaii was crippled when the price of sugar collapsed in the early 1970s. Finally, as managers of investment funds know all too well, falling equity prices immediately worsen fund performance statistics.

How does the third dimension of the exposure management cube work? This dimension examines how a competitor's exposure to market risk might impact the firm. Suppose you decide to sell baseball caps of the team you expect to win the next World Series. You decide to buy and sell these caps locally. Are you exposed to foreign exchange risk? You might not think so, but if a competitor buys baseball caps from abroad and the currency of its source country loses value relative to your home currency, this change may allow your competitor to sell at a lower price than you. This is called *competitive currency exposure*.

QUANTIFY TRADE-OFFS

Another role that accountants play in the risk management process involves the measurement of financial trade-offs. Management may prefer to keep some exposures rather than hedge all financial risks.[7] As an example, an importer who has a firm purchase commitment denominated in foreign currency may prefer not to hedge if he believes the foreign currency will weaken before the delivery date. In similar instances, accountants would measure the benefits from hedging against its costs plus the opportunity costs of foregone gains from speculating in market movements.

ACCOUNTING FOR HEDGE PRODUCTS

Financial hedge products are financial contracts or instruments that enable the user to transfer market risks to someone else. They include, but are not limited to, forward contracts, futures, swaps, options, and combinations of these. Knowledge of accounting measurement rules for hedge products is especially important when designing an effective

---

[7]Froot, Scharfstein, and Stein, for example, suggest that while a firm's shareholders may benefit from hedging, it is not always in their interest for a firm to be completely hedged. Kenneth A. Froot, David S. Scharfstein and Jeremy Stein, "Risk Management: Coordinating Corporate Investment and Financing Policies," *Journal of Finance* (December 1993): 1,629–1,658. 9/7

hedge strategy for the firm. To understand the importance of hedge accounting, we illustrate some basic hedge accounting practices.

First, review the basic components of an income statement (absent taxes).

	Operating revenues	XXX
−	Operating expenses	XXX
=	Operating income	XXX
+	Other income	XXX
−	Other expense	XXX
=	Net income	XXX

Analysts usually focus on operating income in evaluating how well management has operated its core business. However, net income includes the confounding effects of extraordinary or nonrecurring events.

The standard accounting treatment for financial instruments among U.S. corporations is to mark that product to market with any gains or losses recognized as a component of nonoperating income.[8] An exception is permitted if the transaction meets the following hedge criteria:

1. The item being hedged must expose the firm to a market risk.
2. The hedge instrument must minimize that risk.
3. The firm must designate the financial instrument as a hedge with supporting documentation.

If these criteria are met, the firm can use the gains or losses recognized on marking the hedge product to market to offset the gains or losses on the transaction that is being hedged (e.g., sales or purchases). To illustrate, assume that an Irish manufacturer of stout (a dark malt beverage) has a firm sales commitment to deliver X barrels to a buyer in Canada in 2 months. Fearing that the Canadian dollar will devalue before delivery, the Irish manufacturer buys a forward exchange contract that will allow it to sell Canadian dollars in 2 month's time at a price close to the current price. If the dollar devalues before delivery, the gain on the foreign exchange contract will offset the loss on the sales contract. Other things equal, operating income will meet its target.

FOREIGN EXCHANGE RISK MANAGEMENT

Many of the market price movements we have been discussing are interrelated. We confine our analysis to a specific price exposure: foreign exchange rate changes. The risk management concepts and the associated accounting treatments for foreign exchange risk parallel those for interest rate, commodity, and equity price risks.

---

[8]KPMG Peat Marwick, Survey on Current Accounting for Risk Management Activities, New York: KPMG, September 1996, 2.

ACCOUNTING AND CONCEPTUAL ISSUES

Exchange risk management and accounting for exchange rate changes are interdependent. Often, a knowledge of accounting treatments provides a conceptual framework for exchange risk management.

TRANSACTIONS GAINS AND LOSSES

Foreign exchange risk refers to the risk of loss due to changes in the exchange value of national currencies. First let us consider foreign currency transactions. The United States' FAS No. 52 defines a foreign currency transaction as one requiring settlement in a foreign currency (i.e., a currency other than the *functional* currency.) Examples include foreign currency sales, purchases, borrowing, and lending transactions. Thus, a company purchasing inventories denominated in Saudi Arabian riyals suffers an exchange loss should the riyal gain in value before settlement.

A foreign currency transaction may be *denominated* in one currency but *measured* or recorded in another. Assume, for example, that a U.S. subsidiary in Hong Kong purchases goods from the People's Republic of China payable in renminbi. The subsidiary's functional currency is the U.S. dollar. In this instance, the subsidiary would measure the foreign currency transaction—denominated in renminbi—in U.S. dollars, the currency in which its books are kept. From the parent's point of view, the subsidiary's liability is denominated in renminbi but measured in U.S. dollars for purposes of consolidation.

FAS No. 52 mandates the following treatment for foreign currency transactions:[9]

1. At the date the transaction is *recognized*, each asset, liability, revenue, expense, gain, or loss arising from the transaction shall be measured and recorded in the functional currency of the recording entity by use of the exchange rate in effect at that date.
2. At each *balance sheet date*, recorded balances that are denominated in a currency other than the functional currency of the recording entity shall be adjusted to reflect the current exchange rate.

On this basis, a foreign exchange adjustment (i.e., gain or loss on a settled transaction) is necessary whenever the exchange rate changes between the transaction date and the settlement date. Should financial statements be prepared before settlement, the accounting adjustment (i.e., gain or loss on an unsettled transaction) will equal the difference between the amount originally recorded and the amount presented in the financial statements.

The FASB rejected the view that a distinction should be drawn between gains and losses on settled and unsettled transactions, because such distinctions cannot be applied in practice. Two accounting treatments for transactions gains and losses are possible.

Single-Transaction Perspective: Under a single-transaction perspective, exchange adjustments (both settled and unsettled) are treated as an adjustment to the original

---

[9]Financial Accounting Standards Board, FASB Statement No. 52, Stamford, CT: FASB, par. 15.

transaction accounts on the premise that a transaction and its settlement are a single event. The following example illustrates this treatment.

On September 1, 20X2, a U.S. manufacturer sells, on account, goods to a Swedish importer for 1 million Swedish krona (SEK). The dollar/krona exchange rate is $0.14 = SEK 1, the krona receivable are due in 90 days, and the U.S. company operates on a calendar-year basis. The krona begins to depreciate before the receivable is collected. By the end of the month, the dollar/krona exchange rate is $0.13 = SEK 1; on December 1, 20X2, it is $0.11 = SEK 1. (These transactions are posted in Exhibit 11-2.)

In this illustration, until the account is collected, the initial dollar amount recorded for both accounts receivable and sales is considered an estimate to be subsequently adjusted for changes in the dollar/krona exchange rate. Further depreciation of the krona between the financial statement date (September 1) and the settlement date (December 1) would require additional adjustments.

Two-Transaction Perspective: Under a two-transaction perspective, collection of the krona receivable is considered a separate event from the sale that gave rise to it. In the previous illustration, the export sale and related receivable would be recorded at the exchange rate in effect at that date. Depreciation of the krona between September 1 and December 1 would result in an exchange loss (i.e., loss on an unsettled transaction) and currency receivable on December 1, 20X2, at the even lower exchange rate would result in a further exchange loss (i.e., loss on a settled transaction). See Exhibit 11-3.

EXHIBIT 11-2 U.S. Company's Record: Single-Transaction Perspective

		Foreign Currency	*U.S. Dollar Equivalent*
Sept. 1, 20X2	Accounts receivable	SEK 1,000,000	140,000
	Sales	SEK 1,000,000	140,000
	(To record credit sale)		
Sept. 30, 20X2	Sales		10,000
	Accounts receivable		10,000
	(To adjust existing accounts for initial exchange rate change: SEK 1,000,000 × $0.14 minus SEK 1,000,000 × $0.13)		
Dec. 1, 20X2	Retained earnings		20,000
	Accounts receivable		20,000
	(To adjust accounts for additional rate change: SEK 1,000,000 × $0.13 minus SEK 1,000,000 × $0.11)		
Dec. 1, 20X2	Foreign currency	SEK 1,000,000	110,000
	Accounts receivable	SEK 1,000,000	110,000
	(To record settlement of outstanding foreign currency receivables)		

EXHIBIT 11-3	U.S. Company's Record: Two-Transaction Perspective		
		Foreign Currency	*U.S. Dollar Equivalent*
Sept. 1, 20X2	Accounts receivable	SEK 1,000,000	$140,000
	Sales	SEK 1,000,000	$140,000
	(To record credit sale at Sept. 1, 20X2 exchange rate)		
Sept. 30, 20X2	Foreign exchange loss		10,000
	Accounts receivable		10,000
	(To record effect of initial rate change)		
Dec. 1, 20X2	Foreign currency	SEK 1,000,000	110,000
	Foreign exchange loss		20,000
	Accounts receivable	SEK 1,000,000	130,000
	(To record settlement of foreign currency receivable)		

In the interest of uniformity, FAS No. 52 requires the two-transaction method of accounting for foreign currency transactions. Gains and losses on settled and unsettled transactions are included in the determination of income. Major exceptions to this requirement occur whenever (1) exchange adjustments relate to certain long-term intercompany transactions and (2) transactions are intended and effective as hedges of net investments (i.e., hedges of foreign operations' exposed net asset/liability positions) and foreign currency commitments.

TRANSLATION GAINS AND LOSSES

A U.S. parent company operating a wholly owned subsidiary in Ecuador (whose functional currency is the U.S. dollar) experiences a change in the dollar value of its Ecuadoran net monetary assets whenever the exchange value of the sucre changes relative to the dollar. Because foreign currency amounts are typically translated to their domestic currency equivalents for either management review or external financial reporting purposes (see Chapter 6), translation effects have a direct impact on reported profits.

ECONOMIC GAINS AND LOSSES

Fluctuating exchange rates affect the present value of the entire foreign investment by impacting future cash flows, that is, expected sales and cost streams. As we have seen in a previous example, purely domestic companies that face foreign competitors in their domestic markets, or with payables and receivables invoiced in foreign currencies, will also experience cash flow effects whenever the exchange rates in question vary.

RISK MANAGEMENT IN A WORLD OF FLOATING EXCHANGE RATES

In a world of floating exchange rates, risk management includes (1) anticipating exchange rate movements, (2) measuring a firm's exposure to exchange risk, (3) designing appropriate protection strategies, and (4) establishing internal risk management controls.

FORECASTING EXCHANGE RATE CHANGES

In developing an exchange risk management program, the financial manager should have an idea of the potential direction, timing, and magnitude of exchange rate changes. Forewarned of exchange rate prospects, financial managers can more efficiently and effectively arrange appropriate defensive measures. Whether it is possible to accurately predict currency movements, however, remains an issue.

Information frequently used in making exchange rate forecasts (e.g., currency depreciation) relates to *changes* in the following factors:

1. *Inflation differentials*. Evidence suggests that a higher rate of inflation in a given country tends, over time, to be offset by an equal and opposite movement in the value of its currency.
2. *Monetary policy*. An increase in a country's money supply that exceeds the real growth rate of national output fosters inflation, which affects exchange rates.
3. *Balance of trade*. Governments often use currency devaluations to cure an unfavorable trade balance (i.e., when exports < imports).
4. *Balance of payments*. A country that spends (imports) and invests more abroad than it earns (exports) or receives in investments from abroad experiences downward pressure on its currency's value.
5. *International monetary reserves and debt capacity*. A country with a persistent balance of payments deficit can forestall a currency devaluation by drawing down its savings (i.e., level of international monetary reserves) or drawing on its foreign borrowing capacity. As these resources decrease, the probability of devaluation increases.
6. *National budget*. Deficits caused by excessive government spending also worsen inflation.
7. *Forward exchange quotations*. A foreign currency that can be acquired for future delivery at a significant discount signals reduced confidence in that currency.
8. *Unofficial rates*. Increases in the spread between official and unofficial or black market exchange rates suggest increased pressure on governments to align their official rates with more realistic market rates.
9. *Behavior of related currencies*. A country's currency will normally behave in a fashion similar to currencies of countries with close economic ties to it.
10. *Interest rate differentials*. Interest rate differentials between any two countries predict the future change in the spot exchange rate.

Although these items help predict the direction of currency movements, they are usually not enough to predict the timing and magnitude of currency changes. Politics strongly influences currency values in many countries. Political responses to devaluation or revaluation pressures frequently result in temporary measures rather than exchange rate adjustments. These temporary measures include selective taxes, import controls, export incentives, and exchange controls. Awareness of the politics of a country whose currency is under pressure helps financial managers discern whether the government will lean toward market intervention or rely on free-market solutions.

Some claim that exchange rate forecasting is a futile exercise. In a world where exchange rates are free to fluctuate, foreign exchange markets are said to be efficient.[10] Thus, current market rates (i.e., forward exchange rates) represent the consensus of all market participants about future rates of exchange. Information that is generally available is immediately impounded in current exchange rates by the market and thus has little value in predicting future exchange rates. Under these conditions, exchange rate changes are random responses to new information or unforeseen events. Forward exchange rates are the best available estimates of future rates. The randomness of exchange rate changes reflect the diversity of opinions on exchange values by participants.

What do all of these factors imply for management accountants? For one thing, use of exchange rate forecasting as a risk-reduction technique means that accountants must develop systems that can gather and process comprehensive and accurate information on variables correlated with exchange rate movements.

Such information systems can incorporate information provided by external forecasting services, financial publications that track currency movements, and daily contacts with foreign currency dealers. These systems should be online and computer based to ensure managers a superior source of information on which to base their currency forecasts. Financial managers must also clearly understand the consequences of not using other forecasting methods.

If installing such a system is not possible or is too expensive, then financial managers and accountants should arrange their company's affairs to minimize the detrimental effects of rate changes. This process is known as exposure management.

EXPOSURE MANAGEMENT

Structuring a company's affairs to minimize possible adverse effects of exchange rate changes requires identification of its exposure to exchange rate risk. Foreign exchange exposure exists whenever a change in foreign exchange rates changes the value of a firm's net assets, earnings, and cash flows. Traditional accounting measures of foreign exchange exposure center on two major types of exposure: *translation* and *transaction*.

TRANSLATION EXPOSURE

Translation exposure measures the impact of exchange rate changes on the domestic currency equivalents of a firm's foreign currency assets and liabilities. A foreign currency asset or liability is exposed to exchange rate risk if a change in the exchange rate causes its parent currency equivalent to change. Based on this definition, foreign currency balance sheet items exposed to exchange rate risks are those items that are trans-

---

[10]Gunter Dufey and Ian H. Giddy, "Management of Corporate Foreign Exchange Risk," in F. D. S. Choi, ed., *International Accounting and Finance Handbook,* New York: John Wiley & Sons, 1997, 31.1–31.31.

lated at current (as opposed to historical) exchange rates. Accordingly, translation exposure is measured by taking the difference between a firm's exposed foreign currency assets and liabilities. This process is depicted in Exhibit 11-4.

An excess of exposed assets over exposed liabilities (i.e., those foreign currency items translated at current exchange rates) causes a net exposed asset position referred to as a *positive exposure*. Devaluation of the foreign currency relative to the reporting currency (domestic currency) produces a translation loss. Revaluation of the foreign currency produces a translation gain. Conversely, a firm has a net exposed liability

EXHIBIT 11-4   Translation Exposure

Exposed assets > Exposed liabilities = Positive exposure

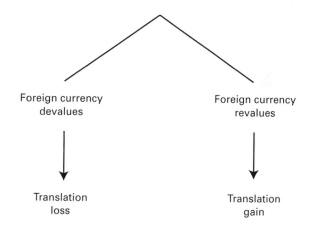

Exposed assets < Exposed liabilities = Negative exposure

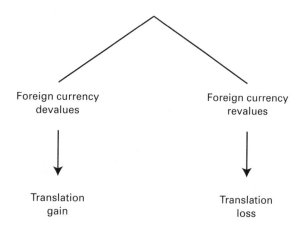

position or *negative exposure* whenever exposed liabilities exceed exposed assets. In this instance, devaluation of the foreign currency causes a translation gain. Revaluation of the foreign currency causes a translation loss.

Accounting measures of exposure vary depending on the translation method adopted. (Chapter 6 distinguished four major translation options.) Exhibit 11-5 illustrates the major translation options described in Chapter 6. The year-end balance sheet is that of a hypothetical Philippine subsidiary of a U.S. parent company. The second column depicts the U.S. dollar equivalents of the Philippine peso (P) amounts at an exchange rate of $0.03 = P 1. The peso is expected to devalue by 33 1/3 percent during the coming period. As inventories are stated at market values under the lower-of-cost-or-market rule, the monetary-nonmonetary and temporal translation methods produce different exposure measures and are treated separately. Assuming the U.S. parent designates the U.S. dollar as the subsidiary's functional currency, its potential foreign exchange loss on a positive exposure of P 1,200 million would be $12 million, determined as shown in Exhibit 11-6.

Alternatively, if the parent company designates the Philippine peso as the subsidiary's functional currency, the potential exchange loss is $23 million based on a positive exposure of P 2,300 million using the current rate method mandated by FASB No. 52. An exposure report format for the income statement is based on similar concepts (suggested by the Management Accounting Practices Committee of the International Federation of Accountants) appears in Exhibit 11-7.

Exhibit 11-6 assumed that the Philippine subsidiary's transactions were denominated solely in pesos. In most foreign operations, however, transactions are done in more than one currency. Exchange risk is a multidimensional issue: For example, a receivable denominated in Finnish markkas is unlikely to have the same future value as a receivable in Portuguese escudos, even if both have the same face value at the time of sale. To account for these situations, management accountants prepare a variety of exposure reports that distinguish among foreign currency assets and liabilities according to the

EXHIBIT 11-5   Accounting Exposure Illustrated (in Thousands)

	Pesos	U.S. Dollars Before Pesos Devaluation ($.02 = P1)	U.S. Dollars After Philippine Peso Devaluation ($.02 = P1)			
			Current Rate	Current-Noncurrent	Monetary-Nonmonetary	Temporal
Assets						
Cash	P 500,000	$ 15,000	$ 10,000	$ 10,000	$ 10,000	$ 10,000
Accounts Receivable	1,000,000	30,000	20,000	20,000	20,000	20,000
Inventories	900,000	27,000	18,000	18,000	27,000	18,000
Fixed assets (net)	1,100,000	33,000	22,000	33,000	33,000	33,000
Total	P3,500,000	$105,000	$ 70,000	$ 81,000	$ 90,000	$ 81,000
Liabilities & Owners' Equity						
Short-term payables	P 400,000	$ 12,000	$ 8,000	$ 8,000	$ 8,000	$ 8,000
Long-term debt	800,000	24,000	16,000	24,000	16,000	16,000
Stockholders' equity	2,300,000	69,000	46,000	49,000	66,000	57,000
Total	P3,500,000	$105,000	$ 70,000	$ 81,000	$ 90,000	$ 91,000
Accounting exposure (P)			2,300,000	2,000,000	300,000	1,200,000
Translation gain (loss) ($)			(23,000)	(20,000)	(3,000)	(12,000)

EXHIBIT 11-6 Calculation of Potential Foreign Exchange Loss (in Millions)

Exposed Assets			
Cash	P 500		
Accounts receivable	1,000		
Inventories	900		P2,400
Exposed Liabilities			
Short-term payables	P 400		
Long-term debt	800		1,200
Positive exposure			P1,200
Pre-depreciation rate ($0.03 = P1)	P1,200	=	$36
Post-depreciation rate ($0.02 = P1)	P1,200	=	24
Potential foreign exchange loss			($12)

EXHIBIT 11-7 Exposure Report Example: Format for an Income Statement Exposure Forecast

Income Statement Category	Items Translated at Current Exchange Rates				Items Tanslated at Historic Exchange Rates				Total Exposure
	Local Currency (amount)	Foreign Currency (amount)	Conversion Rate	Local Equivalent Rate	Local Currency (amount)	Foreign Currency (amount)	Conversion Rate	Local Equivalent Rate	
Revenues (By Category)									
Less: Cost of Sales (By Category)									
Gross Profit									
Less: Expenses (By Category)									
Earnings Before Interest and Tax Expense									
Earnings Before Tax									
Tax									
Net Income									
Net Exposed Position									
Net Covered Position									
Net Uncovered Position									

currencies in which they are denominated. Exhibit 11-8 illustrates a multicurrency exposure report for the Philippine subsidiary, which manufactures a durable good for sales in local, Australian, and American markets. Supplies are imported from Indonesia.

The format of the exposure report in Exhibit 11-8 resembles that in Exhibit 11-5 except that Exhibit 11-8 segregates exposed assets and liabilities by currency of denomination. Balance sheet items are typically expressed in U.S. dollars to facilitate an assessment of the relative magnitudes of the various items.

A multicurrency exposure reporting format offers many advantages over its single-currency counterpart. For one thing, the information provided is more complete. Rather than disclosing a single net positive exposure figure of $120 million, the report in Exhibit 11-8 shows that this figure is comprised of several different currency exposures, each with different exchange risk consequences for the U.S. parent. Also, under a single-currency perspective, the positive exposure of $12,500,000 in Australian dollars is combined with the negative exposure of $12,500,000 in Indonesian rupiahs, suggesting a natural offset. This offset is true only if the Australian dollar and Indonesian rupiah move in tandem relative to the U.S. dollar. If they do not, the translation effects could be significantly different.

A multicurrency report also enables the parent company to aggregate similar exposure reports from all of its foreign subsidiaries and analyze, on a continual basis, its worldwide translation exposure by national currency. This type of analysis is particularly helpful when local managers are responsible for protection against translation exposure. One can easily imagine a situation where local managers in two foreign subsidiaries may face opposite exposures in the same currency. Multicurrency exposure reports enable a parent company to make sure its local managers avoid hedging activities that are disadvantageous to the company as a whole.

TRANSACTION EXPOSURE

Transaction exposure concerns exchange gains and losses that arise from the settlement of transactions denominated in foreign currencies. Unlike translation gains and losses, transaction gains and losses have a direct effect on cash flows.

EXHIBIT 11-8 Multicurrency Translation Exposure (in Thousands)					
	Philippine Pesos	*Australian Dollars*	*Indonesian Rupiahs*	*U.S. Dollars*	*Total*[1]
Exposed Assets					
Cash	$ 50,000	—	—	—	$ 50,000
Receivables	45,000	$15,000	—	$40,000	100,000
Inventories	90,000			—	90,000
Total	185,000	$14,000		$40,000	$240,000
Exposed Liabilities					
Short-term payables	$ 20,000	$ 2,500	$ 12,500	$ 5,000	$ 40,000
Long-term debt	50,000			30,000	80,000
Total	$ 70,000	$ 2,500	$ 12,500	$35,000	$120,000
Net exposure	$115,000	$12,500	$(12,500)		

[1]Stated in U.S. dollars at the spot rate effective on the date of the report.

A multicurrency transaction exposure report for our Philippine subsidiary appears in Exhibit 11-9. It includes items that normally do not appear in conventional financial statements but cause transactions gains and losses, such as forward exchange contracts, future purchase and sales commitments, and long-term leases.[11] The exposure report excludes items that do not directly relate to foreign currency transactions (such as cash on hand). A transaction exposure report also has a different perspective than a translation exposure report. Whereas the translation exposure report takes the perspective of the parent company, the transaction exposure report takes the perspective of the foreign operation. Exhibit 11-9 focuses on what happens on the books of the Philippine affiliate if the peso changes value relative to the Australian dollar, the Indonesian rupiah, and the U.S. dollar. The peso column is of no concern, as peso transactions are recorded and settled in pesos. A devaluation of the peso relative to the Australian and U.S. dollars will produce transaction gains owing to positive exposures in both currencies. A devaluation of the peso relative to the rupiah would produce a transaction loss, as more pesos would be required to settle the Philippine subsidiary's foreign currency obligations. These transaction gains or losses (net of tax effects) directly impact U.S. dollar earnings upon consolidation.

Centralized control of a firm's overall exchange exposures is possible by having each foreign affiliate send its multicurrency exposure reports to corporate headquarters continually. Once exposures are aggregated by currency and by country, the company can implement centrally coordinated hedging policies to offset potential losses.

EXHIBIT 11-9   Multicurrency Transaction Exposure ($ Thousands)

	Philippine Pesos	Australian Dollars	Indonesian Rupiahs	U.S. Dollars	Total
Exposed Assets					
Receivables	$ 45,000	$15,000	—	$40,000	$100,000
Inventories	90,000	—	—	—	$ 90,000
Future sales commitments	—	10,000	—	—	10,000
Total	$135,000	$25,000		$40,000	$200,000
Exposed Liabilities					
Short-term payables	$ 20,000	$ 2,500	$ 12,500	5,000	$ 40,000
Long-term debt	50,000	—	—	30,000	80,000
Future purchase commitments	—	—	10,000	—	10,000
Leases	—	$ 5,000	—	—	5,000
Total	$ 70,000	$ 7,500	$ 22,500	$35,000	$135,000
Net exposure		$17,500	$(22,500)	$ 5,000	

---

[11]These items are normally disclosed in footnotes to the financial statements.

ACCOUNTING VERSUS ECONOMIC EXPOSURE

The reporting framework already described highlights a firm's exposure to foreign exchange risk at a given time. It does not measure a firm's economic exposure—the economic effect of currency value changes on the future operating performance and cash flows of the firm.

Exhibit 11-9 indicates that the Philippine subsidiary is *long* on Australian dollars; that is, exposed Australian dollar assets exceed exposed Australian dollar liabilities. Based on this report, a financial manager might decide to hedge this position by selling $17.5 million Australian dollars in the forward exchange market. Would this be the right decision? Probably not. Although the Philippine subsidiary is long on Australian dollars, not all the items in the exposure report require an immediate inflow or outflow of Australian dollars. The future sales commitment of $10 million will probably not bring in cash until a later accounting period. Also, the exposure report does not include all Australian dollar receipts or disbursements because future sales denominated in Australian dollars are not considered. Although Australian dollar receivables currently total $15 million, this figure will not stay the same for long. From an external reporting perspective, these future cash flows should not be considered. From an internal reporting perspective they cannot be ignored.

More and more companies differentiate between exposures that are static and those that are fluid in nature.[12] Specifically, they prepare multicurrency cash flow statements that enable them to monitor monthly cash receipts and disbursements for each currency in which they do business (see Exhibit 11-10). Whereas a traditional exposure report considers the effects of exchange rate changes on account balances as of the financial statement date, the multicurrency cash flow statement emphasizes exposures generated by exchange rate changes during the forthcoming budget period. Thus, cash receipts for each national currency include the collection of current and anticipated credit sales, asset disposals, and other cash-generating activities. Similarly, multicurrency cash disbursements incorporate those required for current and anticipated obligations, debt service, and other cash purchases.

EXHIBIT 11-10 Budgeted Cash Flows by Currency

Unit/Country: _____   Date: _____

Currency		Budget Periods					
		January	February	March	April	May	June
Philippine pesos	Receipts						
	Payments						
	Net						
Australian dollars	Receipts						
	Payments						
	Net						
Indonesian rupiahs	Receipts						
	Payments						
	Net						
Other	Receipts						
	Payments						
	Net						

---

[12]Business International Corporation, New Directions in Managing Currency Risk: Changing Corporate Strategies and Systems under FAS No. 52, New York: Business International Corporation, 1982.

The notion of economic exposure recognizes that exchange rate changes affect the competitive position of firms by altering the relative prices of their inputs and outputs as well as those of foreign competitors. For example, assume that our hypothetical Philippine subsidiary obtains its labor and material locally. Here, devaluation of the Philippine peso relative to all other foreign currencies could improve rather than worsen the subsidiary's position. A depreciated peso could increase its exports to Australia and the United States by making its goods cheaper in terms of their currencies. Domestic sales could also rise, because the peso devaluation would make imported goods more expensive in local currency. The devaluation would have no appreciable effect on the cost of local-source inputs. Thus, the future profitability of the Philippine subsidiary might increase because of the currency depreciation. Under these circumstances, booking a transaction loss on a positive translation exposure would distort the economic implications of the peso devaluation.

Alternatively, a German manufacturing affiliate of a U.K. parent, organized to serve the German market, may have a positive translation exposure and produce a translation gain upon consolidation owing to an appreciation of the mark relative to the pound. Further, if the German affiliate were to source all of its inputs in Germany, its economic exposure would appear to be shielded from exchange risk. Yet, if a major German competitor obtained some of its manufacturing components from Italy, the competitor may enjoy a cost advantage if the lira were undervalued relative to the deutsche mark.

The foregoing examples suggest that economic or operating exposure has little or no relation to translation and transaction exposure. Accordingly, the management of such exposure will require hedging technologies that are more strategic than tactical in nature.[13] These newer technologies include the following hedging options:[14]

1. Companies may opt for structural hedges that involve selecting or relocating manufacturing sites to reduce the operating exposure of the business as a whole. Such actions, however, may require foregoing economies of scale, which could reduce the expected rate of return of the business.

2. Alternatively, parent companies take a portfolio approach to risk reduction by selecting businesses that have offsetting exposures. In so doing, the operating exposure of the firm as a whole is minimized. This strategy will necessitate careful review of individual business units' operating results after correcting for the effects of operating exposure.

3. A company may opt to exploit exchange rate volatility by configuring its businesses to preserve maximum flexibility in being able to increase production and sourcing in countries where currencies become strongly undervalued in real terms. This will entail additional costs of relocating production facilities and building excess capacity. On the other hand, such strategic posturing should reduce average operating costs across a range of exchange rates.

---

[13]Miller and Reuer provide empirical insight on the relation between strategy and industry structure on a firm's economic exposures to foreign exchange rate movements. Kent D. Miller and Jeffrey J. Reuer, "Firm Strategy and Economic Exposure to Foreign Exchange Rate Movements," *Journal of International Business Studies* 29, no. 3 (3rd quarter 1998): 493–514.

[14]D. R. Lessard and J B. Lightstone, "Volatile Exchange Rates Can Put Operations at Risk," *Harvard Business Review* (July–August 1986): 107–14.

The notion of economic or operating exposure places new burdens on management accounts. Traditional sources will not contain much of the required information. Specifically, the proper measurement of operating exposure will require an understanding of the structure of the market in which a company and its competitors do business, as well as the effects of real (as opposed to nominal) exchange rates. These effects are hard to measure. As operating exposures tend to be long in duration, uncertain in terms of measurables, and not based on explicit commitments, accountants will have to provide information that spans several operating functions and time periods.

PROTECTION STRATEGIES

Once exposures to fluctuating exchange rates are quantified, the next step is to design hedging strategies that minimize or eliminate such exposures. These strategies include balance sheet, operational, and contractual hedges.

BALANCE SHEET HEDGES

A balance sheet hedge attempts to reduce a firm's exposure as much as possible by adjusting the levels and monetary denomination of a firm's exposed assets and liabilities. In Exhibit 11-8, a natural hedge against the $115 million positive exposure would be to increase the Philippine subsidiary's peso borrowings by $115 million. In this case the borrowed cash must be remitted to the parent or invested in nonexposed assets, otherwise the net exposed asset position would not change. Other methods of hedging a firm's positive exposure in a subsidiary located in a devaluation-prone country include:

1. Keeping local currency cash balances at the minimum level required to support current operations
2. Remitting profits above those needed for capital expansions back to the parent company
3. Speeding up (leading) the collection of outstanding local currency receivables
4. Deferring (lagging) payments of local currency payables
5. Speeding up the payment of foreign currency payables
6. Investing excess cash in local currency inventories and other assets less subject to devaluation loss
7. Investing in strong currency foreign assets

OPERATIONAL HEDGES

This form of risk protection focuses on variables that impact foreign currency revenues and expenses. Raising selling prices (for sales invoiced in a devaluation-prone currency) in proportion to the anticipated currency depreciation will help to protect targeted gross margins. One variation of this theme is invoicing sales in hard currencies. Tighter control of costs affords a larger margin of safety against potential currency losses. As a final example, relocating manufacturing sites to reduce operating exposures of the firm as a whole or changing the country in which raw materials or manufacturing components are sourced is called a *structural hedge* and provides an added protection vehicle.

Traditional approaches to eliminating exchange risk exposure, such as operational and balance sheet hedging, are not costless. For example, whenever devaluation is imminent, foreign subsidiaries in the country are urged to minimize their local currency working capital balances (cash and receivables in particular) and to increase holdings of local currency debt. Such actions are often disadvantageous. Increased export potential resulting from a devaluation might call for more working capital rather than less. The opportunity cost in lost sales could far exceed any translation loss. Also, local currency borrowing before a devaluation is usually expensive. Other foreign subsidiaries have the same idea at the same time and, consequently, the local banking system may accommodate such credit demands only at an excessive cost. Furthermore, bank credit during such periods is usually scarce because most countries impose severe credit restraints to counter the problems that cause the devaluation pressures in the first place. The cost of borrowing under these circumstances often exceeds any protection provided. Strategic hedges also have their limits. Vertically integrating operations to minimize a firm's exposure to exchange rate sensitive resources exposes the firm to all of the additional costs connected with setting up a new foreign affiliate and the potential loss of scale economies. Such solutions also take a long time to carry out.

CONTRACTUAL HEDGES

A variety of new hedge instruments have been developed to afford managers greater flexibility in managing foreign exchange exposures. Exhibit 11-11 shows some foreign exchange hedge products that have recently appeared. As you can see, managers have plenty of choices to consider.

Most of the newer financial instruments are *derivative* as opposed to *basic* in nature. Basic financial instruments, such as repurchase agreements (receivables), bonds, and capital stock, meet the conventional accounting definitions of assets, liabilities, and owners' equity. Derivative instruments are formal agreements to transfer risk from one party to another without transferring the underlying instrument. Many are based on contingent events and, therefore, do not have the same characteristics as the instrument on which they are based. An example would be a currency option that transfers currency risk without transferring the underlying instrument.

Financial managers of multinational enterprises should use these contractual hedges to manage their transactions and economic exposures to exchange risk as these exposures directly impact a firm's current and future cash flows. In practice, executives are quite interested in managing translation exposure and risk, as they must report lower earnings to shareholders.[15] In a comparative study of derivative usage among German and U.S. companies, minimizing the variability of reported earnings was rated most important among German companies. While U.S. companies tend to use financial derivatives to minimize the variability of cash flow, minimizing the variability of reported earnings was a close second.[16] In a related study, Swedish companies' use of

---

[15]For example, see C. O. Houston, "Translation Exposure Hedging Post SFAS No. 52," *Journal of International Financial Management and Accounting* 2, no. 2–3 (1990): 145–69.

[16]Reasons for the U.S. emphasis on reported earnings relate to analysts' perceptions and prediction of future earnings and management compensation. In Germany, reported earnings play an important role in taxation and dividend distribution. Gordon M. Bodner and Gunther Gebhardt, " Derivative Usage in Risk Management by U.S. and German Non-Financial Firms: A Comparative Study," *Journal of International Financial Management and Accounting* 10, no. 3 (1999): 153–187.

EXHIBIT 11-11 Exchange Related Financial Instruments

alternative currency option. A currency option which, if exercised, can be settled in one of several alternative currencies at the choice of the option holder.

basket hedging. The use of a basket of currencies (comprising fewer currencies than the hedged portfolio) to offset the risk of all the non-base currencies in a portfolio.

break forward. An option that allows the buyer to fully participate in the movement of a currency beyond a specified level without having to pay an explicit option premium.

combined interest rate and currency (CIRCUS). A transaction in which two counterparties exchange interest payment streams denominated in two different currencies (i.e., exchanging fixed interest payments in one currency for floating rate interest in another).

contingent hedge with an agreement for rebate at maturity (CHARM). A currency option that (1) is exercisable if a bidding company wins the contract or (2) is void if the company loses the contract, where the issuer of the option rebates a portion of the premium. The value of the payoff depends on (1) the buyer's ability to obtain business requiring currency protection, and (2) the movement of the underlying currency.

convertible option contract. An option to purchase or sell foreign currency that converts to a forward contract if the forward exchange rate falls below a certain price.

covered option securities (COPS). Short-term obligations that give the issuer the option to repay principal and interest in the original, or a mutually acceptable, currency.

covered interest arbitrage. An agreement in which two counterparties exchange currencies at both the spot and forward rates simultaneously.

cross-currency basis swap. A floating interest rate swap in two currencies.

cross-currency cap. An option in which the holder is paid the positive difference between the spread on two different currency base rates and a strike spread.

currency coupon swap. A fixed to floating coupon swap in two different currencies.

currency option. The right but not the obligation to buy or sell another currency at an agreed upon strike price within a specified time period.

currency swap. The initial exchange of two currencies and subsequent re-exchange of the same currencies at the end of a certain time period.

currency swap option (swaption). An option to buy or sell a currency swap at a specified exchange rate.

dual option bonds. A bond giving the investor the choice of currencies in which to receive interest and principal repayments.

exchange rate agreement (ERA). A synthetic agreement for forward exchange whose value is correlated with the spread between two forward currency exchange rates.

forward exchange contract. A contractual agreement between two parties to exchange a specified amount of currency for another at a fixed date in the future.

futures contract. An exchange-traded contract calling for delivery of a specified amount of currency at a fixed date in the future.

indexed currency option notes (ICONS). Bonds that are denominated and pay interest in one currency with redemption value linked to the exchange rate of another currency.

look back option. The retroactive right to buy a currency at its low point or sell a currency at its high point within the option period.

principal exchange-rate-linked securities (PERLS). Debt instruments paying interest and principal in U.S. dollars where the principal is pegged to the exchange rate between the dollar and another currency.

range forwards. A forward exchange contract specifying a range of exchange rates at which currencies will be exchanged at maturity.

synthetic position. A combined transaction to produce a security with features that could not be obtained directly (e.g., combining a fixed rate debt with a currency swap).

tailored swap. A currency swap in which the notional principle can be adjusted to meet the changing risk exposure of a business.

Source: Adapted from Gary L. Gastineau, *Swiss Bank Corporation Dictionary of Financial Risk Management,* Chicago: Probus Publishing Company, 1992.

derivatives to hedge the balance sheet (translation exposure) was as prevalent as their use of derivatives for committed and anticipated transactions. While the Swedes tended to hedge balance sheet exposure to a greater extent than their U.S. counterparts, 44 percent of the U.S. sample also did so.[17]

ACCOUNTING AND CONTROL FOR FINANCIAL DERIVATIVES

Accounting and control issues associated with foreign exchange risk management products relate to recognition, measurement, and disclosure. The recognition issue centers on whether hedging instruments should be recognized as assets or liabilities in the body of the financial statements. There is also the question of whether the derivative product should receive the same accounting treatment as the instrument to which it relates.

Closely related to the recognition issue is the question of measurement. How should a derivative instrument be valued? Should it take on the same measurement basis as the hedged instrument or transaction or should it reflect an independent valuation? If an independent valuation, which valuation model—historical cost, market value, lower of cost or market, net realizable value, or discounted present value—is preferable? How should gains or losses related to the derivative instrument be reflected in the income statement? Should they be reflected in income at all? Can and should risks associated with financial instruments be recognized and measured? This last question is especially important because risks attaching to many of the newer financial instruments, such as options and futures, are symmetric; that is, someone's gain is another's loss.

Finally, to what extent should buyers and sellers of financial instruments detail the nature and amounts of financial instruments to which they are a party? What attributes of financial instruments should be disclosed in general purpose financial statements? How much disclosure is necessary to sufficiently inform readers of the nature and magnitude of off-balance-sheet risks associated with corporate financial instruments?

We now examine some basic foreign exchange risk management products. This is followed by a discussion of their appropriate accounting treatments.

FOREIGN EXCHANGE FORWARD CONTRACTS

Importers and exporters generally use forward exchange contracts when goods invoiced in foreign currencies are purchased from or sold to foreign parties. The forward contract offsets the risk of transaction gains or losses as exchange rates fluctuate between the transaction and settlement dates. Forward contracts also hedge anticipated foreign currency payables or receivables (foreign currency commitments) and can be used to speculate in foreign currencies.

A forward exchange contract is an agreement to deliver or receive a specified amount of foreign currency in exchange for domestic currency, on a future date, at a

---

[17]Per Alkeback and Niclas Hegelin, "Derivative Usage by Non-Financial Firms in Sweden with an International Comparison," *Journal of International Financial Management and Accounting* 10, no. 2 (1999): 105–120.

fixed rate called the *forward rate*. Differences between the forward rate and the spot rate prevailing at the date of the forward contract give rise to a premium (forward rate > spot rate) or a discount (forward rate < spot rate). The premium or discount rate multiplied by the amount of the foreign currency to be received or delivered—the *notional* amount of the contract—produces a recognizable premium or discount on the forward contract. The forward contract will also give rise to transactions gains or losses whenever the exchange rate prevailing at the transaction date differs from those prevailing at interim financial statement or settlement dates. The accounting issue here is whether premiums, discounts, gains, or losses on foreign exchange contracts should receive similar or differing treatment for each use identified. Exhibit 11-12 summarizes how these accounting adjustments should be reported under FAS No. 52, now amended by FAS No. 133.

CURRENCY SWAPS

A currency swap involves a current and future exchange of two different currencies at predetermined rates. Currency swaps enable companies to access a capital market that they would not otherwise be able to access at a reasonable cost and/or hedge against exchange rate risks arising from international business. Suppose, for example, that Alpha Corporation (a U.S.-based multinational) wishes to raise $10,000,000 of fixed-rate debt in British pounds to fund a newly formed London affiliate. Alpha is relatively unknown to British investors. Similarly, Beta Company, Ltd., domiciled in the United Kingdom, would like to fund a New York subsidiary with a similar amount of dollar financing. It, too, is relatively unknown in the United States. Under these circumstances, Gamma Bank may accommodate both companies by arranging a U.S. dollar/U.K pound currency swap.

If the swap exchange rate is $1.00 = £.66 (both at inception and maturity), the swap term is 5 years, and the swap specifies interest rates of 10 percent in pounds and 8 percent in dollars, the following cash flow pattern would take place. At inception, Alpha

EXHIBIT 11-12 Accounting Treatment of Forward Contracts		
	Gains/Losses	*Discount/Premium*
Unsettled foreign currency transaction	Recognize in current income	Recognize in current income
Identifiable foreign currency commitment	Recognize in current income	Recognize in current income
Exposed net asset (liability) position		
a. Foreign currency is functional currency	Disclose in separate component of consolidated equity	Same treatment as related gains/losses, or current income
b. Parent currency is functional currency	Recognize in current income	Recognize in current income
Speculation	Recognize in current income[1]	N/A

[1] Gains/losses in this category are a function of the difference between the forward rate available for the remaining period of the contract and the contracted forward rate (or the forward rate last used to measure a gain or loss on that contract for an earlier period).

Corporation exchanges $10,000,000 for £6,600,000 from Beta Company, Ltd. Assuming interest is paid annually, Alpha pays £550,000 to Beta each year and Beta pays $800,000 to Alpha. At the end of the 5-year term, each company would re-exchange the principal amounts of $10,000,000 and £6,600,000. Exhibit 11-13 diagrams this swap arrangement.

As a result of this swap transaction, both Alpha Corporation and Beta Company, Ltd. have been able to access funds in a relatively inaccessible market, have done so without incurring exchange rate risk, and (owing to their comparative advantage in borrowing in their home markets) have achieved their foreign currency borrowings at a lower cost than they could otherwise obtain.

FINANCIAL FUTURES

A financial futures contract (generally recorded in an off-balance-sheet memorandum account) is a commitment to purchase or deliver a specified quantity of foreign currency at a future date at a set price. Alternatively, it may provide for cash settlement instead of delivery and can be cancelled before delivery by entering into an offsetting contract for the same financial instrument. In contrast to a forward contract, a futures agreement is a standardized contract, involves standardized provisions with respect to size and delivery date, is traded on an organized exchange,[18] is marked to market at the end of each

---

EXHIBIT 11-13   Currency Swap Cash Flow Pattern

Initial Exchange of Principal

	$10,000,000			$10,000,000	
Alpha Corporation	———→	Gamma Bank		———→	Beta Company, Ltd.
	←———			←———	
	£6,600,000			£6,600,000	

Annual Interest Payments

	£660,000			£660,000	
Alpha Corporation	———→	Gamma Bank		———→	Beta Company, Ltd.
	←———			←———	
	$800,000			$800,000	

Re-exchange of Swap Principal at Maturity

	£6,600,000			£6,600,000	
Alpha Corporation	———→	Gamma Bank		———→	Beta Company, Ltd.
	←———			←———	
	$10,000,000			$10,000,000	

---

[18]Examples include the International Monetary Market in Chicago and newer exchanges such as the New York Futures Exchange, the London International Financial Futures Exchange, the Singapore Money Exchange (SIMEX), the Sydney Futures Exchange, and the MATIF in Paris.

day, and must meet periodic margin requirements. Losses on a futures contract give rise to a margin call; gains normally give rise to a cash payment.[19]

Corporate treasurers generally use futures contracts to shift the risk of price changes to someone else. They can also be used to speculate in anticipated price movements and to exploit short-term anomalies in the pricing of futures contracts.

How does a financial futures contract work? If Alpha Corporation borrows yen for 3 months and wants to protect itself against an appreciation of the yen before maturity, it could buy a futures contract to receive an equal amount of yen in 90 days. Appreciation of the yen causes a gain on the futures contract offsetting the loss on the yen borrowing.

ACCOUNTING TREATMENTS

The FASB issued FAS No. 133 in June 1998 to provide a single comprehensive approach to accounting for derivative and hedge transactions.[20] Before this pronouncement, global accounting standards for derivative products were incomplete, often inconsistent, and developed in piecemeal fashion. The basic principles of this standard are:

1. All derivative instruments are to be recorded on the balance sheet as assets and liabilities.
2. They are to be recorded at fair value.
3. Gains and losses from changes in the fair value of derivative instruments are not assets or liabilities. They are automatically recognized in earnings if they are not designated as hedges.
4. Only designated items that are effectively hedged by changes in the fair value or cash flows of the hedging instrument or transaction should qualify for special hedge accounting treatment.

The FASB provides guidance for four types of foreign currency transactions or items that are hedged: firm commitments, available-for-sale securities, net investments in a foreign operation (net exposed asset or liability positions), and anticipated transactions.

For hedges of *recognized foreign currency assets or liabilities* and *firm foreign currency commitments*, gains or losses stemming from changes in the fair value of a derivative instrument (and nonderivative financial instruments) are included immediately in earnings. Changes in the value of the foreign currency commitment being hedged are also recognized in current income. A similar accounting treatment is used for *available-for-sale securities*, except that only derivative instruments can be used to hedge.

Gains or losses on hedges of a *foreign currency net investment* (an exposed net asset or liability position) are reported in comprehensive income as part of the cumulative translation adjustment to the extent it is effective as a hedge. Gains or losses on hedges

---

[19]Bruno Solnik, *International Investments*, op. cit., p. 228.
[20]FAS No. 133 supercedes FAS No. 80 and amends FAS No. 52. Financial Accounting Standards Board, "Accounting for Derivative Instruments and Hedging Activities," *Statement of Financial Accounting Standards 133*, Stamford, CT: FASB, October 1994.

of *uncertain future cash flows,* such as forecasted export sales, are initially recognized as an element of comprehensive income. Gains or losses are recognized in earnings when the forecasted transaction affects earnings.[21] IAS No. 39 contains similar guidelines providing, for the first time, universal guidance on accounting for financial derivatives.[22]

Next we next illustrate selected accounting treatments for forward contracts used as hedging instruments.

HEDGE OF A RECOGNIZED ASSET OR LIABILITY OR AN UNRECOGNIZED FIRM COMMITMENT

In our example of the U.S. export to Sweden (see Exhibit 11-2), the U.S. exporter expects to receive $140,000 for the SEK 1,000,000 owed if the spot rate remains unchanged through December 1, 20X2. To avoid the risk of receiving less than $140,000 should the krona lose value before December 1, the U.S. exporter acquires a forward contract on September 1, 20X2 to deliver SEK 1,000,000 for U.S. dollars on December 1, 20X2, at a forward rate of $.13 = SEK 1. In this example, krona can be sold only at a discount, as the spot rate is greater than the forward rate. The total discount on the forward contract is $10,000 [($.14 spot rate − $.13 forward rate × SEK 1,000,000 notional amount] and is the price of reducing uncertainty. In effect, the U.S. exporter turns an uncertain receipt of $140,000 to a certain receipt of $130,000.

At later financial statement dates before maturity, the forward contract amount (krona liability) is multiplied by the spot rate in effect on those dates. Changes in spot rates cause transactions gains or losses on the forward contract. Thus, if the exchange rate prevailing on December 1, 20X2, is $.11 = SEK 1, the U.S. exporter realizes a gain of $30,000 ($.14 spot rate − $.11 future spot rate × SEK 1,000,000 liability). Had the forward contract not been purchased, the exporter would have received only $110,000 upon conversion of the SEK 1,000,000 account receivable. Thus, the forward contract offsets a transaction loss on the foreign currency receivable with a transaction gain on the foreign currency payable.

Exhibit 11-14 provides accounting entries for the forward exchange contract just described, assuming that financial statements are prepared on September 30 prior to settlement of the krona transaction. The exchange rate on September 30 is $.13 = SEK 1.

Similar accounting treatments would take place if our U.S. exporter were to make a sales agreement on September 1 to deliver goods and receive payment of SEK 1,000,000 from the Swedish importer 3 months in the future, rather than immediately delivering goods and waiting for payment. This type of executory contract is known as a *foreign currency commitment.*

If the preceding illustration had taken the form of a forecasted export sale, *an uncertain future cash flow*, the gains or losses on the forward contract to hedge the forecasted krona receipts would first be recorded in equity as a part of comprehensive

---

[21]For additional refinements of SFAS No. 133, see the FASB's Web site at www.fasb.org.
[22]International Accounting Standards Committee, "Financial Instruments: Recognition and Measurement," *International Accounting Standard 39*, London: IASC, December 1998. Also see their Web site at http://iasc.org.uk.

EXHIBIT 11-14 **Hedge of a Foreign Currency Transaction**

Sept 1, 20X2	($) Contract receivable	$130,000
	Deferred discount	10,000
	SEK Contract payable	$140,000
	(To record agreement with foreign currency dealer to exchange SEK 1,000,000 worth $140,000 for $130,000 in 3 months.)	
Sept 30, 20X2	SEK Contract payable	10,000
	Transaction (hedge) gain	10,000
	(To record transaction gain from reduced dollar equivalent of forward contract payable $.14 − $.13 × SEK 1,00,000.)	
Sept 30, 20X2	Discount expense	3,333
	Deferred discount	3,333
	(Amortization of deferred discount for 1 month.)	
Dec 1, 20X2	SEK Contract payable	20,000
	Transaction (hedge) gain	20,000
	(To record additional transaction gain by adjusting contract to new current rate $0.13 − $.11 × SEK 1,000,000.)	
Dec 1, 20X2	Discount expense	6,667
	Deferred discount	6,667
	(Amortization of deferred discount balance.)	
Dec 1, 20X2	SEK Contract payable	110,000
	Foreign currency	110,000
	(To record delivery of SEK 1,000,000 to foreign currency dealer—this SEK 1,000,000 obtained from collecting the amount owed by the Swedish importer per Exhibit 11-3.)	
Dec 1, 20X2	Cash	130,000
	($) Contract receivable	130,000
	(To record receipt of $130,000 cash per forward contract.)	

income. These amounts would be reclassified into current earnings in the period in which the export sales are recognized.

Assuming that the discount is also treated as an element of operating expense, the net effect of the hedge transaction on operating income (ignoring any foreign exchange commissions) is determined as follows:

Dollar equivalent of receivable collected from Swedish importer	$110,000
Transaction gains on forward contract	30,000
Discount on forward contract	(10,000)
	$130,000

Gains on the forward contract have effectively offset the devaluation of the krona. The discount on the forward contract represents the cost of the hedge.

HEDGE OF A NET INVESTMENT IN A FOREIGN OPERATION

When a foreign subsidiary with an exposed net asset position is consolidated with its parent, a translation loss results if the foreign currency has lost value relative to the parent currency. A translation loss also occurs if the foreign subsidiary has an exposed net liability position (possible when the functional currency is the U.S. dollar and the temporal translation method is utilized) and the foreign currency gains value relative to the parent currency. If the company wishes to minimize such bookkeeping losses, one way is to buy forward contracts to offset translation losses with transaction gains on the contracts.

To illustrate, suppose that a U.S. calendar-year foreign affiliate in Japan (whose functional currency is the dollar) has a net exposed liability position of ¥135,000,000 at September 30. Anticipating that the Japanese yen will gain in value by year-end, the U.S. parent contracts with a foreign currency dealer to buy 135,000,000 yen in 90 days at the forward rate of $.008570. Exchange rates to the end of the year are as follows:

September 30 spot = $.008505
September 30 90-day forward = $.008570
December 31 spot = $.008640

Transactional analysis of this hedge appears in Exhibit 11-15.

In this example, which abstracted from tax effects, the expected translation loss of $18,225 (net exposed liabilities of ¥135,000,000 × $.008640 − $.008505) is offset by a transaction gain on the forward contract of $18,225 minus the premium expense of $2,025. If the foreign currency had been the functional currency, any exchange adjustment arising from consolidation would bypass income and appear in consolidated equity. Under these circumstances, *transaction* gains and losses on forward hedges and related premiums/discounts would also be taken to consolidated equity as offsets to the related cumulative *translation* adjustment.

SPECULATING IN FOREIGN CURRENCY

The forward contract in the previous example would not qualify for hedge accounting treatment had it been purchased solely to profit from an expected gain in the value of the yen. Forward contracts bought as speculations are initially recorded at the forward rate. (The forward rate is the best indicator of the spot rate that will apply when the contract matures.) Transaction gains or losses recognized prior to settlement depend on the difference between the initial forward rate and the rate available for the remaining period of the contract.

Suppose that our speculator in yen (Exhibit 11-15) prepares monthly and year-end financial statements. All facts remain the same except that at the end of October the 60-day forward rate for yen is $.008525. The transaction gain on the forward contract at the end of October would be $1,350 or ¥135,000,000 × [$.008570 (90-day forward rate on September 30) − $.008525 (60-day forward rate on October 31)], and is recognized in current income. As the foreign currency contract is recorded at the forward rate, no discounts or premiums are recognized.

Accounting treatments for the other foreign currency instruments discussed are similar to that for forward contracts. The governing criterion as to which accounting treatment is followed is based on the nature of the hedging activity; i.e., hedges of foreign currency denominated firm commitments, available-for-sale securities, forecasted transactions, or net investments in a foreign operation.

EXHIBIT 11-15	Hedge of a Net Exposed Liability Position	
September 30	¥ Contract receivable	$1,148,175
	Deferred premium	8,775
	$ Contract payable	$1,156,950
	(To record contract with foreign currency dealer to exchange $1,021,950 for ¥135,000,000 in 90 days.)	
December 31	¥ Contract receivable	18,225
	Transaction hedge gain	18,225
	(To record transaction gain from increased dollar equivalent of forward contract receivable; $.008640 − $.008505 × ¥135,000,000.)	
December 31	Premium expense	8,775
	Deferred premium	8,775
	(Amortization of deferred premium.)	
December 31	$ Contract payable	1,156,950
	Cash	1,156,950
	(To record purchase of ¥135,000,000.)	
December 31	Foreign currency	1,116,400
	¥ Contract receivable	1,116,400
	Cash	1,116,400
	Foreign currency	1,116,400
	(To record receipt of ¥135,000,000 from foreign currency dealer and its conversion.)	

A major measurement complication arises in measuring the fair value and changes in fair values of hedging instruments when financial derivatives are not actively traded. For example, measurement of the gains or losses associated with an option contract depends on whether the option is traded on or off a major exchange. Valuation of an option is readily done when the option is quoted on a major exchange, but is more difficult when the option is traded over the counter. Here one must generally rely on mathematical pricing formulas. The options pricing model developed by Professors Fischer Black and Myron Scholes, and later refinements, make it possible to value an option at any time.[23]

RECENT REPORTING DEVELOPMENTS

The accounting treatments described previously do not tell readers of a firm's financial statements whether management has made derivative contracts, nor do they indicate the extent of management's use of derivatives or their potential future financial impact on the firm. Consequently, accounting standards setters in many countries are calling

---

[23]Fischer Black and Myron Scholes, "The Pricing of Options and Corporate Liabilities," *Journal of Political Economy* (May/June 1973): 637–659. For recent refinements to the Black and Scholes option pricing formula see, Aswath Damodaran, *Investment Valuation*, New York: John Wiley & Sons, 1996.

for greater corporate financial disclosures of the use of financial risk management products. Required disclosures under FAS No. 133 and IAS 39 include the objectives for using the hedge instruments or transactions, contextual information needed to understand them, strategies for achieving the objectives, risk management policy, and a description of what is being hedged for each of four major hedge categories: (1) fair value hedges, (2) cash flow hedges, (3) foreign currency net investment hedges, and (4) all other derivatives.[24]

There are also required disclosures for each hedge type. They are to be disclosed for each reporting period for which financial statements are prepared.

FAIR VALUE HEDGES

Firms must disclose the net gain or loss included in earnings for the hedged item giving rise to transactions gains and losses under SFAS No. 52 and the designated hedge instrument, where they are reported, and the amounts not qualifying for hedge treatment.

CASH FLOW HEDGES

Disclosures similar to those for fair value hedges are also required for cash flow hedges. Reporting entities also must describe (1) any events that will result in reclassifying amounts in comprehensive income to earnings, (2) the net amounts to be reclassified within the next year, and (3) the duration of any cash flow hedges of forecasted transactions.

FOREIGN CURRENCY NET INVESTMENT HEDGES

For hedges of net exposed asset or liability positions, per SFAS No. 52, firms should disclose the net gain or loss included in the cumulative translation adjustment.

COMPREHENSIVE INCOME

The net gain or loss from derivative instruments serving as cash flow hedges must be separately disclosed under other comprehensive income broken down as follows:

1. Beginning and ending net gain or loss;
2. Net amount of comprehensive income taken to current earnings.

SFAS No. 133 and IAS 39 extend their disclosure requirements to derivative instruments not designated as hedges, in the form of qualitative disclosures on their purpose, particularly in the context of a firm's overall risk management strategies. The tenor of the discussions surrounding the adoption of these two standards suggests that U.S. and international accounting standard setters are gravitating toward the use of fair values for all financial instruments, including liabilities and equity. To this end, representatives from the FASB, the IASC, and standard setters from Australia, Canada, France, Germany, Japan, New Zealand, the Nordic federation, and the United Kingdom are jointly developing a comprehensive international standard on accounting for financial

---

[24]Patrick R. Delaney, James R. Adler, Barry J. Epstein, and Michael F. Foran, *Wiley GAAP 2000,* New York: John Wiley & Sons, Inc., chap. 6.

instruments.[25] The main provisions of this joint working group's effort advocate the following principles:

1. Fair value is the appropriate measurement attribute for all financial instruments.
2. With the exception of foreign currency net investment hedges, gains or losses from marking financial instruments to market are to be recognized in the reporting periods in which they arise.
3. Firms should provide sufficient financial disclosures to enable statement readers to evaluate the risk positions and performance of each of an enterprise's significant financial risks.
4. Financial instruments that are used for hedging purposes should be recognized and measured at fair value with gains or losses recognized immediately in current earnings.

We applaud this international effort. It supports the development of information systems that are more relevant for managerial decision making than historical cost-based reporting.

FINANCIAL CONTROL

Any financial risk management strategy must evaluate the effectiveness of hedging programs. Feedback from a thoughtful evaluation system helps to build institutional experience in risk management practices. Performance assessment of risk management programs also provides information on when existing strategies are no longer appropriate.

FINANCIAL CONTROL POINTS

Arthur Andersen identifies several areas where performance evaluation systems are fruitful. These areas include (but are not limited to) corporate treasury, purchasing, and foreign subsidiaries.[26]

Control of corporate treasury includes assessing the performance of the total exchange risk management program. This assessment includes, for example, quantifying the exposures that were managed, identifying the hedges that were applied to the exposures and reporting on hedging results. Such an evaluation system also includes documentation of how and to what extent corporate treasury aided other business units in the organization.

To illustrate, suppose that the sales manager for a consumer markets division of MNC Company wishes to grant a major customer X a line of credit. As corporate treasury would have to secure the needed funds, it would quote the sales manager an internal transfer price based on current market rates for loans of comparable risk. Assume this rate is 8 percent. The sales manager can then quote customer X a borrowing rate of 8 percent plus a markup to compensate the sales manager for assessing the client's credit risk. In the meantime, corporate treasury will enter the money markets and try to obtain a more

---

[25] Joint Working Group of Standard Setters, *Financial Instruments and Similar Items: Special Report*, Norwalk, CT: Financial Accounting Standards Board, December 2000.

[26] J. P. Morgan & Co., Inc., Arthur Andersen & Co., SC, and Financial Engineering Limited, "The J. P. Morgan/Arthur Andersen Guide to Corporate Exposure Management," *Risk Magazine* (1994).

favorable rate than it quoted the sales manager. The total return on this transaction includes the profit margin on the sale plus the financing spread. Management accountants need to set up a responsibility accounting system that credits the sales manager and corporate treasury for their fair share of the total profit on the sales transaction.[27]

Similar considerations apply to the purchasing function. Here, exchange risk management services are just one piece of the total risk management program. Controls are also necessary to monitor the performance of programs designed to hedge commodity price risk and mix.

In many organizations, foreign exchange risk management is centralized at corporate headquarters to allow subsidiary managers to concentrate on their core business. However, when comparing actual results to expectations, evaluation systems must be able to compare the success of corporate risk protection to risk management programs that local managers could have implemented. (See Chapter 10 for more on multinational performance evaluation systems.)

APPROPRIATE BENCHMARKS

Given that the object of risk management is to achieve an optimal balance between risk reduction and costs, a benchmark against which to judge actual performance is a necessary ingredient in any performance appraisal system. Benchmarks need to be specified in advance of any protection program and should be based on the concept of opportunity cost. In foreign exchange risk management, the following questions should be considered when selecting a benchmark.[28]

- Does the benchmark represent a policy that could have been followed?
- Can the benchmark be specified in advance?
- Does the benchmark provide a lower cost strategy than some other alternative?

Firms that are averse to foreign exchange risk might automatically hedge any foreign exposure in the forward market or borrow local currency. These strategies would be natural benchmarks against which to appraise financial risk management. Thus the performance of a certain hedge product (e.g., a currency swap) or a risk manager would be judged by comparing the economic return earned on the actively hedged transaction versus the economic return that would have been earned had the benchmark treatment been used.

REPORTING SYSTEMS

Financial risk reporting systems must be able to reconcile both internal reporting and external reporting systems. Risk management activities (typically managed by corporate treasury) have a future orientation. However, they must eventually reconcile with

---

[27]If, for example, corporate treasury tries to beat the 8 percent benchmark rate but instead pays 9 percent, the sales manager should not be charged for the reduced spread.

[28]Ian Cooper and Julian Franks, "Treasury Performance Measurement," *The Treasurer* (February 1988): 56.

exposure measurements and financial accounts for external reporting purposes, which come under the corporate controller's department. A team approach is most effective in formulating financial risk objectives, performance standards, and monitoring and reporting systems. Financial risk management is a prime example of where corporate finance and accounting are closely connected.

Selected References

"Accounting for Derivatives," Coopers and Lybrand Capital Markets Accounting Developments Advisory (196-6), July 18, 1996.

Alkeback, Per, and Niclas Hagelin, "Derivative Usage by Non-Financial Firms in Sweden with an International Comparison," *Journal of International Financial Management and Accounting* 10, no. 2 (1999): 105–120.

Barton, Jan, "Does the Use of Financial Derivatives Affect Earnings Management Decisions," *Accounting Review* 76, No. 1 (January 2001): 1–26.

Beaver, William H., and Mark A. Wolfson, "Foreign Currency Translation and Changing Prices in Perfect and Complete Markets," *Journal of Accounting Research* (autumn 1992): 528–50.

Bodnar, Gordon, and Gunther Gebhardt, "Derivative Usage in Risk Management by U.S. and German Non-Financial Firms: A Comparative Study," *Journal of International Financial Management and Accounting* 10, no. 3 (1999): 153–87.

Claiden, Richard, "Accounting for Derivative Products," in *International Accounting and Finance Handbook*, Frederick D. S. Choi, ed., New York: John Wiley and Sons, 1997, 17.1–29.

Copeland, T., and Y. Joshi, "Why Derivatives Don't Reduce FX Risk," *The McKinsey Quarterly*, no. 1 (1996): 66–79.

Damodaran, Aswath, *Investment Valuation*, New York: John Wiley & Sons, 1996.

Eiteman, David K, Arthur I. Stonehill, and Michael M. Moffett, *Multinational Business Finance*, 7th ed., Reading, MA: Addison-Wesley, 1995.

Financial Accounting Standards Board, "Accounting for Derivative Instruments and Hedging Activities," *Statement of Financial Accounting Standards 133*, Norwalk, CT: FASB, October 1994.

Froot, Kenneth A., David S. Scharfstein, and Jeremy Stein, "Risk Management: Coordinating Corporate Investment and Financing Policies," *Journal of Finance* (December 1993): 1,629–1,658.

Gastineau, Gary L., *Dictionary of Financial Risk Management*, Chicago, IL: Probus Publishing Company, 1992.

Houston, Carol O., "Translation Exposure Hedging Post SFAS No. 52," *Journal of International Financial Management and Accounting* 2, no. 2–3 (1990): 145–69.

International Accounting Standards Committee, "Financial Instruments: Recognition and Measurement," *International Accounting Standard 39*, London: IASC, December 1998.

J. P. Morgan & Co., Inc., Arthur Andersen & Co., SC, and Financial Engineering Limited, "The J. P. Morgan/Arthur Andersen Guide to Corporate Exposure Management," *Risk Magazine* (1994).

Joint Working Group of Standard Setters, *Financial Instruments and Similar Items: Special Report*, Norwalk, CT: FASB, December 2000.

Logue, D. E. and G. S. Oldfield, "Managing Foreign Assets When Foreign Exchange Markets Are Efficient," *Financial Management* (summer 1997): 16–22.

Miller, Kent D., and Jeffrey J. Reuer, "Firm Strategy and Economic Exposure to Foreign Exchange Rate Measurements," *Journal of International Business Studies* 29, no. 3 (3rd quarter 1998): 493–514.

Moffett, Michael H., and Jan Karl Karlsen, "Managing Foreign Exchange Rate Economic Exposure," *Journal of International Financial Management and Accounting* (June 1994): 157–175.

Smith, W. S., Jr., "Corporate Risk Management: Theory and Practice," *Journal of Derivatives* 2, no. 4 (1995).

Discussion Questions

1. What is market risk? Illustrate this risk with a foreign exchange example.
2. Active hedging of financial exposures is not generally accepted among financial managers around the world. Some argue that financial management alone cannot increase the value of the firm and that a firm is better off managing its core business risks while leaving itself exposed to some (if not all) financial risks. Do you agree?
3. Consider the statement: "Forecasting foreign exchange rates is futile. You can't outguess the market so you shouldn't try." Do you agree or disagree? What does your stance imply for management accountants?
4. A foreign currency transaction can be *denominated* in one currency, yet *measured* in another. Explain the difference between these two terms using the case of a Canadian dollar borrowing on the part of a Mexican affiliate of a U.S. parent company that designates the U.S. dollar as the functional currency.
5. Assume that you are employed by an investment bank that offers risk management services for corporate clients. In designing a hedge program for a client's exposure to market risk, why is a knowledge of accounting important?
6. Compare and contrast the terms *translation, transaction,* and *economic* exposure. Does FAS No. 52 resolve the issue of accounting versus economic exposure?
7. List ten ways to reduce a firm's foreign exchange exposure for a foreign affiliate located in a devaluation-prone country. In each instance, identify the cost-benefit trade-offs that need to be measured.
8. What is the difference between a *basic* and a *derivative* financial instrument? What accounting issues are associated with the derivative?
9. Explain, in your own words, the difference between a multicurrency translation exposure report and a multicurrency transactions exposure report.
10. Exhibit 11-13 in this chapter illustrated how a currency swap enabled two companies to obtain foreign currency loans at a lower cost. Explain how a company might use a currency swap to hedge its foreign exchange risk on a foreign currency borrowing.
11. What is a financial futures contract? How does it differ from a forward exchange contract?
12. What, in your opinion, do the recent initiatives of the FASB and IASC with respect to accounting for derivatives seem to imply for the future direction of accounting?

Exercises

1. As one of your first assignments as a new hire on the corporate treasurer's staff of Global Enterprises, Ltd., you are asked to prepare an exchange rate forecast for the Mexican peso. Specifically, you are expected to forecast what the spot rate for the peso is likely to be at the end of 20X4. Selected information on which to base

your forecast follows. Be sure to identify any additional bases underlying your forecast and any assumptions.

	19X9	20X0	20X1	20X2	20X3	20X4
Visible trade balance (US$bn)	7.1	6.5	0.6	−7.7	−5.4	
Current account balance (US$ bn)	−1.6	−1.9	−7.3	−15.8	−13.8	
Foreign direct investment (US$bn)	9.5	9.2	12.8	11.3	11.6	
Portfolio flows (US$bn)	−9.7	13.4	5.0	−0.6	9.6	
Foreign exchange reserves (US$bn)	15.25	19.18	28.14	31.46	30.99	
Real GDP growth (% change yoy)	−6.20	5.09	6.80	4.80	3.70	
Consumer prices (% changes yoy)	51.97	27.70	15.72	18.60	12.32	
Nominal GDP (US$bn)	266	335	412	415	479	
Nominal exchange rate to US$	6.42	7.60	7.92	9.15	9.55	?

2. Following is the consolidated balance sheet (000s omitted) of Stern Bank, a U.S. financial institution with wholly owned corporate affiliates in London and Geneva. Cash and due from banks includes CHF 100,000 and a £(40,000) bank overdraft. Loans consist entirely of Swiss franc receivables while consolidated deposits include CHF 40,000 and £15,000. Stern Bank adopts the local currency as the functional currency for its foreign affiliates and so translates all assets and liabilities (including owners' equity) using the current rate. The exchange rate prevailing as of the balance sheet date was (£/$/CHF = 1/2/4).

   Required: Prepare a multicurrency exposure report for Stern Bank.

Stern Bank Consolidated Balance Sheet As of Year-End (000)

Cash and due from banks	$ 20,000	Deposits	$ 50,000
Loans	100,000		
Fixed assets	30,000	Owners' Equity	100,000
Total	$150,000		$150,000

3. Refer to exercise 2. Assume that the Swiss franc is forecast to devalue such that the new exchange relationship after the devaluation is (£/$/CHF = 1/2/8).

   Required: Calculate the consolidated gain or loss that would result from this exchange rate movement.

4. Based on the Stern Bank's exposure to exchange risk identified in exercise 3, corporate management decides to shield reported earnings from FX losses by actively managing its exposure in Swiss francs.

   Required: Prepare a brief report containing suggested hedging strategies to do this, together with any trade-offs that need to be considered.

5. Trojan Corporation USA borrowed 1,000,000 New Zealand dollars (NZ$) at the beginning of the calendar year when the exchange rate was $.50 = NZ$1. Before repaying this 1-year loan, Trojan learns that the NZ dollar has appreciated to $.60 = NZ$1. It discovers, also, that its New Zealand subsidiary has an exposed net asset position of NZ$ 3,000,000, which will produce a translation gain upon

consolidation. What is the amount of the exchange gain or loss that will be reported in consolidated income if:

a. the U.S. dollar is the foreign operation's functional currency?

b. the New Zealand dollar is the foreign operation's functional currency and Trojan Corp. designates the New Zealand dollar borrowing as a hedge of the New Zealand affiliate's positive exposure?

6. On April 1, A. C. Corporation, a calendar-year U.S. electronics manufacturer, buys 32.5 million yen worth of computer chips from the Sando Company paying 10 percent down, the balance to be paid in 3 months. Interest at 8 percent per annum is payable on the unpaid foreign currency balance. The U.S. dollar/Japanese yen exchange rate on April 1 was $1.00 = ¥120; on July 1 it was $1.00 = ¥110.

Required: Prepare dated journal entries in U.S. dollars to record the incurrence and settlement of this foreign currency transaction assuming:

a. A. C. Corporation adopts a single-transaction perspective, and

b. it employs a two-transactions perspective.

7. On June 1, ACL International, a U.S. confectionery products manufacturer, purchases, on account, bulk chocolate from a Swiss supplier for 166,667 Swiss francs (CHF) when the spot rate is $.60 = CHF 1. The Swiss franc payable is due on September 1. To minimize its exposure to an exchange loss should the franc appreciate relative to the dollar prior to payment, ACL International acquires a forward contract to exchange $103,334 for francs on September 1 at a forward rate of $.62 = CHF 1.

Required: Given the following exchange rate information, provide journal entries to account for the forward exchange contract on June 1, June 30, and September 1. The company closes its books quarterly.

June 30 spot rate	$.61 = CHF 1
September 1 spot rate	$.63 = CHF 1

8. What is the effective dollar cost of the Swiss chocolate purchase in exercise 7? Show your calculations.

9. Refer to the Exposure Management Cube shown in Exhibit 11-1. Provide examples of how the various market risks—foreign exchange, interest rate, commodity price, and equity—might affect the value driver "Current Assets."

10. On January 2, Delta Bank has outstanding a $10,000,000, 12 percent fixed interest rate loan it has funded with a 6 percent fixed rate CHF deposit. To protect itself against an appreciation of the Swiss franc, it has arranged a currency swap for its own account with Epsilon Company. Under the swap arrangement, Delta Bank exchanges, for a period of 5 years, $10,000,000 at 10 percent for CHF 20,000,000 at 6 percent. As a result of this transaction, Delta Bank has hedged its currency risk and made money on the spread.

Required: Prepare a flow chart illustrating the pattern of periodic swap cash flows under this arrangement.

11. Provide dated journal entries to account for the transactions described in exercise 10 for the month of January, assuming that Delta bank closes its books monthly. Assume that the dollar/franc exchange rate has not changed during the year.

12. In June, Mu Corporation, a U.S. manufacturer of specialty confectionery products, submits a bid to supply a prestigious retail merchandiser with boxed chocolates for the traditional Valentine's Day. If it secures the contract, it will sign a contract with a large Swiss chocolate manufacturer to buy the necessary raw material. The

outcome of the bidding will not be known for 2 months and the treasurer of Mu Corporation is concerned that the franc may rise in value during the interim, thus reducing (or possibly even eliminating) its planned profit on the fixed-price bid.

To protect his company against an appreciation of the franc, the treasurer buys 25 CHF September 30 option calls at 1.80 (i.e., a premium of 1.8 cents per franc) on a standard contract amount of CHF 62,500. His prediction proves accurate as the franc rises in value to 41.6 cents by the end of August. Rather than await the outcome of the bid, Mu Corporation exercises its call options at the end of August.

Required: Provide the necessary journal entries to record the acquisition and exercise of the options.

Case 11–1 Value at Risk: What Are Our Options?

The scene is a conference room on the 90th floor of One New York Plaza, occupied by InfoTech Enterprises, a small, rapidly growing manufacturer of electronic trading systems for equities, commodities, and currencies.

The agenda for the 8:00 A.M. meeting concerns reporting issues associated with a potential sales contract for the stock exchange in the Slovak Republic, which wants to upgrade its technology to effectively participate in the globalization of financial markets. In attendance are InfoTech's COO Grace Glessing, Controller George Tabback, Treasurer Paul Affuso, and Vice President of Marketing Mary Miller.

Grace: Thank you for agreeing to meet on such short notice. Mary, are you ready to give us an update on Slovakia?

Mary: You mean the Slovak Republic.

Grace: Yes.

Mary: I think there is a 90+ percent chance we'll land the contract. Things move a little slowly over there and they're still concerned about some of the legal details of our sales contract. I think they find the legalese a bit intimidating and I can't say I blame them. I've scheduled another trip next month to go over contract details. This time I'm taking our legal counsel and have asked him to prepare another draft expressed in terms that are easier to understand. They're also waiting for approvals from their Central Bank, which has to approve of major transactions such as this one.

Grace: Good. Are we prepared to deliver on the contract?

Mary: Yes, we've lined up the financing, have done our credit checks, and the equipment and installation teams are ready to proceed on 2 week's notice.

Grace: Given the size of the contract, are we hedged against the possibility of a devaluation?

Paul: Yes, we've written a put option on the koruna for 90 days.

Grace: Do we think we'll close on the deal before then?

Paul: Mary doesn't think so, but you never know. The problem is no one will write an option for a longer term. We'll renew the option as we have other transactions of this extended duration.

Grace: George, are we all right on the reporting front?

George:	Not really.
Grace:	How's that?
George:	It looks like we're up against some new reporting standards that require that gains or losses on cash flow hedges whose maturities do not match that of the underlying be recognized in current earnings.
Grace:	Come again?
George:	The bottom line is that we won't be able to treat gains or losses on our put options as a part of comprehensive income, but we'll have to recognize them in current earnings.
Grace:	Won't that mess up our bottom line?
George:	I'm afraid so. There would be no offsetting gain or loss from our anticipated sale.
Paul:	It's taken me a whole year to get to know the right people and win their trust and friendship. I now have that. There's no doubt in my mind that this sale is a done deal and I anticipate closing the transaction within the next 6 to 9 months.
George:	That may be, but we just can't find anyone who's willing to write an option for more than 90 days at a time.
Grace:	I don't want to think about what the accounting will do to our stock price! I mean, we're about to float our first Euro-equity issue. A lower offering price would be disastrous at this stage of our development, not to mention the effect on our shareholders.
Mary:	Given the nature of our business, I don't think the transactions side of our business will change much.
Grace:	Do you think it would be worthwhile having a consultant advise us on this one?
George, Mary, and Paul (in unison):	Why not?

REQUIRED

As a consultant for InfoTech, identify what you believe are promising hedge accounting options.

Case 11–2   Exposure Identification

You are currently working for a consulting firm that provides risk management products for clients. Your task is to provide your company's sales force with information on prospective clients. Assume that ExxonMobil Corporation, whose financial statements and notes appear at www.exxonmobil.com, is a prospective client.

REQUIRED

1. Using ExxonMobil's 1999 financial statements (especially pp. F6-F39) as a starting point, identify as many exposures as you can that impact the company. Be sure to cross-reference your findings with the specific page number of the financial statements you are referring to.

2. Identify any exposures that the company is currently hedging.

CHAPTER

INTERNATIONAL TAXATION AND TRANSFER PRICING

Of all the environmental variables that financial managers must contend with, only foreign exchange is as influential as taxation. Tax considerations strongly influence decisions on where to invest, what form of business organization to employ, how to finance, when and where to recognize elements of revenues and expense, and what transfer prices to charge.[1]

Consider an example. In Chapter 11, we learned that one way to hedge foreign exchange risk on a new investment abroad is to borrow local currency to fund that investment. However, national tax systems differ in their treatment of exchange gains and losses, and this technique may have unintended cash flow effects. Here, an increase in value of the local currency would produce an exchange gain on the asset and a loss on the borrowing. Where national tax statutes focus on transactions (as opposed to economic substance), any gain arising from the disposal of the investment would be taxable, but any corresponding loss on repayment of the foreign currency loan would not be deductible.

With the possible exception of cost of goods sold, taxation is the largest expense of most businesses. It makes sense for management to minimize international taxes whenever possible, but in contrast to such direct operating costs as labor and materials, management has limited control over tax expense. National tax systems are diverse and complex. The 15 members of the European Union reportedly levy more than 200 different rates on value-added tax alone.[2] Financial managers must also contend with special rules regarding the taxation of foreign source income. Finally, international tax agreements, laws, and regulations are constantly changing. Changes in one country's tax provisions have complex and wide-ranging effects in a multinational tax planning system, and computer-based simulation systems are essential aids to management.

---

[1]For a review of empirical research on the effects of international tax on business decisions, see J. F. Hines, Jr., "Lessons from Behavioral Responses to International Taxation," *National Tax Journal* (June 1999): 305–322.

[2]W. Echikson and D. Woodruff, "One Currency, One Tax? Don't Bet On It," *Business Week* (July 21, 1997): 48E2.

Because it is not possible in a single chapter to provide a working knowledge of the major tax provisions in all the economically important countries of the world, we limit our discussion here to some of the major variables that financial managers need to consider in tax planning for multinational operations. These variables include major differences in national tax systems (i.e., how countries tax businesses operating within their borders), national attempts to address the issue of double taxation (i.e., how countries tax the foreign source income of their business entities), and arbitrage opportunities between national tax jurisdictions for multinational firms. Transfer pricing, in addition to its role in minimizing multinational corporate taxes, should be considered in the broader context of strategic planning and control.

INITIAL CONCEPTS

The maze of laws and regulations that govern the taxation of foreign corporations and profits earned abroad rests on a few basic concepts. These include notions of tax *neutrality* and tax *equity*. Tax neutrality means that taxes have no effect (are neutral) on resource allocation decisions. That is, business decisions are driven by economic fundamentals, such as rate of return, rather than tax considerations. Such decisions should result in an optimal allocation of resources: When taxes influence the allocation of resources, the result will probably be less than optimal. In reality, taxes are seldom neutral.

Tax equity means that taxpayers who are similarly situated should pay the same tax, but there is much disagreement over how to interpret this concept. For example, is a foreign subsidiary simply a domestic company that happens to operate abroad? If so, then foreign- and domestic-source income should be taxed at the same parent country rate. Or, is a foreign subsidiary a foreign company that happens to be owned by a domestic one? In this case, foreign-source income should be taxed the same as other companies in that country, that is, at the foreign country's tax rate. We shall find that actual international tax practices waver between these two extremes.

DIVERSITY OF NATIONAL TAX SYSTEMS

A firm can conduct international business by exporting goods and services or by making direct or indirect foreign investments. Exports seldom trigger a tax exposure in the importing country, because it is difficult for importing countries to enforce taxes levied on foreign exporters. On the other hand, a company that operates in another country through a branch or incorporated affiliate subjects itself to that country's taxes. The effective management of this tax exposure requires an understanding of national tax systems, which differ greatly among countries. Differences range from types of taxes and tax burdens to differences in tax assessment and collection philosophies.

TYPES OF TAXES

A company operating abroad encounters a variety of taxes. *Direct taxes*, such as income taxes, are easy to recognize and normally are disclosed on companies' financial statements. Other *indirect taxes*, such as consumption taxes, are not so clearly recognized or as frequently disclosed. Typically they are buried in "other costs and expenses."

Exhibit 12-1 illustrates the differential impact of direct and indirect taxes on pretax and after-tax income. In comparing investment performance between countries, the focus should be on after-tax returns.

The *corporate income tax* is probably more widely used to generate government revenue than any other major tax, with the possible exception of customs duties. Since the mid-1980s, however, the international trend has been to lower income tax rates. Fueling this trend is the recognition that reduced tax rates increase the global competitiveness of a country's business enterprises and create an attractive environment for international business. Indeed, the integration of the world economy and the increasing ability of businesses to move from high-tax environments to low-tax ones constrain a country's ability to set higher rates than elsewhere.[3] Exhibit 12-2 shows national income tax rates for selected countries.

Withholding taxes are those imposed by governments on dividend, interest, and royalty payments to foreign investors. Thus, a Dutch purchaser of Italian bonds receives only 90 percent of the interest paid by the bonds because Italy has a 10 percent withholding tax on interest payments. While legally imposed on the foreign recipient, these taxes are typically withheld at the source by the paying corporation, which remits the proceeds to tax collectors in the host country. Because withholding taxes may hinder the international flow of long-term investment capital, they are often modified by bilateral tax treaties.

The *value-added tax* is a consumption tax found in Europe and Canada. This tax is typically levied on the value added at each stage of production or distribution. This tax applies to total sales less purchases from any intermediate sales unit. Thus, if a Norwegian merchant buys 500,000 krone of merchandise from a Norwegian wholesaler and then sells it for 600,000 krone, the value added is 100,000 krone and a tax is assessed on this amount. Companies that pay the tax in their own costs can reclaim them later from the tax authorities. Consumers ultimately bear the cost of the value-added tax. Exhibit 12-3 shows how the value-added tax works.

Border taxes, such as customs or import duties, generally aim at keeping domestic goods price competitive with imports. Accordingly, taxes assessed on imports typically parallel excise and other indirect taxes paid by domestic producers of similar goods.

The *transfer tax* is another indirect tax. This tax is imposed on the transfer of items between taxpayers and can have important effects on business decisions such as the structure of acquisitions. For example, business acquisitions in Europe are often made

EXHIBIT 12-1 Earnings Effects of Direct vs. Indirect Taxes		
	Direct	*Indirect*
Revenues	250	250
Expenses	150	190
Pretax income	100	60
Direct taxes (40%)	40	-0-
After-tax income	60	60

---

[3]"Disappearing Taxes: The Tap Runs Dry," *The Economist* (May 31, 1997): 21.

EXHIBIT 12-2	Corporate Income Tax Rates				
Country	*OECD*	*EU*	*Asia Pacific*	*Latin America*	*(%)*
Argentina				•	35
Australia	•		•		36
Austria	•	•			34
Bangladesh			•		35
Belgium	•	•			40.17
Belize				•	25
Bolivia				•	25
Brazil				•	37[1]
Canada	•				29.1[2]
Chile				•	15
China			•		30[3]
Colombia				•	35
Czech Republic	•				31
Denmark	•	•			32
Dominican Republic				•	25
Ecuador				•	25
El Salvador				•	25
Fiji			•		35
Finland	•	•			29
France	•	•			36.66[4]
Germany	•	•			40/30[5]
Greece	•	•			35/40
Guatemala				•	25
Honduras				•	25
Hong Kong			•		16
Hungary	•				18
Iceland	•				30
India			•		38.5
Indonesia			•		30
Ireland	•	•			24
Israel			•		36
Italy	•	•			37[6]
Japan	•		•		30[7]
Korea, South	•		•		30.8
Luxembourg	•	•			30[8]
Malaysia			•		28
Mexico	•			•	35
Netherlands	•	•			35
New Zealand	•		•		33
Norway	•				28
Pakistan			•		43
Panama				•	37
Papua New Guinea			•		25
Paraguay				•	30

EXHIBIT 12-2 (cont.)					
Country	*OECD*	*EU*	*Asia Pacific*	*Latin America*	*(%)*
Peru				•	30
Philippines			•		32
Poland	•				30
Portugal	•	•			34[9]
Singapore			•		26
Spain	•	•			35
Sri Lanka			•		35
Sweden	•	•			28
Switzerland	•				25.1[10]
Taiwan			•		25
Thailand			•		30
Turkey	•				33
Uruguay				•	30
United Kingdom	•	•			30
United States	•				35[11]
Venezuela				•	34
Vietnam			•		14.5-32.5[12]

Note: A simple comparison of tax rates is not sufficient for assessing the relative tax burdens imposed by different governments. The method of computing the profits to which the tax rates will be applied (the tax base) should also be taken into account.

These rates do not reflect payroll taxes, social security taxes, net wealth taxes, turnover taxes, and other taxes not levied on income.

[1] The sum of income tax (25%) and social contribution tax on profits (12%).

[2] Additional provincial income taxes make the effective overall rate approximately 45%.

[3] Additional local income tax makes the overall effective rate 33%.

[4] The sum of income tax (33.33%) and social contribution on profits (3.33%).

[5] The first rate applies to retained profits and the second rate to distributed profits. In addition, there is a trade tax on income that averages 16.32%.

[6] Additional local income taxes make the effective overall rate 41.25%.

[7] Additional business, prefectural, and municipal taxes make the effective overall rate 42%.

[8] Additional municipal business tax makes the effective overall rate 37.45%.

[9] Additional municipal tax makes the effective overall rate 37.4%.

[10] Includes federal, cantonal, and municipal taxes.

[11] Additional state income taxes make the effective overall rate approximately 40%.

[12] Various rates based ownership and type of company.

Source: KPMG Corporate Tax Rate Survey—January 2000. www.kpmg.com/Rut2000_prod/Documents/8/ctrs.pdf

EXHIBIT 12-3	**Value-Added Tax**			
	Producer	*Wholesaler*	*Merchant*	*Consumer*
Cost	Assume 0	€ 12.00	€ 15.60	€ 21.60
Recoverable VAT	—	2.00	2.60	
Net cost	0	€ 10.00	€ 13.00	
Sales price before VAT	€ 10.00	13.00	18.00	
Value added	€ 10.00	€ 3.00	€ 5.00	
Value-added tax (20%)	2.00	0.60	1.00	
Sales price after VAT	€ 12.00	€ 15.60	€ 21.60	
VAT paid	€ 2.00	€ 2.60	€ 3.60	
Recoverable VAT	0	2.00	2.60	
VAT due	€ 2.00	€ 0.60	€ 1.00	
VAT borne				€ 3.60

through the purchase of shares rather than the underlying net assets. More variations in structure are found in U.S. acquisitions because transfer taxes are less important in the United States.

TAX BURDENS

Differences in overall tax burdens are important in international business. Various statutory rates of income taxation are an important source of these differences, as can be seen in Exhibit 12-2. Differences in tax rates tell only part of the story. Many other considerations may significantly affect *effective tax burdens* for multinational enterprises. Differences in national definitions of taxable income are important. While more and more governments are reducing marginal corporate tax rates, many also are broadening corporate tax *bases*.

Consider depreciation. In theory, a portion of the cost of an asset is said to expire as the asset is used up to produce revenue. In keeping with the matching principle, this expired cost is recognized as an expense and deducted from its related revenue. Where the asset is consumed equally in each reporting period, an equal portion of its cost is commonly expensed each period for external financial reporting purposes. In the United States, however, a distinction is generally made between depreciation for external reporting and depreciation for tax purposes. As an incentive to invest in capital assets, including commercial buildings, companies in the United States are allowed to use accelerated depreciation methods. In Germany, tax law specifies depreciation rates, and buildings are depreciated in straight-line fashion. In the Netherlands, firms generally depreciate commercial buildings in straight-line fashion but are granted certain investment incentives that effectively permit a larger depreciation rate. In Latin American countries where inflation rates have been high (such as Mexico and Uruguay), firms are required to adjust their assets for changing price levels, and the higher depreciation charges are deductible for tax purposes (see Chapter 7). Finally, in Japan, companies can take excess depreciation (depreciation beyond that normally taken on depreciable assets) on assets that are deemed important to the national interest. Examples are pollution control equipment and assets devoted to creating alternative energy sources.

Governments also have their own views as to the appropriate transfer prices on transactions between related affiliates of multinational companies. International opinions differ so greatly that parent companies often charge their foreign affiliates for expenditures such as research and development to avoid conflicts with foreign tax authorities.

TAX ADMINISTRATION SYSTEMS

National tax assessment systems also affect relative tax burdens. Several major systems are currently in use. For simplicity, we will only consider the *classical* and *integrated* systems.

Under the *classical system*, corporate income taxes on taxable income are levied at the corporate level and at the shareholder level. Shareholders are taxed either when the corporate income is paid as a dividend or when they liquidate their investment. When a corporation is taxed on income measured before dividends are paid, and shareholders are then taxed on their dividends, the shareholders' dividend income is effectively taxed twice. To illustrate, assume that a parent corporation in Zonolia (fictitious), subject to a 33 percent corporate income tax, earns 100 zonos (Z) and distributes a 100 percent dividend to its sole shareholder, who is in the 30 percent tax bracket. Effective taxes paid on the corporate income would be determined as follows:

Corporate income	Z100.00
− Income tax at 33%	33.00
= Net income	Z 67.00
Dividend	Z 67.00
− Personal income tax at 30%	20.10
= Net income	Z 46.90

Total tax paid on the Z100 of corporate income:

Corporate tax	Z33.00
Individual income tax	20.10
Total	Z53.10

Countries associated with this system include Belgium, Japan, Luxembourg, the Netherlands, and the United States. Except for the United States, the recent trend has been to move away from the double taxation of dividend income by adopting either an integrated or an imputation system.

Under an *integrated* system, corporate and shareholder taxes are integrated so as to reduce or eliminate the double taxation of corporate income. One variant is the *split-rate* system as found in Germany, where a lower tax is levied on distributed earnings (i.e., dividends) than on retained earnings. While corporate income is still subject to a double tax, the lower rate on distributed income results in a lower tax burden than under the classical system.

The *tax credit* or *imputation* system is a more common variant of the integrated tax system. In this system, a tax is levied on corporate income, but part of the tax paid can be treated as a credit against personal income taxes when dividends are distributed to shareholders. This tax system is advocated by the European Union and is found in Canada, Mexico, and many European countries, including France, Germany, Italy, and the United Kingdom.

To see how this tax system works, assume facts similar to that of our Zonolian parent company in the preceding illustration. Here, the Zonolian corporation remits 1/4 (20/80) of any dividends paid to shareholders as an advanced corporation tax (ACT) to the Zonolia Revenue Service. The ACT serves several purposes: (1) it provides the government an immediate cash flow; (2) it operates as a credit against total corporate taxes payable; and (3) it provides a credit for shareholders against personal income taxes payable on dividends received. Based on these assumptions, the total taxes paid would be determined as follows:

Corporate income	Z100.00
− Income tax at 33%	33.00
= Net income and dividend paid	Z 67.00
Corporate income tax	Z 33.00
− ACT	16.75
= Taxes payable	Z 16.25
Dividend income to shareholder	Z 67.00
+ Tax credit (ACT)	16.75
= Grossed-up dividend	Z 83.75
Income tax liability at 30%	Z 25.12
− Tax credit (ACT)	16.75
= Tax due from shareholder	Z 8.37

Total tax paid on the Z100 of corporate income:

Corporate tax	Z 33.00
Individual income tax	8.37
Total	Z 41.37

This example illustrates a *partial* imputation system in which double taxation is reduced but not eliminated. *Full* imputation eliminates double taxation.

The imputation tax system may penalize foreign investors. To yield the same amount of revenue as under the classical system, the imputation system requires a higher marginal tax rate to offset the tax credit (i.e., the ACT in the preceding example) to which domestic taxpayers are entitled. Nonresidents do not get the tax credit and pay the higher rate.

The host country's social overhead is a final item that accounts for intercountry differences in effective tax burdens. To attract foreign investments, less industrialized countries often assess lower corporate income tax rates than their more industrialized counterparts. However, countries with low direct taxes need to fund government and other social services just as any other country. Therefore, lower direct corporate tax rates usually result in higher indirect taxes or in fewer and lower-quality public services.

Indirect taxes often reduce the purchasing power of the local market, and thus reduce its attractiveness to a multinational investor.[4] Fewer and lower-quality public services may impose a higher cost structure on multinational operations. Examples include poor transportation networks, inadequate postal services, ineffective telephone and telecommunications systems, and power shortages. In the real world, effective tax rates seldom equal nominal tax rates. Thus, it is improper to base intercountry comparisons on statutory tax rates alone. Internationally, tax burdens should always be determined by examining *effective* tax rates.

FOREIGN TAX INCENTIVES

Countries eager to accelerate their economic development are keenly aware of the benefits of international business. Many countries offer tax incentives to attract foreign investment. Incentives may include tax-free cash grants applied toward the cost of fixed assets of new industrial undertakings or relief from paying taxes for certain time periods (*tax holidays*). Other forms of temporary tax relief include reduced income tax rates, tax deferrals, and reduction or elimination of various indirect taxes. More industrialized countries offer targeted incentives such as Ireland's reduced corporate tax rate for manufacturing operations (10 percent) through the year 2010.[5] Some countries, particularly those with few natural resources, offer permanent tax inducements. These so-called *tax havens* include

1. the Bahamas, Bermuda, and the Cayman Islands, which have no taxes at all
2. the British Virgin Islands and Gibraltar, which have very low tax rates
3. Hong Kong, Liberia, and Panama, which tax locally generated income but exempt income from foreign sources

Countries that allow special privileges are suitable as tax havens for limited purposes.

HARMFUL TAX COMPETITION

The Organization for Economic Cooperation and Development (OECD) and the European Union (EU) are trying to halt tax competition by certain tax haven countries. The worldwide trend toward lowering corporate income tax rates is a direct result of tax competition. So, is tax competition harmful? Certainly it is beneficial if it makes governments more efficient. On the other hand, it is harmful when it shifts tax revenues away from governments that need those revenues to provide services on which businesses rely. The OECD and the EU are mainly concerned about tax havens that allow businesses to avoid or evade another country's taxes. The main focus of their efforts are the so-called *brass plate* subsidiaries with no real work or employment attached to them. Such subsidiaries lack *substantial activities* and merely funnel financial transactions through the tax haven country to avoid another country's taxes. The OECD and EU es-

---

[4]Gunter Dufey, "Myths About Multinational Corporations," *Michigan Business Review* (May 1974): 15.
[5]By 2003, the Irish corporate tax rate will be 12.5 percent. The 10 percent preferential tax rate for manufacturing companies will be eliminated after 2010.

pecially suspect tax havens that are unwilling to share information with tax authorities elsewhere. Targeted tax havens are being pressured to change their "harmful" practices.[6]

INTERNATIONAL HARMONIZATION

Given the diversity of tax systems around the world, the global harmonization of tax policies would seem to be worthwhile. The European Union is spending much energy in this direction as it works to create a single market. The EU's introduction of a single currency, the euro, highlights the tax disparities among its members. Multinational companies, burdened by disparities of national taxes, also are fueling the pressure for international tax reform.[7]

TAXATION OF FOREIGN SOURCE INCOME AND DOUBLE TAXATION

Every nation claims the right to tax income originating within its borders. However, national philosophies regarding the taxation of foreign source earnings differ, and this is important from a tax planning perspective. A few countries, such as France, Costa Rica, Hong Kong, Panama, South Africa, Switzerland, and Venezuela adopt the *territorial* principle of taxation and exempt from taxation the income of resident corporations generated outside their borders. This reflects the idea that tax burdens of foreign affiliates should equal those of their local competitors. In this view, foreign affiliates of local companies are viewed as foreign companies that happen to be owned by local residents.

Most countries, (e.g., Australia, Brazil, China, the Czech Republic, Germany, Japan, Mexico, the Netherlands, the United Kingdom, and the United States) adopt the *worldwide* principle and tax resident corporations and citizens on income regardless of national boundaries. The underlying idea here is that a foreign subsidiary of a local company is simply a local company that happens to operate abroad.

FOREIGN TAX CREDIT

Under the worldwide principle of taxation, the foreign earnings of a domestic company are subject to the full tax levies of both its host and home countries. To avoid discouraging businesses from expanding abroad, and in keeping with the concept of foreign neutrality, a parent company's domicile (country of residence) can elect to treat foreign taxes paid as a *credit* against the parent's domestic tax liability or as a *deduction* from taxable income. Companies generally choose the credit, as it yields a one-for-one reduction of domestic taxes payable (limited to the amount of income taxes actually paid),[8] whereas a deduction is only worth the product of the foreign tax expense and the domestic marginal tax rate.

---

[6]J. M. Weiner and H. J. Ault, "The OECD's Report on Harmful Tax Competition," *National Tax Journal* (spring 1998): 601–608; F. M. Horner, "The OECD, Tax Competition, and the Future of Tax Reform," OECD Web site: www.oecd.com (January 2000); and "The Mystery of the Vanishing Taxpayer: A Survey of Globalisation and Tax," *The Economist* (January 29, 2000): 16–17.

[7]W. Echikson and D. Woodruff, "One Currency, One Tax?" *Business Week* (July 21, 1997): p. 48.

[8]Indirect levies, such as foreign sales taxes, are generally not creditable.

Foreign tax credits may be calculated as a straightforward credit against income taxes paid on branch or subsidiary earnings and any taxes withheld at the source, such as dividends, interest, and royalties remitted to a domestic investor. The tax credit can also be estimated when the amount of foreign income tax paid is not clearly evident (e.g., when a foreign subsidiary remits a fraction of its foreign source earnings to its domestic parent). Here, reported dividends on the parent company's tax return would be grossed up to include the amount of the tax (deemed paid) plus any applicable foreign withholding taxes. It is as if the domestic parent received a dividend including the tax due the foreign government and then paid the tax.

The allowable foreign indirect tax credit (foreign income tax deemed paid) is determined as follows:

$$\frac{\text{Dividend payout (including any withholding tax)}}{\text{Earnings net of foreign income tax}} \times \text{Creditable foreign taxes}$$

To illustrate how foreign tax credits apply in a variety of situations, assume that a U.S. parent company receives royalties from Country A, foreign branch earnings from Country B, and dividends from subsidiaries in Countries C and D. Withholding taxes on royalty and dividend payments are assumed to be 15 percent in Countries A, C, and D; income tax rates are assumed to be 30 percent in Country B and 40 percent in Country C. Country D assesses a 40 percent indirect sales tax as opposed to a direct tax on earnings within its jurisdiction.[9]

The key variables in this illustration, as shown in Exhibit 12-4, are the organizational form of the foreign activity (e.g., branch versus subsidiary) and relative corporate income and withholding tax rates. In the first column, the royalty payment of $20.00 is subject to a 15 percent withholding tax in the host country. For U.S. tax purposes, the net royalty is grossed up to include the withholding tax, which then forms the base for the U.S. domestic tax of 35 percent. The U.S. tax of $7.00 is offset by the credit for the foreign tax paid to yield a net U.S. tax liability of $4.00.

In the second column of Exhibit 12-4, the foreign branch earnings of the U.S. parent are grossed up to include foreign income taxes paid of $30.00. United States taxes payable on this amount of $35.00 are offset by a foreign tax credit of $30.00, to yield a net U.S. tax payable of $5.00. As with the royalty payment, the effect of the foreign tax credit is to limit the total tax on foreign source income to the higher of the two countries' taxes.[10] In this example, the U.S. tax rate of 35 percent was higher than the foreign tax rate of 30 percent, yielding a total tax on royalty and branch earnings of 35 percent.

Further scrutiny of Exhibit 12-4 is instructive. A comparison of columns 2 and 3 suggests the importance of organizational form on international taxes. A branch operation, viewed as an extension of the parent company, is subject to the full tax rate of the home country. In our example, the foreign branch pays a total tax of $35: $30 of foreign income taxes and $5 of U.S. taxes. Thus, the foreign branch bears the full burden of the U.S. income tax rate. However, it is spared any withholding taxes on earnings distributions to the parent because only a foreign subsidiary can distribute its earnings. On the

---

[9]Note that royalty income and branch/subsidiary earnings are *grossed up*, that is, included in U.S. income, before deducting foreign taxes paid.

[10]However, if the taxpayer is subject to the alternative minimum tax, the credit cannot exceed 90 percent of the alternative minimum tax.

EXHIBIT 12-4 U.S. Taxation of Foreign Source Income

	Royalties from Operation in Country A	Earnings from Branch in Country B	Dividend from Subsidiary in Country C[1]	Dividend from Subsidiary in Country D
Branch/Subsidiary before-tax earnings		100.00	100.00	60.00
Foreign income taxes (30%/40%)		30.00	40.00	-0-
After-tax earnings		70.00	60.00	60.00
Dividend paid (50% of after-tax earnings)			30.00	30.00
Other foreign income	20.00			
Foreign withholding taxes (15%)	3.00		4.50	4.50
Net payment to parent	17.00		25.50	25.50
U.S. income	20.00	100.00[2]	30.00	30.00
Dividend gross-up (30/60 × 40)			20.00	-0-
Taxable income	20.00	100.00	50.00	30.00
U.S. tax (35%)	7.00	35.00	17.50	10.50
Foreign tax credit				
Paid	(3.00)	(30.00)	(4.50)	(4.50)
Deemed paid (30/60 × 40)			(20.00)	-0-
Total	(3.00)	(30.00)	(24.50)	(4.50)
U.S. tax (net)	4.00	5.00	(7.00)[3]	6.00
Foreign taxes	3.00	30.00	24.50	40.00[4]
Total taxes of U.S. taxpayer	7.00	35.00	17.50[5]	46.00

[1] Affiliate owned 10 percent or more.

[2] Grossed up to include foreign taxes actually paid.

[3] Excess foreign tax credits can be carried back 2 years or carried forward 5 years to offset U.S. tax on other foreign source (not U.S. source) income. If unavailable, total taxes = 24.50.

[4] 40% indirect sales tax on 100.00.

[5] Excludes deferred tax on undistributed earnings of affiliate.

other hand, a foreign operation organized as a subsidiary is taxed only on earnings that it remits to the parent company. It can defer taxes on retained income, and thus compete on an equal tax footing with local companies.

Columns 3 and 4 illustrate how a system of worldwide taxation places a subsidiary at a competitive disadvantage when it is located in a country that relies primarily on an indirect tax for revenue. Note that the subsidiary in Country D has a higher total tax burden because the tax credit only relieves direct taxes, not indirect taxes. Similarly, the benefits of tax incentives granted by host governments may also be nullified.

LIMITS TO TAX CREDITS

Home countries can tax foreign source income in many ways. A country may elect to tax income from each separate national source. At the other extreme, all foreign source income from any foreign source may be combined and taxed once.[11] Some countries tax foreign source income on a source-by-source basis with the tax credit for foreign source income limited to the corresponding domestic tax applicable to that income. As illustrated in columns 2 and 3 of Exhibit 12-4, the maximum tax liability will always be the higher of the tax rates in the host or home country. Other countries allow parent companies to pool income from many country sources by income type (e.g., dividends versus interest versus royalties). Excess tax credits from countries with high tax rates (column 3 of Exhibit 12-4) can offset taxes on income received from low tax rate countries (column 2 of Exhibit 12-4).

To prevent foreign tax credits from offsetting taxes on domestic-source income, many countries impose an overall limit on the amount of foreign taxes creditable in any year. The United States, for instance, limits the tax credit to the proportion of the U.S. tax that equals the ratio of the taxpayer's foreign-source taxable income to its worldwide taxable income for the year. Assume that Alpha Company earned $2,000 of foreign-source and $3,000 of U.S.-source taxable income. Its foreign tax credit would be the lesser of the foreign income taxes paid or the foreign tax credit limitation computed as follows:

$$\text{Foreign tax credit limit} = \frac{\text{Foreign source taxable income}}{\text{Worldwide taxable income}} \times \text{U.S. tax before credits}$$
$$= (\$2,000/\$5,000) \times (\$5,000 \times 35\%)$$
$$= \$700$$

Thus, only $700 would be allowed as a tax credit, even if foreign taxes paid exceeded $700. Excess foreign taxes paid can be carried back 2 years and forward 5 years (see footnote 3 in Exhibit 12-4).

A separate foreign tax credit limitation applies to U.S. taxes on the foreign-source taxable income of each of the following types of income (or *baskets*):

- Passive income (e.g., investment-type income)
- Financial services income
- High withholding tax income
- Shipping income
- Dividends from noncontrolled foreign corporations owned 10 percent or more by the taxpayer
- Foreign trade income
- Certain foreign sales corporation (FSC) income
- Other income (general basket)

Foreign-source taxable income is foreign-source gross income less expenses, losses, and deductions allocable to the foreign-source income, plus a ratable share of expenses,

---

[11]David Eiteman, Arthur Stonehill, and Michael Moffett, *Multinational Business Finance*, 7th ed., Reading, MA: Addison-Wesley Publishing Company, 1995, 582.

losses, and deductions that cannot be allocated definitely to any item or class of gross income. The interpretation of this provision is reportedly one of the major areas of dispute between taxpayers and the IRS.[12]

TAX TREATIES

Although foreign tax credits shield foreign-source income from double taxation (to some extent), tax treaties go further. Signatories to such treaties generally agree on how taxes and tax incentives will be imposed, honored, shared, or otherwise eliminated on business income earned in one taxing jurisdiction by citizens of another. Thus, most tax treaties between home and host countries provide that profits earned by a domestic enterprise in the host country shall be subject to its taxes only if the enterprise maintains a permanent establishment there. Tax treaties also affect withholding taxes on dividends, interest, and royalties paid by the enterprise of one country to foreign shareholders. They usually grant reciprocal reductions in withholding taxes on dividends and often entirely exempt royalties and interest from withholding.

FOREIGN EXCHANGE CONSIDERATIONS

The Tax Reform Act of 1986 introduced formal rules regarding the taxation of foreign currency gains or losses in the United States. In keeping with SFAS No. 52 (described in Chapter 6), all tax determinations must be made in the taxpayer's functional currency. The functional currency is assumed to be the U.S. dollar unless the foreign operation is an autonomous unit, or *qualified business unit*. In general, tax rules are similar but not necessarily identical to generally accepted accounting principles described in Chapter 6. Following are examples of tax treatments.[13]

Transaction gains or losses in currencies other than the functional currency are generally accounted for under the two-transactions perspective. Under this approach, any exchange gain or loss recognized when the foreign currency transaction is settled is treated as ordinary income and accounted for separately from the underlying transaction. However, gains or losses on transactions qualifying as hedges of certain foreign currency transactions can be integrated with the underlying transaction. For example, a gain or loss incurred on a forward exchange contract designated as an effective hedge of a foreign currency loan would offset the transaction gain or loss on the underlying obligation.

Foreign exchange gains or losses are generally allocated between U.S. and foreign sources by reference to the residence of the taxpayer on whose books the foreign currency asset or liability is reflected. Thus, for a U.S. corporation, the source of the gain or loss would be the United States.

Taxable profits for foreign branches are initially based on their functional currencies. The functional currency then is converted to U.S. dollars using the weighted average exchange rate for the taxable period. Foreign income taxes paid are translated at the exchange rate in effect when the tax is paid and then added to foreign taxable

---

[12]P. Bodner, "International Taxation," in *International Accounting and Finance Handbook*, 2d ed., F. D. S. Choi, ed., New York: John Wiley & Sons, 1997, 39.11.

[13]P. Bodner, "International Taxation," in *International Accounting and Finance Handbook*, 2d ed., F. D. S. Choi, ed., New York: John Wiley & Sons, 1997, 39.16–39.18.

income or grossed up. The foreign taxes paid are then claimed as a foreign tax credit for U.S. tax purposes.

For foreign subsidiaries, deemed distributions under subpart F regulations (discussed in the next section) are translated using weighted average exchange rates for the foreign corporation's taxable year. Deemed-paid foreign taxes are translated into U.S. dollars using exchange rates in effect on the date the tax was paid.

TAX PLANNING DIMENSIONS

In tax planning, multinational companies have a distinct advantage over purely domestic companies because they have more geographical flexibility in locating their production and distribution systems. This flexibility provides unique opportunities to exploit differences among national tax jurisdictions so as to lower the overall tax burden for the corporation. The shifting of revenues and expenses through intracompany ties also gives MNCs additional opportunities to minimize global taxes paid. In response, national governments are constantly designing legislation to minimize arbitrage opportunities involving different national tax jurisdictions.

We begin our examination of tax planning issues with two caveats:

- Tax considerations should never control business strategy.
- Constant changes in tax laws limit the benefits of long-term tax planning.

ORGANIZATIONAL CONSIDERATIONS

In taxing foreign-source income, many taxing jurisdictions focus on the organizational form of a foreign operation. A branch is usually considered an extension of the parent company. Accordingly, its income is immediately consolidated with that of the parent (an option not available to a subsidiary) and fully taxed in the year earned whether remitted to the parent company or not. Earnings of a foreign subsidiary are not generally taxed until repatriated. Exceptions to this general rule are described in the following section.

If initial operations abroad are forecast to generate losses, it may be tax advantageous to organize initially as a branch. Once foreign operations turn profitable, operating them as subsidiaries may be attractive. For one thing, corporate overhead of the parent company cannot be allocated to a branch, as the branch is viewed as part of the parent. Moreover, if taxes on foreign profits are lower in the host country than in the parent country, profits of a subsidiary are not taxed by the parent country until repatriated (see columns 2 and 3 of Exhibit 12-4). If the subsidiary were organized in a tax haven country that imposes no taxes at all, tax deferral would be even more attractive. National governments know this phenomenon and many have taken steps to minimize corporate abuse of it. One example of this is the U.S. treatment of *Subpart F income*.

CONTROLLED FOREIGN CORPORATIONS AND SUBPART F INCOME

Recall that in the United States, like many other countries adopting the worldwide principle of taxation, income of foreign subsidiaries is not taxable to the parent until it is repatriated as a dividend—the so called *deferral* principle. Tax havens give multinationals an opportunity to avoid repatriation—and home country taxes—by locating transactions and accumulating profits in "brass plate" subsidiaries. These transactions have no real work or employment attached to them. The income earned on these transactions is *passive* rather than *active*.

The United States closed this loophole with the Controlled Foreign Corporation (CFC) and Subpart F Income provisions. A CFC is a corporation in which U.S. shareholders (U.S. corporations, citizens, or residents) directly or indirectly own more than 50 percent of its combined voting power or fair market value. Only shareholders holding more than a 10 percent voting interest are counted in determining the 50 percent requirement. Shareholders of a CFC are taxed on certain undistributed income of the CFC.

Subpart F income includes certain *related party* sales and services income. For example, if a Bahamian subsidiary of a U.S. corporation buys inventory from its U.S. parent and exports the inventory to the European Union, the profits booked by the Bahamian subsidiary are Subpart F income. On the other hand, if the Bahamian subsidiary sells the imported inventory in the Bahamas, income from the local sales is not Subpart F income. Subpart F income also includes passive income such as dividends, interest, and net gains on foreign exchange or commodities transactions; gains from the sale of certain investment property including securities; shipping income derived from the use of any shipping vessel or aircraft in foreign commerce; and certain insurance and oil-related income.

OFFSHORE HOLDING COMPANIES

When provisions of a tax treaty between the parent and host country are not as attractive as provisions of a tax treaty between the parent and a third country, ownership of the foreign investment through a third country holding company affords tax arbitrage opportunities.[14] Advantages of this organizational form include:

1. Securing larger reductions in withholding taxes on dividends
2. Deferring taxes that would otherwise arise in the home country when dividends are distributed to the parent
3. Maximizing foreign tax credits when host countries tax income on a source-by-source basis by converting income from a variety of country sources into income from a single source (i.e., the country of the holding company)
4. Avoiding or deferring capital gains taxes on the sale of foreign subsidiaries

FOREIGN SALES CORPORATIONS

The choice of organizational form for conducting foreign operations is also influenced by country incentives designed to encourage certain types of activities considered beneficial to the national economy. For example, the United States created FSCs to encourage exports and improve a worsening U.S. balance of payments position.[15] Under the FSC provisions, a portion of the earnings from U.S. exports of an FSC is exempt from U.S. income taxes. For example, assume that U.S.-based Parent Corp. contracts with a European buyer for a shipment of inventory. Parent Corp. ships the product directly

---

[14] A. Ogley, *Principles of International Taxation,* London: Interfisc Publishing, 1993, 7–8.
[15] An earlier counterpart of FSCs were DISCs (Domestic International Sales Corporations), which continue to exist but with less attractive features.

from its Oklahoma factory to the European buyer, but also makes a *paper sale* of the goods to its wholly owned affiliate, FSC-Virgin Islands. FSC-Virgin Islands then completes the transaction by another paper sale to the European buyer. The payment is routed through FSC-Virgin Islands, which then forwards it to Parent Corp. Up to 30 percent of the export income of the FSC trade is excluded from U.S. corporate income taxes, and none of the dividend is taxed when FSC-Virgin Islands pays a dividend to Parent Corporation.[16]

In 2000 the World Trade Organization (WTO) ruled that FSCs constitute an illegal subsidy and ordered the United States to repeal its FSC provisions. In response, the United States repealed FSCs, but replaced them with an *extraterritorial income exclusion*. The new law relieves companies from having to set up separate companies to book export sales, but leaves a tax break almost as large as the one under the repealed FSC provisions. As part of its transition procedures, the law also retains the FSC regime until 2002. It is unclear at the time of writing whether this new law will satisfy the WTO.[17]

POSSESSION CORPORATIONS[18]

A U.S. corporation is entitled to a U.S. tax credit equal to the portion of the tax that is attributed to business and investment income from a U.S. possession (i.e., Puerto Rico, American Samoa, Guam, the Commonwealth of the Northern Mariana Islands, and the U.S. Virgin Islands).[19] Thus, if a qualifying U.S. corporation's worldwide income is $10,000,000 and 20 percent of that is derived from a U.S. possession, it is taxed at 35 percent on the $10,000,000 and is entitled to a tax credit of $700,000 ($10,000,000 × 20% × 35%). To qualify for this treatment, the possession corporation must have derived at least 80 percent of its gross income from within its borders during the 3 years immediately preceding the close of its taxable year, and at least 75 percent from the active conduct of a trade or business.

The possession corporation can remit dividends to its U.S. parent with the parent claiming a 100 percent dividends-received deduction regardless of when the income was earned. Accordingly, retained earnings from previous years can be repatriated with virtually no tax on the remittance. As a result of these attractive provisions, many U.S. companies have set up affiliates in Puerto Rico.

---

[16]"How a Foreign Sales Corporation Works," *Business Week* (September 4, 2000): 103. The U.S. company, Boeing, is reportedly the biggest user of the FSC, saving $130 million in U.S. taxes in 1998, 12 percent of its earnings that year. See P. Magnusson, "This Tax Break Could Trigger a Trade War," *Business Week* (September 4, 2000): 103–104.

[17]"FSC Dispute Likely to Resurface, Despite Legislative Fix," *Deloitte & Touche Online,* www.dtonline.com, November 28, 2000; and "U.S. Foreign Sales Corporation Rules Fix," *Accountancy* (January 2001): 116.

[18]For purposes of this section, the term *possession* will also include Puerto Rico.

[19]Payment of income taxes in Guam and the Virgin Islands generally satisfies the U.S. tax liability on such income.

FINANCING DECISIONS

The manner in which foreign operations are financed can also be shaped by tax considerations. Other things equal, the tax deductibility of debt, which increases the after-tax returns on equity, increases the attractiveness of debt financing in high tax countries. Where local currency borrowing is constrained by local governments that mandate minimum levels of equity infusion by the foreign parent, parent company borrowing to finance this capital infusion could achieve similar ends, provided the taxing jurisdiction of the parent allows the interest to be deductible.

In other instances, offshore financing subsidiaries domiciled in a low tax or tax haven country also could be used as a financing vehicle. At one time, U.S. companies wishing to borrow funds in the eurodollar market were constrained from doing so because the U.S. government imposed a withholding tax on interest paid to foreign lenders. To lower the cost of financing, they formed offshore financing subsidiaries in the Netherlands Antilles, a country that has no withholding tax on interest to nonresidents.

As the following diagram illustrates, an offshore financing affiliate also can be used to transfer profits from a high tax country in which either the parent or an affiliate is located to the low tax jurisdiction of the financing affiliate.

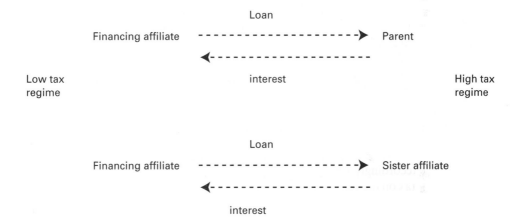

POOLING OF TAX CREDITS

We mentioned earlier that some countries limit tax credits on a source-by-source basis. Pooling income from many sources allows excess credits generated from countries with high tax rates to offset taxes on income received from low tax jurisdictions. Excess tax credits, for example, can be extended to taxes paid in connection with dividends distributed by second- and third-tier foreign corporations in a multinational network. The

United States allows this treatment provided that the U.S. parent's indirect ownership in such corporations exceeds 5 percent. Forward planning in the use of such credits can produce worthwhile tax benefits. Assume for example that a U.S. parent owns 100 percent of the shares of Company X (a first-tier foreign corporation). Company X owns 100 percent of the voting stock of Company Y (a second-tier foreign corporation). During the period, Company Y pays a dividend of 100 to Company X. Company X, in turn, remits a dividend of 100 to the U.S. parent as follows:

	U.S. Parent	Company X (First-tier Foreign Subsidiary)	Company Y (Second-tier Foreign Subsidiary)
1. Taxable earnings	100	200	200
2. Foreign income tax (15%/40%)		30	80
3. After-tax earnings		170	120
4. Dividends		100	100
5. Foreign taxes deemed paid	57 (100/170 × 97)	67 (100/120 × 80)	
6. Total taxes (2. + 5.)		97	

Company X will be deemed to have paid 67 of the foreign income taxes paid by Company Y. In turn, the U.S. parent company will receive an indirect credit against U.S. taxes payable of 57 based on its share of taxes actually paid and deemed to have been paid by Company X (30 + 67). (Refer to our earlier discussion of the calculation of foreign credits.) In this illustration, a dividend from Company Y to Company X increases the allowable U.S. foreign tax credit attendant upon a dividend from Company X to the U.S. parent when the income taxes in Company Y's country of domicile exceed that of Company X's and conversely.

COST ACCOUNTING ALLOCATIONS

Internal cost allocations among group companies is yet another vehicle to shift profits from high tax to low tax countries. The most common of these are allocations of corporate overhead expenses to affiliates in high tax countries. The allocation of such service expenses as human resources, technology, and research and development will maximize tax deductions for affiliates in high tax countries.

LOGISTICS AND TRANSFER PRICING

The locations of production and distribution systems also offer tax advantages. Thus, final sales of goods or services can be channeled through affiliates located in jurisdictions that offer tax shelter or deferral. Alternatively, a manufacturer in a high tax country can obtain components from affiliates located in low tax countries to minimize corporate taxes for the group as a whole. A necessary element of such a strategy is the prices at which goods and services are transferred between group companies. Profits for the corporate system as a whole can be increased by setting high *transfer prices* on components shipped from subsidiaries in relatively low tax countries, and low transfer prices on components shipped from subsidiaries in relatively high tax countries.

Transfer pricing has attracted increasing national attention of late. The dimensions of the problem become obvious when we recognize that transfer pricing (1) is conducted on a relatively larger scale internationally than domestically; (2) is affected by more variables than are found in a strictly domestic setting; (3) varies from company to company, industry to industry, and country to country; and (4) affects social, economic, and political relationships in multinational business entities and, sometimes, entire countries. It could be said that international transfer pricing is the most important international tax issue facing MNCs today.[20]

The impact of intracompany transfer pricing on international tax burdens cannot be examined in a vacuum; transfer prices can distort other parts of a multinational company's planning and control system. Cross-country transactions expose the multinational company to a host of strategic concerns that range from environmental risk to global competitiveness. These concerns often transcend tax considerations.

INTERNATIONAL TRANSFER PRICING: COMPLICATING VARIABLES

Transfer pricing is of relatively recent origin. Transfer pricing in the United States developed along with the decentralization movement that influenced many American businesses during the first half of the twentieth century.[21] Once a company expands internationally, the transfer pricing problem quickly expands. It is estimated that 60 percent of all international trade consists of transfers between related business entities. Cross-country transactions also expose the multinational company to a host of environmental influences that both create and destroy opportunities to increase enterprise profits by transfer pricing. Such variables as taxes, tariffs, competition, inflation rates, currency values, restrictions on fund transfers, political risks, and the interests of joint-venture partners complicate transfer pricing decisions tremendously. On top of these issues, transfer pricing decisions generally involve many trade-offs, often unforeseen and unaccounted for.

TAX CONSIDERATIONS

Unless counteracted by law, corporate profits can be increased by setting transfer prices so as to move profits from subsidiaries domiciled in high tax countries to subsidiaries domiciled in low tax countries.[22] As an example, Blu Jeans-Hong Kong, a wholly owned manufacturing subsidiary of Global Enterprises (USA), ships 500,000 pairs of designer

[20]Ernst & Young, *1999 Global Transfer Survey*, reprinted in R. Feinschreiber, *Transfer Pricing International: A Country-by-Country Guide,* New York: John Wiley & Sons, 2000, 35.4.

[21]Itzhak Sharav, "Transfer Pricing-Diversity of Goals and Practices," *Journal of Accountancy* (April 1974): 56.

[22]For one of the first systematic empirical analyses of the relationship between transfer prices and taxes, see J. T. Bernard and R. J. Weiner, "Multinational Corporations, Transfer Prices and Taxes: Evidence from the U.S. Petroleum Industry," in *Taxation in the Global Economy*, H. Razin and J. Slemrod, eds., Chicago: University of Chicago Press, 1990, 123–54.

blue jeans to a related U.S. sales affiliate, Blu Jeans-USA (also wholly owned by Global Enterprises), for $6 per pair. They cost Blu Jeans-Hong Kong $4.20 per pair to produce. Assuming that each garment wholesales for $12 in the United States, consolidated profits (after eliminating intercompany sales and costs) and taxes would total $1,311,000 and $589,000, respectively. This scenario is shown in Exhibit 12-5.

Given a U.S. corporate tax rate of 35 percent versus 16 percent in Hong Kong, an increase in the transfer price of blue jeans from $6 to $8 per pair would increase total after-tax income as shown in Exhibit 12-6.

In this example, raising the transfer price charged by the Hong Kong affiliate increases taxable income in Hong Kong and reduces taxable income for the U.S. affiliate by $1,000,000. Because the corporate tax rate is 19 percent lower in Hong Kong than in the United States, corporate income taxes for the system as a whole decrease by $190,000 ($1,000,000 × 0.19), with a corresponding increase in consolidated after-tax earnings.

Unfortunately, such actions often create unanticipated problems. Governments often counteract such measures. In the United States, Section 482 of the Internal Revenue Code gives the Secretary of the Treasury authority to prevent a shifting of income or deductions between related taxpayers to exploit differences in national tax rates. This section states in part:

> In any case of two or more organizations, trades, or businesses (whether or not incorporated, whether or not organized in the United States, and whether or not affiliated) owned or controlled directly or indirectly by the same interests, the Secretary or his delegate may distribute, apportion, or allocate gross income, deductions, credits, or allowances between or among such organizations, trades, or businesses, if he determines that such distribution, apportionment, or allocation is necessary in order to prevent evasion of taxes or clearly to reflect the income of any such organizations, trades, or businesses.[23]

Section 482 essentially requires that intracompany transfers be based on an *arm's-length price*. An arm's-length price is one that an unrelated party would receive for the same or similar goods under identical or similar circumstances. Acceptable arm's-length pricing methods include (1) comparable uncontrolled pricing, (2) resale pricing,

EXHIBIT 12-5 Tax Effects of Transfer Pricing			
	Blu Jeans-HK	*Blu Jeans-USA*	*Global Enterprises*
Sales	$3,000,000[1]	$6,000,000	$6,000,000
Cost of sales	2,100,000	3,000,000[a]	2,100,000
Gross margin	$ 900,000	$3,000,000	$3,900,000
Operating expenses	500,000	1,500,000	2,000,000
Pretax income	$ 400,000	$1,500,000	$1,900,000
Income tax (16%/35%)[2]	64,000	525,000	589,000
Net income	$ 336,000	$ 975,000	$1,311,000

[1]Based on a transfer price of $6 per unit.

[2]Income tax rates: Hong Kong 16%, United States 35%.

---

[23]Treasury Regulation, Section 1.482-1.

EXHIBIT 12-6	Tax Effects of a Change in Transfer Prices		
	Blu Jeans-HK	*Blu Jeans-USA*	*Global Enterprises*
Sales	$4,000,000[a]	$6,000,000	$6,000,000
Cost of sales	2,100,000	4,000,000[a]	2,100,000
Gross margin	$1,900,000	$2,000,000	$3,900,000
Operating expenses	500,000	1,500,000	2,000,000
Pretax income	$1,400,000	$ 500,000	$1,900,000
Income tax (16%/35%)	224,000	175,000	399,000
Net income	$1,176,000	$ 325,000	$1,501,000

[a]Based on a transfer price of $8 per unit.

(3) cost-plus pricing, and (4) other pricing methods. Severe penalties are imposed on valuation misstatements in connection with section 482 adjustments.[24]

An emerging consensus among governments views arm's-length pricing as the appropriate standard in calculating profits for tax purposes. However, the rigor applied in monitoring the transfer pricing policies of multinational companies varies worldwide. Multinationals report a low incidence of transfer pricing audits in France, Italy, Japan, Korea, Mexico, Sweden, and Switzerland, but a high incidence in Australia, Canada, Germany, the Netherlands, the United Kingdom, and the United States.[25]

Transfer pricing schemes designed to minimize global taxes often distort the multinational control system. When each subsidiary is evaluated as a separate profit center, such pricing policies can result in misleading performance measures that generally lead to conflicts between subsidiary and enterprise goals. In our earlier example, Blu Jeans-USA would report a lower profit than its sister affiliate in Hong Kong, even though the management of the U.S. subsidiary may be far more productive and efficient than the management in Hong Kong.

TARIFF CONSIDERATIONS

Tariffs on imported goods also affect the transfer pricing policies of multinational companies. For example, a company exporting goods to a subsidiary domiciled in a high-tariff country could reduce the tariff assessment by lowering the prices of merchandise sent there.

In addition to the trade-offs identified, the multinational company must consider additional costs and benefits, both external and internal. Externally, an MNC would have two taxing authorities to contend with: the customs officials of the importing country and the income tax administrators of the exporting and importing countries. A high tariff paid by the importer would result in a lower tax base for income taxes. Internally, the enterprise would have to evaluate the benefits of a lower (higher) income tax in the

---

[24]The penalty is 20 percent (40 percent) of understated income for Section 482 adjustments exceeding $5 million ($20 million) or if the transfer price for services is 200 percent or more (400 percent or more) or property claimed on the tax return is 50 percent or less (25 percent or less) of the amount determined by the IRS to be correct. *Deloitte & Touche Review: Special Supplement* (November 5, 1990): 9–10.
[25]Ernst & Young, *1999 Global Transfer Pricing Survey*, reprinted in R. Feinschrieber, *Transfer Pricing International: A Country-by-Country Guide,* New York: John Wiley & Sons, 2000, 35–23.

importing country against a higher (lower) import duty, as well as the potentially higher (lower) income tax paid by the company in the exporting country.

To illustrate, let us revisit our blue jeans example depicted in Exhibits 12-5 and 12-6. In our revised example (see Exhibit 12-7) assume that the United States imposes an ad valorem import duty of 10 percent. Under a low transfer pricing policy, lower import duties are paid ($300,000 versus $400,000), but the import duty advantage of a low transfer price is offset by the increased income taxes that must be paid ($484,000 versus $259,000). Considering both import duties and income taxes, Global Enterprises is $125,000 better off under a high transfer pricing policy.

COMPETITIVE FACTORS

To facilitate the establishment of a foreign subsidiary abroad, a parent company could supply the subsidiary with inputs invoiced at very low prices. These price subsidies could be removed gradually as the foreign affiliate strengthens its position in the foreign market. Similarly, lower transfer prices could be used to shield an existing operation from the effects of increased foreign competition in the local market or another market; in other words, profits earned in one country could subsidize the penetration of another market.[26] Indirect competitive effects are also possible. To improve a foreign subsidiary's access to local capital markets, setting low transfer prices on its inputs and high

EXHIBIT 12-7 Trade-Offs When Tariffs and Income Taxes Are Considered

	Blu Jeans-HK	*Blu Jeans-USA*	*Global Enterprises*
Low Transfer Price			
Sales	$3,000,000	$6,000,000	$6,000,000
Cost of sales	2,100,000	3,000,000	2,100,000
Import duty at 10%	—	300,000	300,000
Gross margin	900,000	$2,700,000	$3,600,000
Operating expenses	500,000	1,500,000	2,000,000
Pretax income	400,000	1,200,000	1,600,000
Income tax (16%/35%)	64,000	420,000	484,000
Net income	$ 336,000	$ 780,000	$1,116,000
High Transfer Price			
Sales	$4,000,000	$6,000,000	$6,000,000
Cost of sales	2,100,000	4,000,000	2,100,000
Import duty at 10%	—	400,000	400,000
Gross margin	1,900,000	$1,600,000	$3,500,000
Operating expenses	500,000	1,500,000	2,000,000
Pretax income	1,400,000	100,000	1,500,000
Income tax (16%/35%)	224,000	35,000	259,000
Net income	$1,176,000	$ 65,000	$1,241,000

[26]G. Hamel and C. Prahalad, "Do You Really Have A Global Strategy?" *Harvard Business Review* (July/ August 1985): 139–148.

transfer prices on its outputs could bolster its reported earnings and financial position. Sometimes, transfer prices could be used to weaken a subsidiary's competitors.

Such competitive considerations would have to be balanced against many offsetting disadvantages. Transfer prices for competitive reasons may invite antitrust actions by host governments or retaliatory actions by local competitors. Internally, pricing subsidies do little to instill a competitive mode of thinking in the minds of the managers whose companies gain from the subsidy. What begins as a temporary aid easily may become a permanent management crutch.

ENVIRONMENTAL RISKS

Whereas competitive considerations abroad might warrant charging low transfer prices to foreign subsidiaries, the risks of severe price inflation might call for the opposite. Inflation erodes the purchasing power of a firm's cash. High transfer prices on goods or services provided to a subsidiary facing high inflation can remove as much cash from the subsidiary as possible.

Balance of payment problems (often related to inflation) may prompt foreign governments to devalue their currencies, impose foreign exchange controls, and/or impose restrictions on the repatriation of profits from foreign-owned companies. Potential losses from exposures to currency devaluations may be avoided by shifting funds to the parent company (or related affiliates) through inflated transfer prices. With exchange controls (e.g., a government restricts the amount of foreign exchange available for importing a particular good), reduced transfer prices on the imported good would allow the affiliate impacted by the controls to acquire more of the desired import. To circumvent repatriation restrictions, high transfer prices allow some cash to be returned to the parent company each time it sells a product or service to the foreign subsidiary.

PERFORMANCE EVALUATION CONSIDERATIONS

Transfer pricing policies also are affected by their impact on managerial behavior, and are often a major determinant of corporate performance.[27] For example, if a foreign affiliate's mission is to furnish supplies for the rest of the corporate system, appropriate transfer prices enable corporate management to provide the affiliate with an earnings stream that can be used in performance comparisons. However, it is difficult for decentralized firms to set intracompany transfer prices that both (1) motivate managers to make decisions that maximize their unit's profits and are congruent with the goals of the company as whole, and (2) provide an equitable basis for judging the performance of managers and units of the firm. If subsidiaries are free to negotiate transfer prices, their managers may not be able to reconcile conflicts between what may be best for the subsidiary and what is best for the firm as a whole. However, the effect on subsidiary management may be even worse if corporate headquarters dictates transfer prices and sourcing alternatives that are seen as arbitrary or unreasonable. Moreover, the more decisions that are made by corporate headquarters, the less advantageous are decentralized profit centers, because local managers lose their incentive to act for the benefit of their local operations.

---

[27]For a further discussion of this point, see W. M. Abdallah, "How to Motivate and Evaluate Managers with International Transfer Pricing Systems," *Management International Review* (first quarter 1989): 65–71.

ACCOUNTING CONTRIBUTIONS

Management accountants can play a significant role in quantifying the trade-offs in transfer pricing strategy. The challenge is to keep a global perspective when mapping out the benefits and costs associated with a transfer pricing decision. The effects of the decision on the corporate system as a whole must come first.

Quantifying the numerous trade-offs is difficult because environmental influences must be considered as a group, not individually. Consider, for example, the difficulties in measuring the trade-offs surrounding transfer pricing policies for a subsidiary located in a country with high income taxes, high import tariffs, price controls, a thin capital market, chronic high inflation, foreign exchange controls, and an unstable government. As we have seen, a high transfer price on goods or services provided to the subsidiary would lower the subsidiary's income taxes and remove excess cash to the parent company. However, a high transfer price might also result in higher import duties, impair the subsidiary's competitive position (due to higher input prices), worsen the rate of inflation, raise the subsidiary's capital costs, and even cause retaliation by the host government to protect its balance of payments position. To further complicate matters, all of these variables are changing constantly. One thing is clear: Superficial calculations of the effects of transfer pricing policy on individual units within a multinational system are not acceptable.

TRANSFER PRICING METHODOLOGY

In a world of perfectly competitive markets, it would not be much of a problem to set prices for intracompany resource and service transfers. Transfer prices could be based on either incremental cost or market prices. Neither system would necessarily conflict with the other. Unfortunately, there are seldom external competitive markets for products transferred between related entities. Environmental influences on transfer prices also raise questions of pricing methodology. How are transfer prices established? Are standard market prices generally better than those based on some measure of cost, or are negotiated prices the only feasible alternative? Do multinational enterprises the world over use similar transfer pricing methodologies or do cultural factors influence them? Can a single transfer pricing methodology serve all purposes equally well? The following sections shed some light on these questions.

MARKET VERSUS COST VERSUS . . . ?

The use of market-oriented transfer prices offers several advantages. Market prices show the opportunity cost to the transferring entity of not selling on the external market, and their use will encourage the efficient use of the firm's scarce resources. Their use is also said to be consistent with a decentralized profit center orientation. Market prices help differentiate profitable from unprofitable operations, and are easier to defend to taxing authorities as arm's-length prices.

The advantages of market-based transfer prices must be weighed against several shortcomings. One problem is that there is often no intermediate market for the product or service in question. Even if such a market were available, it seldom would be perfectly competitive or internationally comparable. Finally, market prices do not give a firm much room to adjust prices for competitive or strategic purposes.

Cost-based transfer pricing systems overcome many of these limitations. Moreover, they are (1) simple to use, (2) based on readily available data, (3) easy to justify to tax authorities, and (4) easily routinized, thus helping to avoid internal frictions that often accompany more arbitrary systems.

Of course, cost-based transfer pricing systems are not flawless either. For example, the sale of goods or services at actual cost may provide little incentive for sellers to control their costs. Production inefficiencies may simply be passed on to the buyer at inflated prices. Cost-based systems overemphasize historical costs, which ignore competitive demand and supply relationships, and do not allocate costs to particular products or services in a satisfactory manner. The problem of cost determination is compounded internationally, as cost accounting concepts vary from country to country.

ARM'S-LENGTH PRINCIPLE

The typical multinational is an integrated operation: Its subsidiaries are under common control and share common resources and goals. The need to declare taxable income in different countries means that multinationals must allocate revenues and expenses among subsidiaries and set transfer prices for intrafirm transactions.

Tax authorities around the world have developed complicated transfer price and income allocation regulations as a part of their national income tax systems. Most are based on the *arm's-length principle*, which prices intrafirm transfers as if they took place between unrelated parties in competitive markets.[28] The OECD identifies several broad methods of ascertaining an arm's-length price. Resembling those specified by Section 482 of the U.S. Internal Revenue Code, they are (1) the comparable uncontrolled price method, (2) the resale price method, (3) the cost-plus method, (4) the comparable profit method, (5) the profit split method, (6) the comparable uncontrolled transaction method, and (7) other methods.

COMPARABLE UNCONTROLLED PRICE METHOD

Under this approach, transfer prices are set by reference to prices used in comparable transactions between independent companies or between the corporation and an unrelated third party. Although this method is easiest to apply in theory, it is not so in practice. Differences in quality, quantity, trademarks, brand names, and the economic level of the market often make direct comparisons very difficult.

RESALE PRICE METHOD

This method calculates an arm's-length price by starting with the price at which the item in question can be sold to an independent purchaser. An appropriate margin to cover expenses and a normal profit is then deducted from this price to derive the intracompany transfer price. Deciding on an appropriate margin is especially difficult when the purchasing affiliate adds substantial value to the transferred item.

---

[28]Of course, the result is only hypothetical because the parties are related and the markets normally are not competitive. See L. Eden, M. T. Dacin, and W. P. Wan, "Standards Across Borders: Cross-border Diffusion of the Arms-Length Standard in North America," *Accounting, Organizations and Society* (January 2001): 1–23.

To illustrate this pricing method, assume that a company wishes to price a product sold by one of its operating units to one of its foreign distribution units. Income statement accounts and other related facts for the distribution unit are as follows:

1. Net sales (by the distribution unit) of 100,000 units at $300 per unit	$30,000,000
2. Direct manufacturing expenses (DME)	6,000,000
3. DME as a percentage of net sales	20.0%
4. Other expenses (OE)	3,900,000
5. OE as a percentage of net sales	13.0%
6. Imputed financing cost (IFC)[1]	600,000
7. IFC as a percentage of net sales	2.0%
8. Freight and insurance to import (FI)	$1.50/unit
9. Packaging costs (PC)	$2.00/unit
10. Customs duties on F & P (CD)	5.0%
11. Net sales price (NSP) by the distribution unit	$300/unit

[1]Imputed costs to finance the distribution unit are calculated as: Average net working capital × short-term interest rate in local currency ($= \$7,500,000 \times 8\% = \$600,000$). This is designed to avoid overcompensating the distribution unit for having a high interest expense due to a low capitalization or overcharging it for having low interest expenses due to a high capitalization.

The objective is to calculate a transfer price between the two units such that the distribution unit covers all costs and earns a normal profit. As we shall see, the resale price method is a *work backwards* approach. Assuming that the company requires a 5 percent additional margin to cover business risk and provide an appropriate profit, the total product margin would be computed as follows:

1. Direct manufacturing expenses	20.0%
2. Other expenses	13.0%
3. Imputed financing cost	2.0%
4. Additional margin for risk and profit (AM)	5.0%
5. Total margin (TM)	40.0%

Here, the distribution unit must pay freight and insurance costs to import the product and customs duties in addition to the transfer price. (Thus, the distribution unit's cost to import differs from the transfer price.) Given the foregoing information, the transfer price (TP) per unit of product delivered to the distribution unit would be:

$$TP = \{[NSP \times (100\% - TM) - PC]/(100\% + CD)\} - FI$$
$$TP = \{[300 \times (100\% - 40\%) - \$2]/(100\% + 5\%)\} - \$1.50$$
$$TP = \$168.02$$

The foregoing calculation adjusts the net sales price for the total margin, packaging costs, freight and insurance costs, and customs duties to arrive at the transfer price. Specifically, the 1.05 factor reduces the $178 cost-to-import price to a before-duties figure of $169.52. Other dutiable costs are subtracted from this figure to leave a transfer price of $168.02. The cost to import equals (1) the transfer price plus (2) freight and insurance, with duties applied to both. As a check on this result:

	Unit Cost
Transfer price	$168.02
+ Freight & insurance	1.50
Subtotal	169.52
Duties (at 5%)	8.48
Cost to import	$178.00

To work backwards to the transfer price:

Net sales price	$300.00
Margin to cover expenses and normal profit (40%)	−120.00
Packaging	−2.00
Freight & insurance	−1.50
Customs duties	−8.48
Transfer price	$168.02

COST-PLUS PRICING METHOD

Cost-plus pricing is a *work forward* approach in which a markup is added to the transferring affiliate's cost in local currency. The markup typically includes (1) the imputed financing costs related to export inventories, receivables, and assets employed and (2) a percentage of cost covering manufacturing, distribution, warehousing, internal shipping, and other costs related to export operations. An adjustment is often made to reflect any government subsidies that are designed to make manufacturing costs competitive in the international marketplace.

This pricing method is especially useful when semifinished goods are transferred between foreign affiliates, or where one entity is a subcontractor for another. A major measurement issue involves calculating the cost of the transferred item and ascertaining an appropriate markup.

To see how a transfer price is derived employing the cost-plus method, assume that a manufacturing unit in Portugal wishes to price an intracompany transfer based on the following information:

1. Total manufacturing cost per unit (1,000 units)	€200
2. Average net operating assets employed in manufacturing the item	€40,000
3. Average short-term interest rate in Portugal	8.0%
4. Financing cost as a percentage of total manufacturing cost (8% × €40,000/€200,000)	1.6%
5. Government subsidy based on final transfer price	6.0%
6. Credit terms to affiliates	90 days
7. Required profit and other expenses margin	8.0%

The cost-plus transfer price is that which enables the transferring unit to earn a given percentage return above its production costs. That percentage return (the *plus* in cost-plus) is determined in the following manner:

1. Required margin before adjustments:		
Profit and other expenses	8.0%	
Financing cost	1.6%	9.60%
2. Government subsidy adjustment		6.00%
3. Adjusted margin with cash terms [(1.096/1.06) − 1]		3.39%
4. Adjusted margin with 90-day terms		5.46%[1]

[1]This figure is equal to the adjusted margin-cash terms multiplied by 1 plus the short-term interest rate for 90 days, or {1 .0339 × [1 + (0.08 × 90/360)]} − 1. It allows the transferring unit to earn imputed interest for carrying a receivable for 90 days.

This required margin of 5.46 percent, when multiplied by the transferred item's total manufacturing cost, yields the intracompany transfer price to be billed for that item. In this example, the transfer price is €210.92, the result of 1.0546 × €200. This transfer price causes the company to earn its required margin of 9.6 percent plus an 8 percent (annualized compounded) return for carrying the affiliate's receivable for 90 days. As a check on this result:

Compounded return	=	{1.096 × [1 + (.08 × 90/360)]} − 1
	=	11.79%
Transfer price	=	€210.92
Cost		200.00
Margin		€ 10.92
Subsidy (6% × 210.92)		12.66
Total return		€ 23.58
Return as a % of cost	=	(€ 23.58)/(€200.00) = 11.79%

COMPARABLE PROFITS METHOD[29]

This method supports the general notion that similarly situated taxpayers should earn similar returns over reasonable time periods. Thus, intracompany profits on transactions between related parties should be comparable to profits on transactions between unrelated parties who engage in similar business activities under similar circumstances. *Return on capital employed* (ROCE) is a primary profit level indicator. Under this approach, the operating income to average capital employed ratio of a benchmark entity is compared with the ROCE of the entity in question.

Application of this method normally will require adjustments for any differences between comparables. Factors requiring such adjustments include differing sales conditions, cost of capital differences, foreign exchange and other risks, and differences in accounting measurement practices.

PROFIT SPLIT METHODS

These methods are used when product or market benchmarks are not available. Essentially they involve dividing profits generated in a related party transaction between the affiliated companies in an arm's-length fashion. One variant of this approach, the *comparables profit split method*, divides the profit generated by a related party transaction using a percentage allocation of the combined profits of uncontrolled companies with similar types of transactions and activities.

A more sophisticated method, the *residual profit split method*, employs a two-step approach. First, routine functions performed by affiliated entities—the parent and its subsidiary—are priced at each stage of the production process using relevant benchmarks. Any difference between total profits earned by the combined enterprise and those attributable to the routine functions is considered *residual profits*, essentially profits from nonroutine functions. This residual, which resembles a goodwill intangible, then is split on the basis of the relative value of each affiliated party's contribution to the intangible. This value can be determined using fair market value referents or the capitalized cost of developing the intangibles.

COMPARABLE UNCONTROLLED TRANSACTION METHOD

This method applies to transfers of intangible assets. It identifies a benchmark royalty rate by referencing uncontrolled transactions in which the same or similar intangibles are transferred. Like the comparable uncontrolled price method, this method relies on market comparables.

OTHER PRICING METHODS

As existing pricing methodologies do not always reflect underlying circumstances, additional methodologies are now allowed if they result in a more accurate measure of an arm's-length price. To quote the OECD:

> It has to be recognized that an arm's-length price will in many cases not be precisely ascertainable and that in such circumstances it will be necessary to

---

[29]For a more detailed treatment of the following methods, see Walter O'Connor, "International Transfer Pricing," in *International Accounting and Finance Handbook*, F. D. S. Choi. Ed., New York: John Wiley & Sons, Inc., 38.14–38.20.

seek a reasonable approximation to it. Frequently, it may be useful to take account of more than one method of reaching a satisfactory approximation to an arm's-length price in the light of the evidence available.[30]

Section 482 of the U.S. Internal Revenue Code specifies a *best methods rule* requiring the taxpayer to select the best transfer pricing method based on the facts and circumstances of the case. Argentina also has a best methods rule. Other countries, such as Mexico, state no preference for transfer pricing methods. However, most countries with transfer pricing legislation prefer transaction-based methods (comparable uncontrolled price, resale price, cost-plus, and comparable uncontrolled transaction methods) to profit-based methods (comparable profit and profit split methods). These countries include Belgium, China, the Czech Republic, France, Germany, the Netherlands, South Africa, and the United Kingdom. OECD guidelines specify that a *reasonable* method should be chosen, and also prefer transaction-based methods to profit-based methods.[31]

It is not always possible to calculate a precise and accurate arm's-length price. Hence, documentation of any transfer price employed and its underlying rationale is important. This is true regardless of the tax jurisdiction and the transfer pricing methods it may prefer. The following steps are helpful in setting transfer prices:

- Analyze the risks assumed, functions performed by the affiliated companies, and the economic and legal determinants that affect pricing.
- Identify and analyze benchmark companies and transactions. Document reasons for any adjustments made.
- Compare the financial results of the comparable companies to that of the taxpayer.
- If comparable transactions are available, note their similarities and differences with the taxpayer's transactions.
- Document why the chosen pricing method is the most reasonable and why the other methods are not.
- Update the information prior to filing the tax return.[32]

ADVANCE PRICING AGREEMENTS

A major concern is the acceptability of transfer prices to governments. Aware that multinational enterprises use transfer prices to shift income, and worried about their economic and social consequences, governments are increasing their scrutiny of multinational operations. At the same time, the ambiguities and complexities of transfer pricing regulations make it likely that intracompany transactions will be the target of tax audits. Surveys of multinationals consistently show that they regard transfer pricing as

---

[30]Organization for Economic Cooperation and Development, *Transfer Pricing and Multinational Enterprises*, Paris: OECD, 1979, p. 33.

[31]W. G. Dodge, A. M. Shapiro, W. McFarland, and B. J. Mantegani, "Strategy Matrix for Global Transfer Pricing: Comparison of Methods, Documentation, Penalties, and Other Issues," reprinted in R. Feinschreiber, *Transfer Pricing International: A Country-by-Country Guide,* New York: John Wiley & Sons, 2000, Table 36.4.

[32]Alan Shapiro and Arnold McClellan, "New Transfer Pricing: New Rules Give Guidance on How to Avoid Penalties," *Deloitte Touche Tohmatsu International World Tax News* (March 1994): 2.

their most important international tax issue and that facing a transfer pricing audit somewhere in the world is a near certainty.[33]

Advance pricing agreements (APAs) are a mechanism whereby a multinational and a taxing authority voluntarily negotiate an agreed transfer pricing methodology that is binding on both parties. These agreements reduce or eliminate the risk of a transfer pricing audit, saving time and money for both the multinational and the taxing authority. Introduced in the United States in 1991, APAs have been widely adopted by other countries.[34] The agreements are binding for a fixed period of time, for example, 3 years in the United States.

TRANSFER PRICING PRACTICES

Multinational corporations obviously vary along many dimensions such as size, industry, nationality, organizational structure, degree of international involvement, technology, products or services, and competitive conditions. Therefore, it is hardly surprising that a variety of transfer pricing methods are found in practice.[35] Most of the empirical evidence on transfer pricing practices is based on surveys. Because corporate pricing policies are often considered proprietary, these surveys should be interpreted cautiously. Given the dramatic effect of globalization on business operations since the 1990s, we are also cautious about whether transfer pricing surveys before the 1990s are still valid today.[36]

What factors influence the choice of transfer pricing methods? Are transfer pricing effects considered in the planning process? A recent study asked financial executives of U.S. multinationals to identify the three most important objectives of international transfer pricing.[37] Exhibit 12-8 summarizes the findings. Managing the tax burden dominates the other objectives, but operational uses of transfer pricing such as maintaining the company's competitive position and promoting equitable performance evaluation are also important.

---

[33]Ernst & Young, "1999 Global Transfer Pricing Survey," reprinted in R. Feinschreiber, *Transfer Pricing International: A Country-by-Country Guide,* New York: John Wiley & Sons, 2000, 35.6–35.7.

[34]APAs go by different names. For example, they are called an advance pricing arrangement in the United Kingdom and preconfirmation system in Japan. For more on APAs around the world, see S. C. Borkowski, "Transfer Pricing Advance Pricing Agreements: Current Status by Country," *International Tax Journal* (spring 2000): 1–16.

[35]Cost-based transfer pricing methods appear to be used more often than market-based methods. It is also likely that a multinational uses more than one method, depending on the circumstances. See K. S. Cravens, "Examining the Role of Transfer Pricing as a Strategy for Multinational Firms," *International Business Review* 6, no. 2 (1997): 137–138.

[36]For example, one widely cited study [J. S. Arpan, International Intracorporate Pricing: Non-American Systems and Views," *Journal of International Business Studies* (spring 1972): 1–18] found that U.S., French, British, and Japanese managers prefer cost-oriented transfer pricing methods, whereas Canadian, Italian, and Scandinavian managers prefer market-oriented methods; no particular preference was found for Belgian, Dutch, German, or Swiss managers. Although we believe that nationality continues to influence the choice of transfer pricing methods, we question whether this particular conclusion is still valid.

[37]K. S. Cravens, "Examining the Role of Transfer Pricing as a Strategy of Multinational Firms," *International Business Review* 6, no. 2 (1997): 127–145.

EXHIBIT 12-8 Most Important Objectives of International Transfer Pricing (Ranked Using a Weighted Average)	
Manage the tax burden and related objectives	28%
Maintain competitive position	17%
Promote equitable performance evaluation	11%
Promote goal congruence	10%
Motivate employees	10%
Manage tariffs and related objectives	9%
Comply with tax regulations	7%
Mitigate cash transfer restrictions	4%
Manage foreign exchange	2%
Address social and political concerns	1%
Manage inflation	1%
Total	100%

Source: Reprinted from *International Journal of Accounting,* Vol. 6, K. S. Cravens, "Examining the Role of Transfer Pricing as a Strategy of Multinational Firms," p. 136, copyright 1997 with permission of Elsevier Science.

Another study asked a similar question to managers of multinationals from 19 nations.[38] Exhibit 12-9 summarizes these findings. Here, operational issues have a slightly higher priority than tax issues. The study also finds that the operational and tax effects of transfer pricing are most often considered only after the strategic decisions have been made. Only 30 percent of the multinationals indicated that transfer pricing is part of the strategic planning process. Twenty-nine percent consider transfer pricing after strategic decisions have been made, and 37 percent view transfer pricing merely as a tax compliance issue. Four percent do not consider transfer pricing at all in strategic decisions.

EXHIBIT 12-9 Factors Shaping Transfer Pricing				
	Main Priority (%)	*Important but Not a Main Priority (%)*	*Not Very Important (%)*	*Not Important at All (%)*
Maximizing operating performance	40	33	19	8
Documentation in preparation for audit	35	38	20	7
Financial efficiencies	25	45	22	8
Optimizing tax arrangements	23	45	25	7
Performance incentives	12	27	39	22

Source: R. Feinschrelber, *Transfer Pricing International: A Country by Country Comparison* (New York: John Wiley & Sons, © 2000) p. 35. This material is used by permission of John Wiley & Sons, Inc.

---

[38]Ernst & Young, "1999 Global Transfer Pricing Survey," reprinted in R. Feinschrieber, *Transfer Pricing International: A Country-by-Country Comparison,* New York: John Wiley & Sons, 2000, 35-1–35-49.

These results indicate that transfer pricing can play a more important role in the multi-national planning process. The study observes:

> Clearly, the "tax cart" should not come before the "operational horse," but given the levels of taxation around the world, and the profound impact that transfer pricing may have on operations, it is distressing to note the number of companies that do not consider this cost of doing business earlier in the strategic decision-making process. . . . Transfer pricing is a reactive compliance exercise instead of a proactive mechanism to manage downward the organization's worldwide effective tax rate.[39]

THE FUTURE

Technology and the global economy are challenging many of the principles on which international taxation is based. One of these principles is that every nation has the right to decide for itself how much tax to collect from the people and businesses within its borders. Tax laws evolved in a world where transactions take place in clearly identifiable locations, but this situation is increasingly less true. Electronic commerce over the Internet ignores borders and physical location. Commercial events now take place in cyberspace—on a server anywhere in the world.

The ability to collect taxes depends on knowing who should pay, but increasingly sophisticated encryption techniques make it harder to identify taxpayers. Anonymous electronic money is a reality. The Internet also makes it easy for multinationals to shift their activities to low tax countries that may be a long way from customers but as close as a mouse click to access. It is becoming more difficult to monitor and tax international transactions.

Governments around the world require transfer pricing methods based on the arm's-length principle. That is, a multinational's businesses in different countries are taxed as if they were independent firms operating at arm's-length from each other. The complex calculation of arm's-length prices is less relevant today for global companies because fewer of them operate this way.

What do these developments imply for international taxation? Are national taxes compatible with a global economy? We already see greater cooperation and information sharing by tax authorities around the world. This trend will continue. At the same time, many experts foresee greater tax competition. The Internet makes it easier to take advantage of tax havens. Some individuals advocate a *unitary tax* as an alternative to using transfer prices to determine taxable income. Under this approach, a multinational's total profits are allocated to individual countries based on a formula that reflects the company's relative economic presence in that country. Each country would then tax its piece of the profit at whatever rate it sees fit. Clearly, taxation in the future faces many changes and challenges.[40]

---

[39]Ernst & Young, "1999 Global Transfer Pricing Survey," reprinted in R. Feinschrieber, *Transfer Pricing International: A Country-by-Country Comparison,* New York: John Wiley & Sons, 2000, 35-11–35-12.

[40]See "The Mystery of the Vanishing Taxpayer: A Survey of Globalisation and Tax," *The Economist* (January 29, 2000): 1–22; and S. James, "The Future International Tax Environment," *International Tax Journal* (winter 1999): 1–9.

Selected References

Altshuler, Rosanne, and T. Scott Newlon, "The Effects of U.S. Tax Policy on the Income Repatriation Patterns of U.S. Multinational Corporations," in *Studies in International Taxation,* A. Giovannini, R. G. Hubbard, and J. Slemrod, eds., Chicago: University of Chicago Press, 1993.

Aliber, R. Z., "Transfer Pricing: A Taxonomy," in *Multinationals and Transfer Pricing, A. M.* Rugman and L. Eden, eds., New York: St. Martin's Press, 1985.

Bodner, P., "International Taxation," in *International Accounting and Finance Handbook,* 2d ed., F. D. S. Choi, ed., New York: John Wiley & Sons, Inc., 1997.

Borkowski, S., "Transfer Pricing Advance Pricing Agreements: Current Status by Country," *International Tax Journal* (spring 2000): 1–16.

Cravens, K. S., "Examining the Role of Transfer Pricing as a Strategy for Multinational Firms," *International Business Review* 6, no. 2 (1997): 127–145.

Eden, L., M. T. Dacin, and W. P. Wan, "Standards Across Borders: Crossborder Diffusion of the Arm's Length Standard in North America." *Accounting, Organizations and Society* (January 2001): 1–23.

Feinschreiber, R., *Transfer Pricing International: A Country-by-Country Guide,* New York: John Wiley & Sons, 2000.

Hines, J. R., "Lessons from Behavioral Responses to International Taxation," *National Tax Journal* (June 1999): 305–322.

James, S., "The Future International Tax Environment." *International Tax Journal* (winter 1999): 1–9.

Kramer, J. L., and S. S. Kramer, "Foreign Tax Credit Planning," *International Tax Journal* (spring 1992): 82–88.

"The Mystery of the Vanishing Taxpayer: A Survey of Globalisation and Tax," *The Economist* (January 29, 2000): 1–22.

O'Connor, W., "International Transfer Pricing," in *International Accounting and Finance Handbook,* 2d ed., F. D. S. Choi, ed., New York: John Wiley & Sons, Inc., 1997.

Ogley, A., *Principles of International Taxation,* London: Interfisc Publishing, 1993.

Ogum, G., and K. A. Kim, "New U.S. International Pricing Regulations," *Multinational Business Review* (spring 1995): 8–13.

Organization for Economic Cooperation and Development, *Taxing International Business: Emerging Trends in APEC and OECD Economies,* Paris: OECD, 1997.

Razin, A., and J. Slemrod, eds., *Taxation in the Global Economy,* Chicago: University of Chicago Press, 1990.

Tang, R. Y. W., *Intrafirm Trade and Global Transfer Pricing Regulation,* Westport, CT: Quorum Books, 1997.

Weiner, J. M., and H. J. Ault, "The OECD's Report on Harmful Tax Competition," *National Tax Journal* (spring 1998): 601–608.

Weisfelder, Christine J., "Home Country Taxation and the Theory of International Production," *Journal of International Financial Management and Accounting* (October 1994): 193–213.

Yancey, W. F., and K. S. Cravens, "A Framework for International Tax Planning for Managers," *Journal of International Accounting Auditing & Taxation* 7, no. 2 (1998): 251–272.

Discussion Questions

1. What is the meaning of tax *neutrality*? Are taxes neutral with regard to business decisions? Is this good or bad?
2. What philosophies and types of taxes exist worldwide?

3. What role do *tax credits* play in international taxation? What considerations might cause tax credits to not achieve their intended results?

4. Briefly describe the major advantages and disadvantages of the
   a. classical,
   b. split-rate, and
   c. imputation tax administration systems

   from the perspective of a multinational corporate taxpayer.

5. Consider the statement: "National differences in statutory tax rates are the most obvious and yet least significant determinants of a company's effective tax burden." Do you agree? Explain.

6. Carried to its logical extreme, tax planning implies a conscientious policy of tax minimization. This mode of thinking raises an ethical question for international tax executives. Deliberate tax evasion is commonplace in many parts of the world. In Italy, for example, tax legislation is often honored only in the breach. Even when tax laws are enforced, actual tax settlements are usually subject to negotiation between the individual taxpayer and the tax collector. Should multinational corporations operating in such environments adopt a policy of "when in Rome do as the Romans do?" or should they adhere to the taxation norms of their domestic environments?

7. Compare and contrast the role of transfer pricing in national versus international operations.

8. Multinational transfer pricing causes serious concern among various corporate stakeholders. Identify potential concerns from the viewpoint of
   a. minority owners of a foreign affiliate,
   b. foreign taxing authorities,
   c. home country taxing authorities,
   d. foreign subsidiary managers, and
   e. headquarters managers.

9. The pricing of intercompany transfers is complicated by many economic, environmental, and organizational considerations. Identify six major considerations described in the chapter and briefly explain how they affect transfer pricing policy.

10. Identify the major bases for pricing intercompany transfers. Comment briefly on their relative merits. Which measurement method is best from the viewpoint of the multinational executive?

11. Explain the *arm's length price*. Is the United States Internal Revenue Service alone in mandating such pricing of intracompany transfers? Would the concept of an arm's-length price resolve the measurement issue in pricing intracompany transfers?

12. What is an advance pricing agreement (APA)? What are the advantages and disadvantages of entering into an APA?

Exercises

1. You are an investment analyst domiciled in Country Z doing a cross-country comparison of the financial performance of two manufacturing companies in the pharmaceuticals industry. Both companies, X and Y (located in Countries X and Y), have similar expected sales of $400 million. Country X has a corporate income

tax. Country Y has no income tax, but relies on indirect taxes. Selected data for companies X and Y are as follows:

	Company X	Company Y
Pretax income	$100 million	$60 million
Return on sales	15.0%	15.0%

Required: Determine which company promises to have the better financial performance. What tax considerations might affect your conclusions?

2. Using the facts in exercise 1, assume that Companies X and Y have identical dividend payout ratios of 50 percent. Country Z, your country of domicile, has an income tax rate of 35%. Country Z has a tax treaty with countries X and Y so that no withholding taxes are assessed on dividends received. Furthermore, Country Z grants a tax credit for any direct foreign taxes paid.

Required: Show which company now promises the better after-tax investment performance, and why.

3. A Chinese manufacturing subsidiary produces items sold in Australia. The items cost the equivalent of $3.50 to produce and are sold to customers for $4.75. A Cayman Islands subsidiary buys the items from the Chinese subsidiary for $3.50 and sells them to the Australian parent for $4.75.

Required: Calculate the total amount of income taxes paid on these transactions. What are the implications for the company and the taxing authorities involved?

4. Kowloon Trading Company, a wholly owned subsidiary incorporated in Hong Kong, imports macadamia nuts from its parent company in Honolulu for export to various duty-free shops in the Far East. During the current fiscal year, the company imported $1,000,000 worth of nuts and retailed them for $3,000,000. Local income taxes are paid at the rate of 16 percent. Profits earned by the Hong Kong subsidiary are retained for future expansion.

Required: Based on this information, calculate the U.S. parent company's U.S. tax liability under Subpart F provisions of the Internal Revenue Code.

5. A jewelry manufacturer domiciled in Amsterdam purchases gold from a precious metals dealer in Belgium for €1,200. The manufacturer fabricates the raw material into an item of jewelry and wholesales it to a Dutch retailer for €3,000.

Required: Compute the value-added tax from the jewelry manufacturer's activities if the Dutch value-added tax rate is 17.5%.

6. Sweden has a classical system of taxation. Calculate the total taxes that would be paid by a company headquartered in Stockholm that earns 1,000,000 Swedish krona (SEK) and distributes 50 percent of its earnings as a dividend to its shareholders. Assume the company's shareholders are in the 40 percent tax bracket and that the company's income tax rate is 28 percent.

7. Alubar, a U.S. multinational, receives royalties from Country A, foreign branch earnings from Country B, and dividends equal to 50 percent of net income from subsidiaries in Countries C and D. There is a 10 percent withholding tax on the royalty from Country A and a 10 percent withholding tax on the dividend from Country C. Income tax rates are 20 percent in Country B and 40 percent in Coun-

try C. Country D assesses indirect taxes of 40 percent instead of direct taxes on income. Selected data are as follows:

	Country A	Country B	Country C	Country D
Royalty from Country A operations	$20			
Pretax income		$90	$90	$54
Income taxes (20%/40%)		18	36	-0-
Net income		$72	$54	$54

Required: Calculate the foreign and U.S. taxes paid on each foreign source income.

8. Global Enterprises has a manufacturing affiliate in Country A that incurs costs of $600,000 for goods that it sells to its sales affiliate in Country B. The sales affiliate resells these goods to final consumers for $1,700,000. Both affiliates incur operating expenses of $100,000 each. Countries A and B levy a corporate income tax of 35 percent on taxable income in their jurisdictions.

   Required: If Global Enterprises raises the aggregate transfer price such that shipments from its manufacturing to its sales affiliate increase from $1,000,000 to $1,200,000, what effect would this have on consolidated taxes?

9. Using the facts stated in exercise 8, what would be the tax effects of the transfer pricing action if corporate income tax rates were 30 percent in Country A and 40 percent in Country B?

10. Drawing on the background facts in exercises 8 and 9, assume that the manufacturing cost per unit, based on operations at full capacity of 10,000 units, is $60 and that the uncontrolled selling price of the unit in Country A is $120. Costs to transport the goods to the distribution affiliate in Country B are $16 per unit and a reasonable profit margin on such cross-border sales is 20 percent of cost.

    Now suppose that Country B levies a corporate income tax of 40 percent on taxable income (versus 30 percent in Country A) and a tariff of 20 percent on the declared value of the imported goods. The minimum declared value legally allowed in Country B is $100 per unit with no upper limit. Import duties are deductible for income tax purposes in Country B.

    Required:
    a. Based on the foregoing information, formulate a transfer pricing strategy that would minimize Global Enterprise's overall tax burden.
    b. What issues does your pricing decision raise?

11. Lumet Corporation, a manufacturer of cellular telephones, wishes to invoice a sales affiliate located in Fontainebleau for an order of 10,000 units. Wanting to minimize its exchange risk, it invoices all intercompany transactions in euros. Relevant facts on a per unit basis are as follows: net sales price, €900; direct manufacturing costs, €270; other operating expenses, €126; freight and insurance, €2; packaging costs, €3. Also, assume that the French affiliate's net working capital is €4,500,000, customs duties are 5 percent, French short-term interest rates are 8 percent, and Lumet Corporation wishes to earn a profit of 6 percent on the transaction.

    Required: Determine the price at which Lumet would invoice its French affiliate for the cellular phones.

12. The partial income statement of the Lund Manufacturing Company, a Swedish-based concern producing pharmaceutical products, is presented here:

Sales		SEK 75,000,000
Cost of goods manufactured and sold:		
Finished goods, beg. Inventory	-0-	
Cost of goods manufactured:		
(100,000 units)		
Direct materials used	SEK 22,500,000	
Direct labor	11,600,000	
Overhead	6,000,000	
Cost of goods available for sale	40,100,000	
Finished goods, end. Inventory	8,000,000	
Cost of goods sold		32,100,000
Gross Margin		SEK 42,900,000

During the year, short-term interest rates in Sweden averaged 7 percent while net operating assets averaged SEK 45,000,000. The company is entitled to a government subsidy of 5 percent. Its required margin to provide a profit and cover other expenses is 8 percent. All affiliates receive credit terms of 60 days.

Required: Based on this information, at what price would the Lund Manufacturing Company invoice its distribution affiliate in neighboring Finland?

Case 12–1   Muscle Max: Your Very Own Personal Trainer

Muscle Max-Asia, a wholly owned affiliate of a French parent company, functions as a regional headquarters for operating activities in the Pacific Rim. It enjoys much autonomy from its French parent as it conducts its primary line of business, the manufacture and sale of Muscle Max, a commercial grade weight lifting machine that can be used in athletic clubs or in the home. Muscle Max-Asia has manufacturing affiliates in Malaysia and Canton and distribution outlets in Australia, Japan, New Zealand, South Korea, and Singapore. It plans to expand its operations to other Pacific Rim countries in the next several years.

Given the demand for weight lifting equipment in Australia, the company's distribution affili-ate there, Muscle Max-Australia, has been importing its equipment from both Canton and Malaysia, paying a customs duty of 5 percent.[1] Competing suppliers of similar equipment have approached the Australian affiliate for orders. Prices quoted on such machinery have ranged between 650 to 750 Australian dollars (A$). Muscle Max-Australia, which currently retails the jogging machine for A$1,349, has recently complained to Muscle Max-Asia because of differences in the prices it is being charged by its sister affiliates in Canton and Malaysia. Specifically, while the Malaysian affiliate charges a per unit price of A$675, the Canton supplier's price is 26 percent higher. Muscle Max-Asia explains that the transfer price, based on a cost-plus

[1]Assume that the marginal corporate income tax rate in Australia is 36 percent.

formula (production costs total A$540 per unit), reflects several considerations, including higher margins to compensate for credit risk, operating risk, and taxes. As for taxes, Muscle Max-Asia explains that the Peoples Republic of China has provided fiscal incentives to enterprises that promote exports. Although normal corporate income tax rates are 30 percent, Cantonese tax authorities have agreed to a rate of 10 percent on all export-related earnings.

The manager of Muscle Max-Australia remained skeptical and believed that he was paying for the Cantonese manager's inefficiency. In his latest communication, he asked if he could consider alternative suppliers of similar equipment to preserve local market share.

REQUIRED

1. What issues does this case raise?
2. What courses of action would you recommend to resolve the issues you have identified?

Case 12–2   Congress Giveth and Congress Taketh

The tax morality of the multinational corporation has become a popular topic of debate. Opinions range from complete support of the multinational corporation to accusations that it is one of the most exploitative institutions of capitalism ever created. In addition to exporting jobs, adversely affecting a country's balance of payments, and hurting domestic investment, multinationals are accused of not paying their fair share of taxes to either host country or home country governments. Calling the foreign tax credit and foreign income deferral policy "the biggest loopholes in the whole tax law," some members of Congress advocate ending existing international tax provisions for U.S. multinationals. More specifically, proposals have been advanced to eliminate the deferral of taxes on profits held abroad and eliminate the U.S. tax credit on taxes paid to foreign governments. The latter payments would be treated as expenses or reductions in taxable income rather than reductions in the amount of federal taxes owed.

As an impartial observer of the international business scene, you are commissioned by Congress to evaluate the long-run effects of the foregoing proposal on the international competitive position of U.S. multinationals and the implications of your findings for the U.S. economy.

Be sure to consider the effects of the proposals on the profitability of identical investments made in Mexico by U.S.- and German-owned subsidiaries in the country. In your case analysis, assume that a U.S. company and a German company each own 100 percent of the voting shares of a foreign manufacturing corporation in Mexico. The Mexican affiliate of each produces a before-tax income of $500,000 annually and retains all earnings in the business. The income tax rate in Mexico is 35 percent. Germany, with an effective tax rate of 40 percent does not tax unremitted earnings. Book value of the Mexican investment is $3,000,000.

REQUIRED

1. Based on the foregoing assumptions, determine, in comparative fashion, what the effective tax rates and rates of return on equity will be for each investor assuming the United States adopts a policy of taxing unremitted earnings but allows a deemed foreign tax credit for foreign taxes paid.
2. Repeat the analysis called for in requirement 1 but assume instead that Congress only allows a deduction for foreign taxes paid.
3. Discuss the major policy issues stemming from your analysis.

INDEX